D0602396

BOOK
OF
INSIDE
INFORMATION

**By the Editors of
Bottom Line/Personal**

**Bottom Line
Books**

www.BottomLineSecrets.com

Book of Inside Information

Copyright © 2009 by Boardroom® Inc.

10 9 8 7 6 5 4 3 2 1

ISBN 0-88723-508-5

All rights reserved. No part of this book may be reproduced in any
form or by any means without written permission from the publisher.

Bottom Line Books® publishes the opinions of expert authorities in
many fields. The use of a book is not a substitute for legal,
accounting, investment, health or any other professional services.
Consult competent professionals for answers to your specific questions.

Offers, prices, rates, addresses, telephone numbers and Web sites
listed in this book are accurate at the time of publication,
but they are subject to frequent change.

Bottom Line Books® is a registered trademark of
Boardroom® Inc.
281 Tresser Boulevard, Stamford, CT 06901

www.BottomLineSecrets.com

Printed in the United States of America

Contents

16 • SAFETY ALERT

Preface

We are pleased that you've decided to purchase our new book, *Bottom Line Book of Inside Information*. We trust that you will find many helpful ideas and money-saving solutions for everyone in your family.

At Bottom Line Books and Bottom Line Publications, our mission is to provide readers with the best information to help them gain greater wealth, better health, more wisdom, extra time and increased happiness.

When you choose a Bottom Line Book, you are turning to a stellar group of experts in fields that range from banking, investing, taxes, estate planning, insurance, real estate and health care to cars, computers, security, travel and self-improvement. Whether they specialize in the economy, consumer-health advocacy, bargain travel or supermarket shopping, Bottom Line experts are the most knowledgeable and innovative people in the country.

How do we find these top-notch professionals? Over the past 35 years, our editors have built a network of literally thousands of expert sources. We regularly consult with our advisors affiliated with the premier financial institutions, law firms, universities and hospitals. Our sources include entrepreneurs, scientists, physicians and other medical professionals, acclaimed authors, researchers, master craftspeople, nutritionists and chefs and a former IRS agent.

In Bottom Line Book of Inside Information, you will find the latest wisdom from many of these foremost experts distilled into hundreds of carefully researched, up-to-date articles.

We are confident that *Bottom Line Book of Inside Information* can help you and your family enjoy a wealthier, wiser and healthier life.

The Editors
Bottom Line Books®
Stamford, CT
www.BottomLineSecrets.com

Money Manager

Find Money You Didn't Even Know You Had

Government agencies are holding onto more than $60 billion in unclaimed assets and missing money. Some of it may be yours. Life insurance proceeds…bank accounts…tax refunds…government benefits…savings bonds…inheritances—all can go astray without your knowledge.

HOW IT GETS LOST

Assets are considered abandoned when contact with the owner is lost—usually due to a name change after marriage or divorce, an unreported change of address, illegible or incomplete records, or clerical errors.

If you don't promptly get in touch with the holder of a dormant asset, you may lose out.

Banks, stockbrokers and transfer agents, utilities, employers and life insurance companies remit the unclaimed funds to the protective custody of a government trust account in a legal process known as "escheat." There it awaits your claim!

Millions of family members are unaware that they are eligible to collect unclaimed assets owed to relatives who died without leaving updated wills or financial road maps for their heirs.

Important: *You* must initiate the search—the federal government and states holding unclaimed funds will likely *not* contact you.

Caution: There is no central repository or single database containing all unclaimed assets, so don't be fooled by Web sites offering paid access to one.

INSURANCE POLICIES

It's estimated that between one-quarter and one-third of all life insurance policies—amounting to hundreds of millions of dollars annually—go unclaimed upon the death of the insured. Why? Because it's generally up

Mark Tofal, consultant and consumer advocate on matters of escheat and unclaimed property, Palm Coast, FL, *www.unclaimedassets.com.* He is author of *Unclaimed Assets: Money the Government Owes You!* NUPA.

to family members to notify the insurance company when a policyholder dies, and many simply aren't aware that a policy exists.

What's more, many life insurance companies have "demutualized," entitling millions of current and former policyholders to receive stock and cash in addition to policy benefits. Demutualization is the process whereby mutual life insurance companies, which are owned by policyholders, convert to stock ownership. Policyholders become stockholders and receive shares and/or cash in exchange for their ownership interest. *Examples...*

• **John Hancock**—at the time of demutualization (1999), addresses for more than 400,000 policyholders were not current.

• **MetLife**—60 million shares of stock (worth $855 million at the time of demutualization in 2000) went unclaimed.

• **Prudential**—the company was not able to find about 1.2 million policyholders entitled to compensation when it demutualized in 2000.

By law, unclaimed policy benefits and demutualization proceeds are held in trust until claimants come forward. In 2005, trustees took custody of $22.8 billion, of which less than $1 billion has been claimed.

Important: Act fast when making claims. Unclaimed stock from the nearly two dozen other companies that demutualized in the past decade may be sold by a government-appointed custodian. Thereafter, you won't get any dividends or stock appreciation.

For a list of demutualized insurance companies, visit the Demutualization Claims Clearinghouse site, *www.demutualization-claims.com.*

What to do: You may also be in luck if you are the heir of someone who held a policy with one of these companies. Contact the policyholder's company, and ask if you are owed money from an unclaimed policy or demutualization. With demutualization, you will most likely be directed to the company's transfer agent or the government trustee holding the compensation, if indeed it has gone unclaimed for the statutory dormant period, typically one to three years.

SAVINGS BONDS

Contact the Bureau of Public Debt for unredeemed savings bonds. US savings bonds often go missing—they are received as gifts, put in a drawer and forgotten for decades. All US savings bonds stop earning interest at final maturity (now 30 years), and less than 1% of bondholders are notified when their bonds reach that date (only holders of Series H and Series HH bonds that pay interest by check are notified). The value of unredeemed bonds that have reached final maturity currently exceeds *$15 billion.*

Important: Use the right form for your request...

• For undelivered bonds, use Form PD F 3062-4 E.

• For destroyed, lost or stolen bonds, use Form PD F 1048 E.

• For a missing interest check for HH bonds, use Form PD F 5235 E.

Download the form you need from *www.treasurydirect.gov/forms.htm*, call 866-388-1776 or e-mail your request to *savbonds@bpd.treas.gov.*

LOST TAX REFUNDS

Contact the IRS at 800-829-4477. Recently, the IRS had more than 115,000 income tax refund checks totaling $110 million undelivered, mainly due to unreported changes of name and/or address (typically after a move), marriage, death or divorce. In addition, each year an estimated $500 million in IRS refund checks that *are* delivered go uncashed and unpaid.

Upon request to the IRS, checks that were returned will be reissued. If no request is made, the IRS will credit the amount toward any amount due in the succeeding three years. Checks worth about $6 billion have been delivered but never cashed. A check that has been lost, voided (after one year) or destroyed can also be reissued by contacting the IRS.

Important: Generally, no refund can be issued more than three years after the due date of the return to which the refund relates. If you are the heir of a deceased taxpayer who may be owed a refund due to an overpayment made during the year of death, contact the IRS immediately—before the refund period expires.

MONEY HELD BY STATES

Last year alone, states collected $23 billion in unclaimed assets, representing everything from utility deposits, escrow accounts and never-cashed paychecks to the contents of safe-deposit boxes. Every state and the District of Columbia maintains a database of unclaimed property, which may be accessed on-line. For free links to all state unclaimed property databases, go to *www.unclaimed. com/unclaimed_property.htm*. Check every state where you and family members have had a connection—work…business…residence.

Hints: When searching, use your maiden name, any previous married name as well as middle names and initials. Also search for names of deceased relatives.

There's an Extra $300/Month Waiting for You

Jean Chatzky, New York City–based financial editor for NBC's *Today* show and an editor-at-large at *Money* magazine. She is author of *Pay It Down! From Debt to Wealth on $10 a Day.* Portfolio. Visit *www.jeanchatzky.com* for more information.

Finding extra cash each and every month is a great idea, but the most popular ways to save money and cut costs often are not the best…

POPULAR MISTAKES

•**Refinancing your mortgage.**

Problem: Closing costs can be thousands of dollars, so refinancing generally is worthwhile only if your new rate is at least one percentage point less than your current one or if you can get a truly no-cost streamlined refinance deal.

•**Consolidating debt with a home-equity loan.**

Problem: While these loans can reduce interest costs, about one-third of people who use them for this purpose incur heavy credit card debt all over again. Even worse, they put their homes at risk. Also, with declining home values, there may be little or no equity to tap.

SMART MONEYSAVERS

Try several of the following painless ways to free up $300 or more every month…

•**Ask your credit card company to reduce your interest rate.** This works for more than half of callers. *Steps to take…*

•Gather up all the recent preapproved credit card offers you have received in the mail. Call your current card issuer and ask for a rate reduction. Specify which company is offering a better deal.

•Be prepared to counter objections from customer service agents.

Scenario #1: The agent says, "Your card has a fixed rate. It can't be changed."

Your response: "A fixed rate means only that my rate doesn't vary with the prime rate. In fact, your company could raise my rate at any time just by giving me 15 days' notice, right? So, if you want, you can choose to lower my rate today."

Scenario #2: The agent says, "I'm not authorized to lower your rate."

Your response: Ask to speak with a supervisor. Say to him/her, "If I transfer my balance to a new card, your bank probably is going to send me offers to come back at the same lower rate. Why not save the company the cost of that effort by reducing my rate now?"

Potential monthly savings: $20 to $60, assuming an average credit card balance of $8,000 and a rate reduction of three to nine percentage points.

•**Refinance your car loan.** Since there are no closing costs, this strategy can be worthwhile even if you will save only a small amount. *Steps to take…*

•Find out how much your car is currently worth based on its value in Kelley Blue Book, available at most libraries or on-line at *www.kbb.com*. You won't be able to refinance if you owe more than your car's resale value.

•Try to obtain a better interest rate by calling several lenders or checking with *www.bankrate.com,* which pinpoints the best rates in your area.

Potential monthly savings: $35, assuming a car loan of $14,000 and a rate reduction of three percentage points.

•**Haggle for services, not just goods.** Ask for price breaks from your plumber, veterinarian, painter, landscaper—even your doctor. In most cases, it helps to gather prices from several comparable service providers. Then ask your usual provider to match the lowest one. *Other steps to take…*

•Offer to give cash at the time of service. Remind the service provider that he/she won't have to bill you or pay a transaction fee to a credit card company.

•Negotiate a group rate. For example, if you need your chimney cleaned, recruit several neighbors to have theirs done at the same time for a group discount.

Potential monthly savings: $15 to $200.

•**Pay your bills as soon as they arrive rather than near their due dates.** This way, you'll be sure to avoid late fees. These fees have grown so steep that they easily offset any interest you could earn by holding on to your money a bit longer. Typically, a single late credit card payment now means a $35 penalty…an increase in your interest rate to the maximum that the card company charges…maybe even rate hikes on your other credit cards. Of course, if you are wrongly charged a late fee, ask to have it rescinded.

Potential monthly savings: $35 or more.

•**Increase your automatic savings.** Most people never miss the money taken out of their paychecks for 401(k)s. You can use this same technique for personal savings with an automatic investment plan through a mutual fund firm.

•**Stop spending money on high-cost, low-priority items.** Sure, you have fixed costs, but you could probably cut back on some of your habitual spending elsewhere. *Low-priority items might include…*

•Restaurants/take-out food.

Potential monthly savings: $100 and up.

•Unused memberships. Ask your health club to put your membership on hold. In the meantime, take brisk walks…or borrow workout DVDs from the library and exercise at home with a friend. Or decide if paying on a per-class basis would be more cost-effective.

Potential monthly savings: $15 or more.

•A second car. Even if you are done paying for the car, getting rid of it will save on insurance, maintenance and gasoline. Several cities, including New York, offer car-sharing programs, an alternative to rentals in which members can use a car for as little as an hour at a time. Check at *www.zipcar.com* and *www. flexcar.com.*

Potential monthly savings: $100.

•Cell phone calling plans that provide more than you need. On average, people pay for nearly twice as many minutes as they use. *Better:* Gather your recent cell phone bills, and look closely at your calling habits. Then go to *www.myrateplan.com, www.saveonphone. com* or *www.letstalk.com* to find a better rate for your level of usage.

Potential monthly savings: $25 and up.

Smarter Solutions For Common Money Problems

Sheryl Garrett, CFP, founder of Garrett Planning Network, a Kansas City–based international network of hundreds of financial advisers who charge for their services on an hourly (as needed) basis, *www.garrettplanningnetwork.com.* She is author of *Just Give Me the Answer$: Expert Advisors Address Your Most Pressing Financial Questions.* Kaplan.

I oversee a network of more than 250 financial planners around the country who deal with thousands of clients. *Here are some of the recent challenges faced by several customers and how we helped resolve them…*

Problem: Sticking to a budget. A couple in their early 50s, together earning more than $150,000 a year, complained that their spending seemed to run several hundred dollars over the amount they earned each month.

Conventional wisdom: These days, many advisers recommend automatic checking account deductions to maintain better control of mortgage payments, utility and telephone bills, etc.

Our advice: While setting up automatic payments for fixed expenses is a good idea, the best way to achieve financial discipline for discretionary expenses is to make spending less convenient. This couple frittered away money, using high-interest credit cards for restaurant meals, music CDs and expensive clothing.

I recommended that they try the old-fashioned cash-envelope system. Obviously, they didn't want to pay all their bills this way or keep thousands of dollars around the house, but it's very effective for expenses that tend to fall through the cracks.

The couple figured that they could get by with $400 a month for nonessential, nonfixed expenses and stopped paying for these items with credit cards. Each month, they put $400 in an envelope so they knew exactly when to stop or cut back spending. Using cash instead of credit cards also made them think about their purchases so they made them more sensibly.

Problem: **Determining insurance needs.** A husband in his late 40s with two children—a five-year-old and an eight-year-old—was offered the opportunity to buy life insurance for his wife through his job. He didn't know how much coverage to get.

Conventional wisdom: Insure a stay-at-home parent for enough to cover the cost of child care if he/she were not around.

Our advice: I recommended that he purchase at least $250,000 worth of coverage on his wife, who was also in her 40s.

Cost: About $300 annually for a 10-year level-premium term policy. (For slightly more, he could buy a 20-year level-premium term policy.) I also suggested that he purchase the insurance policy privately—not through his employer. It was the same price either way, and if the man left his job, he wouldn't have to leave the coverage behind.

Why purchase so much insurance coverage? If a stay-at-home spouse dies, the financial costs can far exceed child care. What if the children need counseling? What if the husband's bereavement leave of absence from work—typically four to 12 weeks—is not enough? Term life insurance has become so affordable nowadays that it pays to buy the most that you can afford.

Company we recommend based on cost and quality: Banner Life, 800-638-8428, *www.lgamerica.com*.

Problem: **Choosing a mortgage.** A couple in their early 50s was interested in refinancing the $117,000 that was left on their mortgage. Refinancing with a 30-year fixed-rate mortgage at 6% would save them one percentage point on their interest rate, but the couple was concerned that their closing costs would erode most of their savings on the refinancing.

Conventional wisdom: Don't refinance unless you can save at least two percentage points on a fixed-rate mortgage.

Our advice: It still may pay to refinance even if you save only one percentage point on the interest rate. Given the heavy competition in the mortgage lending industry, closing costs often can be negotiated down to a manageable amount—in this case, $1,200. At that level, the couple will break even and recoup their refinancing expenses after only 15 months. Going forward, they will save $77 a month in total payments—$924 a year—and $26,500 over the remaining 28.7 years of the mortgage term.

Helpful: The Web sites *www.mortgage calc.com* and *www.bankrate.com* offer the tools to figure out whether it pays to refinance.

Problem: **Protecting your insurance rating.** A client's car was vandalized. His car insurance included a $500 deductible, and repairs came to $900. It would be his second claim in the past few years, and he was worried that the insurance company would raise his premium because of it. However, he felt that because the damage wasn't his fault, he should file the claim instead of paying for the repair costs out of pocket.

Conventional wisdom: If the cost of a repair exceeds your deductible, file a claim.

Our advice: Stop thinking of insurance policies as savings accounts. Insurance is meant to be used for catastrophic emergencies that could wipe you out financially, not periodic setbacks.

These days, insurance carriers are aggressively trying to limit their losses by screening for people who might present big risks. Filing even a small auto or homeowner's insurance claim could lead to premium increases of 20% or more or even result in nonrenewal of your policy.

Wiser strategies…

•**Raise your deductible.** Since my client decided not to file small claims anymore, there was no reason to maintain a low deductible on his insurance policy. I suggested that he set his auto policy deductible at $1,000 and his homeowner's policy deductible at $2,500 to $5,000. In many cases, the premiums are so much lower due to high deductibles that the money saved exceeds what you would get back from a few small claims.

•**Know exactly what your insurance policies cover.** Keep a copy of the policy handy to check for limitations. Calling your agent after a loss and asking a "what if" question could worsen your risk profile. Some insurers require that such conversations be written up, even if you pay for the damage without ever filing a claim. Reason? The loss shows that you have a propensity for future losses.

•**Beware of making claims for damages that raise the possibility of more claims in the future.** For example, water-damage claims are red-flagged by insurers because they often lead to additional claims later on, such as those for rot and mold.

•**Drop unnecessary add-on coverage,** such as riders for jewelry that is worth $1,000 or less—they encourage you to file small claims.

•**Don't switch insurance carriers just to save a few dollars.** Making a claim within six months might cause a new insurer to drop you, and then you could wind up with a more expensive policy.

Dumb Things People Do…Because Their Financial Advisers Tell Them To

Edward Mendlowitz, CPA, partner in the CPA firm WithumSmith+Brown, 1 Spring St., New Brunswick, NJ 08901. He is author of *The Adviser's Guide to Family Business Succession Planning*. American Institute of Certified Public Accountants.

It is usually worthwhile to hire an accountant or other adviser for financial advice, and most serve their clients well. Unfortunately, even these pros may give advice that isn't suitable for a particular client—or for any client. *Here are some traps that advisers frequently let their clients fall into—or even lead them into…*

REAL ESTATE

•**Pumping up your mortgage.** Your accountant might advise you to take out as large a mortgage as possible because the interest is tax-deductible. Even though it's deductible, mortgage interest must be paid, and payments on a large mortgage might leave you short of cash that you'll need elsewhere. You even could lose your house if you suffer a financial setback and find yourself unable to make the steep mortgage payments.

Some people take out extra mortgage money and plan to save or invest it, but the interest paid on a mortgage is usually greater than what you could earn on personal savings—a gap that can eat up most or all of the mortgage's deductibility advantage. And it's not worth risking a big mortgage in the hope that you can use the borrowed money to earn more elsewhere.

INVESTING

•**Selling mutual fund shares improperly.** Financial advisers often fail to tell their clients that selling fund shares wisely is not as simple as buying them.

To avoid paying unnecessary taxes when you sell all of your shares in a fund, you must tally up any dividends and other fund distributions that were automatically reinvested into the fund and count this amount as part of your "basis" (your cost for tax purposes). Your fund company usually can provide you with the numbers. Then you report your basis on your tax return, along with the amount you receive for the shares when you sell them. Including all of your reinvested distributions in your basis will help you by reducing your taxable gain or increasing your deductible loss.

Trap: If you acquired shares in the fund at different times and want to sell only some of those shares, you can specifically designate that your highest-cost shares be sold. This strategy will minimize your taxes.

How to do it: Write to your broker or the fund company (or have your adviser do so) before the sale takes place, and identify the shares that you would like to sell.

Example: "Please sell the 100 shares of ABC Fund that I bought on January 10, 2005." Keep in mind that any gain on shares held more than one year will be taxed at no higher than 15% federally. Gains on shares held for a shorter time will be taxed at your ordinary income tax rate, up to 35% federally. If you own both short-term-gain and long-term-gain shares, calculate the taxes you would pay in selling each, then sell the shares that result in the lowest tax paid.

•**Disposing of worthless securities without following the tax rules.** If you have invested in a company whose stock has lost all value, you can take a capital loss equal to your entire "cost basis" in the shares. But you must show that the company became totally worthless in the year for which you're filing a return. This may not be easy to do—and many advisers fail to tell their clients that this proof of worthlessness is necessary.

Better: Sell the securities to a sympathetic unrelated party (someone other than your spouse, sibling, parent, child or business partner) for $1, which will enable you to take a normal capital loss without having to prove that the stock became totally worthless. You will probably want to reimburse your helpful friend for any transaction costs.

Alternatively, get a letter from your broker stating that the cost of selling the securities would be greater than the proceeds you would collect. This also enables you to take a capital loss.

TAXES

•**Prepaying estimated taxes.** Some people must pay estimated taxes each quarter to their states, as well as to the IRS. The final payment for any given year is due the following January 15.

Historically, for people who itemize deductions, state estimated tax payments made in the previous December have qualified for a deduction that year on the federal tax return.

Trap: In recent years, exposure to the alternative minimum tax (AMT) has become more widespread. For people who owe the AMT, prepaying state tax can result in "wasting" a large outlay that won't be deductible.

Example: A hypothetical John Morgan, who lives in Buffalo, owes New York State a $5,000 estimated tax payment by January 15, 2009. His accountant tells him to send in a $5,000 check by December 31, 2008, to get a federal income tax deduction for 2008.

However, John winds up owing the AMT in 2008—and state tax payments aren't deductible under AMT rules. John gets no write-off for this $5,000. He would have been better off delaying the payment until 2009, when he might not owe the AMT.

Protection: Ask your accountant to consider the AMT before recommending year-end tax prepayments.

•**Taking unsupported deductions for alimony payments.** This bad advice is commonly given to divorced people by advisers.

The facts: For an alimony deduction to be valid, there must be a written agreement between the two parties spelling out monetary amounts and the rights and responsibilities of each party. Also, you can never deduct child-support payments—so your divorce documents should clearly delineate alimony from child support, if any.

To deduct alimony payments, you must enter on your tax return the Social Security number of the former spouse who received them. This former spouse will owe tax on the alimony income.

ESTATE PLANNING

• **Making unwise gifts.** In 2008, each individual can give away up to $12,000 worth of assets to any number of recipients without owing any gift tax. (For married couples, the amount that can be given away is $24,000 per recipient.) ($13,000 and $26,000 respectively in 2009.) For affluent people, this can be valuable for reducing future estate taxes.

Trap: In these days of long life expectancies and soaring long-term-care costs, too many advisers don't fully evaluate whether their clients might need this money for themselves down the line. Even worse, many advisers fail to set their clients straight on a common misconception—that money given away is tax-deductible. It is *not*. It is merely tax-exempt for the recipient of the gift.

RETIREMENT ACCOUNTS

• **Naming the wrong IRA beneficiaries.** How valuable your hard-earned IRA assets will be after your death is highly dependent on the beneficiaries you designate now. Many advisers don't make clear the extreme importance of naming beneficiaries properly.

Common mistake: Naming your estate as the beneficiary or failing to name a beneficiary at all. This can cost your heirs the benefit of extended tax deferral. The individuals who ultimately inherit the IRA assets will, by law, have to empty the tax-deferred accounts much more rapidly than might otherwise be the case.

Better: Name one or more individuals as beneficiaries. Individual beneficiaries can stretch out required distributions (and defer paying tax on those distributions) over either their own life expectancies or the former life expectancy of the deceased IRA owner, depending on the age of the IRA owner when he/she died.

Also important: Name contingent beneficiaries to allow your primary beneficiaries to decide whether to accept the inheritance or, if more appropriate, to let it go to another beneficiary with its tax benefits intact.

Simple System to Organize Your Finances

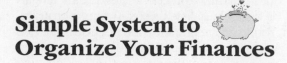

Debbie Stanley, organization coach, founder and principal of Red Letter Day Professional Organizers in Clinton Township, MI, *www.rldpo.com.* She is author of *Organize Your Personal Finances...in No Time.* Que.

Modern financial innovations—credit cards, debit cards and automatic bank deposits and withdrawals—actually make it *harder* than ever to keep tabs on your finances. But it's possible to create a simple system to track your spending and have better control over your records. The key is to use the system consistently. *My strategies...*

FILING

Like most people, I used to file alphabetically by category (Credit Cards...Insurance), but this was labor-intensive. While I was unlikely to ever need most of these papers, I still had to thumb through hundreds of files to put each one away. I put off filing for months until the pile was a foot high. Also, the system relied too much on memory. I could never recall whether I put my cell-phone bills under "C" for cell phone, "S" for Sprint (my provider) or "P" for phone. And if I were to keep a separate index of names, I would need to update it each time I added a new file.

Smart alternatives...

• **File bills by month, instead of by category.** This way, filing can be done quickly. If I do need to retrieve something, it takes longer to find it than if I had filed by category, but I don't need to retrieve most bills and statements. When necessary, I can locate most bills fairly quickly by color and size.

• **Archive filed documents by the year you can discard them.** People spend too much time organizing items they are unlikely to ever need, such as income tax records, insurance documents, utility and credit card bills and investment statements.

My solution: Sort by the year you can throw out the files.

Example: The IRS can audit tax returns as far back as seven years in some situations, so any tax-related documents from 2006 go into a box marked 2014. All of the contents of this box, except the returns, get shredded and thrown out at the end of that year. (Returns and proof of filing should be kept forever in case the IRS says you forgot to file one year.)

●**File receipts for major purchases by room,** instead of by category. I have files for purchases associated with each room of the house, including odd spaces, such as the front porch. For instance, when I buy a new television, I staple all the TV-related documents together—the manual, warranty, receipt, etc. —and place them in a file called "Family Room." I throw out TV-related documents when I throw out the TV. This system feels more natural to many people because they know where all TV-related documents are located, rather than trying to figure out if, say, the warranty should go under "TV," "Warranties" or "Electronics."

Note: This system should be intuitive. Some people keep laptop documents under "Home Office." Others file them under "Bedroom."

●**Record small cash purchases on the backs of ATM slips** if you're trying to keep closer tabs on everyday spending. I often take out $20 or $40 to buy small items. I later jot down the dates and amounts, and add an arrow to the front of the slip to remind myself to look at the back when reconciling my checkbook. It's a great way to track just how you spend your petty cash. I keep my ATM slips in my wallet until I receive my month-end statement.

●**Keep a separate box or filing cabinet for special projects.** Files of special interest that accumulate paper, such as brochures, price lists and news clippings, will choke your main filing system.

Examples: House Hunting…Vacation Plans…Car Buying.

Use words that are comfortable to you when creating folders. I file miscellaneous documents from the Internet under "Web," not "Internet."

●**Don't let a file get thicker than five inches.** At that point, it's better to subcategorize. For instance, when my "Basement" file became too thick, I added subcategories, such as "Basement/Kids' Stuff" and "Basement/Appliances."

BILL-PAYING

●**Arrange for your bills to arrive at the same time.** Many monthly billers, such as credit card issuers, now let you pick your own payment due date for greater convenience. Jot down the date you intend to mail each bill payment on its envelope in the space where the stamp will go.

I keep my envelopes in a small upright file on my desk. If you use financial software, program it to remind you of bill-payment due dates with a pop-up message.

If all else fails, pay bills immediately. I had a client who kept getting late fees on credit cards. Now she pays bills the day they arrive. Sure, she loses out by not leaving money in an interest-bearing account a bit longer each month, but her savings on late fees more than make up for the lost interest.

●**Make sure you and your spouse adhere to the same system.** I had clients who kept miscommunicating about purchases and overdrawing their joint checking account.

My solution: We preserved their joint checking account but also opened a new account for each spouse. Their paychecks were deposited into the main account, and bills were paid from it. Each month, an agreed-upon amount was transferred from the main account to the two individual accounts for their personal purchases and withdrawals. The checking accounts were free, so they avoided extra fees.

If you pay bills electronically: If you use a bank's on-line bill-paying service, you can still control the date the payment is sent. But if you sign up for automatic bill-paying through a vendor directly, you give the company the authority to take money from your account. Many don't remove those funds when they say they will. It could be a few days earlier, which could overdraw your bank account if you maintain a low balance.

Why It Pays to Bank On-Line...And How to Get Started

Jim Bruene, the editor and publisher of *Online Banking Report*, a trade publication located in Seattle. He has spent over 15 years working in interactive financial services, and helped develop US Bancorp's pioneering on-line banking program in the early 1990s.

On-line banking is no longer a novelty. Every major US bank, and many small ones, provide this free service. In just five years, ING Direct—the largest Internet-only bank, with savings account yields nearly 20% higher than the national average—has garnered $40 billion in assets.

Why on-line banking is appealing...

• **It is much faster and more convenient** than going to a bank branch.

• **You can pay bills, transfer money from one account to another,** apply for loans, and view statements and canceled checks from the privacy of your own computer at home—or any computer connected to the Internet.

• **Yields on interest-earning accounts and CDs can be higher** when they are purchased on the Internet.

• **Customer security has been ramped up** to meet 2006 guidelines from federal regulators.

What you need to know...

HOW ON-LINE BANKING WORKS

It's easy to get started. If you already have an account with a land-based bank, go to its secure Web site to register for on-line banking services. There you will be asked to create a user name and password to access your account. No special software or hardware is required, just the computer's Web browser, such as *Internet Explorer* or *Firefox*.

On-line instructions will tell you how to view your accounts and do your banking. For example, in many cases, you can sign up with your monthly service providers—credit card issuers, phone company, etc.—to have them bill you electronically, then schedule your bank to automatically debit your account each month for the amounts. This saves time and eliminates the risk of incurring late fees. (You also can pay bills on-line one by one, if you prefer.) If, for some reason, you want to suspend automatic payments—even temporarily—just contact the creditor and your bank.

CHOOSING THE RIGHT BANK

• **Make sure that your bank has the on-line services you need.** *Look for these features...*

• Free automatic on-line payment of bills and guarantees that the bank will pay the penalties in the event that it sends payments in late or misdirects them.

• Money transfers to and from other banks and brokerages, including automatic debiting to make regular contributions to, say, an IRA at a mutual fund company.

• E-mail alerts when your balance is low, a bill is due or someone tries to access your account with an incorrect password.

• Electronic statements going back at least six months.

• Ability to stop payments on checks, for a charge, and view scanned images (both front and back) of canceled checks.

• Rebates to your checking account if you are charged a fee to use another bank's ATMs. In most cases, there is no fee from your bank and a rebate on up to six fees from other banks each month.

• Some banks offer budgeting reports that organize your expenditures—any payments that you make by check or directly from your bank account, including credit card bills—into specific categories, such as "groceries," "restaurants" and "lodging." Many of these budgeting reports are compatible with on-line features of popular financial software programs, such as *Quicken* and *Microsoft Money*. The reports can help small businesses track tax-deductible expenses.

• **Compare the interest rates on savings accounts and certificates of deposit** at *www.bankrate.com*. They are also listed in Barron's, the financial weekly. Also review the Web sites of various banks for promotions. For example, the London-based global banking giant HSBC is offering US residents an on-line savings account with a 3.05%* annual percentage yield (APY).

● **Consider an Internet-only bank.** These banks provide a variety of traditional banking products but they have no land-based customer branches. You contact bank representatives by e-mail or by calling an 800 number. Checks are deposited by mail and cash can be withdrawn through ATMs.

Where to stash your cash: Internet banks typically provide better deals on interest-bearing accounts, CDs and mortgages and other loans. For example, E*trade offers a one-year CD with a 2.85% APY. And, ING Direct's Orange Savings Account offers 3.0% APY.

Biggest Internet banks: *www.etrade. com...www.ingdirect.com.*

Even if you decide on an Internet-only bank, you should also maintain an account with a local bank. You may want free use of the local ATMs or face-to-face interaction— for example, if you need to cash a check. Some Internet-only banks require you to have a traditional account at another bank.

CAUTION

Don't fall for phishing scams. Con artists send authentic-looking e-mails that appear to come from your financial institution. The messages attempt to trick you into providing account numbers and passwords by claiming to have found "suspicious activity" or warning of the "impending suspension" of your account.

Delete these messages, and never click on the Web links or pop-up ads they include.

No legitimate institution will ask you to supply personal information by e-mail. If you have doubts about any e-mail you receive, look up your bank's phone number and call it. Don't use any phone number in the e-mail—it could be fake.

*Rates subject to change.

Myths About Your Bank Account and FDIC Insurance

Kathleen Nagle, associate director for consumer protection, FDIC's Division of Supervision and Consumer Protection, Washington, DC. If you have questions about FDIC insurance, you can call the FDIC toll-free at 877-275-3342 or go to *www.fdic.gov.*

Americans depend on insurance from the Federal Deposit Insurance Corporation (FDIC) to protect their savings in the event of bank failure, but many bank customers don't understand what's covered. *Common FDIC insurance myths...*

Myth: **Any financial product sold by an FDIC-insured bank is insured by the FDIC.**

Truth: Bank deposits are covered. These include checking and savings accounts, CDs, Christmas club accounts and money market deposit accounts. Investment products, such as stocks, bonds, mutual funds, annuities and money market mutual funds, are not covered even when purchased through an insured bank. Banks must disclose which products aren't covered by the FDIC.

Myth: **FDIC coverage is limited to $100,000 per customer.**

Truth: Your coverage generally is limited to $100,000 per bank and per ownership category—but you can have more than $100,000 in coverage at one bank if your accounts fall into multiple ownership categories. (*Note:* The FDIC has temporarily increased its coverage to $250,000 through December 31, 2009.)

Example: In addition to the $100,000 coverage for individual accounts...

● **Joint accounts owned with a spouse** (or someone else) qualify for an additional $100,000 in coverage per co-owner, as long as all owners have equal withdrawal rights.

● **Individual retirement accounts** (IRAs) held through a bank qualify for $250,000 in coverage. If you have other retirement accounts at the same bank, they may be lumped together with your IRAs before applying this limit.

Example: A man and his wife each have $100,000 in individual accounts at a bank, another $200,000 in a joint account and $250,000 each in IRAs at the bank. All $900,000 is covered by the FDIC at that one bank.

• **Certain kinds of trust accounts qualify** for $100,000 in insurance for each "qualifying beneficiary"—meaning the trust owner's spouse, child, grandchild, parent or sibling.

• **Certain deposits held in a Health Savings Account** (HSA) are covered. Details and limits can vary, so contact the FDIC about your situation.

• **Accounts of certain types of businesses qualify** for $100,000 in separate coverage. However, the accounts of sole proprietors are lumped in with those of their owners for insurance purposes.

If you divide your money among several banking companies, you can protect more. The money must be spread among different institutions, not merely different branches of the same bank.

Myth: I can increase my coverage limits by setting up joint accounts with my young children.

Truth: If your child needs your signature to withdraw money or state law doesn't allow young children to have their own bank accounts, this joint account will be lumped together with your individual accounts and the total coverage will be capped at $100,000.

Myth: I can double the amount of coverage I receive by altering my name on different accounts.

Truth: Using different names for the same person, such as John A. Smith and J. Adam Smith, or changing the order of names on joint accounts will not affect the insurance coverage.

Myth: The FDIC pays pennies on the dollar, and the government can take years to refund my money.

Truth: FDIC insurance pays 100% of the money lost up to the coverage limit and does so within days.

Are the Contents of Safe-Deposit Boxes Insured?

Nancy Dunnan, a New York City–based financial and travel adviser and the author or coauthor of 25 books, including the best seller, *How to Invest $50–$5,000.* HarperCollins.

Unlike money in a bank account, the contents of bank safe-deposit boxes are *not* Federal Deposit Insurance Corporation (FDIC) insured. However, read your box rental contract. Some banks pay up to a certain amount if the box contents are damaged. The amount and the conditions for payment vary widely. Also, check your homeowner's insurance policy to see whether it includes the contents of your safe-deposit boxes. If it does not, talk with your insurance agent about purchasing separate coverage.

Regardless of your insurance situation, take pictures (or videotape) of the box contents and write up a list of the items. If you are insured, this documentation will be helpful in filing a claim.

I also recommend placing paper valuables —such as important documents, a stamp collection and family photographs—in sturdy, waterproof Ziploc bags or Tupperware-type containers before storing them anywhere, including in a vault at a bank.

For the final word on what FDIC bank insurance does and does not cover, contact the Federal Deposit Insurance Corporation at *www.fdic.gov.* Click on "Deposit Insurance." Or, call them at 877-275-3342.

A Bounced Check Can Result in a Criminal Record

The recipient of a bounced check can take legal action against you. If the collection process reaches court and the court rules against you, criminal charges remain on your record forever. However, if you make good on a bounced check immediately, the mistake remains on your credit report for only seven years.

Stephen R. Bucci, president, Money Management International Financial Education Foundation, Houston, and author of *Credit Repair Kit for Dummies.* For Dummies.

Find Good Savings Account Rates On-Line At BestCashCow.com

This site gives free information to people who are trying to get the most interest on savings accounts and other cash-equivalent accounts. Compare the results at this site with ones at other sites providing similar information, such as Bankrate. com and the Motley Fool (*www.fool.com*).

Find a Credit Union

Nancy Dunnan, a New York City–based financial and travel adviser and the author or coauthor of 25 books, including the best seller, *How to Invest $50–$5,000.* HarperCollins.

For years, most credit unions—which often offer higher interest rates on savings and lower interest rates on loans than banks—have allowed spouses to join. But now many have expanded the concept of "family" to include siblings and children and, in some cases, even cousins, aunts and uncles. So, a family member who belongs to a credit union might be your ticket in. And a growing number of credit unions are community oriented—that is, with membership eligibility defined by geography, not by employment.

Begin your search by going to the Web site of the Credit Union National Association (CUNA)—the industry's trade organization —at *www.cuna.org.* On the home page, click on "Consumer Information," then "How to Join a Credit Union."

At the site, you'll find its on-line credit union locator. I typed in the zip code for the town where I grew up and found a credit union that said it had expanded beyond its original membership base and wanted to hear from potential new members. Or, check your city or town's *Yellow Pages.*

More information: Call CUNA at 800-358-5710. You'll be given the name of a contact person in the state where you live who will further help you with your search.

Outrageous Fees— Shrewd Ways to Avoid Them

Greg McBride, CFA, is a senior financial analyst for Bankrate.com, North Palm Beach, FL, which tracks and analyzes interest rates.

The fees *really* add up—bank fees, credit card fees, loan fees, real estate fees and car rental fees. As a consumer, you get dinged at every turn, it seems. Some of these charges may appear to be reasonable—while others are clearly outrageous. *But you can beat the system if you know how...*

BANKING AND CREDIT CARD FEES

Fees charged by banks and credit card companies have skyrocketed in the last several years. *Some of the worst...*

● **Doubled-up ATM fees.** When you use a machine that belongs to a bank other than the one that issued your ATM card, your bank may charge you a fee (usually $1.25 per transaction), *and* the owner of the ATM will charge a fee, as well ($1.64 on average). It's common for banks to charge $2 or even more at ATMs in airports, hotels, sports venues and other places where they know you are under pressure to find cash.

Self-defense: Know your bank's policy regarding ATM fees. Use your own bank's machines or national ATMs—machines within a national surcharge-free network, such as Alliance One (866-692-6771, *www.alliance one.coop*) and Freedom ATM Alliance (412-261-8146, *www.freedomatm.com*)—where there are usually no fees.

Check the free database at my company's Web site, *www.bankrate.com*, for the best ATM fees.

● **Balance-transfer fees.** If you move your credit card balance to another card to obtain a lower interest rate, the new card company can charge you a fee.

Example: Bank of America charges 3% of the balance transferred.

Self-defense: Use a credit card company that has no fees for balance transfers and low interest rates.

Example: Capital One (800-955-7070, *www.capitalone.com*) has no balance-transfer fees on most cards.

● **Credit card late and over-the-limit fees.** Your credit card company may slap on a fee for paying late or for charging beyond your credit limit, even if your payment record is otherwise perfect.

Example: Providian charges a $39 late fee to any customer with a balance of $200 or more who misses a payment deadline, and $39 to those who exceed their credit line by 2% or more.

Self-defense: To avoid these fees…

● Mail your credit card payment 10 days to two weeks before its due date…or if you pay on-line, a few days before it's due.

● Ask to have your payment date moved so that the bill arrives right after a paycheck.

● Contact your issuer and arrange automatic on-line payments. Citibank, MBNA, Discover, American Express and others have on-line sign-ups to do this.

● Pay by phone at the toll-free number on the back of the credit card (there may be a charge from $5 to $15 for this service). The amount will be immediately withdrawn from your bank account and you'll receive a confirmation of the transaction by mail.

What to do: Ask your issuer to waive the fee—many will do so as a courtesy to customers with good payment records.

● **Biweekly mortgage payment fee.** The "magic" of a biweekly (every two weeks) mortgage payment is that you end up making the equivalent of 13 full mortgage payments in a year rather than the usual 12, reducing the time needed to pay down the mortgage and cutting interest payments substantially. But a biweekly payment plan from a bank often includes an up-front fee of several hundred dollars and monthly fees of about $10.

Self-defense: Instead, make extra principal payments with each of your regular monthly mortgage payments. You'll accelerate the payoff and reduce interest as much as you want to with no extra fees (assuming your mortgage allows this).

REAL ESTATE FEES

When selecting a home, the key is location, location, location, but at closing time, the key is fees, fees, fees…

● **Closing costs.** When shopping for a mortgage lender, consider not only the interest rate but also closing costs. By law, you'll receive from the lender up front a "good faith estimate" (GFE) of closing costs. This is an itemized list of estimated costs to be paid at closing (e.g., the lender's fees, appraisal charges, title insurance premium, a partial month's interest payment).

Self-defense: Apply with three different lenders and compare their GFEs. Filling out applications takes some time, but it costs nothing to apply—and you could save thousands of dollars. Use the free search engine at Bankrate.com. Then try to get fees waived or reduced or credited toward closing costs. The lender may not budge—but it's worth asking.

Have your GFE reviewed by an attorney or other professional well before the closing. The privately run National Mortgage Complaint Center (866-714-6466, *www.national mortgagecomplaintcenter.com*) will review it and tell you about any excessive fees.

Cost: $65.

Note: Banks should charge the buyer what they paid in appraisal, credit report and inspection fees. Often, they mark those fees up. Ask the lender to seek good deals on these items and pass along the savings to you. It may not—but it doesn't hurt to ask.

• **Title insurance.** When you get a new mortgage or refinance an old one, you must buy title insurance to protect against such problems as forgery of old title documents and potential interests of missing heirs. The premium is paid once and averages $800.

Self-defense: In some states, such as Texas, premiums are fixed by law. If the premium isn't fixed in your state, search under "title insurance" on the Internet or check the *Yellow Pages*. Call the companies to ask about their rates and coverage. If you're refinancing your mortgage and have lived in the house less than 10 years, ask to get title insurance at the less expensive "reissue" rate.

Beware of "Skip a Payment" Offers From Lenders

Banks and merchants often offer to let consumers "skip" payments on loans, or not make any payments for some months after making a purchase, as a marketing lure.

Trap: The payments aren't really skipped —full interest continues to run. So, in reality, the payment is just put off with interest added until the end of the loan. Even worse, lenders often impose a fee on those who use the skipped-payment option. The result is that the consumer pays extra interest plus a fee for doing so. Don't assume that any "skip a payment" offer is a good deal without reading the fine print.

Mary Hunt, editor, *Debt-Proof Living*, Box 2135, Paramount, CA 90723, *www.debtproofliving.com*.

Closing Accounts May Hurt Your Credit Rating

Don't close unneeded credit lines to improve your rating before applying for a loan. Doing so can hurt your credit score.

Example: You have three credit cards, each with a credit line of $5,000, for a total of $15,000. You've charged a total of $4,000 against two of the cards but nothing against the third. You cancel the third card, thinking that having one less credit card will improve your credit rating.

Reality: Initially you had used 26.7% of your available credit ($4,000 of $15,000). But after canceling the card, you have used 40% of your credit ($4,000 of $10,000). That percentage looks worse to the credit rating agencies, so it may harm your credit score.

Gerri Detweiler, credit specialist, Sarasota, FL, and author of *The Ultimate Credit Handbook*. Plume.

Better Credit Payments

If you pay your credit card bill on-line and send it on the day it is due, you could still be fined. Your credit card issuer may stipulate that payments processed after a *certain time*—such as 3 pm Eastern time, Monday through Friday—will be posted the next business day. Or the bill-paying service you use may not wire payments the same day you authorize them.

If your card issuer has a specific deadline time, notification should be posted on its Web site—or possibly the information was sent to you. If you can't find mention of the deadline among the issuer's documents, call customer service and ask them to tell you where the rule is posted.

Nancy Dunnan, a New York City–based financial and travel adviser and the author or coauthor of 25 books, including the best seller, *How to Invest $50–$5,000*. HarperCollins.

Credit-Counseling Firms Are Not Always Legitimate

Over the past two years, the IRS has revoked the tax-exempt status of at least 41 credit-counseling and debt-management agencies because they abused their non-profit status. Before signing up with a credit-counseling agency, ask questions to be sure it is a reputable firm.

Examples: Does the company get any form of consideration or compensation from the creditors themselves? If the answer is yes, then the company has an incentive to get you to pay back as much as possible—which is not in your favor. *Is the company a member of the Better Business Bureau?* If it is, the company is willing to have its practices scrutinized. *Is the firm licensed and bonded?* Companies that handle money should be licensed and bonded in case a client's funds are mishandled.

Brad Stroh, co-CEO, Freedom Financial Network LLC, which provides consumer debt-resolution services, San Mateo, CA.

Credit Card Smarts

If the interest rate on one of your credit cards is raised because of a late payment, issuers of *all* your other cards may raise your rates. Card issuers often boost rates if you make any late payment or if your credit score drops for any reason. To get a high interest rate reduced, pay future bills on time. The exact number of on-time payments depends on your card issuer—some Capital One cards require 12.

Worth trying: Call the card issuer, and ask for a lower rate. If the person you talk with cannot reduce the rate, ask to speak to a supervisor. Say you will close the account if you don't get the reduction.

Scott Bilker, founder, DebtSmart.com, Barnegat, NJ, and author of *Talk Your Way Out of Credit Card Debt.* Press One.

Low-Rate Credit Cards

With the average fixed rate for credit cards now around 13.1%, cardholders might want to look into these two nationally available low-rate cards—Simmons First Visa Platinum of Pine Bluff, Arkansas, with a fixed rate of 7.25% and no annual fee (800-272-2102, *www.simmonsfirst.com*) and Bank of America Cash Rewards Platinum Plus MasterCard of Charlotte, North Carolina, 9.9% and no annual fee (800-932-2775, *www.bankofamerica.com*).

Devek J. McKinley, CardWeb.com, Inc., 8359 Beacon Blvd., Fort Myers, FL 33907.

Better Overdraft Protection

Apply for an overdraft line of credit or link your checking account to your bank credit card or to a savings account at the same bank. If a check or debit overdraws the account, the bank covers it with an overdraft line of credit loan at an annual interest rate...transfers the amount of the overdraft to the credit card...or moves money from the savings account to cover the overdraft in the checking account. Moving the balance to a credit card gives a grace period of 20 to 25 days interest-free, allowing you time to get things straightened out before you pay back the overdraft. The bank usually charges a transfer fee for both the credit card and the savings account linking, but payment is guaranteed.

Jean Ann Fox, CFA, director, consumer protection, Consumer Federation of America, Washington, DC.

Switching Credit Cards? Money-Saving Strategies

Nancy Castleman, founder of GoodAdvicePress. com, a Web site advocating a better life through taking charge of one's finances, Elizaville, NY. She is coauthor of *Invest in Yourself: Six Secrets to a Rich Life*. Wiley.

I f you carry a balance, transferring to a card with a lower rate can be a great way to save money. But beware of the fine print in credit card agreements. *Balance transfer traps...*

TEASER RATES

Some balance transfer rates last for only two to three months.

Strategy: Make sure an introductory rate lasts for at least nine months before you transfer. Plan to pay off your balance within that time or transfer to a card with an annual percentage rate (APR) that you can live with after the introductory rate lapses. To compare deals, contact Cardratings.com (501-663-0314, *www.cardratings.com*).

TRANSFER FEES

Even a card with no annual fee might charge a fee when you transfer your balance. A few years back, that fee might have been a reasonable 1%, but now it could be as high as 4%. On a $5,000 balance, that's $200.

Strategy: If you're thinking of transferring your balance, call your current credit card company and say that you're going to switch unless it matches the interest rate you've been offered. *About half of cardholders who ask for a better deal get one.* If the issuer agrees, there's no need to transfer your balance and incur a transfer fee. If you decide to switch, call the new card's issuer and get written confirmation that it will waive any transfer fee.

INCONSISTENT RATES

Credit card companies typically charge low interest rates for balance transfers but higher rates for new purchases.

Example: You transfer a $5,000 balance to a card with a 0% introductory rate on transfers and a 29% rate on new purchases. In the first month, you charge $300 in new purchases and make a $300 payment. The credit card company automatically will apply the $300 payment to your transferred balance and charge you the 29% rate on your $300 in new purchases.

Strategy: When you transfer a balance to a new card, don't use that card for new purchases.

UNIVERSAL DEFAULT

The more credit cards you have, the more likely you are to accidentally miss a payment on one of them—and these days, if you're late on a payment on any credit card or other bill, you could dramatically increase the rates you're charged on *all* of your cards. At least half of credit card companies now include a "universal default" clause in their fine print. The clause gives them the right to raise interest rates when a customer misses a payment—even on another company's credit card—and if they decide your debt level is too high.

Strategy: Set yourself up for automatic bill-paying, so you don't miss payments, and keep debt at 30% (or less) of your available credit.

Surprisingly, having too few accounts can hurt your credit score—it is harder for lenders to determine your creditworthiness—so don't be in a rush to close accounts unless they charge an annual fee. Pay credit card bills promptly. Late payments stay on your credit report for seven years.

Low-Rate Credit Card Trap

C redit cards that promise low or zero interest rates on balance transfers often have terms that say—(1) If you use the card for any new charges, the payments you make go to pay off the transferred balance first, while the new charges incur top rates, so your total interest charge goes up every month, and (2) If you are late with a single payment, the interest rate will go up on your entire balance.

Safety: If you transfer a balance to such a card, lock it away and don't use it for new charges and make your payment on it early each month, preferably electronically so it can't get lost in the mail or be delayed in processing.

Curtis Arnold, president and founder, CardRatings.com, which educates consumers about credit cards, North Little Rock, AR.

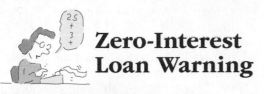

Zero-Interest Loan Warning

Zero-interest loans offered by many retailers can be costly.

Problem: If you fail to repay the loan in full before the term expires, you could be socked with interest charges from the date of purchase. Even if you are only a few dollars short of the balance due, you could be hit with interest—sometimes in excess of 25% a year—on the full amount.

Study the fine print carefully before signing up for this type of loan.

Consumer Reports, 101 Truman Ave., Yonkers, NY 10703.

Get Out of Debt— Simple Steps from Personal Finance Guru David Bach

David Bach, founder and chairman of FinishRich Media LLC, New York City, *www.finishrich.com* and author of six *New York Times* best sellers, including *The Automatic Millionaire Homeowner*. Broadway. He is a featured expert on *The Oprah Winfrey Show*.

Many strategies for debt reduction are ineffective in today's environment, in which short-term interest rates have gone up and stringent bankruptcy laws allow credit card companies greater leverage against cash-strapped customers. *Here are my "guerilla" strategies to get out of debt and turn your financial life around…*

1. CUT CREDIT CARD INTEREST

When you're having financial difficulties and your credit is poor, you might not be able to transfer balances to lower-rate cards. But you can win concessions from card companies. You can ask for a lower rate—often it will be reduced by five or more percentage points.

My suggestion: In a worst-case scenario, ask about a "hardship program"—your interest rate could be reduced to 0%, provided that you repay your debt with an automatic payment plan.

Downside: It will be reflected on your credit report. Ask that your participation not be reported to the credit bureaus. Read all documentation carefully before signing anything.

Credit card companies don't publicize these programs. Be persistent. If the customer service rep can't help you, keep asking for supervisors.

2. PAY OFF CARDS WITH THE SMALLEST BALANCES FIRST

Why not pay off the cards with higher interest rates first? Most people stick to debt-reduction plans for a few months, then become frustrated at their slow progress and give up. You need a series of tangible victories along the way. The sense of accomplishment you get from paying off one of your credit cards—even one with a small balance—can motivate you to pay off other cards in the future.

3. STOP LIVING OFF YOUR HOME EQUITY

If you have a mortgage—especially an adjustable-rate mortgage—and have been taking advantage of soaring home prices in your area by pulling cash out of your home, it's time to stop. Interest rates are creeping up, and home prices are weakening in many areas.

My suggestions: Before rates go higher, take steps to reduce the amount you owe on an adjustable-rate mortgage and other variable-rate loans, such as home-equity lines of credit, by converting to fixed-rate loans.

Also: Pay down your mortgage early by requesting a biweekly payment plan. This can reduce a 30-year mortgage to 23 years or less. On a $300,000 mortgage at 7%, a borrower would save more than $103,000 in interest.

4. IF INCOME DROPS, REDUCE SPENDING, TOO

I've seen many families get into financial trouble because they don't alter their spending habits when one spouse stops working.

My suggestions: If your household goes from having two incomes to one—say, your spouse wants to go back to school—practice living on one income for six months to see if you can. Also, to prepare for layoffs and other losses of income, build up an emergency fund. Otherwise, a minor financial crisis will force you to use credit cards to make ends meet, plunging you into high interest rate debt.

5. BECOME A FEE FIGHTER

If you're like most Americans, you pay hundreds of dollars a year in late fees and other annual charges.

My suggestions: Call and negotiate. A credit card company often will waive or reduce fees if you threaten to close your account.

Negotiate a waiver of your annual fee. Unless your card is affiliated with frequent-flier programs or rebate offers, you should not be paying an annual fee. If you are, ask that the fee be credited back to your account.

If you know you'll miss the due date on a credit card payment, ask the card issuer to add an extra few days to the grace period for that month.

Helpful: Take advantage of new programs that help you save. For example, Bank of America's Keep the Change program (800-900-9000, *www.bankofamerica. com*, click on "Keep the Change") rounds up to the nearest dollar every purchase a customer makes on a Bank of America debit card, then transfers the difference to the customer's savings account. The bank matches 100% of your Keep the Change savings for the first three months and 5% of your savings each year, up to $250 a year.

Bills It's OK to Pay Late

Nancy Dunnan, a New York City–based financial and travel adviser and the author or coauthor of 25 books, including the best seller, *How to Invest $50–$5,000*. HarperCollins.

Many people are finding it difficult to pay all of their bills on time. Helpful: Call companies and lenders to ask if late payments will appear on your credit report. Begin with your electric, gas, water, telephone and cable providers. Find out exactly how late your payments can be, and write down the name of the person you spoke with and the date.

Other ideas…

• **Renters can ask landlords about late payments.** Many will be flexible for one or two months.

• **Personal loans.** If you've borrowed money from family or friends, contact them by phone or in person and ask for some extra time. You will probably be given several months' leeway. (Delinquent personal loans are typically not reported to the credit bureaus.)

• **If you have good credit,** you may be able to transfer credit card balances to a new card with a lower interest rate and even be granted a grace period to make your first payment. *Caution:* A small balance transfer fee may apply, plus lower interest rates may not cover new purchases, so do your research.

• **Retail stores may allow good customers to make late payments on their credit cards.** When you call, state how soon you can make a payment. Then, be sure to stop all unnecessary shopping at that store.

• **Tuition.** Call the school's business office; explain your situation, and work out a schedule for delayed or reduced payments if possible.

Important: You must pay some bills on time, including mortgages, auto loans and leases, American Express bills.

Bottom line: Always get a written confirmation that missed or late payments will not be reported to the credit bureaus.

Having Too Few Credit Cards Can Hurt Your Credit Rating

That's because when a credit record is thin, it doesn't provide lenders with enough evidence to judge creditworthiness.

What to do: If you have only one credit card, open two or three other credit lines—such as another credit card, a consumer installment loan or a car loan—just to establish a solid record of making credit payments on time.

Evan Hendricks, editor, *Privacy Times*, Box 302, Cabin John, MD 20818. He is author of *Credit Scores & Credit Reports*. Privacy Times.

Smart Home Buying

Making an offer on a house? Include the following contingencies, so you can be sure the home lives up to your expectations.

•**Insist on a home inspection** by a professional inspector to uncover defects.

•**Get extra inspections,** if warranted by the general inspector, by structural engineers or other professionals.

•**Make sure the house is insurable—** insurers are reluctant to write policies on homes in certain areas, such as those prone to wildfires and mud slides.

•**Make your offer contingent on finding a willing buyer for your current home—**but you may need to agree to let the house's current owners continue marketing the home until you can make your offer firm.

Elizabeth Razzi, author of *The Fearless Home Buyer*. Stewart, Tabori & Chang.

Buying a Home in a Private Community

Karen Eastman Bigos, real estate broker, Towne Realty Group, Short Hills, NJ.

Before buying a home in a private community, find out the following information…

•**What are the rules?** Ask your agent or seller for governing documents and covenants, conditions and restrictions (CC&Rs). If the rules seem too stringent, keep looking.

•**How much are dues and maintenance fees, and what do they cover?** Fees can range from $100 a year to thousands a month, depending on the community and its amenities. Compare dues in communities similar to the one you are considering.

•**Are there enough cash reserves for future repairs?** Roughly 25% of all dues should go toward replenishing accounts for repairs. It also would help to know the age of the driveways, walkways and common areas and when they will be repaired or replaced again.

•**What are the neighbors like?** Strike up casual conversations with some residents to get a feel for the general atmosphere in the community.

If You're Looking for a Home Abroad…

To find a home overseas—for your personal use or investment purposes—use an Internet search engine such as Google. To get listings, type in "real estate" and the name of the country you want to search. Get listings and information on living and investing abroad at *www.escapeartist.com* and at *www.internationalliving.com*. Search for real estate agents and for real estate listings at *www.worldproperties.com*, sponsored by the International Consortium of Real Estate Associations. Consider agents who are certified international property specialists—they tend to have more expertise than others.

Kiplinger's Personal Finance, 1729 H St. NW, Washington, DC 20006.

Better Research

Prospective home buyers and sellers can learn about a property before looking at it. Zillow.com offers an aerial photo, map and estimated market value for most single and multifamily homes. You also can see lists of what homes recently sold for in the area.

Reduce Costs When Buying a Home

Money, Time-Life Bldg., Rockefeller Center, New York City 10020.

There are ways to reduce costs when you are buying a home. *Here are four of them...*

•**Shop for a mortgage** on your own at local banks and on Web sites, such as *www.bankrate.com*—to save the mortgage broker's fee.

•**Compare title agent fees.** Don't just accept your broker's in-house title agent—the agent has no incentive to reduce costs and may be getting undisclosed commissions.

•**Negotiate all rates and fees,** and ask for any unreasonable ones to be lowered. Find averages for your area at the Bankrate site.

•**Give yourself closing-date flexibility**—that way, you can walk away if a previously undisclosed charge shows up at the closing.

Mortgage Smarts

Jack M. Guttentag, PhD, professor of finance emeritus, aka "The Mortgage Professor," Wharton School, University of Pennsylvania, Philadelphia, *www.mtgprofessor.com.*

Aggressive mortgage service firms may demand that you pay thousands of dollars you don't owe or face foreclosure. The right to handle mortgages—collecting and recording monthly payments, plus insurance and escrow charges—is regularly sold by banks to third-party companies. Those companies then sometimes resell the rights to other firms.

Servicers have the right to foreclose if payments fall far behind, but human and software errors can lead to mistaken charges. Some dishonest firms add charges for services that buyers have not requested...fail to inform the buyers...then deduct a portion of each mortgage payment to pay for the unwanted services. This results in multiple mortgage underpayments—which can lead to foreclosure.

For more information, search for the Real Estate Settlement Procedures Act (RESPA) on *www.hud.gov.*

Secrets of Getting the Best Price on a House In Today's Market

Mark Nash, a real estate broker with Coldwell Banker Residential Brokerage in Evanston, IL (*www.marknashrealtor.com*). He is author of *1001 Tips for Buying and Selling a Home,* Thomson, and a frequent guest on CBS's *The Early Show* and *Dow Jones MarketWatch.*

If you're thinking about buying a house, you have an advantage that most buyers haven't enjoyed in many years—the chance to bargain on the price. The "seller's market" of the past few years has become a buyer's market.

However, while the market is weaker in many parts of the country, it's not in a tailspin.

21

That means you can't start out with an unrealistically low offer.

WINNING TACTICS

As a rule, make your first offer 90% of a reasonable asking price. That might not seem like a big discount, but if you had made a 90% offer a year ago, the seller might have slammed the door in your face—or if you had delayed in accepting the original price, the seller might have *raised* it by 10%.

Today, time is on your side. You have more time, for instance, to look at the houses for sale in the community and weed out the ones that are priced far above average.

A weaker market also means that no matter how impressed you are with a house on your first visit, you can probably wait a day before making an offer. Use that day to consider the financial burden of buying the house, as well as the pluses and minuses of actually living in it—redecorating, leaving old neighbors, etc. Also consider any repairs or improvements that need to be made.

Don't be pressured by a seller who says that he/she expects the property to sell fast. If he didn't want an offer from you, he would simply say good-bye and not discuss how fast he expects a sale.

Note: Do not let how long a house has been on the market affect your bidding strategy.

If, after a day, you still like the house, make your 90% offer. If it's not accepted, tell the seller you'll accept a higher price as long as he makes certain improvements that your first visit showed were needed.

If the seller still holds firm, there may be nothing to change his mind. But take your best shot by saying something like this: "I'm really afraid that my lender's appraisal won't justify your asking price."

Alternatively, you could raise your offer to 95% of the price or back down and offer the full original price. By having thought about the property overnight, you'll be in a better position to know which choice to make.

BITING YOUR TONGUE

When visiting a house where the seller and/or his agent is present, it's tempting to act like a savvy buyer. Even though you and the seller are business adversaries, be cordial without letting the seller know whether or not you like the property. Jot down any problems to discuss later.

And, don't gush when you see a house you like. That only encourages a seller or a seller's agent to hold firm to the asking price.

Be as accommodating as possible with the closing date. By being flexible, you improve the chance of your offer being accepted even if it's below the asking price.

GETTING EXPERT ADVICE

Buying a house can be tricky, even if you've done it before.

Solution: Hire a buyer's representative (instead of a real estate agent) who is accredited by the National Association of Realtors. He can steer you through the purchasing process and help you avoid many of the pitfalls.

Examples: Faults that sellers have concealed or new zoning regulations that could adversely affect property values.

A buyer's representative can be particularly helpful in states where real estate agents represent both the buyer and the seller.

To find an accredited buyer's representative (ABR), contact the association's Real Estate Buyer's Agent Council (800-648-6224, *www.rebac.net*). ABR fees, which you would pay, typically range from 1% to 3% of the sales price. This is in addition to any real estate agent fee—which is paid by the seller.

Ask prospective ABRs for several references. When you speak with references, ask about problems that the ABR helped avoid, such as buying a house with a serious defect.

Caution: In some areas, the seller's real estate agent may try to dissuade you from retaining professional advice on the grounds that state law makes the agent a representative of both you and the seller.

My advice: Disregard the argument if your real estate agent is also the seller's agent. Because of a natural conflict of interest, it's impossible for an agent to fairly represent the interests of a buyer and seller of the same property.

An ABR can be particularly helpful in explaining local laws that regulate the offer-making procedure.

Typically, you make an offer by signing a "contract to purchase" and giving the seller earnest money, usually a check, that will be cashed and applied to the purchase if it goes through. Because of the softening market, earnest money today is rarely more than 5% of the purchase price.

Contracts to purchase, which vary widely from state to state, spell out conditions under which the money will be returned.

Examples: If there's an unresolved building code violation or a snag in the buyer's financing.

ABRs also pinpoint problems that may be difficult to see.

Example: Sellers in most states must give prospective buyers a copy of a recent report made by a state-authorized inspector. If the seller hasn't had such an inspection done, usually the buyer pays to have one done. The seller's inspection report will reveal serious flaws with the property, such as water seepage in the basement.

It won't, however, disclose such potential problems as a heating and air-conditioning system that has only one year left of its service life. ABRs are trained to alert clients to such situations. Often, an ABR might suggest having your own inspection done, which usually costs $300 to $600, depending on the size of the house.

LINING UP FINANCING

Have financing in place before you shop for a house. Ask your bank or mortgage company for a "preapproval" letter that states how much you can borrow to buy property.

Few agents will accept an offer from anyone without this, and the letter can be a valuable bargaining chip with an owner who is selling property without an agent.

Reason: Owner-sellers are often swamped with offers from buyers without financing. With letter in hand, you'll be someone with whom they'll want to do business.

More from Mark Nash...

Protecting Yourself When Buying or Selling Your Home

When buying or selling a home, protect yourself from identity thieves. Ask all parties involved if they have a *Client Identity Protection Program* in place—many loan processors, law firms, title and escrow companies and others have these programs, which use passwords and limited access to help protect financial and personal information. Whether buying or selling, never give your Social Security number by phone, fax or e-mail. Deliver your credit reports in person—don't fax or e-mail them. For the IRS-required W-9 form, which includes your Social Security number, write "do not copy, fax or scan" across the top and bottom.

Live in a Luxury Hotel

Buy rooms that have been converted to condominiums. Purchasers can stay in the hotel whenever they want for as long as they wish. Some hotels allow you to rent out the property and receive a percentage of the rental income. The condo-converted rooms are usually sold fully furnished and are entitled to all hotel amenities, including housekeeping and concierge. Most hotels offering condominium sales are in major cities or popular vacation areas.

More information: Visit *www.condohotels.com.*

 # Home Insurance Smarts

Danny Lipford, syndicated program host of *Today's Homeowner*, regular contributor to CBS's *The Early Show* and remodeling contractor, Mobile, AL.

Home insurance payouts are held by the mortgage lender when a house is destroyed by fire or other disaster.

The mortgage lender pays them to the home owner as the house is rebuilt.

Problem: If the lender doesn't release funds when the contractor insists on payment, the home owner may have to pay out of pocket until the lender releases the money.

Self-defense: Have the contractor put in the contract a statement acknowledging that he will not receive money until the home owner has received it from the mortgage lender.

Also: When buying home insurance, include an ordinance or law provision. This covers the cost of upgrading your rebuilt home to meet codes that were not in effect when your original home was built.

All About Renter's Insurance

Nancy Dunnan, a New York City–based financial and travel adviser and the author or coauthor of 25 books, including the best seller, *How to Invest $50–$5,000*. HarperCollins.

Most people have more possessions than they realize. Before you discuss insuring your belongings with your insurance agent, make a list of what you own, including electronic equipment, clothes, furniture, jewelry, etc.

Here's a brief outline of what you need to know before meeting with your agent…

1. Landlords very rarely cover renter's belongings that are stolen or damaged.

2. Renter's insurance will cover your daughter if her possessions are lost or damaged by fire or smoke, theft, wind or water—but not from damage due to floods.

3. This type of insurance will pay some or all (depending upon the policy) of the cost of a legal defense if someone is injured in your apartment and you are sued.

4. Most policies will reimburse some or all of the additional expense involved if, let's say, there's a fire and you must live elsewhere.

I recommend purchasing a replacement-cost policy. That way, the insurance company will pay the actual cost of replacing lost or damaged items at today's cost. In contrast, with a standard policy, you recover only the current value of items, which can be substantially lower than what it would cost to replace them.

If you have unusual valuables, such as a stamp collection, or you've been accumulating antique jewelry, or own a musical instrument, ask your agent about adding a "floater," a type of rider that covers losses on certain types of movable property wherever the losses occur. The standard renter's policy is unlikely to cover these and other valuables.

Better Real Estate Buying

Here are five strategies to help you organize to buy property efficiently.

• **Get preapproved for a mortgage.** Prequalification letters are meaningless.

• **Negotiate the mortgage origination fee with your lender**—and the commission with your real estate agent.

• **Use the Internet to look for homes**—magazines and other sources go out of date quickly.

• **If a buyer wants to back out after a contract is signed,** let him. It is too costly for the seller to sue to force a closing.

• **Comparable-property listings are only a starting point for valuing a home.** Upgrades and location also must be factored in.

Rhonda Duffy, CEO and broker, Duffy Realty, Atlanta, *www.duffyrealtyofatlanta.com*.

A 50-Year Mortgage?

Some lenders now offer a 50-year mortgage option. These mortgages may be good for first-time home buyers who otherwise couldn't afford the monthly payments and any buyers who plan to stay in a home for three to seven years. A 50-year loan of $300,000 at 6.5% costs $1,691 a month, about $200 a month less than a 30-year mortgage.

Caution: Because the payments stretch out for 20 years longer, the 50-year mortgage will cost $332,040 more in interest over the life of the loan.

John Sauro, president of North Atlantic Mortgage Corp., Stamford, CT, *www.northatlanticmortgage.com.*

Before You Renovate...

Some renovations can actually hurt your home's resale value.

•**Swimming pools,** except in certain hot-weather areas, such as Arizona and Florida —buyers worry about upkeep, insurance and risks for small children.

•**An addition that does not enhance the home's appearance from outside.**

•**Trendy finishes for appliances and hardware**—trends change quickly.

•**A circular tub with massaging jets in the master bathroom**—busy people have little time to spend in a tub, and parents with small children prefer a conventional tub. An oversize shower is more attractive.

Consensus of real estate agents, reported in *Money,* Time-Life Bldg., Rockefeller Center, New York City 10020.

How to Save Thousands On College Costs

Rick Darvis, president, College Funding, Inc., which trains financial professionals in college funding services (*www.solutionsforcollege.com*), 121 N. Main St., Plentywood, MT 59294. He is author of *College Solution—A Roadmap to Selecting the Best Strategy to Fund College.* College Funding, Inc.

If you haven't saved enough for your child or grandchild's college education, cheer up. The official tuition amounts colleges post on their Web sites mean even less than the sticker prices pasted on windows of new cars. If you understand how the financial aid game is played, you can find some generous unadvertised deals at colleges and universities throughout the country.

Here are the strategies that the top college-planning specialists share with their clients...

•**Don't hesitate to apply for financial aid.** Fill out financial aid forms even if you think you won't qualify for needs-based aid. A couple making $130,000 a year, for instance, may still snag a needs-based aid package if their child ends up at a pricey institution, and the income ceiling for aid can rise significantly with more than one child attending college. Besides, the same paperwork often is necessary to qualify for tuition discounts and merit scholarships. Obtain a copy of the standard form, called the *Free Application for Federal Student Aid* (FAFSA), on-line at *www.fafsa.ed.gov* or from your school's guidance department.

•**Ask for tuition discounts.** Whether or not your family qualifies for financial aid, it pays to look for tuition discounts. The nation's private colleges and universities are currently giving incoming freshmen an average tuition discount of 41%, according to CollegeBoard.com. These price breaks may be awarded regardless of the parents' income.

To boost your chances, identify schools where your child's scores on standardized tests and grades put him/her in the top quarter of the applicant pool. You can compare your child's academic standing with that of students enrolled at a school by looking at student profiles posted on *www.collegeboard.com* and *www.princetonreview.com* (click on "College").

•**Play on rivalries.** Even if your child is not athletic, consider applying to schools that face off with one another on the football field or volleyball court. You'll be exploiting their long-standing rivalry, not only in sports but in academics and other extracurricular pursuits. Schools don't like losing good athletes or good students to other schools in their athletic conferences. Competing schools will learn where your child is applying because you list these colleges and universities on your financial aid form. To find out which universities are in the same athletic conference, go to *www.ncaa.org*.

• **Look beyond your own backyard.** The school that most wants your child could be two or three time zones away. Colleges always are looking for students from faraway states to boost the geographic diversity of their campuses. California kids, for example, are in hot demand everywhere in the US except the West.

• **Play the cheap card.** Even if your child would prefer to attend a pricey private school, make sure he applies to at least one in-state public university. When a private university believes it is competing with a cheaper alternative, it's more likely to kick in money to seal the deal.

• **Select a college with empty seats.** Some perfectly fine colleges and universities are rejected by students more than others. You can tell how often a school is spurned by asking about its enrollment yield. For instance, if a school accepts 1,000 students per year, but only 200 accept offers of admission, that's a low 20% yield. Popular schools have yields in the 50% to 60% range. Schools with more seats to fill are motivated to entice a child to attend and often are willing to negotiate tuition based on other offers that the student has received. Your son or daughter also can apply to a school with a lower yield in hope of receiving a fat award package, which he can then use as leverage with schools that he really wants to attend.

• **Try negotiating.** If you're disappointed in the aid package your child receives from a college, don't give up. It is possible to negotiate a better awards package, but don't use the word "negotiate" with financial aid officers—they dislike the term. Instead say, "I would like to appeal the financial aid offer for my child." When making an appeal, send copies of award letters from other colleges to the school your child really wants to attend.

The Independent 529 Plan

The independent 529 plan has the tax benefits of other 529 college savings plans and lets participants lock in private-college tuition rates. The plan was created by a consortium of more than 270 private universities and colleges. If the child doesn't attend a member institution, you can roll the savings into another 529 plan or take a refund.

Information: 888-718-7878, *www.independent529plan.org*.

Is It Important to Go to An Ivy League School?

Only seven CEOs from the top 50 Fortune 500 companies graduated from Ivy League schools.

Also: College students who were accepted at top schools but attended less selective ones earned just as much 20 years later as their peers who attended highly selective colleges.

The Quarterly Journal of Economics, Harvard University, 1875 Cambridge St., Cambridge, MA 02138.

529 Smarts

A single 529 account can be used for several children's or grandchildren's college savings. While there can be only one beneficiary per account, you can open an account for your oldest child or grandchild, pay his/her college expenses, then change the beneficiary designation and save for a younger child. This costs less in maintenance fees than opening several accounts.

However: You might want separate accounts for other reasons—you can invest differently for each child, keep all children's assets separate and put more money into the accounts (you can give away $12,000 per recipient per year) without having to pay gift tax.

Joe Hurley, CEO, Savingforcollege.com, LLC, Pittsford, NY.

A Scholarship at My Age?—Here's How to Get One

Ben Kaplan, author of *How to Go to College Almost for Free.* HarperCollins. His company, ScholarshipCoach.com, sells the *CD-ROM Adult and Non-Traditional Scholarships That Totally Rock! www.scholarshipcoach.com.*

Have you thought about continuing your education but wondered whether it was worth the cost? Before making a decision, consider applying for a scholarship. They're available for people of just about any age.

In fact, there are as many scholarships, grants and other financial incentives available to adult students as to younger ones. Many scholarships don't have age restrictions, and many others are targeted specifically at adults.

A growing number of adults are going back to school to win promotions at work, launch second careers or just for the joy of learning. To compete for these students, many colleges, universities and vocational schools offer scholarships.

Adult scholarships vary from $100 or so to full tuition. But don't ignore small scholarships. If you successfully apply for several of them, they add up.

WHERE TO LOOK

There are a number of sources of scholarships out there…

● **Corporations.** Many companies offer scholarships to the general public, not just employees, to help their communities and also bolster their image.

Example: Talbots, the apparel retailer, annually awards five $10,000 scholarships to women returning to college to seek a bachelor's degree and fifty $1,000 scholarships to women working toward an undergraduate degree.

Information: 781-749-7600, *www.talbots. com/about/scholar/scholar.asp.*

Similarly, insurance giant GEICO annually awards ten $1,000 scholarships to students who achieve academic excellence while balancing additional commitments, such as family and/or a career.

Information: Available from Golden Key International Honour Society, the organization affiliated with the scholarship program, *www.goldenkey.org.*

Many companies also have tuition-reimbursement programs.

Example: United Technologies reimburses employees full tuition for degree programs and also gives them three hours of paid leave a week to take classes that don't have to be work related. On completion of a degree, employees are awarded $10,000 in company stock.

Some companies require that courses be work related, but others don't have such requirements. Check with the human resources department where you work.

● **Business, labor and religious organizations.** If you're a member of one of these groups, ask about scholarships.

Example: The AFL-CIO's Union Plus scholarship program offers a wide range of financial awards for union members and their families.

Information: 301-431-5404, *www.union privilege.org/benefits/education/scholarships/nlcs.cfm.*

Another group, the Business and Professional Women's Foundation, awards scholarships to women over age 25 who've been accepted to an accredited university. Amounts vary according to financial need.

Information: 800-525-3729, *www.bpw usa.org* and go to "Scholarships."

•**Federal, state and local governments.** Federal Pell Grants are the best known among government scholarships, but states and larger cities often offer their own, some of which target older students. Also bear in mind that the Lifetime Learning Credit (a tax credit), which is equal to 20% of the first $10,000 in educational expenses, is open to students of any age.

Information: Contact your state and local education departments. For information on Pell Grants and other federal programs, contact the US Department of Education (800-433-3243 or 319-337-5665, *http://student aid.ed.gov/students/publications/student_ guide/index.html*).

Many government grants are targeted at students with financial need, but this takes into consideration the cost of tuition, so that even someone with relatively high income might qualify for a grant to an expensive school.

The calculation is complex. But you can use a free on-line financial aid calculator, such as the one at my site, *www.scholarship coach.com.* It's best to ask for advice from the financial aid department of the school you're considering.

Many state colleges offer free or discounted tuition to students over a certain age— typically 60. In some states, however, free tuition doesn't apply if a course is taken for credit toward a degree.

Information: Contact your state's education department or local state colleges.

•**Schools.** Colleges, universities and vocational institutions—especially those that have a high percentage of older students on campus, such as commuter colleges—offer more scholarships to adults than ever before.

Example: The University of Wisconsin at Madison offers scholarships of $1,000 and $5,000 a year for adults who return to college.

Information: 608-263-6960, *www.dcs. wisc.edu/info/finanserv/scholarships/osher.htm.*

Schools are also one of the best sources of information about all types of scholarships.

Example: Michigan State University tells prospective adult students about its own scholarships and also helps them find financial awards elsewhere. MSU's Web site recently listed more than a dozen organizations that award scholarships to adult students.

Information: 517-432-6123, ext. 123, *www. lib.msu.edu/harris23/grants/3nontrad.htm.*

Many schools can also tell you about corporations, unions and other organizations that offer scholarships to adult students in their area. When you contact a school, start with the admissions and/or financial aid department or "scholarship" office. Also ask if the school has a department specifically for "non-traditional" students who are resuming their education that may know of scholarships that aren't listed with the financial aid office.

Then contact the departments in charge of the subjects you're interested in studying. They may know of still other scholarships and grants, particularly those for students in their fields of study.

SHOW ME THE MONEY

A great place to expand your search is the Internet. There you'll find dozens of scholarship databases. *Some of the most informative…*

•**College Answer,** a general nationwide database of about 2.8 million scholarships (*http://salliemae.collegeanswer.com/pay ing/scholarship_search/pay_scholarship_ search.jsp*).

•**The College Board's Scholarship Search,** which lists organizations offering scholarships, internships, grants and loans (*http://apps.collegeboard.com/cbsearch_ss/ welcome.jsp*).

•**FastWeb,** which lists scholarships and also part-time jobs (*www.fastweb.com*).

Mistake: Using only one scholarship database. No matter how many scholarships a site lists, it inevitably misses others because new sources of money are being created as older ones are discontinued.

My own site has a free tool, the Scholarship Surfer, that helps you navigate the myriad databases and gives you tips on how to best use each one.

WINNING STRATEGY

Research the organization that sponsors the scholarship program and try to find out what type of recipient they're looking for. Past recipients are often listed on the sponsor's Web site, and dozens of winning entries are featured on my Web site.

Ask former recipients about their winning tactics. In some cases, the scholarship sponsor might have been looking for students who will go into a particular line of work. Others might have sought a member of a minority group or a person changing careers.

A Special Savings Account for Grade School Children?

Nancy Dunnan, a New York City–based financial and travel adviser and the author or coauthor of 25 books, including the best seller, *How to Invest $50–$5,000*. HarperCollins.

With the Coverdell Education Savings Account (ESA), a child, the beneficiary of the account, can be in a public, private or parochial kindergarten, grade school, high school or college. The money cannot be used for preschool expenses. *Other key points…*

• **Annual amount.** You can contribute up to $2,000 a year per child. In addition to parents and other relatives, friends can also contribute. The total from everyone, however, cannot be more than $2,000 per child. Contributions of more than $2,000 will result in the account being charged a 6% annual "excess contribution tax."

• **Taxes.** Contributions are not tax deductible. However, the money in the account grows tax deferred and is not taxed when withdrawn as long as it is used for "qualified" expenses, such as education-related books, computers, equipment, fees, Internet access, room and board, supplies, software, transportation, tuition and tutoring.

• **Child's age.** Contributions can be made only while the child is under age 18. And the money must usually be used by the time the child turns 30. At that point, the money in the account no longer grows tax free, and withdrawals are hit with a 10% tax penalty.

Loophole: When the beneficiary turns 30, he can roll over any money left in the account into a new Coverdell for a sibling, niece, nephew or even the beneficiary's own child.

• **Your income.** To contribute the full $2,000 a year to an ESA, a single taxpayer's modified adjusted gross income must be no more than $95,000…$190,000 if married filing jointly. Limited contributions can be made by single taxpayers who earn up to $110,000 and for married couples up to $220,000— above these caps, you're locked out.

IRS Publication 970, *Tax Benefits for Education*, is surprisingly readable and helpful. Download it at *www.irs.gov* or call 800-829-3676.

Finances After Divorce

Create an emergency fund—figure out how much you would need to live on for eight months, then put that amount in a savings account. If your company offers a 401(k) or 403(b) retirement plan and matching contributions, join the plan and contribute enough to get the maximum match possible. Fund a Roth IRA if your income is below $95,000 per year. You can put in $4,000 if you are under age 50 and $5,000 if you are 50 or older—and when you retire, there is no tax on contributions or earnings.

Edward Mendlowitz, CPA, partner in the CPA firm WithumSmith+Brown, 1 Spring St., New Brunswick, NJ 08901. He is author of *The Adviser's Guide to Family Business Succession Planning*. American Institute of Certified Public Accountants.

Secrets to a Fair Divorce

Gayle Rosenwald Smith, JD, an attorney who specializes in family and divorce law in Philadelphia, *www.divorceandmoneybook.com*. She is author of *Divorce and Money: Everything You Need to Know*. Perigee.

Why do some people receive equitable divorce settlements while others get the short end of the stick? The answer lies in the ability to keep emotions in check. *Based on my legal experience and on interviews with hundreds of judges for my book, here are secrets to getting your fair share...*

• **Hire a top-notch divorce lawyer.** Get referrals from friends and relatives, your accountant or family attorney, or try *www.law yers.com.*

• **Consider the end of your marriage as a business transaction.** This may not be easy emotionally, but tell yourself that your partnership didn't work out. You'll fare better if you wrap up loose ends and separate on good terms.

List dollar amounts for your important financial needs, such as housing, utilities, insurance, transportation, credit cards and other debt payments, retirement contributions and other savings. Refer to this list whenever you sense yourself becoming emotional or irrational. Don't waste time worrying about anything that isn't on your list.

Case study: A nonworking wife was battling her husband for the couple's $12,000, state-of-the-art home theater system. It was a hot button because they had spent months researching it. I pointed out that the top priority on her divorce list was health-care coverage. While federal law (COBRA) ensured that she would continue getting coverage under her husband's plan for 36 months after her divorce, she still would have to pay $200 per month. My client decided to let her husband have the home theater system, which was now worth much less than the purchase price, if he agreed to pay her premiums—potentially more than $7,000 for the three years.

• **Eliminate joint debt.** Pay off credit cards and nonmortgage-related loans from joint funds, or transfer balances to cards in your own name.

Reason: When you reach a property settlement that stipulates who is responsible for joint debts, it won't be binding on a third party, such as a bank. If your ex-spouse defaults on a credit obligation, the bank still can pursue you for the money it is owed.

Important: If you file joint returns, you are liable for your spouse's taxes. If you fear that your spouse has understated income or

overstated expenses, ask your accountant about preparing your returns as "married filing separately." If you trust your spouse, ask your accountant if you can get a tax break by signing a joint return for the year of the divorce.

• **Protect assets you had before the marriage.** In most states, money, securities, property and gifts you brought into the marriage remain yours after the divorce, but you will need proof of ownership of those original assets.

Example: Say you owned a condominium prior to your marriage. After you got married, you sold it and put the sale price toward a home purchase with your husband. In many states, you may be able to get full or partial credit for that down payment when you sell your house, but you will need copies of statements showing withdrawals from your separate bank account that were deposited into a joint account or delivered to the bank or mortgage company. These should be with your closing documents for the home purchase.

List all your joint assets to ensure that they are included in the "marital estate." Include your home, vehicles, bank and investment accounts and often-overlooked assets—prepaid life insurance, frequent-flier miles, club memberships, season tickets to sporting events, upcoming tax refunds, vacation pay and stock options.

Smart: Hire an experienced accountant or a divorce planner to assess your assets and help you propose an appropriate settlement based on your financial situation. For a referral, contact the Institute for Divorce Financial Analysts, 800-875-1760, *www.insti tutedfa.com.*

Caution: If you suspect that your spouse is trying to hide personal or joint assets from you (see the following article), take action.

• **Opt for mediation if you feel that you can negotiate directly with your spouse.** It costs much less than divorce litigation.

How it works: A trained divorce mediator sits down with both parties, negotiates an agreement and prepares a memorandum of understanding, which then is reviewed by a lawyer and submitted to the court for a judge's approval.

Ask your attorney to recommend a local mediator or contact the Association for Conflict Resolution, 202-464-9700, *www.acrnet.org*.

• **Familiarize yourself with your state's divorce laws.** Unless you signed a prenuptial agreement or reached an agreement with your spouse out of court, your property settlement will be governed by the law in your state. In nine of the states—Arizona, California, Idaho, Louisiana, Nevada, New Mexico, Texas, Washington and Wisconsin—all wages, income and property acquired during the marriage are considered community property to be split 50-50, regardless of the length of the marriage or the financial contribution of each spouse.

In most other states, a judge can divide the assets in any way that he/she deems to be fair. To learn your rights where you live, check your state's chapter of the American Bar Association (800-285-2221 or *www.abanet.org*) or check out DivorceNet (*www.divorcenet.com*), a family law advice site with helpful links to state-specific information.

• **Transfer retirement assets in a way that avoids triggering tax penalties.** When figuring out how to divide retirement plans, courts look at the complete marital estate. If there are enough assets, one party can equitably take, say, the house and the sailboat, while the other can take the retirement accounts without having to divide them.

If the estate is small—a house and a pension—and the pension is worth more, it might have to be split. Your attorney may draft a qualified domestic relations order (QDRO), a court order that tells how retirement plan assets will be distributed in a divorce. It must be approved by your spouse's retirement-plan administrator and the divorce judge.

Once you receive your distribution from your spouse's qualified plan, you can roll the money into an IRA. If you take the proceeds in cash pursuant to a QDRO, you will owe ordinary income taxes but not a 10% early withdrawal penalty—even if you are under age 59½.

Resource: Dividing up assets in a traditional (defined-benefit) pension plan may require an evaluation expert. Get a referral from your lawyer or contact Pension Analysis Consultants, Inc., a fee-based service, 800-288-3675, *www.pensionanalysis.com*.

• **Make sure that your spouse purchases term life insurance** if you expect to receive child support or alimony. The insurance benefit should be enough to cover your agreed-upon income stream in the event of your spouse's death. He/she should make you the irrevocable beneficiary of the policy. And, the property settlement should stipulate that the supporting spouse will notify you every time a premium is due and every time one is paid.

• **Don't give up your right to sue.** Most settlements stipulate that each spouse must waive the right to file "known" claims against the other in the future. Don't waive your right to file unknown claims.

Example: After you settle your divorce, you discover that you have contracted a sexually transmitted disease as a result of your spouse's extramarital affair. You want to retain the ability to file a tort claim for money damages for this "unknown claim."

• **Include "cost-of-living adjustment" and "late fee" clauses in child-support agreements.** Otherwise, you will face expensive trips back to court if payments are late or if you want payments increased due to inflation.

More from Gayle Rosenwald Smith, JD…

How Divorcing Spouses Hide Assets

Besides shifting assets out of joint accounts, there are many creative ways to keep money out of the hands of a spouse—some legal and some not. *What to watch out for…*

• **Asking an employer to put off payment of bonuses or raises until after the divorce.**

• **Setting up a custodial account that's in the name of your child,** using the child's Social Security number, and transferring the joint assets to that account.

• **Investing in municipal bonds or Series EE or I US savings bonds.** Interest does not need to be reported on tax returns.

• **"Repaying" bogus debts to friends or to family members,** who hold the money for the spouse until after the divorce.

• **If your spouse has a business,** he/she could pay a "salary" to a nonexistent employee to hide assets.

Self-defense: If you suspect that your spouse is hiding assets, you may need a forensic accountant. Ask your attorney for a recommendation…or when a business is involved, hire a business evaluator. The National Association of Certified Valuation Analysts at 800-677-2009 or *www.nacva.com* is a good place to start.

Protect Your Credit After a Divorce

Refinance the mortgage in the name of the spouse who maintains ownership of the home. Don't rely on a quitclaim deed or divorce decree—these may change the agreement between you and your spouse but not the agreement between you and the mortgage lender. If you don't refinance, your credit may be harmed by your ex-spouse's behavior.

Philip X. Tirone, mortgage broker, United Pacific Mortgage, Los Angeles, and author of *7 Steps to a 720 Credit Score*. Mortgage Capital Advisors.

What to Do If Your Spouse Dies

David W. Latko, president of Latko Wealth Management, Ltd., Frankfurt, IL, which has $100 million in client assets, *www.davidlatko.com*. He is author of *Financial Strategies for Today's Widow* (Fireside) and *Everybody Wants Your Money* (HarperCollins).

In addition to the emotional turmoil that comes with the death of a spouse, few people are prepared for the financial upheaval. *To protect your financial future, here are steps to take immediately, should you experience the loss of a spouse…*

• **Obtain at least 10 to 20 certified copies of your spouse's death certificate.** You will need to present them to financial institutions and other parties. Purchase them through the funeral home or your local health department.

Cost: About $7 per certified copy.

• **Contact your spouse's employer and/or former employer.** If your husband or wife was still working at the time of his/her death, speak with his employer's human resources and/or benefit plan administrator about accrued but unpaid salary, bonuses, profit sharing, commissions, sick days, vacation time, deferred compensation and the value of any life insurance or 401(k) accounts. Also, if you had health insurance through your spouse's employer, decide if you want to continue coverage.

If your husband or wife was retired and receiving a pension, ask if you are entitled to benefits. If your spouse had a 401(k), arrange to have it rolled over into an IRA. Also, ask if you are entitled to any retiree medical coverage.

• **If your spouse had life insurance,** contact the issuer of the policy. I recommend transferring the lump sum into a money market fund until you decide how to invest the money.

If the life insurance was held by a trust as part of your spouse's estate plan, talk to your estate-planning attorney about what the trust language dictates.

• **Contact the Social Security Administration (SSA)** by calling 800-772-1213 or on-line at *www.ssa.gov/survivorplan/index.htm*. As a surviving spouse, you will receive your spouse's SSA payments or your payments (depending on your age)—whichever is greater. If you have unmarried children under age 19, they may be entitled to survivor benefits. You also can receive a one-time $255 death benefit.

• **Contact financial institutions** with which you and your spouse held joint accounts. Change the accounts to your name only.

If your spouse served in the military, you may be entitled to a military pension, death benefits and/or funeral and burial costs, but don't expect quick payment. Contact the US Department of Veterans Affairs (800-827-1000, *www.cem.va.gov*). Ask to get benefits statements in writing.

•**Contact your local motor vehicle department** to cancel your spouse's license and change titles on any vehicles to your name or the name dictated by your spouse's will.

•**Notify issuers of debts held in your spouse's name and debts you held jointly**—with mortgage lenders, credit card companies, auto lenders, etc.—of your spouse's death. Ask the lenders if you or your spouse signed up for "payment protection," guaranteeing that mortgage or car payments or minimum credit card payments will continue for a certain period in the event of death. Some programs pay off the loan. The estate must pay off remaining debts.

•**Consult your tax adviser.** You must report any income your spouse earned in the year of his death. You can file a joint return for that year and claim the standard deduction if you don't itemize.

Web Sites That Monitor Charities

You can research charities before you donate. Several Web sites will help you.

•**American Institute of Philanthropy** (*www.charitywatch.org*) gives charities letter grades based on their efficient use of donations.

•**Better Business Bureau's Wise Giving Alliance** (*www.give.org*) provides reports on compliance with financial and government standards.

•**Charity Navigator** (*www.charitynavigator.org*) rates charities according to financial health and efficiency.

•***www.guidestar.org*** has information on 1.5 million nonprofit organizations and public charities.

The Wall Street Journal.

Form Your Own Charitable Giving Group

A "giving circle" is a group of people, such as friends or coworkers, who get together and pool their money to make charitable gifts. Gift amounts can range from very small to large, and circles can be run informally or regularized under rules the members agree upon. Circles are popular among those who want more control over where their charitable money goes. For more information, visit the Giving Circles Knowledge Center Web site, *www.givingforum.org/givingcircles.*

Scott Simpson, Forum of Regional Association of Grantmakers.

Get Your Parents to Talk About Their Finances

Dan Taylor, an attorney who specializes in elder-care issues. He is president of Wealth Capital Group, a financial advisory firm in Charlotte, NC, *www.parentcaresolution.com*. He is author of *The Parent Care Conversation.* Penguin.

As a financial adviser, I have managed hundreds of millions of dollars for clients. But my own father, a retired railroad foreman, never discussed his finances with me. He didn't want to burden me—and I never pressed the issue.

Then my 74-year-old dad was found by the police wandering the streets at 4:30 in the morning, confused. He was diagnosed with Alzheimer's disease, went directly into a care facility and never returned to his old life.

I had to make wrenching choices about his living situation, his money and his possessions for which I was totally unprepared—because he and I had never spoken about such things.

Based on my personal and professional experience, here are the most common roadblocks put up by parents and other elderly

33

loved ones when you try to discuss their futures—and the strategies to deal with them…

MONEY

Roadblock: Your parents refuse to discuss the details of their financial lives. If you press them, they say, "Don't worry about us. We're fine."

Your immediate goal: To know whether they really are financially safe and secure.

What to do…

• **Break the ice by asking for help with your own financial affairs.** Say, "Dad, I'm planning to withdraw 5% a year from my portfolio when I retire. Is that realistic? How do you do it?" Asking for your parents' advice makes it easier for them to drop their guard and open up. It often leads naturally to discussions about their finances.

• **Acknowledge that they are in control.** Say to your parents, "I appreciate the fact that you've done well financially and that you can—and should—handle your affairs now. But if there comes a time in the future when you can't take care of your investments or other finances by yourselves, who would you like to handle them?"

• **Frame the conversation in terms of accountability.** If your parents expect you to bear any responsibility for their finances in the future, then you need to have enough information to be faithful to their wishes. Say, "Mom and Dad, if you suddenly become sick and can't handle your finances, do you expect me to step into a crisis situation blindly? If you can't open up to me, then don't make me responsible."

• **Ask your parents to go for a second opinion.** If they do open up to you and you're concerned about their financial situation, reserve direct criticism, which may make them feel inadequate. Instead, say, "I appreciate all the work you've done on this. Would you be open to talking to a professional to verify that your thinking is correct here?" I find most parents will reject a son's or daughter's financial advice, even if it is sound—but they will accept and implement an identical proposal from a qualified third party, such as a financial planner.

You even might offer to pay for their visit to the planner. Don't attach conditions, such as requiring them to see a planner of your choosing or letting you sit in on the session.

Helpful: If your parents seem overwhelmed with day-to-day budgeting and bill paying, consider hiring an independent party to help. The American Association of Daily Money Managers is made up of professionals trained to handle budgeting, paperwork and bill paying.

Cost: $35 to $125/hour. 877-326-5991, *www. aadmm.com.*

POSSESSIONS

Roadblock: Your parents complain about, or don't seem to be keeping up with, the clutter in their home. But they refuse to pare down their possessions or even talk about how they would want their possessions dealt with in a crisis.

Your immediate goal: Make life more manageable for them—and for you—as they age.

After my father was hospitalized for Alzheimer's, it took me the equivalent of two full workweeks to deal with his property.

Example: He had hundreds of high-quality tools. I had no idea which ones he wanted to sell or give to family members or friends.

What to do…

• **Initiate a conversation about belongings** as soon as you get clues that your parents may be open to it. Typically, the signal is a comment such as, "I can never find anything in this mess," or "I would like you to have my ring someday."

Your response: "Mom and Dad, why don't you tell me what crosses your mind when you think about what to do with all your stuff in the future?" To start the winnowing-down process, say, "If you had to move next month, what would you keep with you forever? What would you put in storage? What would you give away or sell?"

• **Address faulty solutions.** Elderly people generally offer two rationalizations to avoid dealing in a constructive way with being overloaded with belongings…

"We'll have a big tag sale one of these days."

Your response: "Sorting through a lifetime of possessions, including cherished keepsakes, is going to take a lot of energy and emotion. You'll need plenty of time to do it right."

"If the time comes to move, we'll have the Salvation Army take what we don't want."

Your response: "Charities no longer act as haul-away services. They've become very picky about what they will transport from your home."

• **Ask them to help take a huge weight off your shoulders.** Say, "Mom and Dad, it will be so much harder if I have to go through all your belongings in the future myself."

Rule of thumb: It's natural that your parents will want to keep everything. However, I've found that elders who are downsizing decades of clutter generally need to get rid of one-half to two-thirds of their possessions to make a serious difference in the quality of their lives.

HOUSE

Roadblock: Your parents insist that they plan to remain in their home forever. You know that this may take some real planning—if it's possible at all.

Your immediate goal: To make sure that they can handle the responsibility of staying in place as they age and that their living environment is safe.

What to do…

• **Acknowledge that you really want what they want.** Say, "I'd hate to have to give up my home and move to a smaller place or a care facility. In order to stay here, what changes would you be open to? For example, what would you do if it became difficult to go up and down the stairs?"

Helpful: Your local Area Agency on Aging. This organization helps older adults remain in their homes, aided by services if necessary.

Contact: The National Association of Area Agencies on Aging, 202-872-0888, *www.n4a. org.*

Also: Universal Designers and Consultants offers information about adapting homes for easier living by seniors at *www.universalde sign.com.*

• **Point out realities.** It is common for parents to say, "We've got family and friends who could stop by and check on us if we ever needed it."

Your response: "Yes, you will be checked on some of the time, but there won't be visitors dropping by all the time, and visitors may not want that responsibility."

• **Accentuate the positive.** Instead of focusing on limitations, focus on new possibilities. Say, "You don't have to ever move to a smaller place, but consider how freeing an apartment would be. You wouldn't have to worry about constant upkeep." Or, "The extra money you would have after selling your house and buying an apartment would provide you with more security."

ESTATE PLANNING

Roadblock: Parents usually can be convinced to write a will, but getting them to update their estate plan as the years go by is surprisingly difficult. They say, "Our attorney is taking care of it," or "Why are you so eager to make sure our will is up-to-date?"

Your immediate goal: Making sure their estate plan is current, especially if there is a major tax-law change or a death or change in marital status of a family member. My long experience with estate attorneys is that they tend to be short on follow-up unless the client initiates contact.

What to do…

• **Phrase the task of updating their plans in terms of making your job easier.** Say, "Dad, I know you've done a good job planning your estate. In your view, is there anything that needs to be changed that would make my job (or insert the name of the appropriate party) as the executor easier?"

Important: If your parents are threatened or offended by your interest in their will and other estate documents, say, "I'm sorry that you've interpreted what I said as eagerness to get your money. My eagerness is to make sure that your affairs are the way you want them, regardless of the money."

Helpful: The National Academy of Elder Law Attorneys offers the latest news on legal issues affecting the elderly and can assist in finding an elder-law attorney in your area. 520-881-4005, *www.naela.com.*

2

Smarter Investor

Get the Best Financial Advice

Anyone can call himself/ herself a financial adviser or consultant—a stockbroker, insurance agent, accountant, even a layperson who is good with numbers. In the past five years, the number of financial advisers has risen by almost 40% as consumers—hurt by the last bear market and intimidated by retirement planning—seek professional help.

Unfortunately, financial advisers aren't required as a general rule to act solely in your best interest—a standard known as "fiduciary responsibility."

Common: An adviser may not recommend the best mutual fund for you, but rather the best one for you that also pays him a commission.

Who you choose depends on your needs.

Example: Whether you want someone to draw up a financial plan or provide ongoing investment services.

DECIDING WHAT YOU NEED

To find the right money coach...

•**If you need broad financial guidance**—such as help setting up a portfolio that you will mostly oversee yourself...a plan to pay for your children's educations...a retirement plan...estate planning and tax planning—go with a fee-only planner who has a certified financial planner (CFP) designation.

Fee-only advisers do not accept commissions. CFPs are required to pass a certification exam, have at least three years of financial-planning experience, adhere to a code of ethics, earn continuing education credits and pledge fiduciary responsibility.

Typical cost: One-time fee of $1,000 or more for a comprehensive plan.

Resource: Two associations can make referrals—The Financial Planning Association

Donald B. Trone, president and founder of the Foundation for Fiduciary Studies, which operates in association with the University of Pittsburgh in Sewickley, PA. He is coauthor of two manuals for the financial planning industry, *Procedural Prudence* (Veale & Associates) and *The Management of Investment Decisions* (McGraw-Hill).

(800-322-4237, *www.fpanet.org*)…and the National Association of Personal Financial Advisors (800-366-2732, *www.napfa.org*).

●**If you want a professional to help manage your portfolio** on an ongoing basis, look for a chartered financial analyst (CFA). CFAs undergo rigorous training in stock and bond analysis, financial accounting and portfolio management. They are required to pass a certification exam, adhere to a code of ethics and pledge fiduciary responsibility.

Important: Never give an adviser full discretion over your portfolio, no matter how trustworthy he seems. You should receive at least a phone call or an e-mail when a trade is going to be made.

Typical cost: A fixed percentage of assets under management—0.5% to 2% annually for ongoing market advice and investment recommendations. For example, annual fees for an all-bond portfolio may average 0.5% of assets versus 1.5% for a mix of stocks and bonds.

Resource: For referrals to CFAs, go to *www.cfainstitute.org* or call 800-247-8132.

Important: If you have less than $300,000 in your portfolio, it can be difficult to find a financial adviser to manage it because it is not cost-effective for them.

Alternatives…

●Use a financial planner who charges hourly rates, typically $100 to $300 per hour. For referrals, contact Garrett Planning Network (866-260-8400, *www.garrettplanning.com*), a network of planners who charge by the hour. Or get recommendations from your attorney or accountant.

●Consider the new advisory services offered by large, no-load mutual fund companies. They provide low-cost individualized portfolio advice by CFPs. For example, at Fidelity (800-343-3548, *www.fidelity.com*), counselors will manage a handpicked selection of Fidelity and non-Fidelity funds for clients who have at least $50,000 under management. Fees range from 0.25% of assets to 1.1%. Similar services are available from Vanguard (800-523-7731, *www.vanguard.com)* and T. Rowe Price (800-225-5132, *www.troweprice.com*).

SIZING UP CANDIDATES

●**Conduct a background check of prospective advisers and their firms.** You should work only with firms registered with the SEC. They are subject to government supervision.

Go to *www.sec.gov/index.htm*, click on "Check Out Brokers & Advisers," then on "Research Investment Advisers." Search for the firm you want to investigate, and examine the firm's Form ADV. It contains information on the education and professional backgrounds of the firm's principals, types of clients, compensation, amount managed and disciplinary history.

You can find the same information through the Financial Regulatory Authority (800-289-9999, *www.finra.org*). Any reputable adviser will make his ADV form available to you without your even having to ask.

●**Conduct a 30-minute, in-person interview with each candidate.** (You should not be charged for this.) Ask if the adviser frequently works with other financial specialists on behalf of clients and would therefore be amenable to working with your professionals. For example, if your estate plan is complex, you already may be working with an insurance agent and an estate lawyer.

Find out if the financial adviser will handle your account personally or farm out your assets to managers whom he supervises (you'll need to check the backgrounds of those managers, if that's the case)…how much time you can expect with him…and whether you can monitor your account on-line.

Ask if he will provide a comprehensive analysis of your financial situation, including specific recommendations—he should present you with a sample.

Ask about the firm's typical client, and gauge whether his/her needs are similar to yours. For instance, the firm might deal primarily with corporate executives who need help with stock options or retired people who want to maximize investment income. Ask to see actual performance figures for the clients whose goals are similar to yours.

• **Speak with at least two of the adviser's references.**

Questions to ask: Did the financial adviser educate you on complex financial issues? Did he carefully follow your directives? In particular, did he understand how aggressive/conservative a portfolio you wanted? Did he ever make mistakes or disappoint you? What did he do about it?

• **Once you are ready to hire a firm,** get a written policy. *It should include...*

• A promise that the adviser will act as your "fiduciary."

• List of potential conflicts of interest regarding product-based commissions and a reasonable explanation of how they are addressed.

• Explanation of the fee structure, what constitutes billable work and how fee disputes will be resolved—for instance, if the stock market drops and you make a quick call asking for advice. In this case, an adviser earning an asset-based annual fee should not charge for taking your call.

Lessons from the Master Investors

Mark Tier, an investment analyst and adviser, Hong Kong. He is author of *Becoming Rich*. St. Martin's. The book examines the wealth-building secrets of Warren Buffett, Carl Icahn, Sir John Templeton and other master investors.

For years, my portfolio returns barely kept pace with the major stock market averages. Then I began studying the strategies of legendary investors, such as bargain hunter Warren Buffett, corporate raider Carl Icahn and emerging-markets pioneer Sir John Templeton.

Although they used different strategies, they all had habits that allowed them to implement their techniques with conviction and consistency. After researching their habits for my book, I incorporated their practices into my own strategy. In the eight years since, my personal portfolio has gained an average of 23.7% a year.

Here are the habits of superstar investors and the master who best represents each one...

HABIT: HAVE INFINITE PATIENCE

Master investor: Warren Buffett, Berkshire Hathaway Inc.

If you have stringent investment criteria, there naturally will be extended periods of time when you can't find anything to invest in.

In February 1973, the US economy was in recession and the Dow had fallen by 40% from its highs. Other blue chips also had declined sharply. Stock in The Washington Post Company had fallen so far that Wall Street valued the company at only $80 million. Mr. Buffett estimated that if the company sold its newspaper and magazine businesses to a private publisher, it would get around $400 million, so he began buying shares at an average of $22.75. Even so, the price of the stock kept falling. It took two years before Mr. Buffett even got back to his original purchase price, but he did not care how long he had to wait. His stake is now worth nearly $2 billion.

Lesson: It's not necessary to always be doing something in the market. You get paid for being right, not for actively trading.

HABIT: PASSIONATELY AVOID RISK

Master investor: Carl Icahn, Icahn & Co.

It's hard to believe that an aggressive investor such as Carl Icahn would shun risk, but this has been fundamental to his accumulation of wealth.

He focuses on high-probability situations—for which his analyses indicate that potential profits are large and potential losses minimal. By insisting on this margin of safety, he doesn't always score wins, but the odds are in his favor.

Classic example: In the 1970s, Mr. Icahn set his sights on a real estate investment trust called Baird & Warner. He estimated that the company's liquidation value was, conservatively, $20/share. He started buying this stock at $8.50/share, a nearly 60% discount to his fair value estimate for the stock. This was his margin of safety.

After building enough of a stake to get a seat on Baird & Warner's board, Mr. Icahn launched a proxy battle for control of the company. He vowed not to take a penny in compensation if he won. Meanwhile, managers of the company paid themselves generous salaries while refusing to pay dividends to shareholders.

Mr. Icahn won control of the company and sold off its real estate. Shareholders who stayed onboard made piles of money. (This company still exists, but it is now a real estate brokerage. Mr. Icahn no longer has a stake.)

Lesson: Preserving capital should always be your first priority.

HABIT: ACT INSTANTLY

Master investor: Sir John Templeton, John Templeton Foundation.

Sir John Templeton concentrates on emerging countries—ones with developing stock markets and economies—and refuses to buy any stock that does not meet his rigorous, value-oriented criteria. One of his best-known criteria is to invest based on a "trigger"—a dramatic event that could favorably impact his return. When such triggers occur, he acts instantly.

Classic example: In the late 1990s, Sir John was shocked, like many value managers, to see tech stocks reach absurdly high prices. Based on the stocks' high valuations, many of his peers bet on a price decline by short-selling them. (Short sellers make money when the stock price goes down, and they lose if the price goes up.) But the short sellers suffered huge losses on those positions as tech stocks climbed.

Not Sir John—he waited until he found a specific trigger for tech-stock prices. Typically, corporate insiders are restricted from selling shares they receive in initial public offerings until a 180-day period has elapsed. He used the end of this "lockup period" as his trigger. He figured that the increased supply of stock from insiders rushing to cash out would depress prices. For many technology stocks, the end of the lockup occurred at the beginning of 2000, three months before the tech-heavy NASDAQ composite peaked.

Sir John initiated short positions in 84 different dot-com companies just a few days before the lockup period for each stock expired. Within a year and a half, he had made $86 million shorting dot-com stocks.

Lesson: Do not procrastinate. Once you have made a decision based on thoughtful analysis, take action.

Are Emotions Driving Your Investments?

Richard Geist, EdD, a clinical instructor in psychology, department of psychiatry at Harvard Medical School in Boston, and founding member of the Massachusetts Institute for Psychoanalysis, where he is on the faculty. He is also president of the Institute of Psychology and Investing, Inc., a consulting firm in Newton, MA, and the author of *Investor Therapy*. Crown Business.

Most of us recognize that many investors base decisions on emotion rather than logic. The trouble is that few of us believe we're among them.

To find out how much emotion influences your investments, look back over your stock and mutual fund trades for the past year, and note the reason for each purchase and sale. If trades were motivated by the headlines of the day or your eagerness to make a quick profit, chances are emotion played a key role.

Good news: Once you recognize that emotions are guiding your decisions, you can take steps to separate them from investments. Alternatively, you can choose the stocks and funds suited to your particular psychological bias.

How to deal with psychological traps…

HERD MENTALITY

It is only human to follow the winners. In investing, those are the people who have made money. Unfortunately, by the time an investment sector posts strong returns, there's often little advantage left to plowing money in.

Today, there is a herd mentality concerning short-term investing. Our qualitative research shows that fear of terrorism, anxiety over developments in Iraq and the memory of the recent bear market have made investors more likely to sell for a quick profit —typically, in less than a year—no matter what sector they are in.

Solution: When an investor herd goes in one direction, look for opportunities in stocks and funds that are left behind. Today, these include companies that recently have had problems but have solid fundamentals—good management, a healthy market share, low debt and a history of earnings growth over the last decade.

IMPATIENCE

It's impossible to predict the ideal time to sell a stock, but impatient investors are notorious for selling just before a stock takes off.

Test your own patience: Are you reluctant to start reading long books? In conversations, are you annoyed when people don't get to the point? If you answered yes to either question, there is a good chance that you are an impatient investor.

When you look back over your trading record for the past 12 months, check the price of each position you sold three to six months after you sold it. (If you can't find past transaction statements, ask your financial institution for copies or download them from its Web site.) If you regularly sold shares that continued to rise in price, impatience may have played a role.

Solution: Add up the profits you could have made by holding on longer. Merely seeing the total may be enough to cure you.

If you simply can't break the habit of selling shares prematurely, consider buying stocks that should be sold for a quick profit.

These frequently are in companies that take advantage of new trends—especially technology stocks. If shares in cutting-edge companies rise, the increase is likely to be fast. Holding these risky stocks long after their initial rise can be a mistake if the fundamentals don't support the gain, though there certainly are exceptions to this rule.

FEAR OF LETTING GO

This is the opposite of impatience. It means hanging on to shares long after you should have sold them.

When you look at your trades of the past year, check the price of stocks three and six months before you sold them. Look also at the stocks you own now, and compare current prices with prices three and six months ago.

If you find that you consistently hang on to shares after they rise and then fall, it is likely that you're afraid of selling. Why might this be?

One possibility: If your costliest mistakes always seem to occur at certain times of the year—for instance, around the anniversary of a painful event, such as the loss of a loved one—the memory could be subconsciously influencing your investment behavior.

Solution: Continue to keep records of your trades, and periodically note profits that you missed because you hung on too long.

If this doesn't stop you from keeping losing stocks, stick with stock funds that have performed well in both up and down markets. By following this strategy, you won't be hurt by your fear of letting go.

Helpful: Free fund-screening tools are available at *www.morningstar.com*. If you do not have a computer, research funds at a public library computer.

OVERREACTING TO NEWS

Don't let the headlines determine your stock trades. Individual investors are seldom knowledgeable or dispassionate enough to profit from the news.

Example: Airline stocks suffered after the September 11 disaster as many investors worried about a drop in tourism. Yet very few individual investors got out of the stocks quickly enough to contain their losses.

Professional investors interpret and react to the news more quickly than most individual investors do. As a result, stock prices are affected by news before most individuals have time to respond. In fact, several fund managers did buy airline stocks right after September 11, 2001, and then sold them when they rebounded.

Solution: Before buying or selling a stock, ask yourself whether the decision is influenced by a news event. If it is, review the company's fundamentals—management, competitive position and outlook for its industry sector. Go ahead only if the fundamentals justify the trade.

Think twice before buying or selling shares purely on the basis of trends you see on financial news sites in a day's first hour of trading.

Stock-Picking Secrets— From the Little Book That Beats the Market

Joel Greenblatt, founder and managing partner of Gotham Capital, an investment firm in New York City with $1.6 billion in assets. He is author of *The Little Book That Beats the Market*. Wiley. From 1988 through 2004, a large-cap portfolio based on his strategy had an average annual return of 22.9%, vs. 12.4% for the S&P 500 Index. In 2005, he won the prestigious Graham & Dodd, Murray, Greenwald Prize for Value Investing.

Most professional money managers can't beat the S&P 500 Index over the long term. So how can ordinary investors—who don't have research staffs or financial expertise—possibly earn market-beating returns?

Joel Greenblatt, one of the country's most successful value investors, tells how below. Over the past 20 years, his private hedge fund logged an average annual return of 40% using a low-risk system that doesn't rely on economic predictions.

To carry out this strategy, anyone can use the free stock-screening tool at Greenblatt's Web site, *www.magicformulainvesting.com*, or other financial Web sites...

• **Look for high-return businesses selling at low valuations.** The best companies earn high returns on investments, which might include new equipment or technology. *Screen for high-return stocks using the following measures...*

• Return on capital (pretax operating profit as a percentage of net working capital and net fixed assets) of 30% or higher. My Web site ranks 3,500 companies based on return

on capital, with the highest assigned a rank of one.

• Low stock price in relation to the company's past 12 months of earnings. To find a list of attractively priced stocks, screen for an earnings yield of 12% or more. This is the ratio of pretax operating earnings to market value plus net debt. My Web site also ranks the 3,500 companies by earnings yield, with the highest-rated company assigned a rank of one. Then it combines this rank and the return-on-capital rank (described earlier), assigning top rankings (those with the lowest numbers) to companies that have the best combination of the two factors.

Examples: A company that ranked first in return on capital but 1,150th in earnings yield would receive a combined ranking of 1,151 (1 plus 1,150). A company that ranked 232nd in return on capital and 153rd in earnings yield would receive a combined ranking of 385 (232 plus 153)—a better overall ranking.

• **Narrow the field by selecting companies of a certain size** in terms of value of shares outstanding—known as market capitalization. Stocks of small and midsized companies, with market capitalizations of $1 billion or below, are riskier than stocks of large companies, but they offer higher returns on average. Once you have finished the screening process, invest in at least 20 of the top-ranked stocks. This eliminates virtually all of the risk of owning just one stock but keeps your portfolio to a manageable size.

• **Sell all your stocks after 12 months** (unless they make the grade for the second year in a row), and reinvest the proceeds in the new top-ranked companies. For taxable accounts, make sure that you're eligible for the 15% federal income tax rate on capital gains by holding moneymaking stocks for at least one day more than a year.

Why sell winners after only one year? I have found that for most investors, it's the simplest, most effective strategy. However, money-losing stocks should be sold a few days before one year is up so you can take the stock loss when you file your taxes.

Warning: There will be extended periods of time when your portfolio will trail the market averages, sometimes by double digits. That's why this strategy is intended for investors with time horizons of five years or more.

More from Joel Greenblatt...

Stock-Picking Shortcuts

Here are a few easy ways to make my strategy work for you...

•**Screening.** You can use my Web site, *www.magicformulainvesting.com*, or your favorite stock-screening site. On other sites, you might need to customize the search criteria.

Examples: Use return on assets (ROA) instead of return on capital. Set the minimum ROA at 25%. Use price-to-earnings ratio in place of earnings yield. Eliminate all utilities and financial stocks from the resulting list.

Reason: These industries use different definitions of debt and other financial measures, which make them hard to screen.

•**Trading.** Since the system generates high turnover, keep trading costs down by using a low-cost discount broker, such as *www.foliofn.com* or *www.buyandhold.com*. These firms enable you to buy fractional shares of stock, so you don't need to invest large sums to be well diversified.

Money Myths that Can Cost You Big

Robert J. Reby, CFP, president of Robert J. Reby & Co., Inc., a wealth preservation firm in Danbury, CT. He is author of *Retire Without Worry: Simple, Straightforward Answers to Serious Financial Questions*. Reby.

Falling for an investment myth can cost you big. *Here are the most common myths—about mutual funds, stocks, bonds and gold...*

Myth: Stick with index funds.

Reality: It is true that over long periods (10 years or more), the returns from S&P 500 Index funds exceed the returns from more than 80% of actively managed large-cap funds. However, investors need to consider a mutual fund's risk, not just its return. For example, between 2000 and 2002, a large-cap index fund would have lost almost half of its value. If that fund constituted a major portion of your portfolio, could you have accepted that loss? Would you have kept adding money without bailing out?

Smart strategy: Consider an actively managed fund that is effective at handling downside risk, especially if you invest over periods shorter than 10 years.

Before investing, find out a fund's Sharpe ratio, a measure of risk. The higher a fund's Sharpe ratio, the better its returns have been relative to the amount of risk it has taken.

Sharpe ratios can be found at *www.morningstar.com*. Search using a fund's ticker symbol, then click on "Risk Measures."

Myth: To figure out how much to invest in stocks, subtract your age from 100—so a 55-year-old would keep 45% (100 minus 55) in stocks and the rest in bonds.

Reality: Simple formulas are appealing, but this one won't help most investors meet their goals. In the above situation, the 55-year-old may not have enough in stocks to allow for growth in his/her nest egg, since his life expectancy is 30-plus years.

Instead, decide what return you will need to reach your goal and how much fluctuation you can bear. Then develop an asset allocation that has produced that return over long periods. The wealthier you become, the more conservative you can afford to be.

Helpful: The retirement income calculator at *www.troweprice.com*.

Myth: Gold is a safe investment.

Reality: At its height in 1980, one ounce of gold was worth $870. Today, it is worth approximately $900* in dollar terms and only about $340 in inflation-adjusted terms—even though its price is at a 25-year high.

*Price subject to change.

As a buy-and-hold investment, gold has been disastrous. It costs money to store and insure, yet gold provides no income. And gold-related stocks are extremely volatile. As a hedge against inflation, a weak American dollar and the possibility of worldwide terrorism disrupting oil supplies and wounding Western economies, it has made some sense for large institutional investors with decades-long time horizons to keep a small amount in gold.

For the average investor, there are less risky ways to diversify a stock portfolio—commodity funds, which may have some exposure to gold but also own copper, oil, soybeans and other commodities.

Myth: **Never invest in bonds when the Fed is raising interest rates.**

Reality: Because bond values move in the opposite direction of interest rates, the value of most bonds or bond funds will go down (you will lose principal) when interest rates rise. But it still may make sense to hold bonds as rates rise.

If you plan to hold a bond until maturity, the loss in value won't matter. You also can estimate a fund's sensitivity to interest rates. The rule of thumb is that for every one percentage point rise in interest rates, the value of shares drops by that percentage times the "duration" of the fund. The longer the duration, the more shares will drop in price if rates rise. For example, if interest rates rise by one percentage point and the duration of your fund is six years, your fund shares should decrease in value by about 6%. (Duration can be found at *www.morningstar.com*.)

If you switch to a fund that has a shorter duration, it will lose less if rates rise.

High-yield ("junk") bonds are not as affected by changes in interest rates as comparable Treasury, investment-grade corporate or municipal bonds. They trade largely on the basis of their credit ratings and corporate cash flows. Keeping some money in high-yield bond funds—say, 5% to 10% of your bond portfolio—can soften the effects of rate increases.

Myth: **It pays to invest in foreign stock mutual funds only when the dollar is starting to weaken.**

Reality: It's true that foreign stock funds do well when foreign currencies gain value against the dollar—but not all stocks benefit. And over time, a falling dollar can hurt profits of foreign companies that export heavily to the US because their products become more expensive relative to American-made goods.

Instead of waiting to take advantage of any currency gain against the dollar, investors should always keep 8% to 20% in foreign stocks, especially small- and mid-caps, which don't move in lockstep with US stocks.

You can increase your portfolio's total return over time without increasing your overall risk by adding foreign stocks.

Stocks Are More Predictable than Most People Think

Jeffrey Hirsch, editor of *Almanac Investor*, Nyack, NY, *www.stocktradersalmanac.com*. He is also editor-in-chief of *Stock Trader's Almanac 2008*. Wiley.

Many old-time Wall Street sayings do ring true. That's because they reflect patterns related to seasons, taxes, political changes and even wars. By buying and selling at opportune times, you increase your odds of beating the market. *Here are the most reliable patterns...*

SELL IN MAY AND GO AWAY

The best time to sell, on average, is around May 1. From May to October, what we call the worst six months to invest, stocks tend to stagnate. Market activity slows. After paying taxes in April, people don't have much cash to invest. Then as summer approaches, traders head out of town. Vacationers prefer playing golf to buying stocks.

After Labor Day, investors begin focusing on the markets again. They get nervous about stocks that haven't done well over the summer. Many people worry about October because several major downturns in the past have occurred then, including the Great Crash of 1929. October is when many institutions sell their losing stocks, driving down the market.

By November 1, it often pays to buy stocks again. With the holidays approaching, investors become more optimistic. The stores are crowded, and sales figures show promise. Mutual funds aim to grab winners to improve their year-end returns.

THE SANTA CLAUS RALLY

One of the best periods of the year for stocks tends to include the last five trading days of December and the first two trading days of January. On average since 1950, the S&P 500 Index has gained 1.5% during this period. The Santa Claus rally also can serve as an indicator for the upcoming year. If stocks dip despite holiday euphoria, markets may be headed for trouble.

Example: At the end of 1999, the Santa Claus rally failed to materialize. The S&P 500 lost 4% over the seven-day period. The market went on to fall in 2000, losing 9.1% for the year.

THE JANUARY BAROMETER

In 1972, my father, Yale Hirsch, discovered the January barometer. If the market is up in January, most often stocks will rise for the year. This indicator has been accurate 75% of the time based on data going back to 1950.

January is important because so much happens. Wall Street pundits issue their annual market forecasts. The new president and Congress take office, and the president usually delivers the state of the union address. This sets the tone for many investors.

January is traditionally a strong month. There's a rush of new cash into the market as investors receive year-end bonuses and make contributions to IRAs and other retirement plans.

THE WAR EXCEPTION

In December 2005 and January 2006, the Santa Claus rally and the January barometer were positive, based on investor optimism that the new Federal Reserve chairman would not raise interest rates sharply in 2006.

Wars always act as a drag on stocks. Since its inception more than a century ago, the Dow Jones Industrial Average has never reached a significant new high during a war. In wartime, with the government spending heavily, demand for goods rises and inflation increases. Rising prices erode the value of corporate earnings, hurting stock prices. Investors become pessimistic, and setbacks occur regularly, stopping rallies.

Example: As the Vietnam War escalated in 1966, the Dow attempted to pass 1,000 but failed to stay in that range until 1982, about a decade after peace was announced and the vestiges of wartime inflation began to disappear.

However, while stocks often fall after the initial shock of a war, markets rarely go into a free fall in the midst of a protracted conflict. Government spending and wartime pride help keep stocks afloat. As markets anticipate the end of the war, stocks can rally, but surprisingly, there is a letdown when peace finally appears, causing stocks to dip.

THE PRESIDENTIAL CYCLE

The market often rises during the year before a presidential election because Washington does everything it can to boost the economy and put more money in voters' wallets. After the inauguration, the good times usually stop. Presidents make tough decisions early in their terms, and tax increases, cuts in government programs, etc., can send stocks tumbling. Nine of the last 14 bear markets have bottomed in the midterm year, the second year after a presidential

election—1962, 1966, 1970, 1974, 1978, 1982, 1990, 1998 and 2002.

HOW TO INVEST

Devote a small portion of your tax-deferred portfolio to a seasonal timing strategy. Invest around November 1 in a low-cost exchange-traded fund, such as SPDR Trust (SPY), which tracks the Standard & Poor's 500 Index. Sell the fund around May 1, and shift to cash or a short-term bond fund. Repeat this each year.

The approach does not make money every year, but an investor who followed it since 1950 would have beaten the market. If that individual had invested $10,000 during the best six months—November to April—of each year beginning in 1950, he now would have $534,323. If he had invested $10,000 in May and sold in October of each year, he would have lost $272 during that period. (Figures exclude dividends.)

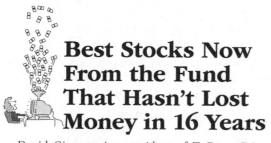

Best Stocks Now From the Fund That Hasn't Lost Money in 16 Years

David Giroux, vice president of T. Rowe Price Group, Baltimore, and manager of T. Rowe Capital Appreciation Fund (PRWCX) since June 2006. When he was a chartered financial analyst covering industrial stocks, Giroux was named to the *Institutional Investor* All-American Research Team for 2005. *www.troweprice.com.*

One of the best ways for a stock mutual fund to deliver consistently strong returns is to never lose much in the first place. However, very few funds achieve this goal year after year. When a fund does accomplish this, investors sleep easier at night knowing that much of their investment in the fund won't be wiped out in a single year.

A stellar example is the $11 billion T. Rowe Price Capital Appreciation Fund. The 21-year-old fund hasn't had a single down year since 1990—its only down year ever—when it lost

only 1.25%. At the low point of the bear market in 2002, a year in which the Standard & Poor's 500 stock index lost nearly one-quarter of its value, the fund *gained* 0.5%.

Over the past 10 years through April 22, 2008, the fund returned an annualized 9.85%, beating the S&P 500 by more than six percentage points. It has delivered annualized returns between 12% and 13% for periods covering the past three, five, 10, 15 and 20 years, even though it has had a succession of five different portfolio managers running it.

Our editors talked with the current manager, David Giroux, about how the fund avoids big losses and what some of his best defensive strategies and favorite stocks are now…

BALANCE OFFENSE AND DEFENSE

Our basic approach has never changed. We focus on a "decent" offense, which means we are willing to trail major indexes in up markets by a few percentage points…as well as a superb defense, often beating indexes in bad times by double-digit percentages.

Lately my stock picks have become more defensive. Although there is reason for optimism—stocks are fairly priced overall, and corporate balance sheets are strong—we have had four consecutive years of positive market returns, and corporate profits are slowing. I'm finding few attractive opportunities in corporate and junk bonds, so in addition to a lot of cash, most of my defensive posture is coming from judicious stock selection. With the recent market pullbacks, I am buying more shares of my favorite stocks. *How I do it…*

• **Start with the basics.** Part of my stock-picking process is not very different from that used by many long-term, value-oriented investors who focus on "fundamentals." I look for undervalued stocks with above-average dividend yield…a low price-to-earnings ratio (P/E) relative to that of the S&P 500…and a low stock price relative to the value of assets minus liabilities.

• **Focus on the downside.** What gives me an advantage is the amount of time I spend trying to learn how badly a stock could hurt the fund.

Example: One candidate I considered for the portfolio this year was the health-care giant WellPoint (WLP), which runs HMOs and managed-care plans. It's a superb business selling at a reasonable P/E, with the ability to grow earnings by 12% to 15% annually for many years.

The downside: If a Democrat is elected president in 2008, that could have negative consequences for the HMO industry. Also, WellPoint's profit margins have reached what I consider a peak. Those factors create far too much potential for error, so the fund has not bought WellPoint shares.

When you hold stocks with very limited downside risk and decent growth prospects, the upside takes care of itself and often surprises you.

• **Buy solid companies facing a temporary challenge or controversy.**

Analyze a Financial Newsletter

Analyze a financial newsletter's record and quality—and the stocks and funds it recommends—with *Hulbert Interactive*, an on-line screening tool based on more than 20 years of data from *The Hulbert Financial Digest*, the newsletter that tracks investment newsletters. The screener provides consensus ratings of thousands of stocks and mutual funds based on the advice and track records of leading investment newsletters.

Annual subscription fee for Hulbert Interactive: $149, with a 30-day free trial.

John Bajkowski, vice president and senior financial analyst, American Association of Individual Investors (AAII), Chicago, *www.aaii.com*.

"Buy Stocks Like You Buy Steaks"…Surprising Strategies from a Top Fund Manager

Christopher H. Browne, managing director of Tweedy, Browne Company LLC, New York City. His flagship mutual fund is Tweedy, Browne Global Value (TBGVX). He is trustee of The Rockefeller University and author of *The Little Book of Value Investing.* Wiley.

I have value investing in my blood. My father was the broker used by Warren Buffett to buy his original shares of Berkshire Hathaway back in the early 1960s. Buffett liked to say that value investing wasn't rocket science. So then, why doesn't everyone who tries it succeed?

Answer: It takes a great deal of patience and discipline. Returns tend to be "lumpy," with extended periods of underperformance compared with the stock market as a whole —such as during the technology-stock craze in the late 1990s. Also, if you're a value investor, you don't have the fun of owning the "hot" growth stocks that your friends and colleagues might be talking about. In fact, my most profitable investments have been in industries that manufactured such "cutting-edge" items as toothpaste and chocolate.

Despite these drawbacks, I've never found a more dependable way to make money on Wall Street. My approach has beaten the international MSCI EAFE index by an average of more than five percentage points a year over the past decade. *My rules of value investing include the following…*

• **Buy stocks as you would buy steaks** —when they're on sale. Most people look at just about everything they buy with an eye on getting the best price—except for investors. They can't resist the lure of exciting, overpriced stocks that everyone else is buying. I avoid these stocks and spend my time applying strict value criteria to a large universe of companies. *I look for…*

• Low price-to-earnings ratio (P/E). This value screen works well in good and bad markets. Many investors look at forward P/Es, which use a consensus of analysts' projected earnings for the coming year. I find these unreliable and recommend using trailing earnings—what a company actually earned in the previous 12 months—that have been audited and reported to shareholders.

• Price below book value. Book value per share is a company's total net worth (everything a company owns, such as buildings, inventory and cash, minus what it owes) divided by the number of its outstanding shares. Book value can consistently lead you to underpriced stocks. You can find many companies' book values per share at *http://finance.yahoo.com*.

• Purchases by corporate insiders. Senior management and directors of companies usually are the first to know whether earnings are going to rise or fall. While insiders tend to sell shares for a variety of reasons, they generally buy on the open market only if they believe the price is going higher. Information on insider buying is also available at *http://finance.yahoo.com*.

• **Don't look for Dr. Livingston.** When I look for international investments, I stick with developed countries and regions with stable economies and procapitalistic, pro-Democratic forms of government.

Examples: Consider Western Europe, Japan, Canada, New Zealand, Australia, Singapore and non-Chinese companies in Hong Kong.

The so-called emerging markets—such as China, Russia, Thailand and Venezuela—remain unsafe and unstable places to invest. To me, the small chance of making a killing isn't worth the risk, the time spent on research and the opportunities elsewhere that are lost.

• **Give your stocks a "physical."** Not every "cheap" stock is worth buying. Once I find companies whose shares are cheap, I determine why they are cheap and throw out the ones that have little chance for recovery.

The balance sheet is like a medical chart—it tells you if the business is healthy enough to survive when times get tough. I scrutinize each company's balance sheet for the past five years. *What I look for...*

• At least twice as much in liquid assets, such as cash and Treasury bills, as short-term debt.

• Declining long-term debt. I define long-term debt as obligations maturing in more than 12 months. The figure should be declining year-over-year in relation to the company's assets, such as real estate, factories and investments in subsidiaries.

I also review the company's annual income statement. *What I look for...*

• Accelerating revenue (sales) growth over a five-year period.

• Steady gross profit margin for the past five years.

• High return on capital (ROC). ROC is a gauge that relates the income of a company to the value of its assets—essentially, it measures how effectively a company uses the money invested in its operations. The higher the ROC in relation to other companies in the same industry, the better.

• **Sift out the fool's gold.** If there is something about a company that I don't understand or that I am uncomfortable with, I reject it. *Red flags...*

• Too much debt—total liabilities are greater than stockholders' equity.

• Serious labor contract issues.

• Risk of product obsolescence.

• Lack of control over expenses, as in the case of airlines' fuel costs.

How Good Is Your Broker? Watch Out For These Red Flags

Daniel R. Solin, JD, an attorney in New York City who has won judgments on behalf of investors against some of Wall Street's most prestigious brokerage firms. He is author of *Does Your Broker Owe You Money?* Perigee. His Web site is *www.smartest investmentbook.com*.

There are many possible danger signs that your stockbroker is not doing a great job for you. *Here's what to watch out for, and what to do if your account is mismanaged...*

RED FLAGS

• **Your portfolio is entirely invested in stocks.** The safest allocation for most investors includes a mix of stocks, bonds and cash. Unless you feel comfortable taking major risks—and unless you and your broker have agreed on such a strategy—you should not be 100% in stocks.

Example: Sally placed $2 million with a full-service brokerage firm and explained that the money was for her retirement. The broker invested nearly everything in high-risk technology stocks. Over three years, her account lost $1.5 million. An arbitration panel awarded Sally only $600,000.

• **Your portfolio seems unusually volatile.** Beware when swings in your stock portfolio's value exceed those of the overall market, as measured by the Standard & Poor's 500 stock index.

Example: Jorge, a man in his 70s, told his broker that he wanted investments suitable for a retiree. The broker picked highly speculative stocks that were five times as volatile as the S&P 500. In 18 months, Jorge's nest egg went from $400,000 to $6,000. Luckily, arbitration awarded Jorge $550,000 in damages.

• **Account expenses seem unusually high.** The annual total you pay in commissions and margin interest (if you buy stocks with borrowed money) shouldn't exceed 3% of the total value of your portfolio. If it does, you need to earn unrealistically high returns, year after year, just to break even.

Example: Kathleen invested $380,000 with a broker at a major national brokerage firm. Over five years, her account lost $275,000. Trading commissions and interest on margin loans amounted to more than 16% of the value of her portfolio—meaning that she would have needed to earn at least that much just to break even. When Kathleen threatened the firm with arbitration, it reimbursed her for 100% of her losses.

WHAT TO DO IF YOUR ACCOUNT IS MISMANAGED

If you are unhappy with your stockbroker, complaining to your brokerage firm is not necessarily the best course of action. Why? When you established your account, you almost certainly signed an agreement requiring any complaint to go to arbitration, rather than to court. If you complain to the firm, you might inadvertently make statements that will hurt you in arbitration.

Even if you have lost money based on a stockbroker's recommendations, you might not have a case against him/her. However, if any of the above warning signs are present, you might be able to bring a successful arbitration claim against your broker. Aim to recover all of your "well-managed account" losses. This term refers to how your portfolio should have performed if it had had reasonable fees and an appropriate asset allocation based on your age and risk tolerance.

• **If your claim is for less than $25,000,** there is a simple procedure to file for arbitration without an attorney. Contact the Financial Industry Regulatory Authority (301-590-6500, *www.finra.org*).

• **If your claim is for more than $25,000,** consult an attorney experienced in securities arbitration law. The Public Investors Arbitration Bar Association comprises more than 750 lawyers who represent complainants in securities arbitration proceedings. Go to *www.piaba.org* and click on "Find an Attorney" or call 888-621-7484.

Ask up front how the attorney expects to be compensated. Some work on a fee basis, but many work on a contingency basis. They take a percentage of what you win in the arbitration.

Don't Get Taken In

Robert Bertsch, founder, Bertsch & Associates, PC, a securities litigation firm, Port Washington, NY, and coauthor of *The Individual Investor's Guide to Recovering Losses* (available at some libraries). His Web site is *www.bertschlaw.com*.

Even savvy investors can be taken in by unscrupulous brokers trying to steal their money.

Look for these warning signs: You get a letter from your broker asking you to sign a form approving your risk level. By signing it, you could be giving up your right to take action against the broker at a later point. Don't sign it unless it accurately reflects your risk level. *Your broker offers perks,* such as IPO shares, to induce you to invest more money or become a "preferred customer." He/she uses hard-sell tactics and such phrases as "you need to move now."

Self-defense: Keep all buy and sell confirmations. Monitor account activity. After you agree to make a trade, ask your broker to call you back with the sell price immediately upon execution.

Looking for an On-Line Broker?

Best on-line discount brokers, based on trade execution, ease of use, research, portfolio reports and help, in order…

- **OptionsXpress**
- **Thinkorswim**
- **Muriel Siebert & Co.**
- **Ameritrade Apex**
- **Fidelity**
- **E*Trade Serious Investor**
- **Scottrade**

Some of these firms have special rates and services for frequent traders. If you are a buy-and-hold investor, look into Muriel Siebert, Fidelity, TD Ameritrade and Scottrade.

Survey and analysis of 27 on-line brokers by *Barron's*, 200 Liberty St., New York City 10281.

Sane Investing in an Insane World from Jim Cramer

Jim Cramer, cofounder of TheStreet.com and host of CNBC-TV's *Mad Money*, located in Englewood Cliffs, NJ and the syndicated radio show *RealMoney*. He is also the author of four books, including *Jim Cramer's Stay Mad for Life*. Simon & Schuster.

You may chuckle at Jim Cramer's outrageous, in-your-face TV antics such as the "lightning round," during which he shouts "buy," "sell" or "hold" for one stock after another. He also adds crazy special effects, such as a man jumping out of a window or strains of the "Hallelujah Chorus." But nobody is denying that this hedge-fund-manager-turned-TV-personality knows how to invest.

During his 13 years running a private hedge fund, Mr. Cramer achieved a 24% compounded return after fees. His secret wasn't so much masterfully picking winners as avoiding losses. *Here are his portfolio defense strategies…*

● **Buy best-of-breed companies.** Amateur investors can be suckers for cheaper alternatives to quality stocks. Too many choose Safeway over Whole Foods Market and pick Hewlett-Packard or Gateway over Dell.

There are very few bargains in the world of second-rate players. When I have the choice of a few companies in an industry, I go with the best one—even if the stock's price-to-earnings multiple makes it more expensive.

Reason: High-quality businesses will hold up much better in downturns. The underdog hardly ever wins the game.

● **Defend your picks.** Take several minutes to explain to someone else—your spouse, a friend, a coworker—why you're buying a particular stock. Having to put your thinking into words this way can help you spot flawed logic and avoid mistakes.

Questions I force myself to answer: What's the catalyst that will make this stock rise? Have I already missed a lot of the move up? Should I wait until it comes down a little in price? Do I like this stock more than every other one I own—and why do I like it more?

This last question is critical because you can keep track of only so many good ideas at once. In fact, many professional investors discipline themselves by refusing to add a stock to their portfolios unless they like it enough to sell one that they already own.

● **Don't buy based on earnings "pre-announcements."** Nothing is more tempting than a stock that has fallen in price after its CEO preannounces that the company's quarterly earnings aren't likely to meet expectations. Professionals know it is foolish to buy one of these.

Reasons: Companies hate to preannounce and aren't required to do so. They won't make negative preannouncements if there is any hope that performance will get better in the month before actual earnings are released.

•**Pay taxes willingly.** Gains can be ephemeral. Never use taxes as an excuse to hold a stock if the price has gone up rapidly. Long-term gains on stocks held for more than one year are taxed at a maximum rate of 15%, while short-term gains are taxed at a rate of up to 35%—but waiting to sell is foolhardy if a stock has weakening fundamentals or has become overvalued.

Helpful: Minimize your taxes by using losses on bad picks to offset gains.

•**When a CEO or CFO leaves suddenly, so should you.** Don't let company press releases fool you. High-level executives don't resign for "personal" or "family" reasons. They got their fabulous jobs after sacrificing much of what other people enjoy.

Competition is so fierce for these positions that a company must have serious problems before a CEO would step down without another equally good situation available. For instance, I wasn't smart enough to cash out of Enron when it was $90 per share, but when CEO Jeffrey Skilling resigned in 2001, I sold immediately at $47. Ultimately, the stock went to zero.

•**Never subsidize losers with winners.** Amateurs hate selling their dogs. Rather than take their medicine—the loss—they rationalize that other investors soon will see the company's hidden value. They raise cash by selling some of their winning shares to buy more of their losers.

My rule of thumb: When a stock's price deteriorates, sell it if the company fundamentals, such as earnings, market share, etc., also are deteriorating. Buy more shares only if such fundamentals are solid or improving.

•**Don't buy all at once.** When I first started as a professional trader, I was arrogant about my stock-picking ability. If I wanted 5,000 shares of Caterpillar, I would buy them all at once.

But after purchasing billions of shares in my career, do you know how often I got in at the very lowest price? Probably once in 100 times—and I'm pretty good at spotting bottoms.

Now I buy and sell in increments, spacing out trades to avoid letting my emotions get in the way. For example, every year for my 401(k) retirement account, I decide how much I will contribute and put ½2 of that to work each month.

Exception: If the stock market is down by 10% one month, I put in the next month's contribution as well. If the market is down by 15%, I put in the entire next quarter's contribution. Should the market decline by 20% in a month—which has happened twice in the past decade—I invest my entire year's contribution.

A Top Trader Tells— "How I Turned $33,000 Into $7 Million"

Michael J. Parness, chief executive officer and founder of TrendFund.com, an advisory and counseling service for active stock traders, New York City, *www.trendfund.com*. He is author of *Rule the Freakin' Markets* (St. Martin's) and *Power Trading Power Living* (Ultimate). He is frequently interviewed by *The Wall Street Journal*, CNBC, *Financial Times*, Fox News and Business Talk Radio. He conducts informational trading seminars around the country.

Eight years ago, Michael Parness, who at the time operated a successful sports-memorabilia business, followed a stockbroker's advice and sunk his $150,000 nest egg into a few recommended stocks. It didn't take long for his portfolio to shrink by nearly 80%. In February 1999, he opened an on-line brokerage account and vowed to get his money back. In just 15 months, Parness's initial balance of $33,000 had soared to $7 million.

While active trading strategies are not for the faint of heart, devoting a small amount of your portfolio to such strategies can boost profits in any market—even when stock prices overall are flat or declining. *Parness's favorite stock-trading techniques…*

TAME YOUR INNER KNUCKLEHEAD

Many investors get into trouble by leaping before they look. For at least a month, try trading stocks "on paper" or start a simulated trading account at *www.stocktrak.com/ trendfund*. Once you begin to see profits, start trading with real money.

Caution: When buying stocks, control your risk. Use a stop-loss order for each of your holdings. This is an order for your brokerage to sell the stock if it drops to a specified price that is below the current market price.

How much should you allow a stock to drop? When setting such a floor, I rely on what I call the 2% rule—no investment should lose more than 2% of the value of your entire portfolio. For example, if you have a portfolio of $100,000 and you buy 500 shares of IBM, set a stop-loss order at a price that ensures you won't lose more than $2,000 on your IBM position.

HEED MY THREE "DON'TS"

Don't invest in just one or two stocks… *don't* invest if you're not confident about a stock's prospects…*don't* buy a stock because a broker, stock analyst or TV personality hypes it—the price may jump immediately after the recommendation, and you'll wind up paying a premium price.

Better strategy: Own at least five stocks, preferably from several sectors, based on careful research. You want to diversify so you're not crushed if one of your positions encounters bad news or is in a sector that gets pummeled.

BUY ON THE RUMOR AND SELL ON THE NEWS

The saying is a cliché, but the strategy makes sense.

Example: When it was first rumored that Sirius Satellite Radio Inc. (SIRI*) was in talks with "shock jock" deejay Howard Stern, investors pushed the stock up from $3 to as

*Prices are subject to change.

high as $9 a share. When Stern actually began broadcasting in January, the news was played out and the stock settled back to $5. Most of those who wanted to invest in the Sirius-Stern play had already done so. Many of my clients made money by selling before Stern started broadcasting.

MAKE THE TREND YOUR FRIEND

This is another cliché but still good advice—and often ignored. I've made most of my money by investing in trends or patterns that I spotted in both bull and bear markets. I look for trends that occur repeatedly in several stocks and use them to anticipate price movements in similar stocks. Trends don't last forever and are continually being replaced by new ones, so you'll need to monitor your portfolio carefully to follow this strategy.

The goal of trend trading is to capture fat profits—5% to 50% or more—within several days or weeks.

Example: There are several stocks that deal in Canadian oil sands. (Crude oil is extracted from oil sands.) The biggest is Suncor Energy Inc. (SU), which I have owned on and off. The idea still is to buy stocks in the same sector that haven't quite caught up to a company whose stock price has moved up rapidly.

KNOW WHEN TO ESCAPE

Not every stock trade will succeed. *Reduce your chances of loss by dumping a stock when…*

• **A trend is no longer working.** In 1999 and 2000, stock splits were a major trend. You could buy a stock within two weeks of an upcoming split, and its price would go up based on the theory that after the split, more investors would buy it at the lower share price. The stock-split play stopped working from 2002 through 2005 but recently began working again.

• **The stock's upward momentum has fizzled** or has been abruptly broken. This might happen without your stop-loss being triggered.

- **The stock is nearing $100 or $200 a share,** which is a major psychological barrier. Historically, investors have resisted pushing stocks above $100 or $200 a share.

Reason: People like to sell at prices that are round numbers, when a stock reaches $100 or $200 rather than, say, $83 or $172.

- **The stock is about to reach a resistance level—**a price that it has been unable to break through before.

Is It Tax-Deductible?

Tax-deductible investment-related items include fees for financial advice…subscriptions to financial publications…software or on-line services for managing investments…safe-deposit-box rental fee if you keep investment documents in the box…transportation to/from the office of a broker or adviser…legal or accounting costs needed to produce taxable income. Trading commissions are not deductible—they become part of your cost basis.

Also not deductible: Travel costs to a shareholders' meeting…investment-advisory fees related to tax-exempt income.

Rande Spiegelman, vice president of financial planning, Schwab Center for Investment Research, San Francisco.

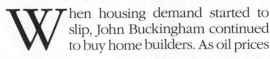

John Buckingham Makes Big Money On Stocks Other Investors Hate

John Buckingham, editor of *The Prudent Speculator* newsletter, Laguna Beach, CA, *www.prudentspeculator.com.*

When housing demand started to slip, John Buckingham continued to buy home builders. As oil prices dropped, he bought energy companies. Such contrarian moves require a strong stomach, but Buckingham's persistence helps explain why his *Prudent Speculator* ranks as the top-performing investment newsletter for the 10 years through March 2008, according to *The Hulbert Financial Digest.*

Buckingham cautions that it is not enough to simply buy unloved stocks. Once they land in the cellar, many troubled companies stay there or go out of business. *To limit the risks, Buckingham suggests that investors…*

- **Seek solid balance sheets.** Big cash holdings and a strong balance sheet can help a company weather hard times. After technology stocks collapsed in 2000–2002, I began recommending Apple Computer. The company had no debt and a $7 share price. With plenty of money in the bank, Apple would have time to develop innovative products, as it had done in the past. I didn't know that Apple's iPod would become an enormous hit or that the company would launch the iPhone in 2007. Based on Apple's history, however, it seemed likely that its researchers would eventually produce another winner.

- **Buy cheap.** My typical holding has a price-to-earnings ratio (P/E) of 12, at a time when companies in the Standard & Poor's 500 stock index average a P/E of 16. For the best bargains, compare a stock's price with its historical patterns or those of its industry. Buy when the price drops so far that history indicates it is not likely to decline much more.

- **Diversify.** All stock pickers make mistakes. About 30% of my choices prove not to be winners. To avoid big losses, hold stocks from more than a dozen industries and own several stocks in each industry.

I am constantly surprised by which of my stocks do best. Recently, I have owned more than a half-dozen pharmaceutical company stocks. The best performer has been Merck & Co., which is up by more than 40%. The company's shares had collapsed following the withdrawal of its drug Vioxx from the market because the painkiller was linked to an increased risk of heart attack and stroke. Since then, the company has beaten back several lawsuits over the drug, and its earnings outlook has improved.

• **Be patient.** On average, I hold a stock for six-and-a-half years. It often takes that long for depressed shares to reach their fair values.

Use Tax Savings to Boost Returns on Your Investments

David Rosenberg, former US head of investment solutions, Citigroup Private Bank. He is currently chief investment officer at the Threshold Group, 590 Madison Ave., NY 10022. He specializes in investment strategies for high-net-worth individuals.

There's a saying that you should not "let the tax tail wag the investment dog." Make decisions based on expected investment results, not merely on tax factors.

Nevertheless, the "tax tail" should not be ignored. With bonds and stocks, tax concerns will greatly affect your ultimate payoff.

BONDS: A GOOD TIME FOR MUNICIPALS

Tax-exempt municipal bonds look quite attractive right now. They have high after-tax yields compared with other bonds.

Suggested: Insured munis maturing in three to five years.

Reasons: Insurance reduces the risk of downgrades and defaults. As for short-term versus longer-term, short-term munis (those maturing in two years or less) have very low yields now, while issues longer than five years may lose value sharply if interest rates rise.

Three- to five-year munis have the best risk-reward profile now.

Comparison: To see the advantages of investing in municipal bonds in today's market, consider the five-year Treasury as a possible alternative. The recent yield was just under 5%.

In a 35% federal tax bracket, you would net less than 3.25% after taxes.

Insured five-year munis, meanwhile, have been paying around 3.8%. You would owe no federal tax on that income, so you would be ahead with the munis.

Strategy: State and local tax might be due on interest from an out-of-state muni. So, when investing in munis, stay with high-quality insured or AA-rated or better munis issued within your state.

AMT trap: If you pay state and local income tax on an out-of-state municipal bond, you increase your chances of being subject to the alternative minimum tax (AMT) because state/local taxes are not deductible under the AMT.

That's another reason to favor in-state muni issues.

High-yield, high-risk: It's true that you can earn higher yields with low-rated US corporate bonds or foreign bonds issued in emerging markets.

However, these issues generate taxable interest. At current yields, the after-tax payoff would not be great enough to justify the risks you assume with such bonds.

Bonds or funds? Knowledgeable investors generally prefer individual bonds to bond funds because fund expenses can eat into yield. With $250,000 or more to invest in bonds, you can purchase a variety of high-quality munis so that you have diversification.

Investors with smaller portfolios can do quite well, though, by using municipal bond funds with unusually low costs. Fund-tracking company Morningstar, *www.morningstar.com*, puts the average muni fund expense ratio at 1.08% per year. But many high-rated funds charge far less. Available funds include some that hold only bonds issued in one state, such as New York or California, and thus can deliver income that's fully tax exempt for residents.

STOCKS: LEARN TO LOVE LOSERS

With a diversified assortment of stocks and stock funds, you probably have some unrealized gains and unrealized losses at any given time.

Strategy: Set limits and take losses whenever those limits are exceeded.

Example: When you buy a stock for $50 a share, tell yourself that you'll sell if the stock drops below $45.

Advantage: Such "loss harvesting" can serve several purposes...

● **Realized losses can offset realized gains** and thus keep your tax obligation down. Losses you take on stocks can offset capital gains from other areas, such as real estate or interests in private companies.

● **If you have net capital losses,** you can deduct up to $3,000 worth of such losses each year.

● **Net losses that you can't deduct immediately** can be carried forward to future years. This will allow you to take capital gains without owing tax, as long as you have sufficient losses in this "bank."

Bottom line: Capital losses can be valuable assets, so you should take them within reason. Taking them sooner rather than later can help prevent modest losses from turning into larger ones.

Trap: Some investors do all their loss harvesting at year-end. If you follow this strategy, you may run into selling pressure that will further depress prices of the equities you're unloading.

Reason: Everyone wants to unload the same stocks—at the same time.

Instead, harvest your losses throughout the year as opportunities arise.

SEPARATELY MANAGED ACCOUNTS

Many financial firms now offer separately managed accounts (SMAs). Tax efficiency is one of the reasons that these vehicles are gaining popularity.

What they are: They have been called "personal mutual funds." Rather than owning shares in a pool of stocks or bonds, as is the case with mutual funds, the investor actually owns the underlying securities. These securities will be picked for you by professional money managers. SMAs usually have a $100,000 minimum investment per account, but some have a $25,000 minimum. Some SMAs use model portfolios (preset assortments of securities), some don't.

Work with your financial adviser to pick an SMA manager. In addition to a good track record, look for an investment strategy that makes you comfortable. For instance, you may choose a manager with a history of selecting dividend-paying stocks. You can request customized portfolios, including the absence of certain companies or industries. You meet with your adviser, who will contact the management company with your instructions.

Gain from losses: The money managers can harvest losses for you when some of your holdings drop in value. You can even have these managers take losses to suit your individual circumstances.

Example: Now that gold prices have shot up, you decide to sell the gold coins you've been saving. This results in a $50,000 taxable gain that would be taxed at 28% under the rules relating to collectibles.

Therefore, you tell your financial adviser about your realized gains. The adviser and the SMA money managers can work together to realize losses so that you won't have to pay such a steep tax bill.

Fee deductions: SMA fees are based on assets in your account. Generally, you would pay 1% to 2% a year.

If this fee is paid with money not in the account, it may be tax deductible. Investment advisory fees are miscellaneous itemized deductions, which are deductible to the extent that they exceed 2% of your adjusted gross income.

Basis advantage: When you put money into individual securities within an SMA, you start out with a fresh basis—your cost for tax purposes.

That's not the case when you invest in a mutual fund.

Example: On July 1, you invest in Fund ABC. Before year-end, the fund takes gains on stocks that it has held for many years.

Those gains are passed through to all shareholders, pro rata.

Result: Although the fund share value drops, which might reduce your future tax obligation, you pay tax immediately on gains you haven't enjoyed. That's true even if you choose to have capital gains distributions reinvested so you don't pocket any cash.

With SMAs, you have control of your investment taxes, which isn't true with mutual funds.

Keep Uncle Sam's Hands off Your Investment Gains

Janice M. Johnson, CPA, JD, A.B. Watley Group, 50 Broad St., New York City 10004. Ms. Johnson has more than 25 years of experience in advising high-net-worth investors, hedge funds, and broker-dealers about the tax consequences of investing.

Careful tax management of your investments can help you keep more of your gains—and suffer fewer investment losses. *Strategies that can help…*

TAX-SAVING RECORD KEEPING

Doing no more than keeping good records can let you reduce the taxes you owe on investments.

For instance, using "specific share" identification on stock trades can enable you to choose whether a trade produces a gain or loss and the size of it, whatever is best tax-wise.

Example: You bought shares of a stock at different times, paying prices of $20, $30 and $40. Today, the stock trades at $35, and you intend to sell a portion of your shares.

IRS rules generally treat the first shares bought as the first sold when computing gain or loss on a stock sale. So, if the $20 shares were the first bought, a sale at $35 will produce a gain of $15 per share (until the $20 shares are all sold).

But, if you've kept records to identify the price of specific shares you own, you can instead select for sale specific shares to generate a loss of $5 per share (selling the $40 shares) or a gain of $15 per share (selling the $20 shares) or any net result in between, whatever is best tax-wise.

For detailed rules on using specific share identification, see IRS Publication 550, *Investment Income and Expenses.*

Other records to keep…

• **Long- and short-term gains records.** It's important to keep records of the long-term holding date for every investment. *If the investment has gone…*

• Up in value, you'll want to hold it more than the full year to get tax-favored long-term-gain treatment for it.

• Down in value, consider selling it before the holding period becomes long term to realize a short-term loss. This can be used to offset short-term gains that otherwise would be taxed at top rates.

Example: You buy a stock that unexpectedly zooms up in value right away—but you fear its value may soon fall. Your dilemma is that if you sell it now, you'll pay 35% federal tax (plus any state/local tax) on the gain, but if you hold it for more than a year to get tax-favored long-term treatment (15% tax), a fall in its value may cost you more than you will have saved.

If your records show that you have an offsetting short-term loss in another investment that you could realize, you have no problem—you can sell both investments right away and pocket the unexpected gain tax free.

Also, keep a running total of your long-term and short-term gains and losses realized to date. This will help you figure out what tax-optimizing offsetting gains and losses to look to take by year-end.

• **Dividend reinvestment records.** One of the most common mistakes investors make is not counting reinvested dividends in the cost of shares sold—erroneously increasing their tax bills. This is most frequently a problem with mutual fund shares where you have your dividends automatically reinvested. But fund companies will supply the information to you on request.

• **Mutual fund basis records.** Know the cost of shares in the order bought and the average cost of all of your shares.

Why: Mutual fund shares can be sold computing gain on an "average cost" basis if doing so produces a better tax result than first-bought, first-sold. See IRS Publication 564, *Mutual Fund Distributions.*

• **Investment-related fee and expense records.** These items are deductible on itemized tax returns. Include the cost of investment publications, advice—even record-keeping ledgers and software.

Key: If you wait until after year-end to tally your investment results, you will miss the chance to make tax-saving moves before year-end, and almost surely make other mistakes in your tax results as well. So start using tax-saving record keeping now.

TAX-LOSS OFFSETS

Reallocate investments using tax-loss offsets. You'll start investing by allocating your holdings among different investments as best for your situation. But varying investment returns over time will drive your holdings away from this "best" allocation.

Example: You decide that your best investment position is 20% risky growth stocks, 40% blue chip value stocks and 40% bonds. You set up your portfolio this way, but after a period of high stock returns, it has shifted to 35% growth stocks, 45% value stocks and only 20% bonds.

Now, you are overweighted in stocks—especially in risky growth stocks that could crash. You should go back to your best allocation by taking gains on your most appreciated stocks, locking in profits and shifting the proceeds to bonds. But you may be deterred from doing so by the tax that will come due on the gains you realize.

What to do: Take offsetting losses at the same time. Find holdings in your portfolio that have lost value and sell them to realize losses that offset gains realized when reallocating—making the process tax free, or as much so as possible.

Bonus benefit: Your portfolio will further improve due to the scrutiny you give its lagging performers in this process.

BIGGER TRADING DEDUCTIONS

If you regularly trade stocks seeking short-term gains, you may benefit from achieving "trader" status and making a Section 475(f) mark-to-market election. *Why...*

• **Trader status provides larger deductions.** Income from trading is reported on the Schedule D of the tax return filed by all investors, but expenses are deducted on a Schedule C.

This gives a full business expense deduction for investment expenses and investment interest, freeing them from normal limitations. It also supports a deduction for a home office and related equipment (computer, etc.).

• **The Section 475 election treats all gains as short term**—traders' gains tend to be short term anyhow—but makes losses fully deductible against ordinary income, exempting them from capital loss limitations.

The election also causes gain or loss to be figured on all open investment positions at year-end.

Strategy: Form a limited liability company (LLC) through which to trade, segregating trading from your other investments. This lets you continue to invest for long-term gains in your personal accounts.

By investing for long-term gains in personal accounts, and having an LLC that manages frequent short-term trades and passes its deductions to you, you get the best tax treatment.

Caution: The mark-to-market election generally is irrevocable. Consult a tax adviser.

PROPER ALLOCATION

Allocate investments wisely between tax-deferred and taxable accounts. *Tax-deferred retirement savings accounts, such as 401(k)s and traditional IRAs, have drawbacks...*

• **All distributions are taxed at ordinary income rates up to 35%**—so they may, in effect, convert tax-advantaged capital gains into highly taxed ordinary income.

• **Distributions usually must start, and be taxed, at age 70½.**

• **Heirs who inherit such accounts owe the same potentially high taxes,** since "stepped-up basis" does not apply to these accounts.

In contrast, investments in taxable accounts receive a top 15% long-term capital gains tax rate, can be held forever and can be bequeathed to heirs with stepped-up basis that eliminates all gains tax on their value as of that date.

Example: You can hold an index mutual fund in a taxable account free of capital gains tax for life, then leave it to heirs tax free with stepped-up basis, eliminating all taxable gain in value to that date. Or you can cash in shares as you wish, paying no more than 15% gains tax.

But the same mutual fund held in a tax-deferred account will be taxed at up to 35%, and must be liquidated starting at age 70½.

Strategy: Construct your portfolio so tax-deferred accounts hold income-earning assets, such as taxable bonds, that benefit from tax deferral to allow pretax compounding. Use taxable accounts to hold your buy-and-hold, long-term-gain investments.

Tax-Smart Way to Choose Mutual Funds

Sue Stevens, CPA, CFP, CFA, director of financial planning at Morningstar Inc., LLC, a financial information provider in Chicago, *www.morningstar.com.* Founder and president of Stevens Portfolio Design, LLC, 500 Lake Cook Rd., Ste. 350, Deerfield, IL 60015, *www.gotospd.com*, she has also been named one of the top 250 financial planners in the US by *Worth* magazine.

With mutual funds, what you see isn't what you get in many cases because of taxes.

Funds report their performance pretax. For investors, the after-tax results can be much different.

Example: In a recent 10-year period, American Century Equity Income Fund (TWEIX) had an annualized return of 12.85%. That return placed it among the top 2% of all funds in its large-company, value-stock fund category.

DWS Dreman High Return Equity (KDHAX) fund, another in the same category, was a cut below, with a 10-year annualized return of 12.06%.

Over those 10 years, the difference in return before taxes would have been more than $2,200 for every $10,000 invested.

But after tax, according to Morningstar Inc., the DWS Dreman fund was ahead in "tax-adjusted" terms, with gains of 9.99% a year, vs. 9.16% for the American Century fund.

Over those 10 years, the DWS Dreman investor would have been *ahead* by about $1,900 for each $10,000 invested, instead of lagging by $2,200.

MAKING A DIFFERENCE

Such differences are by no means unusual. Some mutual funds are more tax efficient than others. Over an extended period, this can make a big after-tax difference to investors.

Crunching the numbers: To arrive at these tax-adjusted returns, Morningstar follows procedures outlined by the federal Securities and Exchange Commission (SEC)…

• **All distributions of income** are assumed to be taxed at the highest federal rate that year (now 35%).

• **Distributions of short-term gains** are taxed in the same manner.

• **Distributions of long-term gains** are assumed to be taxed at the maximum rate for such gains that year (now 15%).

It's true that relatively few taxpayers are in the top federal tax bracket, which doesn't kick in until $336,550 of taxable income this year (on single or joint returns). On the other hand, the SEC formula does not include state or local income tax, which many investors must pay. Ultimately, these hypothetical tax-adjusted returns deliver a reasonable approximation of how investors actually fared and are valuable for comparisons.

LOSING FROM GAINS

Among stock funds, income from dividends now averages only around 0.3%, so they are not the main cause of tax inefficiency.

Instead, capital gains distributions play a key role.

How: Stock funds generally trade their portfolios frequently during the year. Most trades result in a gain or loss for the fund.

Each year, the fund must tabulate its net gain or loss for the year. The law requires a mutual fund to distribute capital gains to shareholders if the fund sells securities for a profit that can't be offset by a loss.

Example: ABC Mutual Fund has 10 million shares outstanding. This year, its trading activities generate a $25 million net gain.

Thus, investors will receive a $2.50-per-share capital gains distribution. If Janice Jefferson holds 1,000 shares of ABC, her distribution will be $2,500.

If some of those gains were from stocks held for a year or less, part of the distribution will be reported as a short-term gain, taxed to shareholders at rates up to 35%.

Otherwise, the gain will qualify for favorable long-term capital gains rates, now generally 15%.

Trap: Tax will be owed on those gains, even if the distribution is reinvested in the same fund or in another security. Thus, investors may have to pay tax on "distributions" even though they haven't received any cash.

What if a fund has net losses from its trading? Such losses are not passed through to shareholders.

However, net losses are "banked" by the fund so they can be used to offset any future trading gains and thus spare investors some tax pain.

TRADE SECRETS

Mutual fund tax inefficiency is caused largely by each fund's trading patterns.

Funds that trade heavily are most likely to incur capital gains that are passed through to investors. A fund that turns its portfolio over rapidly may generate expensive short-term gains.

What's more, buying into a fund at the wrong time can lead to high taxes, as investors learned in the 2000–2002 bear market.

What happened: The technology, media and telecommunications stocks that led the 1990s' bull market fell sharply. Funds holding those stocks sold them off to prevent further losses and also to raise cash needed to pay investors who were redeeming shares.

In many cases, those stocks were bought years earlier, at substantially lower prices, so the funds had huge capital gains on these sales.

Trap: Those gains were passed through to all investors, newcomers as well as those who had been in the funds for years.

Investors who put money into a growth fund in 2000 might have received hefty tax bills, that year and in those that followed, even while suffering sharp losses as the fund's share price fell.

DOWNSIZING DISTRIBUTIONS

To reduce your risk of such lose-lose investing…

● **Evaluate a fund's history.** A fund that has consistently distributed sizable gains to investors in most years may have a management philosophy of heavy trading. Such a fund is likely to continue to distribute taxable gains.

Before you invest, ask your broker or a fund sales representative about its distribution record.

On-line, you can go to *www.morningstar.com* and enter a fund's ticker symbol in the "Quotes" search box. Then click on "Tax Analysis" to find the fund's tax-adjusted return and "tax cost ratio." (There is no charge for this.)

Data also are available in *Morningstar Mutual Funds*, a binder of periodic fund profiles. *Cost:* $599/yr. for 24 issues. But you may also find this at your local library.

Generally, if a stock fund has a tax-cost ratio (which shows how much of its return would have been lost to tax each year) of more than 1.25, it should be held in a tax-deferred retirement account. Bond funds with tax-cost ratios of more than 2.0 also work best in a tax-deferred account.

● **Be wary of built-in gains.** Funds having a portfolio filled with highly appreciated stocks may have a potential capital gains exposure of 40% or more of assets. If those shares are sold, the gains could produce big tax bills for investors.

Conversely, funds with loss carry forwards might be worth considering partly for that reason.

Caution: A loss carry forward should not be the primary reason to buy a fund. A fund's past performance, management expertise and so on, are more important.

Again, information on potential gains and loss carry forwards is available from your broker, the fund company and from Morningstar.

● **Consider tax-managed funds.** Some funds explicitly manage their portfolios to minimize investors' tax bills. They trade little and take losses to offset any trading gains.

Such funds generally have "tax-managed" in their name. Vanguard Tax-Managed Growth and Income Fund (VTGIX), for example, gets three stars* (out of a possible five) from Morningstar.

● **Consider index funds.** Funds designed to track a particular index usually hold the stocks in that index. They tend to trade infrequently and thus don't incur much in the way of taxable capital gains.

So-called exchange-traded funds (ETFs) are index funds that trade like stocks. They're generally tax efficient.

Bottom line: If you hold mutual funds in a tax-deferred account, such as a 401(k) or an IRA, tax efficiency won't matter. You won't owe any tax until you withdraw money.

In a taxable account, taxes count. It's wise to evaluate a fund primarily on its management, philosophy, track record and other fundamentals—but take a hard look at its tax efficiency before you invest.

*Subject to change.

New Fund Manager Warning

Don Phillips, managing director, Morningstar, Inc., 225 W. Wacker Dr., Chicago 60606.

A new fund manager may mean higher taxes for shareholders. Be careful when there are management changes within your fund.

Reason: When a new manager takes over a mutual fund, he/she often sells off unwanted holdings—triggering taxable capital gains distributions for shareholders.

Also: Investors sometimes leave a fund when a new manager comes on board, forcing the manager to make additional sales as people redeem shares. This also may raise

shareholders' tax burden. However, for some types of funds, manager changes don't trigger big distributions.

Example: Index fund holdings are determined by the index the fund tracks, not by the manager's preferences or other factors.

Smart: Hold actively managed funds primarily in tax-deferred accounts and index funds in taxable accounts.

Better Stock Research

Best sources of stock research for investors based on performance of buy and sell recommendations over the last two years: Ford Equity Research, Raymond James, Columbine Capital, Weiss Ratings (now a unit of TheStreet.com), Wachovia Securities, Channel Trend, Citigroup, Argus Research and Bank of America. Costs vary.

Kiplinger's Personal Finance Magazine, 1729 H St. NW, Washington, DC 20006.

How to Choose a Mutual Fund

When choosing a mutual fund, eliminate load funds.

● **Look for a low expense ratio** compared with other funds of the same type.

● **Check portfolio turnover**—the lower, the better.

● **Look at the number of holdings**— fewer means more volatility, while more generally means better diversification.

● **Keep in mind that index funds are the lowest cost,** lowest risk and most tax-efficient way to provide exposure to a certain market.

Frank Armstrong III, founder and principal, Investor Solutions, Inc., investment adviser, Coconut Grove, FL, and author of *The Informed Investor.* American Management Association.

Funds to Avoid

Avoid funds newly available to the public that are sold based on their "long-term" results. These so-called *incubator funds* are started by companies to try out an investment approach and then sold to the public after several years if the approach goes well. But by the time the fund becomes widely available, its management may have changed, fees may be higher than they were in the incubation phase and the investing style may have shifted—so the results from the incubation period may be meaningless.

Karen Dolan, fund analyst, Morningstar, Inc., Chicago.

Emerging Market Warning

For high yields, don't look to emerging-market bonds. Many countries have reformed their economies and have budget surpluses, but yields on emerging-market bond funds average only 6%, according to Morningstar, Inc. For most investors, the spread between this yield and that of US Treasuries would have to widen to three percentage points before the sector would be worthwhile. Even then, no more than 10% of a portfolio should be in emerging-market bonds.

Alternative: T. Rowe Price Spectrum Income fund (RPSIX), a multisector fund that periodically invests in this segment.

Mark Salzinger, publisher and editor of The No-Load Fund Investor, Brentwood, TN, *www.noload fundinvestor.com.*

Help for Load Funds Investors

If you invest in load funds, choose the lowest-cost share class using FINRA's enhanced "Mutual Fund Expense Analyzer" and "Mutual Fund Breakpoint Search Tool" at *www.finra.org.* The Expense Analyzer calculates sales charges, operating expenses and other information for particular share classes. The Breakpoint Search Tool shows at what investment levels your sales charges drop. Both tools are free.

Mary Schapiro, chief executive officer, FINRA, Washington, DC.

Interested in Finding Or Starting an Investment Club?

The National Association of Investors Corporation (877-275-6242, *www.better investing.org*) offers information on how to start your own club or find an established group.

Or: Search for investment groups at *www. meetup.com* by entering keywords, such as "money," "debt" and "investing."

Money, Time-Life Bldg., Rockefeller Plaza, New York City 10020.

Tax-Exempt Bond Trap

William G. Brennan, CPA/PFS, CFP, Capital Management Group, LLC, 1730 Rhode Island Ave. NW, Washington, DC 20036.

A friend of mine was shocked to find he owed a significant tax bill on his "tax-exempt" municipal bonds. How can this happen?

Possible ways…

1. Only interest earned on tax-exempt bonds is tax exempt. If bonds appreciate in value and are sold at a gain, taxable capital gain results, just as from any other appreciating investment.

2. Some tax-exempt bonds pay interest that is taxable under the rules of the AMT, a tax computation that hits more taxpayers each year. These bonds generally are so-called "private activity bonds," issued to support projects (such as sports stadiums) that benefit private parties. Check the AMT status of bonds with their issuer before investing.

3. Tax-exempt bonds are often purchased at a discount, with the amount of the discount taxable as ordinary interest income. Also, not all municipal bonds pay federally tax-exempt interest.

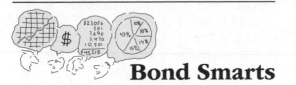

Bond Smarts

Consider selling and repurchasing a bond if its market value is higher than its face value.

Example: A 10-year $100,000 Treasury bond, issued in 2000 with a 6.5% coupon, is now worth about $105,000. After paying long-term tax on your $5,000 gain, you still come out ahead. *Reason?* Selling the bond and then buying it again creates a tax write-off for *amortization of bond premium.* This would allow $5,000 in deductions over the next five years—taken against the five years' interest of $32,500. This approach works best for people in a high federal bracket but a low state bracket. Profits will be reduced by transaction costs.

Helpful: Go to *www.twenty-first.com* and click on "Should You Sell and Repurchase Profitable Bonds?"

Robert Gordon, president, Twenty-First Securities, brokerage and investment firm, New York City.

Helpful Web Sites For Bond Investors

BondsOnline (*www.bondsonline.com*) provides bond-related news, research and other resources. *Yahoo! Finance Bond Center* (*http://finance.yahoo.com/bonds*) provides data such as Treasury bond rates and yields, as well as calculators and screeners for bond yields and returns. Other sites for screening and buying bonds include *www.bondsearch 123.com* and *www.fmsbonds.com*.

Kathy Yakal, electronic-investing columnist, *Barron's*, 200 Liberty St., New York City 10281.

If You Have an Outdated Stock Or Bond

Find the value of an outdated stock or bond at *www.oldcompany.com* or by calling 888-STOCKS6. The site provides a report on a company whose name has changed due to a merger, reorganization, bankruptcy, etc., and tells you how to contact the current company.

Cost: $39.95 per report.

Money, Time-Life Bldg., Rockefeller Center, New York City 10020.

A Low-Minimum Money Market Fund

Money market mutual funds invest in short-term instruments (maturing in less than 13 months). Most funds have opening minimums of $1,000. However, the PayPal Money Market fund will let you in for $1, and there's no fee. So, the full amount you put in your account will be invested. Yield as of press time was 2.61%. Accounts are opened only on-line at *www.paypal.com*. At the top of the page, click on "Sign Up" and then on "Personal Account." To speak with a live person, call 402-935-2050 and when given the taped options, say "Setting up an account."

Nancy Dunnan, a New York City–based financial and travel adviser and the author or coauthor of 25 books, including the best seller, *How to Invest $50–$5,000*. HarperCollins.

The New Oil?

Michael Boyle, former managing director, research and development, Claymore Securities, Inc. The securities mentioned below are currently held in unit investment trusts sponsored by Claymore Securities. Michael Boyle is currently senior vice president of Advisor's Asset Management.

Water, along with other commodities, is gaining new interest from investors as a scarce resource that's experiencing increased demand as the world becomes more urbanized. There are many ways to play the boom, starting with water utilities, such as Aqua America (WTR), the largest US water utility, and Veolia Environnement (ADR:VE), a French company with 110 million customers worldwide, including a large presence in China. Since utilities need to upgrade and enlarge facilities, even better growth potential exists in companies providing the necessary infrastructure, including Ameron International Corp. (AMN), which builds pipes for both fresh and wastewater, and Franklin Electric (FELE), a major pump manufacturer.

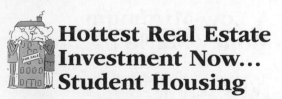# Hottest Real Estate Investment Now... Student Housing

Michael H. Zaransky, co-CEO of Prime Property Investors, Ltd., a real estate investment company in the Chicago area. He is author of *Profit by Investing in Student Housing: Cash In on the Campus Housing Shortage.* Kaplan.

The residential real estate market has cooled, but the outlook for rental properties located near university campuses remains bright.

A record 4.1 million children were born in the US in 1990, and birthrates remain high. In two years, the 1990s generation will start graduating from high school and flooding onto college campuses in unprecedented numbers. Tight budgets make it impossible for many schools to build dorms, so rental housing in university towns should be a solid investment until at least 2020.

A quality apartment building located near a popular campus might produce a return on equity of 8% to 10% per year, based on rental income. If you have less money to invest, consider buying and renting out a co-op or condo apartment or a single- or multi-family home.

Important: Check local zoning laws before you buy a single-family house near a campus to rent to students. Many towns limit the number of unrelated people who can live in one home in areas zoned residential.

If the property appreciates, your total returns will be even higher. Occupancy rates of 100% are common for rental properties near growing campuses, and if you can secure parental guarantees of payment, your rent collection rate should be close to 100%.

The best student housing investment opportunities tend to be found...

•**In states with high population growth rates,** such as Arizona, California, Florida, New York and Texas. Universities in low-growth states can represent opportunities, too, if the schools attract large numbers of non-commuting students.

Example: Iowa's population growth is modest, but the University of Iowa in Iowa City draws enough students from other states that nearby rental properties should do well.

•**Near schools that have dorm space for 30% or less** of students. Contact the university's housing department to find out how many students the school can house on campus versus how many apply for spots. Ask if there is a large-scale dormitory construction project in the works. If there is, invest elsewhere.

•**Within one mile of the student center** or main quad. Anything farther from campus puts you out of easy walking distance, a major turnoff to prospective tenants.

•**Near public universities,** not private ones. Private institutions often encourage or even require students to live on campus, and they're more likely to have the budgets to build additional dorms when needed. There are exceptions, however, so check the housing situation at private colleges in your area.

Examples: Ithaca College and Syracuse University, both in their namesake towns in New York, are private schools that don't have nearly enough dorm space for their students.

• **Near universities with aging housing stock.** When dorms are old and decrepit, many students look for better housing off campus.

CHALLENGES

Students can be tough tenants. Screen all of the roommates—not just the one whose name is on the lease. Many landlords provide a lease to each roommate. Also, ask for one month's rent as a security deposit, plus the last month's rent up front. *Other things to watch out for...*

• **High turnover.** Expect to have close to 100% turnover every year.

• **High maintenance costs.** Plan to spend about $150 per bed per year on maintenance—that's $600 in annual upkeep for a four-bedroom apartment, about 20% more than what is required for nonstudent rentals.

• **Seasonality.** You must rent out all of your apartments by the start of a school year or risk having a vacancy until the next semester. Since most students leave in the summer, getting rents in June, July and August can be difficult. It's a good idea to ask students to pay for these months in advance.

• **Reputational risk.** If you're not attentive to renters' problems, word will spread around campus. Replace broken appliances and unclog drains quickly. It's wise to hire a third-party management company to rent out your units and handle maintenance problems. Expect to pay the management company 5% of annual rental income. If possible, offer tenants high-speed Internet access, air-conditioning, parking and convenient access to washers and dryers. Students expect these amenities.

FAVORITE OPPORTUNITIES

A sampling of schools with attractive housing investment opportunities...

• **Arizona State University,** Tempe.

• **University of Florida,** Gainesville.

• **The University of Kansas,** Lawrence.

• **University of Minnesota,** Twin Cities.

• **The University of Texas at Austin.**

3

Consumer Savvy

Consumer Rip-Offs That Can Cost You Big

he average American consumer spends hundreds of dollars more than he/she needs to each year.

Reason: Corporations use powerful marketing strategies to convince us to spend more or to buy things that we don't need at all. *The most common marketing myths now...*

***Myth:* Bottled water is better than tap water.**

Reality: Tap water is as good as bottled water—and it may even be better. ABC News tested bottled and tap water for bacteria such as *E. coli* and found that there was no difference in purity.

Some people worry about traces of chemicals and minerals in water, such as chlorine, chromium, copper and iron. It's possible that some tap water may contain more of these than bottled water, but trace amounts usually aren't harmful and may even be helpful—that's why iron, copper and chromium are in vitamin pills.

As for taste, ABC's test showed that New York City tap water rated higher than the bottled water Evian. If you still insist upon buying bottled water, think downscale. Kmart's American Fare water finished ahead of imported waters that cost several times as much.

***Myth:* You can save a lot on food at discount shopping clubs.**

Reality: Warehouse clubs, such as Sam's Club and Costco, offer prices as much as 20% to 30% below those of supermarkets on many items—but consumers must buy in large quantities. You'll save money only if you eat what you buy before it spoils...avoid unnecessary impulse purchases...and shop

John Stossel, an investigative reporter with the ABC News program *20/20* since 1981. He has won 19 Emmy awards and written several books, including his most recent, *Myths, Lies, and Downright Stupidity: Get Out the Shovel—Why Everything You Know Is Wrong.* Hyperion.

64

at the club often enough to justify the annual fee of about $40. Many club members come out behind.

To make matters worse, a Cornell University study found that because warehouse club members have more food in the house, they tend to eat more, adding to their waistlines.

Myth: **Discount pet food is bad for your pet.**

Reality: Premium pet food costs more, but it isn't any better than cheap supermarket brands. When selecting a pet food, look for "complete" or "complete and balanced" on the label. That means it has met government standards that say essentially, "If your pet eats this food and nothing else all its life, that's okay, because this is all it needs." You can find this guarantee even on less expensive products.

Myth: **Diamonds are rare, and that's why they cost so much.**

Reality: South Africa's De Beers cartel controls the lion's share of the world's diamond market. By marketing heavily and restricting the supply, the company has convinced consumers that diamonds are much rarer than they actually are.

Truth is, diamonds cost much more than other gems of comparable rarity, and jewelry stores often mark up diamonds by at least 100%, guaranteeing that consumers can never resell them for anything close to what they originally paid.

Bottom line: Even the experts can't tell by the naked eye a real diamond from a well-made cubic zirconia.

Myth: **Baldness cures really work.**

Reality: Most hair-growth potions won't help grow new hair. Rogaine and Propecia are the only exceptions—and even they work only for some people. According to a survey of 20 dermatologists conducted by *20/20*, Rogaine provided noticeable hair growth for fewer than one in 10 of their patients. Propecia has shown more promise, particularly in treating male-pattern baldness, but the new growth often is minimal—and even those gains will disappear if Propecia use is discontinued.

Myth: **Roach motels and roach sprays will solve roach problems.**

Reality: Roach motels effectively trap the roaches that enter the trap…and chemical roach sprays do a good job of killing roaches hit by the spray. The trouble is that the female of the most common indoor species and her offspring can produce more than 30,000 babies in a year. If you have a roach problem, these weapons will hardly make a dent.

Roach baits, such as Raid Roach Baits and Dial Corporation's Combat Roach Baits, are more effective. These small plastic disks contain poisons that roaches eat and carry back to their nests, wiping out whole groups at a time.

The only reason that roach baits haven't pushed roach motels and sprays off store shelves is that sprays and motels leave at least a few dead roaches where we can see them. Roach baits tend to kill roaches while they are hidden away in their lairs. These products do much more, but they don't provide visual evidence that they're doing anything.

Helpful: Ant baits also are more effective than other ant-control techniques.

Myth: **Brand-name foods usually are better quality than store brands.**

Reality: Brand-name groceries typically cost 30% to 50% more than no-frills store labels. People pay this premium because they're squeamish about eating what they perceive to be low-quality food. But in truth, there's no nutritional difference…and taste tests sponsored by ABC News indicate that many people prefer the taste of at least some store brands.

People tend to be more willing to try generic nonfood grocery items, such as soap, paper towels and garbage bags. Ironically, the quality difference between brand-name and generic products tends to be greater with these nonfood items.

Myth: **Internet purchases are riskier than other credit card transactions.**

Reality: Most consumers believe that shopping on-line carries great risks—but your credit card number passes through strangers' hands whether you use the card on an Internet site or in a traditional department store. A survey by the Better Business Bureau found that in 2004, the Internet was responsible for only 11.6% of the cases of identity theft for which the cause was known.

To reduce the risk of on-line identity theft, stick with large, well-known companies… shop only on Web sites that begin "https://" (as opposed to just "http://," which suggests the site doesn't have the same level of security)…use a security program to keep your computer clear of spyware…and check credit card statements for fraudulent charges.

If your credit card number is stolen, your liability is limited to $50 if you notify the credit card company within 30 days of discovering the problem.

***Myth:* Premium brand-name gas is better for your car than discount gas.**

Reality: Unless you drive a car with a high-compression, high-revving engine, high-octane gas offers absolutely no advantage over standard-octane fuel.

Exception: A higher-octane fuel might help cut down on engine knocking and pinging if you drive an older car.

Likewise, no study has ever shown that gas from a big-name chain is any better for your car than gas from a no-name mom-and-pop station. It all comes from the same refineries.

***Myth:* Funeral directors will help you arrange an inexpensive funeral.**

Reality: The average cost of a burial in the US is $6,500, more than three times what it needs to be. You should be able to bury someone for as little as $2,000…buy cremation services for as little as $400…or donate a body to science for free.

The best way to avoid overspending is to shop around before the need arises. Nonprofit memorial societies can help you explore the inexpensive burial and cremation options in your area. The Funeral Consumers Alliance's list of local memorial societies is a good place to start (800-765-0107, *www. funerals.org*, click on "Affiliates Directory").

Area medical schools can tell you how to donate a body to science. Many programs even cremate the body when they're done and return the ashes to you for free.

10 Sneaky Fees and How *Not* to Pay Them

Joe Ridout, spokesperson for Consumer Action, a nonprofit consumer education and advocacy organization based in San Francisco. Consumer Action features a "fee of the week" on its Web site, *www. consumer-action.org/feeoftheweek*.

You shopped around and found a great deal on a hotel room…a checking account…or a rental car—or so you thought. Then fees popped up, inflating the bill way beyond your expectations.

It may be perfectly reasonable for companies to charge additional fees when customers request special services or break established rules. But some companies push fees too far, tacking on hefty charges without warning or legitimate cause.

Several industries are especially notorious for charging unwarranted fees. *Here are some of the worst…*

HOTELS

•**Smoke-odor fees.** Hotel chains impose stiff penalties when they suspect guests have smoked in nonsmoking rooms.

Example: At many Marriott hotels, the smoke-odor cleanup fee is $250. The fee has been imposed even when the only evidence of smoking is a report from a hotel housekeeper who smelled tobacco.

You might be charged a smoke-odor fee if the person who had your room before you smoked and the smell wasn't immediately noticed…or if your clothes picked up a tobacco odor after an evening in a smoky place.

What to do: If the hotel management won't remove the fee, call your credit card provider to protest this portion of your bill and request a "chargeback." The card provider will contact the merchant, which, in many cases, will then reverse the charge.

• **"Resort" fees.** An increasing number of hotels add "resort fees" of $5 to $30 per day to guest bills to cover the cost of maintaining the gym and pool—expenses that most travelers assume are included in the room rate. This fee applies even if you don't use these facilities. Occasionally it is tacked on at hotels that don't even have a gym or pool.

What to do: If a resort fee is unexpectedly added to your hotel bill, ask to have it removed, especially if you didn't use the gym or pool. Point out that it wasn't mentioned when you confirmed your price.

AIRLINES

• **Frequent-flier-mile reactivation fees.** US Airways has begun to erase frequent-flier miles for holders who have not added miles or redeemed them for 18 months, down from the old time limit of 36 months. The only way to get expired miles back from US Airways is to pay a reactivation fee. The fee ranges from $50 for 1–4,999 miles to $400 for 100,000 or more miles.

United Airlines has adopted a similar policy. Other airlines may follow.

What to do: Watch out for rule-tightening by airlines. Always use frequent-flier miles as soon as possible. Keep your US Airways mileage account active by making small transactions before 18 months pass. For example, you can extend your miles by occasionally buying one iTunes song for $1 on the airline's shopping site.

• **Bike transport fees.** Most airlines charge a fee for checking a bicycle as luggage—even if the bike is disassembled and packed in a box that meets luggage size and weight requirements. The bike fee is usually between $50 and $110 per round-trip, depending on the airline.

What to do: Mail your bike to your destination, or rent one when you get there. If you must bring your bike on a plane, pack it in a box with the pedals and handlebars disassembled, and tell the baggage-check employee that it is "exercise equipment." This isn't a lie—and shouldn't trigger a fee, assuming that the box meets luggage size and weight requirements and that the airline employee doesn't open it and discover the bike.

CAR RENTAL FIRMS

• **Airport rental fees.** Rental firms impose hefty surcharges on car rentals at many airports. This can add $10 or more per day to the cost of a rental.

What to do: Ask the car rental agency to confirm your total price before you reserve a vehicle. If the airport fees are significant, check prices at car rental facilities located a few miles from the airport, where these fees might not apply. Off-site car rental companies sometimes even run airport shuttle buses to save customers cab fare.

BANKS AND CREDIT CARDS

• **"Free checking" fee.** So-called free checking isn't always as free as it first appears, and sometimes it doesn't remain free.

Example: Bank of America recently switched customers who had signed up for free checking accounts to new accounts that carry a $5.95 monthly fee unless the customers authorized automatic paycheck direct deposits or made bill payments on-line through the bank.

What to do: Consider closing any accounts that impose unexpected fees, and find a bank that provides really free checking without strings at *www.bankrate.com.* Or you can open a credit union account instead. Credit unions typically charge fewer and lower fees than banks. The Credit Union National Association (800-356-9655, *www.cuna.org*) can help you locate a credit union in your area.

• **Double ATM fees.** When you withdraw cash from an ATM at a bank other than your own, you might expect to pay that bank a fee of $1.50 to $2. In addition, however, your own bank may impose a fee of $1 to $2 for using another bank's ATM. All told, you could be charged $4 or more to withdraw as little as $20.

What to do: If it isn't convenient to use one of your own bank's ATMs, ask for cash back when you make a purchase with your bank debit card—that automatically removes funds from your bank account, and most retailers don't charge a fee for this service.

•**Gift card dormancy fees.** Gift cards with a Visa, MasterCard, Discover or American Express logo often assess an "inactivity fee" of about $2.50 per month if a balance remains on the gift card after six months.

Gift cards issued by specific retailers are less likely to charge this fee, though Amazon, Blockbuster and American Eagle impose dormancy fees where they are permitted by state law.

What to do: Use gift cards quickly to avoid fees. If you don't have a use for a gift card, sell it to a friend or on eBay.

VIDEO RENTALS

•**"No late fee" video rental fees.** Video rental giant Blockbuster has heavily promoted its "no late fee" program, but the late fee is not really gone—it is just hidden. If a movie is seven days late, Blockbuster converts the rental into a sale and charges your credit card the full price of the movie—in some cases, $40 or $50. Blockbuster will let you return the movie for a refund after this charge is imposed, but you will have to pay a "restocking fee" of $1.25. After a month, if the video is not returned, the sale becomes final.

Adding to the confusion is that some Blockbuster franchises are not participating in the "no late fee" program and charge traditional late fees.

What to do: Make sure you understand your video store's late-fee policy, including the fine print—even if the store claims not to charge late fees.

Are You a Savvy Consumer?

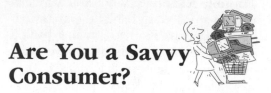

Elisabeth Leamy, an Emmy Award–winning television investigative reporter in Washington, DC. She is author of *The Savvy Consumer: How to Avoid Scams and Rip-Offs That Cost You Time and Money.* Capital.

As a TV investigative reporter, I see even smart people being ripped off for thousands of dollars every day.

To avoid being a target, be the hunter, not the hunted. Ignore any company that pursues you too aggressively—the contractor who knocks on your door claiming to be working on other houses in the neighborhood…the broker who cold-calls you with must-own stocks…the carpet cleaner who sends you a coupon offering steep discounts. Always conduct your own research first, then hire someone that you have sought out.

To test just how knowledgeable you are as a consumer, take my quiz. *Answer true or false…*

•**If your home-improvement contractor rips you off or does shoddy work, some states will pay you back.**

True. Many states have "construction recovery" or "contractor's guaranty" funds that reimburse consumers for as much as $50,000 or more. The fund covers general contractors, plumbers, electricians, etc. Check with the state board of contractors or department of licensing to see if such a fund is available.

Important: To be eligible for a reimbursement, you must have hired a contractor who is licensed in your state. (Thirty-six states require contractors to be licensed, and nearly all states license plumbers and electricians.)

You can present your case yourself at a formal hearing and be reimbursed by your state in as little as 60 days.

Helpful evidence: Photos of shoddy work and an inspector's report.

To avoid unlicensed contractors, know the warning signs…

•An unmarked vehicle. Most states require license numbers to appear on vehicles, estimates and advertising.

•The only contact information for him/her is through a post office box, a pager or an answering service, instead of a permanent street address.

•He has a "business" or "occupancy" license, not a contractor's license. A business license is not proof of competency and requires no testing or apprenticeships. An occupancy license is for zoning—it simply grants permission to conduct a certain type of business at a particular address.

• **If you receive unsolicited merchandise in the mail,** you are legally obligated to send back the product or pay for it.

False. Federal law makes it illegal for companies to send you something that you didn't order and then bill you for it. You are allowed to keep the item as a gift, give it away or throw it out. *Other steps to take...*

• Send a certified letter to the company notifying it that you have received unwanted merchandise and will not be burdened with the time and expense of returning it. While you are not required by law to send such a letter, by doing so you establish a paper trail in case the company ever tries to come after you with collection notices.

• If it does appear that you received a product through an honest error—such as a customer mix-up at a legitimate merchant—write or e-mail the seller saying that you're giving it a reasonable amount of time (15 to 30 days) to send a courier to pick up the product or else you reserve the right to keep it. If you receive a bill for the item, contact your local US Postal Inspector's office to report the company.

• **A coupon to clean four rooms of carpeting for $29.95 is a good deal.**

False. Based on all my investigations of carpet cleaners, initial low prices with these common come-ons always are followed by hefty "upcharges." Typically, you'll be charged extra for pretreatment solutions, deodorizers and protective spray...moving furniture...and cleaning carpeting in closets. *To avoid rip-offs...*

• Use a reputable carpet cleaner. These companies tend to charge by the square foot, not the room. You also may want to hire a cleaning contractor that uses truck-mounted equipment, which is more powerful than the self-contained equipment used by cut-rate carpet cleaners.

• To find a reputable carpet cleaner in your area, contact the Institute of Inspection, Cleaning and Restoration Certification at 800-835-4624 or *www.iicrc.org.*

• **When you get an unwanted telemarketing pitch, you should say, "Take me off your list."**

False. That request has no legal teeth. *Better...*

• Ask the telemarketer to put you on the company's "do-not-call" list. Laws require telemarketers to maintain and honor such lists.

• Have your home and cell phone numbers put on two do-not-call lists—your state's registry (contact your state consumer protection agency office to find out if your state has one)...the FTC's National Do Not Call Registry, 888-382-1222, *www.donotcall.gov.*

• **Parking-garage time clocks always are accurate.**

False. When I investigated parking garages around Washington, DC, I discovered that 75% of them skewed their clocks in their favor by at least six minutes.

Typical result: A customer checks in, returning just before an hour has elapsed, only to be charged for some or all of the second hour.

To avoid rip-offs...

• Make a note of the time on your own watch as you enter and exit, and show the attendant. It doesn't matter whether the garage clocks match yours. What matters is the time elapsed.

• If there is any discrepancy, complain and threaten to contact the department of consumer affairs in your city or town. Most garages will back down rather than risk having an official complaint lodged against them.

• **You can improve or repair your credit score within 24 to 72 hours.**

True. While the credit repair industry is riddled with scams, "rapid rescoring" is a legitimate service offered by local credit bureaus when you apply for a home loan.

How it works: Rescorers work directly with the three major credit bureaus. Not only will they correct errors on your credit report, they restructure your debt in ways that boost your credit score.

Cost: About $200.* This might seem high, but by raising your credit score, you often can qualify for a lower mortgage rate and save thousands.

*Prices subject to change.

How it might work: A rescorer notices that you have three credit cards. One is near its limit, while you hardly use the other two at all. By transferring some debt to the underused cards, you improve your score by 5%. Why would this be? Scoring models are biased against consumers who are near any of their credit limits.

If you want assistance from a rapid rescorer, ask your mortgage broker or lender to refer you to one—rapid rescoring firms don't work directly with consumers. If you get an unsolicited offer for overnight credit repair, it's a scam.

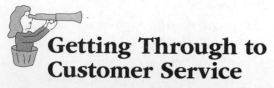

Getting Through to Customer Service

Paul English, cofounder and chief technical officer of the travel Web site Kayak.com, Concord, MA. Out of frustration, Mr. English published on his Web log ("blog") a dozen bypass codes he figured out by trial and error. The rest of them came from other disgruntled individuals. You can view his list at www.gethuman.com *or* www.paulenglish.com. *He is a former vice president of software giant Intuit.*

It is becoming harder and harder to reach live phone representatives at companies. In fact, almost 40% of the phone calls to customer service operations now are handled by interactive voice response (IVR) systems which lead callers through all those annoying, time-consuming series of keypunch menus—"So that we may better serve you, please press or say 'one' for…"

There is an escape from this big maze. I have compiled a list of shortcuts for major consumer companies that allow you to bypass the electronic technology and speak with a human being right away.

GENERAL STRATEGIES

•**Avoid pressing 0 to get an operator.** Callers try this so frequently that many companies have eliminated the option. In fact, hitting 0 just once is likely to send you right back to the beginning of the main menu or in some instances will disconnect the call.

If you want to try guessing at a shortcut, do the following…

•Experiment by hitting 0# or 0* on your phone keypad.

•Press the menu options for opening or canceling an account, such as "sales" or "new service." A human always seems to answer these options promptly. Then ask to be transferred to the department you need.

•Press nothing. The IVR system will think you are calling from a rotary phone and may transfer you to a live person.

•**Ask for the secret code when you reach a customer service rep.** Tell him/her, "I'm a loyal but very busy customer. Is there a way I can navigate your menu to reach a live person directly?"

Also ask about unpublicized toll-free numbers that the company might have that will connect you to an operator immediately.

•**Make sure you are not being charged for speaking with a live person.** Some companies charge customers up to $2 if they talk to an agent more than a set number of times in a month. Most airlines charge $5 to $25 to make a reservation over the phone with a customer service rep rather than on the Internet. Usually, you will be notified about the charge up front, but be sure to ask.

How to Catch Billing Mistakes

Attorney and consumer advocate Edgar Dworsky, JD, creator of the consumer advocacy site Consumer World.org, based in Somerville, MA. Previously, he served as consumer education consultant for the Federal Trade Commission and as assistant attorney general in Massachusetts, where he authored several of the state's consumer protection laws.

Overcharges by companies—cell-phone service providers, credit card issuers, utilities, banks and more—are commonplace. In fact, they could be costing you hundreds of dollars a year.

These errors aren't deliberate. Companies point out that overbilling actually costs them money because customer service representatives must spend valuable time dealing with the resulting billing complaints.

Bottom line: It's up to you to scrutinize what you are charged and then question what you don't understand. *The most common billing mistakes and how to handle them...*

BANKS

Common errors: Misapplied charges, such as check-writing fees when you signed up for free checking...bounced check fees when your account has overdraft protection ...out-of-network automated teller machine (ATM) fees when you didn't use an ATM outside your bank's network.

What to do: Call the number on your statement within 60 days from the date your statement was mailed—most will quickly remove such fees.

UTILITY COMPANIES

Common errors: Reading the meter incorrectly...bills based on estimated usage—when a reading cannot be obtained—that are wildly over the mark. Estimated usage is based on your patterns over the past year, so charges might even reflect errors on past bills.

What to do: Demonstrate that the reading is incorrect by taking a picture of the meter or scheduling a time for the utility company to send a meter reader to your home. Check the reading with him/her, and write down the number yourself. If the amount doesn't match what appears on your bill, report the error to the utility company. If the problem goes unresolved, contact your state public utilities commission (listed in your phone book).

TELEPHONE COMPANIES

Common errors: Charges you paid in the previous month that appear on your bill again because they weren't credited to your account...fees for services you didn't order, such as call-waiting...unreasonably high charges because a discount plan you signed up for was discontinued.

Example: Your plan had a rate of five cents per minute for calls to Canada. Several months later, the plan was discontinued, but you never saw the notice. Your new rate is 25 cents a minute.

What to do: Complain to the phone company. It may correct your bill and offer to switch you to another plan that will save you *some* money—it might charge you less than 25 cents but more than five cents. In general, you should report mistakes and/or overcharges to your phone company as soon as you receive your statement. You have 60 days to dispute unauthorized pay-per-call charges.

Helpful: Consider a one-price plan—for instance, an unlimited monthly domestic calling plan as part of your long-distance service. Anything you can do to simplify the number of charges on your bill will reduce the likelihood of mistakes and save you time when scrutinizing the bill.

STORES

Common error: An item scans for a higher price than the one marked.

What to do: Of course, you should ask for the correct price, but because scanner mistakes happen frequently, it's worthwhile to shop at stores that have "price accuracy guarantees." This means that if there's a mistake, you get the item for free, or in the case of expensive items, you may get $3 to $10 off the correct price. Guarantees are offered by many drugstores and supermarkets, such as Stop & Shop and Shaw's.

HOTELS

Common errors: Mistaken charges for use of the minibar, movie rentals and telephone calls from your room. A recent study by Corporate Lodging Consultants found that 11% of all hotel bills are incorrect. Guests were overcharged an average of $11 per stay.

Reasons: The complex structure of rates and fees...and the hotel industry has become lax about mistakes because business travelers rarely complain. Many business travelers figure it's not worth fighting inaccurate charges if the expenses are going to be paid by their employers anyway.

What to do: If you use a hotel's express checkout service, take a moment to review your bill for obvious mistakes. Get an employee or customer rep ID number when confirming a negotiated rate for a room—or ask to be e-mailed a confirmation.

Caution: Credit card issuers generally won't credit you back the money if a dispute with a travel vendor is over a rate discrepancy.

CREDIT CARDS

***Common errors:* Charges from a former service provider that you no longer use…**extra charges tacked on by your card company, such as credit insurance or other services it sells and you don't want…a merchant's failure to post a credit for returned items…charges for services or goods that you ordered and never received.

What to do: Federal law requires that you first try to resolve the mistake with the company that overcharged you, not the credit card issuer. Technically, to dispute the charge with your credit card company, you must make the request in writing. Practically speaking, many people just call their card issuer.

Review your credit card bills on-line once a week. You're more likely to remember what you bought and spot mistakes than if you wait for paper statements to arrive the following month. Also, you'll have fewer items to check than at the end of the month.

Little Coupons Can Save You Big Money…If You Avoid These Traps

Susan Samtur, author of *Cashing In at the Checkout*. Back in the Bronx. She is editor of *Refundle Bundle*, a newsletter about coupons and refunds (*www.refundlebundle.com*). Using coupons, Samtur saves about $250 on the $500 worth of groceries she buys each month.

Over 80% of Americans used coupons last year to save money at supermarkets, drugstores and mass merchandisers.*

*According to NCH Marketing Services, Inc.

Widespread availability of coupons on-line gives consumers more opportunities to save, but it also creates more confusion—some of which is intentional on the part of manufacturers and merchants.

Here are today's coupon traps—for both paper and on-line coupons…

***Trap:* The fine print is getting more complicated.**

What to do…

•**Read past the picture on the coupon.** Savings may apply to smaller sizes and varieties of products other than the specific item pictured. To make sure you're buying a coupon-eligible item, look for such words as "any variety" or limitations, such as "two 40-ounce bottles or one 100-ounce bottle or larger."

•**Read both sides of each coupon.** Many manufacturers issue double-sided coupons that have a single bar code. You can use the coupon only once, but each side offers different savings. Compare the two sides before deciding which one to use.

***Trap:* Coupons are expiring faster.** Most coupons today expire in one to four months. In years past, coupons typically expired after 12 months or longer.

What to do: Use coupons with upcoming expiration dates first. If your grocery coupons have expired, you can donate them to US military families around the world through the nonprofit organization Overseas Coupon Program (*www.ocpnet. org*). Families are able to use them on military bases for up to six months after the expiration dates.

You may be able to use nongrocery coupons past their expiration dates at certain stores.

Example: Bed Bath & Beyond and Linens 'n Things often will accept their own coupons for 10% or 20% off a single item even after the expiration date. (These stores also accept each other's unexpired coupons.)

***Trap:* Phony coupons are being distributed through e-mail,** chat rooms and on-line auctions. Some include bar codes from expired coupons. Others include doctored numbers—so that, say, a 50-cent discount reads $5 instead.

What to do…

• **Don't buy coupons through on-line auction sites.**

• **Recognize the signs of coupon forgery.** Forged coupons have unusually long expiration dates…lack a bar code below the expiration date…are delivered to you electronically from a party other than the manufacturer or that company's authorized representative.

Trap: **You can't use manufacturers' coupons at warehouse clubs,** such as BJ's and Costco.

What to do: Ask for the club's own booklet of coupons as soon as you enter the store. (You're usually handed one at the store exit—after you've already made your purchases.) Savings can be substantial.

Example: Costco offered coupons for $3.50 off Tylenol PM Extra Strength 225 count…$9 off a 10-pack of Brita water filters…and $30 off a Panasonic 5.8GHz three-handset portable phone.

Trap: **Believing you can't use coupons at local mom-and-pop stores.** These stores typically don't have big marketing budgets, so they don't offer coupons. However, don't assume that they won't accept coupons from a competitor or a manufacturer.

What to do: Ask the owner or manager if he/she will accept a coupon from a similar business in town or a national manufacturer. Many will.

FAVORITE WAYS TO SAVE

These are the best sites for saving on groceries, restaurants and more…

• **Groceries.**

• Boodle.com offers coupons from newspapers around the country.

• CoolSavings.com has coupons for groceries and retail stores.

• Upons.com takes you to CoolSavings—a free resource for printable coupons, discounts and special offers from a wide range of brands and stores. You can also browse money-saving tips and articles, free newsletters and recipes, sweepstakes, free trials and samples and more.

• Grocerygame.com tracks advertised and unadvertised products on sale at select grocery stores nationwide, then tells subscribers where to find coupons for those items.

Cost: $1 for a four-week trial period…$10 for two months.

• **Coupon codes.**

These sites provide codes to use for discounts, usually 5% off the purchase price, or free shipping when shopping on the Internet—Couponmountain.com…Couponmom. com…Keycode.com…Currentcodes.com… and Smartsource.com.

• **Restaurants.**

You can print out retailer and restaurant coupons at Myclipper.com, Valpak.com and Hotcoupons.com. Purchase gift certificates with discounts of 50% off meals at Restaurants.com.

When you book through reservation services—such as Opentable.com and Dinnerbroker.com—you receive points based on the number of reservations you keep. They can be redeemed for restaurant gift certificates and bonus points for dining at off-peak hours.

Also, the restaurant rebate program Rewardsnetwork.com gives you cash back—up to 20%—on restaurant meals. Rewards are issued to the credit card of your choice, so your dining companion need not know about the discount.

How to Haggle Like a Pro… Even If You Hate Haggling

Max Edison, a pawnshop owner for 10 years in Owatonna, MN, and author of several books on personal finance, including *How to Haggle: Professional Tricks for Saving Money.* Paladin.

Haggling is the secret to paying less for goods and services. Haggling isn't just unseemly horse trading;

it's a form of negotiation—and it's perfectly respectable. *What you need to know to haggle successfully…*

PREPARATION PAYS

There is room for negotiation in virtually every purchase, even at large department stores where you can get a discount if you can point out a defect in a product.

Important: Good hagglers always carefully inspect items that they're interested in.

Biggest mistake made by hagglers: Lack of preparation. A seller who is aware that you are guessing or bluffing will be unlikely to give an inch.

The most important thing you need to know: What constitutes a fair price for what you want to buy. When making a major purchase, it's a good idea to go to several places first to make price comparisons…

•**For items such as appliances, electronics and jewelry,** visit several stores. Also, since prices are lower on the Internet, check on-line to see what comparable merchandise sells for—that's the price you want to beat.

•**If you are house hunting,** learn the prices paid recently for comparable houses in similar neighborhoods. To get this information, ask a real estate agent or visit your county tax office and look at sales records.

•**For automobiles,** find out how much the dealer paid for the vehicle. Edmunds (*www.edmunds.com*) is a good place to learn the invoice price of a car as well as other pricing information, including how true market value (TMV) is calculated.

Second-biggest mistake made by hagglers: Not knowing the tricks used by salespeople. Since you can't avoid a salesperson's negotiating ploys, your best defense is to recognize what he/she is doing. You then have the chance to use some of those tactics yourself. *Examples…*

•A car salesman says, "I'd love to make this deal with you, but my manager says no way." Counter that with, "Let me speak with the manager."

•When offering you a loan, a banker says, "You've got to take this insurance policy for death or disability for us to approve the loan."

Counter that with, "I know that I don't have to have insurance for you to make the loan."

HOW TO HAGGLE

Haggling can be courteous and even friendly, but it's essentially psychological warfare. *Helpful…*

•**Play hard to get.** If a seller can tell that you're in love with an item, he knows that he will be able to get top price. Pretend to be only mildly interested and don't go back too many times to look at the item.

•**If you make an offer, let it stand.** If you make an offer and it's accepted, the deal is done. If a counteroffer is made, you can then make another offer. This is how the game is played. If the seller accepts your offer and you say that you'll be back next week, you may not have a deal the next week.

•**If you and the seller can't agree on the price of an item,** ask the seller if he's got anything that he can throw in on the deal.

Examples: Ask automobile dealers to throw in floor mats, a bicycle rack or free service for six months…with computer and stereo equipment, ask the seller for free cables and free installation…with DVD players, ask for free movies.

•**Never tip your hand.** If you are willing to pay $100 for an item, offer $80 or even $60. You never know—the other guy might take it. Even if he passes or counteroffers, he'll feel like some progress is being made.

•**Nail down early whether or not sales tax is included.** Why go through 20 minutes of haggling only to start over when it comes to sales tax?

•**Ask for the cash price,** if you are able to pay cash for an item.

Background: Merchants lose about 2% when a credit card is used, so they may be willing to take a 2% bite if you pay cash.

•**Take advantage of a seller's weaknesses.** *Examples…*

•Politely point out any flaws in the merchandise. If the item is outdated in any way, let him know that. This works best with digital cameras, flat-screen televisions and computers where new models are introduced seemingly every day.

• Be aware that people will be more or less willing to haggle under different circumstances. The two main factors are time and attachment to the object. A home owner who is having a two-day garage sale knows that whatever doesn't sell is going back to the attic or to the dumpster. On the other hand, there may be an emotional attachment (this was Grandma's dresser!). If someone won't part with his stuff for a reasonable price, look elsewhere. Seasonal merchandise, such as patio furniture and fur coats, can be bought at huge savings for buyers who can think (and haggle) months ahead.

WHO BEST TO HAGGLE WITH

You can haggle with just about every seller, but you may find the greatest success with…

• **Small-town merchants or stores that are independently owned.** Their owners are much more likely to dicker than a large outlet like Best Buy or the Home Depot. Make sure that you talk to a decision-maker, such as the owner or at least the store manager. Many times, a mom-and-pop store will try to match their larger competitor's sale prices.

• **Jewelry stores.** They have markups that are usually 300% to 400% above wholesale, so they have lots of room to haggle.

• **Car dealers.** Haggling with car dealers works best when bad weather keeps other customers away, near the end of the month (when their sales quotas are due) and from August to September (when the new models are coming out).

• **Banks.** They will argue over percentage points on loans, services such as free checking and even fees from bounced checks. Always ask to have fees waived. Go up the chain of command until you find someone who has the power to say yes.

• **Chains and discount stores** will cut prices under the right circumstances, such as buying a display model, an item with very slight damage or an air conditioner in October.

• **Individuals who place ads in the paper using the words "best offer" or "OBO"** (or best offer). These people expect a counteroffer to the price they're asking— and they're doing you the favor of saying so!

Avoid Those Fees On Credit Cards, Cell-Phone Plans, Airline Tickets, More

Linda Sherry, director of national priorities at Consumer Action, a national nonprofit advocacy and education organization headquartered in San Francisco. For free consumer protection reports, go to *www.consumer-action.org*.

Americans are facing a wave of fees and surcharges for almost every service. Credit card holders recently paid more than $15 billion a year in penalty fees. Many retailers can't raise their prices because the business environment is so competitive. Instead, they bury high fees in the fine print of contracts or simply neglect to inform you about additional costs until your bills arrive. The charges can be outrageous.

Example: A typical bank overdraft, or "insufficient funds," fee on a bounced check runs $25 to $35 (*estimated cost to the bank: $1*).

Not only do such fees siphon hundreds of dollars a year from your wallet, they make it harder to know the true cost of purchases so that you can comparison shop for the best deals.

How to avoid being overcharged for common products and services…

ON-LINE TRAVEL

• **Penalty fees.** When you need to change an airline ticket, many airlines charge $25 to $100. Canceling a hotel reservation may trigger a fee as well. If you book through travel Web sites, such as *www.expedia. com…www.travelocity.com…www.orbitz. com…*or *www.cheaptickets.com*, you also will be hit with their penalty fees (*amount:* $30 to $50 per ticket).

Self-defense: To avoid a double penalty, book your hotel or airline directly if you think you might have to make changes.

SHOPPING

• **Restocking fees.** Many retailers charge a fee if you purchase an item and then return it.

Amount: 10% to 20% of the cost of the original item.

Example: Electronics store Circuit City charges a 15% fee for returns of digital cameras, desktop PCs, notebook PCs and printers and a 25% restocking fee for home-theater equipment.

Self-defense: Ask about restocking fees. For instance, you may not have to pay if you return the merchandise unopened within 14 days.

• **Handling and/or packing fees.** Most Web sites require you to purchase a hefty dollar amount of products—say, $100 worth —to be eligible for free shipping. Some sellers on the on-line auction site eBay offer free shipping but may charge for such extras as insurance (*amount:* $5 to $15 per item), making any shipping savings negligible.

Self-defense: Look skeptically at "free shipping" offers. Check the total amount that you have to purchase to be eligible. If you shop on eBay, find out about additional fees, or go to *www.free-shipping.com* to shop from a directory of items with free standard shipping and handling.

BROKERAGES & INVESTMENT COMPANIES

• **Account maintenance charges.** Investors with less than a certain amount in their brokerage accounts—typically $10,000 to $25,000—are charged about $25 per quarter. Investors who trade infrequently (less than three times a quarter) also may face a $10 or higher "inactivity" fee per quarter. Mutual fund firms often charge annual administrative fees of $10 to $25 for any accounts, including IRAs, that fall below a certain minimum.

Self-defense: It's best to choose brokerages that don't charge maintenance fees for most accounts, such as Etrade.com and Siebertnet.com. Also, maintain all your taxable and nontaxable accounts at the same investment firm or brokerage—your combined account total might allow you to avoid maintenance fees. Inquire about linking accounts that are not listed under the same Social Security number. For example, if three members of your family have IRAs at the same firm and the total for your combined accounts surpasses the minimum, you all may be able to avoid fees.

OVERNIGHT MAIL

• **Remote surcharges.** The major carriers—Federal Express and UPS—bill extra for "out-of-the-way" areas (*amount:* $1.50 and up). But many of these locations are actually residential areas in cities such as San Diego, Miami Beach, Phoenix and Atlanta. To find out if a zip code is considered remote, call 800-463-3339 or 800-742-5877.

Self-defense: Whenever possible, send the package to an office instead of to a home.

Reason: UPS and FedEx apply the remote surcharge only to shipments to residences. Or send the package by overnight mail through the US Postal Service. The rates are comparable, and remote surcharges are not levied.

CELL-PHONE PLANS

• **"Federal Recovery" fees.** Wireless companies advertise a low base price without mentioning that your bill will be inflated by government-mandated charges, such as the Federal E911 Fee (*amount:* $1 to $3 per month)* and Number Portability Service Charge (*amount:* $1 to $3).*

Some companies even tack a Regulatory Cost Recovery fee on bills to high-speed Internet customers (*amount:* about $3).* This fee sounds as if it is required by law. Not true. It's just a way for companies to increase their revenues.

Self-defense: Factor in additional fees when you comparison shop for cell-phone plans. These fees will increase a plan's base cost by 10% to 25% each month. Negotiate for reduced charges before you sign up. Cell-phone companies are so competitive nowadays that even if they won't eliminate the fees, they may be willing to give you more minutes or throw in a better phone.

Helpful: *www.saveonphone.com/wireless. html* (enter your zip code and click on "Shop by Plan" to compare wireless plans).

*Amounts vary by state.

CREDIT & DEBIT CARDS

•**Late penalties.** Credit card companies try to trick you into paying late, such as cutting the grace period (from the time of the charge to when payment is due) from 31 days to as little as 20 days (*amount:* $15 to $39).

Self-defense: You must be notified about any changes to grace periods at least 15 days before the changes take place. Federal law requires that you receive your bill at least 14 days before the due date. If it doesn't arrive on time, complain to the bank's regulator—FDIC for banks (877-275-3342) or Office of Thrift Supervision (800-842-6929) for savings and loans.

You must pay on time even if you don't receive a bill. If you can't pay in full, pay the minimum amount due immediately. If you sometimes do pay late, consider Providian's Real Rewards program (800-775-8382, *www.providian.com*). Cardholders can use the points earned by making purchases to offset late fees and fees for exceeding the credit limit. They also get 500 points for paying on time for six consecutive billing cycles. Your points also can be redeemed for rewards, such as gift cards at Barnes & Noble and Macy's.

•**Convenience fees.** Some merchants charge you this 3% fee on your total purchase for using a credit card.

Self-defense: Tell merchants that you prefer using your debit card and its PIN—rather than signing by hand—so you can avoid this fee.

GENERAL STRATEGIES

Poorly trained phone representatives often pass along misinformation. You will have a better chance when you dispute a charge if you have jotted down notes. Include the date and time of the call…full name/ID number of the phone representative…the phone number you called and the rep's extension…and what you were told. *Other smart strategies…*

•**Get it in writing.** Always request that fee information you receive over the phone be e-mailed or faxed to you.

•**Request that late fees be waived.** They often are waived, as a courtesy, the

first time if you ask or if you haven't incurred any penalty fees within the past two years.

•**Skim the inserts.** Notices of higher fees and changes of terms usually are tucked into a packet of solicitations or in hard-to-read disclosure paragraphs. You don't need to read everything. Just focus on the numbers amid the legalese, and read those sections.

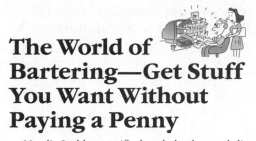

The World of Bartering—Get Stuff You Want Without Paying a Penny

Natalie Ladd, a certified trade broker and director of The Trade Exchange, based in Portland, ME, *www.thetradeexchange.com*, which has been in business for 30 years. The Exchange, which has more than 300 members, brokers barter deals nationwide on goods and services, including auto repairs, bookkeeping, hair styling and medical care.

Barter—the cashless exchange of goods and services—is enjoying new popularity. Hundreds of Internet sites and barter exchanges around the country let you swap for everything from travel accommodations to dental care. Even people who think they don't have anything worth bartering might be surprised to find their skills—perhaps a knack for gardening or interior decorating—in demand.

Here's how to get started…

ONE-ON-ONE BARTER

How it works: You join a low-cost online barter service, where you can list or respond to offers. Or you can barter on your own by personally contacting people whose goods or services you need.

Best for: Individuals who want to trade occasionally for a specific item or service, such as trading baby-sitting for lawn services.

Sample savings: A high school tennis coach needed to pay for his daughter's wedding. The coach went around to local businesses and offered to trade tennis lessons for goods and services. In this way, he was able to get all the flowers for his daughter's wedding and the alterations to her wedding dress.

Important: Make sure you and your trading partner are bartering at the same value level. You don't want to trade your goods at wholesale, while he/she is charging you retail prices.

Also, many professionals are willing to barter their labor, but they still might need to charge you in cash for certain fixed costs, such as paying their staff or buying raw materials.

My favorite sites: *www.craigslist.org*, click on your state, then "Barter" under "For Sale" (free)...*www.targetbarter.com* ($2.50/transaction for items presumed to be valued under $25...10% of the transaction for trades valued over $25...free to place a listing).

Drawbacks: You're limited to trading with people who live nearby—an optician in New York has little to offer a landscaper in California.

You do all the leg work—evaluating the quality of goods and services.

There is no governing body with a code of standards or ethics and little recourse, other than small-claims court, if something goes wrong.

TRADE EXCHANGE BARTER

How it works: A barter exchange acts as a broker, a third-party recordkeeper and, in cases of disputes, a mediator for your transaction.

People who use the service are called "exchange members" and trade in "credits." (One credit typically equals $1.) Members receive statements monthly. Traders (referred to as "brokers") who work for an exchange can tap into an international network and put together deals for almost anything.

There are barter exchanges nationwide. You can research them as you would any business. Check the Better Business Bureau for complaints. Make sure the exchange has been in business for at least three years and belongs to a governing body, such as the International Reciprocal Trade Association (585-424-2940, *www.irta.com*), which has a

code of ethics, a peer review board and a certification program for traders.

Resource: To get a state-by-state listing of exchanges, go to *www.barternews.com* and click on "Barter Contacts."

Best for: Small-business owners or people looking to trade regularly and save cash for nontradable items and overhead.

Sample savings: A New England radio station wanted to do an on-air promotion for which it needed 2,000 pairs of socks. The station was willing to barter $1,000 worth of advertising airtime. A trade broker for a national exchange found a local barter exchange in Kansas that had a sock manufacturer among its members. That manufacturer didn't need radio ad time in New England, so he traded him the socks for a white-water rafting trip offered by one of the exchange's other members, a travel company in Maine. The travel company used its exchange credits from the deal to purchase the advertising airtime from the radio station.

Drawbacks: Higher costs, including annual dues of $120 and up, and transaction fees (for example, a fee of 6% of the transaction value) each time you buy or sell. You generally need to offer at least $500 worth of goods or services to open a barter account.

TAXES

According to the IRS, barter "income" is treated the same as cash income. You must list the fair market value of goods or services received through barter on your federal tax return, Form 1040, *Schedule C.*

For federal rules on barter income, call 800-829-1040 or go to *www.irs.gov/taxtopics/tc420.html.*

Best Place to Buy Electronics

For the best prices on electronics, buy on the Web. Consumers report that they are more satisfied with the prices and service when they purchase digital cameras, MP3 players, TVs and other types of electronics from on-line retailers, such as Amazon.com, Costco.com, Buydig.com and Buy.com.

Before you buy: Check the retailer's return policy. There often are strict time limits and packaging requirements. Instead of taking an extended warranty, use a credit card that doubles the manufacturer's warranty, such as American Express, Visa or MasterCard.

Consumer Reports, 101 Truman Ave., Yonkers, NY 10703.

Credit Card Smarts

Merchants who accept Visa and Master-Card cannot require a minimum purchase. Card companies want their cards to be used for purchases of any size. If a merchant insists on a minimum purchase amount, contact your card issuer to complain.

Greg McBride, CFA, senior financial analyst, Bankrate.com, 11760 US Hwy. 1, North Palm Beach, FL 33408.

Convert Unused Gift Cards into Cash

Auction gift cards off on eBay, where cards can sell for 90% or more of their face value.

Or: Use the Web site *www.cardavenue.com* to trade an unused card for one you want. Even expired cards still may have value. The issuer may well be willing to reactivate the card for a modest fee ($10 to $15)—after which you may be able to sell the card on the Web for cash.

Money, Time-Life Building, Rockefeller Center, New York City 10020.

Real-World Shopping Using the Internet

Mary Hunt, editor, *Debt-Proof Living*, Box 2135, Paramount, CA 90723. *www.debtproofliving.com.*

Before leaving home, search on-line for the item you want, to be sure the store has a competitive price.

• Go to *www.shoplocal.com* or *www.salescircular.com* for current prices and sales at stores near you.

• For comparison shopping, try *www.froogle.google.com,* which includes items offered on eBay.

• Carry a cell phone with text messaging capability to the store. Before buying an item, send its name or UPC number to 466453 ("GOOGLE" in numbers) and use the word "price" in your message. An automated response will show the item's current best price on-line. *Details:* Visit *www.google.com/sms.*

Financing Folly

Interest-free store financing—which often is available on home appliances, computers, furniture, etc.—is a bad deal unless you plan to pay down a significant portion of the debt every month.

Reason: If you do not completely pay off the debt by the end of the interest-free promotional period, you will owe accrued interest charges that could be as high as 20%. If you have financed the purchase of a $1,200 item, interest on that amount could reach $750 or more after 18 months.

Money, Time-Life Building, Rockefeller Center, New York City 10020.

When to Buy an Extended Warranty

James Sebastian, managing partner, Safe, LLC, warranty consultancy firm, Las Vegas, NV, *www. safellc.biz.*

Product warranties for manufactured goods are growing ever shorter while manufacturers and retailers try to make money by selling extended warranties instead.

Shrewd buying: Manufacturers' extended warranties tend to be a better buy than those from retailers, both in price and by being more comprehensive.

Beyond that, for some kinds of products, buying an extended warranty is a good idea—while for others, it just adds to the seller's profit.

Products for which warranties are worthwhile…

• **Plasma TVs.** These are expensive to replace and use advanced technology prone to need repair—30% of plasma television sets need service in the first three years.

• **Laptop computers.** They are more costly, more delicate and more expensive to fix than desktop computers—and more likely to be dropped and damaged.

• **Wristwatches.** Standard warranties usually exclude the parts most likely to be broken, such as the face and the band. Extended warranties that do cover them often are inexpensive.

Keep your money rather than spend on warranties for…

• **White goods,** such as refrigerators and washing machines. These usually are reliable, and a warranty is liable to cost as much or more than any repairs you'll actually need.

• **Desktop computers.** Most failures occur early on, within the term of the original warranty.

• **Digital cameras.** Few need repairs, and those that do usually need them during the original warranty.

Save Hundreds On Electronics, Appliances, Cell Phones and More

Robert Silva, an expert on consumer electronics based in La Mesa, CA. Since 1999, he has written for About.com and currently serves as its home theater guru (hometheater.about.com). He tests and reviews hundreds of new products each year and has worked in electronics sales, video production and computer animation.

Each year, there are billions of dollars worth of brand-name appliances and electronics returned to the retailers and manufacturers. Consumers return items because of shipping damage and minor problems or simply because they changed their minds. In past years, since these products could no longer be marketed legally as "new," they were destroyed or sent to liquidators. But retailing has become so competitive that manufacturers now "refurbish" the goods that are returned—repairing and repackaging them—and then sell them as high-quality, used merchandise.

Savings: Up to 80% off retail price.

"Refurbs"—from cameras and laptop computers to DVD players and golf clubs—come with a limited choice of features and colors and may not have the latest technology, but their prices make them attractive bargains.

The best deals can be found in January.

Reasons: Holiday returns pile up. And, electronics retailers must clear shelves of old demo models and stock to prepare for new products following the industry's Consumer Electronics Show, held every January.

HOW TO SHOP FOR "REFURBS"

• **Find out how the manufacturer or retailer defines "refurbished."** There are no federal regulations for labeling these goods, which also may be called "factory reconditioned," "open-box" or "preowned," but many sellers will tell you if you ask.

The best refurbs are…

•Items that have been returned unused. Most major retailers have a 30-day return policy for their products.

•Otherwise-sound goods that had cosmetic damage, perhaps scratches or dents. The original internal components usually are put into a new cabinet or casing.

•Overstock items. These typically are older models that need to be cleared off store shelves.

Less desirable refurbs…

•Demonstration units. These floor models are used in stores, at trade shows or for product reviews. They often have suffered substantial wear and tear.

•Defective products. These items already have been repaired, which may or may not have fixed the problem.

•**Look for a strong parts-and-labor warranty and return policy.** The product should come with a 45-day warranty and a 14-day return policy.

Caution: You may be able to get a warranty only if you buy through the manufacturer or a manufacturer-authorized reseller.

•**Make sure the refurb comes with all the basic components of a new product.** Check the model and configuration of the newest version of the product on the manufacturer's Web site or in the owner's manual to make sure that your model comes with everything you need. For instance, some refurbished electronics may be sold without necessary cables, headphones, software, etc.

POPULAR SOURCES FOR REFURBISHED GOODS

My favorite Web sites for refurbs…*

•**Electronics…**

•Apple, *store.apple.com* (see "Special Deals")

•Dell, *www.delloutlet.com*

•Hewlett-Packard, *www.shopping.hp.com*

•The Palm Store, *store.palm.com*

•Frys, *shop1.outpost.com*

•*www.smalldog.com*

*Click on "refurbished" or enter "refurbished" plus the product in the search window unless the site is just for refurbs. In most cases, you also can enter "refurbished" plus the brand in an Internet search engine.

•**Appliances…**

•*www.kitchencollection.com*

•*www.shopkitchenaid.com*

•**Sports gear…**

•Callaway Golf, *callawaygolfpreowned. com*

•**General merchandise…**

•*www.amazon.com*

•*www.ebay.com*

•*www.costco.com*

•*www.nextag.com*

•*www.overstock.com*

•*www.refurbdepot.com*

•*www.shopping.com*

•*www.ubid.com*

•**Cell phones…**

•Find them at cell phone stores or at *www.ebay.com*.

Get Newspaper Coupons Over the Internet

You can get money-saving coupons from your regional newspapers without getting the newspapers themselves (or after you've thrown the newspapers out) over the Internet. The Boodle.com Web site presents printable coupons from more than 380 newspapers. Visit *www.boodle.com*.

Low-Cost or FREE Vision Care

Jim Miller, a writer based in Norman, OK, whose syndicated column "The Savvy Senior" is published in 400 newspapers nationwide, *www.savvysenior.org*.

Free or discounted vision care is available for people with limited incomes. *Key resources…*

•**EyeCare America's Senior Eye-Care Program.** Coordinated by the American

Academy of Ophthalmology, this program provides free medical eye care to all US citizens or legal residents, age 65 and older, who have not seen an ophthalmologist in three or more years and who don't have coverage through an HMO or the Veterans Administration. The program also offers a diabetes and glaucoma eye-care program. 800-222-3937, *www.eyecareamerica.org.*

•**Knights Templar Eye Foundation.** This charitable foundation provides financial assistance for eye care to people under age 65 who don't qualify for Medicaid or who have private insurance but can't afford to pay for care. 847-490-3838, *www.knights templar.org/ktef.* Knights Templar also co-sponsors EyeCare America's program.

•**Mission Cataract USA.** This program provides free cataract surgery to people of all ages who don't have Medicare, Medicaid or private insurance and have no other means to pay. 800-343-7265, *www.mission cataractusa.org.*

•**Vision USA.** Coordinated by the American Optometric Association (AOA), Vision USA provides free eye-care services to uninsured and low-income workers and their families who have no means of obtaining care. 800-766-4466, *www.aoa.org* (click on "AOA Public Programs").

•**New Eyes for the Needy.** This international program distributes new prescription eyeglasses to people with limited incomes. 973-376-4903, *www.neweyesfortheneedy.org.*

•**Local Lions Clubs.** This is a top referral resource for eye-care and eyeglasses programs that are available in your area. Programs and eligibility requirements vary by community. Call your local Lions Club chapter or contact Lions Clubs International, 800-747-4448, *www.lionsclubs.org.*

•**"Give the Gift of Sight" program.** Sponsored by Luxottica Retail and in partnership with Lions Clubs International, this program provides free screening and glasses to people who can't afford them. 513-765-6000, *www.givethegiftofsight.com,* or contact LensCrafters. To find a nearby store, call 800-541-5367 or visit *www.lenscrafters.com.*

Low-Cost Health Care

Low-cost health care is available at mini-clinics. These facilities are found in retail outlets, such as grocery chains and drugstores. They are staffed by nurse practitioners, who can write prescriptions and handle basic procedures. Clinics can save you 50% over full-service doctors. Consider using them for minor ailments, such as bronchitis and rashes. Many of these clinics also accept insurance.

Time, 1271 Avenue of the Americas, New York City 10020.

Are You Being Overcharged for Medical Care? How to Fight Back

Sid Kirchheimer, an investigative reporter and author of the "Scam Alert" column in AARP Bulletin. He is author of *Scam Proof Your Life: 377 Smart Ways to Protect You and Your Family from Ripoffs, Bogus Deals & Other Consumer Headaches.* Sterling.

Three-quarters of hospital bills have overcharges, and the average overcharge is about $1,000, according to People's Medical Society, a nonprofit medical consumer rights organization. Doctors, too, are handing inflated bills to patients.

Good news: It's simple to fight back.

If your health insurance completely covers hospital and doctor visits, these steps might not be necessary, though making the extra effort to eliminate overcharges can help bring down medical costs for everyone. Also, be aware that your insurance coverage might not be as comprehensive as you think—call your insurance carrier or review the exclusions section of your policy.

DOCTORS' BILLS

To avoid paying more than you should...

•**Negotiate.** If you have no health insurance, ask your doctor for a discount. Only 13% of patients ever make this request, but when they do, the majority secure a lower price, according to a survey of 2,118 adults conducted by Harris Interactive.

Ask the doctor in person. Requests made by phone or to an office assistant rarely work.

Keep in mind that insurance companies typically pay doctors one-half to two-thirds of the billed amount. If you will be paying out-of-pocket, you can offer to pay somewhere in that range when negotiating a price.

• **Get blood tests done at a lab.** When your doctor does a blood test, he/she charges you for the office visit…plus an added fee for drawing your blood…plus the amount a lab charges to run the test.

Ask the doctor to waive his fees, or go directly to a lab to have the test done and pay only for the test (ask the doctor to supply any necessary paperwork).

Look in your local *Yellow Pages* under "Laboratories—Clinical, Medical, Diagnostic" or "Laboratories—Testing" for labs in your area.

• **Don't pay for the follow-up visit.** When you see a doctor about a health problem, you often have to see him again a few weeks later to confirm that the treatment was successful. Chances are, your doctor will look you over for a few seconds during this follow-up, pronounce you well—then bill you another $50 to $100 for the second appointment.

During your initial appointment, tell the doctor that you're paying out-of-pocket and ask if he'll waive or reduce the charge for the follow-up visit, assuming that it takes only a moment. Many doctors will agree to this, particularly for regular patients.

• **Confirm that tests are necessary.** Doctors often order unnecessary medical tests out of fear that not conducting these tests might open the door for negligence lawsuits later. Unless your health insurance is picking up the entire bill, question whether recommended tests—including MRIs, CAT scans and X-rays—really are necessary. Ask what these tests will determine.

HOSPITAL OVERCHARGES

Here's how to spot overbilling on hospital bills…

• **Ask for a daily itemized bill.** When you check into the hospital, tell the staff member who takes down your insurance information that you want an itemized bill brought to your bed every day. Hospitals are required to provide this upon request.

When you receive these daily bills, review each listing (or ask a family member to do so for you). Were you billed for two doctor visits yesterday even though you saw a doctor only once? Were you billed for tests that you don't recall getting? Are there vague entries, such as "miscellaneous costs" or "lab fees"? Are there listings you can't understand? Tell the nurse you would like to speak with the hospital's patient advocate, then ask the advocate to explain any charge that isn't clear. You might be appalled by what you're told.

Examples: Some hospitals have been known to call a box of tissues a $12 "mucus recovery system" and a bag of ice cubes a $30 "thermal therapy kit."

Save the daily bills so you can reconcile them later with the final bill.

If the patient advocate won't help remove the mistakes and reduce egregious overcharges from your bill, hire an independent medical billing advocate. He/she will examine your bill and fight to remove any overcharges, usually in exchange for a percentage—typically 35%—of the amount he saves you.

To find a medical billing advocate: Contact Medical Billing Advocates of America (540-387-5870, *www.billadvocates.com*)… American Medical Bill Review (530-221-4759, *www.ambr.com*)…or Edward R. Waxman & Associates (877-679-7224, *www.hospitalbill auditing.com*).

• **Bypass the hospital pharmacy.** Hospitals dramatically overcharge for drugs. A patient might be billed $5 to $10 for a pill that retails for 10 cents elsewhere.

If you are taking medications on an ongoing basis and are not fully covered by insurance, bring your drugs with you to the hospital.

When you consult with your doctor prior to entering the hospital, find out which drugs you're likely to be given during your stay. Ask the doctor to write you prescriptions so that you can buy these drugs at your local pharmacy in advance and avoid the hospital markup. Even if your doctor won't do this, you can bring any nonprescription pills you're told you'll need, such as vitamins.

If you must get drugs through the hospital pharmacy and your insurance isn't footing the bill, ask your doctor to specify generics whenever possible. When you get your itemized daily bill, double-check that you weren't charged for brand-name drugs instead.

• **Watch for double billing.** Hospitals often bill patients twice for certain things. If your bill lists sheets and pillows, ask the hospital's patient advocate if these items are included in your daily room rate. If you're billed for the scrubs, masks and gloves worn by surgical staff, find out if these were included in your bill for operating room time.

Also double-check the times on your operating room bill. Hospitals charge from $20 to $90 for every minute you're in the operating room, so if the time you spent in surgery is padded even a little, it will add a lot to your bill. Your anesthesia records will say how long your operation really lasted.

• **Don't pay for your last day.** Hospital patients are charged the full day's room rate for the day they check in—even if they arrive at 11:59 pm. In exchange, patients are not supposed to be charged for their last day, but hospitals often try to bill for the final day anyway. Sometimes these last-day room bills are simply removed when you complain, but there are hospitals that insist the last-day charge is legitimate for patients who aren't discharged by a certain hour, often noon.

During your hospitalization, ask the hospital's patient advocate whether you'll be billed for your room on the final day of your stay. If the answer is, "Yes, if you're not out by a certain hour," ask your doctor on the next-to-last day of your stay to give you your final checkup and discharge the following morning, rather than waiting until the afternoon. If the doctor says this doesn't fit his schedule, tell the patient advocate that you shouldn't have to pay because the delay is the doctor's fault.

Free Health Care Made Easy

Matthew Lesko, Kensington, MD–based best-selling author of more than 70 books on how to get free services and products, *www.lesko.com*.

I f you don't have insurance coverage, even a very brief hospital stay can easily cost you tens of thousands of dollars and put you on the edge of bankruptcy.

FREE HOSPITAL CARE

Fortunately, now there is something you can do. If you need hospital care but cannot afford it and have no insurance or if you have already been in the hospital and cannot afford to pay the bill, try calling the Hill-Burton Hotline. Through this program, hundreds of participating hospitals and other health facilities provide free or low-cost medical care to patients who are unable to pay.

You could qualify for this assistance even if your income is double the poverty-level income guidelines and even if a medical bill has already been turned over to a collection agency.

For more information: Hill-Burton Hotline. 800-638-0742, *www.hrsa.gov/hillburton/compliance-recovery.htm*.

FREE MEDICAL CARE

How would you like to have the finest medical care money can buy…and not spend one penny for it? That is exactly what thousands of people are doing every year thanks to the National Institutes of Health (NIH) Clinical Center. The NIH is funded by the federal government and is one of the nation's leading medical research centers.

At any one time there may be more than 1,000 programs under way where researchers are studying the latest procedures in the treatment of every imaginable disease, including all types of cancer, heart disease and diabetes, to mention a few.

If your condition is one that is being studied, you might qualify for free medical care at the NIH hospital located in Bethesda, MD.

For more information: National Institutes of Health, Mark O. Hatfield Clinical Research Center, Bethesda, MD 20892. 800-411-1222, *www.cc.nih.gov.*

FREE EYE CARE

The community service pages of your local newspaper occasionally will run announcements by organizations such as the Kiwanis or Lions Clubs. They offer free eyeglasses and eye examinations to elderly people who couldn't afford them otherwise.

Also, check with your state's Office of the Aging. There is a wide variety of eye-care programs offered, and many include free eye exams and free eyeglasses.

To locate your state's office along with other resources, call 800-677-1116 or go to *www.eldercare.gov.*

CONTACT LENSES FOR FREE

If you wear contact lenses or are thinking of getting them, Johnson & Johnson would like you to try their Acuvue contacts for free. Go to *www.acuvue.com,* fill out the information requested and a free-trial pair certificate will be sent out to you.

FREE OR ALMOST-FREE DENTAL CARE

There are more than 50 dental schools in the United States. All of them operate clinics that provide basic services at great savings. Services include checkups, cleaning, X-rays and fillings.

More advanced services such as fitting bridges, dentures and implants may also be available. Student dentists do the work but are closely supervised by their professors.

Bonus: Care may even be free for conditions the professors are studying.

For more information: To locate a list of dental schools, go to the American Dental Association's Web site at *www.ada.org* and click on "Dental Schools" under "Dental Professionals." Or call local universities and ask if they have dental schools.

Also, the dental society or association in each state has a list of dentists who volunteer their services to assist people who cannot afford proper dental care.

How to Save Big on Medications

Charles B. Inlander, a consumer advocate and health-care consultant based in Fogelsville, PA. He was founding president of People's Medical Society, a consumer health advocacy group. He is the author of more than 20 books, including *Take This Book to the Hospital with You.* St. Martin's.

Everyone wants to save as much money as possible on medications, but some of the best ways for doing so are not well known. *My advice...*

• **Stay up to date on generic drugs.** Generic drugs are as safe as brand-name medications and can sometimes cost 50% to 70% less. Unfortunately, most people—even many doctors—are not aware when drugs become available in generic form. In the past year, the popular cholesterol-lowering drug Zocor (generic name *simvastatin*), the antidepressant Zoloft (*sertraline*) and the allergy-control nasal spray Flonase (*fluticason*) became available in much less expensive generic forms.

• **Shop around for generic drugs.** Pharmacies are now in a price war over generic drugs. It started recently when Walmart announced that it would sell 300 commonly prescribed generic drugs at $4 per 30-day supply. Other chains, including Target and Kmart, and food stores, such as Wegmans and Price Cutter, have similar programs now.

Look at the generic drugs you take to see if any are on the discount list of a store near you. These lists are available on store Web sites or you simply can call the pharmacy. If the generic medication you take is not listed, ask your doctor if you can switch to one that is. Your savings will be significant. For example, the popular generic blood pressure drug *lisinopril* is $4 for 30 10-mg tablets at Wal-Mart, compared with $12.99 at Drugstore.com and $30 at several community pharmacies I called. Even if you have medication insurance, the $4 price is probably lower than your current copayment.

• **Ask about older brand-name drugs.** Of course, not all drugs are available in generic form. More than half of all medications dispensed are brand-name drugs. But you still can save money if you ask your doctor to consider prescribing an older drug rather than one of the newer, more expensive drugs. Brand-name drugs on the market for seven or more years are often up to 40% cheaper than newer ones. Studies show that most older drugs are just as effective as new ones. It's also smart to shop around. Regardless of the drug, prices vary by up to 25% from pharmacy to pharmacy. There are even price variations within the same chain!

• **Opt for medication insurance.** If your employer offers drug coverage, get it. It will save you up to 90% in out-of-pocket expenses. When you become eligible for Medicare, unless you have private insurance from a previous employer, sign up for one of the many Medicare drug programs available in your state.

Warning: Even if you use no drugs at the time you sign up for Medicare, get the insurance. If you do not and decide to buy the drug insurance later, you will pay a 1% penalty on your premium for every month you were not in the program. So if you wait four years to enroll, your premium will be 48% higher than if you had enrolled when you first became eligible for Medicare.

Cut Your Grocery Bill by 75%

Susan Samtur, author of *Cashing In at the Checkout*. Back in the Bronx Press. She is editor of *Refundle Bundle*, a newsletter about coupons and refunds (*www.refundlebundle.com*). Using coupons, Samtur saves about $250 on the $500 worth of groceries she buys each month.

If you clip coupons from the Sunday newspaper, your average savings per coupon is 81 cents. That's not bad—but if you look beyond the obvious places, your savings can be extraordinary. I use coupons to reduce my weekly spending for food and household items from $100 to less than $25.

I often get staples such as toilet paper, spaghetti sauce and razor blades for free. *My best savings now...*

ON-LINE DISCOUNTS

On-line coupons have a greater average face value (97 cents per coupon) than store coupons and a longer average time until expiration (4.8 months versus three months). There are many discount resources, so it's very easy to be overwhelmed. Some require you to provide your name and e-mail address. To save time, bookmark a few Web sites that you'll use regularly.

• **Coupon clearinghouses.** These provide coupons from many manufacturers. Print and use them when you shop. When you have the time, visit several sites—one may offer bigger discounts than another for the same product. *Best sites...*

- *www.coolsavings.com*
- *www.refundsweepers.com*
- *www.smartsource.com*

• **Retail savings sites.** Some of these sites feature savings at Old Navy, Eddie Bauer and Payless ShoeSource, among other stores...

- *www.keycode.com*
- *www.couponparadise.com*
- *www.eversave.com*

• **Manufacturers' Web sites.** Look on the packages of favorite products for the manufacturer's Web sites. See if the sites offer promotions, coupons and/or rebates. *A few that are particularly generous...*

- *www.chickenofthesea.com*
- *www.clairol.com/brand/blonding/offers/trymefree.jsp*

Example: Full purchase price refund of up to $10.99 on any product from the Clairol Perfect Highlighting and Blonding Collection.

- *www.colgate.com*
- *www.cottonelle.com*

Example: $1.50 off the price of any two packages of Cottonelle Fresh Folded Wipes.

• **Discount codes for on-line shopping.** Stores depend on weekly sales, coupons and shopper's clubs to attract buyers. On-line merchants provide discounts using promotional codes. You type in the code when you go to the checkout page.

Recent example: www.barnesand noble.com gave $5 off any purchase of $50 or more, plus free shipping on two or more items after I registered for its on-line newsletter. Since the purpose of a discount code is to attract buyers to on-line stores, you may find them on Web sites other than the ones where the coupons will be used.

Some sites with generous coupon codes and promotions...

• *www.couponmountain.com*
• *www.currentcodes.com*
• *www.dealcatcher.com*

• **Manufacturers' rebates.** Some retailers have taken all the hassle out of getting manufacturers' rebates. Simply register at their Web sites—for example, log on to *www.riteaid.com...www.walgreens.com... www.truevalue.com...*and *www.officemax. com*. When you make an eligible purchase at one of these stores, enter the transaction number listed on your receipt. The manufacturer will mail you a check in four to six weeks. These rebates can total more than $100 a month, so check back frequently.

• **Free products.** Check manufacturers' Web sites for free products. You'll also find lots of free products at *www.all-free-samples.com*.

DOUBLE AND TRIPLE YOUR SAVINGS

I try to combine discounts from different sources. I'm able to get many products for free or close to it because I create "triple plays," combining savings from store sales, newspaper coupons and Web sites.

Example I: A 12-pack of Pepsi was advertised at my local supermarket for $2. A rebate sticker on the cans offered $10 back if I mailed in proofs of purchase for three 12-packs and three bags of Lay's potato chips. I purchased the three bags on sale for $5, less 75 cents off because I used three 25-cent coupons that I found on the Frito-Lay Web site. *Final cost for the soda and chips:* 25 cents—$10.25 minus the $10 rebate.

I love "double coupons." If I had made my purchases using double coupons at the supermarket, the soda and chips would have cost me nothing.

Example II: I could get two 96-tablet economy packages of Sudafed nasal decongestant at my neighborhood Rite-Aid drugstore for $7. I went to *www.eckerd.com* to get an additional $1 rebate. I also had a newspaper coupon for $1 off each package. *Final total:* $4—a saving of more than 40% off the sale price.

Send Packages For Less

Compare the delivery prices and pickup options from the top carriers at RedRoller.com. Setting up an account and comparing pricing are free. You can also print your own shipping labels and track the packages after you send them.

How to Save Money On Organic Food

Ronnie Cummins, national director of the Organic Consumers Association, a nonprofit organization that promotes food safety, children's health and environmental sustainability, Finland, MN, *www. organicconsumers.org*. He is author of *Genetically Engineered Food: A Self-Defense Guide for Consumers*. Marlowe & Company.

Many people who would like to eat organic fruits, vegetables, dairy, meat and poultry are put off by the high prices. Organic foods can cost 25% to 100% more than regular foods—but if you're willing to do a bit of sleuthing and look beyond traditional grocery stores, you can find organic products for much less.

My organization's Web site, *www.organ icconsumers.org*, has links to most of the resources suggested below...

• **Compare prices** of conventional and organic foods when shopping at regular grocery stores. Occasionally, the price gap narrows dramatically, or organic foods may even be cheaper.

• **Shop at a farmers' market.** You can find bargains if you prowl around the stalls of your local farmers' market. You'll save even more if you haggle. Farmers may be especially willing to negotiate prices if produce is misshapen or closing time is approaching.

Sample savings: Organic apples at a farmers' market often are 25% to 50% cheaper than organic apples at grocery or natural-food stores.

• **Consider purchasing a share in a community-supported agriculture program (CSA).** There are more than 1,000 of these programs around the US. Through a CSA, you purchase produce from an organic farmer in a region near you. You'll receive a weekly basket that contains produce, flowers and perhaps even eggs and milk. A share in a CSA typically costs several hundred dollars for one growing season, which could last half a year (prices vary dramatically depending on location). In mild regions, such as California, you can receive just-picked produce year-round. Each week, it's fun to discover what goodies are in the basket.

Sample savings: In rural Minnesota, where I live, I pay $450 for the season and split my weekly harvest with another family. This is at least 50% cheaper than store prices.

Helpful: Most CSAs deliver produce orders to a central location. You may be able to reduce the price of your weekly delivery if you allow your front porch to serve as a delivery spot for your neighborhood.

CSAs can be found at the Web site of Local Harvest (*www.localharvest.org*), as well as on my Web site.

• **Join a food co-op.** Co-ops typically offer high-quality organic food and produce at a discount for members. You may be required to volunteer your time for a certain number of hours each month. For a list of co-ops, see my organization's Web site.

• **Buy in bulk.** This is a great way to save money on long-lasting and nonperishable organic food, such as dried beans, lentils, pasta, rice, cereals, trail mix, nuts and even peanut butter. Health-food stores, Whole Foods, and even some supermarkets sell bulk items.

Cheaper still: Join a wholesale buying club (regular yearly membership fee is between $35 and $50). The minimum order for the club I belong to is $1,000 every three months, so I share a membership with several families in my area.

Typical savings: 30% to 50% off retail.

There is no national directory of buying clubs. Ask your local natural-food store for the names of its organic-food suppliers and contact them.

• **Eat seasonally.** You're sure to overpay if you buy organic fruits and vegetables off-season. That's when you want to buy frozen or canned. When produce is bountiful and cheap, you may want to can, freeze or dry it for the coming months.

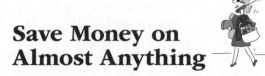

Save Money on Almost Anything

Linda Bowman, author of *The More for Your Money* series of guides, including *Free Food and More* and *Freebies (and More) for Folks Over 50.* COM-OP Publishing.

It's easy to cut costs by taking advantage of discounts and freebies, provided you know where to find them.

UTILITIES/ENERGY

• **For free evaluation of your energy usage,** call your local utilities company. In addition, many utilities companies give away free energy-saving devices, such as low-flow shower heads, water-heater blankets and fluorescent bulbs.

• **Repair major appliances yourself** instead of paying for a costly service call.

How: Call manufacturers' customer-service repair hotlines for instructions.

- *General Electric*, 800-626-2000.
- *Whirlpool*, 800-253-1301.
- *Electrolux*, 800-245-0600.

• **Gather free firewood from any of our 155 national forests.** Contact your regional office of the US Forest Service for a permit, which allows you up to six cords of downed or dead wood. At the going rate of about $150 a cord, this will save almost $1,000.

• **Install a water restrictor for your shower head.** That saves an average family thousands of gallons of water a year. Check with your local utility for a free water-restrictor head.

HOME- AND HEALTH-CARE PRODUCTS

• **Coupons are not just for food.** Some of the very best coupon savings are for cleaning supplies, tissues, toothpaste, shampoo, batteries and other home-care and health-care products. Keep an eye out for "Free with Purchase" offers…stores that pay double coupon values…coupons printed on product packaging.

• **Take advantage of refund/rebate offers.** You must take the time to save UPC symbols, labels and receipts, but the savings can easily reach hundreds of dollars a year.

Good source of offers: Supermarket and drugstore bulletin boards.

• **Ask for free samples at department store cosmetics counters.** Just say you need to try products before you buy, and you'll walk away with handfuls of high-priced makeup, skin-care products and fragrances.

Watch for: Fine print in magazine ads offering free samples of perfume or moisturizer simply by writing or calling an 800 number.

• **Have your hair cut, colored, permed or styled at a cosmetology school.** Students have spent hundreds of hours working on mannequins and each other and are closely supervised by expert instructors. Customers are usually pampered.

Savings: About 60% less than a salon. The average American woman spends $325 a year at hair salons, so expect to save $195.

• **Get routine dental care at a dental school.** Services at the country's 57 dental-school training clinics, including orthodontics, are high quality and 60% less expensive than normal dentists' fees. To find one, check the phone book for your local dental society.

• **Ask your doctors for free samples of medications** whenever you are given a prescription. Most doctors have plenty to give away.

HOME ENTERTAINMENT

• **Take advantage of free magazine offers.** Don't throw away subscription invitations from periodicals. Most publications will send you a free issue, then begin your subscription unless you cancel.

Key: Remember to write "cancel" on the invoice they send, and mail it back to them. The postage is almost always paid, and you owe nothing.

• **Use your public library** to borrow books, records, audiotapes, videotapes, even posters and artwork.

• **Order free publications from your favorite manufacturers.** Almost every food product company offers a free cookbook, including Quaker Oats, Dannon, Kikkoman, Goya's Seasonings and Nestlé…as does almost every trade organization, including the American Mushroom Institute in Kennett Square, PA, the California Raisin Advisory Board in Fresno and the Idaho Potato Commission in Boise.

Examples: Eastman Kodak of Rochester, NY, offers free booklets on photography…Gerber Baby food provides a quarterly magazine and coupons for each stage of your baby's life…Crayola Products offers a 50-plus page booklet on stain removal tips.

To find others: Check package labels for the location of company headquarters, or call 800-555-1212. Then contact the company's customer-service department.

Inexpensive Way To Get Books

Two Web sites let you trade your old paperback books for different ones. List the books that you have to trade, then browse for a new read. You pay only the postage on the books you send, which is usually less than $2.

More information: *www.paperback swap.com* and *www.frugalreader.com.*

Money-Saving Secrets From America's Cheapest Family

Steve and Annette Economides, founders and publishers of *The HomeEconomiser Newsletter*, Box 12603, Scottsdale, AZ 85267, *www.homeeconomiser. com*. They have five children ranging in age from 12 to 23. They are the authors of *America's Cheapest Family Gets You Right on the Money*. Three Rivers.

Many people think it is stressful to keep an eye on spending, but being frugal *reduces* the stress in our house. Unexpected financial setbacks, which rarely occur, can be remedied without major lifestyle changes. Our family members have learned to work together toward common goals. *Our favorite strategies...*

•**Plan and save in advance for all expenses.** We divide our checking account into 20 subaccounts on paper—though it could be done using a computer—to save for all regularly occurring household expenses, such as mortgage and auto insurance payments, as well as such categories as recreation, gifts, home repair, savings and even pets.

Every other week, we spend two hours recording our expenses and dividing our total paycheck into the subaccounts. For instance, we anticipate the cost for gas and maintenance on two cars is about $2,700 a year, so we set aside $103 per paycheck for those needs. Money in a subaccount that is not completely spent accumulates with each paycheck. This way, it's never a financial strain when the car needs new brakes—we have the money saved to cover it.

This system takes discipline, but it gives us peace of mind. We know exactly how much money we have to spend in each category. No more robbing Peter to pay Paul.

•**Plan how to spend large sums.** People often squander large payouts, such as work bonuses and tax refunds. Instead, determine the most effective use for the money before it comes in. For instance, when we were paying off our first house (within nine years), we decided that extra money would be divided as follows—30% to extra payments of our mortgage principal, 30% to retirement and other savings accounts, 20% for house projects, 10% for charitable giving and 10% for recreation. We always allow some money for fun while working toward a goal. It makes it easier to stick with the plan.

•**Budget and pay bills together as a couple.** Many financial experts suggest that spouses keep their money separate. We don't. Working together has built incredible unity in our marriage, as we have worked toward and accomplished our financial goals. We both know exactly where we stand financially. There are fewer arguments and more determination to persevere.

•**Avoid the ATM.** This cash usually evaporates as quickly as ice on a hot griddle. Instead, to take control of the most common areas of overspending—food, recreation and clothing—we withdraw predetermined amounts in cash from each paycheck. Putting a set amount of cash into three separate envelopes minimizes overspending. When the cash is gone, the spending stops. It is amazing to see how easy it is to get control of your money this way.

•**Plan dinner menus for the coming week.** This habit will encourage you to eat dinner at home more often, rather than at restaurants. With practice, a weekly menu can be created in as little as 15 minutes. You will make fewer trips to the grocery store and will save time and money. We have a list of more than 90 different dinner meals that we rotate from month to month. A favorite resource is *The Good Housekeeping Illustrated Cookbook*, which includes pictures of many of the dishes.

●**Give up your "sacred cows" for a month to reach your goals.** Sacred cows are the little extravagances that you refuse to forgo even when you're under financial pressure. If you're comfortable enough without your sacred cows for 30 days, consider giving them up for good. For many people, these include premium cable channels, bottled water and Sunday brunches at restaurants.

We had a friend in financial trouble who insisted on continuing his newspaper subscription for $30 a month. He couldn't imagine living without it. We challenged him to give it up for 30 days, just to see what happened. When you let go of something, you often find a creative way to meet that need. In this case, our friend discovered that someone at his office brought the paper each day and left it in the break room.

●**Make a game of being thrifty.** Find a creative solution that costs less than the obvious one.

Example: We saved $400 for a dishwasher. After consulting *Consumer Reports*, we called several appliance stores in our area looking for a particular brand and model. We discovered that most large distributors have "scratch and dent" and discontinued units, so we called more stores looking for these deals. We struck pay dirt at Maytag and walked out of its downtown warehouse with a brand-new, $800 stainless steel dishwasher (in an open box) for $400. We stayed within our budget and got a much better quality dishwasher than we expected.

●**Keep your eyes open**—deals are everywhere. Most Sam's Club warehouses have discount/closeout areas in the back of the store. We always check there for deals. One day, we found a twin pack of Xerox Toner cartridges for our copier. They retail for $130 each. We have bought them on eBay for as little as $60, but Sam's Club had discontinued this particular item and marked it

down to $10. Of course, we scooped them up. The deal got even sweeter when we remembered that inside each box was a certificate for a $5 rebate when we mailed in our empty toner cartridge (postage paid).

●**Decide on your "time versus money" threshold.** If one phone call will resolve a small error on our bank statement, we go for it, but we're always careful to balance our drive to save money with our time for family and friends.

Our rule: If the resolution of an issue can't yield us at least $10 to $15 per hour of our time, then it probably isn't worth pursuing.

Look Great for Less

Kathryn "The Budget Fashionista" Finney, author of *How to Be a Budget Fashionista: The Ultimate Guide to Looking Fabulous for Less*. Ballantine. She served as a fashion and shopping expert for CNN, NBC's *Today* show and FOX Television Network. Her Web site is *www.thebudgetfashionista.com*.

S hopping at off-price and discount retail stores, such as Target, TJ Maxx and Marshalls, is a great way to save money on clothing, but you can't count on fashion-savvy salespeople to help you find what looks good on you. *Here's how men and women can look their best for less...*

●**Emphasize quality over price.** Cheap clothes almost always look cheap. If you care about looking good, find quality garments that have been marked down, rather than cheaply made pieces.

Clues: If a garment has patterns, make sure they're matched up throughout the garment...look for lining in slacks and jackets... buy natural fabrics, such as wool/gabardine and cotton—it's hard to find high-quality synthetics unless you pay top dollar.

●**Dress monochromatically.** Wearing one color from head to toe is an easy way to impart a classy look with inexpensive clothing, and it's slimming. It also makes it much easier to dress—just look for matching colors.

• **Add a high-end accessory.** Adding a high-end accessory from a major designer is a surefire way to upgrade an outfit, especially if the accessory has a visible logo. Wear Calvin Klein loafers with your affordable Levi's Dockers pants…put on your high-end watch with your Old Navy shirt.

What Your Dry Cleaner Won't Tell You

Steve Boorstein, a dry cleaner for more than 30 years and a national dry-cleaning consultant, Boulder, CO, *www.clothingdoctor.com.* Boorstein has served customers ranging from a US Supreme Court justice to leading clothing designers. He is author of *The Ultimate Guide to Shopping & Caring for Clothing* (Boutique) and *The Clothing Doctor's 99 Secrets to Cleaning and Clothing Care* (Fashion Media Group).

Almost everyone has a horror story about dry cleaning. Dry-cleaning complaints, ranging from lost garments to damaged items, regularly top lists at many Better Business Bureaus.

My suggestions for resolving the most common problems…

Problem: **The dry cleaner damaged my wool blazer.**

Solution: If a garment can't be repaired to your satisfaction and the cleaner acknowledges responsibility for the damage, the cleaner should replace it with a similar item or, as is more often the case, a cash settlement within a week.

Reality check: Some cleaners go by the item's depreciated value as listed in the *Fair Claims Guide,* published by the Drycleaning & Laundry Institute (DLI), the main association for dry cleaners. But most responsible cleaners try to do anything they consider reasonable to keep the customer happy. For more information, go to DLI's Web site, *www. ifi.org/consumer/disagreement.html* or call 800-638-2627.

Guidelines: For a damaged year-old skirt or shirt that was in average condition, expect to be paid about 40% of the cost of replacing it with a new one. But if that five-year-old wool blazer is in excellent condition, the cleaner should pay nearly full replacement cost.

Important: Examine your clothing for damage before you leave the dry cleaner. If you take it home, put it in your closet and notice something two weeks later, you may have trouble getting compensation.

Problem: **The cleaner can't find my favorite sweater.**

Solution: Try to avoid this by taking precautionary measures. Don't bring in single items, such as one shirt or one tie. Single items sometimes get tacked onto other people's orders by mistake and are more likely to be lost. Also, ask the cleaner to put specific details on the claim check when valuable items are dropped off. Have him/her mark something such as "Ralph Lauren cashmere sweater" instead of just "sweater." Otherwise, the value of the lost item may be disputed.

If a garment is missing, give your dry cleaner a few weeks to find it. After that, the protocol for getting compensated is the same as for damaged items.

Problem: **The stain on my tie didn't come out.**

Solution: Your dry cleaner should be willing to try to reclean a still-stained item at no additional charge, but some stains may not come out. What you did to the stain before bringing the item to the cleaner can have a big impact. *In the future…*

• **Don't try to get out a stain yourself** on clothing that says "dry clean only." You can blot it lightly with a dry, white cloth or napkin, but never rub it or use soap or club soda, especially on oily stains, such as salad dressing or mayonnaise. This could set the stain permanently and pull out dye.

• **Get to your cleaner within 24 hours.** The longer a stain sets, the more difficult it is to remove. When you drop off an item, give your cleaner detailed information about what caused the stain. Lipstick or ink marks, for example, may need to be cleaned differently from coffee, depending on the material.

Problem: **My shirt is returned with a cracked or missing button.**

Solution: There are at least 100 varieties of shirt buttons, so cleaners don't stock them all. And broken buttons are common even at the best cleaners. But all cleaners should seek to provide a good match or move the mismatch to a less prominent position.

IF ALL ELSE FAILS...

If you can't resolve a problem with your dry cleaner, contact your local Department of Consumer Affairs or Better Business Bureau, listed in your telephone directory.

QUESTIONS ABOUT PRICES

• **One cleaner charges $3.50 to clean a pair of pants...the other one charges $12. Is the more expensive one worth it?** A higher price usually correlates with higher quality. That may include hand ironing, which lessens the chance of "shine" or "impressions" from buttons, rather than machine-pressing garments...more skilled stain removal...and accommodating your particular needs, such as "rolling" the lapels of your suit instead of flattening them.

• **The cleaner charges twice as much to launder my wife's cotton blouses as he/she does to launder my shirts. Is that fair?** Pricing by gender does have some legitimacy. Women's garments tend to have more complex details, construction, fabrics and delicate finishes that require greater attention and time. Also, the machines that press men's shirts often do not accommodate women's blouses, which then require hand pressing.

Unhappy with Your Cell Service Provider?

Consumers who are dissatisfied with their cell-phone service can avoid early termination fees by swapping service contracts with dissatisfied consumers from other providers. Celltradeusa.com arranges swaps of contracts and services among cell users.

The contract is legally traded, leaving your credit record and cell number unaffected.

Cost: $19.99.

Best: Start with a free "Get Out" profile to see if there is any demand for your offer before you pay the $19.99 activation fee.

Money, Time-Life Building, Rockefeller Center, New York City 10020.

Choose Short-Term Cell Phone Contracts

Service providers entice new customers with free or discounted phones and lots of free minutes if they sign two-year contracts—but these customers pay a premium to replace lost phones and penalties if they cancel the contract. A shorter contract might mean paying more for the phone and a higher activation fee, but you won't be locked into one provider and can take advantage of other providers' lower rates.

Web sites to find the best deals: *www. myrateplan.com...www.wirefly.com...www. saveonphone.com.*

Kiplinger's, 1729 H St. NW, Washington, DC 20006.

Be Sure You're Not Leasing Phones

Too many US households needlessly pay a monthly rental charge for phones. Most renters are older people who may have had their phones since before the breakup of the Bell telephone system in 1984. A phone that you can buy for just $20 may cost hundreds in rental fees over many years.

Self-defense: Check your phone bill. If it shows a charge for "leased equipment," you are leasing your phone.

Chris Baker, senior policy adviser, consumer team, AARP Public Policy Institute, 601 E St. NW, Washington, DC 20049.

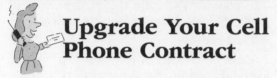

Upgrade Your Cell Phone Contract

Richard Nardone, president and CEO, Cellular Express Phone Rentals, Inc., an international cell-phone rental company, Englewood, NJ, *www.cellularphone rentals.com.*

You can upgrade your cell phone while still in the middle of your current contract. Any cell-phone carrier will let you upgrade your phone midcontract—for example, if you want e-mail access or Bluetooth technology. In fact, carriers are usually happy to see customers do this, since it may generate additional fees for special services, such as Web browsing by phone, and may trigger more phone usage.

To upgrade your phone, visit a store operated by or associated with your carrier, such as Cingular, Sprint or Verizon. After you buy the new phone, the store will communicate with your carrier, if necessary, and activate the new phone. You probably can keep your existing phone number, especially if you stay with your current carrier.

But do make it clear that you don't want your contract changed—unless you choose to extend your contract to get a discount on the new phone.

Caution: Be sure to ask if there are any upgrade or activation fees.

Secrets of a Hassle-Free Move

Christopher Noblit, owner, Avatar Moving Systems, Inc., a moving and storage company based in Yaphank, NY, *www.avatar-moving.com.* Within the Web-based consumer advocacy community, he is a recognized supporter of fair pricing in moving.

Using a moving company to relocate from one city to another—or even within the same town—doesn't have to be the nightmare that many people expect it to be.

While the moving industry is different from most other service industries—it has its own ground rules, and some of them are counterintuitive—once you understand the system and its traps, your next move is likely to go very smoothly.

What you need to know about hiring a mover...

SELECTING THE RIGHT MOVER

•**Don't rush.** Take your time in selecting a mover—a bad choice can be very expensive.

Example: A mover delivers your goods and presents a bill that's far above the agreed-upon price. If you refuse to pay the full amount, a disreputable mover might drive off with your property, essentially holding it hostage for money it claims you owe. (There's a federal law aimed at stopping this practice, but it's rarely enforced.)

•**Get recommendations from friends and neighbors** who have had positive experiences with movers. Other good sources of recommendations are your current or previous employers. Few moving companies will risk losing a corporate client by overcharging someone who has a relationship with it.

•**Check out movers with the Better Business Bureau** (*www.bbb.com*) and your state department of transportation. Don't deal with companies that have more than two or three complaints over the last year.

•**Contract directly with the company** that will actually be doing the moving, if possible. In many cases, the booking agent—the one who gives you a quote—isn't necessarily the one who operates the truck that moves your possessions. If it isn't, check out both companies.

•**Make unannounced visits to the companies,** once you've identified a few promising candidates. Say that you're considering a move, and ask to see the premises. Don't deal with a mover that doesn't welcome you in and show you an operation that appears clean and well organized.

•**Check out the mover's insurance certificate.** This shows that its insurance company is liable for mishaps, such as property damage or worker injury, during the move. Don't deal with a mover that doesn't have insurance coverage, especially workers' compensation. If you have any doubts about the authenticity of the certificate, check with the insurance company shown on it.

• **Visit Web sites that post the latest advice** for customers of moving companies. One of the most popular sites is *www.mov ingscam.com*. Among other types of information, the sites often list movers with high rates of reported customer satisfaction.

Caution: Don't use any of the growing number of Internet sites that let you enter details about your move and then compare on-line bids from moving companies.

Reason: Though most of these sites try to keep disreputable companies out of the bidding procedure, they're rarely successful.

Example: I recently went to a Web site and entered information about my upcoming move from a village on Long Island to another that was only a few miles away. I said I had 18,000 pounds of household items, which I knew should cost about $4,500 to move.

About a dozen moving companies responded—with bids that ranged from $1,000 to $4,000. The low bids were scams in the sense that if I chose any of them, the company would still bill me for around $4,500. I know that because I'm in the business, but the average home owner doesn't.

REALISTIC ESTIMATES

The biggest problem with moving nearly always involves a final bill that's higher—sometimes much higher—than the original estimate.

Ironically, the disparity usually happens because the customer asked for quotes from several movers and then selected the one with the lowest estimate. It's often smarter to pick the mover with the highest weight estimate.

Here's why: When you tell a mover what you want to ship, the sales rep uses an industry formula to estimate the total weight of items you name—a six-foot sofa, a 19-inch television, etc. But, because the moving business is highly competitive, sales reps are under pressure to give you the lowest possible estimate.

Example: You're relocating from Baltimore to Miami and ask for bids from three movers. You receive bids based on three different weight estimates—8,000, 12,000 and 16,000 pounds. You take the low bid based on 8,000 pounds that would typically be about $4,000, depending on insurance and packing costs.

Result: Your goods arrive in Miami, where the company presents a bill for $8,000—twice what you expected to pay. When you ask for an explanation, you're told that the actual weight of your goods was 16,000 pounds. What the company doesn't tell you is that, in order to get your business, it based its estimate on a deliberately understated weight.

That's also why a "binding estimate" can be an advantage—or can be completely useless. The term implies that the final bill won't vary from the estimate. However, the binding estimate is only good for the items listed on the inventory, which often does not accurately reflect the final count of articles that you want to move. If you put more onto the truck, the mover will charge for the additional weight—or refuse to move the items.

To prevent these problems: Go with the company that makes the highest weight bid. High bidders are more likely to give honest weight estimates while many low bidders intentionally understate the weight or try to cut costs by not carrying insurance.

Ask to witness the actual weighing of the truck on moving day. Most home owners are unaware that they have a legal right to see the truck being weighed before and after loading.

When you tell a moving company that you want to exercise this right, it will tell you when and where the van will be weighed—usually at a state-certified site on the outskirts of town.

Go to the site before the van picks up your goods, watch it being weighed and ask for a copy of the weight certificate. Then return to the site after your goods are loaded, and again watch the scales and get a written record of the added weight.

Movers usually put more than one customer's goods on a truck, but you'll still know the weight of your own goods because the truck is put on the scales immediately before and after it's loaded.

Moving companies that know the customer is aware of the actual weight will rarely try to bill for a higher amount.

Another smart move: Always take out "full-replacement loss or damage liability," offered by the company that moves you, on goods that you ship.

Typical price: About $300 to insure the full-replacement value of a shipment valued at $50,000, with a $250 deductible.

You may also want to check out what moving coverage is offered by the company that carries your homeowner's or other insurance.

Caution: If you ship any high-priced items, such as antiques, jewelry, a stamp collection, etc., always have proof of value, such as receipts or a letter from a licensed appraiser.

Supermarket Guru's Very Smart Shopping Strategies

Phil Lempert, food trends editor and on-air correspondent for NBC News and host of the nationally syndicated radio show *Shopping Smart.* He is editor of SupermarketGuru.com and *Facts, Figures & the Future,* a free monthly e-newsletter, Santa Monica, CA. *www.factsfiguresfuture.com.*

S upermarkets keep coming up with new ways to get you to spend more—by stocking costly nongrocery items and overpriced snacks. *Here are my latest smart shopping strategies…*

SAVINGS IN THE STORE

•**Avoid nonfood items.** Supermarkets now sell everything from books and kitchen appliances to hardware and pet supplies.

You almost always can find these items cheaper elsewhere.

•**Ask for the sale price on an item** even if you buy less than the "required" minimum. Most stores don't want you to know that if a product is on sale at, say, four for $6, you almost always can purchase just one item and still get the sale price, in this case, $1.50 for one.

•**Buy fruits and vegetables in season.** It is more important than ever now. *Reason?* Spikes in fuel prices have driven up transportation costs—this especially affects the price of produce when it is out of season in a particular region. For a list of what's locally in season, go to *www.foodnetwork. com* and click on "Cooking," then "Cooking Guides," then "Produce Guides."

•**Shop with friends at Costco and Sam's Clubs.** The drawback of warehouse clubs is having to buy large quantities, especially if your family is small.

My suggestion: Visit the clubs with a few friends. As you walk the aisles separately, discuss over your cell phones what bulk items you would like and who will get them. (This saves money and time.) Meet in the parking lot afterward to divide your purchases and split the cost.

•**Avoid trendy, expensive foods.** Here are the hot—and overpriced—items on shelves now…

•Food pumped up with supplements, including eggs enhanced with omega-3 fatty acids, to help maintain vascular health, and juices and cereals with antioxidants and phytochemicals that combat cellular damage.

My suggestion: Have ordinary eggs and juices, as well as whole-grain cereals, to get the nutrients you need. If your doctor thinks you're not getting enough from food, it is more cost effective to take supplements in a pill form.

•Portion-controlled snacks. Treats such as Oreos and Pringles come in 100-calorie packages for people who crave snacks but lack the discipline to control portions. These snack packages often are more than twice as expensive per ounce than the larger version.

My suggestion: Buy a larger box, and subdivide portions yourself.

SAVINGS USING TECHNOLOGY

• **Plan purchases on-line** before you go to the market. Most major chains have sophisticated Web sites that let you browse on-line circulars for promotions so you can decide which items to buy. You also can create shopping lists, which shortens your time in the supermarket. Some sites allow you to order on-line for home delivery (at an extra cost based on the total of your order) or pick up at the store at no extra cost.

Favorites: *www.albertsons.com...www.safeway.com...www.kroger.com...www.publix.com...www.stopandshop.com.*

Or check out Internet-only supermarkets that deliver.

Examples: *www.freshdirect.com* (New York City metro area) and *www.simondelivers.com* (Twin City area, Minnesota).

To find a delivery service in your area, go to an Internet search engine and type in "supermarket food delivery" and the name of your city.

• **Print out coupons and rebates** from your computer.

My suggestion: Search for coupons for items that you buy regularly at Web sites such as *www.coolsavings.com* (click on "Grocery Coupons") and *www.couponcart.com.* Some sites let you specify the coupons you want to receive and then e-mail them to you, but read the small print—you may have to allow the coupon sponsor to share your e-mail address with other parties.

• **Shop at supermarkets that offer "scan" technology.**

How it works: You use your cell phone to scan a bar code for more information, such as customer ratings, about a product. Just download the free software from *www.scanbuy.com.* Then you are connected to the Internet to get price comparisons for that product from nearby retailers. For more information, go to the Scanbuy.com Web site and click on "ScanLife."

Another innovation: Several hundred Stop & Shops offer cart-mounted minicomputers that keep a running total of your purchases and let you order ahead from the deli counter.

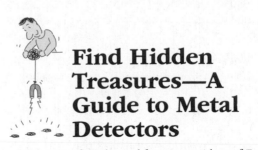

Find Hidden Treasures—A Guide to Metal Detectors

Dick Stout, founder and former president of Federation of Metal Detector and Archaeological Clubs, Inc., McClellandtown, PA. He is author of several books on metal detecting, including *The New Metal Detecting...the Hobby.* White's Electronics.

Have you ever wondered if those people scanning the ground with metal detectors find anything valuable? Take it from me, a longtime "detectorist," we do. I have unearthed Civil War uniform buttons and cannon balls...gold and diamond rings appraised for as much as $1,500...and, while visiting Europe, Roman coins more than 2,000 years old. It's not unusual for an experienced user to find more than $10 in coins per hour at the beach the Monday after a sunny summer weekend.

However, metal detecting is a bit like fishing—one day you get dozens of hits, the next day nothing at all. It takes patience and is worth doing only if you enjoy the search and are looking for a hobby that gets you outside on nice days. It's also a way to further an interest in coin collecting or local history.

BUYING A METAL DETECTOR

There are metal detectors on the market for as little as $50, but these bargain-basement models don't work well. A decent entry-level metal detector costs $200 to $400 and will find a dime as far down as eight inches and a quarter down to 12 inches. *Reliable brands include...*

• **Fisher,** 915-225-0333, *www.fisherlab.com*

• **Garrett,** 800-527-4011, *www.garrett.com*

•**Minelab,** 702-891-8809, *www.minelab. com*

•**Tesoro,** 928-771-2646, *www.tesoro.com*

•**White's Electronics,** 800-547-6911, *www.whiteselectronics.com*

You'll also need a good set of headphones. Get the type that completely covers your ears so you don't miss faint signals.

Cost: $20 to $50.

Dealers often rent metal detectors for about $20 a day. If you're not certain that metal detecting is for you, rent before you buy.

When you select a detector, lighter is better. Every pound counts when you're carrying it around for hours.

Your metal detector should let you switch between an "all-metal" setting and a "discriminate" setting. Use the all-metal setting to search wide areas, then switch to discriminate when you get a hit to weed out the garbage. The discriminate setting is adjustable—you'll want to set it so that it's sensitive enough to react to a pull tab from a soda can. If a detector skips over pull tabs, it also might skip over gold rings.

Some metal detectors have ID meters that tell you what you have found—but these identification systems are right only about two-thirds of the time.

SEARCH STRATEGIES

Where to search depends on what you hope to find. If you're looking for modern objects, such as coins and jewelry, search soon after the crowds have departed—at the beach the Monday after a nice weekend or on a fairground the day after a concert.

Bring along a garden trowel with serrated edges for grassy areas and a sieve for the beach.

If you're looking for old coins or other historical items, read about the region's history to learn where buildings once stood and people gathered.

The best time to search is the day after a heavy rain, because metal detectors can "see" farther down into moist earth than dry.

Cut Pet-Care Costs

Woman's Day, 1633 Broadway, New York City 10019.

Here are seven ways you can cut pet-care costs. You can start saving today by following the suggestions below.

•**Leash, fence and/or supervise your dog**—dogs often sustain injuries while running loose.

•**Skip fancy premium foods sold by vets,** and use name-brand pet food labeled "complete and balanced" or one with the Association of American Feed Control Officials seal of approval.

•**Spay or neuter.** Spayed and neutered dogs have fewer health and behavioral problems.

•**Make wellness a routine.** Pet stores, humane societies and veterinary schools often offer on-site clinics that provide inoculations and wellness exams. Keep careful records of all pets' inoculations and treatments.

•**Don't buy pet insurance.** Instead, put the amount you would have paid in premiums into a savings account for future medical bills. Or enroll your pet in a discount wellness plan, such as the one offered by Banfield, The Pet Hospital (866-277-7387, *www.banfield.net*), a national chain of pet-care facilities.

•**Get a second opinion** if the estimate for a pet's medical care is for more than a few hundred dollars.

•**Shop around for medications.** Ask your vet for prescription drug samples to get started, and then call retailers and pharmacies to compare prices. Last year, pet owners spent more than $38 billion on food, supplies, services and medical care for their 358 million pets.

An Insider's Secrets to Getting More Financial Aid for College

Ben Kaplan, founder of ScholarshipCoach.com, which provides information on how to obtain college financing. He graduated from Harvard University debt-free in 1999 by using $90,000 in scholarships. He is also the author of 12 books and CDs on paying for college, including *How to Go to College Almost for Free: 10 Days to Scholarship Success.* Collins.

Many families fail to take full advantage of the financial aid available to them and lose out on tens of thousands of dollars in grants, scholarships and subsidized loans. Even households that have considerable incomes and assets can qualify. (Merit scholarships are available regardless of income.) *Here's how to get the most financial aid you can...*

•**Defer your income in the calendar year before your child graduates from high school.** The financial-aid eligibility clock starts ticking sooner than most parents expect.

Example: If your student graduates high school in 2009, your income during 2008 will serve as the basis for freshman-year financial-aid calculations.

Strategy: Ask that employers give year-end bonuses in early 2009 rather than during 2008. If you're self-employed, accelerate or postpone customer billing to minimize 2008 income. Avoid selling assets, such as stocks, bonds and rental property, in 2008 if proceeds will be taxed as income. (Delaying income from 2008 to 2009 might cause your aid to drop in the student's sophomore year, but you'll come out ahead, since the freshman "base" year sets the precedent for financial aid allocations.)

•**To reduce cash reserves, make major expenditures**—on home renovations, cars, computers, entertainment systems, etc.—before you apply for aid.

Reason: Colleges take most financial assets into account when they determine your need for aid but not other personal assets, such as cars or home electronics.

If your child has significant savings, urge him/her to spend his own money first—as opposed to yours—on big-ticket items.

Reason: When figuring out an aid package according to the federal methodology, colleges expect students to contribute 20% of their assets to college costs. Parents are expected to pitch in only about 5% of all their assets. (You could, of course, pay the child back later without incurring gift tax as long as you do not exceed the maximum annual gift limit of $12,000 per recipient— $24,000 for couples in 2008.)

•**Apply for aid as soon as possible.** Many colleges distribute financial aid on a first-come, first-served basis, so money might be substantially depleted long before the official end of the application period. Submit the federal government's *Free Application for Federal Student Aid* (FAFSA) form—as well as any additional forms required by private colleges—by January or early February of your child's senior year in high school to ensure the biggest share possible.

To assemble the necessary information, you will need to finish up your tax forms well before April. If you can't, use estimates on your college aid forms (identifying them as estimates) and follow up with actual figures as soon as possible.

•**If a school's aid offer is lower than you expected, explain special circumstances** that are not considered by the aid formulas—hefty medical bills...private-school expenses for your other children in grade-school...graduate school costs for your older kids, if you pay some of their bills...or an unusually high income year that is not representative of your typical earnings. Follow up with evidence, such as invoices, establishing that, for example, you are paying Grandma's hospital bills, or the last five years' tax returns to show that your income last year was much higher than normal.

•**Apply for merit-based scholarships from corporations,** foundations, associations, unions and community groups. Links to award databases can be found at my site, ScholarshipCoach.com.

Note: These scholarships may affect other financial aid.

•**Leverage offers from other schools.** If your top choice is X University, but Y University offers more aid, call X and ask to speak to the financial aid officer responsible for your file. Explain that your child really wants to attend, but Y's aid package makes going there more financially feasible. X might increase its offer. This works best when the schools involved are rivals or the student is particularly appealing to the college because of special credentials or talents.

Wedding Insurance

Wedding insurance can be a good buy now that the average cost of a wedding is close to $30,000. Different policies cover different contingencies.

Examples: Cancellation because of a death in the family…a natural disaster…the deployment of one member of the couple on military assignment. Cost ranges from a few hundred dollars to $1,000 or more. Available at WedSafe.com (877-723-3933) and Bridal AssociationofAmerica.com (661-633-1949).

Christa Vagnozzi, senior editor, TheKnot.com, New York City.

Tons of Free Stuff

There is such a thing as a free lunch and much more. You can shop on-line for full-size products and samples of all kinds of snacks, over-the-counter medications, household items, cosmetics and even electronics like computers, game consoles, flat-screen TVs and iPods—all for free. Availability varies.

Web sites with the best deals: *www.freestuffhunter.com…www.totallyfreestuff.com…www.thefreesite.com.*

4

Retirement Report

It's Not Too Late! You Can Still Build a Solid Nest Egg

 Only 18% of American workers have retirement savings of more than $100,000. Less than half have even calculated how much they will need for retirement.

Rectifying this situation has become a personal mission for economist Ben Stein. Notoriously frugal, he based his Emmy Award–winning TV game show, *Win Ben Stein's Money*, on his passion for saving. More recently, he served as spokesman for National Retirement Planning Week, sponsored by a coalition of financial education organizations, and testified before Congress about America's retirement savings problem.

Mr. Stein discusses America's growing retirement problems and how he likes to invest his money...

● **Can Americans count on the Social Security privatization plan to boost their savings?** Privatization does not look probable. It is actually a distraction from real retirement planning. Squeezing extra returns from your government benefits—the average payout for retirees currently is just $958* per month—is not going to enable you to retire comfortably. That will happen only if you make saving an everyday priority.

● **How much do you put away?** I have been worrying about my retirement since I was 13. I am 61 now, and although I expect a modest pension from the Screen Actors Guild, I'm also trying to save very aggressively on my own—about 20% of my annual income.

● **Few people can afford to save that much. How can the average person**

*Rates subject to change.

Ben Stein, an economist, attorney, actor and comedian who resides in Beverly Hills, CA, with his wife and teenaged son. He was a speechwriter for Presidents Richard Nixon and Gerald Ford. His most recent book is *Yes, You Can Become a Successful Income Investor! Reaching for Yield in Today's Market.* Hay House.

squirrel away more money? Look, people in China, which has only 14% the gross domestic product per capita that we have, save 40% of their incomes. Americans save roughly just 1%, so we can do a lot better.

A clear-cut goal makes it easier to deprive yourself of indulgences. You can calculate how much you will need in retirement at the AARP Web site, *www.aarp.org/money/ financial_planning*. Be sure to use 100% of your current living expenses as your goal.

You can live on less—but a man of 65 today is likely to live to 80...a woman of 65 is likely to live to 83½. Prices could increase by 75% or more by then, so you must generate income in excess of what you need today.

●**Where do you invest additional money after you have maxed out retirement plan contributions?** Any additional money is put into variable annuities. That advice came from my father, who served as chairman of the Council of Economic Advisors under Presidents Nixon and Ford. He did not earn a lot of money in his lifetime, but he had a comfortable retirement because owning annuities meant that he never had to worry about outliving his money.

●**Haven't a lot of people been burned by variable annuities?** Annuities have taken a lot of heat in recent years because of overaggressive selling by the insurance industry and lots of hidden fees. But if you do your homework, you'll realize that transferring the financial risk of living a long life to the insurance company and away from yourself is worth a look. To get a primer on annuities, visit *www.sec.gov/investor/pubs/ varannty.htm* or research all the inexpensive offerings from TIAA-CREF (800-842-2252, *www.tiaa-cref.org*) and at The Vanguard Group (800-522-5555, *www.vanguard.com*).

●**How do you invest your retirement money?** I have always been very diversified, so I have never suffered a catastrophic loss. I spread my money around the way a large institutional investor does. I use a variety of brokerage firms. I manage some of my accounts myself...I hire money managers for others. I own wide-ranging global

asset classes—from emerging-market bonds to real estate investment trusts (REITs).

●**What mistakes have you made?** Most of the mistakes I have made as an investor have come from ignoring my own advice. I bought Berkshire Hathaway when it was cheap—$900 a share—but I didn't buy with conviction and should have scooped up a lot more. It's now worth $131,290* a share. I also got caught up a bit in the quest for Internet stock riches, even though my indicators told me that the market was overvalued.

●**You detailed those indicators in your book,** *Yes, You Can Time the Market.* **How do you use this strategy for retirement investing?** My definition of market timing bears no resemblance to that of most financial gurus. No one can consistently predict what will happen in the stock market within the next year or the next five, but you can identify when stocks are cheaper by historical standards. If you buy stocks in those periods, your likelihood of making money over 20 years or longer is far better than if you dollar cost average into stock investments year after year, as many advisers recommend.

●**Tell us more about your research.** I sifted through 100 years of stock market data and found four simple measurements, or "metrics," that indicate with uncanny consistency when the S&P 500 was over- or undervalued. They include the current inflation-adjusted average price of stocks in the index...the index's average price-to-earnings ratio based on the trailing 12 months...average dividend yield...and average price-to-book value. You can see current figures, along with historical returns, on my book's Web site, *www.yesyoucantimethe market.com*.

Next, I compared each of these measurements to their own 15-year moving averages. The optimal time to buy is at market lows—when the dividend yield is above its moving average and the rest of the metrics are well below theirs. You avoid stocks when the situation reverses itself.

By following this strategy, you would have bought stocks in 15 out of 15 of the

*Prices subject to change.

best years to invest since 1926 and would have avoided the worst 15 years.

•**What do you do during overpriced stock market cycles?** Stay invested in the stocks I own, but I use new money to buy bonds (or bond funds), REITs (or REIT funds) and shares in a money market fund.

Money Mistakes Seniors Are Making Now

Alexandra Armstrong, CFP, chairman of the financial planning firm Armstrong, Fleming & Moore, Inc., 1850 M St. NW, Washington, DC 20036, *www.afmfa.com.* She is author of *On Your Own: A Widow's Passage to Emotional and Financial Well-Being.* Dearborn.

A young person who squanders his/her nest egg may have decades to recover. But seniors cannot afford to make big financial errors.

Common financial mistakes—and how to avoid them...

Mistake: **Taking Social Security too soon.** Many people begin collecting Social Security when they turn 62. But the earlier you start taking benefits, the smaller your monthly check. It is usually better to postpone taking Social Security until you reach the full retirement age. That age varies—for instance, it's 65 years and 10 months for those born in 1942.

Example: If you were born in 1950 and currently earn $70,000 annually, according to the Social Security calculator (*www.ssa.gov*), you would receive monthly benefits of about $1,307 starting in 2012, when you turn 62. If you wait until age 66 (your full retirement age) in 2016, you will get $1,780 a month. You'll get $2,407 at age 70 in 2020.

Besides receiving smaller payments at 62, you run the risk of having your checks further reduced if you decide later to go back to work. That's because if you're under full retirement age and earn more than a certain

threshold amount ($13,560 in 2008), you lose $1 of benefits for every $2 of earnings over this limit. But if you are above your full retirement age, your payments will not be cut—no matter how much you earn at a job.

If you wait to collect until you are age 70, you will receive the maximum monthly check. But you are taking a larger gamble on your longevity—that is, you may not live to age 70.

Calculated risk: If you wait until age 70 to start receiving Social Security payments, therefore getting the highest payments, and then live past 78, you will have received more total income from Social Security than if you had begun receiving checks at age 65 and 10 months. Nonetheless, my advice is generally to take the checks as soon as you reach full retirement age. If you don't need the money, you can invest it for a rainy day.

Mistake: **Failing to take the required minimum distributions from retirement accounts.** When you turn 70½, you must begin taking payouts from your traditional IRAs. If you fail to take withdrawals on time, the IRS can impose a 50% penalty. This means that if you are late to withdraw $10,000, the government will charge you $5,000. The rule is so tough because Washington doesn't want money to stay tax sheltered indefinitely.

The IRS Web site (*www.irs.gov*) spells out correct withdrawal amounts. There, you can find your life expectancy according to IRS tables.

Example: If you are 70 in May, the IRS figures you will live another 27.4 years. The government wants to spread your withdrawals evenly over your life span. Say you have $100,000 in your IRA. You must divide that figure by 27.4. The result is $3,649.63—the amount you must withdraw the first year. Consult the table each year because this withdrawal figure changes as you age.

If you forget to take a withdrawal the first year, correct the mistake and send a written notice to the IRS. The IRS is often lenient with someone who is struggling with the tables for the first time. The tax collectors may let you off with a warning about not making the same error next year.

Best: To avoid problems, contact the custodian of your IRA to have the withdrawal amount paid directly to your bank well before the end of the year—then check to make sure it happens.

Mistake: **Paying off mortgages too soon.** As they approach retirement, some people feel that they must pay off their mortgages. For peace of mind, this may be important. But if you plan to sell off other assets to accomplish this, you may do better by keeping the mortgage debt.

Example: You have a $100,000 mortgage with an interest rate of 5.75%. Because you can deduct the mortgage interest (even if you pay the alternative minimum tax), the after-tax cost of the mortgage if you are in the 25% tax bracket is about 4.3%. You could pay off the mortgage by selling $100,000 worth of investments to raise the cash.

Better: Instead of selling your assets to pay off the mortgage, keep the money invested in a portfolio that is expected to earn more than 5.75%. That way, you can use the earnings to cover the mortgage and still have some investment income left.

Mistake: **Ignoring inflation.** Many people figure that inflation won't erode the value of their investments in a significant way. After all, the consumer price index (CPI) has historically risen at an average annual rate of only 3%, and a well-constructed investment portfolio should do much better than that over time. But over time, even small price increases whittle away at your purchasing power.

Example: Your investments earn 8% annually, while inflation runs at 3%. So, you will only have 5% left after inflation. And there is a chance that you can face above-average inflation rates. A sudden spurt in energy or health costs can wreck your budget. (Historically, people who live in big cities on the coasts have faced inflation rates that are much higher than the long-term averages.)

For protection, emphasize dividend-paying blue-chip stocks in your portfolio. These tend to appreciate over time, and many raise

their dividends at annual rates that are well above the long-term average increases in the CPI. Don't rely exclusively on income from fixed sources, such as bonds or pensions, which can be eaten away by inflation. If inflation is at 3% and you receive $50,000 a year from a pension or annuity, during your second year of retirement your purchasing power will have dropped to $48,500. The third year, the real value of the income will be $47,045.

Mistake: **Paying bills by check.** Many retirees insist on paying by check because they don't trust electronic systems. But the more important danger is that you will forget to pay on time—incurring penalties. That can hurt your credit rating and increase borrowing costs. *What to do...*

•**Automate deposits.** Have your Social Security checks automatically deposited into your checking account. If you are working, ask your employer to also make automatic deposits. This saves time and reduces errors. If the account is interest bearing, automatic deposits will boost your income, since payments will spend more time in your account and less time in the mail.

•**Automate payments.** Pay as many bills as possible automatically. That way, you won't miss payments—even if you take a trip overseas.

Examples: Many cable TV companies and Internet service providers allow you to charge your monthly bill automatically. Many banks and brokerages offer electronic systems that enable regular payments—such as utility bills—to be withdrawn automatically from your account. For extra efficiency, do all your business with one bank or brokerage. There is no reason to have six different accounts spread around town.

Mistake: **Holding stock certificates personally.** Many people insist on holding paper stock certificates in their bank safe-deposit boxes because they are afraid of losing the securities. When they need to make sales, these investors run to the bank vault, retrieve paper shares and mail them to their brokers. Investors who hold old-fashioned paper certificates must round up individual records of dividends and transactions for each stock or bond—a time-consuming and error-prone process. This is a throwback to the Great Depression, when many stock brokers went bankrupt, and investors found that their securities had vanished. But all reputable brokers are members of the Securities Investor Protection Corporation (SIPC) and covered for up to $500,000 for stocks, bonds and other securities and up to $100,000 for cash. Most firms also have additional coverage.

It is now very efficient to have your broker hold the certificates. That way, you can sell shares immediately with a phone call or computer key stroke. At the end of the year, the broker will send you a record of all dividends and transactions. At tax time, you have one convenient record.

Finance Your Dream Retirement Home

Martin M. Shenkman, JD, CPA, estate planning attorney, Teaneck, NJ. Author of 34 books, including *The Complete Living Trusts Program*. Wiley. *www.laweasy.com*.

With the softening real estate market—especially in areas where many people buy second homes, such as near the shore or in the mountains—now may be a good time to shop for a home that you would like to retire to eventually. Even though prices have dropped, it may not be easy to finance the retirement home you want. The most straightforward and tax-efficient strategy is to purchase a new home with the proceeds from the sale of your current home. If your current home has been your primary residence for at least two of the previous five years, you'll be able to shield from tax $250,000 in capital gains on the sale ($500,000 if you're married).

Even though it might be a good time to buy, you might not be quite ready to move out of your home yet. *If that's the case, consider these financing alternatives…*

• **Liquidate your life insurance.** Are your children grown and living independently? Have you accumulated a large enough retirement fund to support your spouse or life partner after your death?

If so, you may no longer need your life insurance policy. The cash from selling or surrendering the policy can be used to help pay for a retirement home. The money that you would otherwise use for insurance premiums can go toward upkeep, taxes and other costs associated with owning the new home.

Strategy: Ask your insurance company about your policy's cash-surrender value. That will let you know how much you would pocket if you terminated the policy. Then look into whether you would fetch a higher price by selling the policy to an outside investor. Ask your agent to obtain multiple bids. The older you are, the more the policy will be worth, especially if you have had some health problems. An investor will keep the policy in force and collect on it upon your death.

One reason *not* to get rid of life insurance is to provide liquidity in case of an estate tax obligation. However, under current law, couples with estates of up to $4 million may not be subject to much federal estate tax at all.

Check with your tax professional to see whether surrendering your policy or selling it will put you ahead on an after-tax basis.

• **Borrow.** Either refinance the mortgage on your existing home or take out a home-equity loan, assuming that you have enough equity to finance the second purchase and enough income to make the loan payments.

If you wish, you can eventually sell your primary residence, use the capital gains exclusion, repay the mortgage and move into your retirement home.

Caution: This strategy can greatly increase your debt, and interest on a mortgage you refinance above your old mortgage might not be deductible. Speak with your tax professional.

• **Rent.** Sell your principal residence on the condition that you can rent it from the new owner for a certain amount of time—

say, two years. At the same time, the sale proceeds can go toward your purchase of a retirement home.

Loophole: You can enter into a sale-leaseback with a family member, such as a grown son or daughter. As long as the entire transaction is at fair market value (based on comparable prices in the area), you'll get the capital gains exclusion, while the buyer will get the tax benefits of owning rental property, such as depreciation and a property tax deduction.

Top Six Places to Retire

Warren R. Bland, PhD, professor of geography, California State University at Northridge, and author of *Retire in Style: 60 Outstanding Places Across the USA and Canada*. Next Decade. Professor Bland intends to retire this year to Ithaca, NY.

When choosing a place to retire, it is easy to neglect features of a town that might not seem immediately important but that could be significant later on. In my studies of retirees, I have discovered that the happiest ones nearly always live in areas with certain characteristics in regard to climate, community services, crime rate, cost of living, cultural and educational activities, employment and volunteer opportunities, health care, landscape, recreational activities, retail services and transportation. *Based on these criteria, here are six of the leading cities for retirement, selected to represent different geographical areas...*

PORTLAND, OREGON

The Portland metropolitan area has a population of roughly 1.95 million, but the city often seems much smaller because of its uncongested downtown and its beautiful residential neighborhoods. Many retirees are also drawn to the city because of its excellent public transportation and medical facilities.

Apart from a wide range of cultural and recreational activities, Portland has first-rate

basketball and hockey teams, making it a great town for sports fans.

Located between two mountain ranges in the Willamette Valley, Portland averages only about 36 inches of rain a year, far less than the deluge that many newcomers might expect. Temperatures vary from an average daily high of 46°F in January to 81°F in August.

A house in an upscale neighborhood near public transportation typically costs about $350,000,* and retiree living costs are slightly above the national average.

Smaller houses and those in less fashionable neighborhoods are, of course, less expensive, as are condominiums.

Information: Portland Oregon Visitors Association, 800-962-3700, *www.pova.com.*

BOULDER, COLORADO

Unlike many other US cities, Boulder has a low-crime downtown area where people stroll among upscale shops, street markets and restaurants. Parking is easy, and there's little traffic congestion.

Recreational opportunities include skiing and nature hiking, and the University of Colorado provides an abundance of cultural activities for this city of just over 100,000 residents. Boulder is only 35 miles from Denver, where a major airport and Amtrak trains make it easy to reach other parts of the country.

The city gets about 83 inches of snow a year, but temperatures are surprisingly mild. In January, the daily high averages about 45°F, and in July, it's 88°F.

Drawback: Boulder is expensive. A house suitable for a retired couple can easily cost $500,000, and the cost of living is about 20% above the US average.

Information: Boulder, Colorado Convention and Visitors Bureau, 800-444-0447, *www.bouldercoloradousa.com.*

ASHEVILLE, NORTH CAROLINA

Located on a 2,100-foot-high plateau near the Blue Ridge Mountains, Asheville is a sophisticated city that has attracted retirees for many decades. The city, which has about

*Prices and rates subject to change.

70,000 residents, provides excellent health care, shopping and entertainment, and a wide variety of outdoor activities.

Using a variety of data, I estimate that the cost of living in Asheville is near the national average. A three-bedroom, 1,800-square-foot house in great condition in an upscale neighborhood costs about $275,000.

Many Northerners enjoy Asheville because it has the familiar four seasons but without the bitter cold. Southerners like the city because summers are not oppressively hot. In January, the average daily high is 47°F, and in July, it's 83°F.

Drawback: To fly from Asheville to many major cities, you must transfer in Atlanta or take a plane at the Greenville-Spartanburg International Airport in South Carolina, which is about 50 miles away.

Information: City of Asheville, 828-251-1122, *www.ashevillenc.gov.*

SAN ANTONIO, TEXAS

This riverside city of 1.8 million has first-class health care, and there's excellent transportation within the city and to other regions of the country, including Amtrak routes to Chicago, Los Angeles and points in Florida.

Retirees are attracted to San Antonio's upbeat rhythm and friendly people. Its vibrant Mexican heritage is reflected in local restaurants and music festivals in many of San Antonio's cultural centers, including the San Antonio Museum of Art.

The city is a bargain. The cost of living is 7% below the national average, and houses suitable for retired couples cost about $200,000.

Drawbacks: Temperatures climb to 90°F or more on an average of 116 days a year. Air pollution in the summer can be a problem for people with respiratory ailments.

Information: San Antonio Convention and Visitors Bureau, 800-447-3372, *www. sanantoniocvb.com.*

VICTORIA, BRITISH COLUMBIA

Just across the border on Vancouver Island, off Canada's west coast, Victoria is a sophisticated city with excellent museums, theater and recreation opportunities. Three colleges in the area provide a wide variety of cultural activities.

Nearby mountain ranges act as a barrier to rain clouds, so Victoria averages only 30 inches of rain a year. The average high temperature is 44°F in winter and 70°F in summer. The greater metropolitan area has a population of approximately 325,000.

Drawbacks: The cost of living is about 20% above the average for North America. A three-bedroom house located in an upscale neighborhood typically costs about $400,000.

Information: City of Victoria, 250-385-5711, *www.victoria.ca/common/index.shtml.*

TALLAHASSEE, FLORIDA

The capital of Florida is only 30 miles from the Gulf of Mexico, but is high enough above sea level to protect it from flooding in the event of a hurricane.

Population 151,000, Tallahassee combines old Southern charm with a variety of cultural and recreational activities at Florida State University. Tallahassee also has excellent health-care facilities. Its cost of living is near the national average. The typical price of a three-bedroom house is as low as $200,000.

Information: Tallahassee Visitor's Guide, 800-628-2866, *www.visittallahassee.com.*

More from Warren Bland, PhD…

Four Lesser-Known Great Cities

Below are some frequently overlooked cities that are wonderful places to live for retirees…

BLOOMINGTON, INDIANA

Located in the rolling hills of southern Indiana, Bloomington is the epitome of a university town—in this case, Indiana University. Retirees like the city's many outdoor activities and cultural and athletic events.

Population: 70,000.

Cost of living: About 5% below the national average.

Housing: An upscale house costs as little as $200,000.

Information: City of Bloomington, 812-349-3400, *www.bloomington.in.gov.*

THOMASVILLE, GEORGIA

Retirees are rediscovering this southern Georgia city. They like its antebellum charm, outdoor activities, downtown boutiques and architectural remnants of the late 19th century. It has first-rate health-care facilities.

Population: 18,000.

Cost of living: About 10% below the national average.

Housing: Three-bedroom homes start at about $150,000.

Information: Thomasville/Thomas County Conventions & Visitors Bureau, 866-577-3600, *www.thomasvillega.com.*

ITHACA, NEW YORK

Sure, it's cold in the winter, but the city offers lots to compensate for the climate. Ithaca is located at the south end of Cayuga Lake and close to scenic mountains. Cornell University and Ithaca College provide many free and low-cost activities, including theater, concerts and classes.

Population: 30,000.

Cost of living: Just above the national average.

Housing: An upscale house typically costs $275,000.

Information: City of Ithaca at 800-284-8422 or *www.visitithaca.com.*

BURLINGTON, VERMONT

Situated on the shore of Lake Champlain with the Green Mountains in the background, Burlington offers many outdoor activities as well as the boutiques, cafés and craft vendors at the Church Street Marketplace. And, health-care facilities are excellent.

Population: 40,000.

Cost of living: About 12% above the national average.

Housing: About $300,000 in an upscale area.

Information: City of Burlington at 802-863-3489 or *www.ci.burlington.vt.us.*

Simple Steps To a Much Happier Retirement

Nancy K. Schlossberg, EdD, a counseling psychologist and professor emerita at University of Maryland, College Park. An expert in the areas of adult transitions and retirement, she is author of *Retire Smart, Retire Happy: Finding Your True Path in Life.* American Psychological Association. She is now working on a new book about retirement.

Most people look forward to retirement as a time to relax, discover new sides of themselves and enjoy life without the constraints of a job. Retirement can bring all of these pleasures, but some new retirees are shocked to find that retirement is uncomfortable and stressful.

Retirement causes dramatic changes in your daily routine and your social network. Like any transition, it goes more smoothly when you are prepared.

To create a smoother transition…

•**Think about how you enjoy contributing.** One secret to a happy retirement is feeling appreciated and depended upon. What causes are you passionate about—arts, education, politics? See how you can be more active in those areas once you retire. Begin to set the stage before you retire.

Examples: Enroll in training to become a museum docent. Apply to tutor a school-age child. Get involved in a political campaign. Sign up for a class in memoir writing.

Another way to get in touch with your passion is to ponder your regrets. What do you wish you could do but never had time for? You can use retirement as an opportunity to do those things.

Examples: Learn another language… play a musical instrument…sail a boat…scuba dive.

•**Develop a support system.** Before you retire, begin to meet and network with people who can help you achieve your dreams and cheer you on during this next phase of your life.

Example: A woman who wanted to open a bed-and-breakfast began attending meetings of the B&B association in her area. She made a new circle of friends and got valuable ideas about how to get started.

• **Talk with your spouse** about how your roles might change. How much time will the two of you spend together? You probably will want to pursue shared interests (such as travel), but also consider lining up independent activities.

One newly retired couple was arguing because they weren't used to being together so much, so each of them took a part-time job—the husband at a jewelry store, the wife at a flower shop. Harmony returned, and they kept their part-time jobs for several years until they got used to the transition.

Another couple decided that each person would have a room that was "his/hers" so they could comfortably retreat when one of them wanted time alone.

Roles also may shift if one spouse continues to work while the other is retired. Will the retired spouse be expected to do more around the house? Will he feel more dependent on the other for emotional support? Discuss these potential shifts before they happen, and be willing to try different ways of dealing with them.

• **Create structure** for your post-retirement day. You may love the idea of a life with a free-form schedule, but too little structure leaves some people listless and unmotivated. Instead of switching suddenly from a scheduled life to an unscheduled one, plan at least one activity a day during the first few weeks of retirement.

Examples: Consider exercise class, reading groups, gardening clubs. These activities also provide social contact.

WHICH TYPE ARE YOU?

Not everyone approaches retirement the same way, but most people fall into one of four types. It may take some experimenting before you discover the path that is right for you.

• **Adventurers** look for challenging new projects and want to develop skills that are very different from those they used on the job.

Examples: A retired government consultant enrolled in massage school and became a licensed massage therapist. A former pharmacist joined a senior baseball league.

• **Continuers** stay connected with the skills and activities they used on the job, through part-time or related volunteer work.

Example: After selling his paper company to retire, the former owner missed the paper business. He and his wife started a shop that sold handmade paper and gave classes in paper crafts.

Some retirees become consultants in the fields in which they previously worked on staff.

• **Easy gliders** are comfortable with the unstructured life and content to go with the flow. They may be happiest on the golf course or playing with grandchildren.

Example: A retired TV producer enjoys being able to visit her grandchildren whenever the whim hits her.

• **Searchers** need time to find their niche. They are separating from their past but are not sure what they want for the future. They tend to explore a number of different pursuits before finding one or more that feels right.

Example: It took one man two years of trying out different volunteering organizations until he found the right spot for himself.

Great Second Careers— Have Fun Working After You "Retire"

Howard Stone, a professional life coach and founder of 2young2retire.com, an on-line community for people interested in retirement alternatives, Palm Beach Gardens, FL. He is coauthor of *Too Young to Retire*. Plume.

The concept of retirement in this country is about to fundamentally change. Waves of baby boomers will turn 60 over the next decade and redefine this phase of life. Advances in health care will keep many of us healthy and vigorous into our 90s and beyond. We will need to stay challenged to be fulfilled, and we'll have to generate income to ensure that our nest eggs last for 30-plus years.

The new "rehirement" will combine work, volunteering and leisure activities. Some retirees will work for their former employers as independent contractors. Others will train for new careers—certification programs, such as those listed below, will be particularly popular.

Good news for older workers: By 2010, a severe labor shortage will occur because there will be fewer younger workers. *Here, rehirement opportunities...*

PROFESSIONAL CERTIFICATIONS

Many preretirees and retirees want to expand their professional abilities but are reluctant to commit to a graduate degree program. A certification lets you work as an accredited professional in a specialty field. Generally, the part-time training takes less than a year and costs significantly less than graduate school.

These opportunities are in growing fields and allow flexible schedules...

●**Life coach.** Help clients achieve their goals for careers, relationships, etc.

Earnings potential: $75 and up for a 45-minute session, or a monthly fee of $200 and up.

More information: *www.coachfedera tion.org.* Certification costs $300 to $600 and requires a minimum of 125 hours of training and experience, which generally costs $5,000 to $10,000.

●**Financial gerontologist.** Counsel older people on how to achieve their financial goals. Course and examination requirements are lighter than those for a certified financial planner (CFP). (You need to already have a license in a financial advisory field, such as accountancy, law or insurance.)

Earnings potential: You can charge the same rates as a certified financial planner, $100 per hour and up.

More information: The American Institute of Financial Gerontology offers certification after six three-day courses.

Cost: $1,500. 877-277-2434, *www.aifg.org.*

●**Horticulturist.** Design landscape for residential properties. Certification is by state and helps you obtain employment with a nursery or greenhouse or start your own business.

Earnings potential: $50 per hour and up.

More information: Inquire at your state's nursery and landscaping association. Links can be found at the Association of Professional Landscape Designers Web site, *www. apld.com/education/for_students.asp.*

●**Family business consultant.** Help family-owned businesses function well and deal with succession planning.

Earnings potential: $100 per hour and up. Certification is available to service professionals—management consultants, psychologists, therapists, educators.

More information: Family Firm Institute, 617-482-3045, *www.ffi.org.*

●**Hypnotherapist.** Hypnosis has become an increasingly popular option in mental health.

Earnings potential: $75 per hour and up. You need a graduate degree in a health discipline, such as nursing, social work or chiropractic, plus 60 hours of classroom training, which costs $1,000 to $1,500. Some states require a license in addition to certification.

More information: The National Board for Certified Clinical Hypnotherapists, 800-449-8144, *www.natboard.com.*

●**Massage therapist.** In most states, you need just 500 hours of training to be licensed.

Cost: $5,000 to $10,000.

Earnings potential: $50 to $75 per hour.

More information: The American Massage Therapy Association, 877-905-2700, *www. amtamassage.org.*

●**Relocation specialist.** Manage employee transfers on behalf of large real estate brokerages and/or chambers of commerce.

Earnings potential: $50 per hour and up.

More information: Worldwide Employee Relocation Council, 703-842-3400, *www. erc.org.*

• **Yoga instructor.** Most gyms now offer classes. You need at least 200 hours of training for certification.

Cost: $2,000 to $2,500.

Earnings potential: Yoga instructors can charge $50 to $75 per hour.

More information: Contact your local gym or *www.yogasite.com.*

OTHER OPPORTUNITIES

The following rewarding jobs for seniors don't require professional certification...

• **Caretaker.** Care for homes, often in exotic locales, in exchange for a free room. In some cases, board, a salary and health insurance are offered as well. Jobs can last a few weeks to a year or more. Travel expenses are usually covered.

More information: The Caretaker Gazette, 830-755-2300, *www.caretaker.org.*

• **Cruise ship lecturer.** A good fit if you like to speak in public and have expertise in a popular lecture topic, such as health or money. The cruise is free for you and your spouse. Usually no cash is offered, but lecturers use these trips as a calling card to attract clients who need their advice.

More information: www.lynnseldon. com/article312.html for an overview...*www. webstrategies.cc/acruise.html* offers an E-book on how to apply, select in-demand topics and make connections.

• **Senior move manager.** Help the elderly and their families with the emotional and physical aspects of relocation, including selling belongings, arranging shipments and storage. Move managers often find clients through family members, attorneys, senior housing communities and real estate agents.

Earnings potential: $25 per hour and up.

More information: National Association of Senior Move Managers, 877-606-2766, *www.nasmm.com.*

• **Virtual assistant.** Provide administrative support or specialized business services for companies from home, via Internet, fax and telephone.

Earnings potential: $20 per hour and up.

More information: International Virtual Assistants Association, 888-259-2487, *www. ivaa.org,* or search for "virtual assistant" at *www.businessweek.com.* For current job openings, try *www.virtualassistants.com.*

BEST WEB SITES

• **On-line job sites.** Post your résumé and search for jobs at *www.seniorjobbank.com.*

• **Best companies for older workers.** AARP provides its ranking of the top 50 US employers—with 50 employees or more—at *www.aarp.org/bestemployers.*

Some of the best: Mercy Health System, Volkswagen, Massachusetts General Hospital.

The Instant Pension Plan

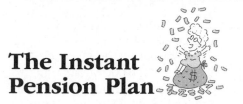

Stacy L. Schaus, CFP, senior vice president and lead strategist, defined contribution practice, PIMCO, Newport Beach, CA.

In the past, retirees could rely on pensions and Social Security to replace most of their preretirement income. A 401(k) plan or IRA and personal savings provided additional support.

Today, with fewer companies providing pension plans, nonpension resources often are the sole support. Unfortunately, 401(k)s don't guarantee a steady income stream. *To ensure that retirees will not outlive their savings, most need to create their own pensions...*

HOW IT WORKS

You can simulate your own pension plan by purchasing an immediate annuity. In exchange for your lump-sum payment, an insurance company agrees to provide a stable, guaranteed income every month for the remainder of your life.

There is no right or wrong age at which you should purchase an immediate annuity. Consider buying one when you need to replace or supplement your income. *Smart strategy...*

• **Ask whether your employer offers an annuity option** via your retirement plan

—it may offer a more generous payout than an annuity you would purchase privately.

• **Compare annuity payout rates** and request free reports at *www.immediateannuities.com* (800-872-6684). There can be big differences among providers.

Also: Whether you're buying through your employer or on your own, make sure the company's claims-paying ability is rated A+ or better by A.M. Best (908-439-2200, *www.ambest.com*) or AA by Standard & Poor's (212-438-2400, *www.sandp.com*).

• **Factor in expenses.** Compare net results or monthly income amounts from different providers.

ANNUITY OPTIONS

Your monthly annuity income depends on your age, the size of your lump-sum payment and any special features you choose. For instance, for a $100,000 straight life annuity purchased directly from a financial institution, a typical 65-year-old male could get about $650 a month. (Purchasing one via an employer might generate a higher payout.)

Payments from a straight life annuity stop when you die, whether death occurs in the first year of the annuity or 30 years later. In the example above, the retiree would get $7,800 a year and so would have to live about 13 years to recover his initial investment without interest. *There are features you can add that adjust for these and other uncertainties...*

• **Life income for a fixed period.** If you die soon after the annuity payouts begin, your beneficiaries continue to receive payments for the period contracted—say, for 10 or 20 years. This feature will decrease the monthly payout—so, with a 20-year fixed period, the 65-year-old male in the example above and, subsequently, his beneficiaries, might receive a monthly payment of $550.

Who should choose this option: People who want expenses to be covered whether they are living or not, for an established period of time, possibly until other income sources kick in. This feature is not for people who want to ensure payment for the life of a coannuitant, such as a spouse.

• **Fixed period only.** This type of annuity pays income only for a specific length of time—for instance, exactly 10 years. This approach provides you with the highest monthly payout—for example, the 65-year-old male might receive a check for $950 every month for the 10 years.

Who should choose this option: Someone whose main concern is having income for a specific period and who knows that future income sources will be available after that period.

• **Cost-of-living rider.** If you're concerned that inflation will erode the value of your annuity payment over time, you may want to shop for a provider that will build in a cost-of-living adjustment. Some insurers allow you to increase your payout by, say, 3% each year. Others base increases on changes in the Consumer Price Index. Of course, this feature will mean a reduced monthly payout at first, depending on the extent of the increase or the inflation protection, but you'll come out ahead if you live long enough.

Who should choose this option: People who don't think they can hedge against inflation in less costly ways—for instance, by combining an immediate annuity with equity investments. Such a strategy can hedge against inflation effectively while maximizing current income.

• **Joint-and-survivor.** This annuity continues paying a percentage of income—typically, 50% to 100%—to your spouse or beneficiary after your death. The higher the percentage earmarked for your beneficiary and the younger he/she is, the smaller the monthly payout.

Important: Seek advice from a fee-only adviser (not a commissioned salesperson) to determine the best approach. For instance, purchasing a life insurance policy along with an immediate annuity may be more tax efficient for your situation than a joint-and-survivor annuity.

Many of the above features can be combined, so it's critical to compare apples to apples when choosing an annuity.

WHEN TO BUY

With interest rates higher than they were, you may be concerned that now is not the best time to purchase an annuity. It's true that higher interest rates may mean a higher annuity payout if you wait, but in the meantime, you might earn less on your cash than required to meet your needs.

If your income need is immediate but you are concerned about the level of interest rates, consider dollar cost averaging annuity purchases over the next two to three years and/or purchasing some inflation protection.

Best strategy: Consider buying an annuity now with some of your money to cover your fixed cash needs. Then invest the remainder of your savings for the longer term. You may rest more comfortably investing in stocks or other securities knowing that your fixed expenses will be covered. Don't forget to set aside some cash for emergencies and, if you wish, for your heirs.

Keep in mind that annuities aren't for everyone. If you can live comfortably on the income from your investments without worrying about exhausting your principal, then an annuity may not be appropriate. Seek the counsel of a trusted adviser to set up a retirement income strategy. Since purchase of an annuity is an irrevocable decision, it's critical for you to understand what you're buying and how it fits with your overall financial and estate plan.

Guaranteed Retirement Income Myths...And Reality

Mark Cortazzo, CFP, senior partner, Macro Consulting Group, 1639 Rte. 10 E., Parsippany, NJ 07054. A member of the Financial Planning Association and the Estate Planning Council of Northern New Jersey, he has been named one of the best financial advisers in the US by *Worth, Registered Rep* and *Research* magazines.

Many people want an income stream in retirement that will last as long as they do—guaranteed. *That's possible, as long as you can separate fact from fiction about guaranteed retirement income...*

SOCIAL SECURITY

Myth: **Social Security won't be around for long.**

Reality: Social Security is immune from annulment.

But: Taxes on earned income may be increased to keep the system intact...taxes on benefits may be increased...cost-of-living adjustments may be curtailed. Any or all of these might occur, but you'll receive at least some lifetime income from Social Security.

Myth: **Social Security will provide income sufficient to maintain a lifestyle similar to the one you now enjoy.**

Reality: The average Social Security check is about $1,000 a month...the average retired couple receives around $1,700.

Even for someone who paid the maximum amount of Social Security taxes over the years, the current maximum benefit at normal retirement age (around age 66) is just over $2,100 a month, about $26,000 a year. That will be much less than such a person would be used to taking home.

Myth: **Social Security benefits are so small as to be inconsequential.**

Reality: Receiving $25,000 a year from Social Security is equivalent to getting a 5% yield from $500,000 worth of bonds. That's not bad at all.

By considering those benefits as a bond equivalent, you can hold more stocks in your portfolio, which likely will help your long-term investment returns.

Another positive: Benefits will rise with inflation.

PENSIONS/ANNUITIES

Myth: **Pensions hardly exist anymore.**

Reality: Lifelong pensions are still offered to government workers, many union members and some employees of large organizations, provided that they worked the required number of years.

Many other workers have accumulated substantial amounts in employer-sponsored retirement plans.

Often, retiring employees are given the choice of receiving their retirement funds in the form of an annuity. Such an annuity can provide income for a retiree or for a retiree and spouse as long as either is alive.

Myth: **Taking the annuity offered by an employer is a good way to lock in guaranteed retirement income.**

Reality: There may be times when this is a good choice. At some companies, there is a "sweet spot" in which particular annuities are very attractive.

Example: The company might subsidize annuities that pay a 50% benefit to an employee's surviving spouse, making it more attractive than similar annuities sold directly to investors by insurers.

In other cases, though, the payout offered by an employer might be on the low side compared with what you could get commercially. And a company-provided annuity might be inflexible, lacking newer features, such as access to money and investments that provide growth potential.

Myth: **If you don't take the annuity offered by your employer, you won't get guaranteed retirement income to supplement Social Security.**

Reality: You can buy an annuity.

One option: Roll the money in your employer-sponsored retirement plan into an IRA, which will maintain the tax deferral of the assets. Then purchase an annuity with some or all of that money. Alternatively, you can use non-IRA funds to buy an annuity.

Myth: **No matter where you purchase your annuity, the rates will be about the same.**

Reality: Annuity payment rates can vary greatly.

Myth: **When you buy an annuity, you lose access to your money, you lock yourself in to a given payment amount and the issuer will reap a windfall if you die soon.**

Reality: Immediate annuities, sometimes called "payout" or "income" annuities, have added new features in recent years…

•**Some allow access to the principal.** This flexibility does, however, come at the price of lower payouts.

•**Some are *variable* rather than *fixed*,** so your payments can rise or fall, depending on investment account performance.

•**Some offer payments for at least a certain number of years to a beneficiary,** if necessary.

Myth: **An immediate fixed annuity is always the best way to lock in guaranteed retirement income.**

Reality: Some immediate *variable* annuities have minimum ("floor") payout rates that are as high or higher than immediate fixed annuity rates, in today's low-yield environment. You can get guaranteed minimum income from the floor plus potentially higher returns, if your investments do well.

Myth: **You must purchase an immediate annuity to get guaranteed retirement income that doesn't come from a pension or from Social Security.**

Reality: *Deferred* annuities also may provide guaranteed lifelong income. In a deferred annuity, investment income is untaxed until the investor takes out money. There's usually a 10% penalty, in addition to income tax, for withdrawals before age 59½. These annuities come in two varieties—fixed or variable. Fixed annuities pay a specific return for a specific time period. Variable annuities have varied returns, depending on the performance of chosen investment accounts.

Deferred variable annuities, in particular, usually offer some form of guaranteed income.

Myth: **You have to "annuitize" a deferred variable annuity—meaning convert the account value into a payment stream—to get guaranteed income.**

Reality: From one deferred variable annuity to another, guarantees contain different terms. *They generally fall into one of two categories…*

•**Guaranteed income benefits.** You are promised an income based on whichever is higher—a minimum guaranteed return or the actual performance of your investment accounts.

•**Guaranteed withdrawal benefits.** You are permitted to withdraw a certain percentage of your investment for a fixed number of years or for your lifetime.

Either way, you can invest in stock funds, for upside potential, while being protected against loss.

Myth: **Variable annuities are always overpriced rip-offs.**

Reality: Variable annuities can differ tremendously.

Some are very expensive with limited benefits and virtually no access to your money for years without significant penalties.

Others are issued by reputable firms. The fees are comparable to what you would pay for other financial products and the guarantees may provide peace of mind.

These products aren't for everyone. However, if you want guaranteed retirement income, they are worth considering.

Strategy: Ask your financial adviser if you need to invest in a type of account that generates guaranteed retirement income. Before you buy, request a full explanation of the costs. Also determine whether your adviser has a widespread array of products from which to choose. Ask to see a spreadsheet showing how several of these offerings compare. That way, you'll have a greater chance of getting generous retirement income and a short surrender period (the time during which you'll pay a penalty for taking money from an annuity), for more access to your money.

Social Security Know-How

A widow or widower can receive full Social Security benefits at age 65 or older (if born before January 2, 1940) or reduced benefits as early as age 60. Full benefits also are available earlier if a widow/widower is caring for the deceased's child who is under age 16 or disabled before turning 22.

More information: 800-772-1213, *www. socialsecurity.gov.*

Jane Zanca, senior public affairs specialist, Social Security Administration, New York City.

Don't Get Shortchanged By Social Security— Catch Mistakes Now

Donna A. Clements, manager of Social Security Information Services for Mercer Human Resource Consulting, which helps some of the country's best-known companies solve Social Security and other benefits problems, Louisville, KY, *www.mercerhr.com.*

I s the government calculating your Social Security benefits correctly? If it isn't, you may not get the amount to which you are entitled once you retire. If you have already retired, you may not be receiving as large a monthly check as you should.

How to prevent mistakes and correct them if they occur...

Mistake: **Faulty earnings data.**

Social Security benefits are based on your 35 highest-earning years, as reported to the government by your employers. If an employer has given the government incorrect salary data or if the government has erred in recording the information it received, you may miss out on full benefits.

A $100 mistake early in your career is unlikely to have much impact on benefits, but a $10,000 error made during a peak-salary year could lower benefits by several hundred dollars a year.

What to do: Look at the Social Security Administration (SSA) statement that the government sends you each year around your birthday. For each year of employment, the statement lists the earnings on which Social Security taxes were based. It also estimates your benefits if you retire at the earliest age of eligibility (62) or if you wait for full benefits.

Compare earnings listed in the SSA statement with income listed on W-2 forms in your tax records. If you spot a discrepancy, call the nationwide number (800-772-1213) to contact your local SSA. Most corrections can be made by phone. You also can use this number to request a statement.

It helps to have your W-2 (or tax returns if you are self-employed) for the incorrect years. If you don't, the SSA can use your employment information to search its records and correct the mistake. If the SSA can't find your records, contact your employer for the year in question to obtain a copy of your W-2.

Once your earnings data is corrected, the SSA will send you a confirming notice. If you don't receive one in three to four months, contact the SSA again. It is best to make an appointment with a staff member, but it is also possible to handle problems by phone. Regardless of how you communicate, ask the staffer for a direct phone number so you can easily get back in touch. Then double-check the correction by making sure it appears on the following year's SSA statement.

If the SSA fails to make this or any other type of correction, start an appeals process by writing a letter within 60 days (plus five days after the postmark for mailing time) of the date of the SSA decision notice. It also is wise to contact your US representative. Many members of Congress have staffers who help constituents in their dealings with the SSA. As a last resort, hire an attorney with experience in Social Security matters. To research attorneys, go to *www.lawyers.com.*

Mistake: **Faulty calculations.**

Even when it has the correct earnings data, the SSA occasionally errs in calculating benefits. It is wise to suspect a miscalculation if you have already discovered other errors in your annual statement.

What to do: Tell the SSA about your misgivings, and ask that your benefits be recalculated. If you still have doubts, you can make the calculation yourself using the SSA's formula, which is available on its Web site, *www.socialsecurity.gov.*

Since the math is complex, consider asking a knowledgeable accountant to do the calculation or ask your employer's human resources department for assistance.

If you find an error, point it out to the SSA in the same way that you would notify it of a mistake in your earnings data. Make sure you receive a confirming letter and that the correction appears on next year's statement. If you're already receiving benefits, the SSA will reimburse you for the amount of the error.

Mistake: **Incorrect address.**

If the SSA doesn't have your correct address, earnings may not be recorded. You also may miss important correspondence. You should suspect a problem if you fail to receive an annual statement. Even if you do receive one, make sure that the address includes your exact street number and zip code.

What to do: If there is a mistake in your address, contact the IRS—the SSA depends on the IRS for addresses. To make the correction, ask for IRS Form 8822, *Change of Address.* (You can request the form by calling 800-TAX-FORM or download it from the IRS Web site at *www.irs.gov.*)

Mistake: **Wrong personal data.**

Benefits are in jeopardy if your name or date of birth in SSA records isn't the same as it appears in IRS files. Mistakes often occur after a marriage or divorce.

When women marry, for example, their employers routinely start reporting their earnings under their married names. Social Security records, however, still may be listed under their maiden names. This can result in lower benefits.

What to do: Whenever you change your name, ask the SSA for Form SS-5, *Application for a Social Security Card,* and submit it with the correct information. The form can be downloaded from the SSA Web site.

If you suspect that you have forgotten to notify the SSA of a name change earlier in your career, review the earnings data on your annual SSA statement for the years immediately following a marriage or divorce. The earnings should match the amounts on your W-2 forms for the same years.

Though less frequent, mistakes occur with dates of birth. If IRS and SSA records don't match, your full earnings may not be reported. Benefits can be delayed if SSA records show the date of birth is later than it actually is. Use Form SS-5 to correct this type of mistake.

***Mistake:* Missing benefits from a spouse.**

Check for errors in your spouse's Social Security account as well as your own.

Reason: If you outlive your spouse, you are entitled to a portion of his/her benefits, depending on your age.

What to do: If your spouse is deceased and you suspect a mistake in the benefits you are receiving, check the accuracy of your spouse's last annual statement. If you don't have it, ask the SSA to send you one. (You may be asked for a copy of your marriage certificate.)

If you believe that the error lies in calculating the proportion of your spouse's benefits that you're receiving, phone the SSA to verify the amount, or go to the Web site *www.socialsecurity.gov/survivorplan/ifyou5. htm*. The site includes a table for determining the proportion of benefits to which surviving spouses are entitled.

Often-overlooked benefit: At full retirement age, you may be entitled to as much as 50% of benefits from a former spouse who is age 62 or older, even if the spouse has not applied for Social Security benefits. (You must be unmarried, and your former marriage must have lasted at least 10 years.)

What to do: For an estimate of what you're entitled to from a former spouse's earnings record, call the SSA.

How to Unlock Your Retirement Accounts Before Age 59½

Ed Slott, CPA, editor, *Ed Slott's IRA Advisor*, 100 Merrick Rd., Rockville Centre, NY 11570, *www.ira help.com*. Mr. Slott is a nationally recognized IRA distributions expert and author of *Parlay Your IRA into a Family Fortune*. Penguin.

The tax law encourages you to build up money in your retirement plans by imposing a 10% penalty on withdrawals taken before age 59½. But what if you need the money before then? Can you get your hands on it without paying a penalty? And how can you avoid tax?

BORROW FROM THE PLAN

If you need money quickly—for a down payment on a home, to cover large medical bills or for other major expenditures—consider borrowing from your company retirement plans, including your 401(k). Most plans permit borrowing. Since the money you receive is a loan, not a plan distribution, you aren't taxed on it. Nor are you penalized.

Limit: You can borrow up to half of your account balance or $50,000, whichever is less.

Example: Your 401(k) shows a balance of $82,000 and you don't have any other outstanding plan loans. You can borrow up to $41,000.

Contact your plan's administrator to request the loan. You'll be required to repay the funds in level payments within five years—longer if the money is used to buy a home. If you fail to repay, it's a taxable distribution and may be subject to penalties.

The interest that you pay is credited back to your account. As long as you're not a "key employee" (owner or executive earning more than $145,000 in 2007), the interest may be deductible, depending on how the money is used. *If you use the money...*

• **To buy a home,** the interest is fully deductible if the loan is secured by the home.

• **For investment purposes,** the interest is deductible to the extent of your net investment income for the year.

• **For personal reasons**—including payment of medical expenses—you cannot deduct any of the interest.

You can't borrow from your IRA. But you can take distributions before age 59½ without a 10% penalty to pay for...

• **Medical expenses exceeding 7.5%** of your adjusted gross income.

• **First-time home-buying costs**—up to a maximum of $10,000.

• **Health insurance if you're unemployed** and have received unemployment benefits for at least 12 consecutive weeks (or would have received benefits but for the fact that you're self-employed and aren't entitled to unemployment benefits).

The tax-free Roth way: If you funded your Roth IRA in 2002 or earlier, either through contributions or a conversion of your existing IRA, you can withdraw the earnings tax free because five years have passed—as long as you are at least 59½, or disabled, or use the funds to pay first-time home-buying expenses up to $10,000. Contributions to the Roth IRA can be withdrawn penalty free at any time for any purpose.

RETIRE EARLY

If you retire early, but after you have reached age 59½, and find that you need more income, consider taking distributions from your retirement accounts. They can tide you over until you start collecting Social Security benefits. While you won't pay a penalty, the withdrawals are taxable.

You can withdraw as much as you need. But keep in mind that your savings—in both personal and retirement accounts—must provide you with income for the rest of your life.

There's no early distribution penalty for…

• **Withdrawals from your traditional IRA** after you reach age 59½.

• **Distributions from company plans,** including 401(k)s, after age 55 following separation from your job.

• **Pre-59½ withdrawals from an IRA** or company plan taken in a series of substantially equal periodic payments. The payments must continue until you reach age 59½ but for no less than five years.

Example: You're age 57 and want to tap into your IRA for extra retirement income. You must continue distributions under this method until age 62—five full years.

There are three ways to calculate substantially equal periodic payments. These rules are complex, so it's best to work with a tax or benefits expert. If you make a mistake—for instance, if you stop distributions too early or take too little or too much—you can be subject to the early distribution penalty on all the distributions you've taken.

DIVORCE

If you divorce, and your retirement accounts are a marital asset subject to a property division, don't simply withdraw funds from the accounts and pay them to your spouse. Doing so will result in a taxable distribution, even if you owe your spouse money under the terms of your divorce. *To avoid taxes, follow these rules when transferring funds to your ex-spouse…*

• **For company plans,** the transfer must be pursuant to a qualified domestic relations order (QDRO). This is a court order that directs the plan administrator to pay the benefits to your ex-spouse.

• **For IRAs,** transfer funds into your spouse's IRA incident to the divorce. By having your IRA custodian make a direct transfer to the custodian of your spouse's IRA, you never have control over the funds, so you're not taxed on them.

INHERITANCE

If you inherit a retirement account, you must take distributions even if you do not need the money and you would prefer to let the funds continue their tax-deferred compounding. You can, of course, take all of the funds immediately in a lump sum and pay the resulting tax. But if you don't want to do so, in most cases, you can spread distributions over your single life expectancy at the time of the decedent's death. The first distribution must be made by the end of the year following the year of death.

Exception: If you're a surviving spouse and inherit an IRA, you can roll the funds over to your own retirement account. Ordinarily, distributions would begin the year following the year of death. But, in this event, you can delay taking distributions until age 70½. And you can name your own beneficiaries to inherit the account after you die.

Turn Your IRA Into a Family Fortune

Ed Slott, CPA, editor, *Ed Slott's IRA Advisor*, 100 Merrick Rd., Rockville Centre, NY 11570, *www.ira help.com*. Mr. Slott is a nationally recognized IRA distributions expert and author of *Parlay Your IRA into a Family Fortune*. Penguin.

Your individual retirement account (IRA) can do much more than provide funds for your retirement—it can be stretched to provide millions of dollars in payouts to your children, grandchildren or others you choose to be beneficiaries.

Example: An IRA balance of only $100,000 may provide more than $8 million in future distributions when left to a young child.

What you need to know...

STRETCHING AN IRA

Most IRA owners think of their IRAs as providing savings only for themselves—and their spouses, if married.

This is largely because traditional IRAs are subject to annual required minimum distributions (RMDs) that begin at age 70½ and cause the IRA's funds to be distributed over the life expectancy of its owner.

IRA owners typically believe that if they live to their full life expectancies (or longer), there will be little or nothing left in their IRAs to leave to heirs.

Surprise: The life expectancies that govern mandatory IRA distributions as given in IRS tables are not actual life expectancies. The IRS life expectancies are much longer than actual average life expectancies.

The following table shows the life expectancies as provided by the IRS's "Uniform Lifetime Table" for IRA distributions, which is used by most IRA owners (single persons and married persons with spouses not more than 10 years younger) to determine the size of RMDs, versus actual average life expectancies as given by the National Center for Health Statistics...

LIFE EXPECTANCIES

Age	IRA Table Years	Actual Years
70	27.4	14.9
75	22.9	11.8
80	18.7	9.0
85	14.8	6.8
90	11.4	5.0
95	8.6	3.6
100	6.3	2.6

Key: As a result of the difference, you may be able to leave funds in an IRA for much longer than you expect.

Moreover, initial RMDs may be so small that your IRA will continue to grow in value for years after distributions begin.

Explanation: At age 70½, when RMDs start, life expectancy under the IRS table is 27.4 years.

Each year's RMD is determined by dividing the IRA balance by the number of years in life expectancy—so at age 70½, the RMD is $\frac{1}{27.4}$, or 3.6%, of the IRA's value. If your IRA earns more than this, it will continue to grow in value in spite of the distributions.

So, if you take only minimum distributions each year from your IRA and it earns 8% annually, it will continue to grow until you reach age 88! (Under the IRS table, the RMD won't reach 8% of the IRA's value until then.)

THE STRETCH

Once a beneficiary receives an IRA, its value may resume growing at a much faster rate.

Rule: A beneficiary can take required distributions over his/her life expectancy starting in the year after the inheritance. But if the beneficiary is young, life expectancy may be 50, 60 or 70 years, or even more, making initial RMDs so small that the IRA can grow rapidly.

Example: A grandparent leaves a $100,000 balance in an IRA that earns 8% annually to a one-year-old grandchild. The child's life expectancy under the IRS single life tables used by beneficiaries is 81.6 years, so the initial RMD is only 1.2% of the IRA balance.

Under the applicable IRS life expectancy table, the RMD won't reach 8% of the IRA balance until the grandchild is 70 years old. If the child takes minimum distributions, the IRA balance will grow for 69 years—even with the child taking minimum distributions from it all that time.

In total, over the 82 years of the child's life expectancy, the IRA will pay the child $8,167,629 dollars—more than eight million dollars from the initial $100,000.

HOW TO DO IT

Steps to make the most of your IRAs...

• **Roll over funds from other retirement accounts into IRAs.** This will let you use the "stretch IRA" strategy for as much of your retirement savings as possible.

• **Open Roth IRAs or convert traditional IRAs to Roths if eligible.** These are even better to stretch than traditional IRAs. Distributions from them are tax free and there are no required minimum distributions for the original IRA owner. (Beneficiaries must take RMDs.) This lets you save funds in them for longer periods to earn more compounding.

• **Plan retirement spending to preserve IRAs.** Build your investment portfolio for your retirement years.

Best: Plan to consume IRA funds last. This will provide more tax-favored compounding within the IRA for you, and help you leave a bigger IRA balance to heirs.

RULES FOR THE STRETCH

• **The beneficiary who takes a stretch IRA must be a named person,** not your estate.

• **Be sure the custodial agreement with your IRA trustee provides for allowing a stretch IRA**—not all do.

• **Either have separate IRAs for each beneficiary or formally "split" your IRA among them,** such as by designating a set percentage as going to each. *Traps...*

• If an IRA with multiple beneficiaries isn't split up, the life expectancy of the oldest governs distributions for the others.

• If a non-person (such as a charity) is co-beneficiary of an IRA, its life span of zero applies to all other co-beneficiaries, forcing

them to take rapid distributions—and eliminating the stretch.

• **When an IRA is left to a spouse,** to use its funds to set up a stretch IRA for a child (or other beneficiary), the spouse must first convert the inherited IRA into his own IRA (only a spouse can do this), and then name the child (or other party) as beneficiary.

• **After the spouse dies,** the inherited IRA must be retitled with the deceased owner's name in it, or the IRS will deem it distributed and taxable.

Example: "Frederic Jackson, IRA (deceased June 15, 2006) for the benefit of Sandra Jackson, beneficiary."

Important: Convince your beneficiaries of the importance of taking minimum "stretch" distributions. If they empty your IRA of cash as soon as they inherit it, all the potential decades of future compounding will be lost.

Saver: A trust can be named as beneficiary of your IRA to pass through payments to an heir, assuring that only minimum RMDs are taken (unless the trustee deems there is good reason to take larger distributions) so compounding is maximized.

Many technical rules apply to trusts and IRAs generally, so consult an IRA expert.

More from Ed Slott...

How to Get Millions From $100,000

The power of compound interest over time has been called "The Ninth Wonder of the World." *IRA examples...*

Facts: Steve is age 65, his wife, Deb, is 62 and their son Jeff is 27. Steve has $100,000 in a traditional IRA that earns 8%.

Steve takes RMDs from the IRA from age 70½ until he dies at 85. Deb, as his IRA beneficiary, inherits the IRA, converts it into her own IRA, names Jeff as beneficiary and takes RMDs until she dies at age 92. Jeff inherits the balance of the IRA at age 57 and takes RMDs over the 28 years of his life expectancy.

Result: The original $100,000 IRA balance pays out $1,020,366—$153,132 to Steve, $176,523 to Deb and $690,711 to Jeff.

Variation #1: The same facts, except that Steve has saved the $100,000 in his IRA when he was age 50 and Deb age 47, so 15 more years of compounding occur before distributions begin. Now the IRA pays $3,236,841—more than three times as much. Of this, $485,766 goes to Steve, $559,973 to Deb and $2,191,102 to Jeff.

Variation #2: Steve is age 50 as above, but the IRA is a Roth IRA, so there are no RMDs. Steve and Deb don't take any distributions, letting all IRA funds compound for Jeff. Jeff's distributions will total more than $11 million.

Variation #3: The IRA is a Roth from which neither Steve nor Deb take distributions—but Deb names her newborn granddaughter, Victoria, as beneficiary (instead of Jeff).

If Steve has $100,000 in the IRA at 65, Victoria receives distributions of more than $88 million.

If Steve has $100,000 in the IRA at 50, Victoria receives more than *$281 million*, of which more than $193 million came from Steve having accumulated his savings at age 50 instead of 65.

When Do You Need to Start Making Regular IRA Withdrawals?

Nancy Dunnan, a New York City–based financial and travel adviser and the author or coauthor of 25 books including the best seller, *How to Invest $50–$5,000*. HarperCollins.

You must start taking out money by April 1 of the year after the year in which you turn 70½. Your accountant can run the numbers to determine how much you need to take out. Or, check the life-expectancy tables and other required information in IRS Publication 590, *Individual Retirement Arrangements* (IRAs), available free by calling 800-829-3676 or from *www.irs.gov*.

Tax saver: If you will still be working after age 70½, ask your accountant or financial adviser whether your income plus the required IRA withdrawals are likely to push you into a higher tax bracket. To prevent this, you might want to begin taking out money before age 70½ to reduce the impending tax bite. Doing so could reduce the value of the account and thus the required annual withdrawal.

Note: You are allowed to make withdrawals after age 59½ without a penalty.

Real Estate in Your IRA? Yes! But Be Careful...

Diane Kennedy, CPA, founder, TaxLoopholes, LLC, 821 N. Fifth Ave., Phoenix, AZ 85003, *www.taxloopholes.com*. She is author of *The Insider's Guide to Tax-Free Real Estate Investments*. Wiley.

When choosing your types of investments for your IRA, real estate can also be a valuable choice.

Result: Many people have been shifting investment assets to real estate—and they would like to hold real estate in their IRAs, too, to increase the amount earned, tax deferred.

Assessment: Placing part of your IRA in real estate may make sense, especially if you have experience in investment property.

But, doing this the proper way is necessary if you want to avoid these dangerous traps...

• **Self-dealing.** The Tax Code allows you to defer tax in your IRA in order to provide for your retirement. If you take steps that can enrich you personally right now (before retirement), you may have to pay a penalty or even have your IRA annulled.

• **Unavailability of leverage.** Most IRA custodians don't let you borrow money with your IRA assets. However, the biggest profits from investing in real estate come when you make a down payment and use a mortgage for most of the purchase price.

How can you dodge these traps? *Use the following plan...*

SELF-DIRECT YOUR IRA

You must first hold your IRA (or one of your several IRAs) as a self-directed IRA.

What this means: This is an informal term rather than one found in the Tax Code. It means that you, the IRA owner, have greater control over your IRA than is typically the case.

With more control, you can access a wider range of investments, such as private companies and real estate.

Required: You must use an IRA custodian that's willing to let you hold real estate in your IRA (not every bank or trust company is willing to handle them). PENSCO (*www.pensco.com*), for example, is a trust company specializing in self-directed IRAs. Other custodians can be found on-line. For example, six others are listed at *www.1040tools.com*—click on "professional tax links."

Once you find a custodian, you can transfer your IRA to an account there. Fees vary among IRA custodians, but you can expect to pay more than you would pay for an IRA of comparable size at, say, a no-load fund company.

FORM AN LLC

The limited liability company (LLC) structure is best used for holding real estate in an IRA.

Advantage: As the name suggests, an LLC can protect property owners from liabilities that arise from operating real estate. But an LLC can also protect you from the self-dealing trap when owning real estate in an IRA.

Strategy: Don't use a "member-managed" LLC. Instead use a "manager-managed" LLC.

Reason: With a member-managed LLC, all the business owners (the members) have a say in the management. But your IRA cannot actively be involved in real estate ownership. (The rules governing retirement plans prohibit retirement plans from being actively involved in owning and operating investment real estate.)

Instead, you can be the manager of a manager-managed LLC while your IRA is the other member. As long as you're not taking any compensation or pulling out profits for your personal use, you won't run afoul of the self-dealing rules.

Restriction: You can't move a property you already own into an IRA. That's considered self-dealing. Instead, your IRA has to acquire a property from an unrelated party.

Another restriction: You can't buy a property from your IRA. But you can distribute real estate out of your IRA in the same way you would make any other retirement plan distribution. If it's from a tax-deferred IRA, you'll pay tax...if it's from a Roth IRA, you may avoid any tax.

CREATE LEVERAGE

As noted above, most IRA custodians don't let you borrow money with your IRA.

To solve the leverage problem, the LLC, not the IRA, borrows the money and the loan is secured by the property, not by the IRA. You can use money from your self-directed IRA to fund your LLC. Then, the LLC can make a down payment on a property you select.

Required: Generally, your LLC will have to put up at least 30% of the purchase price.

Lenders may be willing to put up the other 70%, secured by the property. (By law, your IRA can't be used as collateral.) Shop around local lenders or go on-line to find a loan.

Suggestions: North American Savings Bank (*www.iralending.com*) and Fremont Bank (*www.fremontbank.com*) are among the lenders willing to back selected properties held in this type of LLC.

Caution: You're prohibited from directly buying, selling or renting to or from your IRA. Thus, you can't put money down on a property from your personal account and then have your IRA involved in the deal.

If any of your personal assets touch the deal, it's tainted for your IRA. You can't even personally guarantee the loan if your IRA is investing in the property.

DEALING WITH DEBT

You'll owe a tax on debt-financed property. This is known as an unrelated business income tax (UBIT).

Example: Your IRA invests $100,000 in a rental property, financed with borrowed money. This year, that property throws off $10,000 in income.

Even though your IRA is a tax-deferred account, it still will owe tax on this $10,000 in income.

Tax treatment: The first $1,000 of UBIT each year is tax free. Then taxes kick in at trust tax rates.

In 2008, taxable UBIT over $11,450 is taxed at 35%.

Strategy: One approach in dealing with the UBIT issue is to just live with it. In practice, leveraged real estate is not likely to throw off much taxable income each year, after deductions for mortgage interest, operating expenses and depreciation.

Endgame: If the property appreciates, you will owe capital gains tax when you sell it. However, if you also hold cash in your IRA, you can use this cash to pay off or pay down any remaining debt 12 months before the sale. (UBIT is calculated based on average indebtedness for the previous year.)

Twelve months without debt will reduce or eliminate the UBIT due on the sale. What's more, selling after the property has been held for a year will allow the profits to be taxed at favorable long-term capital gains rates.

Loophole: Some types of retirement plans are exempt from the UBIT rules.

Examples: Solo (one-person) 401(k) and solo Roth 401(k) plans.

Strategy: If you have your own business, with no participating employees, you may be able to set up one of these plans and roll your IRA funds into it.

Then invest in leveraged real estate through your solo 401(k) or solo Roth 401(k), instead of through your IRA, using the steps outlined above.

Outcome: You won't owe UBIT. Moreover, if you use a solo Roth 401(k), you'll be investing with after-tax dollars and any profits will be completely tax free.

The Tax Code is very unforgiving when it comes to mistakes made investing with pension money. Worst-case scenarios could mean penalties of up to 50% and/or the entire tax-deferred amount becoming immediately taxable. There are big potential benefits, but you have to follow the rules. Check with an experienced CPA or attorney and a qualified custodian to avoid these costly mistakes.

IRA Smarts

Don't hold foreign dividend-paying stocks in an IRA.

Reason: The tax hit can be higher than it would be if they were held in a taxable account. Dividends on foreign stocks, held directly or through a mutual fund, may be subject to tax in the foreign country, and the tax usually is withheld by the IRA's custodian (the bank, broker or other institution handling the account). Unlike an owner of a taxable account, however, an IRA owner cannot claim a US foreign tax credit to offset this tax, nor may a deduction be claimed. Thus, the actual return from the foreign dividend in the IRA can be lower than you might otherwise earn.

Ed Slott, CPA, editor, *Ed Slott's IRA Advisor*, 100 Merrick Rd., Rockville Centre, NY 11570, *www.ira help.com*. Mr. Slott is a nationally recognized IRA distributions expert and author of *Parlay Your IRA into a Family Fortune*. Penguin.

What to Do with an IRA When You Leave a Job

If your employer is going to hand you a check for the lump sum in your retirement account when you leave the job, then he/she must withhold 20% for taxes—it's the law.

Best approach: To make certain that the assets in your account maintain their tax-deferred status and avoid the 20% withholding tax, open a "direct rollover" IRA with a brokerage firm, bank or mutual fund company. Have the money transferred by your employer directly into this account, from one plan to the other. In other words, make it a company-to-institution transaction. All financial institutions are set up to handle such transfers.

Nancy Dunnan, a New York City–based financial and travel adviser and the author or coauthor of 25 books, including the best seller, *How to Invest $50–$5,000*. HarperCollins.

How to Make Sure Your Nest Egg Lasts

William Bengen, CFP, Bengen Financial Services, Inc., 844 Singing Heights Dr., El Cajon, CA 92019. His latest book is *Conserving Client Portfolios During Retirement*. FPA Press.

A key goal for many people is determining when they'll be able to stop working and enjoy a comfortable retirement. Extended life expectancies have made this harder to establish.

Another factor: How your investments are held. The more of your investing that is done in a tax-deferred account, such as a 401(k), the more you may be able to withdraw each year—making for a real difference in your usable wealth.

BRIDGING THE GAP

To determine how much you can withdraw from your retirement funds without running short of money, crunch some numbers.

Begin your retirement planning by deciding how much you would like to spend after you stop working.

Starting point: Many early retirees will spend about as much as they did during their working years. Career-related costs will go down, but there will be more time for leisure activities, which can be expensive.

Pretax or after-tax dollars? Precise planning would focus on after-tax dollars because that's what you'll be spending. For simple, back-of-the-envelope projections, though, it may be easier to use pretax dollars.

Example: Jane Smith, who is beginning to plan for her retirement, earns $100,000 a year and invests $20,000 a year. She doesn't expect to keep investing after she retires and starts to draw down her portfolio. Therefore, her initial retirement goal is to have an $80,000 income, which will maintain her lifestyle.

Jane expects to start receiving Social Security benefits of approximately $20,000 a year as soon as she retires.

Shortfall: Jane does not expect any other type of income in retirement. Thus, she will need to take $60,000 a year from her portfolio.

THE $60,000 QUESTION

How large a portfolio will Jane need to withdraw $60,000 per year? *Some assumptions that need to be made…*

- **Life expectancy.** Jane is in good health and her parents are still alive. Thus, Jane thinks there is a good chance that she could live for 30 years after retiring at 65.

- **Asset allocation.** The more of a portfolio that is in stocks, the higher the returns are likely to be over a long retirement. However, one has to be able to stand stock market volatility.

Recommended: Hold at least 50% in stocks to generate adequate returns. A 60/40 stocks-to-bonds allocation may be ideal.

The 4% solution: Given those assumptions, a 4% to 4.5% initial withdrawal rate is likely to allow annual inflation adjustments over a 30-year retirement without depleting the portfolio. (This assumes pretax earnings on average of 10.4% for stocks and 5.3% for intermediate-term government bonds, based on annualized returns from 1926 through 2005.) To be on the safe side, use a 4% rate in your planning.

Example: Jane builds up a $1.5 million portfolio. That's enough so that a 4% first-year withdrawal will give her the $60,000 she wants.

If inflation in year one is 4%, Jane can increase her second-year portfolio withdrawal by 4%, to $62,400, and so on, each year, so that her income keeps up with inflation.

Result: Assume that Jane keeps her fairly conservative portfolio split 50/50 between stocks and bonds and follows the plan described above, with a 4% initial withdrawal increased annually by the inflation rate.

Such a strategy, implemented any time since 1925, would have kept a portfolio intact for at least 33 years. Therefore, Jane feels comfortable with a 4% withdrawal rate. If she starts with a 4.5% withdrawal, there'll still be a good chance that her portfolio will last 30 years or longer.

TAKING MORE

What if Jane decides to increase her first-year withdrawal rate to 5% instead of 4% or 4.5%?

Reasoning: The goal is to start with a $60,000 draw from the portfolio. With a 5% withdrawal, Jane will need to accumulate only $1.2 million—her $60,000 first-year withdrawal will be 5% of $1.2 million rather than the $1.5 million mentioned above.

Caution: The smaller amount of retirement savings must earn more if Jane wants it to last for a lengthy retirement.

Strategies: Starting with a smaller portfolio and a higher draw increases your risk of running short of money, but taking that risk might make sense as long as…

• **You have ample exposure to stocks.** More stocks mean more volatility during your retirement but also is likely to boost portfolio accumulation over a long time period.

• **You do most or all of your retirement investing in a tax-deferred account.** The tax deferral probably will result in a larger, longer-lasting pool of funds.

TAXABLE VS. TAX DEFERRED

Since the chances of success with a 5% withdrawal rate are greater if Jane does all or nearly all of her investing in tax-deferred retirement accounts, she might invest in a 401(k) plan during her career and roll the money to an IRA when she retires.

Reason: Inside a retirement account, all investment income will be tax deferred. That

investment income might be substantial if Jane holds 40% to 50% of her portfolio in bonds, an allocation that may comfort retirees.

Because of the tax deferral, Jane's portfolio will grow faster in an IRA, year after year, than it would in a taxable account. Again, higher growth may permit a higher withdrawal rate.

We can't know what the tax rates will be in 2018 or 2028 or whenever a retiree is eventually drawing down an IRA. We also don't know what the spread will be—the tax rate on long-term gains in the future versus the tax that a retiree will pay on ordinary income after he/she stops drawing a paycheck. We do know that deferring tax results in a greater buildup inside an IRA than in a taxable account.

DRAWING DOWN

Many people will have a portfolio divided between taxable and tax-deferred accounts.

Strategy: Tap taxable accounts first so that your IRA can remain intact as long as possible. You might set a retirement goal of building a total portfolio that's 20 times your first-year withdrawal target. Then take a 5% first-year withdrawal from your taxable account. Keep withdrawing taxable funds as long as you can.

Result: Your IRA may be larger when you start to take withdrawals, and your life expectancy will be shorter. So your portfolio may well last your lifetime, even though you started at 5%.

After you reach 70½, you'll have to take minimum required distributions from your IRA of around 3.8% the first year (for most people). So, take the minimum from your IRA, if practical, and take the balance from your taxable account, as long as it doesn't run dry.

More from William Bengen…

Tax-Deferred Accounts Pay Off

Can you withdraw more from a tax-deferred account than from a taxable account? Yes, if your retirement fund lives up to historic expectations.

Assume that an individual has $4,000 of income available annually (on a pretax basis) to save for retirement. He is in a 25% combined federal and state tax bracket, so, after taxes, he can only afford to contribute $3,000 annually to a taxable account. Naturally, if the individual contributes to a 401(k) account, and receives the full benefit of his tax deduction, the entire $4,000 will be contributed to the account.

Let's also assume that inflation is 3% annually, and that contributions will grow with inflation. We also assume typical rates of return (10% stocks, 5% bonds) and a 70% stock/30% bond portfolio, rebalanced each year.

After 30 years of contributions, a taxable account would have grown to $149,800, and a 401(k) account to $215,800—almost 50% larger!

Result: The retirement withdrawals from a tax-deferred account can be about 10% (or more) larger than those from a taxable account. For example, let us say that one can withdraw 4.5% from the 401(k) account and only 4% from the taxable account. That means for the first year, the individual can withdraw $9,100 from the tax-deferred account, and only $6,000 from the taxable account.

Even though withdrawals from a tax-deferred account are taxed, the individual will likely end up with considerably more after-tax spending money if his assets grew in the tax-deferred account. This is particularly true if his marginal income tax rate during retirement is significantly lower than it was during his working years.

Smart Retirement Spending

Bob Carlson, editor, *Bob Carlson's Retirement Watch*, Box 970, Oxon Hill, MD 20750.

When you retire, you are likely to hold savings in a mix of investment accounts that are taxable, tax deferred (such as 401(k) accounts and traditional IRAs) and tax free (Roth IRAs). As a rule, it's best to spend down savings in your taxable accounts first.

Why: Tax-favored accounts receive more long-term benefit from tax-free compounding. Employer plans and IRAs also receive legal protection from creditor claims, adding extra long-term security as long as you have them.

After spending down taxable accounts, spend tax-deferred ones. Save Roth IRAs and Roth 401(k)s until last—they benefit the most from tax-free compounding, and if you die, they will be of most value to heirs because of the totally tax-free income they provide.

This general rule for retirement spending may be affected by the types of specific investments in your various accounts. Consider the details of your best spending strategy with a financial adviser.

Protection for Retirement Accounts

The Federal Deposit Insurance Corporation (FDIC) has increased insurance to $250,000 from $100,000 for self-directed retirement accounts held at banks.

Protected: Traditional and Roth IRAs, simplified employee pension plans, "Section 457" deferred compensation plan accounts, Keogh plan accounts, and defined-contribution plan accounts such as 401(k)s.

A self-directed retirement account is one for which the owner, not a plan administrator, has the right to direct how the funds are invested.

Limit: Each person's deposits in such accounts at the same bank are added together with their total insured up to the $250,000 limit. So, if you have funds in both an IRA and a Keogh at the same bank, the $250,000 limit applies to their combined balance, not to each account separately.

Federal Deposit Insurance Corporation, *www.fdic.gov/deposit/deposits/deposit/faqs/faqs2.html.*

Section 529 Plans Are for Seniors, Too

Although 529 college savings accounts usually are used to save for children's college costs, they can pay for *anyone's* education. If you are thinking of taking classes, even after retiring, you can save in a 529 plan for yourself.

For a list of qualifying schools, go to *www.savingforcollege.com*. Click on "eligible institutions" under "Learn About 529 Plans."

Benefits: Income earned in the account is tax free when used to pay qualified education costs, and contributions are tax deductible in some states. If you end up not using the savings yourself, you can transfer the account to children or grandchildren.

More information: College Savings Plans Network, *www.collegesavings.org*.

Barbara Weltman, an attorney based in Millwood, NY. *www.barbaraweltman.com*.

Funds for Retirement

Target-date funds are pegged to the year you will retire. The allocations of the investments in the funds are adjusted as the retirement year approaches. The investments are in funds offered by the fund group. Groups use different approaches.

Example: For an investor planning to retire in 2030, Vanguard currently puts 80% in stock funds, but T. Rowe Price puts 90% in stock funds. Some fund companies charge additional fees for target-date funds.

Three that offer target-date funds at no additional cost: American Century, T. Rowe Price, Vanguard.

Vern Hayden, CFP, president, Hayden Financial Group, investment advisory firm, Westport, CT, and author of *Getting an Investing Game Plan*. Wiley.

Downside of Retiring Early

Early retirement may lead to premature death.

Recent finding: People who retire at age 55 are twice as likely to die by age 65 as those who keep working. Until recently, it was generally thought that retiring early increased longevity.

Shan P. Tsai, PhD, manager, department of epidemiology, Shell Health Services, Shell Oil Company, Houston, and leader of a study of 3,500 Shell Oil retirees, published in *British Medical Journal*.

Should You Finance Your Retirement With A Reverse Mortgage?

Barbara Stucki, PhD, project manager specializing in reverse mortgages for the National Council on the Aging, a nonprofit educational organization in Washington, DC, *www.ncoa.org*.

There has been a dramatic increase in the number of reverse mortgages—a type of loan that enables home owners to raise cash. Unlike with a standard mortgage, you don't have to pay back a single penny of a reverse mortgage as long as you live in the house.

In a reverse mortgage, you borrow against the equity in your home, often taking a line of credit or a lump-sum payment. In 2000, about 6,000 loans were originated. By the end of 2007, the number had increased to slightly over 100,000 loans.

Part of the increasing appeal can be attributed to the general financial environment. In recent years, interest rates have been relatively low, while home prices have climbed. That has enabled home owners to borrow more against equity, while paying fairly low costs.

At the same time, the pressure to raise cash has increased, as retirement nest eggs have suffered following the recent tech-stock crash. In addition, attitudes about reverse mortgages have changed.

Now more middle-income home owners see reverse mortgages as a routine financial-planning tool. The mortgages are particularly valuable for people who can pay regular expenses but require help with special needs, such as home health aides, that may make it possible for the borrower to continue living in his/her own home.

HOW THE LOANS WORK

A reverse mortgage is a loan against a home. The home owner has several options for how to receive the cash (see below). You can receive a line of credit, a lump sum or regular payments for up to the length of time you live in the home.

About 90% of reverse mortgages are originated under the Home Equity Conversion Mortgage (HECM) program of the US Department of Housing and Urban Development (HUD). Other loans come under programs from Fannie Mae, the government chartered mortgage company, and Financial Freedom Senior Funding Corp., a private lender. The HECM loans require paying mortgage insurance premiums, while the other lenders don't require mortgage insurance. But HECM is more popular because it enables many people to borrow bigger sums.

The amount of money that you receive depends on the value of your equity in the home and the age of the youngest borrower. Older people can borrow more because their life expectancies are shorter and there is less chance that the loan will eventually exceed the value of the home. The exact borrowable amount also depends on where you live. For a guide to how much you can borrow, see the reverse mortgage calculator at *www.rmaarp.com.*

Example: You are 73 and own outright a $200,000 house in Columbus, Ohio. With an HECM loan, you can get a line of credit or lump-sum advance of about $105,000.

If the house is worth $300,000, you can borrow $124,000. If you are 70, you can only borrow $115,000.

As with any mortgage, the borrower must pay interest and the loan is secured by the house. But you need not make any payments at all until you leave the house. Then you or your estate can sell the house and pay the principal and interest. Any appreciation belongs to the home owner or heirs. Many home owners or their heirs elect to prepay the interest and principal—and keep the house. There are no penalties for prepayments. Throughout the process, the home owner owns the house—not the lender.

PAYMENTS TO YOU

Besides a lump sum, there are several other ways to take your cash from a reverse mortgage…

• **Line of credit.** You use the reverse mortgage credit line when you need it. You could spend some of the money to pay routine bills and use the rest for home repairs. You owe interest and principal only on money that is actually drawn down.

• **Monthly advances.** Under this option, the home owner in Columbus could receive monthly payments of about $735 for as long as he stays in the house. If the home owner dies after one year, the heirs need only pay the interest and principal of the payments already received.

• **Fixed period.** Instead of electing income for your life in the home, you can elect to receive monthly checks for a fixed period, such as five years. This could help you survive a difficult time, say, until pension payments start or until you sell the house and move to a retirement home.

• **Combinations.** You can select more than one payment option. You might take a lump sum of $25,000 to make repairs on the house. At the same time, you could receive monthly payments to cover living costs.

PAYING OFF MORTGAGES

About 78% of older Americans own their own homes without any debt, according to the US Department of Health and Human Services. But those with a conventional mortgage can use a reverse mortgage to pay off the debt. This relieves the pressure of meeting monthly payments and enables the owner to avoid foreclosure worries.

Costs: Interest rates on reverse mortgages are typically adjustable annually. The recent rate was 6.6%, a bit more than the interest on an average fixed-rate 30-year mortgage.

Besides interest, an HECM borrower must pay an origination fee equal to 2% of the value of the home or $2,000, whichever is greater. In addition, there is an up-front HECM mortgage insurance fee equal to 2% of the value of the home.

Most of the fees can be included in the value of the loans. So the borrower does not face sizable out-of-pocket costs at the closing. Instead, the fees can be paid along with the rest of the mortgage when the house is sold.

WHO SHOULD USE A REVERSE MORTGAGE

To decide whether it is worth paying the costs of a loan, meet with a financial planner to discuss all aspects of your situation. Under the rules, all borrowers must attend a counseling session with an independent expert. This process is worthwhile, because borrowers may decide that other alternatives are more attractive.

If you are in chronic bad health and may not be able to live in the house much longer, a reverse mortgage could be the wrong choice. In addition, a reverse mortgage could be unsuitable if the home is in bad shape. In an extreme case, the property may cost more to repair than it is worth. From the reverse mortgage, you might get a lump sum of $100,000, but have to spend $80,000 to make the house suit your needs.

You May Need Less Than You Think for Retirement

Ty Bernicke, CFP, a principal at Bernicke & Associates, Ltd., an investment advisory firm in Eau Claire, WI. He gained national attention for his June 2005 study in *Journal of Financial Planning*, which concluded that Americans are overestimating how much they need in retirement.

You hear it all the time—most Americans are not saving nearly enough money for their retirement.

But what if that warning is based on faulty assumptions? A growing number of economists and researchers say that this is often the case, even though the idea that you could save less for retirement and spend a greater amount now is heresy to the financial services industry.

Investment adviser Ty Bernicke is among the leading proponents of the view that financial firms routinely overestimate the retirement needs of their clients. Their incentive is obvious—the more that people save, the higher the fees these firms collect.

While it's still necessary for you to save aggressively and plan conservatively, you may be better prepared for retirement than you think…

WRONG ASSUMPTIONS

Most retirement planners and on-line retirement calculators assume that you will spend at an increasing rate throughout your retirement, but that's not what my real-life clients—both married and single—end up doing.

Most of my older retirees spend far less than younger retirees. For instance, my clients in their 50s and 60s often travel more, go out to eat with friends often and enjoy the freedom that retirement brings. My clients in their 70s and 80s are less likely to socialize or go to restaurants, especially because they have a harder time driving at night. They also often have health problems and lower energy levels. These tendencies decrease food, travel, entertainment and other spending.

In fact, the latest US government statistics reveal a similar pattern. People ages 55 to 64 spend an average of $50,789 a year…those 65 and older spend $35,058…those 75 and older spend just $28,904. Except for health-care costs, which rise with age, that drop in spending holds true for all individual categories—including food, clothing and entertainment.

Strategy: Sit down with your financial planner, and run some scenarios based on the premise that your spending may decrease as time goes by, even when you account for inflation.

You might find that you can splurge a little bit more now on things ranging from home improvements to travel to eating out—and yet still be comfortable during your retirement. Or you may decide to retire earlier than you had planned.

HOW TO PLAN
MORE REALISTICALLY

A married couple had contributed the maximum allowed to their 401(k)s and IRAs for the past 20 years. Now they were both planning to retire at age 55 with a combined nest egg of $800,000, and Social Security payments of $12,000 each per year, which would begin when they reached age 62 and presumably would increase by about 2% a year.

Traditional retirement planning calls for withdrawing 3% to 4% of your savings at first and then increasing that annually to keep up with inflation. That supposedly allows investors to keep their lifestyle consistent throughout retirement, but it does not reflect how people really spend as they age.

Using a traditional 30-year retirement plan, the couple expected to start out spending $60,000 a year in retirement, the same as they had been spending...earn 8% per year on their nest egg...and withdraw enough to fill in for any income needs not covered by Social Security. Using traditional retirement calculations and assuming an average inflation rate of 3%, the couple would run out of money by the time they reached age 85.

They weren't sure how to solve this dilemma. They would either have to keep working for several years...or boost their savings rate dramatically.

They didn't have to worry. If they could agree to spend at a declining level as they aged, in line with the US Bureau of Labor Statistics' Consumer Expenditure Survey, the couple would not run out of money. Their nest egg would grow to $1.7 million in 26 years, rather than be completely depleted.

Reality: Many investors should consider withdrawing 6% of savings in the early retirement years, when they are most likely to travel and pursue hobbies. Over time, as activities decrease and expenses drop, that rate of withdrawal can be reduced.

Your housing situation also will have a big impact on your withdrawal rate. If you pay off your mortgage or downsize to a less expensive home when you retire, your expenses could immediately be lower than they were before retirement.

THE BIG EXCEPTION

In contrast to other categories, health-care expenses tend to jump as you age. *Steps to take...*

•**Budget annual increases** of at least 8% for health-care expenses. Unexpected medical bills are, by far, the biggest threat to keeping your retirement plans on track.

•**Watch the gap.** If you retire early, budget enough money to pay premiums for private medical-care insurance after you retire and up to age 65, which is when you become eligible for Medicare coverage.

If you already have a medical-care insurance policy and are healthy, you can probably find a cheaper one.

Example: A couple, both age 56, had obtained a policy in 1998 with premiums of $5,000 per year and a $5,000 deductible for the two of them. By 2005, they both were still in excellent health, but their premiums had nearly doubled to almost $10,000 with the same deductible. That's because in many states when you initially purchase insurance, you're thrown into a pool along with other people who buy insurance that same year. Over time, the unhealthy people from your original pool make the policy more expensive for everyone.

By shopping around for insurance, this couple was able to save $5,000 per year in premiums because the couple was put in a pool of healthier insured people.

•**Plan to enroll in a Medicare supplement plan.** Medicare does not cover everything.

Examples of things that are not included: Hearing aids...dental care...emergency care during foreign travel. There are 10 standardized supplemental Medicare plans to choose from, each varying in the extent of coverage and costs. Contact the Centers for Medicare & Medicaid Services, 800-MEDICARE, *www.medicare.gov,* for more information in your state.

How to Avoid The Six Major Retirement Mistakes

Jeri Sedlar, cofounder of Sedlar & Miners, a New York City–based executive search and transition coaching firm. With husband and business partner Rick Miners, she coauthored *Don't Retire, REWIRE!* Alpha. *www.dontretirerewire.com.*

Most Americans think of retirement as just a financial target. Once they have enough saved, they assume that they are ready to retire. For many people, however, that's not the case. The psychological transition from working to not working can be so much harder than anticipated.

We interviewed more than 300 retirees and preretirees to learn what makes some retirements more satisfying than others. *Among the most common mistakes that can sabotage a retirement...*

• **Not realizing what you are giving up.** Careers provide us with more than just income. They can be a source of companionship and provide a sense of achievement and self-worth.

Example: Dr. Hill, a small-town physician, retired at age 75 because of the increasing paperwork involved in running a medical practice. Only then did he realize how much he missed being "Doc," the trusted friend on whom the community relied for medical care.

Give some thought as to what makes your workday gratifying. You might not enjoy your retirement if you can't find a new source for that gratification.

• **Full-time travel and leisure.** Many assume that retirement will be one long vacation or never-ending golf game—but that can lose its allure in as little as two years.

Be honest about how much relaxation you can handle. You might want to work part-time or seasonally.

Example: Andy, age 59, soon to retire from a successful career in sales, is looking forward to indulging his passion for fly-fishing. He's aware that it might not sustain him for the rest of his life, so he also plans to start a fly-fishing camp for kids.

• **Retiring for the wrong reason.** Hating a particular job is not the same as being ready for retirement. Nor is it necessarily time to stop working simply because someone else's schedule says so. Do not retire just because you are offered an early retirement package or because your spouse wants to retire.

If you're not certain that you're ready to retire, don't. Look for a new job—you always can retire at a later date.

Example: Renee retired at age 60 from a career in education administration because she didn't like her new boss. Until the change in leadership, she had loved her job. Years later, she realized her dissatisfaction would have been better solved by finding a different employer.

• **Falling out of the loop.** A retired executive I spoke with said that the hardest thing about retiring was not getting any phone calls. No one seemed to want or need his opinion anymore. He felt totally disconnected from his old life.

Five years prior to retiring, take steps to ease the transition—mentor young executives so that they have a reason to come to you with future problems...look into becoming a consultant...join organizations or associations with an eye toward future leadership positions.

Example: When Jerry saw retirement on the horizon, he then persuaded his company to name him its representative to the industry association. When he left his job five years later, he had enough friends in the association to win a term as president. The nonpaying position did not demand much time, but it kept him connected to his old life.

• **Expecting to spend all your time with your spouse.** With many couples, the wife manages the social calendar. The husband then expects his wife to keep him occupied after he retires. But millions of women continue to work after their husbands retire. Even when a woman does stop working, she shouldn't be expected to plan her husband's day.

Example: One wife said of her husband's upcoming retirement, "I don't want twice the husband for half the pay." She had her friends and activities and wanted her husband to have his own friends and activities.

Before you retire, develop activities separate from your spouse that will interest you after you leave work.

• **Ill-considered relocations.** People often move when they retire. The result can be loneliness and boredom.

Example: Dan, a former attorney, and his wife, Arlene, a former accountant, moved from New York City to a villa in France. They were back within a year. The couple missed their friends, clubs, grandkids and even racquetball.

Before you sell your current home, rent in the region you're considering for several full seasons. You may love Florida in the winter, when the weather's mild and your friends are down for the season, but not in the summer when it's hot and no one is around.

How to Ace a Job Interview When You're Over 50

Todd Bermont, president, Ten Step Corporation, a Chicago-based company that counsels job seekers. He's also a business development manager at Lee Technologies, a computer security provider for corporations and other large organizations. His latest book is *10 Insider Secrets to a Winning Job Search.* Career.

As you grow older, you need to change your job interview tactics. Once you learn the strategy, it's as easy to ace an interview when you're over 50 as it was when you were in your 20s.

First move: Weed out the losers—the companies that probably won't hire you because of your age.

You might persuade a biased company to hire you, but you can greatly improve your job chances by concentrating on businesses that welcome older applicants. The best way to find them is to be up front about age on your résumé. Most companies with an age bias won't even schedule an interview.

Too often, however, older applicants try to hide their age by omitting dates, especially those of college graduation and/or early jobs.

My advice: Put the dates in, and don't worry. The companies that call you back to schedule an interview are usually those that know the value of older employees.

LAYING THE GROUNDWORK

Your résumé is likely to be the interviewer's only information source before talking with you in person. That's why it pays to research the company and tailor your résumé accordingly. The object is for the person who schedules interviews to read your résumé and say something like: "Here's a perfect candidate! I'll schedule an interview immediately."

Visit the company's Web site and download brochures and the annual report, or phone and ask the firm to send them to you. If possible, talk with someone you know who has worked for the business, and also look for information on the company in magazines, newspapers and on the Internet (using Google or another search engine). Also check the AARP Web site of the best companies to work for at *www.aarp.org.*

What to look for: Information about the company's goals and what it values—technology, customer relations, growth in certain geographical areas, etc. With this information in hand, you can write a résumé so it shows that you possess the skills a company values.

Examples: If applying for a job at a retail chain that values customer relations, mention how your experience in this area benefited previous employers. Or if a company is targeting the Hispanic market, emphasize how a previous employer profited from your knowledge of Spanish.

Keep your résumé to one page—many human resources (HR) managers don't read the second page. If you need a second page, list several major accomplishments near the top of the first page.

Examples: Saving an employer a large sum of money or making a crucial sale.

Explain these and other achievements at greater length later on in the résumé. It's unlikely that résumés of competing job candidates—particularly younger ones—will start with a list of attention-grabbing accomplishments.

When you find an opening at a company you would like to work for, phone the HR department and ask about the position.

Helpful question: "What are some characteristics of people who have succeeded on your team?"

Most companies designate a person in the HR department to answer questions about specific job openings. But even if you reach a low-ranking assistant, it pays to ask, "What kind of person is your boss looking for?" You'll often pick up facts about the job that other candidates don't know and that will be useful in the interview.

Examples: The job requires traveling, computer skills aren't important or the company would consider a part-time employee.

GETTING PSYCHED

Hiring managers—the people who decide whether to employ an applicant—rarely admit it, but the first minutes of an interview are crucial. It's then that they decide whether to consider the candidate seriously or just get the interview over with as quickly as possible.

With that in mind, it pays to prepare to make a great first impression for the interview...

• **Wear standard business attire—** even if most employees dress informally. That means a dark suit and tie for men and a professional business suit for women. Above all, don't make the mistake of wearing clothes that, in your mind, will make you look younger. They usually have the opposite effect.

• **Wear your hair in a traditional style**—nothing unusual.

• **Practice in front of a mirror.** Do this several times during the days before an inter-view. Smile and say to yourself, "I'm great!" It sounds corny, but the technique actually works. It shows you how much better you look with a smile on your face and lets you practice the smile so it comes naturally when you walk in for the interview.

• **Practice shaking hands firmly** and looking the other person in the eye when you speak. That's what to do at the beginning of an interview, and the gestures should also come naturally.

• **Visualize the interviewer** extending a hand and offering you a job. Doing that puts you in a positive frame of mind that you'll automatically telegraph with body language during the interview.

PLAYING YOUR ACES

Get the edge on other job candidates by asking questions that let you talk about ways in which the company will benefit by hiring you. *Examples...*

• **What are the characteristics of your ideal candidate?** Many interviewers will be delighted by the question, and the answer gives you an opening to point out how many of the characteristics you have.

If the interviewer mentions a qualification you lack, it may turn out that the company can help you with it—learning a computer program, for example. Immediately stress the point that someone with your accomplishments couldn't have succeeded without a willingness to learn and adapt to change.

• **What projects or challenges are involved with this job?** The answer gives you another opportunity to relate your skills to the work that will be expected of you.

• **What accomplishments will I have to make in order to get a perfect score on my yearly performance review?** This works because it assumes you're already hired and shows a positive attitude. And again, use the answer to talk about your qualifications and skills.

It's best to keep your statements short and to let the interviewer do most of the talking. If the interviewer fidgets, avoids eye contact or crosses his/her arms, you're talking too much.

The interviewer is interested in what you're saying if he smiles, nods frequently or moves forward in his chair. But even then, don't drag out your answers. If there's any doubt, ask the interviewer if you've given enough information.

Don't ask about salary or benefits (unless the interviewer brings up the subject). If you need information, ask HR after the interview. If you have problems with the compensation package, wait until you get an offer and then negotiate.

More from Todd Bermont...

When Discrimination Starts

The federal *Age Discrimination in Employment Act* of 1967 (ADEA) makes it illegal to put an employee or job seeker at a disadvantage because he/she is over 40. Some state laws set the threshold as low as 21. Vulnerability to discrimination usually increases when an employee reaches the age of 50.

Discrimination is illegal in all but a few situations where the job requires a person of a certain age, such as a movie role for a teenager.

More information: Go to the US Department of Labor Web site at *www.dol.gov* and click on "Workers."

5

Tax Facts

Get the Fastest Tax Refund of All

If you are owed a tax refund from the IRS for 2008, you'll want to get it as quickly as you can. *How to get the fastest refunds possible on your income taxes...*

PERSONAL REFUNDS

To get the fastest refund on your personal tax return, file electronically (e-file) on the earliest date possible and elect to have your refund sent via electronic direct deposit into a bank or investment account that you designate. Your refund will arrive within two weeks, says the IRS.

The first date on which the IRS will accept e-filed 2008 tax returns is the middle of January 2009.

Contrast: The IRS says that when...

•**A paper return is filed by mail and the refund is mailed back by check,** the refund can take six to eight weeks to arrive.

•**A paper return filed by mail requests a direct-deposit refund,** or an e-filed return requests a mailed refund check, the refund should take three to four weeks to arrive.

E-filing is becoming routine for millions of Americans—86 million tax returns were e-filed during the 2008 filing season (for 2007 returns), with 26 million filed from home computers and the rest filed by tax professionals on behalf of clients.

Most taxpayers can e-file through the Free File program, a joint effort of the IRS and commercial tax-preparation firms, that provides for electronic preparation and filing of tax returns at no charge. Details about the 2008 version of Free File will be announced on the IRS Web site in January.

Direct deposit: Refunds may be sent directly not only to checking and savings

Barbara Weltman, attorney based in Millwood, NY, and author of *J. K. Lasser's Small Business Taxes.* Wiley. She is publisher of the on-line newsletter *Big Ideas for Small Business.* Monthly. Free at *www.barbaraweltman.com.*

accounts, but also to IRAs, Coverdell Education Savings Accounts, Health savings accounts and Archer medical savings accounts —and each refund can be divided among up to three of these. File Form 8888, *Direct Deposit of Refund*, if deposits are to be made to more than one account.

Moreover, after you e-file your return, you can check up on the status of the refund after only seven days by using the "Where's My Refund?" utility on the IRS Web site or calling the IRS's Automated Refund Hotline at 800-829-1954. This is the fastest way to learn whether your requested refund is on its way to you—and whether there is a problem that may be slowing it down. If you file a paper return, you won't be able to verify your refund's status for four to six weeks.

To learn the details about e-filing, direct deposit and Free File, go to the IRS Web site, *www.irs.gov*, and click on the e-File logo.

Some things are beyond your control. For instance, employers and other payers of income must provide Forms W-2 and 1099— their deadline for providing these is January 31. If you haven't received an expected form by early February, call your employer or other payer and alert them.

More early refund strategies…

• **Start preparing your 2008 tax return early.** Pull together records and numbers to be able to finish your return as soon as possible after year-end.

• **Even better than getting a fast refund is not overpaying your taxes.** Estimate your tax position for the year now. If you think you've overpaid, you may still be able to reduce wage withholding on your last paychecks of the year. Similarly, take care not to overpay a quarterly estimated payment due for 2008 on January 15, 2009, on the basis of an earlier-in-the-year tax liability projection that has been overtaken by events.

How to Earn Invisible Income the IRS Can't Touch

Edward Mendlowitz, CPA, partner in the CPA firm WithumSmith+Brown, 1 Spring St., New Brunswick, NJ 08901. He is author of *The Adviser's Guide to Family Business Succession Planning*. American Institute of Certified Public Accountants.

Not all the money you receive is taxable income, even though the IRS might like you to think it is.

• **Gain on the sale of your home.** You're not taxed on gain up to $250,000 ($500,000 on a joint return) from the sale of your principal residence. You qualify for this exclusion if you owned and used the home for two out of five years before the date of the sale, regardless of your age.

• **Life insurance proceeds.** The beneficiary receives the proceeds of life insurance policies free of tax. However, the decedent's estate may be liable for estate tax on the proceeds.

• **Gifts and inheritances.** You do not pay income tax on money or property you receive as a gift or inheritance. Any gift tax owed is the responsibility of the person who gave the gift. In the case of an inheritance, federal estate tax is paid by the decendent's estate, not by the beneficiaries.

If you inherit property that has increased in value, such as the family home, you receive it at its stepped-up estate value. This enables you to avoid tax on the gain. When you sell the property, you use its stepped-up value, rather than the original cost, to calculate your taxable gain—another big benefit.

• **Borrowed money.** You can borrow up to $50,000 from your company pension plan tax free.

Trap: If a debt you owe is canceled, the amount of debt forgiven might become taxable income to you.

• **Grants for education.** Scholarships and fellowship grants are tax free—provided you are a degree candidate and the money is used strictly for tuition, fees, books, supplies and required equipment. (Grants for room and board are taxable.)

• **Employee awards.** Awards of tangible personal property (not cash) for length of service or safety achievements—up to $400 per employee or $1,600 provided the employer has a qualified plan—are tax free. (Awards for suggestions to an employer are generally taxable.)

• **Damages.** Any damages received in a lawsuit due to personal physical injury or sickness are tax free.

• **Rollovers.** No taxes are payable on a lump-sum payout for a company pension plan directly transferred into an IRA or another qualified plan within 60 days.

• **Property settlements.** Settlements between spouses in a divorce are not taxable to the recipient. However, the recipient does take over the tax cost (basis) in the property and will be taxed on any gain when the property is sold.

• **Child support and alimony.** Child-support payments are tax free to the recipient. Alimony is generally taxable, but it can be tax free if both spouses agree.

• **Municipal bond interest.** Generally, the interest is exempt from federal income tax and sometimes from state and local tax as well.

Exception: Interest from certain "private activity" municipal bonds is subject to the alternative minimum tax (AMT). Also, municipal bond interest is taken into account in figuring your income level to determine whether any of your Social Security benefits are taxable.

• **Return-of-capital dividends.** Some companies pay dividends that are considered a return on your investment in the company. These are wholly or partially tax free. However, your tax cost in the stock has to be reduced by the amount of untaxed dividends.

• **Life insurance policy dividends.** These are generally considered a partial return of the premiums you paid and are not taxable. You don't have to pay tax on these dividends until they exceed the accumulated premiums paid for the policy.

• **Long-term capital gains and qualified dividends.** If you are in the 10% or 15% tax bracket, you pay zero tax on this income.

• **Annuity payments.** The part of an annuity payment that represents the return of your investment in the annuity contract is not taxed.

• **Education savings bonds.** Interest on US Series EE and I savings bonds that were issued after December 31, 1989, is tax free to many taxpayers if the bonds are later redeemed to pay for education expenses.

Limits: This exclusion is not available for taxpayers with income in excess of certain annually determined amounts.

ALSO TAX FREE

• **Workers' compensation.**

• **Social Security payments**—provided your income is less than $32,000 if married filing jointly, or $25,000 if filing singly.

• **Federal income-tax refunds.** (However, any interest the IRS pays on a late refund is taxable.)

• **State income-tax refunds,** provided that you did not itemize deductions on your federal tax return for the previous year. If, however, you itemized your deductions for the year, your state refund is taxable. State refunds are not taxable if you were subject to the AMT the previous year and got no tax benefit for your state tax payments.

• **Disability payments** from any accident or health insurance policies paid for by the taxpayer are generally not taxable. But they're usually taxable if your employer paid the premiums.

• **Foreign-earned income.** The first $87,600 of salary earned in another country in 2008 is excluded from US tax if you were a resident of that country for the entire tax year. Some of your housing expenses are also excluded from US tax.

• **Certain fringe benefits from your employer.**

Examples: Health and accident insurance, pension plans, up to $50,000 of life insurance coverage, child- and dependent-care expenses, adoption assistance, meal money, employee discounts and transit passes not exceeding $100 per month.

• **Reimbursed medical expenses** that are not claimed as itemized deductions.

• **Reimbursed travel and entertainment expenses** that you adequately account for to your employer (unless the reimbursement is included on your W-2 form).

• **The amounts received for insurance reimbursement** up to the amount of your original cost for the property that was lost or damaged.

AMT ALERT

The AMT prevents the taxpayers who benefit from special credits and deductions from paying too little or no taxes. You may have to pay the AMT if your taxable income with adjustments in 2008 is above a certain level ($69,950 for married filing jointly and $46,200 for single or head of household). These figures are not adjusted annually for inflation, and are set to decline after 2008 unless Congress takes action.

Beware of These Common Filing Mistakes

James Glass, a tax attorney based in New York City and a contributing writer to *Tax Hotline*.

Don't let an avoidable mistake on your tax return cause your refund to be delayed, your tax bill to be recomputed by the IRS or your return to earn extra attention from an IRS auditor. *Mistakes made most frequently on tax returns, according to the IRS itself...*

EXPERTS' MISTAKES

The most common mistakes made by paid tax return preparers...

• **A dependent's last name doesn't match Social Security Administration (SSA)** or IRS records, so a dependency exemption is disallowed.

• **Earned income credit (EIC) errors...**

• The EIC amount is figured or entered incorrectly.

• A child's Social Security number (SSN) and/or name on EIC forms do not match SSA or IRS records.

• IRS Form 8862, *Information to Claim Earned Income Credit After Disallowance*, is not filed when reapplying for the EIC after the IRS has questioned eligibility for it—so the credit is disallowed again.

• An SSN is not reported at all for a child.

• The taxpayer or spouse was not at least 25 years old, but less than 65, within the tax year, as required to claim the EIC, if there is no qualifying dependent.

• **The IRS has to refigure tax due on investment income using a computation from the Schedule D tax worksheet or the qualified dividends and capital gains worksheet**—because computations on the return are wrong.

• **An SSN or a tax identification number** (TIN) is not provided for a dependent, so an exemption is disallowed.

• **Child tax credit errors...**

• A child's age exceeds the eligibility limit (under age 17 at year-end) for the credit.

• The credit is figured incorrectly because of math errors.

• The amount of the credit as computed on IRS Form 8812, *Additional Child Tax Credit* (used by low-income individuals who have three or more children to obtain a refundable credit), is incorrectly figured or incorrectly transferred to the return.

• **The taxable amount of Social Security benefits is figured incorrectly.**

• **The amount of tax reported as owed isn't correct** based on taxable income and filing status.

• **The amount of tax due or to be refunded is figured incorrectly.**

• **The taxpayer's or spouse's name,** SSN or TIN doesn't match SSA or IRS records, so a personal exemption is not allowed.

• **Self-employment tax from Schedule SE is incorrectly computed or transferred to Form 1040.**

• **The total exemption amount on page two of the return is incorrect.**

• **Net profit or loss from a business is incorrectly computed** or transferred to Form 1040.

Safety: Check the information given to your preparer (such as exact names and SSNs), then double-check the information on the return when you get it back before you sign and file it. Don't fail to check the items mentioned earlier.

INVESTORS' MISTAKES

Top mistakes made by investors...

• **1099-B errors.** Individuals who receive a late or corrected Form 1099-B reporting the result of a securities transaction often fail to amend their returns accordingly. Or they do not receive a 1099-B and fail to report the transaction at all.

Safety: Be sure that you receive all expected 1099s and check that the amounts shown on them are correct.

• **Capital gains holding period.** Taxpayers misclassify capital gains and losses as either short-term or long-term when reporting them on Form 1040, Schedule D.

Key: Remember to include the "date acquired" and "date sold" for each securities sale to document eligibility for short-term (held for one year or less) or long-term (more than one year) treatment. It's required.

• **Purchase and sale amounts.** Taxpayers fail to report on Schedule D both the original purchase price and later sale price for securities sold. Instead, they report only a net amount of gain or loss.

The original purchase price must be reported in order to compute gain or loss from the subsequent sale. If records are inadequate, individuals may be able to reconstruct original purchase price information through their brokers, or by conducting research to discover it at a business library or on the Internet.

• **Misidentifying investments.** When reporting income from stock sales made through a broker in the space on Schedule D for "description of investment," taxpayers often write the name of the brokerage that remitted the sale proceeds and issued the 1099-B reporting the sale.

What should be done instead: List the stock ticker symbol or abbreviation to describe the investment sold.

• **Omitting transactions.** Taxpayers fail to list all their transactions, omitting those that resulted in no net gain or loss.

The rule: The sales of all stocks, bonds, mutual fund shares, stock options, etc., are required to be reported on Schedule D, regardless of whether they result in any gain or loss.

Details: See IRS Publication 550, *Investment Income and Expenses.*

RETIREE TROUBLE SPOTS

• **Using the wrong deduction chart.** The standard deduction amount is different if you and/or your spouse are age 65 or older and/or blind. If you are completing a paper form, make sure that you are using the proper chart to determine your standard deduction.

• **Taxable Social Security calculations.** Double-check your taxable Social Security worksheet if you are filing a paper form.

• **Income reporting.** Be sure to report all sources of income, including interest income, which taxpayers often overlook.

Note: Tax-exempt interest income from municipal bonds does have to be included when calculating the taxable portion of Social Security benefits, and is now reported on Form 1099-INT, *Interest Income.*

SELF-PREPARED PAPER RETURNS

These are *especially* likely to contain simple mistakes, such as incorrect or missing SSNs...incorrect tax entered from tax tables...computation errors regarding the child- and dependent-care credit and earned income credit...missing or incorrect identification numbers for child-care providers...withholding and estimated tax payments entered on the wrong line...basic math errors.

Good idea: Prepare your return using commercial software or a tax-preparation Web site, which will catch most of these errors automatically.

SMALL BUSINESSES

Owners of small businesses are subject to making a wide range of errors on their tax returns—varying by the type of business, its form of organization and the type of return being filed.

For an IRS listing of the top errors to avoid, enter "common errors" in the search box at *www.irs.gov.*

CHARITIES, ETC.

Charities and noncharitable tax-exempt organizations (such as social clubs) have return-filing obligations even though they usually don't owe any taxes. If you participate on the board or in the management of such an entity, you should know about them.

More information: Enter "common errors made by exempt organizations, filing tips for Form 990," in the search box at *www.irs.gov.*

Beat the Tax Man Legally

Bernard S. Kent, Esq., CPA, human resource services partner, PricewaterhouseCoopers LLP, 400 Renaissance Center, Detroit, MI 48243. He is past chairman of the personal financial planning committee of the Michigan Association of Certified Public Accountants and coauthor of *PricewaterhouseCoopers Guide to Tax and Financial Planning, 2007: How the 2006 Tax Law Changes Affect You.* Wiley.

When you retire, the paychecks stop but the taxes don't. Your income may be fixed, or nearly so, if you rely on Social Security, a pension, an annuity, etc. Meanwhile, taxes can eat up more and more of the money you need for living.

Here are ways to fight the tax hit...

PROPERTY TAXES

For many people on modest incomes, property taxes can be higher than income taxes. *Take these steps...*

•**Apply for a senior property tax break.** Many states offer such programs. There may be income or other limitations. Contact your state's revenue (tax) department to find out what's available and how to apply.

Example: Some Illinois seniors can cut their property taxes by as much as $3,000 per year, thanks to a "senior citizen's homestead exemption."

Resource: Federation of Tax Administrators (*www.taxadmin.org/fta/link*) has links to every state's tax authority.

•**Appeal your property assessment** if you think you pay much higher taxes than your neighbors for a similar house. If successful, you may be able to reduce your annual tax bill.

How to do it: Contact your town or county assessor's office to get the information on which it based your assessment. Look for outright mistakes about your property, such as the wrong square footage, number of bedrooms or lot size. There also may be external factors that reduce the property's value, such as heavy traffic and/or noise near your house.

Deadline alert: Each jurisdiction has an "appeal season," generally several months early in the year. Contact your jurisdiction to determine your window of opportunity.

You may be able simply to show your evidence to the county assessor to have your assessment reduced. If informal procedures don't work, go before the local assessment board to make your case.

•**Sell your house.** As long as you have owned and occupied the house for at least two of the last five years, you'll owe no tax on up to $250,000 worth of profit from the sale ($500,000 for married couples). You then can move into an apartment or buy a house with lower taxes.

If you would like to remain in your house, you can sell it to a grown son or daughter and pay him/her rent to live there. You'll pocket your tax-free gain, and, as long as you pay fair market rent, the new owner will be entitled to the tax benefits of owning rental property—such as deductions for depreciation.

FEDERAL INCOME TAXES

If your taxable income is below $50,000 and your finances are relatively straightforward, it might pay for you to take the standard deduction on IRS Form 1040EZ or Form 1040A for your federal tax return. These forms are short and simple. Otherwise, using these forms might lock you out of certain deductions and/or credits and cause you to overpay your taxes.

Example: If your unreimbursed medical expenses come to more than 7.5% of your adjusted gross income, you can itemize and deduct them—but only on Form 1040, the regular "long" form.

To further cut your taxes…

• **Use borrowing power.** The IRS taxes *income*. Money that you *borrow* can provide cash flow without raising your tax bill. Use borrowed money, tax-free, for some of your expenses. Today's low interest rates make such an approach practical.

Examples: You might use a home-equity line of credit with a very favorable interest rate. The interest you pay probably will be deductible if you itemize on Form 1040.

For information on home-equity interest deductibility, see IRS publication 936, *Home Mortgage Interest Deduction*, available from the IRS at 800-829-1040 or *www.irs.gov.*

Another possibility is to take out a loan against your cash-value life insurance or your securities portfolio.

Strategy: Keep the bulk of your long-term noncash savings in assets that do not generate much taxable income, such as growth stocks or tax-managed mutual funds.

Warning: Don't borrow at high interest rates or to excess. You might endanger your core assets—your investment portfolio, insurance policies, even your house.

• **Let your house pay you.** If you are at least 62 years old and your home is not heavily mortgaged, consider taking out a reverse mortgage. You'll get tax-free cash, and the money doesn't have to be repaid until you die or move out of the house.

Information: AARP, 888-687-2277, *www. aarp.org/revmort.*

STATE AND LOCAL INCOME TAXES

Some state and local governments provide seniors with income tax breaks that shelter pension and/or Social Security benefits. For information, contact your tax adviser or state tax authority.

Example: Michigan offers married couples an income tax exclusion for up to $84,480 of annual private (nongovernment) pension income. Single filers can exclude up to $42,240.

If your income is high and/or you live in an area that has high taxes even for seniors, you might want to move to a less taxing jurisdiction. Before you pick a new place to live, be sure to take all of its taxes into account. A state might have low income tax, but the area you like might have high property tax. For help comparing overall tax burdens in various states, call the Tax Foundation at 202-464-6200 or visit *www.taxfoundation.org.*

Caution: States chase down residents who try to illegally avoid taxes by claiming they've moved, perhaps by buying or renting a second home or even using a relative's address.

If you move, be sure to sever your connections to your old state. Move your bank accounts, turn in your driver's license after you get one from your new sate, register to vote in your new jurisdiction, etc.

File a final income tax return with your former state, and subsequently file returns with your new state if required. Use your new address on all tax documents, and file federal returns with the IRS Service Center for your new state.

Is Your Tax Return Asking For an Audit?

Barbara Weltman, attorney based in Millwood, NY, and author of *J. K. Lasser's Small Business Taxes.* Wiley. She is publisher of the on-line newsletter *Big Ideas for Small Business.* Monthly. Free at *www. barbaraweltman.com.*

An IRS audit. It's what taxpayers most dread as they prepare their returns and what more than 1.3 million of them faced in 2007—up 7% from the year before.

As the White House and Congress look for more ways to shrink the federal budget deficit, your chances of being audited are likely to grow, especially if your income tops $100,000.

Although there are no foolproof methods to avoid an audit—and many returns are chosen randomly—there are certain red flags that draw the attention of IRS computers and auditors.

Here are mistakes that could cause your return to stand out and suggestions on how to avoid an audit...

1. Omitting or underreporting income. Employers and financial institutions sometimes report income incorrectly to taxpayers and the IRS on W-2 forms (for employees) and 1099 forms (for independent contractors).

Safest: If you receive an incorrect W-2 or 1099, don't just substitute a different figure on your tax return. Get the mistake corrected by the source, and ask for a new W-2 or 1099.

2. Failing to fill out an alternative minimum tax (AMT) schedule. This year, more than 3.5 million individuals are expected to owe this tricky tax, which kicks in when deductions push the regular tax below a certain minimum amount. Taxpayers who live in "high tax" states, such as New York and New Jersey, are particularly vulnerable, because state and local income tax and sales tax are not deductible for AMT purposes.

Safest: Use the IRS AMT assistant, an online calculator at *www.irs.gov* (put "AMT Assistant" in the search window), to determine whether the AMT applies to you.

3. Messing up the math or leaving blanks. IRS computers easily detect math errors and omissions.

Safest: Print out your calculations so that you can double-check them. Review all lines, as well as blanks, to make sure that you didn't leave out required information or put it in the wrong place. That includes the signature lines—remember that both spouses must sign a joint return.

Better yet: File electronically. It cuts down on math errors—e-filed returns have an accuracy rate of more than 99%, compared with 80% for paper returns, because the program checks the math.

4. Claiming too many deductions and/or credits. The IRS is on the lookout for excessive deductions and credits.

Example: The IRS has said that some taxpayers asked for too much in refunds for certain taxes they paid in the past on long-distance phone bills. Those taxes had been ruled illegal, and the government offered to refund to each taxpayer a "standard" phone tax amount of $30 to $60, depending on the number of exemptions claimed on the tax return, without requiring any proof. For higher amounts, proof of what was paid in phone taxes was required. IRS commissioner Mark W. Everson said that "people requesting an inflated amount will likely see their refund frozen, may have their entire tax return audited and even face criminal prosecution where warranted."

If you request more than the standard phone tax refund, be sure to have on hand the phone bills that prove what you claim.

Safest: In general, don't claim deductions that far exceed what tax preparers say is reasonable for your income bracket, or if you do, attach an explanation. Attach copies of bills for unusually high medical expenses. Have proper documentation for donations to charity. For used clothing and household items, take pictures of the items to show that they were in good used condition or better.

Guidelines: There are no "standard" deduction amounts. Based on IRS statistics for 2005, taxpayers with adjusted gross incomes (AGIs) of $50,000 to $100,000 itemized an average of $2,703 in charitable contributions and $6,144 in medical costs. Those with AGIs of $100,000 to $200,000 itemized an average of $4,057 for charity and $9,727 for medical costs.

5. Claiming losses on hobbies. Deductions for a fun activity, such as coin collecting, may be rejected if the activity results in losses that don't make commercial sense year after year.

Safest: Don't claim deductions for hobby expenses unless you are prepared to show that you are engaged in the activity for profit.

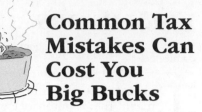

Common Tax Mistakes Can Cost You Big Bucks

Martin S. Kaplan, CPA, 11 Penn Plaza, New York City, *www.irsmaven.com*. He is a frequent speaker at insurance, banking and financial-planning seminars and is author of *What the IRS Doesn't Want You to Know*. Wiley.

The Internal Revenue Code is published in two jam-packed volumes that take up several inches of shelf space. It's no wonder that taxpayers make so many big mistakes when it comes to their taxes.

Here are some of the most costly mistakes...

CLAIMING DEPENDENTS

Mistake: **Not having any money withheld from your paycheck.**

It is true that you can reduce or even eliminate income tax withholding by increasing the number of dependents you claim on the Form W-4 you file with your employer. However, you'll have to settle up with the IRS when you file your tax return for the year. At that point, having withheld too little will cost you interest and possibly penalties.

What to do instead: If possible, increase income tax withholding toward year-end to make up for shortfalls, since all withholding is considered to be paid evenly throughout the year.

Caution: If you are self-employed and owe $1,000 or more in federal income tax, failing to make equal quarterly payments of federal income tax, Social Security and Medicare taxes can lead to penalties.

SOCIAL SECURITY

Mistake: **Thinking that you won't have to pay any tax on Social Security benefits once you reach your full retirement age.**

Most people have to pay this tax, unless they have low "provisional income." *Provisional income is the total of...*

- **Adjusted gross income (AGI).**

- **Tax-exempt interest income** from municipal bonds and municipal bond funds.

- **One-half of your annual Social Security benefits.**

On a joint return, if your provisional income is more than $32,000 (but less than $44,000), up to 50% of your benefits can be taxed. For single filers, the threshold is $25,000 to $34,000.

If provisional income is greater than $44,000 on a joint return ($34,000, single), up to 85% of benefits will be taxed.

What to do instead: Reduce your AGI to help lower the tax on Social Security benefits. You might, for example, postpone taking withdrawals from your IRA.

SELF-EMPLOYMENT

Mistake: **Not paying tax if you don't receive a Form 1099.**

If you're self-employed, even part of the time, you are supposed to receive an IRS Form 1099 from every party who paid you $600 or more during the prior year. Those forms also are sent to the IRS. Some people think that if they don't receive a 1099 form, they don't have to declare the income.

What to do instead: You must report all of the income that you earn. Some employers will send a 1099 to the IRS even if they do not send you a copy. Any discrepancy may trigger an audit. Even if a 1099 was not sent to the IRS, if your tax return is examined for any reason, the IRS agent may ask to go over your bank records. Deposits may be considered taxable income unless you can prove that they should not be.

DEDUCTIONS

Mistake: **Taking any deductions you want as long as they are not in excess of the "average" amount.**

The IRS publishes the average itemized deductions for certain levels of income. For those who had AGIs of $50,000 to $100,000 in 2005, for example (the last year for which figures were published), average deductions included $8,946 of interest expenses and $5,812 for taxes paid.

What to do instead: Take only the deductions that you can corroborate with supporting documents, such as receipts.

PERSONAL EXPENSES

***Mistake:* Transferring assets to a trust so that you can deduct your personal expenses.**

Some trust promoters promise that personal expenses can be paid by the trust, which will effectively make these expenses tax deductible. Not true.

When a trust is created, any income generated by the trust is taxable to the creator ("grantor"), the beneficiaries or the trust itself, depending on the circumstances. Income that is taxable to the trust is taxed at higher rates than on a personal tax return.

What's more, personal expenses do not become deductible just because they're claimed by a trust. Only expenses that are legitimate can be deducted.

What to do instead: Use a trust for legitimate purposes only, such as an irrevocable life insurance trust for paying estate tax or a credit-shelter trust to pay income to your spouse for life and then pass the remainder tax free to other beneficiaries.

FOREIGN TAX SHELTERS

***Mistake:* Holding investments offshore in order to shield them from US income taxes.**

Some people even get foreign credit cards because they believe that they can then spend the money without Uncle Sam finding out. Some unethical advisers tell clients to have earned income paid to an offshore bank, where it won't be reported to the IRS.

What to do instead: Report any income you earn anywhere in the world to Uncle Sam—that is what is legally required. You might get an off-setting credit for income taxes paid to foreign governments, but you must first report offshore income to the US.

Having an offshore credit card won't shelter money either—the IRS now requires credit card issuers to report activity by US residents holding offshore cards.

Inside the IRS

Ms. X, Esq., a former IRS agent who is still well connected.

The date you file your tax return can mean the difference between getting audited and not getting audited, though the IRS will never admit there's a connection. But my understanding, as a former IRS insider, is that the IRS fills its quota of tax returns to audit on a "first-in basis." This means that the vast majority of the returns selected for the next audit cycle will have already been identified by the end of September in any given year.

Impact: The safest time to file your return is as close to the October 15 extended filing deadline as possible.

CLAIMING TOO MANY DEDUCTIONS CAN SPELL BIG TROUBLE

There's a distinct line between taking all the deductions you are entitled to and overstating or inflating the deductions to materially reduce your tax liability. Many taxpayers who find themselves in serious trouble with the IRS do not realize that their troubles could have been avoided by being less aggressive. Making up numbers or encouraging your tax preparer to make up numbers is a recipe for disaster.

Example: Suppose claiming an additional $10,000 of deductions you know you can't prove will save $2,500 in tax. This extra $10,000 of deductions could very well trigger an audit, resulting in interest and penalties on tax not paid.

Best advice: Don't be greedy or allow your tax preparer to get you back any more money than you are entitled to.

WHAT IF YOU DON'T SHOW UP FOR YOUR AUDIT APPOINTMENT?

Not appearing for a scheduled appointment could be the smartest approach to a tax audit, especially if you failed to report a substantial amount of income or overstated your expenses and the IRS doesn't know this. Generally, if you don't appear for an appointment, the auditor assigned to your case will submit a report disallowing all of the expenses he was prepared to examine.

Strategy: You can always appeal the findings contained in the report. Meanwhile, the auditor will not have the opportunity to ask you questions.

Best approach: Contact a knowledgeable tax attorney if you have failed to report income and are being audited.

Beneficiary Loopholes

Edward Mendlowitz, CPA, partner in the CPA firm WithumSmith+Brown, 1 Spring St., New Brunswick, NJ 08901. *www.withum.com.* He is author of *The Adviser's Guide to Family Business Succession Planning.* American Institute of Certified Public Accountants.

As a general rule, beneficiaries of trusts and estates have the right to receive income and other payments, but have no control over the management or distribution of the money or when it is taxed. *But there are techniques for getting around these limitations...*

TRUST LOOPHOLES

Loophole: **Provide current income to your beneficiaries with a grantor trust (also called an intentionally defective trust).**

These trusts are set up under Sections 671–679 of the Tax Code. The grantor, who sets up the trust, is considered the owner of the assets solely for income tax purposes, and trust income is taxed on the grantor's tax return.

For estate tax purposes, these trusts remove assets from the grantor's taxable estate and can provide current income to the trust beneficiaries. Tax paid by the grantor on trust income creates a "tax-free" gift from the grantor to the trust beneficiaries in the amount of income tax paid.

Note: Transfers of assets to a grantor trust create a taxable gift, subject to annual gift tax exclusions and lifetime exemptions.

Loophole: **Irrevocable life insurance trusts avoid estate tax on insurance proceeds and provide income to beneficiaries.**

These trusts typically are funded only with an insurance policy on your life, so they provide no cash flow until your death. At that point, the death benefit can be fully distributed to the beneficiaries or retained in the trust with any future income distributed.

Typical arrangement: Income is distributed to the surviving spouse and, after that, to the grantor's children when they attain certain ages. Assets remaining after these income beneficiaries die or upon some other event, such as the children reaching a specified age, are distributed according to the terms established in the trust. The insurance benefits are received free of estate tax.

Loophole: **Provide for your surviving spouse with a qualified terminable interest property (QTIP) trust.**

The assets in a QTIP trust qualify as a marital bequest. This means that no estate tax is payable until the death of the surviving spouse, and delaying taxes means more money in the QTIP to generate cash flow to the surviving spouse.

Surviving spouses (the income beneficiaries) have the right to all the trust income and can request that the trust invest to have more income if they feel that the trust is underperforming the market. It's up to the trustee to determine if the request is valid.

Surviving spouses also have the right to request a distribution of principal if the trust income is insufficient for their needs. This is also subject to the approval of the trustee.

Loophole: **Make life easier for your beneficiaries by setting up a revocable trust ("living trust").**

These trusts avoid or eliminate much of the probate process so that the assets or the income can be distributed sooner to the beneficiaries upon the death of the grantor. Living trusts, which can be revoked by the person who sets them up—the grantor—provide no income- or estate-tax advantages. All income is attributed to the grantor, who is usually the sole beneficiary.

Strategy: Use a living trust to fund a prenuptial agreement.

How this works: The trust supplies cash flow to the surviving spouse and, later, trust assets are distributed to children from a prior marriage.

BREAKS FOR BENEFICIARIES

Loophole: **Beneficiaries can deduct estate tax paid on "income in respect of a decedent" (IRD).**

IRD is income from an asset taxed on a federal estate tax return, including IRA accounts, accrued US savings bond interest, and the decedent's rights to unpaid commissions earned before death. The federal estate tax allocable to the IRD when the beneficiary receives the payments is deductible as an itemized deduction on the beneficiary's tax return.

Note: IRD is subject to both estate tax (if the estate is taxable) and income tax. The income tax deduction mentioned above mitigates some of this double taxation. However, the deduction applies only to federal estate tax, not state estate or inheritance taxes.

Loophole: **Beneficiaries who sell inherited property at a loss can deduct the loss on their tax returns.**

Example: Your parents leave you a house with an original purchase price of $50,000 that is worth $300,000 when both parents have died. You inherit the house free of estate tax and receive a "stepped-up" basis (tax cost) of $300,000. The house is sold for $270,000 after brokers' commissions and selling costs. You can deduct $30,000, subject to annual loss deduction limits, as long as you didn't use it as your personal residence and immediately offered it for sale or rental.

Note: Capital losses are deductible dollar for dollar against capital gains and can offset up to $3,000 of ordinary income each year. Excess losses are carried forward to subsequent tax years.

More from Edward Mendlowitz...

Forms that Mess Up Your IRA

I'm a mild-mannered guy, but one aspect of how banks and brokerage firms treat their IRA customers infuriates me. I get clients all the time who are forced to pay ridiculously high taxes when they inherit an IRA because a bank or broker gave the IRA owner badly prepared forms to fill out.

Especially upsetting: Customers rely on these bank trustees/custodians to know the IRA rules. Many trustees don't.

Most IRA beneficiary designation forms—the forms that you fill out to indicate the person or people you want to inherit your IRA—are inadequate. They don't leave room for secondary beneficiaries to be written in or for the Latin phrase *per stirpes* to be added after a primary or secondary beneficiary's name. The forms don't prompt you to do this and you're not likely to get help from the trustee. *These provisions are important...*

- **Secondary beneficiaries** are the ones that you want the IRA to go to if your main beneficiary dies before you do. If you don't name a secondary beneficiary, the IRA could go to your estate. Your heirs will lose the ability to "stretch out" the IRA over their lives, meaning that they will have to cash it out sooner and lose decades of tax deferral.

- **Per stirpes** means that the children of a beneficiary who dies before you do will receive their parent's share equally.

Now, don't get me wrong, some trustees/custodians get it right. But in my experience, most foul it up. Be alert. Remember that it doesn't matter what you might say about your IRA in your will—only the beneficiary forms that you file with your IRA trustee govern where your IRA goes. *What you need to do...*

- Always name an individual or individuals as your primary beneficiary or beneficiaries—never your estate.

- Always name a secondary, or contingent, beneficiary in case your primary beneficiary dies before you.

- If you have children and you want to leave their shares to their offspring if any of your children die before you do, just write the words "per stirpes" after your children's names where they are listed as beneficiaries. Otherwise, the IRA is distributed according to your state's law.

Important: The concerns for Roth IRA, 401(k) and 403(b) beneficiary designations are the same as for traditional IRAs.

Throwing Away Old Tax Records

Generally, tax records should be maintained for three years after the date the return was filed.

Exception: Records relating to cost basis (stocks, mutual funds, real estate) should be held until three years after the property has been sold. Don't keep tax records longer than required, since a summons issued by the IRS could require you to produce those records. The records could be used to help strengthen a case against you (for instance, you have a 10-year pattern of overstating your charitable contributions).

Caution: If your computers contain sensitive financial information relating to old returns, consult a computer technician to ensure that deleted information can't be reconstructed.

Ms. X, Esq., a former IRS agent who is still well connected.

More from Ms. X...

Volunteer Preparer Foul-Ups

According to a recently released report by the Treasury Inspector General, 44% of the tax returns prepared by the federal government's Volunteer Income Tax Assistance (VITA) program during the 2007 filing season were inaccurate. The Inspector General based his report on the results of a test sample of 39 tax returns. Seventeen of the 39 were found to contain errors. In recent years, the IRS has been criticized for delegating too

much of its own responsibility for taxpayer service to volunteers who lack the experience to gather the proper information and apply the appropriate tax law.

Lesson: You get what you pay for.

Also from Ms. X...

Private Collection Agencies

Now that the IRS has outsourced a portion of its collection work, a private debt collector may contact you.

Limits: These collection agencies can only negotiate installment payment agreements of up to $25,000 and 36 months.

Good news: A private collection agency cannot issue a summons for financial information and cannot make third-party contacts—with your bank, employer or neighbors, for example.

Strategy: You may have an easier time getting an agreeable installment plan with a private collection agency since they're paid a commission on anything they collect, whereas the typical IRS collection employee has no financial incentive to let you pay off your liability over time.

Note: If you can't or won't accept an agreement with the private agency, your case gets sent back to the IRS, which will then pursue collection in the normal manner.

Also from Ms. X...

Pay Attention to IRS Notices

It is not uncommon for the IRS to send a notice to an individual explaining that it believes that dividends, interest or stock sales occurred but were not included on the individual's income tax return. If the letter is ignored, the IRS will eventually issue a notice of deficiency and, if you can't resolve the matter within 90 days of the issuance of the notice of deficiency, you must file a petition with the US Tax Court to protect your rights. Sometimes, the items the IRS is questioning go back more than two years, so getting your hands on the records might be tough.

Suggestion: Make sure that when you respond to the IRS, you send correspondence to a specific person so that you can follow up if you don't hear from him/her within a reasonable period of time.

Also from Ms. X...

How Long Does the IRS Have to Come After You...?

The answer depends on the amount of unreported income and why it was not reported on your return.

Statute of limitations rule: Unless the IRS issues an assessment within three years from the date the tax return was filed, it is out of luck.

Exception 1: If you understated your income by more than 25% of the gross income reported on your return, the three-year limitation period is extended to six years.

Exception 2: If the IRS can prove that the understatement of income was attributable to fraud (that is, you *intended* to underreport your income—it was not a simple mistake), there is no statute of limitations and it can make an assessment at any time.

Inside information: Even in fraud cases, it is unlikely that the IRS will go back for more than six years.

Also from Ms. X...

The IRS Cuts Costs by Relying on Volunteers

One way that the IRS is seeking to reduce its overhead is in its taxpayer service function. For many years, the IRS spent considerable sums staffing walk-in sites during tax season to assist low-income taxpayers in preparing their income tax returns. Today, the people who devote their time in the volunteer income tax assistance (VITA) program fill much of the role previously assumed by paid seasonal employees.

Problem: As poor as the advice sometimes is from the IRS, at least standards were in place to monitor the advice being given by paid employees to the public. Volunteers, although well intentioned, are not subjected to formal IRS supervision, and the advice could be spotty.

Finally from Ms. X...

What Happens If You Are Arrested by the IRS?

Many times, a grand jury will be presented with the aspects of a case (as portrayed by a government attorney), an indictment will be issued and an arrest warrant will be executed. IRS special agents will show up at your home or place of business and inform you that you are under arrest. You will then be handcuffed and transported to a federal district courthouse for processing—fingerprinting and mug shot—and a bail hearing. The entire process takes about a day and, if you have no prior criminal convictions, bail will be set and you'll probably be able to go home that night. In more complicated cases, you might have to stay overnight in jail until a bail package can be negotiated with the assistant US attorney assigned to your case.

Caution: During the car ride to the courthouse, the special agents will encourage you to make incriminating statements. Be polite, but tell them that you don't want to talk to them until you have met with your attorney.

Make Tax Time Easier—Steps to Take Right Away

Christopher R. Williams, JD, Ernst & Young LLP, New York City, *www.ey.com*. He is senior manager in the firm's Personal Financial Services area specializing in income tax and financial planning for high-net-worth individuals.

Don't wait until the last minute to get started on this year's tax return. It can take several weeks—possibly even months—to assemble all the necessary documents. Now is the time to get your paperwork in order. *Here is a list of the records you will need—and where to find them...*

SECURITIES/MUTUAL FUND SALES

When you sell stocks, bonds or mutual fund shares held in a taxable account, it is

a taxable event. You must compare the sale proceeds with the "cost basis" (what you paid). The difference will be a taxable gain or a tax-deductible loss (different rules apply to securities acquired by gift or inheritance).

What to do: To find out a stock's price on a certain date, including splits, for free, visit *www.bigcharts.com*. To find bond prices, check with your broker or the bond issuer. For fund prices, check the fund company or your broker. You also can check your year-end statements and original purchase orders.

Where to find records: The cost basis for the security or fund you sold may be reported on IRS Form 1099-B, *Proceeds from Broker and Barter Exchange Transactions*, which you receive from your mutual fund company or brokerage firm. This form also reports income and capital gains distributions, which are taxable if the fund is not held in a retirement account. If you haven't received this form by the end of January, call your financial institution.

HOME IMPROVEMENTS

If you sell a home that you have occupied as your principal residence for at least two of the previous five years, up to $500,000 worth of capital gains is not taxed for married couples filing jointly. (Single filers get a $250,000 exclusion.) However, many homes have appreciated so much in recent years that tax still might be due on a sale.

Example: The house you and your spouse purchased many years ago for $50,000 now can be sold for $900,000—a gain of $850,000. After the $500,000 exclusion, you would owe tax on $350,000 worth of profits.

What to do: You can increase the cost basis of your home by counting all the expenses incurred in buying, improving and selling it. Buying expenses might include legal and recording fees. Selling expenses that can be added to your basis might include sales commissions and advertising fees.

Improvements might include adding a bathroom or a fence...new landscaping... plumbing or wiring upgrades...a new roof... or paving an unpaved driveway. Additions to your home—such as a deck, sunroom or garage—also are considered improvements.

Caution: Money you spend on repairs does not count toward your cost basis.

IRS Publication 523, *Selling Your Home*, has details on basis-increasing buying and selling expenses, as well as home improvements.

Where to find records: Look for receipts from contractors for home improvements. If you didn't save receipts, the canceled checks and credit card statements relating to the work can be used. You also might ask contractors for records of what you paid.

TAXES AND INTEREST PENDING A HOME SALE

When you buy or sell a property, generally each party usually will pay property taxes and mortgage interest for the period the person owned the home during the month of the sale. These amounts are reported to the US Department of Housing and Urban Development (HUD) by the settlement agent, who might be the lender, title insurance company, escrow company, real estate broker or attorney for the buyer or seller. This agent takes care of the title search, property survey, etc. The amounts are reported on a HUD-1 statement. Hold on to this statement. These amounts, which are tax-deductible, often are overlooked at tax time because they may not be reported on any other form.

IRA WITHDRAWALS

With a traditional IRA, most contributions are tax-deductible. That's why when you withdraw the money, distributions are taxed. In addition, there is generally a 10% penalty for taxable withdrawals made before age 59½.

Since 1987, nondeductible IRA contributions made with after-tax dollars have been permitted. If you haven't accounted for such contributions and you have made withdrawals, you may be paying double tax on some IRA withdrawals. That's because withdrawals of the nondeductible contributions should be tax-free.

What to do: If you have made contributions with after-tax dollars, use the "cream in the coffee" method to reduce your tax.

Example: You are 60 years old and have $200,000 in your IRA. Of the total, $20,000—or 10%—came from nondeductible contributions. That is the cream.

Say that you withdraw $30,000 this year. Without good records, you might pay tax on the full $30,000 withdrawal. With records, you can avoid tax on the "cream"—10%, or $3,000—and owe tax only on the "coffee"—$27,000.

Where to find records: Go over previous financial statements or ask your IRA custodian for copies to determine after-tax contributions. With your tax return, file Form 8606, *Nondeductible IRAs*, on which you can enter cumulative after-tax contributions on line 2. File this form each year to keep track of the "cream" in your "coffee."

If you have overpaid tax on withdrawals in any of the prior three years, you should consult a tax adviser to see if it makes sense for you to amend any of the three prior years' returns.

Separate but Equal

Spouses who file separate returns must treat deductions in the same manner. If one spouse itemizes, so must the other. This is sometimes a problem with estranged spouses.

Peter Weitsen, CPA/PFS, partner, WithumSmith+ Brown, 1 Spring St., New Brunswick, NJ 08901.

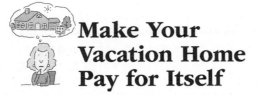

Make Your Vacation Home Pay for Itself

Albert Ellentuck, Esq., CPA, of counsel to the law firm King & Nordlinger, LLP, 2111 Wilson Blvd., Arlington, VA 22201. Past chairman of the tax division of the American Institute of Certified Public Accountants (AICPA), he writes a monthly column for the AICPA publication, *The Tax Adviser*.

If you own a second home used purely for your own getaways, the tax implications, federal and state, are fairly straightforward. You probably can deduct outlays for mortgage interest and property tax, just as you can with your primary residence. (Property tax deductions won't be deductible, though, if you are subject to the alternative minimum tax.)

Mixing business with pleasure: The rules change—and become considerably more complex—if you sometimes receive rental income from your second home.

Opportunity: Knowing how to mix rental use with personal use can result in substantial additional tax savings.

14-DAY RULE

If you rent out your vacation home occasionally, you can qualify for a prime tax break.

Loophole: You can rent out your home for up to 14 days a year and owe *no tax at all* on that income.

This can result in thousands of dollars of tax-free income if your home is near a major sports event, such as when the Super Bowl was in Miami, or in a desirable vacation area.

Caution: It probably won't make sense to rent your home for just over 14 days in a year. If you do, all the income will be taxable, not just the excess from the fifteenth day on. You might pocket less after taxes than if you had rented the place out for fewer days.

14-DAY 10% RULE

Once you rent out your home for more than 14 days in a given year, things become complicated.

Rental vs. residence: If you use your vacation home for personal purposes* for no more than the greater of (1) 14 days or (2) 10% of rental days, the home will be considered rental property. In this case, losses may be deductible.

Example: Jim Smith rents out his beach house for 100 days a year and uses it personally for 13 days. He can treat his beach house as rental property. If he uses it for 14 days, however, it is considered a residence.

Janice Jones has the beach house next to Jim's, which she rents out for 200 days a year.

*You must count as personal use any day that the residence is used for personal purposes by you or by a relative, even if you used it for only part of that day.

She can use it up to 19 days (less than 10% of 200 days) and still treat it as rental property.

Why this matters: As explained above, when you rent out a property for more than 14 days a year, the rental income is taxable. But at the same time, expenses related to that rental income can be tabulated. Such expenses might include management fees and marketing costs. You also can allocate expenses, such as insurance, repairs and depreciation to the property's rental use.

Outcome: A portion of your vacation home expenses will become business-related, and this will reduce the net income you'll report from the property. You'll owe less tax on your rental income.

In some cases, business-related expenses will exceed rental income. The resulting loss will fall under the "passive-loss" rules if you can treat your vacation home as rental property.

How this works: If you have a passive loss, it can offset taxable income from un-related passive activities. This could include other rental property you own or income from a limited partnership.

Even better: In addition, net passive losses may be deductible from your taxable income (the income you report on your tax return after deductions).

Required: If your adjusted gross income (AGI) is less than $100,000 on a single or joint return, you can deduct up to $25,000 worth of net passive losses.

To deduct passive losses against your taxable income, you also have to take part in some management decisions, such as approving tenants and authorizing repairs.

Phaseout: If your AGI is between $100,000 and $150,000, you can deduct a lower amount of net passive losses.

Example: Your AGI is $145,000 this year, so you are 90% through the phaseout range. You are entitled to 10% of the maximum passive-loss deduction, so you can deduct up to $2,500 in net passive losses (10% of $25,000).

Looking ahead: Net passive losses you can't deduct right away can be used in the future if your AGI permits a write-off at that time or if you have passive income from other sources. Otherwise, all of your deferred passive losses can offset any gains when you sell the property.

Bottom line: If you think that you'll have a passive loss from renting out a vacation home and you'll be able to deduct such a loss, keep personal use down to the level where the home is classed as rental property.

If you use the vacation home for so many personal days that it is classed as a residence rather than a rental property, no losses can be deducted.

SEVEN-DAY RULE

Yet another rule comes into play for vacation home owners.

In some areas, especially resorts, your average rental period for a vacation home may be less than seven days. If so, you face different requirements. You divide the number of days you rented by the number of your paying customers.

If your vacation home rentals average less than seven days, you may be able to avoid the passive-loss rules and deduct your losses currently, in the year that you have the loss. *To do so, you must "materially participate" in the venture by either…*

• **Devoting more than 500 hours per year** to gaining revenues from the property or…

• **Devoting more than 100 hours to this effort,** as long as this is more time than anyone else spends.

Strategy: If your vacation home rentals will average less than seven days and you expect to have net losses from this activity, consider not using a management company. By spending more than 100 hours per year yourself on this business, you will probably be able to deduct those losses.

What if your vacation home usage qualifies you for the seven-day rule, but you do not materially participate in running the business? You'll be subject to the passive-loss rules, without the opportunity of deducting up to $25,000 worth of net losses.

DISAPPEARING DEDUCTION

As explained, it may make sense to restrict personal use of a vacation home to qualify it as rental property so that a loss can be deducted.

Trap: A home classified as rental property is no longer a residence. Mortgage interest payments allocable to your personal use won't be deductible.

Example: You rent out your vacation home 190 days in a year and use it for 10 days. Therefore, the home is considered rental property.

However, 5% of the usage (10 days out of a total of 200 days) is allocable to your personal use. Consequently, 5% of the mortgage interest you pay is not deductible.

Reasoning: That 5% can't be allocated to your rental activities because it's attributable to personal use. Yet the home does not qualify as a residence, so that 5% is not deductible home mortgage interest, either.

Strategy: Crunch the numbers to see which will produce the best after-tax result—a deduction for home mortgage interest or a passive-loss deduction.

Then adjust your personal use to have your vacation home fall into the category that works best for you, rental property or residence.

Best: Talk with an accountant experienced in helping clients maximize the tax benefits of owning a second home.

Turn the Hobby You Love Into Great Tax Breaks

Laurence I. Foster, CPA/PFS, consultant and former partner at Eisner LLP, 750 Third Ave., New York City 10017. Mr. Foster is former chairman of the Personal Financial Specialist Credential Committee for the American Institute of Certified Public Accountants.

With longer and healthier retirements, more and more people want to stay financially productive. But they also want to do something fun—something that is both personally and financially rewarding.

Perfect solution: Turn a hobby or pastime you enjoy into a moneymaking sideline or second career. The IRS will even help you do it. *Here's how...*

FOR STARTERS

Most new businesses incur start-up losses. You can write these off against income from other sources, such as bond income or salary from your day job, so your business acts as a legal tax shelter.

Starting a business can provide valuable new deductions, too—for home-ownership costs, previously nondeductible commuting, travel and other items.

Then, when your business becomes profitable, you can use some of the profit to generate tax-favored income. You can fund retirement accounts, for example, that will reduce your current tax bill while building future wealth.

A BUSINESS IS A BUSINESS

Many different kinds of hobbies can be developed into sideline businesses or second careers—collecting (antiques, pottery or stamps), photography, writing, gardening, jewelry making—practically anything.

Key: To qualify a hobby as a business, you need to demonstrate a profit motive. Without a profit motive, it will still be deemed a hobby, and loss deductions and other business deductions won't be allowed.

You do not have to actually make a profit from an activity to qualify it as a business—but only show that you *intend* to make a profit. When courts have been satisfied that taxpayers had profit motives, they have allowed many consecutive years of loss deductions, even for businesses that *never* made a profit.

Of course, courts are not mind readers, so they look for evidence of profit motive in the way an activity is conducted—whether or not it operates in a businesslike manner. *Evidence of profit motive...*

• **Complete business books and records are kept.**

• **Business funds are segregated from personal funds** by using separate bank accounts.

- **The business is registered with the local authorities.**

- **There is a formal business plan** that maps out how the business intends to make a profit.

- **It advertises its product or service.**

- **The owner consults with experts in the field.**

- **The owner spends a significant amount of hours working in the business.**

- **If profits don't result, the business plan is modified in light of experience.**

The IRS publishes audit guides for dozens of businesses. See the IRS Web site at *www.irs.gov*. The guide will tell you what the IRS is looking for in a particular business.

No one item is determinative, but the more businesslike the manner in which an activity is run, the more likely a profit motive will be deemed to exist—even in the face of continuous losses.

Helpful: If an activity shows a profit in three out of five years, it is presumed to have a profit motive. (Separate rules do apply for breeding, showing and racing horses.)

When starting a new business, you can file IRS Form 5213, *Election to Postpone Determination*, to postpone determination of business status for five years.

Pro: This filing gives you five years to show your activity's profit motive, and allows you to deduct all losses and business deductions in the meantime.

Con: You notify the IRS that you are conducting such an activity, and so increase risk of an audit five years in the future. If the IRS then decides you had no profit motive, it can disallow all five years of deductions and charge you interest. By contrast, in a normal audit, the IRS can go back only three years.

Bottom line: If you are very certain that you won't have a profit for the first three years, file a Form 5213. Otherwise, it's better not to.

Once you can show a genuine profit motive, you can then reap a host of tax breaks from your new business.

HOME-OFFICE DEDUCTION

If you run your business out of your home, you can deduct those expenses associated with the part of your home used for the business, which would otherwise be nondeductible…

- **Equipment used in your home office,** such as computers, copiers, phones, furniture, chairs, desks and other items, are subject to generous deduction rules. Their total cost may be fully tax deductible when purchased under Tax Code Section 179 expensing rules. If you convert personally owned equipment to business use, the equipment cannot be expensed but it can be depreciated (using the lower of cost or fair market value at the time of conversion).

- **Commuting to a regular job may become deductible.** Travel between two work locations is tax deductible—so if your home qualifies as a work location, travel between it and other work sites (formerly nondeductible commuting) becomes deductible.

Other write-offs can include insurance, repairs and maintenance, utility bills and depreciation on that part of the home you own that is used as an office—a noncash expense that produces cash tax savings.

Deduction requirements: A home office must be used exclusively for business, as the primary place you conduct your business or as a place needed to maintain records for a business activity conducted elsewhere due to the lack of any other office. The home office needn't be an entire room—a portion of a room may qualify.

Safety: Take photos of the office or work area so that you can show an auditor who may inquire about it years later.

TAX-FAVORED BENEFITS

A sideline business can provide the same tax-favored benefits as a full-time business. *For instance…*

- **A solo 401(k) account** that you set up can receive up to the first $15,500 of business income ($20,500 from a person age 50 or above) plus 25% of additional amounts, up to $46,000 ($51,000 if age 50 or older) in total in 2008. That much income becomes tax free today while increasing future retirement wealth. Other kinds of retirement plans are available, too, such as Keogh plans and SIMPLE IRAs.

• **Health insurance** is 100% deductible when it's obtained through your own unincorporated business.

TRAVEL DEDUCTIONS

When you take a trip primarily for business, the cost of travel and lodging and 50% of meals is deductible even if the trip has a pleasure element. Only separate "pleasure" expenses (such as theater tickets) are nondeductible.

If you travel with someone else, the cost you would incur if traveling by yourself is still deductible—the extra cost for the additional person is not. But the extra cost may be slight. If a single room costs $100 and a double costs $120, you can deduct the $100.

SHIFTING INCOME

When you have your own business, you can hire children and other low-tax-bracket family members, and deduct their wages at your high-tax-bracket rate while having them taxed at their low bracket. They can then use the wages to fund Roth IRAs or deductible retirement savings plans, increasing their financial security.

LEGAL PROTECTION

You can protect yourself against the business's potential liabilities by organizing it as a limited liability company or a similar entity under your state's laws and by getting appropriate insurance. These measures shouldn't be complicated or expensive, but always consult legal and tax advisers before starting a business.

SECURITY AND HAPPINESS

The best benefits of a new business may be the additional financial freedom and personal satisfaction it provides—and it is entirely yours, to do with as you please.

More from Laurence I. Foster...

Don't Miss These Surprising Medical Expense Deductions

The IRS and courts have approved many surprising and unusual deductions for medical expenses. Keep these possible opportunities in mind when planning your tax strategies or preparing your tax return.

TOPPING THE HURDLE

Medical expenses for items and services prescribed by a doctor for a specific condition are deductible, but only to the extent that their total exceeds 7.5% of adjusted gross income (AGI), and 10% of AGI if you are subject to the alternative minimum tax. *To get over this hurdle, you can deduct "big ticket" items such as...*

• **Home improvements.** If you improve your home to mitigate a diagnosed medical ailment, the cost is deductible to the extent that it exceeds any resulting increase in the value of your home.

Example: Central air-conditioning to alleviate a respiratory condition. If you spend $12,000 putting it in, but it increases the value of your home by only $8,000, then you've got a legitimate $4,000 medical deduction.

To determine how much an improvement increases the value of your home, see a real estate appraiser. *Other examples...*

• A lap swimming pool—when swimming was prescribed by a doctor as treatment for a condition, and the individual was allergic to chemicals in the water of a public pool, and no other public pool was available.

• An attached garage, when a doctor advised the home owner to avoid cold winter air.

• An elevator for a person with a heart condition or arthritis.

Improvements to accommodate a *disability* are fully deductible without regard to any increase in value. *Included...*

• Modification or lowering of kitchen cabinets and counters.

• Certain bathroom modifications, including railings and support bars.

• Rampways into a home.

• Widening of doorways and halls.

• Grading the ground around a home to ease access to it.

Medically related improvements to a property you rent are fully deductible if you are not compensated for their cost by your landlord.

Example: On your doctor's advice, you install a bathroom on the ground floor of a house you rent to avoid having to climb stairs. Your landlord permits you to do so but does not pay any of the cost. You can deduct as a medical expense the full cost that you pay.

Operating costs, including electricity, maintenance and repair of air-conditioners, elevators and chair lifts, and other improvements that qualify for medical deduction also are 100% deductible.

• **Expenses paid for others.** You can deduct medical costs you pay for persons who qualify as your dependents. For tax years after December 31, 2004, the definition of a medical dependent was changed. It now includes married individuals even with their own dependents. There is no test for gross income. (See the *Working Families Tax Relief Act of 2004.) Examples...*

• A retired parent who doesn't live with you, when you pay more than half the parent's support—such as when the parent is in a nursing home.

• A person for whom you obtain a dependency exemption by filing Form 2120, *Multiple Support Declaration.* This enables a group of individuals who jointly support a person to obtain a dependency exemption and assign it to one among them, even when no one member of the group pays more than half of the recipient's support.

• A child after divorce, even when the dependency exemption for the child is claimed by your former spouse.

Rule: When either divorced spouse claims a dependency exemption for a child, each spouse can deduct medical expenses that each spouse actually pays for the child.

Note: Gifts of medical payments on behalf of anyone in any amount paid directly to health-care providers are not subject to gift tax.

• **Travel.** If you or a dependent must travel for medical reasons, the cost of travel and lodging is deductible as a medical expense. (The cost of meals generally is not deductible.) *Examples...*

• A person who was advised by a doctor to move to a different part of the country with an environment better for the person's medical condition found that he could claim a medical deduction for some moving costs. If you think that you have a similar situation, check with your accountant.

• Parents who sent a child to boarding school in Arizona to alleviate the child's respiratory ailment were allowed by the Tax Court to deduct the child's travel and room and board costs.

• The costs of attending a conference that presents information about a chronic disease affecting the taxpayer or a dependent are deductible.

• When one stays at a hospital or other medical facility, meal charges imposed by the facility may be deducted.

• In deducting medically related travel costs, airfares and other travel fares, including taxis, are deductible at their full cost. Driving in 2008 is deductible at 19 cents per mile for the first half of the year and 27 cents per mile for the second half of the year, or at actual recorded out-of-pocket cost if higher, with parking and tolls also deductible.

FREQUENTLY OVERLOOKED

Don't miss deductions for the cost of...

• **Equipment used to alleviate a medical condition,** such as portable air-conditioners, humidifiers and dehumidifiers—and their operating costs.

• **Weight-loss programs,** when prescribed as treatment for a specific medical condition such as high blood pressure.

• **Smoking cessation programs.**

• **Cosmetic surgery** when utilized to alleviate a medical condition rather than merely improve appearance.

Example: Hair transplant surgery to improve one's appearance is not deductible. But surgery to remove skin folds that remained after a formerly obese person lost a large amount of weight is deductible as part of the treatment for obesity.

• **A wig purchased on the advice of a physician** for the mental health of a patient who lost hair due to disease.

• **Clarinet lessons,** when prescribed to alleviate a child's overbite.

• **Lamaze** and other childbirth preparation classes.

• **A child's special education costs,** when on a doctor's recommendation you pay extra for a teacher who is specially qualified to work with children who have learning disabilities caused by mental or physical impairments. If the child is advised to board at a school providing special education, medical expenses may include the cost of tuition and room and board.

• **Psychoanalysis,** psychologist fees and psychiatric care costs.

• **Trained animals** used to alleviate disabilities.

Examples: Cats trained to react to sound for the deaf…seeing-eye dogs for the blind.

• **Special controls for automobiles,** such as hand controls instead of foot pedals.

• **Meals,** when special foods are prescribed by a doctor, to the extent that their cost is greater than regular foods.

• **Eyesight correction,** including contact lenses and related solutions and cleaners, eyeglasses, and laser surgery for sight correction.

• **Dental treatments,** including X-rays, fillings, braces, extractions and dentures (but not teeth whitening).

• **Blood sugar test kits** and other diagnostic devices for specific maladies.

• **Hearing aids** and special audio equipment attached to televisions, phones and other items to compensate for a hearing impairment.

• **Insurance premiums** used to cover medical care costs, including Medicare drug coverage.

Included: Insurance on contact lenses… other insurance that pays for prescription drugs.

• **Medicare Part B.** This is supplemental medical insurance. Premiums for it are a deductible medical expense.

• **Laboratory fees** incurred in receiving medical care or a diagnosis.

• **Acupuncture.**

For more information, see IRS Publication 502, *Medical and Dental Expenses*, available free at *www.irs.gov.* You might have a unique medical situation that could qualify for a deduction. Check with your tax adviser.

The Greatest Loopholes of All Time

Edward Mendlowitz, CPA, partner in the CPA firm WithumSmith+Brown, 1 Spring St., New Brunswick, NJ 08901. He is author of *The Adviser's Guide to Family Business Succession Planning.* American Institute of Certified Public Accountants.

With all these great tax-saving methods most everyone can uncover big money. *Here are some of the best loopholes I have encountered throughout my more than 40 years of working with taxes…*

***Loophole:* Convert a regular "taxable" IRA (individual retirement account) to a "nontaxable" Roth IRA** in a year in which you have business losses and very little income.

Advantage: You can use the business losses to offset taxable income created by converting a traditional IRA. The money in the Roth IRA and its income will then become tax free (unless withdrawn prematurely).

***Loophole:* Donate appreciated long-term stock in place of cash to all your favorite charities.**

When you do this, you can deduct the full fair market value of the shares and owe no capital gains tax on the stock's buildup in value since you bought it.

Example: You own 100 shares of stock, purchased 10 years ago for $15 per share. When you donate the shares, now worth $50 each, to charity, you deduct the full $5,000 fair market value—not your $1,500 cost. You also avoid capital gains tax on the $3,500 of appreciation.

Loophole: **Shelter business or freelance income with tax-deferred retirement plans.**

You can shelter income, whether from a full- or part-time job, in a retirement plan. For example, self-employed workers (including full-time workers who run sideline businesses) can contribute up to 20% of net business income to the Keogh and simplified employee pension (SEP) plans—up to $46,000 in 2008. (Corporate employees can contribute up to 25%.)

Strategy: Business owners and self-employed workers who are older than age 45 should consider setting up a defined-benefit plan that permits larger contributions than those available in defined-contribution plans.

Caution: Defined-benefit plans can be more expensive and less flexible than defined-contribution plans. Talk to your tax adviser about the pros and cons.

Double benefit: Maximize your overall contributions by setting up a 401(k) plan as well. The maximum deduction for a 401(k) plan in 2008 is $15,500 ($20,500 if age 50 or older), and no percentage limitations apply to the contributions for 401(k)s.

Example: You work full-time for a company but operate a sideline business. If you earn $22,000 from the business, you can contribute nearly all of this—$21,000—to retirement plans. You can put away $15,500 in a 401(k) plan, assuming you do not contribute to the company 401(k) plan, and $5,500 additional in another defined-contribution plan (25% of $22,000).

Loophole: **Avoid paying alternative minimum tax (AMT) by exercising some of your incentive stock options (ISOs)** each year instead of waiting until just before the expiration date to exercise all of them.

When you exercise ISOs, the difference between the fair market value of the stock and the exercise price is a "tax preference" item included in the AMT calculation if the stock is not sold in the year acquired.

Result: You may owe AMT for the year because of exercising the ISO.

Strategy: If you want to hold the stock, you can avoid the AMT by exercising small amounts of ISOs each year, just below the amount that would require you to pay the AMT.

Loophole: **Replace personal debt with a home-equity loan to maximize deductible interest payments.**

Interest paid on automobile loans, credit card charges and other personal debt is not deductible, but interest paid on home-equity loans is deductible on loan amounts of $100,000 or less. You can use the proceeds from a home-equity loan for any purpose, such as paying off personal loans—and still deduct the interest—as long as you are not subject to the AMT.

Loophole: **Use your IRA, 401(k) or pension plan money to buy rental real estate.**

How to do it: The property must be purchased directly by your retirement account (not in partnership with the plan participant). The plan can borrow funds, using the real estate and other plan assets as collateral, but then some of the real estate income will be taxed inside the plan.

Caution: By law, you cannot manage this property yourself. You need to hire a property manager to collect the rents and pay the mortgage, real estate taxes, utility bills, etc.

Benefits: Profits remain in the plan tax deferred. Any gains from the sale of the property are deferred until you begin taking distributions from the plan. However, those gains, like all plan distributions, are taxed at ordinary income rates, not capital gains rates.

Loophole: **Operate your own business as a cash-basis S corporation.**

In general, C corporations (except personal service corporations) with average annual sales for three years of more than $5 million cannot use cash accounting. Instead, they must use the accrual method of accounting, paying taxes on money not yet received. This rule does not apply to S corporations that have inventory.

Benefits: You defer tax until income is received, not when it's booked as accounts receivable.

Before You Move Cash Or Other Assets Out of Your Name

Many taxpayers in debt to the IRS think nothing of transferring assets to another family member to "protect" those assets from the IRS.

Problems: The IRS can take the position that you have engaged in a fraudulent conveyance and file a lawsuit against the person who is now in possession of your assets. A more immediate step the IRS can take is to impose a "nominee lien" on the person to whom the assets were transferred. A nominee lien is developed by the IRS by creating a lien document, without any court approval, which is then filed with the county clerk imposing another taxpayer's liability on the transferee's real and personal property. Before you transfer assets, speak to a knowledgeable tax professional.

Ms. X, Esq., a former IRS agent who is still well connected.

Addicted Gambler's Losses Are Deductible

Francis Gagliardi won a lottery paying $1.3 million per year for 20 years, and soon became a "pathological gambler." He won hundreds of thousands of dollars that the casinos reported to the IRS, but always re-bet his winnings until he lost them. On his tax return, he deducted losses matching his winnings, but because he kept no diary of losing wagers, the IRS disallowed most of his deduction.

Court: Both a psychiatrist and an expert on gambling mathematics testified that it was impossible for Gagliardi not to have lost more than he won—so the losses are deductible.

Francis M. Gagliardi, TC Memo 2008-10.

Better than Paper Receipts

Scan receipts into your computer, and store them in appropriate files. Electronic images are increasingly considered equivalent to paper records—even the IRS accepts them if you can show that you have controls, such as passwords, in place to prevent modification of your records. For easy storage, consider putting each year's worth of tax receipts on a CD—reducing needed storage space significantly.

Barbara Weltman, attorney based in Millwood, NY, and author of *J. K. Lasser's Small Business Taxes*. Wiley. She is publisher of the on-line newsletter *Big Ideas for Small Business*. Monthly. Free at *www.barbaraweltman.com*.

Turning Betting Losses into Business Losses

You may not have to be a full-time professional gambler to get a tax break from gambling losses. In a recent Tax Court decision (*James Castagnetta*, TC Summary Opinion 2006-24), the court ruled that an individual could deduct losses from horse race betting as business losses.

How: The taxpayer pursued the activity regularly and with continuity and operated it in a businesslike manner.

Essential: For any business loss to be deductible, the taxpayer must prove a profit motive. As long as you continue to try something new to make a profit, it is hard for the IRS to argue that you lacked a profit motive. It may be possible to sustain a tax-deductible loss from casino activity if you keep very accurate records, visit casinos on a regular basis and can establish via your records that you changed betting strategies in an effort to generate profits—even if you are not a "professional" gambler.

Ms. X, Esq., a former IRS agent who is still well connected.

Gamblers and The IRS—Keep The Most and Avoid Trouble

Wayne Hagendorf, an attorney and CPA with offices in Las Vegas and Los Angeles who specializes in estate planning and asset protection for business owners.

Gambling is a $50 billion business in this country, and the IRS must love it. Winnings are taxable and may be subject to withholding, and deductions for losses are restricted. *Here are some ways to make the most of both winning and losing…*

THE WINNERS

If you are lucky enough to have had a good year at the track, casino or other gambling venue, your winnings will have both a direct and an indirect impact on your taxes…

• **Direct impact.** Gambling winnings are taxable as ordinary income. This includes sweepstakes, lotteries and winnings through illegal betting (e.g., the office football pool or on-line poker—now a $10 billion industry).

Even if you *sell* the right to collect your winnings, you get no break. The IRS says that you received ordinary income in this case—not capital gains.

Example: Suppose that you win a state lottery payable over 25 years. After collecting your first-year share, you sell the right to your 24 other payments. The amount you get from the third party is ordinary income—just as it would be had you received the payments directly from the state.

Casinos and other venues must report gambling winnings to you—and to the IRS—on Form W-2G, *Certain Gambling Winnings*, when your winnings are more than the following amounts…

• $600 or more at one time if this is at least 300 times the amount wagered.

• $1,200 or more from bingo or a slot machine (regardless of the size of the wager).

• $1,500 or more from a keno game (net of the wager).

Income tax withholding: Winnings from any source are subject to mandatory withholding at the rate of 25% if they exceed $5,000 and the take is at least 300 times the amount wagered.

It's the total amount of the winnings that determines withholding. This is the case even if the purse is split between two or more winners and each winner receives less than the threshold amount for withholding.

Example: Two people buy a winning lottery ticket together for $1 and win $5,002. Withholding is required, even though each person received less than $5,000.

Caution: Watch out for increased withholding ("backup withholding"). If a winner gives a taxpayer identification number at the time of the winning, 25% will be withheld. If not, 28% will be withheld. This includes winnings from bingo, keno and slot machines.

For noncash winnings, such as an automobile, withholding is based on the fair market value of the item. *If the fair market value exceeds $5,000, there are two ways withholding on noncash items is figured…*

• The winner pays the withholding tax to the casino, lottery authority or other payer. The withholding rate is 25% of the value of the item minus the amount of the wager.

• The payer pays the withholding tax. The withholding rate is 33.33% of the value of the item minus the amount of the wager.

• **Indirect impact.** Gambling winnings are reported in full on your tax return. They increase your adjusted gross income (AGI), and this can adversely affect other items on your return. *It may...*

• Increase the amount of Social Security benefits subject to tax.

• Reduce itemized deductions for medical expenses, casualty and theft losses, and miscellaneous expenses.

• Prevent a Roth IRA conversion if gambling winnings push AGI over $100,000.

RESTRICTIONS ON LOSSES

Gambling losses are deductible to the extent of winnings and only as miscellaneous itemized deductions—so you must itemize to get any tax benefit from losses. But losses are not subject to the 2%-of-AGI floor that applies to most other miscellaneous write-offs.

Professional gamblers can treat losses as a business expense on Schedule C rather than as an itemized deduction on Schedule A.

The amount of deductible losses cannot exceed total winnings for the year. Thus, if you win $1,000, but lose $15,000 throughout the year, your total deduction for the year is only $1,000. The balance of your losses ($14,000) is lost forever and does not carry forward to be used in a future year.

Record keeping for losses: While winnings are reported by the casino or other payer to the IRS, it is up to you to keep track of your losses for the year. If you are a regular gambler, it's a good idea to keep a log or diary—written or electronic—tracking your betting activities. Records should show the date and type of wagering activity, the name and location of the gambling establishment, the names of other gamblers present if applicable, and the amounts won and lost. Retain all losing tickets for lottery games and bets at the track.

Suggestion: If you fail to do this, you can follow the lead of a couple who used their credit card, debit card, and bank statements showing cash withdrawals at a casino to help substantiate their losses (see *Traci A. Tomko*, TC Summary Opinion 2005-139).

PLANNING STRATEGIES

What can you do to make the most of your luck? As when you receive any income windfall, it is advisable to minimize taxes through tax-planning measures that include...

• **Charitable giving.** Reduce your taxable income by being generous to worthy causes. Note, however, that your charitable contribution deduction for the year for cash donations is limited to 50% or less of AGI.

• **AGI planning.** Keep AGI low by using salary reductions where possible—maximize contributions to your 401(k) and flexible spending account (FSA). Realize capital losses in excess of capital gains up to $3,000. Take advantage of above-the-line deductions (e.g., traditional IRA contributions).

For sizable purses, consider using "partnerships" or trusts for family income splitting. This will allow payments to be spread among family members and, where applicable, taxed at lower rates. Reduce oral partnerships— loose agreements to split winnings—to a written agreement before collecting the prize money to avoid fighting among the parties later on.

Important: While tax planning may be a prime concern after a sizable win, asset protection, such as by using an LLC (to hide your identity) or a Nevada Spendthrift Trust (which gives the trustee control of the money), should also be considered. Publicized winners, such as those who win a big state lottery, often become targets of the unscrupulous. Work only with trustworthy advisers—those you already know or for whom you have sound recommendations.

Also take into account state and local income taxes, if applicable, when planning.

Smart People Fall for Tax Scams, Too

Becky Schmitz, enrolled agent, certified tax resolution specialist and owner, Centsable Accounting, 2680 Overland Ave., Billings, MT 59102, *www.centsableaccounting.com*. She was named the 2006 Top Practitioner by the American Society of Tax Problem Solvers.

The Internal Revenue Code is filled with legitimate ways to reduce your tax bill. Even so, many people look for more aggressive tax shelters—and the Internet has opened a whole new world for tax scammers in search of prey.

If you go beyond tried-and-true tax-reduction techniques, such as deducting home mortgage interest or making pretax 401(k) contributions, you may make yourself vulnerable to con artists. Not only might you pay for bogus advice, you could wind up owing interest and perhaps penalties and back taxes.* *Here are tax schemes—new and old—to watch out for...*

- **Cheating accountants.** While there are many conscientious tax preparers, there also are plenty willing to inflate your personal or business expenses, encourage you to take false deductions and/or include excessive exemptions and apply impermissible credits.

You may think it's wonderful to have a tax preparer who is willing to "bend the rules" for you, but returns prepared by third parties are subject to the same scrutiny as self-prepared returns—and you still are responsible for their accuracy. Moreover, the IRS keeps a list of "problem preparers"—their returns get extra attention.

Don't work with tax preparers who promise you substantial tax savings that you haven't achieved in the past.

Example: I had a client who was advised by a tax preparer to set up a fake business so he could take substantial business deductions. The taxpayer was issued a hefty

*If you think that you have been a victim of a tax scam, call the IRS at 800-829-0433.

refund from the IRS, and the tax preparer took a portion of the refund as payment. The IRS ultimately audited the taxpayer's return and assessed him penalties and interest on top of the balance due. The taxpayer attempted to get money back from the crooked tax preparer, but the IRS had already issued the preparer a cease-and-desist order and the tax preparer had filed for bankruptcy. The taxpayer ended up paying far more than he had gotten back as a refund.

- **Bogus abatements.** With this gimmick, a genuine IRS form (Form 843, *Claim for Refund and Request for Abatement*) is misused. People file these forms, claiming to deserve a refund for paying too much tax in the past. In truth, this form doesn't even apply to income tax—it is meant for refunds of employment, gift, estate and excise taxes. By filing such a form incorrectly, you're inviting an audit by the IRS.

- **Offshore tax havens.** Many tax scams involve "hiding" income in a foreign bank, brokerage account or certain types of trust, but moving money offshore doesn't excuse you from your responsibility to pay income tax. Indeed, the IRS has beefed up its enforcement efforts in this area. The post-9/11 security environment makes it much more difficult to keep foreign financial maneuvers from detection.

- **Bogus charities.** Donating cash or other assets to charity is among the long-standing tax-reduction tactics available to taxpayers who itemize deductions. There are limits, though.

For example, John Johnson can't simply create the Johnson Foundation and then write checks to this self-directed organization and take deductions. To be deductible, a charitable donation must be made to a tax-exempt organization recognized as such by the IRS.

The tax-exempt organization, in turn, must engage in qualifying activities. If the entire venture is a sham and you retain control of the money for personal use, deductions will be disallowed—and you could face criminal charges.

URBAN LEGENDS

As absurd as they sound, these age-old pitches still dupe many people…

• **Frivolous arguments.** In this rip-off, taxpayers are told that there are constitutional grounds for claiming that paying taxes is voluntary. You might be led to believe that the Sixteenth Amendment—the one that gives Congress the right to collect income taxes—was never ratified.

There is no validity to such contentions. The IRS has been collecting income tax for nearly a century and will continue to do so.

• **Zero wages.** Here, you're provided with a fake IRS Form 1099-MISC (*Miscellaneous Income*) that replaces the real form you received. You're told to attach the substitute form, which shows little or no income, to your tax return.

On the substitute form is a supposed "correction" of information already reported to the IRS. Not only will the IRS not accept corrections showing zero wages, but such a submission is likely to generate an audit.

The scammer may charge an enormous amount for the fake form. One client paid more than $12,000.

• **Zero returns/zero gains.** In this type of fraud, a promoter advises you to enter nothing but zeros on your federal tax return. Then, of course, you'll owe no tax. In a variation on this scam, you fill out page one of Form 1040, computing your adjusted gross income (AGI). Then you deduct your entire AGI amount on Schedule A by writing, "No gain realized."

• **Employment tax.** If you are a business owner, it's your responsibility to see that income tax, Social Security taxes and Medicare taxes are withheld from employees' paychecks and paid to the proper taxing authorities.

Don't be fooled by promoters hawking an incorrect interpretation of the tax code, which states that withholding is not required. If you attempt to evade your withholding obligations, the IRS may be able to seize your assets and put your company out of business.

Timely Strategies to Deal with the Horrible Housing Market

Julian Block, Esq., tax attorney and nationally syndicated columnist, 3 Washington Sq., Larchmont, NY 10538. He is author of *The Home Seller's Guide to Tax Savings: Simple Ways for Any Seller to Lower Taxes to the Legal Minimum*, available from the author at *www.julianblocktaxexpert.com*.

Are you ready to move, but worried about selling your house in today's brutal market? *Keep these points in mind…*

• **Selling a house is tough today and likely to get tougher.**

• **Tax breaks can offer you an exit strategy.**

After years of sharp gains, home prices are retreating. In the first quarter of 2008, the S&P/Case-Shiller US National Home Price Index fell more than 10%, compared with the first quarter of 2007.

In some areas of the US, prices have fallen more steeply.

Worse to come: As foreclosures mount, more and more houses are coming onto the market. The National Association of Realtors already has reported that the supply of unsold homes is the largest on record.

While more houses are being offered for sale, tightening by mortgage lenders has taken many prospective buyers out of the market. With less demand and more supply, home prices are likely to continue to drop.

Bottom line: This may not be a good time to sell a house. Although the future is unknown, it might take two or three years for home prices to recover.

Strategy: Instead of selling now, convert your house to rental property. You'll still have up to three years to sell your house and use the generous tax breaks for home sellers. *Here's how to do it…*

UP WITH RENTALS

As mentioned, mortgage lenders have tightened their standards. This tightening is reverberating all the way to the residential rental market—in a way that you might be able to take advantage of if you are a home owner.

Subpar results from subprime loans: In the past few years, millions of loan applicants with poor credit ratings received so-called subprime mortgages. Many of these borrowers have been delinquent with payments.

Therefore, lenders are less likely to make home loans to marginal borrowers these days. Many of those would-be home owners, unable to obtain mortgages, are being forced to rent houses or apartments.

Result: With more demand, rental rates are firming—in some areas, they're moving up. This may be a better time to be a landlord than to be a home seller.

So, if you rent your current home to tenants, where will you live? Shop among the many homes now on the market. A poor time to be a seller can be a good time to be a buyer.

As long as you have a solid credit rating and enough cash for a down payment, you probably can get a mortgage loan for most of the purchase price. This will allow you to move, perhaps to change locales…to be closer to family…to downsize…or even to upsize to a more luxurious home, if that's your goal, without taking a bath on your current home.

RESIDENCE TAX BREAK

Even after you convert your home to rental property, you still can qualify for a home-owner's tax break. Rental markets are local. To see if you are likely to benefit by taking advantage of this strategy, contact your local landlords' association and ask what the market is in your area.

How it works: If you sell your principal residence, you can exclude a capital gain up to $250,000. For married couples filing a joint tax return (and certain surviving spouses), the exclusion goes up to $500,000.

Required: You must have owned the house and used it for your principal residence for at least two years of the five-year period ending on the sale date.

Loophole: **Those two years do not have to be immediately before the sale.** You can rent the house for a while, but for less than three years, and you would still qualify for the exclusion.

Example: Paul and Paula Smith own a house where they've lived for 10 years. They have three young children, so they would like to move to a larger place.

However, they fear that they won't get a good price for their house. On December 15, 2008, they rent out their house, thus converting it to investment property. (The start date for the exclusion is the day you rent out your residence.)

Deadline: In this scenario, the Smiths have until December 15, 2011, to sell their house. By that time, they may get a better price than they would get today. If they sell by this date, they will qualify for the home-sale exclusion.

Counting the days: Assume that the Smiths sell on December 15, 2011. The five-year period before the sale will run from December 15, 2006, to December 15, 2011.

The Smiths will have owned the house for the entire five years, so they will pass the ownership test.

In addition, the Smiths will have used it as a principal residence for two of those five years—from December 15, 2006, to December 15, 2008. This will pass the use-of-house test.

Warning: Under new law, gain on non-personal use of a home (such as rental or vacation use) after 2009, cannot be excluded from income and cannot be sheltered by the exclusion.

TALLYING THE TAX BILL

If you follow this strategy, be aware of a quirk in the Tax Code.

How it works: At the time a residence is converted to rental property, the home gets a new tax basis. This new basis will be whichever is lower, the owner's current basis or the fair market value.

Strategy: You want your basis to be as high as possible, because with a higher basis, the home will generate lower profit on a sale, and more depreciation deductions while the property is a rental. Have a knowledgeable real estate broker provide a timely appraisal in writing, showing the market value on the conversion date to support your basis for future tax calculations. The appraisal will help to counter a possible IRS argument that the residence was worth less on the conversion date than what you paid for it.

DOUBLE TAX BREAK

The Smiths may decide to pay the tax on the remaining unsheltered $132,000 gain. Assuming current tax rates are still in effect, their $32,000 in depreciation deductions will be recaptured at a 25% tax rate, and the other $100,000 will be taxed at 15%, as a long-term capital gain.

But they don't have to sell *at all*.

Loophole: **In this example, the Smiths have been using the house as investment property.** Therefore, the house qualifies for a tax-deferred exchange under Section 1031 of the Tax Code. (Tax-deferred exchanges must not involve personal residences.)

To exchange properties, you don't have to make a direct swap. Instead, most swaps today are multi-party deferred exchanges, often involving the services of a qualified intermediary.

In a typical exchange, you find a buyer for your property and close the sale. The proceeds go to the intermediary, who puts the money into an escrow account.

After you transfer your property, you have 45 days to identify potential replacement property, in writing, to the intermediary. Several properties may be identified, so you're covered in case an intended acquisition falls through.

You have 180 days from the time you relinquish your property to actually close a deal for replacement property. After you have finalized the replacement purchase, the intermediary uses the money held in escrow to buy the replacement property.

You've disposed of one property and acquired another. As long as you have received neither cash nor debt reduction, capital gains taxes are deferred.

Strategy: Instead of paying tax on $132,000, the Smiths can have that portion of the sales proceeds collected by a qualified intermediary. A qualified intermediary can be any party with no family or business relationship to the seller. Then the Smiths can identify replacement investment property within 45 days. A letter to the intermediary can serve this purpose.

Reminder: The replacement property must be used as investment property. The Smiths can't live there.

Within 180 days of the sale of their house, the Smiths can direct the intermediary to use the $132,000 to buy the replacement investment property, which they rent out.

Result: No tax will be due on the sale, thanks to the use of both the home-sale exclusion and a tax-deferred exchange.

6

Career Coach

Success Secrets from Mike Wallace, J.K. Rowling and More...

ow did Mike Wallace of *60 Minutes* become one of TV's most celebrated investigative reporters? How did Mary Higgins Clark become one of the world's highest-paid writers? How did Diane von Furstenberg come to head a multimillion-dollar fashion empire? Certainly they all have talent, but plenty of talented people never reach the top. Talent leads to extraordinary success only when it is paired with smart decision making. As J.K. Rowling wrote in *Harry Potter and the Chamber of Secrets* (Scholastic), "It is our choices...that show what we truly are, far more than our abilities."

How do successful people make the right choices and manage to see things through? *By doing the following...*

1. Get more credit for accomplishments. We might get a bonus or a promotion for an idea that makes our employer money, but most of the spoils go to the company. Capturing a significant share of those gains for ourselves can mean the difference between a solid career and a hugely successful one.

Example: Michael Flatley, star of the hit Irish step-dancing show *Riverdance*, left in 1995 to start his own show, *Lord of the Dance*. He had seen the money other people were making from his dancing and risked his savings to make those profits his. He gives his net worth now as close to half a billion dollars.

2. Stand out from the pack. Doing what everyone else is doing rarely leads to extraordinary success. Making the leap from talented to spectacularly successful often involves a decision to take the untrodden road.

Example: Shoe designer Kenneth Cole spent his entire advertising budget for 1986

Dyan Machan, an award-winning financial journalist, based in Ridgewood, NJ. She is researching a forthcoming book about decision-making.

on an ad about AIDS that ran on billboards and in 23 magazines. His advisers warned him that it could kill his company to be associated with the disease. Instead, the ad campaign generated so much buzz that it helped him stand out in the crowded shoe market.

3. Discover what is really important. Sometimes a crisis or tragedy can force us to reevaluate our lives.

Example: In the 1950s and early 1960s, Mike Wallace made a good living reporting the news, hosting game shows and appearing in commercials. Only after his 19-year-old son, Peter, died in 1962 did he devote himself to investigative reporting. The tragedy convinced him to make a change despite the financial risks.

4. Find a role model for facing fear. Diane von Furstenberg, founder of a hugely successful clothing company, reminds herself that her mother survived a Nazi concentration camp. Compared with that, what is there to be afraid of in a career decision?

Successful people tend to understand that it isn't our failures we'll regret at the end of our lives—it's the opportunities we let slip away.

Example: Drew Nieporent, founding chef of famed New York restaurant Nobu, learned to take risks because his parents could not. His father talked for years about buying New York City real estate but was too scared to take the plunge. His indecision cost him millions of dollars in potential profits. Nieporent decided that when he had an idea he believed in, he would act.

5. Know what's worth the risk for you. Successful people don't always know that their crucial decisions will work out when they make them, but they are willing to take the risks to pursue their dreams.

Example: Singer Sting had a burning desire to be a musician, so he left a secure job with Inland Revenue (England's IRS) for a job as a teacher. The shorter hours gave him time to pursue his music.

6. Remember, there are second chances. The old saying about opportunity knocking only once isn't always correct. If we work hard and interact with a wide circle of people,

we might get multiple shots at making life-changing decisions.

Example: Mystery writer Mary Higgins Clark's first book, a biographical novel about George Washington, was a commercial disaster. She determined that thrillers sold better and got back to work. She now makes more than $12 million per book.

Billionaire's One-Word Secret to Success

Sir Richard Branson, chairman of Virgin Group, a London-based conglomerate of more than 350 companies. In 2007, *Time* listed him among the world's 100 most influential people. He is author of *Screw It, Let's Do It: Lessons in Life*. Virgin.

English entrepreneur Sir Richard Branson founded Virgin, a hugely profitable mail-order record retailer, while still in his 20s. He launched Virgin Atlantic, a successful airline, in his 30s. Now, at 57, Branson has expanded the Virgin Group to include literally hundreds of other businesses, including a mobile phone service provider and Virgin America, his new US-based airline.

Branson is known for his adventuring as much as for his business savvy. He has made headlines by racing speedboats across the Atlantic and attempting to circle the Earth in a hot-air balloon.

We spoke with Branson about his success strategies for business and life...

•**Your employees call you "Dr. Yes" because of your propensity to greenlight ideas. What's the advantage of this go-for-it mentality, and what are the risks?** The principal advantage is that it makes life more interesting. Saying yes means there's always a new challenge. Saying yes also spreads the risks. Virgin started as a music business, but because we said yes to new opportunities, we now have more than 350 other businesses around the world. That's fortunate because the music industry is on the decline.

The negative side of being a "Dr. Yes" is that you always are in danger of spreading yourself too thin. This can be overcome, but only if you are good at delegating. You cannot do it all on your own.

● **You are known for taking chances, but you say that you don't believe in gambling.** How do you define the line between sensible risk taking and foolish gambling? I believe in making bold moves— but I also believe in making sure that my downside is protected. Let me give you an example. When we were turning our music business into an airline, we struck a deal with Boeing that allowed us to lease a plane for 12 months. That way, if we had miscalculated and travelers were not so fed up with the other airlines that they would fly with us, the most we could have lost was the $10 million rental cost. Because our music business was then making $20 million a year, there was no way that the airline could destroy us.

● **You wrote that you will never say, "I can't do this, because I don't know how to."** What's the secret to doing things you don't know how to do? When I started Virgin in the 1970s, I chose that name because I was a virgin in business. If I had waited until I was an expert, I might have missed the opportunity. You don't have to be a pilot to run an airline…or an astronaut to run an aerospace company. When I enter a new industry, I spend three months completely immersing myself in it. Then I find the best people I can find, trust their input and learn what I need to know as I go.

● **You also write that you will never let a silly rule stop you.** How can you tell what's a silly rule and what isn't? A silly rule is any rule that isn't a safety rule—a rule that protects people from injury. Of course, you also have to follow the law. All other rules should be broken. Most rules only reflect the ways things always have been done, not the way they are best done.

● **What's an example of how you have changed the way things have always been done?** I noticed that check-in desks at airports always look awful. There is no reason that check-in desks have to look so unappealing—that's just the way it is. I decided that Virgin America's check-in desks would be beautiful, with a unique design and fresh flowers.

● **You stress the importance of making work fun.** How can people make their careers more fun? A successful businessperson might spend 90% of his waking life at work, so if you're trying to balance work and fun, fun will always lose. It's better to make sure your work is something enjoyable and entertaining.

One way to do that is to select a job that provides the proper amount of human interaction for you. Some people are not particularly sociable, so they will never be happy in management or sales. Other people are happy only when they are around other people, so they won't be happy sitting in front of a computer. And all this is true no matter how much money they make.

● **You tell a story in your book about a childhood attempt to make money by growing Christmas trees.** Rabbits ate all the seedlings, yet you still turned a profit by shooting the rabbits and selling them to butcher shops. The moral of the story was the importance of flexibility in life and business. What's your advice for identifying new opportunities? The first thing they teach you in business school is to specialize in what you know. At Virgin, we believe the opposite. Our approach is to try something, and if it doesn't work, then try something else…and if it *does* work, try something else anyway. I find opportunities by identifying things that aren't working well now.

I entered the airline business because I had companies all around the world and found that traveling between them on the existing airlines was a dire experience. I thought that other travelers must find it a dire experience as well, so I set up an airline to serve them. When you board our planes, you'll feel as though you've stepped into the most beautiful room imaginable, with mood lighting and the most comfortable leather seats—even in economy class.

● **In your book, you warn that regrets can weigh us down.** How do you stop that from happening? I believe that as long as I have learned something from my mistakes, they are useful experiences. Even if things go horribly wrong in life, we don't have to let it get to us. Real success is having people we love in our lives—family and friends. If we have this, then we have everything.

Secrets to Finding A Job When You're Over 50

Richard Nelson Bolles, a leader in the field of career development for more than 30 years. He is based in the San Francisco Bay Area. He is author of *What Color Is Your Parachute? 2008*. Ten Speed. The book is in its 35th edition and has sold more than nine million copies. *www.jobhuntersbible.com*.

Finding a job is always a challenge—a typical bout of unemployment lasts at least four months. A job search can be particularly frustrating for those who are over age 50. Some employers don't like to hire older workers, for fear that they'll lack energy…retire soon…strain the company's pension or health-care plan…or demand hefty salaries. Laws designed to protect older job applicants from age-based discrimination are relatively ineffective.

Older job hunters need not become discouraged, however. Though rejection is an unavoidable part of the job-search process, there are plenty of employers who are happy to hire workers of any age if they are qualified to do the work that the employers need.

Job applicants over age 50 can learn to minimize the concerns that some employers have about hiring older employees while emphasizing the advantages of age. *Smart ways to do this…*

● **Show enthusiasm.** Employers often worry that older hires have lost their energy and enthusiasm for work. The best way to show that you are not the type to coast through your remaining years until retirement is to display some passion during the interview.

Review your skills and job-related interests prior to the interview. Make a list of your "transferable skills"—the abilities that would be useful in virtually any job.

Are you an expert at analyzing data? Gathering information? Leading teams? Do you love solving problems? Helping people? Building things? Being creative? Review this list immediately before your interview, and you're more likely to exude enthusiasm.

Also, lean forward slightly in your chair when the interviewer is speaking. Respond with an intelligent question about some detail. Your age is irrelevant if you convey energy and enthusiasm. Every employer is looking for someone like that.

● **Take advantage of your large grapevine.** Jobs generally aren't found through the want ads. They're found by tapping our contacts—the networks of friends, acquaintances and colleagues who like and respect us.

Older workers have a major advantage here because after decades in the workplace and community, there might be hundreds of people who know them and their abilities. This grapevine might include business owners, division presidents and others in a position to offer them work. Younger people typically know mostly other young people in low-level jobs.

Even the contacts who are not in a position to offer work can open doors and arrange meetings with those who can. At the very least, your contacts can provide advice or background on a company or industry. Don't underestimate the value of background information—the more you know, the more attractive a candidate you become.

● **Don't overlook small companies.** If a firm has only a handful of employees, it's often possible to just walk in the door and chat with the owner—this isn't feasible with large corporations.

Don't immediately volunteer the fact that you're looking for work. Instead, ask intelligent questions about the industry or company. Take no more than 10 minutes of the owner's time. He/she may even offer you a job out of the blue.

Example: I know a former librarian who walked into every business on a busy commercial street and started a conversation with each business owner about what his/her company did. These were mostly clothing stores, lawyers' offices, etc. By the time she reached the end of the street, she had three job offers.

Older people do particularly well with this walk-in-the-door strategy because their curiosity is less likely to be viewed with suspicion—and they're more likely to find common ground when they encounter older company owners.

•**Tell yourself this is just like dating.** It's easy to feel desperate when you're over 50 and out of work, but desperation makes job seekers feel like job beggars, and that will hurt your chances of landing a job.

A job interview isn't just a chance for an employer to size you up—it's also a chance for you to size up the employer. Try to feel as though you're on a first date, and you're trying to decide if you want to "go steady." The final decision is as much up to you as it is to the interviewer. Job applicants who adopt this attitude have more confidence and a greater sense of self-worth, which vastly improves their odds.

•**Watch to see the time frame of the questions the employer is asking.** It is very favorable to you if these questions are more and more about the present and future ("How would you handle the following type of problem?"…"Where do you see yourself three years from now?") instead of the past ("What have you done at previous jobs?").

If the interview doesn't seem to be progressing from questions about the past to questions about the present and future, try to steer the discussion toward what you intend to do for this company in the future.

Example: "Yes, I did help XYZ Corporation launch its Widget product line—and I know that your company expects to start two new product lines in the next 18 months. Let me tell you how I might help with those new projects…"

•**Don't ramble.** Older people sometimes speak for longer than they realize. This will raise concerns that you might have trouble focusing on deadlines.

Keep each interview answer to between 20 seconds and two minutes in length for each question the employer asks. Practice speaking in two-minute stretches before the interview so that you get a good feel for how long this is. *If you have more to say after two minutes, conclude with, "I could say more if you wish…"*

•**Play up the positive stereotypes.** There always will be some employers who judge job applicants based on age, perhaps without even realizing they're doing so. Play up the positive aspects of the older-employee stereotypes. Older workers are generally considered loyal, responsible, hardworking and dependable.

Demonstrate that you have these virtues by how you conduct the interview. If you want to claim that you're dependable, show up on time or ahead of time. If you want to claim that you are thorough, be sure to find out as much as you can about the company before you go into the interview.

Helpful: Always send a thank-you note. Ideally, it should be e-mailed immediately, followed by a printed version sent through the mail. Most job hunters ignore this advice, so you will stand out from the crowd if you send thank-you notes to everyone you met that day.

Get Your Graduate Degree On-Line from A Top University

Thomas Nixon, coauthor of *Bears' Guide to Earning Degrees by Distance Learning, 16th ed.,* Ten Speed, based in Fresno, CA. He is founder of CollegeoftheWeek.com, an e-mail service showcasing schools, and featured columnist for About.com's Continuing Education Web site (*adulted.about.com*), where he writes about on-line learning, accreditation and educational programs.

Only a handful of universities granted graduate degrees over the Internet five years ago. Today, on-line graduate school programs number well into the hundreds and include some of the world's best-known universities. On-line study is attractive for would-be grad students who don't want to leave careers, families and homes to return to campus.

HOW ON-LINE PROGRAMS WORK

It's generally more difficult to get into programs at traditional schools than ones specializing in distance learning. However, entrance requirements are similar to those of on-site programs—strong college transcripts and scores on tests, such as GMATs and GREs. Many master's programs are moving away from requiring essays and references.

On-line courses are as academically rigorous as those taken on campus. On-line grad students typically "attend" classes by watching a video feed over the Internet, either in real time or by accessing a stored file. Exams are sometimes administered at a high school or college in your area. (Of course, you do have to leave home for these.)

The degrees earned are the same ones awarded to students who attend in person. No difference is noted on the diploma or anywhere else.

Important: Choose a school that is accredited by one or more of the agencies listed on the Web site of the Council for Higher Education Accreditation (*www.chea.org*, click on "Databases and Directories," then "CHEA Recognized Accrediting Organizations Directory"). For discussion groups of legitimate, accredited on-line distance learning programs, go to *www.degreeinfo.com*.

On-line degrees typically cost the same amount per credit as on-campus programs, but on-line students save on room, board and travel, and expand their options to include distant universities that may offer quality educations for far less than local schools.

The downside is the lack of college atmosphere—networking and studying with other students, attending lectures by guest speakers and chatting with professors. Some on-line programs try to replicate these experiences through on-line access to professors and classmates or by organizing groups of students who can meet in person.

MBA PROGRAMS

• **Duke University Fuqua School of Business–Cross Continent program.** Fuqua's program is not 100% on-line—students spend nine weeks on campus during the two-year program. (919-660-7804, *www.fuqua.duke.edu*)

• **Indiana University Kelley School of Business** consistently ranks among the 20 best MBA programs in the US. (877-785-4713, *www.kd.iu.edu*)

• **Penn State University MBA program.** This is a well-designed on-line program from a well-known university. (800-252-3592, *www.worldcampus.psu.edu*)

• **Edinburgh Business School.** Though the school is based in Scotland, MBAs from Edinburgh are well-respected by American employers. If you have extensive work experience, you might not even need a bachelor's degree to attend. Tuition for the entire program is less than $15,000. (011-44-131-451-3090, *www.ebsmba.com*)

Note: British schools are not accredited by US accreditation agencies. Instead, they receive a "Royal Charter."

ENGINEERING AND COMPUTER SCIENCE PROGRAMS

• **Carnegie Mellon School of Computer Science, Distance Education.** Software engineering and information technology degrees. (412-268-5067, *www.distance.cmu.edu*)

•**Rochester Institute of Technology Online.** Highly regarded RIT offers a wide range of on-line graduate degrees, including information technology, software development and telecommunications engineering. (800-225-5748, *www.distancelearning.rit.edu*)

•**Stanford Center for Professional Development** offers electrical and mechanical engineering, management science and computer science degrees. (650-725-3000, *scpd.stanford.edu*)

MASTERS OF EDUCATION

•**Drexel University e-Learning Program** offers an on-line MS in higher education. (877-215-0009, *www.drexel.com/field_of_studyeducation*)

•**University of Illinois, Urbana-Champaign,** offers an on-line MS in curriculum, technology and education reform. (217-244-3315, *cter.ed.uiuc.edu*)

MASTERS OF SOCIAL WORK PROGRAMS

•**Florida State University Online MSW Program** was among the first MSWs to be offered on-line. (800-378-9550, *ssw.fsu.edu/index*)

•**University of North Dakota MSW Program** combines lectures and discussion. It also includes a fieldwork component. (877-450-1842, *www.conted.und.edu/ddp*)

The One Simple Habit That Leads To Success

Michael Masterson, publisher of *Early to Rise* (*www.earlytorise.com*), a free e-zine with advice on wealth-building and career success, Delray Beach, FL. He is author of several books, including *Seven Years to Seven Figures*. Wiley.

In the past 30 years, I have started dozens of successful businesses, including two that grew to more than $100 million in revenues. The single habit that has been invaluable to my success is getting to work one hour earlier than everyone else.

EARLY TO RISE

"Early to rise" is not an absolute mandate for success (Thomas Edison was a night owl), but most successful people I know get to work before their colleagues. Getting to work early provides you with quiet time that can be profitably spent before the rest of the world starts working. Arriving early also sends a strong message to colleagues and bosses that you are on top of your game. Early birds are viewed as energetic, organized and ambitious. People who arrive late and leave late look as if they're not in control.

Arriving early will have a significant and enduring effect on your career only if you use that extra hour to accomplish something important. *Here's how to make the most of it...*

DON'T PLAN YOUR DAY IN THE MORNING

Over the years, I have found it much more effective to plan my next day's tasks at the end of each day. That way, I can begin the next day by focusing on something important.

When planning each day, ask yourself, "Of all the things I must do tomorrow, which are the three or four that will best help me achieve my most important long-term goals?" Don't allow yourself to say, "Everything is very important," because everything isn't. I limit my selection to three or four tasks and then highlight them in my daily planner. Finally, I select one task to attack first thing the next morning.

FOCUS ON GOALS

When I arrive at work—usually between 6:30 and 7:00 am—I close my door (to prevent interruptions) and get to work on my most important goal. I know that focusing on what is important will have a profoundly positive effect on my future.

One hour a day, subtracting weekends and a two-week vacation, is about 250 hours a year. It's possible to accomplish many career-changing objectives in that time. *Sample goals...*

•**A great new product idea you want to develop.**

• **The clever marketing plan you want to test.**

• **High-level networking activities you want to engage in.**

• **A financing proposal you have been meaning to create**.

HOW I SPENT MY HOUR

The first thing I did when I started getting to work early was write a book about wealth, which I had been meaning to write for 10 years. At 500 words a day—a comfortable pace for me, since I was writing about something I was familiar with—I wrote a 60,000-word book (288 pages) in just over six months. That book went on to become a bestseller, and it encouraged me to write three more books over the next several years.

AVOID DISTRACTIONS

Don't listen to the radio or make any unnecessary phone calls.

Don't even open your e-mail. If you spend the extra hour in the morning responding to e-mails, you'll end up wasting time and energy on insignificant matters, including things that you probably shouldn't get involved in.

Dealing with Difficult People at Work

To get along with a self-centered coworker, try these techniques.

• **Butter him/her up.** Compliment him into not being so difficult.

• **Let him be the center of attention.** Self-absorbed coworkers tend to be below-average performers, but they may do more than their share of the work when they can show off.

• **Keep a sense of humor.** Self-centered workers can be a pain, but if you keep a sense of humor, they can begin to seem entertaining.

Psychology Today, 115 E. 23rd St., New York City 10010.

Career Smarts

After you are warned or suspended for an infraction at work, use the *three-contact rule* to develop a more positive relationship with your boss. Pick three reasons to ask for your supervisor's advice each week for at least three weeks. Choose a safe subject on which you will have no problem following whatever advice he/she gives. Ask the supervisor's opinion, be receptive to it, follow the advice—and be sure to let him know later that you appreciated the advice and followed it. By doing this, you should convince the supervisor that he can work with you, despite the earlier disciplinary action.

Richard C. Busse, Esq., senior partner, Busse & Hunt, plaintiff's employment law firm, Portland, OR, and author of Fired, Laid-Off or Forced Out! *Sphinx.*

Your Career

It is better to work for a bad boss at a good company than for a good boss at a bad company.

Reasons: A good company's leaders will eventually identify and get rid of a bad boss, and you may be rewarded for staying. And the experience you get at a good company will look better on a résumé.

BusinessWeek, 1221 Avenue of the Americas, New York City 10020.

To Stand Out in Meetings...

Use assertive language in meetings. Don't ask to ask a question. Make sure everyone can hear you. Look at others as you speak, not at your notes. Support people with whom you agree—to show you are a team player.

Barbara Pachter, president, Pachter & Associates, workplace communication consultants, Cherry Hill, NJ.

Keep Business Meetings Under Control

If you are the one in charge and one of the participants is talking too much or causing the meeting to be sidetracked, break in when there is a pause, compliment the speaker or thank him for his contribution and then move the meeting along with a transitional phrase.

Examples: "Let's put it aside for now" …"Let's talk more about this at our next meeting"…"Let's stick to the agenda so we can finish on time."

If you are not running the meeting, it may not be appropriate to try to move things along—except perhaps by introducing a more relevant topic if things go very far off track.

Peggy Post, great-granddaughter-in-law of etiquette pioneer Emily Post and spokesperson, The Emily Post Institute, Burlington, VT. *www.emilypost. com.* Her latest book is *Excuse Me, But I Was Next… How to Handle the Top 100 Manners Dilemmas.* HarperCollins.

Increase Your Chances Of Getting the Job

Contestants who perform later in competitions are rated more positively by judges than those who perform earlier. Known as the "serial position effect," this can be applied to daily life.

Example: When scheduling a job interview, ask to be one of the last candidates seen to increase your chances of getting the job.

Wändi Bruine de Bruin, PhD, research faculty, department of social and decision sciences, Carnegie Mellon University, Pittsburgh, and leader of a study of singing and ice-skating contests, published in *Acta Psychologica.*

If Another Company Wants You…

If you get a job offer from another company, negotiate a counteroffer with your current employer only if you are seriously thinking of leaving the company. Be clear about what would entice you to stay, such as a raise, a different work assignment or a promotion.

If you accept your current company's counteroffer: Be prepared to work harder and demonstrate your loyalty—your employer will expect to see results.

Steve Gross, worldwide partner, Mercer Human Resource Consulting, Philadelphia.

 ## The Art of Compromise

Sonya Hamlin, president, Sonya Hamlin Communications, New York City, trains corporate executives, trial lawyers and business school students to communicate effectively. She is author of *How to Talk So People Listen: The Real Key to Job Success* (HarperCollins) and *What Makes Juries Listen Today* (Glasser LegalWorks).

The key to successfully handling a difficult situation is thinking through not only your goals and needs but also the other person's goals and needs. How can both of you come out with some "wins" instead of ending with "I win, you lose"? *Helpful…*

• **Begin with a question to engage the other person** in arriving at a solution rather than giving the solution yourself.

Example: "We're having a problem getting reports out on time. What's needed to turn this around? Can you help?" Sincerely asked questions help keep situations from becoming accusatory and adversarial.

• **Use the word "I" instead of "you."** "I must not have explained that well," rather than, "You got this all wrong." This helps others save face, which allows them to hear you and change what's wrong.

- **Look down rather than making eye contact with the other person.** Do this when presenting a problem that needs solving. This helps him/her get over his embarrassment and focus on the issue. Avoiding eye contact makes the problem objective, not personal. Resume eye contact after you have outlined the problem.

- **Edit what you say.** Some people give so many details when they talk that the main points get lost. Simply refer to what the other person already knows, then add your point of view about the situation.

- **Ask another question** if the person seems to have stopped listening to what you are saying. The secret to giving and getting information is dialogue, not monologue.

Genuine Work-at-Home Opportunity

Companies such as J. Crew and Sears outsource call centers to people who work at their homes in the US, rather than overseas. The number of home-based call center agents has tripled since the year 2000 to 672,000 workers in the US and Canada. Pay is typically between $25,000 and $40,000 a year, and the jobs usually don't include benefits. Legitimate jobs are available through established outsourcing firms, such as West Corporation, LiveOps, Alpine Access and Working Solutions.

Caution: Ignore work-at-home offers on the Web—they are almost always scams.

The Wall Street Journal.

Small Business Alert

What are small-business owners going to jail for these days? Filing false payroll tax returns, indicating smaller salaries.

Restaurant owners, in particular, seem to be a good target for IRS investigators. These businesses tend to have at least some employees who are on the books for a portion of their salaries, with the balance of their compensation paid in cash.

Defense: There is not much of a defense that can be mounted if the IRS can put together five or six employees who will testify that they were paid in cash—even though the employees will admit that they did not report the cash on their own income tax returns.

Best bet: Clean up your act now. The payroll taxes saved by paying employees with cash is not worth the legal expenses and potential time in prison.

Ms. X, Esq., a former IRS agent who is still well connected.

Time for a New Career? The Best Home-Based Businesses Now

Paul and Sarah Edwards, California-located cohosts of the *Entrepreneur Magazine Home-Based Business Show* on WSRadio.com and columnists for *Entrepreneur*. They are also coauthors of 16 books, including *The Best Home Businesses for People 50+* (Tarcher). Their Web site is at *www.pinemountaininstitute.com.*

Whether you are searching for a different or more interesting work life or looking for a way to supplement your income, a home-based business can be a wise option.

Other big advantages: By owning a home-based business, you turn your maturity into an advantage—even people as young as 40 may face discrimination when they apply for jobs. Ageism works in favor of older business owners—potential clients and lenders consider age a sign of reliability and experience.

There are financial benefits, as well. You can keep expenses down—there is no need to rent office space—and enjoy generous tax breaks.

To boost your chance of success, choose a business that is suited to your skills, schedule and interests. Is there a hobby that you could turn into a full- or part-time profession? Do you have a skill that is highly coveted, a service that companies might want to outsource?

If nothing springs to mind, look into one of these ideas that are in big demand in today's marketplace...

• **Errand service.** There are 29 million two-career couples in the US. Most of these families have little time for such everyday tasks as taking vehicles in to be serviced... waiting at home for repairmen to arrive...or picking up clothes from the dry cleaner. Small businesses also might outsource such tasks for certain busy executives or the company as a whole during hectic times.

Getting started: Most of your business will come through word of mouth, but you can attract clients initially by taking out inexpensive ads in local publications...posting flyers on community bulletin boards...and/or soliciting work directly from small businesses.

Helpful: Ask a friend with a flexible schedule to help you out occasionally when you get two rush assignments from important clients at the same time.

Potential earnings: $15 to $25 per hour.

Important: Purchase insurance for liability to protect you in the event of a lawsuit, particularly if you'll be driving other people in your own car or theirs. The cost of auto insurance varies greatly from state to state, but your insurer should be able to add an appropriate business rider to your policy for $1,500* or less per year. A special driver's license should not be necessary.

• **Medical coder.** Medical coders translate physicians' written diagnoses and lists of procedures into the codes that insurance companies use for billing. Most medical coding is done at hospitals or clinics, but outsourcing is becoming more common.

The job requires a good memory, a meticulous personality and the unique ability to read bad handwriting.

You'll need to pass the Certified Professional Coder (CPC) exam before you get into the

*Prices subject to change.

profession. The best way to prepare for this test is to enroll in a 12- to 18-month course, typically through a community college. Expect to spend at least 20 hours per week studying. The Medical Training Directory site has links to reputable colleges that offer coding courses. At *www.medicaltrainingdirectory.com,* click on "Become a Medical Coder" under "Medical Career Guides" on the right-side menu.

You'll need to get liability insurance, which should cost between $250 and $700 per year, depending on your state. Contact the American Academy of Professional Coders (AAPC) for additional information about the profession (800-626-2633, *www.aapc.com*).

Getting started: Contact doctors' offices and hospitals in your area to find out if they need freelance coders, or check the AAPC's on-line job database.

Potential earnings: $20 to $45 per hour, or $1 per item in piecework from hospitals, though this varies by region.

• **Caretaker.** House-sitting for home owners who are out of town can be an easy way to earn extra money. It is also fun, because most people who hire caretakers live in big, attractive homes. Caretakers over age 50 are in particular demand because of their perceived reliability—older married couples all the more so because clients consider them stable, honest and dependable.

Liability insurance generally is not necessary, though if a home is full of expensive antiques or other valuables, insurance or bonding could help to reassure the home owner and clinch the job for you.

Getting started: Post ads on Web sites such as *www.caretaker.org* or *www.craigs list.org.* Or place classified ads in your local newspapers.

Potential earnings: Most caretaking jobs provide only free housing, but some pay hundreds of dollars or more per month. If the home owner does offer to pay you, get the deal in writing. The paying jobs also generally involve garden or pet care. The more effort the job requires, the more you can charge.

You can distinguish yourself from other applicants if you have specialized knowledge of plants, animals or home maintenance.

Helpful: Some successful caretakers decide to sell their homes and furniture, freeing up cash and slashing expenses. This only makes sense if you have someplace to stay between jobs or if business takes off and you land consecutive assignments that last six months or longer.

- **Résumé writer.** Résumé writing is a wonderful part-time business, especially if you have experience in human resources and/or communications. Clients expect customized work, not computer-generated résumés.

Unlike most home-based businesses, résumé writing is recession-proof—when the economy falters and people lose their jobs, high-quality résumés are in particular demand.

You must have very strong writing skills and a firm grasp of what employers like to see on a résumé. People skills are important as well—a résumé writer must interview clients to draw out crucial information about them.

Getting started: Network with professional or trade organizations. The more active you are in the organization, the more likely others will steer potential clients your way. If you have a Web site or advertise your services on-line, focus on a particular profession. To stand out, buy an ad on the industry association Web site rather than on general job search sites. Leave your business cards with print shops, such as Kinko's, that handle résumés…make contact with executive recruitment or placement firms…and/or place an ad in the Yellow Pages.

Potential earnings: A flat fee of $50 for the typical résumé, but as much as $150 per hour for an executive résumé. Cover letters can bring another $30 to $65 apiece.

- **Personal coach.** Successful people can market their experience. Coaches help clients make decisions. Some coaches specialize in life decisions, others in career decisions. Many coaches concentrate on a particular industry or on a type of decision.

Examples: A corporate coach might specialize in supply-chain issues or in management training…a personal coach might specialize in parenting skills or retirement goals.

The job requires strong interpersonal skills, good judgment and an impressive life or career history that will convince clients that your advice has merit. For example, you might have risen to a high position in a well-known corporation.

Getting started: To find clients, network in professional or social organizations…volunteer to speak before professional or community groups or give free workshops and seminars…and offer free 30-minute initial consultations during which you either focus on one specific issue or speak in broader terms to get to know a potential client.

Potential earnings: Coaches typically charge $200 or more for three or four 30- to 50-minute sessions, either in person or on the telephone. If you meet in person, it might make sense to do so at the client's home or office so that you don't have to have a special rider added to your homeowner's insurance in case a business visitor is hurt on your property. The more coaching experience you have and the more impressive your résumé is, the more you can charge. Business coaches generally earn more than personal coaches.

- **Home inspector.** Home inspectors examine houses that are on the market for any hidden flaws or problems that could affect the value. Most inspectors have backgrounds in home building or maintenance, but if you're a longtime home owner with the skills to do a remodeling job on your own and a willingness to study up on what you don't know, that should be sufficient.

Home inspectors must have knowledge of all of the systems in a home—heating, plumbing, electric, etc.—and must be physically fit enough to inspect attics and crawl spaces and to climb ladders to examine roofs. They must pass an exam to be certified by the American Society of Home Inspectors.

Liability insurance is a must and could cost thousands of dollars each year, depending on your state.

Getting started: After being certified, develop relationships with local real estate agents. Visit open houses, and introduce yourself when the host agents have a slow moment. Let them know that you'll deliver your reports quickly. Advertise in the real estate sections of all local newspapers. Also, join the American Society of Home Inspectors (ASHI) and take part in its "Find an Inspector" program (call 800-743-2744 or go to *www.ashi.org*).

Potential earnings: $250 to $300 per day, assuming one inspection per day.

Google Your Problems Away

If your computer is experiencing a problem, just type the error message or explanation of the problem into Google.com. You'll bring up a list of sites that could help. It may take some digging to locate a fix for your problem, but it's a good first step before calling technical support (or while on hold with technical support). You also can try this for household or other problems—just type your question into Google.

David Boyer, research editor and resident computer guru, Bottom Line/Personal, Boardroom Inc., 281 Tresser Blvd., Stamford, CT 06901.

Between Jobs and Need Health Coverage?

Your cheapest health insurance option might be a short-term policy if you're between jobs. It is almost always less expensive than federally regulated COBRA, which extends your former employer's coverage.

To compare prices: Shop at sites such as *Insurance.com* and *eHealthInsurance.com*.

Important: If you have a preexisting condition, get COBRA and then see if you can get a short-term policy. After you get one, cancel COBRA.

Robert Hurley, vice president of corporate communications at eHealth Insurance, a leading site for finding, comparing and buying health insurance, Mountain View, CA. www.ehealthinsurance.com, 800-977-8860.

Thorny Home-Office Deduction Questions... And Answers

Barbara Weltman, attorney based in Millwood, NY, and author of J. K. Lasser's Small Business Taxes. Wiley. She is publisher of the on-line newsletter Big Ideas for Small Business. Monthly. Free at www. barbaraweltman.com.

Home-office deductions are one of the reasons home-based businesses can be so profitable. When you run a business out of your home, you can write off a portion of your home-related personal expenses, such as mortgage interest or rent, utilities, insurance, repairs and real estate taxes.

But home-office deductions aren't always straightforward. *Here are some special situations that can easily arise in a home-based business context—together with ways to maximize the home-office deduction in each of them...*

SIDELINE BUSINESS

The rules for the home-office deduction are exactly the same whether a business is full-time or part-time. *Key tests...*

• **Principal-place-of-business test.** The home office must be used as the principal place of business for a particular activity.

• **Exclusive-use test.** The space must be used regularly and exclusively for business—occasional or mixed use (business and nonbusiness) won't do.

Problem: The IRS may view a sideline business as a hobby and limit overall business deductions to the extent of income from the activity for the year. If the activity is a hobby and income is modest, this could mean the loss of a home-office deduction.

Worse: Deductions currently barred by this hobby loss rule are lost.

Solution: Regardless of income, a sideline business can overcome the hobby loss rule by showing that its operators run it with a reasonable intention of making a profit.

Telling factors: Keeping good books and records...having a separate business bank account and credit card...writing a business plan showing how profit will be derived.

Once the hobby loss rules no longer apply, any unused home-office deduction for the year can be carried forward.

THE DAY CARE EXCEPTION

The Small Business Administration reported that for businesses owned by women, child day care was the second most-common type of the top 10 types of businesses for the years it examined. (The most common was door-to-door sales.) Those who care for children (or, increasingly, seniors) in their homes are called "family day care workers" by the Department of Labor.

Problem: The customers (children or adults being cared for) usually are not confined to a single part of the home. They generally have access not only to a living room or family room, but also the bathroom, kitchen, and other parts of the home. These areas are not used exclusively for business (the provider's family uses the living room, kitchen, etc., after hours) and fail the exclusive-use test.

Solution: There is a special home-office rule for day care providers. As long as the home is used regularly for day care, a portion of the home's expenses is deductible even though the same space is used for nonbusiness purposes. To qualify, you must be in the business of providing day care for children, people age 65 or older, or people who are physically or mentally unable to care for themselves, and you must have the appropriate license or certification for your locality (or be exempt from having it).

Figuring the deduction: Expenses relating to any portion of the home used exclusively for day care are deductible under the normal rules. For example, if one bedroom is devoted exclusively to day care use and it accounts for 10% of the home's square footage, then 10% of the home's expenses are part of the home-office deduction based on that use. The portion of expenses relating to the part of the home not used exclusively for business is deductible according to a time ratio.

How: Compare the total time the area of the home is used for the business with the total time available for use for all other purposes. Base this on an hourly comparison per week (168 total hours) or per year (8,760 hours for 2007).

Example: Ms. Y uses the basement in her family home for paid child care an average of 12 hours a day, five days a week, for 50 weeks a year. During the balance of the time, the basement is available for use by her family. The portion of home-related, basement-related expenses she can deduct is 34.25%, which is the number of hours used for day care (12 hours per day × 5 days × 50 weeks = 3,000) divided by the total number of hours in the year (8,760). Since the basement comprises 50% of the total square footage of her home, the percentage applied to the deductible costs for the home is 17.13% (34.25% × 50%). So, if Ms. Y's rent, utilities, maintenance, and other related costs total $12,000 for the year, her home-office deduction related to the basement is $2,056.

Bonus: If she paints the basement or incurs another expense solely for the basement, she can include 34.25% of the cost as part of the home-office deduction. So, if it cost $500 to paint the room, $171 is added to $2,056, for a total deduction of $2,227.

TELECOMMUTERS

Today, more than 5% of the workforce telecommutes—that is, they are employed by a company but perform their duties from home.

Problem: An employee can claim a home-office deduction only if use of this office is for the convenience of the employer—not the employee.

Solution: Satisfying this requirement is often not easy to do. Usually, the convenience of the employer means that the company does not have office space for you, so you *must* work from home.

Even companies that provide office space may have policies that mandate working from home in certain situations (e.g., no office access after business hours, no showing up sick). In these situations, telecommuters who work from home because of the company's preference should obtain a letter from the employer to this effect. They can attach the letter to the tax return to deter any IRS inquiry about why an employee's return includes a home-office deduction.

Suggestion: Don't wait until the IRS sends an audit letter to ask your employer for its policy letter—by then, you may no longer be with the same company, and it may be difficult to obtain the required employer letter.

UNPROFITABLE BUSINESSES

Businesses, even those run from home, may not make money every year. This is especially so when businesses are just getting started.

Problem: The home-office deduction cannot exceed gross income from the business conducted from the home office. "Gross income" for this purpose means net profit reduced by the portion of expenses that could have been deducted as itemized personal expenses (i.e., the allocable portion of mortgage interest, real estate taxes, and, where applicable, casualty losses that have been included as part of the home-office deduction).

Solutions: Recognize this limitation and try to increase business income, if possible, or shift other deductible expenses to a later year. For example, a home-based business owner whose income for the year is modest may want to maximize the current home-office deduction by waiting until the following year to reorder supplies or renew business association dues.

If income cannot be increased, any unused loss can be carried forward and used in a future year when there is gross income from the activity. There is no limit on the number of years for this carryforward. You do not even have to be in the same home. However, if you start another home-based business, you cannot use the loss from the old activity that was carried forward.

7

Winning Ways

How to Win Anyone Over with Charm

Charming people are generally more successful than their less charming counterparts. And, in fact, charm is the single most important quality you can possess if you want to be a leader. But what is it that charming people do differently from everyone else? They are not necessarily wittier or better-looking or more sophisticated. All charming people simply have taught themselves a few interpersonal skills—skills that anyone can master.

Surprisingly, the point of these interpersonal skills isn't primarily to make us seem more appealing to others—it is to make the individuals we interact with seem more appealing to themselves. People are attracted to any person who increases their self-esteem. They are inclined to help him/her and predisposed to believe what he has to say—even if they do not completely understand why.

To be more charming...

• **Greet everyone you meet as if he were very special.** Do this with strangers and longtime acquaintances alike. If you cannot muster the necessary enthusiasm naturally, tell yourself that each person you meet is a dear childhood friend whom you haven't seen in decades. Act as though you are absolutely thrilled to have this old friend back in your life.

It can be particularly difficult to smile and seem thrilled to meet people when you are nervous. If a situation fills you with anxiety, mentally rehearse being warm and genial.

Example: Before a job interview, imagine that you are smart and charming and that everything goes very well.

Brian Tracy, chairman and CEO of Brian Tracy International, a leadership and success consulting company, Solana Beach, CA, and president of Brian Tracy University, a private on-line university for sales and entrepreneurship, *www.briantracy.com*. He is also author of several books including *Speak to Win: How to Present with Power in Any Situation* and coauthor of *The Power of Charm: How to Win Anyone Over in Any Situation* (both from Amacom).

•**Be free with a "thank you."** Thank everyone for every reason you can find. Thank your spouse for listening to your problems, even when your spouse is the problem. Thank your employees for their work, even when they are just doing their jobs. Thank the maitre d' for trying to find you a table, even if it was he who lost your reservation in the first place.

A heartfelt "thank you" lets people know that we appreciate what they've done, which boosts their faith in their own importance and competence. They feel better about themselves and are drawn to us for making them feel that way.

Saying "thank you" inflates our self-esteem, too, because it reminds us of our ability to help others. The higher our self-esteem climbs, the more comfortable we are around others and the more charming we become.

Helpful: Before visiting a foreign country, learn to say "thank you," "you are welcome," "please" and "good morning" in the language.

•**Pay attention.** Listen to people as if you are hanging on every word. And, lean forward slightly, nod every minute or two, focus on the speaker's eyes, occasionally "flicking" your gaze from one of his eyes to the other. There is no such thing as too intense a gaze when you are listening—imagine that your eyes are sunlamps and your goal is to give the speaker's eyes a tan. When people feel listened to, they feel happier and will tend to associate you with those happy feelings.

The longer you can keep a conversation partner speaking on subjects that interest him, the more charming he'll consider you. If you don't know what topics are of interest to this person, inquire about his family or ask, "What sort of work do you do?" Be sure you use the phrase "sort of work." The vagueness lets people who are currently unemployed discuss their fields in general rather than admit that they're out of a job. Follow this up with "How did you get into that line?"

At some point, the person will pause to make sure you are still listening. Prompt him with an encouraging question, such as "What did you do then?"

•**Praise people's efforts.** Humans have an unquenchable need to be reassured that they are worthy of praise. If you feed this need in people, they will repeat whatever behavior earned them your praise, hoping that they will get more. Almost like addicts, they will return to you for a praise fix again and again.

Some people will try to downplay your praise, claiming that their efforts were nothing special. Don't let them stop you. People who aren't good at accepting praise still love to receive it.

•**Find something to admire.** Compliment something about everyone you meet. Your compliments need not be about big things—sometimes we score more points by noticing the little things that everyone else tends to overlook.

It is sometimes tricky to compliment people we have just met, since we don't know much about them yet. Consider complimenting something they are wearing.

Example: The famously charming former president Bill Clinton often would say in receiving lines, "I like your tie."

Best Ways to Make Better First Impressions

Camille Lavington, international communications consultant, 160 E. 38th St., New York City 10016.

First impressions aren't formed in the first ten minutes of a conversation—or in the first half hour. They are formed in the first few seconds.

Of course, a one-hour meeting with someone you've never met before gives you ample time to refine and embellish the first impression you make. But what occurs in the last few minutes of a first encounter is deeply influenced by the experience of the first few seconds.

The lesson for businesspeople is that you can prepare beautifully for a favorable first impression and blow it by paying too little attention to the instantaneous perception people get based on your posture, your eye contact, the way you hold your head and your general expression and demeanor.

POLISHING THE FIRST IMPRESSION

Your attitude has a great deal to do with your expression and demeanor. To make a positive impression, you must be sincere and sensitive to what makes others feel comfortable. There's a kind of natural graciousness that some people have. But anyone can learn to think of the other person first.

When you are going to an important meeting with strangers, concentrate on putting others around you at ease, instead of focusing only on driving home your agenda. Helpful: Pretend you are the host of the meeting, and treat everyone accordingly.

Self-restraint is a virtue today. The time is long gone when Americans could get away with arrogant or overbearing behavior around the world. Projecting self-esteem does not mean projecting arrogance.

Much better: Exhibit the strength to be considerate of others, the deference to hold a door open or write a note to thank someone who has helped you and the generosity of spirit that leaves others with something after your meetings with them.

PROPER ATTIRE

Dress as if you are always on stage—because you are. While the dress code varies widely from company to company, depending on climate and other factors, there are certain wardrobe guidelines that will stand you in good stead anywhere in the world...

•**Strive for a well-groomed,** coordinated look. This means conservative suits or dresses of simple lines and solid colors, such as navy, gray, beige or black. Women can branch out to brighter shades, such as yellow, green and red, as long as the outfits have a conservative cut. Because good tailoring is expensive, many women are now turning to softer clothes and knits. These allow them to look professional without having to pay for costly alterations.

Men should have at least a few custom-tailored shirts for important first-impression occasions. They fit better and look much neater than traditional button-downs. Choose fabrics that breathe, but at the same time look crisp and unwrinkled. Choose a straight or spread collar. They are appropriate anywhere in the world.

Most executives will always feel right in a conservative tie with small or repeat prints. If you want to stand out, shop for patterns from Hermes, Ferragamo or Gucci. A sassy Nicole Miller tie makes a creative statement. (*Caution:* Not for everyone.)

Important: Be sure that your tie does not have spots or stains around the edges of the knot. And put away ties that have a width that has gone out of fashion. Width styles change every few years.

•**Wear the outfit that is appropriate** to the role you are in or that you aspire to. Influential decision-makers really do look different. Pattern your wardrobe after those in the company or social circle you admire and hope to emulate.

Creative entrepreneurs do not have to follow tradition as much as corporate managers do, and they often want to signal that by dressing less conventionally. Even they, however, are wise to suit up—or at least wear a blazer and gray slacks—when they are meeting with influential bankers, lawyers or shareholders.

•**Concentrate on your head** because that's your power center. It's the place where much of the other person's attention will focus first. Note: Women with long hair are too often not taken seriously in business. For men, it's essential to be clean shaven, especially for those who travel internationally. In Asia and certain other countries, facial hair indicates lower class or servitude.

Women should wear some makeup, but not too much. The same goes for jewelry, where a simple gold necklace or pearls (real or not) and nondangling earrings effectively frame the face. A colorful silk scarf tied around your neck is also flattering.

Avoid wearing anything that jingles, such as a charm bracelet or too many bangles. One piece of good gold jewelry is much more impressive than a lot of costume jewelry.

•**Avoid exposing the skin on your legs.** Women should always wear stockings, and men's hosiery must be of a length so as to avoid showing skin if they cross their legs.

Don't ever show the soles of your shoes. In Middle Eastern countries that is a terrible insult. When you do cross your legs, do it in such a way that the soles are not facing another person.

•**Invest in accessories.** Shoes are perhaps the most important accessory. People around the world size you up by your shoes. Ferragamos are so well made that they will keep their shape even after a thorough soaking. Moreover, they are recognized everywhere as a standard of good taste and quality.

Be sure to carry your papers and laptop computer in a handsome tote or briefcase. A briefcase does not have to be brand new, but it should be in good shape. It should not look like a leftover from school days. That marks you as a worker bee rather than a decision-maker.

Don't think people don't notice these details of your bearing. Conclusions are drawn quickly.

By the same token, wear a quality watch and carry a distinguishing pen. Never put your Montblanc in your shirt pocket. That signifies an order-taker, rather than an order-giver. Do, however, use the pen for personal messages to capture attention.

A CAPTIVATING VOICE

Gain and hold someone's attention by speaking clearly and slowly. If a dialogue goes off track, try not to ever interrupt, disagree or offend the other person. At times it may help to add a little humor to relieve the tension.

Top off all of these tips with a warm smile and a gracious farewell. If you want to walk away knowing that you've made a great first impression, plan ahead. It doesn't mean that you are trying to be someone other than yourself. It just means that you are willing to discipline yourself to make someone with certain expectations more comfortable in your presence. This gives you the edge when you are trying to land—or keep—a job or influence a client.

Do You Have a Short Fuse? Five Ways to Break the Anger Habit

Brenda Shoshanna, PhD, a psychologist and therapist for more than 25 years, *www.brendasho shanna.com*. She is author of *The Anger Diet: 30 Days to Stress-Free Living* (Andrews McMeel) and *Zen Miracles: Finding Peace in an Insane World* (Wiley). She has an active therapy practice in New York City.

Expressing anger at your spouse, your boss or the driver in front of you may make you feel more powerful and less vulnerable—but only for a short time. It rarely resolves feelings and often intensifies them. Over time, anger can become addictive. You don't even recognize that you are angry or investigate why.

Even if you don't outwardly express your anger, it can be destructive. Repressed anger can be a root cause of anxiety, depression, overeating and other problems. *To reduce anger...*

1. GAIN CONTROL

The moment you begin to sense anger rising in you...

•**Regain your physical equilibrium.** Stop talking, break eye contact with the other person and/or breathe deeply.

•**Avoid personalizing the situation.** That cashier isn't just being rude to you—she is rude to everybody. If her parents, teachers and bosses couldn't teach her to be polite, how are a few words from you going to change anything? It's a waste of your emotional and intellectual energy to confront her.

•**Gain perspective** by placing your anger in a larger context. Imagine yourself looking back at the incident a year from now. Would it matter?

Example: I had a patient who had a wonderful new wife. She had a habit of talking to her friends on the phone late at night. He felt she was taking time away from him, and he would blow up at her. The next morning, he would apologize profusely, but she was left feeling wounded. He had tried asking his wife to spend less time on the phone, but she felt he was being unreasonable. I suggested that whenever he was in a rage, he write down five great things he got out of their relationship. This helped remind him of what was really important.

2. TURN A FOE INTO A FRIEND

Change your perceptions by thinking about what you can do to turn a perceived "enemy" into a friend.

Example: I had a patient who was furious because a particular employee of his kept showing up late for work. My patient saw this as a conscious refusal to be a team member and submit to the established channels of authority.

I suggested that instead of reprimanding the employee, my patient ask what he could do to help the employee arrive at work on time. It turned out that the employee was a single parent who was struggling with child-care issues but was too proud to admit it. My patient altered the man's working hours and earned an ally in his office.

3. STOP OBSESSING

Anger builds when you dwell on an incident, playing it over and over in your mind in an obsessive loop. Instead, direct your mental attention elsewhere.

Example: One patient was a hardworking manager at an insurance company. He was convinced that his boss didn't like him. The loop in his head kept saying, "You're going to be passed over for promotion." His resulting anger expressed itself in cold and distant behavior toward the boss. He turned down social invitations, kept conversations short and never smiled. In reality, his boss valued my patient's work but was turned off by his curt actions. When my patient realized how he was fueling this negative situation, he changed his self-talk. He told himself that he was doing a fine job and that his boss recognized it. He also became aware of the boss's needs and began to reach out to him and offer support. A promotion followed naturally.

4. TAKE THE HIGH ROAD

Avoid responding to an insult with an insult. It only escalates situations and can inflict long-term wounds. Realize that the other person is probably acting out of pain, fear or weakness. Respond with, "What do you need from me right now?" This cuts through the other person's anger.

Example: I worked with a couple whose arguments would escalate quickly and viciously. I suggested to the woman that the next time her husband insulted her, she not lash out but ask her husband what he needed. The next week, the woman agreed to meet her husband at a cocktail party after work. When she arrived, he snapped, "You're late." Instead of snapping back, she asked her husband what he needed. That stopped the argument cold. It turned out that he was angry because he had been uncomfortable waiting at the party alone. He didn't feel as capable as she did in social situations. He wanted her company and the warm, engaging manner in which she met people. Simply communicating this diffused the anger between them.

5. LET GO OF A GRUDGE

We like to nurture old hurts because it legitimizes our ill thoughts or bad behavior.

Example: One patient had held a grudge against her husband for decades. At their engagement party more than 20 years earlier, her husband had commented in front of the entire family how beautiful her sister looked that night, but he hadn't commented on my patient's appearance. She felt deeply hurt and thought that forgiving her husband would mean she was weak and lacked self-esteem. I told her that dropping the grudge would be healing, giving her the freedom and clarity to improve their relationship. *How to let go of a grudge...*

• **Think about times when you might have behaved in a similar way.** My patient realized that she had hurt her husband's feelings in the past by talking negatively about him in front of his own family.

• **Figure out what you need to do to release your grudge.** My patient wanted her husband to acknowledge that she was beautiful to him.

• **Ask for what you want.** Express your needs clearly. My patient discussed her grudge with her husband. He responded, "I think you are the most beautiful woman in the world!" After hearing that, her anger disappeared.

Why Men Never Remember and Women Never Forget

Marianne Legato, MD, FACP, a physician and professor of clinical medicine at Columbia University and founder of Columbia's Partnership for Gender-Specific Medicine, New York City. She is author of several books, including *Why Men Never Remember and Women Never Forget.* Rodale.

Neither men nor women can claim that their brains are "better." Even though men's brains are 10% larger on average, women's brains have more elaborate connections that make them more efficient. Male and female brains unquestionably are different, in terms of both structure and chemistry, and that can trigger problems when we try to communicate with one another.

Most of us speak to our spouses just as we would speak to members of our own sex—then wonder why they don't seem to understand.

Here's how to communicate more effectively with the opposite sex...

NONVERBAL CUES

The female brain is good at decoding nonverbal signals, including facial expressions and tone of voice, perhaps because mothers must understand the needs of children too young to speak. When women send nonverbal signals to men, women are often dismayed to find that these signals are ignored.

Women do not realize that the typical male brain is not very skilled at interpreting nonverbal communications. And, men are particularly bad at identifying signs of sadness in women—though men are pretty good at spotting signs of anger and aggression.

Women: Tell him verbally when something is bothering you. A sad expression or the silent treatment won't get you anywhere. It's not that he is ignoring your feelings—he is just unaware of them.

If a man asks you what he can do to make you feel better, tell him. If you say "nothing," he'll assume that you mean nothing and he'll do nothing. He isn't trying to hurt you—men's brains just work in a more linear, literal manner. Because men often like to be left alone when they're upset, he might conclude that he is doing you a favor by giving you some space.

Men: Search for the clues beyond her words when she seems unusually quiet or terse. She might be sending signals that you're not picking up. If you can't figure out the signals and she won't tell you what she needs, remind her that you really want to help, but it's hard for you to pick up her nonverbal cues.

LISTENING

The female brain seems to be better at listening than the male brain—women have more nerve cells in the areas known to process language and put a larger percentage of their brains to work when they hear someone speak.

The more elaborate wiring of the female brain also makes women better multitaskers than men. Evolution likely made women this way so that mothers could keep an eye on the children and still get other things done. Evolution shaped the male brain to focus on one very difficult task at a time. Tiger hunts were more successful when the hunters focused on the tiger.

Add men's inferior listening ability to their superior focus, and the result is a phenomenon most wives know well. Tell a man something important while he's watching a ball game, and he might not remember a word of it. He is not purposely ignoring you—his brain simply isn't wired to hear what you said.

Women: Put him on alert that what you are about to say is important. If it's particularly vital information, begin with a gentle, "I need you to look me in the eyes." If there are too many distractions in your present location, ask him to go with you for a walk or out to a quiet restaurant.

Men: Don't be insulted if she doesn't stop what she is doing when you want to talk to her. Chances are that she can pay attention to you even if she is occupied. If you want her undivided attention, ask for it.

PROBLEM SOLVING

The structure of the male brain makes men straight-ahead thinkers—when they see a problem, their instinct is to try to solve it.

Women are more likely to ruminate over a decision. They will verbalize a problem and talk through all of the implications and issues before they proceed. When women try to talk through their problems with men, they're often dismayed and insulted that the men try to tell them what to do. This confuses the men, who thought they were being asked for a solution.

Women: Tell a man the specific type of response you want before you share a problem. Are you asking the man for a solution, or do you just want to talk through the issue so it's clear in your mind? If you don't specifically tell him that it's the latter, he'll assume it's the former. If he tries to solve your problem anyway, understand that this is just how his brain responds.

As for how to respond to a man's problems, this rarely comes up. Men tend not to share their problems with anyone.

Men: Understand that women like to verbalize their thinking and don't always want you to solve their problems. Instead, wait for a question before providing an answer. Ask what you can do to help rather than assume you know. And if your wife starts crying, hold her quietly. Don't tell her she's being too emotional.

DIFFERENT INTERESTS

Women tend to expect their male partners to be interested in every subject they wish to discuss. That isn't fair. A woman wouldn't expect her female friends to chat about a subject that she knows bores them.

Women: Customize the conversation to your partner's interests. (Men should do this, too, but because men talk less, it isn't as often

an issue.) Find other conversation partners for topics that don't interest him.

Men: Encourage your partner to spend time with female friends so there's another outlet for the conversations that don't interest you. Don't get upset if she's busy with friends.

BETTER ARGUMENTS

During an argument, women are more likely to bring up previous events. Estrogen increases the amount of *cortisol*, a memory-boosting hormone, that is released during stressful moments. Because a female brain has more estrogen, the memories of old fights remain fresher in a woman's mind. The male brain finds it easier to forget emotional situations and move on. Maybe forgetting a close call on the tiger hunt made it easier for men of the past to continue to hunt.

Women: Use simple, declarative sentences, and state what you want in outline form when imparting important information to men. Leave out anecdotes and unnecessary adjectives. Take advantage of your ability to read his emotions to spot the signs of boredom. When you see them, sum up your argument with a closing statement and end the conversation. Try not to rehash old arguments.

Men: Try to keep a woman focused on the point under discussion. If during an argument she brings up a fight you had five years ago, tell her, "We've discussed that already and it isn't going to help to go over it again. Let's focus on the current problem."

How to Find Lost Objects—Fast

Michael Solomon, a writer based in Baltimore, MD, *www.professorsolomon.com*. He refers to himself as a "findologist" and is author of five books, including *How to Find Lost Objects*. Penguin.

One of life's persistent aggravations is misplacing everyday objects, such as keys, cell phones and reading glasses. You wind up wasting time ransacking the house in a frenetic search. Michael Solomon has studied how things get lost and how best to find them. *His strategies…*

● **Identify the Eureka Zone.** The majority of lost objects tend to travel no more than 18 inches from their last known locations. I call this the Eureka Zone.

Examples: A pencil that has rolled beneath your computer. Eyeglasses hidden under today's newspaper.

Whenever I lose something, I explore the Eureka Zone meticulously.

● **"Lose" another object.** If you happen to drop and lose sight of an object that has one or more identical counterparts (such as a screw or an earring), try purposely dropping a second one and watching where it goes. This gives you an estimated radius for how far the first object might have rolled or bounced.

● **Make sure you are not staring right at it.** When you're feeling rushed and agitated, your vision literally narrows. This is why your spouse or a friend often finds the lost object as soon as he/she joins in the search. You can improve your focus by taking a few deep breaths and repeating to yourself the name of the lost object over and over—"car keys, car keys, car keys"—which keeps you from becoming distracted from the task at hand.

Also, the object may look different than you imagine.

Example: My friend couldn't find a hardcover book that he needed. We searched his apartment in vain until I grew suspicious of his description and began to examine the paperbacks on his bookshelf. There was the book, a paperback, in plain sight.

● **Check whether you've substituted one routine motion for another.** Instead of being where it's supposed to be, your object may be where something else is supposed to be. This often happens in the kitchen.

Example: You normally keep scissors in a jar on the kitchen counter, but you mindlessly returned them to the tool drawer.

It's also a problem when filing items.

Example: You file your Bruce Springsteen CD under "B," instead of "S."

● **See if the object has been borrowed.** Is it something that your spouse or your coworkers may have used since the last time you saw it? Ask before you drive yourself crazy looking.

Get More Done in Less Time

Susan Martin, founder of Business Sanity, a coaching and consulting firm that helps business owners and independent professionals increase profits, avoid burnout and run their businesses and lives more effectively, Brooklyn, NY, *www.business-sanity.com.*

Do you have trouble getting things done? Often miss deadlines? Show up late for appointments? If so, your time-management skills need significant improvement.

Five simple steps that can help…

● **Identify time wasters.** Most people who struggle with time management tend to get caught up in activities that waste time, such as surfing the Internet or making long phone calls. Pinpoint these habits, and post a list to remind yourself not to do them.

● **Trim your to-dos.** Many of us have to-do lists that are full of tasks that don't really help us reach our goals and thus aren't priorities. Review your list, and decide what really needs to be done.

● **Value your time.** Many people misjudge how much they can accomplish and think they can do everything themselves. This makes it impossible to manage time. Be sure you're doing things that can be done only by you. Try to delegate or outsource everything else to family members, colleagues and people you hire, such as gardeners and cleaning people.

● **Get real.** Probably the biggest time-management trap is underestimating how much time things really take. Estimate how long you think a task will take and then double or triple the amount of time until you're better able to accurately judge how much time is needed.

• **Make an appointment with yourself.** Schedule focused work periods to accomplish specific tasks. During these periods, let voicemail pick up your phone, turn off the Internet and e-mail, and tell others that you won't be available.

Hidden Benefits Of Being Messy

David H. Freedman, a business and science journalist based in Needham, MA, who has written books on the management principles of the US Marines and the structure of modern computers. He is coauthor, with Eric Abrahamson, of *A Perfect Mess: The Hidden Benefits of Disorder.* Little, Brown.

Society isn't kind to messy people. Parents punish children who won't clean their rooms, and bosses question the competence of employees who have messy desks. But is messy really so bad?

Professional organizers claim that clutter costs us hours each day by making it harder to find things. Our surveys, however, suggest that messy people spend only nine minutes per day, on average, trying to find things in their homes and another nine minutes trying to find things in their offices. Most messy people can locate what they need fairly quickly—they just look where they last had the item. When a mess has been cleaned, it often takes longer to remember where the item has been stored.

Some experts believe we need schedules and plans to stay headed in the right direction, but people with plans often stick to those plans long after it should have been obvious that their plans were not working. Disorganized people usually are better at rolling with the punches and seizing serendipitous opportunities.

Example: Scottish biologist Alexander Fleming discovered penicillin when samples he had carelessly left exposed in his mess of an office were contaminated while he was on vacation.

For many people, a certain amount of messiness can be beneficial...

MESSY HOUSE

What does a tidy home actually do for you? It will not make you more productive—the hours spent cleaning won't save you much, if any, time finding things later. It will not make you healthier—if anything, exposure to the chemicals in household cleaners tends to be worse for our health than living in a cluttered home, unless the mess is extreme and dust and mold accumulate. Finally, a tidy home probably will not make you happier—perhaps you feel better when your house is neat, but if your family does not share this passion for spotlessness, your demands for cleanliness are likely to lead to arguments and unhappiness. *What to do...*

• **Allow certain sections of the house to be messy.** Let your messy spouse have a disorganized den...allow projects to pile up on the otherwise unused dining room table... don't worry if the kids' rooms are a mess.

• **Permit mess cycles.** Don't try to keep the home spotless all the time. Let the mess build, and pick up every few weeks or when guests are coming.

CLUTTERED DESK

Neat people tend to equate messy desks with inefficiency, but for a naturally messy person, a messy desk might be the most efficient arrangement.

Helpful: Messes don't look as messy when they're arranged in stacks. Things will be easy to find because they will be piled close to where they were last used, and stacking is quicker than organizing and filing. It doesn't take substantially longer to dig through a pile of papers on a desk to find an item than it does to sort through a filing cabinet trying to remember where the item was filed.

UNTIDY YARD

Tending to a lawn absorbs hours of our time, wastes hundreds of gallons of water and often involves drenching the yard in pesticides. We all would be better off if "neat" lawns were replaced with "messy" fields of native plants.

You can make a naturally landscaped lawn more palatable to fussy neighbors by placing a border of neat grass around the edges. Also, explain to your neighbors what you're doing and why. You might even get them thinking about their own lawns.

Help for E-Mail Overload

Marjory Abrams, publisher, *Bottom Line* newsletters, Boardroom Inc., 281 Tresser Blvd., Stamford, CT 06901.

Recently I heard about a financial news correspondent who had 23,276 new e-mail messages waiting for him when he returned from vacation.

My situation has never been that horrific—but e-mail often places overwhelming demands on my time. *I have a number of tricks to keep it from ruling my life, including…*

• **Limiting the number of times a day that I check my new mail**—and closing the e-mail window and turning off the sound on my computer in between so that I am not tempted to take a look.

• **Categorizing my e-mail address book by color**—coworkers, personal, e-letters, etc.—so I know immediately which messages are important and which ones can wait. (You also can set up rules so that e-mail is automatically filtered into folders. Your "Help" file will show you how to do this.)

• **Promptly stopping e-mail subscriptions** that I no longer want.

• **Printing out long e-mails** so I can read them at a more convenient time.

• **Using the phone** for questions that are better suited to conversation than a lot of back and forth messages.

There is an even more drastic step—opting out of e-mail completely. Trends forecaster Edie Weiner bit that bullet after her e-mail in-box spiraled out of control. Ms. Weiner, president of the firm Weiner, Edrich,

Brown, Inc., New York City, is a futurist, so you might expect her life to be filled with the latest technology. Wrong! Besides not having e-mail, she also doesn't have a BlackBerry, PalmPilot, iPhone or pager. She keeps a paper calendar. She doesn't have a computer at home. And, she leaves her cell phone off except when she is making a call.

When Ms. Weiner gives one of her frequent speeches, her "no e-mail policy" will generally pique the strongest interest from the audience. She says, "Some people enjoy technology and find that it works well for them. If not, no one should feel forced to use it in order to remain part of the human race."

Although Ms. Weiner misses the ease with which e-mail crosses multiple time zones, she has no real regrets. Her clients know how to get a hold of her. Phone calls, "snail mail" and even faxes keep things more personal, which is just how she likes it.

Memorize While You Sleep

To memorize speeches and other material, review them before going to bed.

Reason: Most of memory consolidation happens during sleep, so what you read immediately before going to bed is more likely to be encoded in your long-term memory, making it easier to recall when you need it.

Candi Heimgartner, MS, instructor, department of biological sciences, University of Idaho, Moscow.

Lucky Seven Helps You Remember

Because the average person's brain can store up to seven chunks of information at a time, the best way to remember something is to break it down into groups of seven or less.

Examples: To remember a phone number with area code, separate the number into two pieces—the area code and the seven-digit number. To remember a poem, focus on the first seven words—then, after you memorize them, the next seven, and so on.

Women's Health Letter, 7100 Peachtree Dunwoody Rd., Atlanta 39328.

Exercise to Improve Memory

Exercise boosts the brain's working memory. That is the part that stores and manipulates information on which you are currently focused, such as looking up a phone number and remembering it while you walk to the phone. To strengthen working memory, get at least 30 minutes of moderate activity, such as brisk walking, most days of the week. Or have three 20-minute sessions of more intense exercise weekly, such as swimming laps or lifting weights.

Kate Lambourne, MS, research assistant, kinesiology department, University of Georgia, Athens.

To Remember a Word, Get Physical

If a word is on the tip of your tongue, but you just can't recall it, try gesturing. Physical movement can sometimes unlock a temporary memory block. If possible, move your hands in a shape related to the word.

Example: When trying to remember a type of bird, shape your hands like wings.

Elena Nicoladis, PhD, associate professor of psychology, University of Alberta, Edmonton, Canada.

Get People to Do What They Don't Want To

To get someone to do something you think they don't want to do, say: "I know you don't want to do this, but…" People are 29% more likely to grant a favor when the person asking for it uses this phrase.

Why: Showing that you understand that someone is reluctant empowers him/her to feel that he/she has a choice—and to decide it might not be so bad to grant your request.

Eric Knowles, professor of psychology, University of Arkansas, Fayetteville, chief scientist at Omegachange.com and co-editor of *Resistance and Persuasion*. LEA.

Six Ways to Spot a Liar—Secrets from a Trainer for the FBI

Paul Ekman, PhD, author of *Emotions Revealed* (Times) and *Telling Lies* (Norton). He has taught FBI and other security agents and has developed two CDs that teach lie-detecting skills through games and tests. His Web site is *www.paulekman.com*.

No matter how hard they try, liars nearly always give themselves away with words or expressions. New research—used by the Department of Homeland Security and the FBI—can help you spot these signs of deceit.

MICRO-EXPRESSIONS

These are flashes of true feelings that escape when people lie. Watch for brief expressions that run counter to a person's dominant facial gestures. They last less than a second and can occur during any part of a conversation.

Examples: When a colleague explains why he is too busy to help you on a project, look for a flash of discomfort. Or when a guest compliments the host on a lousy roast beef, watch for the brief grimace that doesn't belong on the face of a delighted diner.

GIVEAWAY EYELIDS

You can see through a disingenuous smile by watching the area between the upper eyelid and the eyebrow, known as the *eye cover fold*. When someone is enjoying himself/herself, it is slightly tightened and pulled down. It's nearly impossible for someone to lower the eye cover fold if he is not experiencing true enjoyment.

EXAGGERATED GESTURES

Whenever people fake emotion, they often go overboard. Keep an eye out for exaggerated gestures or emotions to spot a cover-up.

Example: You ask your teenage son what happened to the $10 on the table. He gets very angry—an over-the-top response that suggests he is lying.

HESITATIONS IN SPEECH

Hesitations and stammering often indicate a lie—but only if the person does it more than usual on a familiar topic.

Example: If a lawyer talks about astrophysics, he might hesitate because he is unfamiliar with the topic. If you're shopping for a computer and ask a salesperson if he has any for less than $1,200, he should have a speedy answer. Be suspicious if he hesitates. He might be thinking of selling you something that is more expensive once you pay for add-ons.

OTHER BODY LANGUAGE

The probability of a lie also increases when gestures don't match a person's words. *Suspect a lie if someone...*

...says he's interested in your ideas but does not make steady eye contact.

...says he agrees with you and then presses his lips together, a gesture that can indicate discomfort or anger.

...moves away from you while professing his friendship.

...says he's glad to see you but gives you an abbreviated handshake.

PRACTICED PHRASES

When people lie, they often memorize one or two pat phrases but rarely prepare for follow-up questions. Questioning someone closely is the most effective way to get the truth.

Example: Your real estate agent says he has a "great house" that's a "real steal." *What to do:* Pin him down by asking questions. You'll gain important information if he hesitates when he describes the house or flashes a phony smile when he says it is perfect for you. The more he talks, the better. When faced with really having to discuss a matter, most people resort to telling the truth.

How to Deal with People You Can't Stand

Rick Brinkman, ND, a naturopathic physician and public speaker on communication based near Portland, OR, *www.rickbrinkman.com.* He is co-author of *Dealing with People You Can't Stand: How to Bring Out the Best in People at Their Worst.* McGraw-Hill.

Many of us have people in our lives whom we can't stand. Often, there's no escaping interaction with these difficult people. However, even the most unpleasant situations can be made tolerable.

Most difficult people fall into one of the following categories, though some jump from category to category depending on the situation. *Strategies for dealing with each type...*

• **Tanks.** Pushy and confrontational, tanks come at us with guns blazing when they think we're causing them problems. Explanations won't calm them, and counterattacking could lead to all-out war.

What to do: Let the tank vent for up to 60 seconds. Remain calm and maintain eye contact—looking down or backing away might make you seem weak or fearful, which will make the tank respect you even less. If the attack still hasn't ended, firmly repeat his/her name until he quiets. Then summarize his main point to show that you were listening, and explain why his interest is best served by calling off the attack. Tanks tend to be pragmatists, so this should work.

Example: "Dad. *Dad.* I know you don't like my long hair and the way I dress. But I flew all the way here for us to enjoy each other as a family. We can do that. Or I can leave right now. Your choice."

• **Snipers.** Snipers make rude or sarcastic comments or engage in malicious gossip. Their behavior often stems from suppressed anger or resentment that's unrelated to a specific encounter.

What to do: Call attention to their unpleasant behavior in front of a group. When a sniper insults you, immediately stop whatever you're doing, look right at the sniper, repeat the comment, then ask, "What's going on? What are you really trying to say?" If the joke or insult is irrelevant to the situation, add, "What does that have to do with this?" Keep your tone of voice innocent, not sarcastic or annoyed.

Important: Most snipers back down when confronted, but a few transform into tanks. Should this occur, use the strategy for dealing with tanks, above.

If the sniping continues, pick a private moment to ask, "All of this sniping at me…is something the matter between us?" If your question seems sincere, the sniper might open up and explain the underlying problem…or realize that he's gone too far and stop the behavior.

• **Know-it-alls.** Know-it-alls are sure that they're always right. In fact, they often *are* right—but they have little regard for the opinions of others.

What to do: Though it may be hard to swallow, the only way to get anywhere with a know-it-all is to treat him with respect. Frequent use of lines like "Obviously you know your stuff," and "You always have something intelligent to say," should reduce his need to prove his brilliance to you. Repeat know-it-alls' opinions back to them so that they know you grasp them. Rather than offer your opinion to a know-it-all, ask questions that lead him to the answer you want. Never question a know-it-all's views directly, because this will only make him defensive and cause him to dig in his heels. If you think he's wrong, cite irrefutable outside sources, then ask how that affects his conclusions.

Example: Your know-it-all spouse says that there's only one island worth visiting for scuba diving, and only one time of year worth going. Your research suggests that there's a jellyfish problem on that island at that time of year. You say, "August sounds wonderful there, but I read an article in last June's *Scuba Diving* magazine about the August jellyfish problem. Should we consider a different island or month to avoid jellyfish?"

• **Think-they-know-it-alls.** These people act like know-it-alls, but they're usually wrong. They just enjoy the attention that acting like experts brings them.

What to do: Ask these people for specific examples until their lack of insight becomes obvious to all…or ask them follow-up questions. Then explain that anyone could have made this mistake so the would-be know-it-all doesn't feel backed into a corner.

Example: "I know your idea won't work because my friend considered doing the same thing. Turns out there are complex tax consequences that only an accountant would know about."

• **Grenades.** Grenades explode unexpectedly, with little provocation. A grenade might begin a rant by blaming you for a specific problem, but by the end, he's likely to be venting about things that seem unrelated or even irrational. Unlike tanks, who focus on specific problems, grenades are mainly in search of attention.

What to do: Fight fire with fire. Get the grenade's attention by raising your voice to match his, calling his name and waving your hands in front of you (without getting too close to him). Keep your tone friendly as you do this. Use rant-interruption statements, such as "I don't want you to feel that way. No one should have to feel that way." Address the portion of the grenade's rambling rant that matters most to him, if it can be identified. (Often this central problem will be that he's not getting the attention he feels he deserves.)

Example: "We care about all the effort you put into this."

If appropriate, add that you love this person. Grenades need to cool off before they can talk rationally, so suggest meeting later if more discussion is required. If you must deal with a grenade regularly, learn to avoid the topics that tend to set him off.

• **Yes-people.** Yes-people want so badly to be loved and valued that they automatically agree to every request. Then they become overcommitted and can't deliver.

What to do: The key to living or working with a yes-person is providing reassurance that no one will hold his decisions against him. When necessary, walk these problem people through the decision-making process.

Example: A yes-person who already is spread too thin volunteers to assist with yet another project. Walk this person through each step that would be involved and how it would fit into his schedule until he understands that it isn't feasible for him.

• **Nothing-people.** Nothing people offer no feedback, and won't voice an opinion even when one is needed.

What to do: To drag a response out of a nothing-person, ask questions that require more than yes or no answers, such as "How do you want to proceed?" Then put on your best expectant look, and stare at this person—for an uncomfortably long period of time, if need be. If staring fails, try guessing.

Example: "Are you mad at me because I got home late on Tuesday? Because I forgot to wash the dishes? Because of something I said?" Toss out guess after guess until one triggers a response.

If the nothing-person's only answer is "I don't know," ask him to guess. If he refuses, supply greatly exaggerated choices. When faced with exaggerations, most people supply an accurate answer.

Example: A contractor tells you he doesn't know how much a job will cost. You ask, "Well, is it $50? $50,000?" Inserting numbers that are way too low and way too high often will prod such a person into a reasonable response.

• **No-people/whiners.** No-people are defeatist...whiners feel overwhelmed by an unfair world. Oddly, these people become more defeatist or whinier when we try to solve their problems for them...or tell them that their problems are not really so bad.

What to do: Get these people to solve their own problems. Begin by getting to the specific problem. No-people/whiners will claim that the whole world is the problem. Insist that they name a concrete, relevant issue, then ask, "What do you think we should do about it?"

If no useful response is given, come up with an exaggerated solution to lighten the mood.

Example: "You say that the president of your bridge club doesn't respect you. OK—let's have her killed. I'll start interviewing hit men on Monday."

If humor fails, establish a boundary. Say, "You don't want to think about solutions. When you do, let me know and I'll help."

Strategies for a Better Marriage from a Leading Divorce Lawyer

Robert Stephan Cohen, Esq., founding partner of the law firm of Cohen Lans LLP in New York City. His clients have included New York City Mayor Michael R. Bloomberg, supermodel Christie Brinkley and Donald Trump's former wives Ivana Trump and Marla Maples. He is author of *Reconcilable Differences: 7 Keys to Remaining Together from a Top Matrimonial Lawyer.* Simon & Schuster.

I n my 30 years as a matrimonial lawyer, I have listened to countless men and women tell me why their marriages have failed. Disagreements over money and lifestyle, and, of course, infidelity lead all kinds of couples to divorce court. Divorce is so common nowadays—expected, even—that couples start thinking about it at the first sign of trouble.

I have seen enough divorce battles up close to have a good handle on the marital mistakes couples make. Many issues can be worked out—if there's a real desire on both *sides. Here are the most common problems that endanger marriages and strategies to deal with them...*

• **Parallel lives.** A couple might live in the same house and share the same bed, but their communication may be perfunctory. They could go for days without really talking.

Both spouses are so busy with their "own" lives that they more or less forget they're married. Whether because of busy careers, child-rearing or even time-consuming hobbies, they never make time for each other.

Strategy: Carve out time for each other by picking one night a week to go on a "date." That means time together—no phone calls or kids. Also, don't let a day go by without having a conversation, even if it is by phone.

I recall one professional couple who had little free time for each other. They decided to share part of every day by walking their dog together. This simple change helped get their marriage back on track.

• **Infidelity.** Cheating spouses who want to save their marriages need to stop cheating and—assuming that they haven't been discovered—keep their mouths shut.

Strategy: That's right—don't tell. Telling a spouse about a one-night stand or an affair that has ended may make you feel less burdened and more virtuous, but you'll have created an enormous obstacle that the marriage may never overcome. Marriages fail not because of an affair, but because of the aftermath.

Warning: If the cat is out of the bag, don't try to fix things alone. Couples who successfully get past a known affair almost always do so with the help of a neutral party, such as a member of the clergy or a therapist.

• **Sexual incompatibility.** Most people who have been married for a while have sex less frequently than they once did. Some people are fine with that. For others, a lack of sex colors their view of the entire marriage.

How powerful is the sexual aspect of a marriage? In three decades, I have never had anyone come into my office wanting a divorce even though sex at home was great.

Strategy: Couples must discuss their sexual needs and wants. The increasing popularity of sexual topics in mainstream media may make it easier to broach the subject. One spouse could refer the other to a relevant article, for example, or they could go to a therapist together.

• **Problem children.** I have seen a number of marriages collapse over differences in how to deal with troublesome children. In the cases that I have dealt with, the children were heavy drug users or had serious mental illness, but even minor problems with children can damage a marital relationship.

If spouses already are leading parallel lives, they begin to line up in separate camps with their children. For instance, one spouse might hide a child's misconduct from the other. Then when the misconduct becomes impossible to ignore, the parents take opposite positions. In my experience, mothers frequently think that love and affection will alter their children's behavior, while fathers are more apt to take a tough stance. The fierce arguments that follow can destroy a marriage.

Stepparents have a particularly tough time. The children often try to undermine the new marriage because they see it as a threat to their own relationships with their parents, and they still hold on to the hope that their parents will get back together.

Strategy: Enlist the help of a neutral authoritative third party. When doctors or therapists take over much of the decision-making in terms of the child's treatment, the husband and wife can address marital issues and comfort each other, which often brings them closer together.

• **Money matters.** Financial disagreements can cause serious trouble for any couple, no matter how well-off they are. Historically, wives often have been in the dark about a couple's finances—and this is true even today.

Whether the husband insists on handling the money alone or the wife is willfully ignorant, the result often is heated arguments about finances that spiral into personal attacks on each other's values, common sense and honesty. It can undermine a marriage when, for instance, one spouse simply tells the other that the couple can't afford a trip this year.

Strategy: For the best chance of marital success, both spouses should be familiar with the household's finances and have a say in spending and investing. Then the couple's expectations will be similar and, in many cases, more realistic.

Some people think a prenuptial agreement is unromantic, but I'm a big fan of them—and the lessons I've learned through using prenups can be applied at any time during a marriage.

I recommend that engaged, newlywed or even long-married couples talk to an accountant, financial planner or even a divorce lawyer to get a sense of how the economics of the marriage can work. Then they should continue talking about money so that things stay out in the open at home.

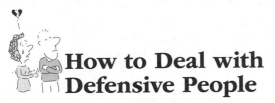

How to Deal with Defensive People

James Tamm, former judge and current managing director of the international consulting firm Business Consulting Network, Inc. He mediated more than 1,500 employment disputes during his 25 years as a senior administrative law judge for California's Public Employment Relations Board, San Francisco. He is coauthor of *Radical Collaboration: Five Essential Skills to Overcome Defensiveness and Build Successful Relationships.* HarperCollins.

A coworker responds with anger whenever someone disagrees with him. A husband retreats into silence whenever he gets into an argument with his wife. An employee buries her boss in piles of irrelevant information whenever she is asked a question.

These behaviors might appear different, but they're all just variations of the same problem—defensiveness. Additional forms of defensive behavior include habitually claiming, "I already knew that," when corrected…rationalizing or explaining away every misstep…or chronically making fun of others to deflect criticism from oneself.

Defensive people believe that their reactions protect them from outside attack. In fact, defensive people are unconsciously trying to shield themselves from their own doubts about their significance, competence or likeability.

We all get defensive sometimes and to some degree, but most of us learn to limit our defensive tendencies. Those who don't curb their defensiveness make life difficult for themselves and those who live and work with them. Their chronically defensive behavior promotes conflict and divisiveness…encourages rigid thinking that stifles creativity…and brings out the defensiveness in others.

Here's how to control your defensiveness —and better deal with the defensiveness of those around you…

DEALING WITH DEFENSIVE PEOPLE

The best way to blunt other people's defensiveness is to not become defensive yourself, even when provoked (more on that later). If you start to get upset, remind yourself that this person's defensiveness is rooted in his/her insecurities and has little to do with you. Arguing back will only make the person more insecure. *Instead…*

• **Be a good listener.** After the emotional moment has passed, offer the defensive person a chance to speak with you about the situation that led to the defensiveness. During the conversation, resist the urge to evaluate, criticize or suggest. Just listen intently, and take both the words and emotional content into account. Every now and then, summarize what you're hearing to make sure you understand—and to make sure the person knows that you're really listening.

Example: A coworker is upset with you because you criticized his proposal in a meeting. Rather than defend your position, listen to what your coworker has to say, then summarize—"You felt I misunderstood your recommendations" or "You were embarrassed in front of your colleagues."

By listening, you help the defensive person feel understood and accepted, easing his insecurities and making future defensive reactions less likely.

• **Change the way you argue.** Try "interest-based negotiation." With this strategy, your first goal is to state your opponent's underlying interests to his satisfaction. Your second goal is for him to do the same to you. Only then do you start proposing solutions. This creates an atmosphere of understanding that makes defensiveness less likely.

Example: I once mediated a labor strike in which the union insisted on a 7% raise, though the union leaders knew that management couldn't go past 4%. The discussions became adversarial. Through interest-based negotiation, management learned that the underlying goal of the union negotiators was not the 7% raise itself, but to make good on a promise they had made to their members to deliver a 7% raise. The parties agreed to a 7% raise for six months of the year, the equivalent of a 3.5% annual raise, which was within management's budget. Union members were happy with the 3.5% increase overall and pleased to have the negotiations resolved.

MANAGING YOUR OWN DEFENSIVENESS

The most difficult step in overcoming defensiveness in yourself is acknowledging that you are indeed defensive.

You probably consider your responses to perceived criticisms to be rational and justified when they occur. Reconsider them after the moment of confrontation has passed. Do they still seem appropriate, or were they unwarranted and unhelpful? If you're not certain, ask your spouse or a trusted friend—and try not to get defensive at the reply.

If you feel you tend to be defensive, identify the form your defensiveness takes. Are you belligerent? Uncommunicative? Overly talkative?

Other warning signs of defensiveness: Tightening in the gut…general sense of paranoia…adrenaline rush…feeling that you lack allies…a sense that you have been personally rejected, though the subject under discussion is only tangentially related to you.

To cut off defensive reactions…

• **Intercept the physical symptoms of defensiveness,** such as rapid, shallow breathing and a quickened pulse. It will be easier to alter your behavior if you can alter these physical reactions. Head to the rest room and splash cool water on your face…take a short walk to calm down…or if there's no time for a break, take a few long, deep breaths.

• **Monitor your thoughts.** If your mind is telling you, "This guy is out to get me," or "She doesn't think I'm very smart," you're likely to become increasingly defensive. Respond to negative thoughts with positive self-talk.

Examples: "I know this is difficult, but I can get through it"…"They're entitled to a different opinion"…"If I listen carefully enough, maybe I can learn something."

• **Develop a reaction appropriate to your particular form of defensiveness.** If you tend to flood others with information when you feel attacked, force yourself to remain quiet for a full minute. If you tend to shut down, push yourself to say something. If you counterattack when you feel confronted, take a few deep breaths and find something that you can agree with in what's being said.

There are times when we must defend ourselves against verbal attacks, but these times are rare—and knee-jerk defensiveness isn't effective anyway. Defensive reactions make us feel temporarily better about ourselves but rarely paint us or our opinions in a favorable light. Defensiveness provides no defense—it only makes us seem less credible.

Great Conversation Starters

Marjory Abrams, publisher, *Bottom Line* newsletters, Boardroom Inc., 281 Tresser Blvd., Stamford, CT 06901.

Whether in business or social settings, asking the right questions is key to getting people to open up, says communications expert Dorothy Leeds. In fact, she sees it as so important that she has written two books on the topic—*The 7 Powers of Questions* and *Smart Questions: The Essential Strategy for Successful Managers* (*www.dorothyleeds.com*).

Many people have a hard time making conversation, particularly with strangers. When counseling her clients, Dorothy affirms the value of open-ended questions for eliciting valuable information, promoting critical thinking and leading to genuine connections. (Closed-ended questions are those that can be answered with just a word or two.)

According to Dorothy, the average person asks 39 closed-ended questions for every one open-ended question.

Here are some common conversation starters that typically go nowhere—and alternatives that are more likely to open up a discussion...

●**"Isn't the temperature ghastly?"**

Better: "It's been so hot lately that I'm thinking of putting in central air-conditioning. How do you cool your home?"

●**"Have you seen the latest Tom Cruise movie?"**

Better: "I'm thinking of going to the movies this weekend. What have you seen lately that you liked—or hated?" A conversationally challenged person might just give you the name of the movie—but follow-up questions are easy. ("What did you like about it?")

Dorothy has her own tricks for starting conversations in situations where many people blunder...

On an airplane: Dorothy introduces herself to her seatmates, asks whether they are heading home or going on a trip and takes the conversation from there. (She also will ask whether they would prefer to talk or to stay quiet, adding something like "which is fine with me.")

At a party: She might first ask how a guest knows the host and follow it up with a more creative question. For example, at a graduation party (or other milestone event), "Tell me about the best gift you ever received." On New Year's Eve, "What's your most outrageous fantasy for the New Year?"

Conducting a job interview: "What were the tasks you most enjoyed on your last job and why? What were the tasks you least enjoyed and why?"

Even well-phrased questions will not get people to open up if your body language communicates that you don't truly want a conversation. *Dorothy's dos and don'ts...*

●**Don't cross your arms.** That posture suggests that you don't really want to talk.

●**Don't be a "space invader."** Most people are comfortable with a one-and-a-half-to-two-foot distance from new acquaintances. A very funny episode of the *Seinfeld* TV series involved a character who kept leaning in until he was about six inches away from the person to whom he was speaking, making that person very uncomfortable.

●**Do use a gracious tone.** Don't ask questions in a terse, combative or interrogative way.

●**Do give your full attention.** Shifting eyes make people think that you are not interested. Don't stare, but do try to maintain lots of eye contact.

The person asking questions automatically controls the conversation, so beware of monopolizing. Managers interviewing job candidates say that they spend 70% of the interview time listening—but research shows that they actually talk 70% of the time.

Shy? How to Come Out of Your Shell

Martin M. Antony, PhD, director and founder of the Anxiety Treatment and Research Centre, St. Joseph's Healthcare, and professor of psychiatry and behavioral neurosciences at McMaster University, both in Hamilton, Ontario, Canada, *www.martinantony.com*. He is the author of *10 Simple Solutions to Shyness: How to Overcome Shyness, Social Anxiety & Fear of Public Speaking*. New Harbinger.

I t's normal to feel nervous before attending a party, giving a speech or meeting with new people. But for shy people, social engagements can be fraught with anxiety.

Shyness is the tendency to be withdrawn or uncomfortable in situations that involve contact with others. Anyone, whether shy or extroverted, may sometimes experience the more intense form of shyness called social anxiety—extreme nervousness in situations that involve being observed or judged by others. You may experience both mental distress and the physical symptoms, such as a pounding heart or shaking hands.

More than five million of Americans, almost equally divided between women and men, have social anxiety disorder. In extreme cases, a person with social anxiety disorder may stop going out altogether. Millions more are shy. They cope socially, but with difficulty.

If shyness disturbs or disrupts your life, be assured that the pain can be conquered. Standard treatments for social anxiety disorder will likely work for shyness, too.

GETTING STARTED

Use a journal to record your experiences...

•**Note your general observations about what's happened before.** Then describe anxious thoughts as they occur or as soon as possible afterward. Think about where these thoughts came from and how to refocus them.

•**Classify what alarms you.** Do you fear big gatherings...one-on-one encounters...perhaps public speaking?

•**Identify all your symptoms.** *Shyness has three components...*

•*Physical*: Blushing...perspiring...shaking...palpitations...shortness of breath...dry mouth.

•*Cognitive:* Negative thoughts, such as, "I will make a fool of myself" and "No one will like me."

•*Behavioral:* Avoidance of all social situations...hiding out in a corner...increased consumption of alcohol.

•**Assess the situation.** In your journal, write a page on how shyness interferes with your life.

•**Set a goal.** Your immediate goal may be long term or short term, general or specific.

Example: A shy woman sought help from our clinic to increase her social comfort level three months before her daughter's wedding.

STRATEGY #1: EXPOSURE THERAPY

Shy people often fear rejection and can feel uncomfortable even during personal encounters that do not faze others. By deliberately exposing yourself to low-threat versions of alarming social situations, you'll learn that even if things don't work out this time, the consequences will be minimal and you'll be OK. Building your confidence over time will encourage you to break out of your shyness.

In developing exposure exercises for yourself, recall situations that created unacceptable levels of distress. List them from most distressing to least distressing. Address one of the least upsetting scenarios first and work your way up.

First, expose yourself to situations in a safe environment through role play. Ask friends to be your simulated audience at a group presentation...a relative can pretend to be a stranger at a party where you both arrived early.

Before the role play, imagine everything about such a situation—sights, sounds, smells...your thoughts, emotions and feelings. Record these in your notebook. What anxious thoughts, predictions or assumptions do you have regarding this exposure? What do you expect to happen during the exposure practice? What evidence do you have that your fearful thoughts are true?

After the role play, write up what happened and how accurate your original thoughts and predictions were.

When it feels safe, face your fear in the real world, but in a low-key way.

Example I: If you strongly dislike drawing attention to yourself, do just that by intentionally dropping your keys in a mall. People will look up for a second, then ignore you. That wasn't so bad. Slowly, you'll condition yourself to relax.

Example II: If making small talk intimidates you, say hello to a neighbor.

STRATEGY #2: SOCIAL SKILLS TRAINING

People who spend most of their time alone may feel anxious around others. At gatherings, they stand in the corner, talk quietly and look down. They remember parties as negative experiences and may stop going.

Start fitting in better: Talk to an amiable stranger, making eye contact, at the gym …give a short presentation at your book club.

Be patient with yourself. Give yourself assignments and follow them. (A therapist can help with this.) If one attempt does not work out, another will.

STRATEGY #3: COGNITIVE THERAPY

Cognitive therapy with a professional therapist makes you more aware of the beliefs and the assumptions that influence your emotions…helps you learn to view your negative beliefs as hypotheses, not facts…replaces your assumptions with more realistic, more positive ways of thinking. As you explore your reactions to ordinary situations, you will discover ways to protect yourself from anxiety. Working with a therapist can be very useful for beating shyness.

What a therapist might suggest: When you notice your anxiety level shifting up or down, ask yourself, "What am I thinking right now? How did my thoughts just change?" Record these observations in your notebook.

Most anxious thoughts can be phrased as predictions. Ask: "What do I think will happen? What might this person be thinking about me? How does that make me feel?"

Criticism and comparisons assail us from all sides. You may be afraid you aren't perfect, but can you name anyone who is? The same traits that make one person like you will make another person dislike you.

Example: Susan fears returning shoes to a store because "the saleswoman will think I'm an idiot." I ask Susan, "Can everybody like everybody? Does it matter what the sales clerk thinks of you?"

Assess the probable consequences of others' negative judgments—"Even if my friend never goes on vacation with me again, is that the end of the world?"

STRATEGY #4: MEDICATION

Drugs, best when used along with psychological approaches, can reduce even severe cases of social anxiety.

Advantage: Medication will often work more quickly than psychological therapies, which may not take effect for a couple of months.

Disadvantages: Medications may cause side effects, sometimes including weight gain, low sex drive and fatigue…may have to be taken for years, eventually becoming much more expensive than a few months of counseling…may interact with other drugs or alcohol…may have unpleasant withdrawal effects.

Three medications have been approved by the Food and Drug Administration for treating social anxiety disorder—*paroxetine* (Paxil), *venlafaxine* (Effexor XR) and *sertraline* (Zoloft). All are antidepressants, an umbrella term covering five drug classes. (The word "antidepressant" was coined for their initial use, to treat depression. They can do much more.)

Also effective: *Clonazepam* (Klonopin), *alprazolam* (Xanax) and other *benzodiazepines*. For some people, a combination of drugs works best. Ask your doctor whether any such drugs are appropriate for you.

SLOW BUT STEADY IMPROVEMENT

If you follow these winning strategies, you'll probably notice improvement in a few weeks or months. You may still be anxious at the end of treatment, but far less than before.

Don't be shy. Try.

Easy Way to Boost Your Mood

Lift your own mood by giving someone a compliment. Compliments tend to be passed on—people who receive them are more likely to give them to others. Aim for five positive encounters for every negative one… look for things people do right…support your friends…and give real recognition with a sincere smile.

Tom Rath, global practice leader, Clifton Strengths-Finder, Gallup, Inc., Princeton, NJ, and his late grandfather Donald O. Clifton, PhD, inventor of the Clifton StrengthsFinder, an analysis tool. They are the coauthors of *How Full Is Your Bucket?* Gallup.

A New Twist On the Power Of Positive Thinking

Joe Vitale, PhD, president of Hypnotic Marketing, Inc., a marketing consulting firm based outside Austin, TX. He is the author of more than 20 books, including *The Attractor Factor: 5 Easy Steps for Creating Wealth (Or Anything Else) from the Inside Out.* Wiley. *www.mrfire.com.*

W hen an Australian production company released *The Secret*—a documentary created by Rhonda Byrne, a former television producer, about the "law of attraction"—it soon became a self-help sensation. According to this theory, people can make their own realities through their thoughts.

Millions of DVDs and books based on it have been sold. Oprah Winfrey devoted two broadcasts to *The Secret*, telling her audience that she had been living her whole life according to the law of attraction, without even knowing it.

We asked one of the self-help gurus featured in the documentary, who has written his own book on the law of attraction, to tell us more about what this concept is and how we can make it work for us...

UNDERSTANDING THE LAW

The idea that we attract things to ourselves with our thoughts might seem controversial, but at a certain level, it's just common sense.

Is there any doubt that people who have positive thoughts about their careers are more likely to attract promotions and raises than those who think of their work as an unpleasant chore? Or that people who have upbeat, positive attitudes about their fellow man are more likely to attract friends than those who think everyone is against them? Medical science has shown that patients who think they will recover are more likely to do so. Our thoughts and attitudes unquestionably affect our world.

The law of attraction takes this a step further. Our thoughts shape every aspect of our existence. It isn't our boss, our family, bad luck or the economy that is holding us back—it is our own thoughts. The idea is to awaken and take conscious control—choose what we want to be or have. It's up to us to make things right.

ONE WAY IT WORKED FOR ME

I always wanted to have an audio program in the well-known Nightingale-Conant catalog of self-help audiotapes. Its roster of greats includes Tony Robbins, Deepak Chopra, Brian Tracy and Wayne Dyer. Despite the fact that I always sent the editors of Nightingale-Conant my new books as soon as they were published, I couldn't interest them in my work.

But I didn't give up. I simply held on to the dream, picturing my work in the catalog and trusting that something would give sooner or later. In the meantime, I kept writing books that I hoped would inspire and help people. One day, a man began sending me e-mails related to my book *There's a Customer Born Every Minute* (AMACOM), based on P.T. Barnum's life. I answered all his questions, glad to help.

Eventually he sent me an e-mail that said, "If you ever want your material considered by Nightingale-Conant, let me know. I'm their marketing project manager."

I immediately sent him my books, which he loved. He then proceeded to convince others at the catalog company to include my work. It did take nearly 11 months, but Nightingale-Conant now carries my audiotape *The Power of Outrageous Marketing*, and it is a best seller for them.

This story illustrates many lessons. One is the power of the Internet—my contact found me at my Web site. Another is that I was willing to be helpful to someone who wrote to me out of the blue—if I had ignored his e-mail, I never would have found out where he worked. Still another is the importance of having someone believe in you. But certainly one key lesson is the true magic of the power of a dream.

THE FIVE STEPS

•**Step 1.** Know what you want. It is easy to become fixated on the pain of a bad back...the mental strain of a mountain of bills...or the frustration of a go-nowhere job or challenging relationship. But our bitterness about our problems only attracts more problems to us.

Replace negative thoughts about your problems with positive thoughts about the way you would like things to be, and you'll draw those things to you instead. "I'm fed up with these interruptions" becomes "I want a quiet, peaceful place where I can read a book." "My feet are killing me" becomes "My foot pain will go away soon, and I will be just as mobile as ever." "My marriage is failing" becomes "I have a wonderful spouse whom I love, and I'm going to make this work."

●**Step 2.** Think big. Decide what your goal is. What would make your heart sing? What would you do if you knew you could not fail? What would you want if you could have anything?

Most people feel bound by the limits of what they consider feasible for their lives. They hope to get through a difficult day...or to find enough money to pay the bills. They don't dare hope for a truly fabulous, life-changing day...or to make enough money to put them on easy street. But even your biggest dreams are not big to the universe. There are trillions of dollars worth of wealth floating around the world—who's to say you can't be a millionaire? Set aside the constraints, and think about what you would want if you could have anything at all.

Write your goal on a card, and put it in your pocket or purse. By doing so, you will unconsciously remind yourself of your intention. Your own mind will then nudge you in the direction of making your goal a reality.

●**Step 3.** Clear all negative or limiting beliefs. It's crucial to rid ourselves of any negative beliefs we have about ourselves. Common examples include variations of "I'm not good enough"..."If it hasn't happened yet, it never will"..."Somebody (or something) always will stand in the way of my success"...and "If I get my hopes up, I'll only get hurt."

Example: If your weight-loss attempts always fail, the reason could be a negative self-belief. You might believe that since your parents were overweight, you are destined to be overweight, too...or that the failure of your earlier weight-loss attempts is proof that you're incapable of sticking to a diet. You might believe that looking better will change who you are...damage your relationships with your friends...or inspire new romantic relationships that will end in heartache.

Once you find a negative belief, confront it. Clear it from your mind, and replace it with a positive thought, one based on the idea that you are capable and worthy of achieving your goal.

●**Step 4.** Feel what it would be like to have, do or be what you want. Just imagine that you already have what you want. If you are a salesperson and your goal is to make $200,000 in sales commissions this year, think about how you would feel if you achieved that. Pretend you are a movie director, and write a script for what you want to experience. Really get into it as you write it. Feel it. Sense it.

Instead of writing, "I want a customer to call me with a big order," write, "A brand-new customer just phoned and ordered $100,000 from me. I feel fantastic! I'm still smiling about it. The customer was so pleased."

Visualizing your goals and desires can set the process in motion, drawing close to you people and things that help you get what you want.

●**Step 5.** Let go as you act on your intuitive impulses and allow the results to manifest. Once you start thinking, "I'm going to be a millionaire," then ideas, contacts and opportunities capable of making you a million dollars will be pulled toward you. You will notice a societal need that you could fill by starting a company...or see the perfect way to promote the skills or ideas you already have...or realize that the person you just met could help put your career on the fast track.

Once you start thinking, "My spouse (or boss) will treat me wonderfully," you'll begin to see ways to give your spouse (or boss) what he/she wants from you. When you learn to give these people what they want, they will start to treat you wonderfully.

The Art of Friendship—Easy Steps to Lasting Relationships

Roger Horchow, a Tony Award–winning Broadway producer and founder of The Horchow Collection, the first luxury mail-order catalog, which was bought by Neiman Marcus in 1988. Famed for his ability to build relationships, he is coauthor, with his daughter, Sally Horchow, of *The Art of Friendship: 70 Simple Rules for Making Meaningful Connection.* St. Martin's.

Money, possessions and jobs come and go—family and friends are what have true meaning. We have limited control over who is in our family, but we can choose our friends. In fact, our willingness and ability to cultivate meaningful friendships can have a greater impact on our quality of life than anything else we do. It's important to view each encounter as an opportunity to start a new friendship and each day as an opportunity to deepen the friendships we already have. *Here are six secrets to making and developing new friends...*

1. Alter your habits. People are prone to falling into ruts. We find a way of doing things that works, then repeat it over and over for the rest of our lives. But repeating the same patterns every day makes it unlikely that we will meet anyone new or start any new friendships.

Pick a different coffee shop, a different walking path or a different evening activity. Join a new club, or take a new class. Greet every new person you encounter with a friendly hello, and remain open to the possibility of further conversation. If you decide that you prefer your old way of doing things, you can always return to it tomorrow. Nothing is at risk but a few hours of your time.

2. Prepare some conversation starters. Before you go to a place where you're likely to meet new people, think up a few all-purpose conversation-spurring lines that you feel comfortable using. *The top conversation categories include...*

- **Compliments.** If you're trying to start a friendship, not a romance, your compliment shouldn't be too personal—compliment an article of clothing, not someone's looks or personality.

- **Opinions.** Give people an opportunity to share their views, and they'll love you for it. Avoid topics that are controversial, such as politics or religion.

    Example: "I'm sorry to interrupt, but I heard you mention the new James Bond movie. My wife and I were thinking about seeing it. Do you recommend it?"

- **Information requests.** People like to be helpful, and asking for information gives them a chance to do so at no cost to themselves. Ask someone if he/she can recommend a restaurant or provide driving directions.

3. Don't assume that you don't have time for new friends. Many people feel overscheduled with the commitments and relationships they have and fear that adding new friends means devoting more time to social engagements. However, the potential friendships you turn down for time reasons could become the most meaningful friendships of your life.

Go ahead and add new friends even if you're busy. If time is really tight, invite a prospective friend to a party or include him in larger get-togethers, where adding one more person (or couple) to the group won't add to your time commitments.

4. Follow up. Will a new acquaintance become a close friend? That likely depends on whether one of you follows up on the initial meeting within a few weeks. A good follow-up should show that you remember something personal about him. *Examples...*

- **Clip an article about a topic the two of you discussed,** and mail it to the prospective friend. Jot a note on it, saying, "We chatted about this at the MacGregors' party. I thought the article might be of interest to you."

- **If you discussed a specific restaurant or a type of cuisine,** call or e-mail this person and mention that you and your spouse are planning on dining at this restaurant soon. Would he care to join you?

5. Don't keep score. There's a natural tendency to expect a quid pro quo in friendships. Relationships often suffer when this doesn't occur.

Example: "We have invited the Smiths over three times, and they have never had us to their house. Maybe we should stop calling them."

Consider that there might be a reason these friends don't invite you over. They may not be comfortable entertaining or their home might not be as impressive as yours. Being a friend means enjoying the time you spend together, not expecting payback.

It is smart to keep score yourself, however. If you can't have friends over to your home, find another way to repay their hospitality—for example, take them out to dinner. And when you do fall behind on invitations, apologize and explain the reason.

6. Don't confuse a business relationship with a friendship. Some business acquaintances become true friends, but others act like friends only for the good of their careers.

Example: A colleague might seem like your best buddy, but he stops talking to you as soon as you're transferred to another department.

Don't take this personally. The coworker's actions speak only to his own priorities, not to your worth as a friend. Let this relationship go, and think no more of it.

Better Listening

Listen quietly when someone is talking. Don't spend the time formulating your response or you will miss some of his/her message. Welcome his ideas with an open mind. This helps you personally and professionally—people want someone to care about what they say.

Gary D. Danoff, executive coach, Rockville, MD, *coachgaryd@aol.com.*

Identifying True Friendship

Laverne Bardy-Pollak, author of the humor column titled "Laverne's View" for *50 Plus Monthly*, a regional NJ newspaper, and a columnist for the nationally syndicated Senior Wire news service. Her essays, articles and poems have appeared in many magazines and anthologies. A resident of Newton, NJ, she is compiling a book of her columns and working on a memoir.

Potential friends are attracted much as lovers are—through both chemistry and body language...the recognition of similar temperaments, intelligence, sense of humor, experiences, tastes and interests. The more that two people have in common, the deeper their relationship promises to be.

How you will know a true friend...

● **Friends are people you genuinely look forward to sharing time with** and miss when you're apart for too long.

● **Friends reveal their weaknesses.** At 50 and over, we (finally) know we're not perfect. Recognizing the same faults in ourselves strengthens the bond.

● **Friends accept each other's quirks and value their strengths.**

Example: My friends know that as a writer, I have an inordinate personal and professional craving for solitude. An old pal confided, "It's a good thing I understand your needs. Otherwise, this relationship wouldn't have lasted so long."

● **Friends reveal truths that you may not want to hear.** In turn, you can say what's on your mind without being hurtful or insulting. A solid friendship can withstand well-intended criticism.

Bonus: Those who know us best may offer better personal advice than anyone else could.

● **Friends are generous and flexible.**

Example: Two old pals and I choose activities to share on our own birthdays. They love museums, plays and visits to the big city...I prefer craft shows, antiquing and being pampered at a spa. Obliging each other is part of the fun—and opens us to new experiences.

Two Top Executives Reveal Their Success Secret—Being Nice

Robin Koval, president, and Linda Kaplan Thaler, CEO and chief creative officer, of The Kaplan Thaler Group, Ltd., a New York City advertising agency responsible for such successful campaigns as the award-winning Aflac duck. They are coauthors of *The Power of Nice: How to Conquer the Business World with Kindness.* Currency.

Nice has an image problem. Nice people often are assumed to be wimpy and naïve—and not particularly successful. We're told that nice guys finish last. In truth, nice wields amazing power. *Here's how...*

• **Nice people live longer.** People who volunteer their time typically outlive nonvolunteers, according to a study conducted by researchers at the University of Michigan.

• **Nice people are more productive workers and more effective bosses.** Each 2% increase in the cheerfulness of an organization's employees leads to a 1% increase in revenue, according to research by psychologist Daniel Goleman, PhD, co-chairman of Rutgers University's Consortium for Research on Emotional Intelligence in Organizations.

• **Nice people have happier love lives.** Low-key, congenial people are 50% less likely to divorce than the population as a whole, according to a University of Toronto study.

• **Nice people stay out of court.** Doctors who spend more time positively interacting with their patients are less likely to be sued, according to health-care researchers.

HOW TO BE NICER

• **Make small gestures of kindness** to those often treated poorly. The worse the treatment someone tends to receive, the more he/she will appreciate even the smallest kindness.

Example: An airline passenger offered a cookie to a harried flight attendant—and was rewarded with an upgrade to first class.

• **Share credit.** Turn your victories into triumphs for your colleagues. Not only is this a nice gesture, it creates a group of people who have an interest in seeing your ideas succeed.

• **Be free with compliments.** People worry that frequent compliments make them seem phony or smarmy, but they rarely do if given sincerely.

• **Help your rivals.** A rival need not be an enemy. Today's competitor might be tomorrow's ally.

Example: Magician Tony Hassini shared blueprints for some illusions he wasn't using with a promising young magician. That young magician, Doug Henning, went on to tremendous success and ended up hiring Hassini to help with his Broadway show.

• **Give people a little more than they expect.** Making small, unanticipated gestures sends the message that you really care.

Example: The service department at a Lexus dealership in California puts chocolate candies in vehicle cup holders when customers retrieve their cars. Business has climbed 20% since this policy began.

• **Show vulnerability.** Admit that you're new at something and even a little scared. Your admission of weakness makes those around you feel better about their own insecurities. It also could win them to your side, because people generally root for beginners and underdogs.

• **Make connections for others.** When you meet someone new, ask yourself if someone you already know would benefit from making his acquaintance. Then make the introduction.

• **Repair lapses in niceness.** We all have days when we speak rudely or treat people poorly. Acknowledge your mistake. And do so promptly—the longer you wait, the more the hurt grows.

Get What You Want— Secret from a Former White House Negotiator

Martin E. Latz, founder and president of Latz Negotiation Institute, a training company in Scottsdale, AZ, whose clients include Eli Lilly & Co., Honeywell Aerospace and many of the nation's largest law firms. During the Clinton administration, Mr. Latz worked as a member of the White House advance negotiating team. He is author of *Gain the Edge: Negotiating to Get What You Want.* St. Martin's.

Everything is negotiable—from division of household chores to the price of a car. Many people believe that they are good negotiators because they have a comprehensive knowledge of the subject at hand and know what they want to achieve—but they often fail to gain an edge because they haven't thought about the process itself. They apply pressure or make compromises when it feels right on a gut level, rather than use battle-tested strategies that can sway the other party.

Here are the common mistakes that prevent good negotiators from being great...

Mistake 1: **Not being aggressive enough.** You fail to negotiate aggressively because a particular situation or environment is awkward or even intimidating.

Examples: Buying a car...asking for a severance package.

It's hard to think clearly and strategize when you are up against an expert who has greater knowledge or experience...or if the issue has much greater bearing on your emotional well-being and future than on your counterpart's. *What to do instead...*

●**Gather facts that can help your cause.** Facts and statistics empower you and help to level the playing field.

Example: Joe was laid off from his law firm. He asked for two months' severance because he figured it would take him that long to get a new job.

Instead, don't ask for what you would like or need. Ask for what you *deserve.* Had Joe talked to former employees, he would have learned that the company's severance packages ranged from four to six months' pay. Knowing there was wiggle room, he could have bolstered his demands—for example, with statistics on how much revenue he had brought into the organization.

●**Let someone negotiate for you.** There's nothing wrong with admitting that certain situations rattle you.

Example: Mary is a business owner and an excellent negotiator. When her father died, she had to go to the funeral home to purchase a coffin. She knew she would overpay because she was too upset and preoccupied to do the proper research. So, she asked another family member who had experience in funeral planning to step in.

Mistake 2: **Not negotiating with the ultimate decision maker.** You spend 30 minutes haggling with an electronics salesman over the price of a top-of-the-line home-entertainment system. After you agree on the price, the salesman reveals that he needs approval from the store manager. Inevitably, the word comes from the manager that you need to make some minor price concessions. *What to do instead...*

●**Get your counterpart to disclose the full extent of his/her authority early on.** If he is not in a position to make the decision, ask to speak to someone who has sufficient authority. Stress the importance of integrity—if you can't trust his word, it's a deal breaker. Don't accept the explanation that the underling is in charge of the deal and the manager's approval is just perfunctory.

Also, ask your counterpart several times if all issues are on the table.

Reason: The decision maker often requests concessions on issues that were not brought up during the negotiations.

Example: Many car dealerships impose a "document-preparation fee" or similarly named charge that really is just more profit for them. It magically shows up after a deal has already been struck.

●**Turn the tables.** Tell a salesperson that you need to run the store manager's last-minute requests by your spouse for his/her final approval. You then can come back and demand additional concessions. Turning the tables this way will encourage the salesperson to stop playing games and reach a quick deal.

***Mistake 3:* Offering to split the difference.** Almost everyone has used this closing technique when a negotiation drags on. Both parties compromise and give an equal amount—but if you make the initial offer, you will tend to lose more in the end.

Example: Steve had set the price for his used BMW at $12,000. The buyer was offering $10,000. Steve said they were close enough that he would accept $11,000 to be fair. In fact, what he did was make an oral commitment to accept $11,000 without the buyer having to concede anything. The buyer called back later and said, "I still prefer to pay $10,000, but I'm willing to split the difference and offer you $10,500." Of course, Steve insisted on splitting the difference again. The car sold for $10,750—$250 less than the "fair" compromise that he initially offered.

Instead, play it cool…rather than pushing for a quick deal, wait for your counterpart to offer to split the difference.

***Mistake 4:* Talking too much.** The person in charge of the discussion is the one doing all the talking, right? Actually, you lose leverage if you monopolize the conversation. You give yourself a false sense of control and wind up revealing more information than you want. Conversely, quiet negotiators present information only at the most strategic times. *What to do…*

• **Aim to ask twice as many questions as your counterpart**—exploring his needs, interests and goals and establishing a rapport—and spend twice as much time listening as speaking.

• **Use information-blocking techniques.** These let you withhold sensitive information without lying or acting so evasive that your counterpart loses trust in you.

Example: Allison was interviewing for a position as a marketing manager. During her third interview, the CEO asked her outright, "Are you seriously considering a position with any other firm right now?" The

truth was that she wasn't. She didn't want to lie, however, she knew that admitting this information would weaken her leverage in the salary negotiations. *Her alternatives…*

• Answer a different question. *Response:* "I've interviewed with many companies over the past few months, and yours is my favorite." You are addressing the issue, but in an indirect fashion.

• Discount the question's relevance and ask for clarification. *Response:* "I am not sure I understand how that makes a difference to your interest in me. If we're a good fit, this will work. That's more important than anything, right?"

• Apologize for not being able to answer due to integrity, legal issues, etc. *Response:* "I'd like to tell you, but it wouldn't be fair to the other companies with which I've talked. Naturally, I would never reveal the discussions that you and I have had to your competitors."

Dr. Joy Browne on Getting the Help You Need

Joy Browne, PhD, licensed clinical psychologist in New York City and host of a daily syndicated radio show. She is author of several books, including *Getting Unstuck: 8 Simple Steps to Solving Any Problem* and her newest, *Dating Disasters and How to Avoid Them* (both from Hay House).

As a psychologist, I am struck by the way people tend to isolate themselves during painful times. Whether dealing with losing a job, the end of a relationship or any major disappointment, it seems that when we most need other people, we find it most difficult to ask for help.

One reason is that people believe—erroneously—that they should be able to handle problems themselves. They don't want to impose or be a burden.

The truth is that most people like being asked for help. Think about how you feel when a friend needs your help. It's flattering. It means that your friend is taking the relationship seriously. Giving and receiving make friendships stronger.

BE SPECIFIC

Some people feel it's up to friends and loved ones to recognize distress and offer help without being asked, but it's unrealistic to expect others to read your mind or catch your hints. *Here are ways to ask for the help you need...*

- **Problem solving.** "I can't figure out what to do. Would you mind brainstorming options with me?"

- **A sympathetic ear.** "It's been a tough week. Can I tell you about it?"

- **Reassurance.** "I'm discouraged. I'd love it if you could remind me of the things I'm doing right in my life."

- **Perspective.** "I'm not sure if the problem is me or him. Can I get your take on the situation?"

- **Sympathy.** "My boss is on a rampage. I don't need to hear about how I should handle him—I just want someone to take my side for a few minutes."

- **Affection.** "I could use a hug."

- **Company.** "Would it be OK if I came over for a few hours? I don't want to be alone this afternoon."

- **Suggestions.** "My computer crashed. Can you recommend a good repair service?"

- **Physical assistance.** "I'm too sick to go out. Could you stop by the deli and pick up some soup for me?"

PRACTICE

Don't wait until you're in a crisis to ask for help. Practice in situations that aren't so traumatic.

Example: When your car is in the shop, call a friend and say, "Would you be able to give me a ride to work?"

SHOW APPRECIATION

Helping isn't something you contract for. Treating your request as a quid pro quo ("If you do X for me, I'll do Y for you") is likely to offend. Instead, be generous with your thanks.

Examples: Send a thank-you note... flowers...or a small gift.

Help for Anxiety

Nervous about stressful situations, such as public speaking? Have sexual intercourse the night before.

Recent finding: Participants who engaged in intercourse before stressful events had lower blood pressure levels and felt less stressed the next day than those who abstained from intercourse.

Stuart Brody, PhD, professor of psychology, University of Paisley, Scotland, and leader of a study of 50 people, published in *Biological Psychology*.

Lay on the Guilt

Fear-and-guilt combination provides the best motivation for improving behavior. Researchers find that this combination is much more effective than a hopeful or positive message at changing behavior.

Example: The message, "Smoking pot may not kill you but it will kill your mother," proved much more effective than positive and educational messages at deterring drug use among teenagers.

Conclusion: Making people feel hopeful, good or informed is much less important for changing behavior than making them feel accountable.

Kirsten A. Passyn, PhD, assistant professor of marketing, Salisbury University, Salisbury, MD, and Mita Sujan, PhD, Woldenburg professor of marketing, Tulane University, New Orleans.

Rational Responses To Irrational Verbal Attacks

Nando Pelusi, PhD, clinical psychologist in private practice, New York City.

There are reasonable ways to resolve conflicts with less-than-logical foes. *Try...*

- **Ask the person what he/she is upset about.** This shows that you want to communicate, not argue—and it puts the responsibility back on him.
- **Concede one kernel of truth,** if there is one, but deny the generalization.

   Example: If your sister-in-law calls you a screwup, admit to one specific error but say that it does not represent everything you do.
- **Take a stab at what you think the person is feeling:** "You sound angry right now. I'm sorry you feel that way." Do not place blame.
- **Resist the urge to win.** Instead, listen and ask questions, which will ultimately help the other person independently arrive at a workable solution.

The Gift of Peace

Marjory Abrams, publisher, *Bottom Line* newsletters, Boardroom Inc., 281 Tresser Blvd., Stamford, CT 06901.

I recently had dinner with my friend the Reverend Ann Schmidt, who is director of pastoral care at Stamford Hospital in Connecticut. She has been involved with end-of-life counseling for more than 30 years. I'm continually amazed at how she is able to remain so positive in the face of such constant sadness. Ann mentioned that most of the patients (and their loved ones) whom she counsels are looking for peace. "How do you help them find that?" I asked.

One of her strategies is to ask her patients what helped when they were faced with difficulties in the past. Was it a particular friend? A prayer? Pouring out their feelings on paper? Through poetry or art? Journaling on a computer?

Remember that during hard times, you are not alone. To find out about local support groups and other resources, ask a hospital social worker or chaplain, or contact a community or social service agency. *There are many national organizations that can provide information and support, including…*

- **American Cancer Society.** 800-227-2345, *www.cancer.org.*
- **American Stroke Association.** 888-478-7653, *www.strokeassociation.org.* (Ask for a free subscription to its bimonthly magazine, *Stroke Connection Magazine.*)
- **The Compassionate Friends,** which assists families following the death of a child of any age. 877-969-0010, *www.compassionatefriends.org.*
- **Gilda's Club,** which helps people living with cancer and their loved ones. 888-445-3248, *www.gildasclub.org.*

Ann observes that we all need someone to lean on—but when dealing with loss and grief, it should be someone who can enter into the experience and not try to "fix" things. If someone you know is suffering because a loved one is ailing, let him/her feel whatever he is feeling. Don't say that you understand or that you know what he is going through. You don't. Simply be present and listen.

The grieving process is different for everyone. Cleaning out your parents' home with your sibling may stir up memories of when your younger brother got more cookies than you did. Suddenly you may feel as if you are seven years old again—and start squabbling as if you were, unless you understand what is going on.

Often, spouses are at odds. According to Ann, women tend to cry, express fear or talk through their emotions. Men traditionally want to fix things (find the best doctor, treatment center, "do, do, do"). Heavy conversation may occur not over coffee but during a golf game or other activity, where talking is secondary. Neither way is right or wrong.

When I asked Ann which books she recommends as a source of help and inspiration, she cautioned me that no one book is right for everyone. *Here are some excellent ones representing a variety of approaches…*

- *The Art of Happiness* by the Dalai Lama and Howard C. Cutler (Riverhead).
- *A Grief Observed* by C.S. Lewis (Harper One).
- Hazelden Meditation Series (Hazelden), which includes *The Promise of a New Day, Each Day a New Beginning* and *Touchstones.*

- *Healing After Loss: Daily Meditations for Working Through Grief* by Martha W. Hickman (Collins).
- *Kitchen Table Wisdom: Stories That Heal, 10th Anniversary Ed.*, by Rachel Naomi Remen (Riverhead).
- *When Life Becomes Precious: The Essential Guide for Patients, Loved Ones, and Friends of Those Facing Serious Illnesses* by Elise Babcock (Bantam).
- *Sabbath: Finding Rest, Renewal, and Delight in Our Busy Lives* by Wayne Muller (Bantam).

All of our lives are touched by loss—but as Ann pointed out, the human spirit is extraordinarily resilient.

How to Help Someone Who Is Mourning

Don't ask if he/she needs help—he may be unable to focus on what he needs. Assume that nothing has been done. Help with errands, dog walking, laundry, baby care, housecleaning and even bring in a meal. People in mourning may be overwhelmed. Anything you do will be appreciated.

Rabbi Aryeh Markman, executive director, Aish HaTorah Los Angeles, part of a worldwide network of Jewish educational centers with programs in 200 cities, *www.aish.com.*

The Right Way to Handle Difficult Conversations

Barbara Pachter, business consultant and executive coach, based in Cherry Hill, NJ. She is author of several books on communications issues, including *New Rules @ Work: 79 Etiquette Tips, Tools, and Techniques to Get Ahead and Stay Ahead.* Prentice Hall.

It is not fun to confront a neighbor about his barking dog...inform a coworker that he has bad breath...or tell a friend her behavior is inappropriate—but sometimes something must be said. *Here's how best to say it...*

- **Ask permission before you stick your nose in.** You think a close friend needs to rethink his comb-over, but you are unsure how he'll react if you suggest it. The odds that he'll respond favorably improve dramatically if you first get his go-ahead to raise a difficult subject.

Example: "There's something I've been thinking about. I don't know if it's really my business to bring it up, but if it were me, I'd want someone to say something. Is it okay if I raise a sticky subject?"

- **Pick a calm moment.** Your neighbor doesn't mow his grass for weeks at a time. You have been stewing over the situation all day and decide to confront him when he gets home from work. However, people tend to be tightly wound when they first get home, making a tricky conversation that much more challenging. It is better to wait until he is relaxed. People tend to be calmer on weekends than on weekdays...after an hour or more at home than immediately after fighting traffic...and soon after a meal than when hungry. In the workplace, people are calmest when they are not facing deadlines.

If you're worked up over the problem—or even about an unrelated problem—postpone the conversation until you're calm, too.

- **Act as though it's no big deal.** A coworker has food on her face at an important lunch meeting. Minimize her embarrassment by sharing this information without judgment or embarrassment on your part. When the messenger seems embarrassed, the message inevitably seems more embarrassing. Simply describe the situation—"Mary, you have a little piece of broccoli on your cheek."

If this person still acts embarrassed, add, "Don't worry, it happens to everyone"...or "I don't think anyone noticed but me."

Whenever possible, tell the person in private. If there's no way to escape the crowd, whisper or write a note to keep things confidential.

- **Don't just raise a problem**—also propose a solution. Your natural inclination when you share difficult information might

209

be to blurt out the problem and escape the conversation as soon as possible, but this might leave the other party feeling confused or angry. After saying there's a problem, mention a potential solution (unless it's obvious), then check that everything is still okay between you and this person. By ending with a question, you help turn a confrontation into a conversation.

Example: "Jack, your dog's been doing his business on my lawn and digging up my wife's garden. Could you tie him up when you put him out back or keep an eye on him? Would that be okay with you?"

•**Assume the best.** A neighbor's loud music has been keeping you awake every night for a week. You feel like telling the jerk what you think of him. Instead, enter the conversation under the assumption that this person is unaware of the problem and would genuinely want to know. If people sense our dislike for them, they're less likely to change their behavior for us.

•**Mix the good with the bad.** The text in a coworker's slide presentation is so small that no one can read it. Share this problem, but include good news.

Example: "I loved your presentation. You really covered all the facts. One thing—you might consider using a larger font next time. It was hard to read from the back of the room."

•**Keep it focused.** You finally get up the nerve to confront a relative about something that has been bothering you…then you mention a few other problems as well. Better to discuss only one tough issue per conversation. Presenting a list of quibbles might make the other person feel as if you're piling on bad news—and the secondary issues could detract from your main point.

•**If someone confronts *you*, respond with grace, not anger.** Let's say a neighbor asks you to replace your rusty old mailbox. Even if you don't think this is any of his business, say something positive, such as, "Thank you for letting me know. I'll think about that." If you decide you want to keep the mailbox, you may want to explain why—"It's been in my family for years."

•**Know how to duck a difficult conversation.** When a problem is likely to resolve itself if we do nothing…the time isn't right for confrontation…or you want to avoid an issue…

•Suddenly "remember" a previous responsibility and excuse yourself.

•Say, "Oh, I just remembered, I wanted to ask you about…" then raise a completely different matter.

•Answer a difficult question posed to you with "Well, what do you think?"

•Dodge the issue when asked your opinion about something you dislike with "I bet everyone will love it."

Everyday Etiquette

Peggy Post, great-granddaughter-in-law of etiquette pioneer Emily Post. She is a director and spokesperson for the Emily Post Institute in Burlington, VT, and author of *Emily Post's Etiquette, 17th Edition.* HarperCollins. Their Web site is *www.emilypost.com.*

D o you ever find yourself in a sticky situation and don't know what to do or say? *Here, renowned etiquette expert Peggy Post gives advice on how to handle rude kids, nosy coworkers and much more…*

CELL PHONE BLABBERMOUTH

•**When I'm near a person who is speaking loudly on a cell phone, what's the best way to ask him/her to be quiet?** It's hard to enjoy a meal, a train ride or any other activity in public when your ears are held hostage by a cell phone blabbermouth. Sometimes, simply a pointed look at the talker will get your message across. Speaking directly to the offender usually is not a good idea—it could lead to a very unpleasant confrontation.

Your best bet is to seek help from an authority—a restaurant manager, for example. He might ask the caller to move to the lobby or restroom area. If the cell phone user is on a train, speak to the conductor.

FORGETTING A NAME

• **What should you do if you're about to introduce someone and suddenly can't remember his name?** We've all been there—that awkward moment when we're starting to make an introduction but cannot remember a name. Just say, "I'm very embarrassed. I have completely forgotten your name."

If you suspect someone has forgotten your name, one of the kindest gestures that you can make is to simply extend your hand to them and say, "Hello, I'm Jane Smith. It's so wonderful to meet you."

E-MAIL RULES

• **What's the most polite way to ask someone to stop e-mailing jokes, cards or other frivolous messages?** Individuals who are inundated by e-mails often feel bothered, not flattered, by pass-along e-mails. If you're a victim of "friend spam," speak up politely and honestly, asking the friend to stop. Say, "John, I love hearing from you, but please stop sending me jokes via e-mail. I'm so busy at work that I don't have time to keep up with my personal e-mail."

• **Is it OK to e-mail a condolence note? What about a wedding or birthday party invitation?** Any invitation that you would extend over the phone can be done with e-mail, assuming that the person you are inviting looks at e-mail regularly.

E-mail also is great for confirming invitations that you've already made over the phone. *Sue, we're looking forward to having you and Dan join us at the cookout at our house on Saturday at 6 pm.*

For condolences, it's acceptable to send an e-mail first, but it always should be followed by a handwritten note. Think of the e-mail as replacing the phone call, not the handwritten note.

Very informal or last-minute baby or bridal shower invitations can be extended via e-mail, but it is better to issue traditional invitations through the mail. Ditto for wedding invitations. Only if you're getting married at the last minute in a small, informal ceremony can you send an e-mail. For any other type of wedding, a mailed invitation is appropriate.

PERSONAL HYGIENE PROBLEM

• **An acquaintance has awful body odor. What, if anything, can I do?** Since you are just an acquaintance, it would be best not to say anything to him about his problem. Speaking up directly could embarrass him greatly.

The only way that you could try to help is to mention the problem discreetly to someone who knows him well. You could suggest to the good friend that he say something like, "Matt, I've noticed that you have the same problem I do with perspiration. I didn't know what to do until I tried this product. It worked for me, and it might work for you, too." Even if Matt is embarrassed initially, he probably will appreciate his friend's concern.

If the acquaintance is a coworker and his problem is hindering his ability to interact with others, you might say something in confidence to his supervisor, who in turn could speak to him discreetly.

DINNER PARTY DILEMMA

• **I'm a vegetarian. When invited to a dinner party, should I let the host know this ahead of time? What about my husband, who is allergic to particular foods?** Upon accepting the invitation, mention any allergy that could cause a serious reaction. Explain to your hostess, "We'd love to come for dinner, but I must tell you that Bob is deathly allergic to shellfish."

Dietary preferences, such as vegetarianism, should be handled on a more individual basis, depending upon the event.

If it is a large party or a buffet, the guest should try to "make do" since a variety of foods will be served.

If the gathering is small, the dinner is in your honor or you're going to be an overnight houseguest, you should mention your restrictions to the host and offer to bring a dish to share. Say, "Thanks so much for the invitation, Joan. I should let you know that I am a vegetarian. I'd love to bring a zucchini casserole if that's OK with you."

This way, your host won't work hard only to make something you can't eat, and you'll be providing a solution to your restriction.

RUDE KIDS

• **What should I do if a child is rude and his parents are not present?** It depends on what type of behavior you have witnessed. A simple correction or explanation from a well-meaning adult whom the child knows well usually is fine—as long as the comment is made in a way that doesn't embarrass the child or criticize his parents.

For example, it would be fine to say, "Jack, in our house, we don't use language like that." Or when it's just you and your grandchild sharing a meal, you might say, "It's so much nicer when you chew with your mouth closed, Maryanne."

You needn't discuss the behavior with the child's parent unless it's particularly disruptive or outlandish. If the child's parents are there and do or say nothing, generally you will have to bite your tongue.

If you feel you must respond to the behavior, do so genially. If the child talks back, you could say something like, "I really don't appreciate the way you are speaking to me. Could you use a nicer tone?" You want to say it in a friendly way that expresses your sincere concern for how the conversation is going.

NOSY COWORKERS

• **What is the best way to keep the nosy coworkers who drop by my cubicle from reading confidential papers on my desk or e-mails on my computer?** Tell them to get lost—in a polite way, of course. While cubicle-style offices may encourage some coworkers to participate in this kind of space invasion, it is unprofessional and intrusive. Simply say, "Frank, I'll have to ask you to step back from my desk. I'm working on a confidential project. I'm sure you understand. Thanks."

8

Fitness News

The Simplest Diet Ever

Don't be misguided by the glowing testimonials from people who have lost lots of weight with some of today's popular diets.

Fact: Nearly everyone who starts a new diet loses weight initially. Up to 95% of these dieters fail to maintain their weight loss after one year. Some people gain back even *more* pounds than they lost.

Most diets are too complex or restrictive to stick with for very long. People get frustrated counting calories or carbohydrates…shifting between confusing food phases at different weeks…or giving up the foods they love.

The basic diet that works best for my patients—one that's recommended by the prestigious Institute of Medicine—consists of 40% carbohydrates, 30% protein and 30% fat. You don't need to be exact—just checking food labels will keep you in the target zone. Over the past five years, hundreds of

patients who followed my basic diet program lost an average of one pound every one to two weeks, and a majority of these patients sustained their weight loss for a year.

My story: When I hit 210 pounds at age 46, I knew it was time to get serious about losing weight. I exercised almost fanatically at first, but managed to lose only about 10 pounds in six months, since I did not change my diet. When I started researching and implementing commonsense dietary principles, I lost 35 additional pounds.

Based on my experience, I developed three basic rules for weight loss. *I wrote these basic instructions on prescription blanks for patients who found most of the popular diet plans too complicated…*

RULE #1: EAT THREE MEALS A DAY

Approximately 70% of people who end up at weight-loss clinics have never made

---

Bill Gavin, MD, cardiologist and director of the Heart Program at St. Peter Hospital in Olympia, WA. Dr. Gavin is also the author of *No White at Night: The Three-Rule Diet*. Riverhead.

a habit of eating breakfast, and many skip lunch as well.

Result: They're ravenous by 5 pm and often consume more calories at dinner than they would if they ate three sensible daily meals.

Sample meals…

Breakfast: Two tablespoons of natural peanut butter on half a bagel.

Lunch: Nonfat yogurt and two sticks of string cheese…chicken caesar salad…or nonfat cottage cheese and fruit or tomatoes.

Dinner: Lean meat, fish or fowl of your choice and all the salad and vegetables you like.

Snack: Stick of string cheese and an apple or a protein bar.

Dinner is the largest daily meal for most of Americans. That is the opposite of what you need for weight loss.

In laboratory studies, rats that consume most of their calories at night gain more weight than animals who are given an equal number of calories spread throughout the day.

The body secretes more insulin for the same carbohydrate intake as the day progresses. This may cause calories consumed late in the day to be stored as fat.

It is acceptable to distribute all your calories equally at each meal, but you'll lose weight more efficiently if you get most of your calories at breakfast and lunch and fewer at dinner.

Helpful: Do not eat anything within three hours of going to sleep. That is when your body's metabolism is slowest. The calories that you consume at that time are not burned for energy, so they have a greater tendency to go into storage.

RULE #2: EAT LEAN PROTEIN WITH EVERY MEAL

It curbs hunger more effectively than fat or carbohydrates.

Try this: On one morning, have a bagel for breakfast. Slather it with all the jam you want. Write down how many hours after breakfast you get hungry.

The next day, eat another bagel topped with two tablespoons of natural peanut butter.

You will discover that you do not get hungry for an additional two hours because of the protein in the peanut butter.

Eat at least 10 to 15 grams (g) of protein with each meal. That's roughly the amount in three egg whites…two tablespoons of natural peanut butter…one-half cup of nonfat cottage cheese…one-half cup of cooked soy beans…or one-and-a-half ounces of turkey. This is the minimum amount that is needed to curb hunger. The average person requires more overall—about 1 g of protein daily for every two pounds of body weight.

Self-test: If you're hungry one to two hours after eating, you probably are not consuming enough protein.

RULE #3: EAT NO WHITE AT NIGHT

This means no white rice, bread, potatoes or pasta at your evening meal. You'll also want to avoid red potatoes, brown rice, whole-wheat bread and starchy vegetables, such as corn and peas. Dinners should consist of lean meat, fish or poultry, and all the salad and nonstarchy vegetables, such as green beans, carrots and broccoli, you want.

The "white" carbohydrates tend to have a high glycemic index, a measurement of how fast blood sugar rises after eating. Foods with a high glycemic index produce a high insulin response. They can increase your blood sugar about 90% as fast as pure sugar.

The increased insulin response causes your blood sugar to decrease rapidly, which in turn causes more hunger. Eating these high-glycemic foods at night causes higher insulin levels than if the foods are eaten earlier in the day. This almost guarantees weight gain.

During the initial few months of your diet, you might want to give up white, starchy foods altogether. Once you have reached your target weight, you can reintroduce them into your diet—but never at night, and not as a substitute for fruits and vegetables.

Self-test: If your energy slumps within one to two hours after eating, you've probably had too many carbohydrates.

DR. GAVIN'S OTHER SECRETS

Nearly everyone who follows these three simple rules will lose weight. *To lose weight more quickly, do the following…*

• **Drink at least one-and-a-half to two quarts of water daily.** Water, along with oxygen, is needed to burn body fat. When you are trying to lose weight, it is important to have an adequate water intake so that your body will continue to burn fat for needed calories.

• **Exercise at least 30 minutes seven days a week.** Exercise, such as walking, bicycling and swimming, burns fat and builds muscle tissue. Muscle is metabolically more active than any other tissue in the body. That's why muscle burns more calories per hour, even while you are sleeping.

Helpful: When you're trying to lose weight, exercise in the morning. Your body is less efficient in the morning, which causes a higher calorie burn. Morning exercise also boosts metabolism throughout the day.

Important: Don't restrict *all* fats in your diet. The traditional advice to cut back on all fats is helpful for weight loss, but it is not optimal for cholesterol control. Restricting your intake of beneficial fats, such as olive oil, can decrease levels of HDL "good" cholesterol.

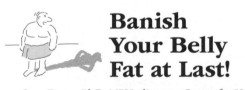 # Banish Your Belly Fat at Last!

Gary Egger, PhD, MPH, director, Centre for Health Promotion and Research, Sydney, and adjunct professor of health sciences, Deakin University, Melbourne, Australia. He is coauthor of *GutBuster: Waist Loss Guide.* Allen & Unwin.

Whether it's called a potbelly or a spare tire, fat deposits concentrated around the middle of a man's body have long been the butt of jokes.

But mid-body fat is no laughing matter. It raises the risk for heart disease, type 2 diabetes, high blood pressure, back pain, knee problems, snoring and even impotence.

Almost every man develops at least a bit of a paunch as he grows older. How can you tell if yours is just a few harmless extra pounds or a reason for concern?

Do not rely on your bathroom scale—either to check yourself now or to monitor your weight loss later. A scale can tell you if you weigh more than most other men your height. But muscular men are sometimes overweight without being fat.

Your waist measurement is a more reliable indicator of potential health problems. Any man whose waist spans 39 inches or more should take immediate steps to lose his belly.

To find your waist size: Place a tape measure around your waist at the level of the navel. Do not suck in your gut. That will only give you an artificially small number—reassuring, perhaps, but dangerously misleading.

SIX WAYS TO SHRINK A BELLY

The good news for men is that it's not especially difficult to lose a potbelly. Abdominal fat tends to be more "mobile" than weight deposited at the hips and thighs—as women's fat often is.

Follow these guidelines, and you should lose an inch of fat in your waist measurement every two to three weeks…

1. Cut fat consumption dramatically. Most health experts continue to recommend getting about 30% of total calories in the form of fat. But it's not really the percentage of dietary fat that counts. It's the total amount of fat that you eat that controls how fat your body is.

Important: Eat no more than 40 grams (g) of fat per day. Pick up a fat-count book, such as Karen J. Bellerson's *The Complete & Up-to-Date Fat Book* (Avery).

Recent research suggests that dietary fat is actually addictive—the more you eat, the more you crave. Stop eating fatty foods for just two weeks, and you should lose most, if not all, of your craving.

2. Eat small, frequent meals. Doing so boosts your metabolic rate, speeding the rate at which the body burns calories and helping you avoid the hunger that sometimes leads to uncontrolled eating.

Never go more than four hours without eating. Do not skip breakfast. If you have no appetite upon rising, start the day with toast and juice.

3. Focus simply on moving more—not necessarily getting more exercise. Vigorous exercise is unnecessary. Your goal should be simply to boost the amount of time you spend in motion—going up stairs, walking the dog, mowing the lawn, etc.

Stomach exercises do firm the abdominal muscles. But they have no special magic against belly fat. Walking is actually more effective, since it's a more efficient way of burning calories.

4. Cultivate a caffeine habit. Too much coffee or any other caffeinated beverage can cause health problems, including anxiety. But it's now clear that a little caffeine each day constitutes a safe way to speed your metabolism and lose weight.

Because the body quickly develops a tolerance to caffeine, drinking coffee, cola, etc., is most effective after a period of abstinence.

If you're a habitual coffee, tea or cola drinker, go "cold turkey." After two weeks, gradually reintroduce caffeine into your diet. Limit consumption to two cups of coffee—or four cups of tea or cola—per day.

5. Season your food with hot peppers. *Capsaicin*, the compound that makes hot peppers hot, fights body fat in two ways. It boosts your metabolism…and helps reduce the amount of food eaten at each meal. It does the latter by curbing your appetite.

Sources of capsaicin: Red and green chili peppers, cayenne pepper, Tabasco sauce and jalapeños.

6. Observe your drinking habits. Contrary to popular belief, alcohol is not a significant contributor to a potbelly. It's the chips, cheese, etc., that you eat while drinking alcohol that add on the pounds.

Raisins Before a Workout

Although exercise offers many health benefits, a strenuous workout can trigger the formation of free radicals. The damage caused by these harmful molecules can contribute to cancer or heart disease.

Helpful: Eating a handful of raisins (approximately one ounce) 15 minutes before a workout can significantly lower levels of free radicals—and the damage they cause. Raisins are rich in antioxidants, powerful compounds that protect the body.

Gene A. Spiller, PhD, director, Health Research and Studies Center, Los Altos, CA.

Best Time to Exercise

Exercise in the late afternoon to achieve the best results.

New finding: Lung performance, which is governed by circadian (24-hour) rhythms, drops in the early morning and again at about noon. In the late afternoon (4 pm to 5 pm), lung function is about 15% to 20% more effective than at noontime.

Important: Although your lungs may function most effectively in the late afternoon, it is still advisable to exercise whenever you can fit it in.

Rubin Cohen, MD, codirector of the Asthma Center at Long Island Jewish Medical Center, New Hyde Park, NY.

Fitness Secrets from Exercise Legend Jack LaLanne

Jack LaLanne, author of *Revitalize Your Life*, Hastings House, and creator of eight exercise videos and DVDs. His new book is *Cooking with Jack*. His Web site is *www.jacklalanne.com*.

When Jack LaLanne began his fitness career more than 70 years ago, most Americans were not even aware of the health benefits of exercise.

LaLanne, now a legend in the fitness world, opened the first modern health club in 1936, invented many of the kinds of equipment used in gyms today, such as the first leg extension machine and pulley machine using cables, starred in his own fitness show on television for 34 years and became known as the "Godfather of Fitness." Today, his goal remains the same as it always was—to help people stay fit and healthy.

Jack LaLanne's latest secrets to staying fit...

YOU DON'T HAVE TO GO TO THE GYM

It's great to belong to a gym and have a personal trainer, but many people don't have the time or money for this. Fortunately, there are many activities you can do at home that take only minutes to complete.*

What you can do: Walk up and down the stairs until your muscles tire. This is one of my favorite exercises. It works your leg muscles and your heart and lungs. If you feel unsteady, use a handrail.

• **Standing around?** Run or walk in place by bringing your knees as high as you can toward your chest. This gets your heart beating and targets your abdominal muscles.

• **Do you sit in a chair behind a desk?** Stand up and sit back down 10 times quickly. Now, slow it down and do it five more times.

Also: Stand up with your feet shoulder-width apart. Make a fist with your fingers and raise your fists to shoulder height. Punch your arms toward the ceiling, bring your fists back to your shoulders and repeat. Start with 10 repetitions and work up gradually until you can do three sets of 10.

 • **Watching television?** Scoot down in your chair and hold on to the sides. Bring one knee to your chest, then the other, alternating and pumping like you're riding a bicycle. This works your abs, back, thighs, heart and lungs. Remember to start slowly and rest when your muscles tire.

Illustration by Shawn Banner.

*Check with your doctor before starting this—or any—exercise program.

Also: Do sit-ups. Lie on the floor or your bed so that your back is flat. Bend your knees, keeping your heels as close to your buttocks as possible. With your hands either behind your head or across your chest, try to sit up. Exhale as you raise up. Inhale as you lie down. Start slowly with five repetitions and work up to 10.

Important: Increase your workout intensity gradually.

MIX UP YOUR WORKOUTS

Sticking to the same old routine can become boring, making it harder to stick to regular exercise. Also, by doing the same routine your muscles eventually stop getting stronger.

What you can do: Change your workouts every three to four weeks, so that you are challenging your muscles to work harder. Without resistance, your muscles become complacent.

Example: If you walk regularly, walk up hills after you become used to walking on a level surface.

Also helpful: Try walking a short distance with your feet turned inward. Then repeat with your feet turned outward. All of these strategies provide resistance, which strengthens your muscles.

ADOPT HEALTHFUL EATING HABITS

You are never too old to learn to eat more nutritiously. You must replace bad habits with good ones.

What you can do: Avoid foods with added sugar and salt.

Also: Instead of cooking with oil, sauté in chicken or vegetable broth to cut calories. If you use oils, canola, olive and peanut oils are the best—they contain healthier fats. Eat plenty of whole grains, fresh fruits and raw vegetables. If raw vegetables are difficult for you to digest, lightly steam them.

How I do it: My wife, Elaine, and I eat out regularly. For lunch, I usually have four hard-boiled eggs and eat only the egg whites. I also have soup with no cream and four pieces of fresh fruit. For dinner, a usual meal consists of a salad with eight to 10 raw vegetables, fresh fish and brown rice. Whenever I can, I bring my own salad dressing—a mixture of vinegar, canola oil, honey, soy sauce and a little sesame oil. On the road, we stick to oil and vinegar.

SET NEW GOALS

Keep challenging yourself by making gradual increases in your fitness routine. For example, if you don't get much exercise, aim to walk a block the first day, a block and a half or two the second day, etc. Each day, walk a little farther, and before you know it, you'll be walking a mile. If you miss a day, reset your goals.

Exercising for 20 to 30 minutes three to four days a week is adequate to keep most people healthy and fit. Remember, our body is the only machine where the more you work it, the stronger it gets.

How I do it: My personal workout consists of one hour of weight lifting in my gym and one-half hour of exercises and/or lap swimming in the pool each day. I do not expect everyone to follow my regimen—but I have been doing this for more than 70 years, so I want to see how long I can continue.

JACK'S CARROT AND GINGER SOUP

I love soup and have it at least once a day, sometimes twice. My mother made delicious soup, and her specialty was carrot soup. *Her recipe, which follows, is my favorite…*

1   medium onion, diced

4   garlic cloves, minced

2   Tbsp. olive oil

2   lbs. carrots cut into 1" chunks

2   Tbsp. gingerroot, peeled and chopped

1   quart chicken stock, defatted

Plain yogurt and sesame seeds for garnish.

Sauté the onion and garlic in oil for five minutes. Add carrots, cover and cook for 15 minutes. Add half of the ginger and all of the stock. Simmer 15 minutes. Add the rest of the ginger. Purée soup in a food processor or blender. Pour into bowls and garnish with yogurt and sesame seeds. Serves six.

Before a Workout

Drinking coffee before exercise may be dangerous.

New finding: The equivalent of two cups of coffee 50 minutes before exercise reduces by 22% the body's ability to boost blood flow to heart muscles.

Theory: Caffeine blocks the release of adenosine, a compound produced during exercise that opens the arteries.

This finding is especially important if you have coronary artery disease or other conditions that reduce blood flow to the heart.

Philipp Kaufmann, MD, professor of nuclear medicine and cardiology, University Hospital, Zurich, Switzerland.

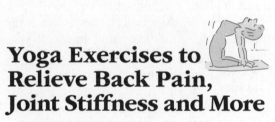

Yoga Exercises to Relieve Back Pain, Joint Stiffness and More

Susan Winter Ward, a Pagosa Springs, CO–based yoga instructor and author of *Yoga for the Young at Heart: Accessible Yoga for Every Body.* New World Library. She has taught yoga for 15 years and is the creator of the *Yoga for the Young at Heart* video series, which can be ordered on her Web site, *www.yogaheart.com.*

Many people assume that they could never practice yoga because it requires so much flexibility. The truth is, inflexibility is actually one of the *best* reasons to do yoga.

Traditional yoga can be more challenging for people who suffer joint stiffness due to osteoarthritis or inactivity—the stretching as well as getting up and down from the floor, where some yoga poses are performed, can be difficult. But there is an alternative.

I've created a series of yoga exercises designed to be performed while seated in a chair.* These poses are accessible for people with physical handicaps, such as multiple sclerosis or muscular dystrophy. Chair yoga

*Check with your doctor before beginning this or any exercise program.

also can be done at your desk, or while traveling on a plane or a train.

The following series of exercises require little space and no equipment other than a firm, steady chair. When combined with cardiovascular exercise, such as brisk walking, and strength training, such as weight-lifting, chair yoga helps create a well-balanced exercise program. All inhalations and exhalations for these exercises should be done through the nose for a count of five.

For maximum benefits, practice the following exercises daily...

•**Breathing for relaxation.** Deep breathing brings extra oxygen into the lungs and bloodstream, and is both relaxing and energizing for the body, and calming for the mind.

What to do: Sit up straight. Place your right hand over your heart and your left hand over your stomach. Close your eyes and breathe in deeply. Exhale, then breathe in again, while focusing on lifting your chest and expanding your ribs. Inhale, then exhale while maintaining a straight spine. Repeat five to 10 times.

•**Butterfly curls.** These stretch the back of the neck, the spine, rib cage and arms.

What to do: Sitting toward the front of your chair, straighten your back and clasp your hands behind your head. Breathe in deeply and lengthen your spine while pulling your elbows back and letting your rib cage expand. Keeping your back flat, exhale and curl your head forward, pulling your elbows gently toward each other. Take a few deep breaths, lifting your chest toward your chin as you inhale and dropping your chin toward your chest as you exhale. Repeat five times.

•**Windmill.** This relaxes the shoulders, neck and arms.

What to do: Sitting up straight, inhale as you raise your right arm overhead. Bend your right elbow so that it points upward and your fingers touch your upper spine or neck. Exhale, then inhale again.

Next, stretch your left arm out to your left side and bend your elbow, bringing the back of your left hand to your spine. Exhale, pressing your hands gently toward each other while keeping your back and shoulder blades flat. Inhale, lifting your chest and gently pressing your hands toward each other as you exhale. If you like, you can hold a belt or strap between your hands. Repeat three to five times.

•**Expand your heart.** This pose relaxes the back, shoulders and chest, and aids breathing by creating space in the rib cage for the lungs to expand.

What to do: Sitting toward the front of your chair, clasp your hands behind you at the waist. With your elbows bent, press your shoulder blades together, lifting your chest. Inhale, drawing your elbows toward each other. Lengthen your spine as you inhale and lift your ribs away from your hips. Exhale as you press your knuckles down toward the chair seat. Repeat three to five times, taking long, deep breaths.

•**Seated push-ups.** This exercise strengthens the arms, back and shoulders.

What to do: Sit near the front of your chair and put your hands on the front corners of the seat. Inhaling deeply, with your elbows in toward your sides, straighten your elbows and lift yourself off the seat of the chair. Keep your legs and shoulders relaxed and avoid pushing with your feet. Exhale as you slowly lower yourself. Repeat at least five times.

•**Spinal twist.** This stretches the rib cage and spine and eases back strain. It also aids digestion by massaging the stomach and intestines.

What to do: Sitting up straight, cross your right leg over your left and place your left hand on the inside of your left knee. Inhale deeply as you twist to the right, pulling your right elbow and shoulder around toward the back of the chair. Keeping your back straight, take three to five deep breaths as you hold the pose. Lengthen your spine by lifting through the top of your head with each inhalation, and twist a bit farther to the right with each exhalation. Return to center, then repeat on the opposite side.

• **Cervical stretch.** This pose stretches and relaxes the arms, wrists, hands, shoulders, back and chest. It counteracts the effects of typing and eases headaches due to shoulder tension.

What to do: Sitting near the front of your chair, inhale deeply and raise your arms overhead. Interlace your fingers, palms facing the ceiling. Exhale, pressing through the heels of your hands. Inhale again, tucking your chin in toward your throat. While holding this position, exhale and let your chin drop toward your chest. Breathe deeply three to five times, feeling the stretch down to your shoulder blades with each exhalation.

• **Hamstring stretch.** This stretches the backs of the thighs, releases low back tension, strengthens the back and abdomen, and improves digestion.

What to do: Sitting toward the front of your chair, place both feet flat on the floor. While keeping your back flat and chest lifted, clasp your left knee just below the kneecap with both hands and pull your thigh toward your rib cage. Hold for three to five breaths. Switch legs and repeat.

Illustrations by Shawn Banner.

Strength Training Is the Best Exercise for Your Health...Really!

Wayne Westcott, PhD, fitness research director for the South Shore YMCA in Quincy, MA. He is the author or coauthor of 20 books, including *Strength Training Past 50*. Human Kinetics.

Thirty minutes of aerobic exercise, such as walking or cycling, three to five days per week has long been known to help prevent cardiovascular disease.

Latest development: A recent study published in *Circulation*, the journal of the American Heart Association, concluded that strength training is equally important for maintaining healthy cholesterol levels and blood pressure—and even more critical for preventing diabetes and boosting the body's metabolism, which helps burn calories and prevent weight gain.

Why is this type of exercise so important? Researchers have found that regular strength training is the *only* way to prevent the five- to seven-pound loss in muscle mass that all adults—except trained athletes—experience each decade beginning in their mid-20s.

That's why the American College of Sports Medicine (ACSM) now recommends that, in addition to regular aerobic workouts, all adults perform two or three strength-training sessions per week. Each workout should last 20 to 40 minutes and consist of eight or more exercises that work all the major muscle groups of the body.

There's just one problem: If you walk into a health club or local YMCA, you're likely to encounter a bewildering array of strength-training classes that claim to "firm and tone your body," "build lean muscle mass" or some combination of the above. Which type of class is right for you?*

Any class you're considering should be supervised by a trainer who has been certified by a national fitness organization, such as the ACSM or the American Council on Exercise. When properly supervised, strength training is one of the safest forms of exercise there is—even among elderly and frail adults.

Caution: Your muscles require 48 to 72 hours to recover from each strength-training workout. Adults age 50 or older should strength train every three days.

What you need to know about strength-training classes...

*If you prefer at-home exercise, Tufts University and the Centers for Disease Control and Prevention (CDC) have created a strength-training program called "Growing Stronger." It can be downloaded for free from the CDC Web site (*www.cdc.gov.*) Type "Growing Stronger" into the "Search" box. Or you can buy "Growing Stronger" for $9.95 at *www. tuftsbooks.com.*

BODY SCULPTING

What it does: Tones muscles, while moderately increasing strength and muscle tissue.

These classes include a variety of strength-building exercises, using elastic resistance bands, dumbbells, medicine balls (handheld, weighted exercise balls) and calisthenics. A typical body-sculpting class consists of eight to 15 different exercises that work all the body's major muscle groups. Each exercise should involve 20 repetitions or less, and take no more than two minutes.

While body-sculpting classes don't produce as much gain in strength and muscle mass as other types of strength-training exercises, they will increase lean muscle tissue somewhat, and are highly effective at increasing functional muscle strength (used for lifting and carrying).

PILATES

What it does: Strengthens the "core" muscles of the low back, front abdominal muscles and oblique muscles that run from the back of the abdomen to the front.

Pilates classes use slow-moving stretches and resistance exercises to increase flexibility and strength. These moves are performed using Pilates equipment (pulleys and weights set on a frame) or without equipment on a floor mat.

Caution: If you have back pain, check with a doctor before taking Pilates classes to be sure you have no structural abnormalities that might be exacerbated.

Note: Core-training classes offer benefits that are similar to those of Pilates and typically consist of a variety of resistance exercises using calisthenics, medicine balls, lightweight dumbbells, resistance bands and inflated stability balls (which you sit on while exercising)—all designed to activate and strengthen the low-back and abdominal muscles.

WEIGHT TRAINING

What it does: Builds strength and muscle mass.

When it comes to increasing strength and muscle mass, no other form of strength training comes close to matching standard weight training. Weight training typically involves about 10 different resistance exercises covering all the major muscle groups. They can be performed with weight machines (such as those made by Nautilus or Cybex) or free weights (barbells and dumbbells). In each exercise, a weight is lifted eight to 12 times in a slow, controlled fashion.

Research has found that weight training increases the glucose uptake of the body's muscles by nearly 25% (reducing the risk for diabetes), and lowers blood pressure by an average of 4 mmHg systolic (top number) and 2 mmHg diastolic (bottom number) over periods of two to four months. By stimulating the skeletal system, it also can help maintain bone density.

CIRCUIT TRAINING

What it does: Combines the maximum strength- and muscle-building benefits of weight training with an aerobic workout that benefits the cardiovascular system.

In a circuit-training class, exercisers perform about 10 weight-training exercises for one minute each. Between these strength exercises, a minute or two of aerobic activity (such as riding a stationary bicycle or walking/jogging on a treadmill) is performed.

These classes are excellent time-savers, since they offer the benefits of weight training and an aerobic workout in a single session of 30 to 45 minutes. Due to the aerobic component, circuit training also burns about 50% more calories per workout session than standard strength-training classes.

Best Fitness Equipment For the Over-40 Crowd

Patrick Netter, the "Gear Guru," an independent sports and fitness equipment expert and consultant based in Los Angeles, *www.gearguru.com.*

After age 40, we need exercise equipment that reduces pressure on the back and joints and is equipped with easy-to-read displays. *Here, some of the best exercise products for this age group...*

ALL-IN-ONE

• **Continuing Fitness CFC-100 Resistance Chair.** This replicates most of the functions of a home gym, all from a safe and comfortable seated position. It's ideal for seniors (and those recovering from injuries) who want to maintain flexibility, balance, and muscle and joint strength without significant risk of exercise-related injuries from falls or overexertion. An optional minibike exercise-cycle attachment is available for cardio training.

Cost: $239.70,* plus $69.95 for the optional minibike. 877-368-6800, *www.continuing fitness.com.*

COMPACT TRAINER

• **The Intermediate Cross-Trainer Burn Machine.** Forget bulky barbells. This device replaces them, yet it's small enough to fit into a briefcase and weighs just 12 pounds. The center bar has a sliding weight that can be positioned to the left, right or center. You can perform 21 exercises, including curls, presses and knee bends, for a full-body workout. 24" x 7".

Cost: $159. 800-380-6527, *www.theburn machine.com.*

EXERCISE BIKE

• **Ironman 430r Recumbent Exercise Bike.** This bike is very comfortable. The seating position is low, rather than upright. The seat itself is oversized and designed for proper lumbar support. The bike is relatively quiet and has the easy-to-read display and low-impact, smooth-pedaling action that older exercisers need. There's even a built-in cooling fan. 55" x 24" x 50".

Cost: $599.99. 888-559-8810, *www.iron manfitness.com.* Sold through Costco (*www. costco.com*).

TREADMILL

• **Bladez Fitness 715-ME Treadmill.** The most common reason people don't stick with their exercise programs is that they get bored while exercising. The BF-715-ME includes a 15-inch LCD cable-ready touch-screen TV built right in to ward off boredom. Exercisers can easily toggle with the touch

*Prices are subject to change.

of a finger between a full TV picture or a nine-inch version with statistical information, such as running speed and heart rate. This model's shock-absorbing deck makes running easier on the back and legs than most other treadmills. 71" x 31½" x 52".

Cost: $3,199. 866-325-2339, *www.ebladez. com.*

ELLIPTICAL MACHINE

• **KeysFitness CG2 Elliptical.** The CG2 is the smoothest, least-jarring elliptical available, with the most natural striding motion. Unlike many ellipticals, it is designed for proper spine alignment and posture, reducing the risk of back pain. It's also surprisingly compact. 68.4" x 31" x 69.3".

Cost: $2,499. 800-683-1236, *www.keysfit ness.com.*

The Right Shoe for Walking Workouts

Buy a shoe specifically designed for walking—it should be flexible at the ball of the foot, but not the arch. The heel should be cushioned. Buy in person, not on-line—from a knowledgeable salesperson at a store oriented toward runners and walkers. Buy a large-enough shoe—the listed size does not matter, but the fit does. Make sure there is at least a thumbnail's width from the end of your longest toe to the end of the shoe. The best time to have shoes fitted is at the end of the day because your foot swells during the day. Buy a new pair once the padding inside starts to lose its cushioning and stability—usually after about 500 miles.

Melinda R. Reiner, DPM, Syracuse, New York.

Vitamin C Helps You Burn More Fat When You Exercise

In a recent study, people who took 500 milligrams (mg) of vitamin C daily burned

39% more fat while exercising than people who took less. Since it is difficult to get enough vitamin C just from fruits and vegetables, take a vitamin C supplement to be sure you get at least 500 mg per day.

Carol Johnston, PhD, professor and chair, department of nutrition, Arizona State University, Mesa, and leader of a study published in *Journal of the American College of Nutrition.*

Simple Ways to Walk 10,000 Steps a Day

By walking 10,000 steps or more each day, you'll be able to build and maintain fitness. *Here's how...*

• **Measure how much you walk** with a pedometer.

Cost: $15 to $30. Less-expensive ones are often not accurate, and more-costly ones are unnecessary.

• **Take a walk at lunchtime every day.**

• **Park in an *inconvenient* spot.**

• **Get together with friends to walk,** not to drink coffee.

• **Use stairs instead of an escalator or elevator.**

• **If you bike, row or swim,** count every 10 minutes of exercise as 1,000 steps.

Katrien De Cocker, staff academic assistant, department of movement and sports sciences, Ghent University, Belgium.

Mind Over Muscles

While stretching, imagine moving the limb that is being stretched—*mentally* seeing and feeling the limb moving helps make the stretch more comfortable. If done vividly, this can also enhance the effectiveness of the stretch.

Ineke Vergeer, PhD, lecturer, School of Applied Social Sciences, University of Durham, Stockton-on-Tees, England.

"The Less You Eat, the More You Lose"...and Other Diet Myths

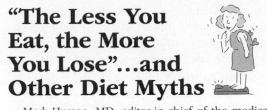

Mark Hyman, MD, editor-in-chief of the medical journal *Alternative Therapies in Health and Medicine* and medical editor of *Natural Solutions* magazine. He is author of *Ultrametabolism: The Simple Plan for Automatic Weight Loss* (Scribner) and coauthor of the best-seller *Ultraprevention: The Six-Week Plan That Will Make You Healthy for Life* (Atria). Formerly co–medical director of Canyon Ranch, a health spa resort in the Berkshires, in Massachusetts, he is in private practice in Lenox, MA.

Losing weight can be hard work. People feel they have to count calories, endure hunger pangs and work up a sweat. It's no wonder so many give up and regain their hard-lost pounds. It doesn't have to be that way. The reason we are losing the battle of the bulge is that we have bought into some common myths about weight loss. Here, six of those myths and what to do instead...

Myth 1: **The less you eat, the more weight you'll lose.**

Our bodies are made up of hundreds of genes that protect us from starvation. That's why we end up gaining weight if we start out eating too few calories. You can starve yourself for only so long before your body engages a primitive response that compensates for starvation by making you overeat. In my experience, the average person who goes on a diet actually gains five pounds.

What to do: Never go on a diet. Instead, eat foods that turn on your metabolism. These are whole foods that come from nature, such as vegetables, fruits, whole grains, nuts, seeds, beans and lean animal protein. If you eat only these foods, you won't have trouble with your appetite—it will self-regulate, and the triggers that drive overeating will be under control.

Myth 2: **It doesn't matter what kind of exercise you do, as long as you exercise.**

It's true that any kind of exercise is better than no exercise, but interval training is the most effective for weight loss. Interval training

223

consists of short bursts of intense activity followed by longer periods of lighter activity. This kind of training tunes up your metabolism so you burn more calories all day and while you sleep, not just when you are exercising.

What to do: Aim for 20 to 30 minutes of interval training two to three days a week. Exercise as vigorously as you can for 30 to 60 seconds, and then slow your pace for three minutes, repeating this pattern for about a half hour.

If you are over 30, have a physical before you start interval training. If you are out of shape, ease into a regular exercise routine first—you might start by walking for 30 minutes five times a week.

Myth 3: You can control your weight by counting calories.

Many people believe that all calories are the same when it comes to weight control—that if you substitute 100 calories' worth of, say, cookies for 100 calories of carrots, you'll come out even. But food isn't just about calories. Everything that you eat contains "instructions" for your DNA, your hormones and your metabolism. Different foods contain different information.

For instance, the sugar in soda enters your blood rapidly, increasing insulin levels. Insulin is a hormone that promotes more fat storage around the middle and raises inflammation levels in the body, which in turn promotes more weight gain.

On the other hand, the same amount of sugar from kidney beans enters your blood slowly. Because the sugar is absorbed over time, your insulin levels remain stable and more of the calories are burned and fewer are stored.

What to do: Don't focus on the number of calories you are consuming. Losing weight is not about counting calories—it's about eating the right calories.

Myth 4: Eating fat makes you fat.

Dietary fat does not correlate with excess body fat. Any weight loss resulting from a low-fat diet is usually modest and temporary. The amount of fat Americans eat has dropped from 42% to 34% of total calories on average, but we still are getting fatter.

That's because all fats are not created equal. There are good fats, bad fats and ugly fats. Good fats actually can help you lose weight, but many of us have nearly eliminated them from our diet.

Two examples of good fats are omega-3s and monounsaturated fats. Omega-3s are found in fish, flaxseed and flax oil, and nuts and seeds, such as walnuts and pumpkin seeds. Monounsaturated fats are found in olive oil, avocados and nuts.

Bad fats include refined polyunsaturated vegetable oil—such as corn and safflower—and most saturated fat, found in meat and animal products, such as butter.

The ugly fats are trans fats, often found in snack foods and packaged baked goods. Trans fat comes from adding hydrogen to vegetable oil through a process called hydrogenation.

What to do: Eat good fats. These improve your metabolism by activating genes that help you burn fats. Saturated and trans fats turn off fat-burning genes. The Inuit people of Greenland used to eat a diet that was very high in fat—primarily omega-3 and monounsaturated fats—and they were thin and healthy. Now they have shifted to a diet that is lower in fat and high in carbohydrates from junk food, and many are obese, with higher rates of heart disease and other illnesses.

Myth 5: Going low-carb will make you thin.

Carbohydrates are the single most important food you can eat for long-term health and weight loss. They are the source of most of the vitamins, minerals and fiber in our diet—and all the phytonutrients, plant compounds that are key regulators of our health. Phytonutrients turn on the genes that help us burn fat and age slowly. They contain disease-fighting nutrients. Some examples are the *isoflavones* in soy foods, *polyphenols* in cocoa and *glucosinolates* in broccoli.

However, just as there are different fats, there are different types of carbohydrates.

What to do: Eat complex carbohydrates—vegetables, fruits, nuts, seeds, beans and whole grains. These tend to have low glycemic loads, which means they are absorbed slowly and don't raise blood sugar quickly, so you feel full longer. Refined carbs, such as white flour, rice and pasta, along with sugary foods, make your blood sugar spike so that you feel hungry sooner.

***Myth 6:* It doesn't matter what time you eat.**

Sumo wrestlers look the way they do because they fast during the day, then overeat at night and go to bed. Like Sumo wrestlers, we eat most of our calories late in the day. When you eat late, calories are stored instead of burned.

What to do: Don't eat within two to three hours of going to bed, because you need to give your body time to digest and burn off your food. Also, eat throughout the day to keep blood sugar levels stable. Breakfast is important. I can't tell you how many people I have helped to lose weight by having them eat breakfast. The National Weight Control Registry, which is tracking long-term weight-loss maintenance in more than 5,000 people, has found that 96% of those who have maintained weight loss for six years eat breakfast regularly.

Keep Track of Calories

Know how many calories you're burning with a glance. The *BioTrainer* clips onto your waistband and with a small motion detector keeps track of how active you are. It instantly calculates the amount of calories you're burning and displays it on a small digital screen in real time. Stores up to nine days of data. Great for keeping track of your exercise goals.

Information: 561-208-6906, *www.bio trainerusa.com.*

Cost: $49.

Fish Curbs Appetite

In a study of 23 men ages 20 to 32, those who ate fish (salmon) for lunch consumed 11% fewer calories at dinner than those who ate beef for lunch. The lunches contained the same number of calories and the same ratio of proteins, carbohydrates and fats.

Theory: Fish protein takes longer to digest than beef (or chicken) protein, so eating fish may help you feel full longer.

Stephan Rossner, PhD, obesity unit, Karolinska University Hospital, Stockholm, Sweden.

Eggs for Weight Loss?

In a new study, overweight women ages 24 to 60 ate either eggs or a bagel-based breakfast of equal calories followed by a lunch of pasta with marinara sauce and sliced apples.

Result: The women who ate eggs at breakfast reported feeling more satisfied and consumed an average of 420 fewer calories than the bagel group over the next 28 hours.

Theory: High-protein foods, such as eggs, tend to induce feelings of fullness better than foods rich in simple sugars, carbohydrates and fats.

Caution: Eggs should be thoroughly cooked.

Jillon S. Vander Wal, PhD, assistant professor, department of psychology, St. Louis University, St. Louis, MO.

Herbal Weight-Loss Aid

Mice injected with ginseng berry extract consumed 15% less food and burned 35% more calories than animals that didn't get the herb. This extract is being sold as a weight-loss aid in health-food stores.

The Medical Post, One Mt. Pleasant Rd., Toronto, Ontario.

Vitamins May Fight Food Cravings

In a recent study, people who had taken multivitamins, B vitamins or chromium regularly for the past 10 years gained less weight than people who did not take them.

Possible reason: The body's craving for certain essential nutrients may cause hunger. Vitamin/mineral supplements may lessen hunger by supplying nutrients that would have been supplied by food.

Best: Take a multivitamin/mineral that provides chromium and the daily recommended intake of B-6 and B-12.

Emily White, PhD, epidemiologist at Fred Hutchinson Cancer Research Center, Seattle, and coleader of a survey of 15,000 men and women, presented at a recent meeting of the American Association of Naturopathic Physicians.

10 Surprising Ways to Stay Healthy and Control Your Weight

Mehmet C. Oz, MD, medical director of the Integrated Medical Center and director of the Cardiovascular Institute at NewYork–Presbyterian Medical Center and professor and vice chairman of surgery at Columbia University, all in New York City. He is coauthor, with Michael F. Roizen, MD, of *You on a Diet: The Owner's Manual for Waist Management.* Free Press.

Whether you're trying to lose weight or simply find a healthful eating plan you can stick with, you're bound to fail if you try to stay on a diet. Invariably, people on diets end up depriving themselves of certain foods and/or scrupulously counting calories.

Problem: Virtually no one can maintain long-term deprivation because our bodies are programmed to avoid this type of ongoing discomfort. And calorie restriction causes your metabolism to slow down in order to preserve energy, often resulting in *more* stored fat.

The secret is to work with your body's chemistry rather than against it, so healthful eating becomes automatic, not forced.

Recent development: Body weight used to be considered one of the best indicators of overall health.

Now: Research has shown that your waist measurement (at or just below your navel) may be more reliable. That's because abdominal fat is especially harmful due to its proximity to your vital organs, where it can lead to harmful increases in cholesterol and triglyceride levels. Fat in this area has been linked to heart disease, cancer and diabetes. Studies have found that men should strive for a waist measurement of 35 inches or less, while women should aim for 32½ inches or less. When these measurements are exceeded, health risks increase. For example, risk for metabolic syndrome (a group of conditions, including hypertension and abdominal obesity, that raises diabetes and cardiovascular disease risk) increases by 40% at 40 inches for men and 37 inches for women.

Important: Even if your weight is ideal, you still can benefit from some of the strategies described below because they promote healthy cholesterol and blood pressure levels. *My recommendations...*

1. Spice up your morning eggs. Cayenne and other forms of red pepper contain *capsaicin*, a substance that suppresses appetite signals, increases metabolism and decreases the desire for food later in the day. In addition, eggs are high in protein, which tends to induce feelings of fullness.

2. Consume fiber early in the day. Fiber increases levels of appetite-suppressing signals in the small intestine. Eating fiber early in the day makes people less hungry in the afternoon—the time when most of us tend to eat snacks and other calorie-dense foods. Consume about 30 g of fiber daily in the form of high-fiber cereals, fruits and vegetables, and 100% whole grains.

3. Eat nuts. The monounsaturated fat in nuts stimulates the production of *cholecystokinin* (CCK), a chemical messenger that slows the rate at which the stomach empties and reduces appetite without putting your body into starvation mode—that is, the point at which it starts conserving calories, rather than burning them. Before lunch and/or dinner, have about six walnuts, 12 almonds or 12 hazelnuts.

4. Drink coffee instead of soft drinks. Coffee (caffeinated and decaffeinated) is a rich source of antioxidants, and Americans consume more of it than any other antioxidant-rich food. Coffee is much lower in calories (if you don't add a lot of sugar and/or creamer) than sugary soft drinks.

Bonus: Caffeine stimulates the release of *norepinephrine*, a hormone that suppresses appetite and promotes calorie burning by increasing heart rate and metabolism. Green tea also is a rich source of antioxidants and caffeine.

5. Supplement with 5-hydroxytryptophan (5-HTP). Related to the amino acid *tryptophan* and sold as a weight-loss supplement, 5-HTP increases brain levels of serotonin, a neurotransmitter that controls appetite. In one study, people taking 5-HTP for six weeks lost an average of 12 pounds, compared with only four pounds in a control group.

Recommended dose: 300 mg daily.

Bonus: 5-HTP has mood-enhancing benefits.

6. Turn up the thermostat. One reason that people tend to eat more during the cold months is that cold temperatures stimulate appetite. Also, people with naturally low body temperatures tend to have a slower metabolism and are more prone to weight gain. Staying warm may be a natural form of appetite control, particularly if you increase body temperature with exercise. Every one degree increase in body temperature increases metabolism by 14%.

7. Ask your doctor about Tagamet. The active ingredient (*cimetidine*) in this heartburn drug is thought to activate appetite-suppressing CCK. One 12-week study found that people taking a prescription form of Tagamet (400 mg, three times daily) had about a 5% decrease in waist size.

Important: Tagamet is unlikely to cause significant side effects, but should be taken to aid weight loss only if you have heartburn symptoms.

8. Consider using nicotine. It's common for people who quit smoking to gain weight, probably because the nicotine in tobacco suppresses appetite, increases metabolism and damages taste buds, which makes food less appealing. Studies have shown that nicotine—in the form of patches and gum, *not* from cigarettes—when combined with small amounts of caffeine, can help some people lose weight.

If you've hit a weight plateau: Talk to your doctor about combining a nicotine patch with two cups of coffee daily. Even for nonsmokers, this approach can be used temporarily (to avoid possible addiction risk) to jump-start weight-loss efforts.

9. Smell grapefruit. Grapefruit oil, available from aromatherapy shops, emits an aroma that is thought to affect liver enzymes and help promote weight loss. In preliminary research, animals exposed to grapefruit scent for 15 minutes, three times weekly, had a reduction in appetite and body weight.

10. Control emotional stress. People who live with chronic stress (due to family pressures, a fast-paced job, etc.) produce high levels of cortisol, a stress hormone that increases the propensity for the *omentum*—a structure located near the stomach—to store fat. Excessive fat in the omentum can significantly increase waist size.

Important: Exercise is among the best ways to lower stress—and curb accumulations of omentum fat.

Recommended: A 30-minute walk and five minutes' worth of stretching daily…and three weekly sessions that include basic exercises, such as push-ups, shoulder shrugs, abdominal crunches, etc.

More from Dr. Oz…

What Type of Taster Are You?

Everyone likes some foods more than others, but genetic factors also determine whether we eat—or avoid—the foods that play a key role in weight management.

•**Supertasters** tend to avoid fruits and vegetables because these foods may taste very bitter to them. Low intake of produce may put these people at greater risk for certain diseases and colon polyps. To ensure adequate nutritional intake, supertasters should take a daily multivitamin.

•**Undertasters,** on the other hand, often eat too many sweets because they require a lot of sweet foods to feel satisfied. Therefore, undertasters should carefully monitor their intake of sweets.

To determine your type...

Mix a 1 g-sized pack of saccharin (Sweet'N Low) in two-thirds of a cup of water, then sip. If it tastes mostly bitter, you're probably a supertaster. If the taste seems more sweet than bitter, you're probably an undertaster.

Healthy or Not? The Whole Truth About Coffee, Eggs, Sweeteners...and More

Marion Nestle, PhD, MPH, professor of nutrition, food studies and public health at New York University, New York City. She is author of several books about food, including, most recently, *What to Eat.* North Point.

We're bombarded with conflicting information about foods and health. The result is confusion. Is milk good for our bones or bad for our hearts? Is fish a source of healthful fats or dangerous toxins? Are artificial sweeteners smart low-calorie alternatives to sugar or dangerous chemicals?

Here, a closer look at the controversies about common foods...

FISH

Fish is a wonderful source of protein, vitamins, minerals and omega-3 fatty acids, but the nutritional benefits of omega-3 fatty acids fall short of their hype. Some scientists claim that they are great for the heart as well as for children's ability to learn, but all we can say for sure is that omega-3s may be beneficial.

Also, because of water pollution and some fish-farming techniques, fish can contain *methylmercury* and PCBs. High amounts of these chemicals can cause children to have muscle weakness, fatigue, headaches and severe developmental problems.

Bottom line: Eat fish if you enjoy it, with certain caveats...

•**Limit consumption of large predatory fish** likely to contain the most methylmercury (shark, swordfish, king mackerel, albacore tuna and tilefish) to no more than twice a week. Do not eat the fish at all if you are or might become pregnant—and don't feed these fish to children.

•**Select wild fish over farm-raised.** Farm-raised fish, salmon in particular, can have higher concentrations of PCBs than the same fish raised in the wild.

•**Don't regularly eat fish caught in freshwater** without checking first with state health or wildlife officials. Unless you know that the water the fish came from is safe, assume it's not. Consuming a few fish a year from a local lake or stream should be fine, but the health risks climb the more you eat.

COFFEE

It's full of caffeine, a mild "upper," and millions of people down it by the quart every day—surely coffee must be bad for us. In fact, there's little evidence that there's anything in coffee that's harmful to our health, and it may even be good for us. Coffee contains antioxidants believed to promote good health.

Bottom line: You can enjoy coffee without guilt, but don't load it with sugar, milk or cream. A 12-ounce caffe latte breve at Starbucks has 420 calories and 23 grams of saturated fat—more fat than you should consume in a day. If you become nervous or shaky when you drink coffee, you may be sensitive to caffeine. Reduce your intake or switch to decaf.

EGGS

Eggs are widely considered unhealthy because they're high in cholesterol—higher than any other food. But when eaten in limited quantities, eggs are good for you. They're relatively low in calories and are a good source of protein.

Some producers feed the hens flaxseed and fish oil to boost the eggs' omega-3 content—but these "omega-3 eggs" cost more, and it's not clear that they actually are any better for you. *Note:* There's no difference between a brown egg and a white egg aside from the color of the shell.

Bottom line: The American Heart Association recommends no more than one egg per day from all sources. If your doctor has warned you to watch your cholesterol, cut down on eggs or eat egg whites, which have no cholesterol.

MARGARINE

Margarines do have significantly less saturated fat and cholesterol than butter, so a nonhydrogenated (no trans fats) margarine is a healthy alternative. It certainly is cheaper than butter. But if you are not eating much of either, this decision isn't going to have a major effect on your health. Personally, I prefer butter. I just don't eat much of it. If you like margarine, you can choose from vegan or organic margarines, omega-3 margarines and "light" low-calorie/low-fat margarines—but these cost significantly more than standard margarines, and the difference they make to your health will be small, at best.

Bottom line: If you like margarine, choose one with no trans fats.

ARTIFICIAL SWEETENERS

The FDA has approved artificial sweeteners because there is no compelling evidence that they cause harm at current levels of intake. But I am not a fan of them. I can't believe any food with that kind of chemical taste can be good for you. Their single virtue is the absence of calories, but there is not much evidence that their use has helped people lose weight. Perhaps people who use them compensate by eating more calories from other sources, or artificial sweeteners reinforce our preference for sweets. Personally, I prefer sugar—just not much of it.

Bottom line: If you are trying to lose weight, it is best to eat less, move around more and avoid junk foods.

MILK

For decades, dairy trade associations and lobbying groups have told Americans that drinking milk strengthens bones. Now they claim that dairy helps us lose weight. As with many aspects of nutrition, the evidence linking dairy foods to health conditions is complicated and contradictory. Dairy foods may have lots of calcium and other nutrients, but they are high in saturated fat (the bad kind) and calories.

Bottom line: If you want to avoid the fat and saturated fat, choose nonfat options. If you don't like or can't tolerate milk, you can get the nutrients it contains from other foods. Consuming dairy foods is not the key to bone health. The best advice for bone health—and for just about any other health condition—is to eat a diet with plenty of fruits, vegetables and whole grains, don't smoke cigarettes, be active and don't drink alcohol to excess.

These good habits mean more to your health than the effects of any one food that you might choose.

Tricks to Make Yourself Eat Less

Lisa R. Young, PhD, RD, adjunct professor of nutrition at New York University and a nutritionist in private practice, both in New York City. She is the author of *The Portion Teller Plan: The No-Diet Reality Guide to Eating, Cheating and Losing Weight Permanently.* Morgan Road.

The "supersize" portion phenomenon is fooling you into eating more than you think—even at home. Here's how to beat it.

The food industry knows a powerful truth about one of your human weaknesses: The more food that is put in front of you, the more you will eat. This is generally true even for people who are weight-conscious, or who just feel better when they eat less.

It's easy to spot the "supersize" portion trend at a restaurant when you receive a giant bowl of pasta or a six-inch-high pile of onion rings—less easy to escape the same mindset when you eat at home.

Problem: Because Americans are eating more food than ever before, 66% of them are overweight or obese.* Being overweight or obese increases risk for diabetes, heart disease, high blood pressure, joint problems and even some types of cancer.

Childhood admonitions to "clean your plate!"…the desire to get what you pay for… and the time lapse between eating and feeling full (about 20 minutes) are some of the factors that make most people eat whatever food is in front of them.

Even worse: The degree to which typical portion sizes have increased over the years is astounding. For example, fountain sodas during the 1950s and 1960s were about seven ounces, compared with 12 to 64 ounces these days. A typical bag of popcorn at the movies was once about five to six cups. Now a large bucket with butter flavor contains up to 20 cups and 1,640 calories. A pasta entrée at a restaurant? Double what it used to be. Eating at home? Standard plates, bowls and glasses are bigger, too—so we fill them up with more food.

HOW MUCH ARE YOU EATING?

The first step toward eating sensibly is to know how much you're consuming. This is much harder than it sounds. In one informal experiment conducted by a food writer in New York City, four expert nutritionists were given heaping plates of food (including pasta, risotto and sandwiches) and asked to estimate calorie and fat content. No one came even remotely close.

Nutritional guidelines generally suggest eating a set number of "servings" of meats, vegetables and other food groups. But a serving, which is usually defined in ounces, tablespoons or cups, is not the same as a portion, which is the actual amount of food served—at home or at a restaurant.

*Overweight is defined as a body mass index, or BMI, above 25…obesity is a BMI above 30. To determine your BMI, multiply your weight in pounds by 704.5. Divide that number by your height in inches squared. For a BMI calculator, visit the National Heart, Lung and Blood Institute Web site (*http://nhlbisupport.com/bmi*).

Examples: For grain products, a "serving" equals one slice of bread, one cup of ready-to-eat cold cereal or one-half cup of pasta. A restaurant order of linguine is likely to be three cups—nearly a whole day's recommended intake of grain! And a single bagel, in today's standard size of five ounces, equals *five* slices of bread.

DEVELOP PORTION AWARENESS

The problem with dietary guidelines is that measurements, such as cups, ounces and tablespoons, aren't easy to eyeball.

Helpful: Measure out the portion you ordinarily take. Then measure out a standard serving of meat, vegetables, pasta, etc. See what each looks like in comparison.

Important: If your usual portion of meat is actually two servings, you don't necessarily have to cut back during that meal—just know that you have consumed nearly a day's allocation of meat and adjust the rest of the day's intake accordingly.

RESTAURANT SMARTS

Portion inflation is most out of control in restaurants—where the average American eats four times a week. *To defend yourself against today's supersize restaurant meals, follow these steps…*

• **Have a snack at home.** About an hour before eating out, eat some fruit, low-fat yogurt or vegetable-based soup (made without milk or cream), so you won't arrive at the restaurant famished.

• **Have the right appetizer.** Many people skip the appetizer in an attempt to cut down on the size of their meal. That's a mistake. Order a soup, salad or a vegetable appetizer to fill up, and tell the waiter not to bring the bread basket. A Pennsylvania State University study found that starting lunch with a low-calorie salad cuts the total caloric intake of the meal by as much as 12% because the fiber contained in the salad is filling.

• **Order small entrées.** Or order a half-size portion, if available. Or share a full-size entrée with your dining companion—in most restaurants, it will be enough (especially if you add a salad or a side order of vegetables).

• **Eat only half of the meal.** When you order an entrée for yourself, eat half and ask the waiter to wrap up the rest to take home. This way, you'll be eating about as much as restaurant-goers did 20 years ago.

Helpful: Don't rely on willpower alone—when the entrée first arrives, set aside what you plan to eat and ask the waiter to wrap up the rest.

•**Slow down!** Eat at a leisurely pace to give your body time to catch up with your appetite, and stop before you're full—no matter how much is left. If you're tempted to finish off the plate or go back for seconds, stop and wait 20 minutes. That's usually all it takes to feel satiated.

PORTION CONTROL AT HOME

Portion sizes are set not only by restaurants, but also by food and even dinnerware manufacturers. *Here's how to protect yourself...*

•**Choose smaller dinnerware.** We're conditioned to think that a meal-size portion is what fills a plate. That's why you should set your table with eight- to 10-ounce (not 20-ounce) glasses...10-inch (rather than 12-inch) dinner plates...and bowls that hold two cups rather than four.

Helpful: One woman I know found a simple way to downsize her portions—she bought a charming set of 1950s dishes at a flea market.

•**Divide your plate.** Allocate space on your plate to meet healthful dietary recommendations—fill half with vegetables and fruit...one-fourth with meat, fish or another protein source...and one-fourth with grains or starchy vegetables.

Helpful: Plates marked with portion reminders for adults and children are available from BeBetter Networks, 304-345-6800, *www.theportionplate.com.*

Cost: About $12** per plate.

•**Create your own snack portions.** To control your consumption of pretzels, chips and other snack foods, read the label to see how many servings the package contains—and portion it out into that number of plastic, resealable bags. Do the same with three-ounce portions of deli meats.

**Price subject to change.

•**Substitute foods.** Three cups of popcorn is just as filling as three-quarters cup of pretzels—and popcorn is a healthful whole grain, while pretzels are typically refined. Three cups of puffed wheat go a lot further than one-quarter cup of granola. Fresh fruits typically leave you feeling more satisfied and with fewer calories than juices or dried fruit.

More from Dr. Young...

Serving-Size Guide

It may help to visualize proper portions. *One serving looks like...*

VEGETABLES AND FRUIT

Daily intake: Three or more servings of vegetables...two to four servings of fruits.

1 cup of raw fruit or vegetables = fist
1 medium fruit = baseball
½ cup of cooked fruit or vegetables
  = ½ baseball
¼ cup of raisins = large egg

GRAIN PRODUCTS

Daily intake: Four to eight servings of grains and starchy vegetables.

1 cup of cereal flakes = fist
½ cup of cooked rice, pasta or potato
  = ½ baseball
1 slice of bread = cassette tape

MEAT AND ALTERNATIVES

Daily intake: Two to three servings of meat, poultry, fish or a meat alternative.

3 oz. of meat, fish or poultry
  = deck of cards

DAIRY/CHEESE

Daily intake: Two to three servings of dairy products.

1 oz. of cheese = 4 dice

FATS

Daily intake: One to three servings.

1 tsp. of butter or other spread = 1 die
1 Tbsp. of peanut butter
  = ½ Ping-Pong ball

Natural Supplements That Help You Drop Pounds

Harry G. Preuss, MD, CNS, FACN, professor of physiology, medicine and pathology at Georgetown University Medical Center, Washington, DC. He is a certified nutrition specialist, fellow of the American College of Nutrition and author of more than 300 scientific studies. He is coauthor of *The Natural Fat-Loss Pharmacy.* Broadway.

Weight-loss "pills" often are viewed with skepticism and for good reason. Many are ineffective…some even are dangerous. But a few nutritional and herbal supplements do work. Some offer bonus health benefits, too. These natural substances have been scientifically shown to aid weight loss by helping the body burn more calories and fat…reducing appetite…improving how the body handles blood sugar…and blocking absorption of fat and carbohydrates.

Laboratory, toxicological and clinical studies—and years of everyday use by millions of people—demonstrate that these supplements are safe. However, it is prudent to take any supplement under the guidance of a qualified health professional. All of the following are available in health-food stores unless otherwise noted.

GREEN TEA EXTRACT

Green tea contains *catechins,* a class of powerful antioxidants. EGCG is short for *epigallocatechin gallate*, the most abundant catechin in green tea.

In a study published in *British Journal of Nutrition*, Canadian researchers gave one group of men a supplement containing EGCG and caffeine and another group a placebo. Those who took the supplement burned 180 more calories a day—a level that could help a person shed 22 pounds in a year. For those already at their normal weight, studies show an EGCG/caffeine supplement can help maintain weight. (Previous studies had shown that an EGCG/caffeine combination burns more calories than either EGCG or caffeine alone.)

The combination works by stimulating the sympathetic nervous system, which helps regulate appetite, temperature and many other metabolic processes, including calorie burning and fat burning. However, unlike potentially heart-damaging weight-loss herbs, such as ephedra, which also stimulate the sympathetic nervous system, a therapeutic dose of EGCG/caffeine doesn't increase heart rate or significantly boost blood pressure.

Dose: 575 milligrams (mg) of green tea catechins (with 325 mg from EGCG) and 100 mg of caffeine a day. Supplements with this mixture include Schiff-Natural Green Tea Diet and Universal Nutrition-Thermo Green Tea Caps.

Bonus: EGCG may be neuroprotective in humans—it has reduced the severity of Alzheimer's disease in laboratory animals genetically programmed to develop the disease.

CLA

Conjugated linoleic acid (CLA) is a type of fatty acid—a building block of fat. It is found in small quantities in meat and milk. CLA can help the body lose fat and build muscle.

In a study conducted in Norway and published in *The American Journal of Clinical Nutrition*, 149 women and 31 men received either CLA or a placebo daily. Within three months, the CLA group lost an average of five pounds of body fat and gained two pounds of firming muscle—without dieting or exercise. The placebo group had no change in body composition.

In a study published in *International Journal of Obesity*, people who took CLA for six months experienced no weight gain during the November–December holiday period. People who didn't take CLA gained an average of 1.5 pounds during the holidays.

Researchers don't yet know exactly how CLA works, but it may stop dietary fat from entering fat cells.

Dose: 3.4 grams a day.

Bonus: In a study conducted at the University of British Columbia, people with mild-to-moderate asthma experienced a complete normalization of their airways when they took CLA, which decreases inflammation.

MCTs

Medium-chain triglycerides (MCTs) are a type of fat. Triglyceride molecules are typically arranged in chains, with carbon atoms as the links. Most triglycerides you eat are long-chain triglycerides, with up to 24 carbon links. MCTs have only six to 12 carbon links. During digestion, long-chain triglycerides combine with transport molecules and travel in the circulatory system, where they're deposited in fat cells. Because of their unique length, MCTs don't require transport molecules—they move directly from the stomach to the liver, where most are instantly burned for fuel (and very few are stored as fat). This unusual digestive process increases calorie burning.

In a study conducted at University of Manitoba in Canada and published in *The American Journal of Clinical Nutrition*, 24 men who took MCT supplements burned an average of 100 more calories per day, compared with men who took a placebo.

Dose: MCT is derived from coconut oil, a saturated fat. There have been concerns that MCT supplements could increase cholesterol levels. The MCT formulation used in the study above includes cholesterol-lowering plant sterols—and lowered total cholesterol by 13% and LDL (bad) cholesterol by 14%. This supplement, Slim Smart, is available at *www.nfh.ca*.

CHROMIUM

The trace mineral chromium increases the number of insulin receptors on muscle and fat cells, helping those cells utilize blood sugar more effectively. The body uses blood sugar to build muscle, storing less of it as fat.

In a study of overweight women, those who took chromium supplements while on a diet and exercise program lost weight the healthy way—84% as fat, 16% as muscle. Those who didn't take chromium lost weight but 8% as fat and 92% as muscle.

Losing muscle rather than fat is the sad fate of many dieters. (Evolutionarily, your hunter-gatherer body is programmed to lose muscle, to preserve fat stores in case of famine.) Muscle burns many more calories a day than fat, so you end up with a body that burns fewer calories. Postdiet, you return to a normal level of eating but gain weight. Chromium can help prevent this common metabolic problem.

Dose: 600 micrograms (mcg) daily, until you reach your weight-loss goal. The maintenance dose—for lifelong blood sugar balance—is 200 mcg a day.

Caution: Too much chromium can cause major side effects, such as anemia, kidney failure and liver damage. Ask your doctor if chromium is right for you.

Bonus: Because it regulates blood sugar, chromium can help prevent or normalize type 2 diabetes.

STARCH-BLOCKER

An extract of white kidney beans, a starch-blocker limits the action of *alpha-amylase*, the digestive enzyme that breaks down starch in the intestines. In a study conducted in Italy, 60 overweight but healthy people received either a starch-blocker or a placebo for 30 days while on a diet of 2,000 to 2,200 calories per day that included lots of starch, such as bread and pasta. Those taking the starch-blocker lost an average of seven pounds… those taking the placebo didn't lose weight.

Dose: A dose of 300 mg, taken right before each meal, with eight ounces of water. Look for a product with Phase 2 as the starch-blocker. It's the most widely studied starch-blocker.

HOW TO CHOOSE

With a health professional's guidance, choose one or two supplements that fit your weight-loss goals and lifestyle.

Example: A person eating a lot of carbohydrates might take a starch-blocker to cut absorption and chromium to balance blood sugar.

If after two months or so the selection doesn't seem to be working, stop taking those and try another one or two supplements.

Secrets of Thin People

Stephen Gullo, PhD, health psychologist and president of the Center for Healthful Living at the Institute for Health and Weight Sciences, New York City. He is former chairman of the National Obesity and Weight Control Education Program of the American Institute for Life-Threatening Illness at Columbia-Presbyterian Medical Center and author of *The Thin Commandments Diet*. Rodale.

Do you know people who never gain an ounce and yet don't seem to have to watch what they eat? Good genes play a role—if your parents were thin, more than likely you will be, too. But in helping thousands of patients slim down, Stephen Gullo, PhD, author of *The Thin Commandments Diet*, has found that though most of us assume thin people never give their weight a second thought, they actually rely on a number of strategies to keep the pounds from accumulating. *Here, the secrets of thin people, which can help anyone who is trying to lose weight or maintain a healthy weight...*

•**Thin people don't skip meals.** They don't allow themselves to get so hungry that they become compulsive eaters rather than selective eaters. Thin people have structured eating habits. They eat three meals and one to two healthful snacks a day to keep blood sugar stable and prevent the body from secreting large amounts of *insulin,* the hunger hormone. Stable blood sugar levels also help prevent cravings for sweets.

•**Thin people eat the right breakfast.** The National Weight Control Registry, which monitors people who have lost weight and successfully kept it off, found that 78% of those who have maintained their weight loss eat breakfast every day. But the wrong breakfast isn't helpful. A breakfast high in simple carbohydrates, such as a sugary cereal, stimulates appetite. That's because blood sugar is low in the morning. If you eat a sugary breakfast, blood sugar levels rise and then crash rapidly, making you hungry. A breakfast that contains protein and fiber—such as oatmeal and skim milk or low-fat yogurt with fresh fruit—is better. It satisfies your appetite, keeps blood sugar levels on an even keel and helps you feel full longer.

•**Thin people act quickly.** If they gain a few pounds, they immediately cut back on portion sizes and exercise more. I tell my patients that a mark of a winner at weight control is to own only one size of clothing. When thin people think their clothing is getting too tight, they don't buy larger clothes. They change the habits that are creating the problem. It's far easier to lose three or four pounds than it is to lose 20.

•**Thin people weigh themselves regularly.** Most people who have lost weight and kept it off weigh themselves at least once a week. A gain of even two to three pounds motivates them to shift into a more restricted eating plan for a few days. I weigh myself on Monday, right after the weekend, when my eating habits tend to be more liberal, and again on Friday. If I don't like what I see on Monday, I make changes in my diet. I eat lighter meals, such as broiled fish and chicken, egg white omelets and steamed vegetables without oil or butter, and I don't eat sweets. I weigh myself again on Wednesday to see if my weight is coming down.

•**Thin people don't deprive themselves.** They devise creative strategies to limit consumption of high-calorie foods. They don't stock the house with them. When they do buy them, they select individual portions or serve them only when they have company or on weekends. A patient of mine only buys her children cookies containing peanuts because she doesn't like peanuts. Other people eat desserts only in restaurants.

•**Thin people get enough sleep.** Being sleep-deprived stimulates the appetite, especially carbohydrate cravings. Researchers at the University of Chicago studied young men who got only four hours of sleep per night for two nights. The researchers measured levels of the hormone *leptin.* An increase in leptin signals the brain that no more food is needed...a *decrease* triggers hunger. The sleep-deprived men had an 18% decrease in leptin. The researchers also found that levels of *ghrelin*, a hormone that causes hunger, increased by 28%.

The sleep-deprived men were not only hungrier, they also craved carbohydrates, such as sweets, and salty foods, such as chips. They may have wanted sweets because of lower blood sugar levels. The salt cravings may have been because salty foods temporarily made the young men feel more energetic.

• **Thin people move a lot.** Studies show that people who lose weight and keep it off exercise regularly. They may not work out in a gym or have a structured program, but they walk a lot, garden or take the stairs instead of the elevator. The National Weight Control Registry found that people who keep off weight burn about 11,830 calories per week through physical activity—the equivalent of walking more than 20 miles.

Researchers at the Mayo Clinic have reported that lean people expend about 350 more calories per day, on average, than sedentary obese people—and not just through exercise, such as walking. They fidget, tap their toes and so on.

• **Thin people exercise portion control.** They know which foods they can eat in generous amounts, such as lean protein, fruits and vegetables. If they overeat, they do it at a special restaurant or on a holiday. There's nothing wrong with overeating on Thanksgiving, but there is something destructive about consuming a pint of ice cream every night. Thin people also consider how food is prepared. They know that a healthy, low-calorie filet of sole, for example, is neither healthy nor low-calorie if it's fried in oil or sautéed in butter.

• **Thin people don't use food to deal with emotion.** Many of my patients don't really enjoy the foods that are making them heavy. They use food to cope with anger, depression and stress. People who stay trim over a lifetime don't use food as therapy. They also don't eat because of boredom or out of habit, such as when they go to the movies or they're watching TV.

Instead, they have other ways to deal with their emotions. They may go for a walk, take a bath, play a computer game or browse in a store. Mental diversion turns off the food switch. If they associate watching television with food, they chew on a stick of gum or eat cut-up vegetables. Or they allow themselves a sensible portion of a low-cal snack, such as a small bag of low-fat popcorn.

A Drink a Day May Keep the Pounds Away

In a recent study, people who drink one alcoholic drink a day, including wine, beer and mixed drinks, are 54% less likely to be obese than those who don't drink at all. Those who have two drinks are 41% less likely to be obese.

But: Don't overdo it—people who drink four or more drinks a day are 46% *more* likely to be obese than nondrinkers. Binge drinkers, who sometimes have five or more drinks per day, are 80% more likely to be obese.

Ahmed Arif, MD, PhD, assistant professor of family and community medicine, Texas Tech University Health Sciences Center, Lubbock, and leader of a study of the link between obesity and alcohol consumption in 8,236 nonsmokers, published in *BMC Public Health*.

9

Everyday Health

Natural Remedies for Fatigue and Heartburn And More

It is a little-known truth that an estimated 50% of all hospital admissions are currently the result of adverse reactions to prescription drugs, and over-the-counter medications as well.

But aren't drugs the only alternative for some medical conditions? Certainly—but not as often as you might think.

Many natural remedies are effective, inexpensive *and* safe. Dietary supplements, herbs and simple lifestyle changes are available for most health problems.*

Important: Some natural remedies can bring immediate relief, but others may take

weeks. Be prepared to wait up to one month to experience the full effect.

To see what works best for you, try one of the following remedies, available in health-food stores, for two weeks. If you don't begin to see a beneficial effect during that time, try a different remedy for the condition.

FATIGUE

A persistent lack of energy is common in our age of too little sleep, too much stress, lack of exercise and inadequate nutrition.

Natural approach: The dietary supplement coenzyme Q10 (60 milligrams [mg] daily) fights off fatigue by strengthening the heart muscle…and dehydroepiandrosterone (DHEA), taken as a supplement first thing in the morning (25 mg for women and 50 mg for men daily), increases energy. Levels of this hormone naturally decline after age 40.

---

*To find a naturopathic physician in your area to monitor your use of natural remedies, contact the American Association of Naturopathic Physicians, 866-538-2267, *www.naturopathic.org. Please note:* Pregnant and breast-feeding women should avoid many natural remedies.

Earl Mindell, RPh, PhD, emeritus professor of nutrition at Pacific Western University in Los Angeles. He is also the author of more than 50 books, including *Natural Remedies for 150 Ailments* (Basic Health) and *Bottom Line's Prescription Alternatives* (Bottom Line Books at *www.bottomlinesecrets.com*).

If you are over age 40, ask your doctor to measure your DHEA level with a saliva test to confirm that you are deficient. This hormone should not be taken by people with a hormone-sensitive cancer, such as breast or prostate cancer.

Also helpful: The herbs astragalus and ginseng are natural energy boosters. Drink a cup of astragalus or ginseng tea daily.

GLAUCOMA

This condition is marked by increased pressure within the eyeball. Regular eye exams should include a check for glaucoma. If it is detected, you may need prescription eyedrops and should be under an ophthalmologist's care.

Natural approach: If glaucoma is detected early, dietary supplements can help to decrease eyeball pressure. I recommend to my patients a combination dietary supplement of methylsulfonylmethane (MSM) —1,000 mg daily—and vitamin C for its anti-inflammatory effect. I also advocate two additional dietary supplements—alpha lipoic acid (50 mg daily), which protects against free radicals that can exacerbate eye pressure…and L-arginine (1,500 mg, twice daily) to increase circulation.

Also helpful: The herbs grape seed extract (200 mg daily) and green tea extract (200 mg daily), both of which help prevent eye damage.

HEARTBURN

This fiery pain behind the breastbone is caused by stomach acid backing up into the esophagus. There are drugs that can shut down stomach acid production, but a natural approach aims to improve digestion.

Natural approach: The probiotic acidophilus (one to three capsules before each meal) adds "friendly" bacteria that fight heartburn by aiding digestion…and the hydrochloric acid supplement betaine (150 mg once daily, with a meal) increases stomach acid levels in people who have a deficiency. Both supplements help the body break down protein and other food elements.

Also helpful: Aloe vera juice (one tablespoon, twice daily with meals) heals the intestinal lining, which helps prevent heartburn.

If heartburn develops, chew one to three papaya tablets or eat fresh papaya for quick relief.

HEMORRHOIDS

These inflamed veins in the rectum can be painful and often bleed.

Keep bowel movements regular to prevent straining on the toilet, which worsens hemorrhoids. Get at least 25 grams (g) of fiber in your daily diet. In addition to eating plenty of fruits and vegetables, add unprocessed wheat bran to soups, stews and salads…or take a fiber tablet. Be sure to drink eight to 10 glasses of water daily—otherwise, fiber can be constipating.

Natural approach: Vitamin C (500 to 1,000 mg daily) helps strengthen capillaries, including those in the rectum. Acidophilus (one to three capsules before each meal) aids bowel regularity.

Also helpful: Apply vitamin E oil or cream to hemorrhoids to ease the discomfort and promote healing.

PSORIASIS

The scaling, itchiness and inflammation from psoriasis can be tormenting, but dietary supplements bring substantial relief for many people.

Natural approach: Fish oil capsules (500 mg, twice daily) and selenium (100 to 200 micrograms [mcg] daily) have been shown to reduce symptoms of psoriasis. Natural mixed carotenoids—5,000 international units (IU) to 10,000 IU daily—which convert to vitamin A in the body, if it is needed, and vitamin D (400 to 800 IU daily) promote healthy skin and protect against infection. Allow 30 days for this program to take effect.

Also helpful: Aloe vera gel, applied twice daily, soothes affected skin and relieves itching.

TINNITUS

This incessant ringing or buzzing in the ears is often worse at night and frequently interferes with sleep.

Natural approach: Calcium (500 mg daily) and magnesium (200 mg daily) help to promote sleep if taken before bedtime… coenzyme Q10 (60 mg, twice daily) and a multivitamin-mineral complex rich in antioxidants protects against cell breakdown that can worsen the condition.

Also helpful: The herb ginkgo biloba (60 mg, three times daily) reduces tinnitus by improving circulation to the inner ear.

Scents that Boost Energy, Mood and Memory

Alan Hirsch, MD, founder and neurological director, Smell & Taste Treatment and Research Foundation, Chicago. He is a neurologist and psychiatrist, and author of *What Flavor Is Your Personality?* Sourcebooks.

Scents stimulate important mental and physical functions. They trigger the release of neurotransmitters, chemicals that send signals to the brain. *What scents can do for you…*

CONTROL APPETITE

In a study of 105 people, we found that those who inhaled a chocolate-like aroma whenever they felt like eating lost nearly three pounds in two weeks. Another study of 3,193 volunteers found that sniffing banana, green apple or peppermint scents resulted in an average weight loss of 30 pounds in six months.

Sniff these scents often, and remember to smell every food before you eat it. Your brain will perceive that you're eating more, thus suppressing your appetite.

INCREASE ENERGY

These odors stimulate the part of the brain that promotes wakefulness…

• **Jasmine** causes an increase in beta waves in the brain, a sign of alertness. Jasmine tea is a great pick-me-up.

• **Strawberries and buttered popcorn** will cause exercisers to burn more calories.

• **Peppermint** works on sensory nerves and increases alertness. Try a peppermint candy or chewing gum.

• **Freshly brewed coffee** is very stimulating, probably because we associate the aroma with the energizing effects of caffeine.

BOOST ROMANCE

Both men and women are sexually stimulated by scents, but the odors that arouse them aren't the same.

For men: The smell of lavender or pumpkin pie increases blood flow to the penis by about 40%. The smell of doughnuts, black licorice, vanilla or women's perfume (any scent) also is sexually stimulating to men.

For women: The odors of cucumber and licorice are stimulating. Women are turned off by the smells of cherries, barbecued meat and men's cologne.

REDUCE ANXIETY

Fresh, natural scents generally induce calm. In one study we conducted, volunteers became extremely anxious when they were confined in coffin-like tubes, but then calmed down when the tubes were infused with the smells of green apple and cucumber. These odors seem to have an impact on the limbic system, the emotional center of the brain.

If you anticipate a situation in which you will feel anxious, wash your hair that morning with a green-apple–scented shampoo and/or put a dab of the shampoo in a cloth to take with you.

IMPROVE MEMORY

People who sniff floral scents increase retention of new material by 17%.

Sniff a floral odor when learning new material, then smell it again when you want to recall it. This is known as *state-dependent learning.* The material you learn in one state—while smelling roses—will be more accessible when you replicate that state in the future.

Folk Remedies that Really Work—for Fatigue, Insomnia And Other Conditions

Joan Wilen and Lydia Wilen, folk-remedy experts located in New York City. The sisters are the coauthors of many books, including *Bottom Line's Secret Food Cures & Doctor-Approved Folk Remedies*, from which this article is adapted (Bottom Line Books, 800-678-5835, *www.bottom linesecrets.com*).

Expensive medications aren't the only solution for certain health conditions. The following folk remedies have stood the test of time—and many have received a measure of acceptance from the scientific community. They are much cheaper than prescription medications, are available without a prescription and typically involve familiar ingredients known to be safe, reducing the odds of side effects. Consult with your doctor if a health condition persists or seems potentially serious.

FATIGUE

If you've lost some of your get-up-and-go and your doctor can't find an underlying medical explanation, try...

• **Figs.** Dried figs contain slow-burning natural sugars for a lasting energy boost. They are also full of potassium and calcium and low in fat, cholesterol and sodium.

• **Cayenne pepper.** Mix ⅛ teaspoon of cayenne pepper into a cup of water and drink it down for a spicy eye-opener.

• **Chia seeds.** Chia seeds, a staple of Native American cultures, are high in beneficial omega-3 fatty acids, and they seem to aid the circulatory system, even reducing high blood pressure. Available at health-food stores, they can be ground and sprinkled on salads or soups.

INSOMNIA

Pharmaceutical sleep aids often leave users feeling drowsy or drugged the following day. *Consider these natural cures instead...*

• **Socks.** Keep your bedroom cool, but wear warm socks to bed, or rest your feet on a hot-water bottle when you climb into bed. A Swiss sleep experiment conducted in 1999 confirmed that while most people prefer to sleep in cool rooms, we fall asleep faster when our feet are kept warm.

• **Chamomile tea.** Drink a cup of chamomile tea next time you can't sleep. Recent experiments on mice indicate that this herb is indeed a mild sedative.

• **Nutmeg.** The oil in nutmeg can act as a sedative. Steep half of a crushed nutmeg (no more) in hot water 10 minutes, strain and drink a half hour before bedtime. Or, stir a half teaspoon of powdered nutmeg into a glass of warm milk. Milk contains the amino acid *tryptophan*, which may encourage sleep by increasing serotonin levels in the brain.

ARTHRITIS

There are many types of arthritis, and no one treatment can improve them all. *But the following are worth trying...*

• **Cherries.** Cherries are rich in anthocyanins, a class of chemical known to suppress the production of inflammation-related compounds in the body. Eat fresh, canned or frozen cherries daily, or drink 100% pure cherry juice. A dozen cherries a day and a glass of cherry juice is a good starting point, but feel free to eat more if your body doesn't protest.

Note: Excessive cherry consumption causes diarrhea in some individuals.

• **Cod-liver oil.** Cod-liver oil acts as an anti-inflammatory, and studies suggest that it might limit cartilage damage caused by osteoarthritis. Cod-liver oil is also rich in vitamin D. People who consume diets rich in vitamin D have been shown to be less likely to develop rheumatoid arthritis.

Take one tablespoon daily with a meal. Emulsified Norwegian cod-liver oil is less fishy-tasting than other cod liver oils.

Important: If you take supplements that contain vitamin D, adding a daily tablespoon of cod-liver oil is not likely to push you beyond the maximum recommended intake. However, it's best to check with your doctor.

• **Avoid all nightshade foods.** Eliminate the nightshade family of plants—white potatoes...eggplant...all peppers (including table pepper and cayenne pepper)…and tomatoes—from your diet for a few weeks. If your arthritis improves, give them all up permanently. Consumption of these foods might create a buildup in the body of the inflammation-causing enzyme known as *cholinesterase*.

CARPAL TUNNEL SYNDROME

This swelling of tendons in the wrist can compress the median nerve, causing pain, numbness or other unpleasant sensations in the hands. The problem is most common among people who regularly use their hands in rapid, repeated motions, such as for typing. Proper ergonomics can reduce the risk of carpal tunnel syndrome, while prescription drugs can lessen the pain and surgery can correct very serious cases. *Some home remedies that also might ease the discomfort…*

• **Willow bark.** Willow tree bark contains *salicylates* that reduce pain *and* inflammation and was the original source of aspirin. Steep one to two teaspoons of dried, powdered willow bark (or five teaspoons of fresh bark) in hot water for 10 minutes, then strain out the plant material. Drink three cups a day. If it is too bitter, mix it with lemonade.

Warning: Don't take willow bark if you are using blood-thinning medications or are allergic to aspirin.

• **Chamomile tea.** The herb chamomile contains the anti-inflammatories *alphabisabolol* and *chamazulene* and has long been used to treat ailments that involve swelling. Consume several cups daily.

• **Pineapple, ginger and papaya.** Pineapple and papaya contain enzymes that serve as anti-inflammatories. Compounds in ginger known as *gingerols* have a similar effect. Eat at least one of these daily.

URINARY PROBLEMS

Bladder and kidney ailments can be serious, so always consult a doctor. *With your doctor's permission, also try the following…*

• **Parsley.** This diuretic can help treat urinary tract infections and kidney and bladder stones. Drink parsley tea or juice three or four times daily until the condition improves, or sprinkle fresh parsley flakes on your food.

Parsley tea bags can be found in health-food stores, or you can steep fresh parsley leaves in hot water. Combine fresh parsley and water in a food processor to make parsley juice (add carrot juice to dilute the taste).

• **Cranberry juice.** Cranberries contain a compound called *proanthocyanidin* that makes it difficult for the strains of bacteria responsible for certain urinary tract infections, kidney infections and bladder infections to adhere to cells in the body. Drink two ounces of pure cranberry juice (no sugar or preservatives added) diluted in six ounces of water at room temperature three times a day as long as urinary discomfort persists.

• **Buchu leaves.** Used for centuries to treat incontinence, painful urination and bladder inflammation, Buchu's effectiveness has not been scientifically demonstrated. It's available in health food stores if you would like to give it a try. Steep three to four tablespoons of dried buchu leaves in hot water, strain and drink three times a day until the condition improves.

VARICOSE VEINS

Surgery isn't the only way to minimize varicose veins…

• **Apple cider vinegar.** Twice a day, soak a cheesecloth bandage in apple cider vinegar and use it to wrap the affected area for 30 minutes. After wrapping, recline with your legs at heart level or above. Vinegar is believed to encourage varicose veins to contract. Some folk remedies suggest drinking two teaspoons of apple cider vinegar in a cup of warm water at the end of each session.

• **Bromelain.** This collection of enzymes in pineapples has anti-inflammatory properties believed to inhibit the uncomfortable and unattractive swelling that often occurs around varicose veins. It's available at health-food stores in pill form. Take 500 mg to 1,000 mg with each meal.

Note: Check with your doctor before drinking vinegar or taking bromelain if you have ulcers or gastritis.

• **Sit with uncrossed legs.** Crossing the legs puts unnecessary strain on the veins. Also avoid high heels, knee-high stockings and tight socks.

Dangerous Medical Myths— Protect Yourself

Michael F. Roizen, MD, chair of the division of anesthesiology, critical care medicine and comprehensive pain management at The Cleveland Clinic.

Mehmet C. Oz, MD, medical director of the Complementary Medicine Program and director of the Cardiovascular Institute at NewYork–Presbyterian Hospital—Columbia University in New York City.

Dr. Roizen and Dr. Oz are coauthors of *You: The Owner's Manual* (HarperCollins) and *You: The Smart Patient* (Free Press).

Most people unintentionally increase their risk for sickness, premature aging and even death just because they lack key facts about their own bodies.

Problem: Because doctors don't have time to educate patients about everything that could possibly go wrong with their health, you need to have a basic understanding of what kinds of symptoms to watch for...and which medical advice can be trusted.

Some of the most commonly held beliefs are the most dangerous...

Myth: **Ulcers are not contagious.** Nearly all ulcers are caused by *Helicobacter pylori* (H. pylori), a spiral-shaped bacterium which penetrates the stomach lining. A blood test can detect H. pylori in people with ulcer symptoms, including pain in the abdominal area just above the navel. Doctors can successfully eradicate H. pylori with a two-week course of antibiotics, but ulcers often return.

Reason: Kissing can transmit the bacterium. Even when an ulcer patient is successfully treated with antibiotics, he/she can later reacquire the bacterium—and the ulcer—from H. pylori-infected saliva.

Recommendation: If you or your spouse or partner has ulcers due to H. pylori, ask your doctor about *both* of you taking antibiotics to avoid reinfecting one another. Also, get a new toothbrush to avoid reinfecting yourself.

Myth: **High blood pressure begins only at 140/90.** Until recently, doctors didn't consider blood pressure to be elevated unless it climbed above 140/90. According to the National Heart, Lung and Blood Institute, a patient with a reading as low as 120/80 has *prehypertension*—and is at an increased risk for heart disease.

Optimal blood pressure is 115/76 or below. The difference of just a few points might seem insignificant, but patients who maintain blood pressure readings at this level or lower have *half* the cardiovascular risk of those at the higher level.

Recommendation: Because many physicians don't flag blood pressure readings that are only slightly elevated, ask the nurse/technician taking your blood pressure what your reading is. If it is above 115/76, ask your doctor how to bring it down.

Slight elevations can almost always be controlled with lifestyle changes, such as losing just five to 10 pounds, exercising and increasing fruit and vegetable intake.

Myth: **If your cholesterol levels are normal, you won't have a heart attack.** Most heart attack sufferers have normal cholesterol levels. Few people realize that heart attacks are typically caused by blood clots that form on top of irritated, inflamed areas of plaque (a mixture of cholesterol and other substances) on artery walls. When these clots grow, they can lodge in an artery and cause a heart attack.

Lowering LDL "bad" cholesterol creates a less favorable environment for clot formation. If your doctor says your LDL cholesterol is elevated, implement lifestyle changes, such as diet and exercise.

Still, some researchers speculate that statins, such as *atorvastatin* (Lipitor), work not so much by lowering cholesterol but rather by reducing the arterial inflammation that promotes clots. In fact, studies have shown that statins reduce heart attack risk even in patients with normal cholesterol levels.

Important: Do *not* take more than 100 milligrams (mg) of vitamin C or 100 international units (IU) of vitamin E daily if you are taking a statin, as these vitamins inhibit the drug's anti-inflammatory effects.

In addition to statins, these natural strategies help prevent inflammation and clots...

241

Recommendation 1: Care for your teeth. Brush *and* floss daily. Get a professional cleaning twice a year. The bacteria that cause gum disease also can promote inflammation and plaque in the arteries.

Recommendation 2: Consider aspirin therapy. Ask your doctor about taking two 81-mg "baby" (or half an adult) aspirin daily to reduce arterial inflammation and inhibit clots.

Helpful: Buy regular, cheap aspirin. Drink one-half glass of water before and after taking the aspirin. This will aid absorption and make the aspirin less likely to cause gastrointestinal bleeding.

Important: Some recent studies have questioned whether aspirin really does help prevent heart disease, but we recommend this therapy for patients who are candidates because it also helps curb the risk for colon, breast, prostate and other cancers.

***Myth:* Fiber prevents colon cancer.** Eating fruits and vegetables can help to prevent colon malignancies and other cancers, but research shows that it isn't the fiber in these foods that does the trick—it's the antioxidants.

Although there are many reasons to get plenty of dietary fiber—for example, it prevents constipation, improves digestion and helps lower LDL cholesterol levels—other approaches have been proven to be more effective at preventing colon cancer.

Recommendation 1: Ask about aspirin. Two baby (or half of an adult) aspirin daily reduces your risk for colon cancer by 40%, possibly due to its anti-inflammatory effect. Ask your doctor if aspirin is right for you. It should not be taken with blood thinners.

Recommendation 2: Boost intake of folate and calcium. People who take at least 400 micrograms (mcg) of folate daily and/or 500 mg of calcium twice daily reduce their colon cancer risk by 30%. The reason for this effect is unknown, but researchers believe these supplements may slow the harmful breakdown of DNA that is associated with cancer.

***Myth:* The more you exercise, the better your health.** The human body isn't designed to withstand constant stress. People who exercise vigorously more than about an hour a day don't live longer or healthier lives than those who exercise at moderate levels.

Recommendation: Get one hour per day of moderate exercise—fast walking, swimming, bicycling, etc. Research shows that this level of activity can make you feel and behave younger.

Regular physical activity will promote weight loss, improve cardiovascular conditioning and bone strength and decrease the risk for diabetes. Exercising for more than one hour at a time doesn't provide additional health benefits, however, it does increase the risk for muscle, bone or joint damage.

***Myth:* Diarrhea should run its course.** A common misconception is that it's best not to treat diarrhea in order to promote the removal of organisms/toxins that lead to this potentially dangerous condition.

Not true. Untreated diarrhea is more than just uncomfortable. It can remove quarts of water from the body and cause dangerous dehydration within 24 hours, especially in children and older adults.

Recommendation: Eat chicken soup with rice. The broth and rice provide protective sugars to cells that line the intestine. Drink two quarts of water or juice daily to prevent dehydration. Also, take readily absorbable, calcium-containing tablets (such as Tums) several times daily. Calcium slows down muscular movements in the intestine.

Hiccup Cures That Work

Here are four ways to cure hiccups. Try them, and get rid of your hiccups fast.

• **Stick a finger into each ear**—this stimulates the vagus nerve, which runs from the brain to the abdomen and controls hiccups.

• **Use a cotton swab** to draw a line gently down the roof of your mouth—the tickling stops the throat spasm that causes hiccups.

• **Breathe into a paper bag** to produce carbon dioxide, which helps calm the diaphragm—but do this only if someone is with you, in case you get light-headed.

• **Get distracted**—have someone ask you a nonsensical question or try to make you hiccup at an exact moment.

Health, 2 Embarcadero Center, San Francisco 94111.

The Right Food Can Fight Headaches

Elaine Magee, MPH, RD, registered dietitian, Pleasant Hill, CA, and author of 25 books on nutrition, including *Tell Me What to Eat If I Have Headaches and Migraines*. New Page.

More than 45 million individuals in the US annually seek medical treatment for either frequent or severe headaches. Doctors have identified dozens of headache triggers, including stress, air pollution and weather changes, but one of the primary triggers—especially for migraines—is diet.

At least 30% of migraine patients have one or more food triggers. In some cases, a single food may be responsible. Most patients have combination triggers—for example, red wine plus a high level of stress plus an extra cup of coffee in the morning.

Everyone who experiences migraines and/or other types of headaches should keep a food and lifestyle diary. Write down all the foods and beverages you consume. Also note patterns that precede headaches—exercise activities, changes in sleep, stress level, menstrual cycle, etc. After a few weeks, review your diary and identify likely connections.

WHAT TO AVOID

• **Caffeine** is one of the main headache triggers. Some patients get headaches when they consume any caffeine. And others get headaches when they consume less than they usually do and then need caffeine to relieve the headache.

If you drink coffee or other caffeinated beverages regularly, blood vessels in the brain become sensitized to the caffeine's effects. Eliminating or cutting back on caffeine causes rebound headaches in about half of patients.

People who have chronic headaches often are advised to eliminate caffeine completely. Instead of quitting abruptly, gradually taper off. If you're used to drinking three cups of coffee a day, drink only two cups daily for a week. For several days after that, substitute decaf for one of your daily servings. Then dilute your regular coffee with decaf until you quit entirely.

• **High-fat foods.** Significantly reducing dietary fat decreases the frequency and intensity of headaches. Try to limit total fat intake to 20% of total calories. In particular, avoid saturated fats (mainly found in meats, fast food and full-fat dairy products) and trans fats (often called "partially hydrogenated oils" on product labels and found in margarines, snack foods and packaged baked goods).

• **Tyramine** is a natural by-product of the amino acid *tyrosine*. Foods that are aged or fermented tend to be high in tyramine, which can cause vascular spasms that result in migraines.

Main offenders: Red wine, aged cheeses including blue and cheddar, deli meats and overripe bananas.

Stick with the fresh meats and cheeses such as cottage cheese, ricotta and fresh mozzarella. White wine and beer have less tyramine than red wine—but any alcohol can trigger headaches.

• **Food additives,** such as *monosodium glutamate* (MSG), nitrates and nitrites, dilate blood vessels and trigger migraines in people who are sensitive to these additives. Nitrates and nitrites are found mainly in processed meats, such as hot dogs, bacon and salami. MSG is added to literally thousands of processed foods. Check food labels, and avoid products that contain any of these additives.

FOODS THAT HELP

• **Omega-3 fatty acids.** The healthful fats in fish, flaxseeds and olive oil can reduce migraines by stimulating the production of body chemicals that inhibit inflammation in blood vessels located in the brain.

Recommended: Two to three fish servings every week. Also, have one tablespoon daily of ground flaxseed (you can add it to your cereal or smoothies or sprinkle on salads or yogurt). Cook with olive oil or canola oil, which contain more omega-3s than other vegetable oils.

• **Magnesium.** There is some evidence that adequate magnesium intake can help women prevent headaches (including migraines) associated with menstruation. The recommended daily intake for most women is 320 milligrams (mg). Foods high in magnesium include whole grains, nuts, seeds, soy foods, legumes and dark green vegetables.

Examples: Almonds, two tablespoons (86 mg of magnesium)...artichoke, one medium (180 mg)...brown rice, two-thirds cup (57 mg)...peanut butter, two tablespoons (51 mg)...pumpkin seeds, two tablespoons (152 mg)...cooked spinach, one-half cup (78 mg)...tofu, one-half cup (118 mg).

• **Water** helps prevent dehydration—a common cause of headaches. Try to drink eight eight-ounce glasses every day.

• **Stinging nettle** (*Urtica dioica*) is a flowering plant found in most temperate regions of the world.

In a clinical double-blind trial of 69 hay fever sufferers, 58% taking freeze-dried stinging nettle leaf daily for one week experienced a reduction of symptoms, such as sneezing and itchy eyes, compared with 37% of those receiving a placebo. The mechanism for stinging nettles' beneficial effect is unknown.

Typical dose: 450 mg in freeze-dried stinging nettle leaf capsules two to three times daily...or 2 ml to 4 ml of tincture three times daily. Take at the onset of symptoms and continue as needed.

Side effects are rare, but some people taking oral stinging nettle formulations experience mild gastrointestinal upset.

Stinging nettle should be avoided by people taking blood-thinning medication, such as *warfarin* (Coumadin). Stinging nettle has a diuretic (water-excreting) effect, so it should not be used by people with kidney disease.

Because herbs can interact with medication, consult an allergist or herbalist before trying stinging nettle.

Hay Fever— An Herbal Defense

Ara DerMarderosian, PhD, professor of pharmacognosy (the study of natural products used in medicine) and Roth chair of natural products at the University of the Sciences in Philadelphia. He also is the scientific director of the university's Complementary and Alternative Medicines Institute.

O ver-the-counter and prescription antihistamines and decongestants are heavily advertised and are a mainstay of treatment for most of the 20 million to 40 million Americans who suffer from hay fever. The fact that herbal therapy also can be effective as a treatment for hay fever is less well known.

Natural Cures for Nasal Congestion

Jamison Starbuck, ND, a naturopathic physician in family practice and a lecturer at the University of Montana, both in Missoula. She is past president of the American Association of Naturopathic Physicians and a contributing editor to *The Alternative Advisor: The Complete Guide to Natural Therapies and Alternative Treatments.* Time Life.

W hen cold weather arrives, decongestants and boxes of tissue are familiar standbys for people with stuffy, runny noses. The common cold is often the culprit. With a cold, the nose can become congested as the body tries to eliminate the virus that is causing the illness. But there are other irritants that also cause nasal congestion. *Fortunately, you can get at the root cause of your nasal congestion and avoid taking decongestants, which only temporarily mask symptoms, by following these steps...*

• **Identify respiratory irritants**. One of my patients recently complained of congestion when she vacuumed her house. Although she has a cat, she claimed to not be allergic since she does not sneeze or get congested when she spends time with her pet. As an experiment, I asked her to visit a friend who doesn't have pets and spend a little time vacuuming. When she did not become congested, my patient agreed that the cat dander released in the air from the vacuum could be the problem. A simple dust mask worn while vacuuming prevented any other bouts of congestion. Dust masks made of paper (about $1 each) work nicely for reducing sneezing and/or runny noses triggered by dust, pollen, pet dander, smoke, grass, hay or fallen leaves. If potentially harmful vapors, such as fumes from paint, varnish or cleaning compounds, bother your nose, use a carbon-filtration mask, available in paint stores for about $35. They trap vapors, removing them from the air breathed.

• **Test for food allergies.** If you're chronically congested, or regularly get a stuffy nose after eating, ask your doctor for a food allergy blood test to check for IgG mediated—or delayed sensitivity—food allergens. These allergies cause generalized inflammation, leading to congestion.

Most common food allergens: Dairy, wheat, peanuts and soy.

• **Eat the right foods.** To soothe and strengthen the mucous membranes of your nose and upper-respiratory tract, eat lots of proanthocyanidins, a type of plant pigment with anti-inflammatory, antiviral and antiallergenic properties. Blueberries, blackberries, Marion berries or raspberries (fresh or frozen) are great sources of proanthocyanidins. If you suffer from chronic nasal congestion, eat one-half cup daily.

• **Drink hot tea.** For a gentle decongestant, try a tea made from equal parts dried linden, elder and chamomile flowers. Combine the herbs and use three teaspoons of the mix per 10 ounces of boiling water. Steep, covered, for 10 minutes. Strain and flavor the tea with honey and lemon, if desired. Drink one cup twice daily until congestion is eliminated.

• **Use a neti pot.** In Ayurvedic (Indian) medicine, neti pots, which cost about $20 and resemble small watering cans, are used to pour a saline solution through each nostril, to reduce congestion. You can buy saline solution at drugstores or make your own (follow the instructions that accompany the pot). Use once or twice daily—upon waking and/or at bedtime, when congested or exposed to allergens.

A Simple Plan to Get Rid of Back Pain...for Good

Miriam E. Nelson, PhD, associate professor and director of John Hancock Center for Physical Activity and Nutrition at the Gerald J. and Dorothy R. Friedman School of Nutrition Science and Policy at Tufts University, Boston. A fellow of the American College of Sports Medicine, she is author, with Lawrence Lindner, of *Strong Women, Strong Backs.* Putnam.

As many as 90% of all adults suffer back pain at some point in their lives. Back pain—lower back pain, in particular—ranks fifth among the most frequent reasons for hospitalizations.

Worse for women: Their musculoskeletal systems—ligaments, vertebrae, spinal disks, etc.—are more delicate than men's and more vulnerable to injury. Women also tend to be less active, on average, than men, and a sedentary lifestyle is a common cause of back pain.

Most back problems are caused by prolonged sitting or by lifting heavy objects the wrong way, but other factors contribute to back pain, including excess body weight, stress and depression. Even smoking is a factor for reasons that aren't exactly clear.

Simple lifestyle measures—maintaining a healthy weight, not smoking and controlling stress and depression—can prevent many cases of back pain. Most important, though, are exercises that strengthen muscles in the back, chest, abdomen, hips and sides. These are the core muscles—the scaffolding that supports the spine and enables the back to flex and twist without injury. Strengthening these muscles can relieve pain and also prevent it.

A FIVE-STEP PLAN

The following workout, which takes no more than 20 minutes, targets all of the core muscles. It can be done three to five times weekly (unlike most strength-training workouts, which should be done no more than three times a week, because muscles need time to recover between sessions). These exercises can be done more often because the intensity is lower—and they're less likely than traditional workouts to cause back pain or other injuries.

For each of the following exercises...

• **Complete 10 repetitions,** rest for one minute, then complete another 10 reps. If you can complete only five or six reps, the intensity is too high and you should do only what you can comfortably manage.

• **Work up to an advanced progression.** This is a way to increase the exercise intensity by making the movements more difficult.

• **Always warm up**—by taking a brisk walk around the block or stepping quickly in place—for five minutes before doing the exercises.

STEP 1: ABDOMINALS

Most people's abdominal muscles are weaker than they should be. Strengthening the abdominals is among the best ways to prevent back pain.

Starting position: Lie on your back on the floor with your knees bent and the soles  of your feet flat on the floor. Lightly rest your hands on the lower part of the stomach.

The movement: Contract the abdominal muscles until you feel the small of the back pushing toward the floor. Imagine that you're pulling your belly button downward. Hold the "tense" position for three seconds, then relax.

Progression: Do almost the same exercise as above, with this difference. While the abdominal muscles are tight, raise the still-bent right leg a few inches off the floor and hold it up for three seconds, then place that leg down and raise the left leg for three seconds. The entire move will take 10 to 12 seconds.

STEP 2: CHEST MUSCLES

Along with abdominal exercises, chest workouts protect the back by strengthening the "front" of the core muscle groups.

Starting position: Stand facing a wall or a counter, about an arm's length away, with your feet hip-width apart and knees slightly bent. Put your palms on the wall (or lightly hold the edge of the counter).

The movement: Holding your body straight, bend at the elbows until you are leaning forward toward the wall or counter about 30 degrees. Pause in this position for a moment, then push with your arms until you're back in the starting position.

Progression: Work the same muscles with more intensity with a modified push-up. Lie facedown on the floor, with your palms directly next to your shoulders, elbows bent.

Keeping your knees on the floor, slowly push up only your chest. Keep your trunk in a straight line from your head to your knees. Push up until your shoulders are over your hands, but don't lock the elbows. Pause for a moment, then lower back down until your nose is about four inches from the floor. Keep your trunk in a straight line throughout the movements.

STEP 3: MIDBACK

Many exercises target the upper/lower back, but relatively few target the middle back—a common area for problems.

Starting position: Lie facedown on an exercise mat or carpet, with your  arms straight out to the sides, perpendicular to the body.

The movement: Contract your shoulder blades to lift the arms up and slightly back. Hold the arms in the lifted position, and make four figure eights with the hands. Then lower your arms to the starting position.

Progression: Make the figure eights with the thumbs down or up…or while holding a balled-up sock in each hand…or with the little finger up or down. Varying the movement works different parts of the muscles.

STEP 4: UPPER BACK

This exercise increases shoulder strength as well as back strength.

Starting position: Tie a knot in the middle of an elastic exercise band (available at  sporting-goods stores for $2 to $3). Place the knot over the top of a door, and then close the door to anchor the band in place. The two ends should be hanging down on the same side of the door. Sit in a chair facing the door, with your toes against the door. Hold one end of the band in each hand.

The movement: Slowly pull your hands down and in toward your chest. Keep your elbows pointed down and close to your body. Pause for a moment, then slowly let your arms extend back to the starting position.

Progression: When the exercise starts feeling easy, change to a higher-resistance band.

STEP 5: LOWER BACK

This is the area that gives most people problems.

Starting position: Lie facedown on an exercise mat or carpet. Reach your right hand in front of you, palm down. The left arm should be down alongside your body, with the palm up.

The movement: Slowly raise your right arm, chest and left leg about five inches off the floor. Keep your face down, so your spine is in a straight line. Keep your right leg and left hand on the ground. Pause for a moment, then return to the starting position.

Reverse the movement, raising your left arm, chest and right leg, and keeping the left leg and right hand on the floor.

Progression: Kneel on all fours. Raise your right arm straight in front of you while simultaneously raising the left leg straight behind. Keep the abdominal muscles contracted. Pause, return to the starting position. Then reverse the movement.

OPTIONAL EXERCISE: THIGHS, HIPS AND MORE

This optional exercise is a complex move that targets the upper legs as well as the trunk. It is good for improving stability and balance. The exercise requires the use of a stability ball, available at sporting-goods stores for about $20.

Starting position: Stand with your back to a wall, with the stability ball positioned between your back and the wall. Lean back against the ball, with your feet a bit more than hip-width apart. Hold your arms straight in front of you or crossed over your chest.

The movement: While keeping light pressure on the ball with your lower back, bend at the knees and slowly squat down—the ball will roll with the movement. Squat down as far as you comfortably can. The ball will then be positioned at about the midback.

Keeping pressure on the ball, contract the buttocks and slowly "roll" yourself up and back to the starting position.

Illustrations by Shawn Banner.

Better Back Pain Relief

For 12 weeks, adults with persistent low back pain either took gentle yoga classes, performed conventional aerobic and strengthening exercises or followed advice from a back pain self-help book.

Result: After 12 weeks, the participants who performed the gentle yoga poses showed the most improvement in back-related dysfunction, such as difficulty walking up stairs.

Caution: Vigorous styles of yoga could worsen chronic back pain. To find a yoga instructor experienced in helping people with back pain, consult the International

Association of Yoga Therapists, 928-541-0004, *www.iayt.org*.

Karen J. Sherman, PhD, associate scientific investigator, Center for Health Studies, Group Health Cooperative, Seattle.

Herbal Relief For Low-Back Pain

In an analysis of 12 studies involving more than 1,000 people, devil's claw relieved back pain as effectively as the standard dose of *rofecoxib* (Vioxx), the COX-2 inhibitor that was taken off the market due to increased risk for cardiovascular complications.

Theory: Devil's claw contains iridoid glycosides, substances believed to have strong anti-inflammatory effects.

Self-defense: Take 60 mg daily of harpagoside, the active compound in devil's claw. It is available in most health-food stores.

Caution: Do not use devil's claw if you currently take a blood thinner or you have a clotting disorder.

Joel J. Gagnier, ND, postgraduate fellow, Institute of Medical Sciences, University of Toronto.

Secrets to Pain-Free Sitting

Rebecca Shannonhouse, editor, *Bottom Line/Health,* Boardroom Inc., 281 Tresser Blvd., Stamford, CT 06901.

At one time or another, we've all heard the admonition to "sit up straight." Now, new research shows that this advice may not be sound. Using magnetic resonance imaging (MRI) scans, researchers in Scotland found that spinal disks became more compressed—indicating increased pressure—when people sat straight up. When study participants leaned back, however, the disk compression was much less pronounced.

Joseph Weisberg, PhD, a physical therapist and dean of Touro College School of Health Sciences in Bay Shore, NY, explains it this way: "The more you lean back, the more the weight of your body is supported by the chair, rather than putting pressure on the spine."

Standing puts less pressure on the lower back than sitting, but it isn't a practical solution for people who spend their days in seated positions, such as working at computers or watching television. What's the answer? *Dr. Weisberg advises…*

• **Sit in an adjustable chair** that allows you to lean back—and that also provides good lumbar support. Padding at the base of the spine creates a natural arch and reduces pressure.

Good brands: BackSaver, 888-388-2225, *www.backsaver.com*…and Healthy Back, 888-469-2225, *www.healthyback.com*.

Typical cost: $200 to $1,700.

• **Use a sliding keyboard tray** if you work at a computer. Adjust the keyboard/mouse so that you can work while leaning back. Or position a laptop so that you can work without sitting straight.

• **Take a break at least every 45 minutes.** Stand up…stretch your back…and walk around a little to keep the spinal ligaments loose.

You Don't Need Pills to Get a Good Night's Sleep

Peter Hauri, PhD, a consultant emeritus to the Sleep Disorders Center at the Mayo Clinic in Rochester, MN. He is coauthor of *No More Sleepless Nights*. Wiley. Dr. Hauri is one of the founders of the American Sleep Disorders Association, now the American Academy of Sleep Medicine, *www.aasm net.org*.

More Americans than ever are now taking sleeping pills. Last year, about 42 million prescriptions for sleep medication were filled.

Insomnia is more than an annoyance. It can wreak havoc on the immune system, contributing to serious illnesses.

The newer sleep medications, such as *zolpidem* (Ambien), *zaleplon* (Sonata), *ramelteon* (Rozerem) and *eszopiclone* (Lunesta), are believed to be safe.

However: Even these medications can cause headaches, daytime drowsiness, dizziness and other adverse symptoms. Older adults, who are most likely to use sleeping pills, are particularly sensitive to them.

Is there a better alternative? Absolutely. New studies have found that natural treatments are just as effective as sleep medication for mild to moderate insomnia.

GETTING STARTED

Most people require eight hours of sleep per night to feel refreshed and to stay healthy, but some of us need as many as 10 hours and others as little as four.

If you have trouble getting to sleep, staying asleep or regularly awaken much earlier than you'd like, schedule an appointment with your primary care physician. Medical problems, including thyroid disorders, pain and allergies, can compromise sleep. Treating such conditions can improve sleep.

Depression, anxiety, a panic disorder or even everyday stress also can disturb sleep. If you suspect that psychological issues may be causing sleeplessness, mention it to your doctor and consider consulting a mental health professional.

If your doctor can't find a medical problem, you can begin a natural self-help treatment plan. To determine whether natural approaches will be effective, you must try them for at least one or two weeks—one at a time.

Helpful: Keep a log of your sleep quality for at least a week, preferably two. Use a rating scale from one to 10, with 10 being optimal. Rate your sleep each night—preferably about a half hour after you get out of bed in the morning.

When you introduce one of the strategies described below, rate your nightly sleep again for about a week or two. If the ratings improve, then you know that the technique you're trying works for you.

BEHAVIORAL APPROACHES

During my 40-year career, I've treated thousands of adults with sleep complaints. *Here are the simple strategies that I've found to be most successful…*

•**Create a sleep-inducing environment.** Keep your bedroom at a temperature that is comfortable for you (cooler is typically better)…turn out all the lights (darkness promotes the body's production of a sleep-promoting hormone called melatonin) —some people, however, sleep better with a night-light…and, if necessary, adjust your sound level—some people like total quiet, while others prefer soft background noise, such as a radio or a "white noise" machine.

•**Go to bed at about the same time each night so that your body gets into a rhythm.** Some insomniacs are kept awake all night worrying what time it is, so putting a clock where you cannot see or reach it is often helpful. It is counterproductive to lie in bed desperately trying to fall asleep. Distract your mind by reading.

•**Get more physical activity.** Physically fit people tend to sleep more deeply. If you have been sedentary, start performing aerobic exercise, such as brisk walking or bicycling, three times a week.

Some sleep research indicates that it's best to exercise four to six hours before going to bed. If you exercise too close to bedtime, your body may be too stimulated for you to fall asleep.

•**Meditate.** Studies indicate that a period of meditation during the day or the early evening helps fight insomnia by promoting physical relaxation and/or slowing the mind.

SUPPLEMENTS

If the behavioral approaches described above don't work as well as desired, consider also trying a sleep-promoting supplement (available at health-food stores).* *Effective supplements…*

*The FDA does not regulate herbal and other natural supplements. Do not take these supplements if you are pregnant or nursing.

• **Melatonin** has been shown to help restore a more normal sleep cycle—but it rarely lengthens the amount of time you sleep. If you have problems falling asleep, take it two hours before bedtime. If you wake up too early or in the middle of the night, take it when you awaken.

Recommended dose: Three milligrams (mg) once per day. If this doesn't work, gradually increase the dosage over a month to a maximum of 9 mg daily.

Possible side effects: Headache, digestive upset and depression. Long-term use of melatonin has not been studied, so consult your doctor if you need to use this hormone for more than a few months or you develop side effects.

• **Valerian** helps many people fall asleep faster and stay asleep longer.

Recommended dose: Take one-half to one teaspoon of liquid extract or 300 to 500 mg in capsule form 20 minutes before bedtime.

Possible side effects: Stomach upset.

• **5-hydroxytryptophan (5-HTP)** is a compound derived from the seed of an African plant called griffonia. 5-HTP is best known for treating mild to moderate depression. The scientific evidence on 5-HTP's efficacy as a sleep aid is inconclusive at this time, however, the compound may be worth trying if you don't get relief from the other supplements listed above. 5-HTP has helped some of my patients.

Recommended dose: Ask your doctor.

Possible side effects: Mild nausea.

• **Vitamin B-12 and/or calcium** can help improve your sleep if you have a deficiency. Both vitamin B-12 and calcium calm the nervous system and have a mild sedative effect in some.

Recommended dose: Ask your doctor.

Possible side effects: None are known.

Important: If you are taking any medications, including prescription sleeping pills, consult your doctor before taking these supplements.

Rub Out the Ache! The Very Best Pain-Relief Creams and Ointments

Beth E. Shubin Stein, MD, sports medicine and shoulder surgeon with the Women's Sports Medicine Center at the Hospital for Special Surgery in New York City.

If you suffer from chronic arthritis pain or have aching muscle strains or spasms after exercising, chances are you regularly take aspirin or another nonsteroidal anti-inflammatory drug (NSAID), such as *ibuprofen* (Advil) or *naproxen* (Aleve).

There is another option. Over-the-counter (OTC) topical pain relievers can be very effective without causing the stomach upset or gastrointestinal bleeding that may accompany oral pain medication.

Latest development: A topical form of the oral prescription NSAID *diclofenac*, Voltaren Gel received US approval in October of 2007 as the first topical prescription treatment for pain associated with osteoarthritis.

Meanwhile, a variety of OTC topical pain relievers are available now. The products below relieve arthritis, backache and muscle strain. Most are used three to four times daily. Follow label instructions.

Helpful: If one type of topical pain reliever doesn't work for you, try one from another class until you find a product that provides relief.

Caution: Keep these products away from your eyes, nose and other mucous membranes.

SALICYLATES

These aspirin-based products dull pain and curb the inflammation that often accompanies and worsens pain.

How they work: Topical salicylates inhibit the production of *prostaglandins*, substances in the body that cause pain and swelling when they are released in response to strains, sprains and other injuries. *Salicylates include...*

• **BenGay Ultra Strength Pain Relieving Cream.**

•**Aspercreme Analgesic Creme Rub with Aloe.**

•**Sportscreme Deep Penetrating Pain Relieving Rub.**

•**Flexall Maximum Strength Pain Relieving Gel.**

Warning: Do not use salicylates if you are sensitive or allergic to aspirin or take blood-thinning medication that might interact with them. Consult a doctor before applying a salicylate to a large area several times a day.

COUNTERIRRITANTS

These pain relievers give the sensation of warmth or coolness to mask pain.

How they work: Creating a secondary stimulus to diminish the feeling of pain reduces physical discomfort. It's what you do instinctively when you stub your toe, then grab it to apply pressure. Both competing sensations travel to your brain at the same time—but because only a limited number of messages can be processed at one time, the initial feeling of pain is diminished. *Counterirritants include...*

•**Icy Hot Pain Relieving Balm, Extra Strength.**

•**Tiger Balm Extra Strength Pain Relieving Ointment.**

•**Therapeutic Mineral Ice.**

In most cases, coolness is beneficial for acute injuries, such as sprains, while warmth eases stiffness.

Caution: People sensitive to heat or cold should avoid counterirritants.

CAPSAICINS

These products, which are a type of counterirritant, contain capsaicin, an extract of hot peppers that causes a burning sensation.

How they work: Unlike most other counterirritants, capsaicin inhibits the production of substance P, a chemical that sends pain messages to the brain via the nervous system. *Capsaicins include...*

•**Zostrix Arthritis Pain Relief Cream.**

•**Capzasin HP Arthritis Pain Relief Creme.**

LIDOCAINE

Lidoderm is a prescription-only patch that contains *lidocaine*, a topical anesthetic similar to the *novocaine* that dentists often use to numb the gums.

How it works: Lidocaine blocks signals at the skin's nerve endings. The Lidoderm patch (lidocaine 5%) is worn for 12 hours a day over a period of days. It slowly releases medication, so it has longer-lasting effects than other pain relievers and helps with pain that emanates from nerves near the surface of your skin, such as that caused by shingles or diabetic neuropathy.

Caution: Side effects include dizziness, headache and nausea. Allergic reactions are rare but may occur.

My Aching Feet! Relief from Three Common Foot Problems

Crystal M. Holmes, DPM, clinical instructor in podiatry, University of Michigan Medical School, Ann Arbor. Dr. Holmes is a member of the American Podiatric Medical Association and its Public Education & Information Committee, *www.apma.org.*

Foot problems grow more common with advancing age, as a lifetime of wear and tear takes its toll.

But three very common problems—bunions, fungal nail and a painful heel—won't slow you down or keep you from activities you enjoy if you know how to deal with them.

BUNIONS

If the big toe goes awry where it joins the foot and angles back toward the smaller toes, it is a bunion. The characteristic bump—actually the out-of-place head of the first metatarsal bone—typically starts decades before increasing pain brings the bunion to a doctor's attention.

Many people believe that bunions are caused by years of ill-chosen shoes, high heels in particular. The truth is that heredity is the prime culprit—if you have pronounced bunions, it is likely that other family members do, too. Shoes may speed up a bunion's progress and make it more painful by rubbing against and irritating the bump, or by changing the way you walk. Injury can throw muscles and tendons out of alignment (a likely explanation if you have a bunion on just one foot). Arthritis can worsen bunion pain and cause the toe joint to degenerate.

Whether due to injury or heredity, bunions are the result of a flaw in the structure and mechanics of the foot—a muscle imbalance pulls the big toe out of line.

You might keep a bunion from getting worse by avoiding aggravating factors—don't wear shoes that are too tight, narrow or short for your foot, or that have excessively high heels. If you have arthritis, get appropriate care.

Bunions need treatment when they are painful, particularly if the pain makes it difficult to wear normal shoes or participate in your usual activities, or when other toes start pushing up or down or get jammed together by the big toe.

• **Nonsurgical treatment.** An orthopedist or podiatrist will usually evaluate a bunion with X-rays to clarify the structure of the foot, and use this information along with the size of the bunion, its history and the pain it causes in choosing a treatment.

Nonsurgical options are preferable. These include orthotics—shoe inserts to correct the imbalance and change the forces exerted on your feet as you stand and walk—and possibly anti-inflammatory medications.

• **Surgery.** When nonsurgical measures don't work, it's best to consider surgery. There are a number of different procedures—most of which usually involve cutting one or both of the bones at the joint where the toe meets the foot, and holding the bone or bones in place with a pin or other implanted device. In severe cases, the joint must be fused—the space between the two bones is closed and the bones are held together with screws, plates or both. The right procedure for you depends on the severity of the bunion and the structure of your foot, and whether arthritis is present, among other factors.

Recovery is generally lengthy. Bone takes four to six weeks to heal, so you must keep weight off the foot altogether for at least some of this time, and restrict your activity for longer. After more extensive procedures, healing can take months.

What about laser? Laser surgery is sometimes advertised as a simple, comfortable way to correct bunions, with a quick recovery. This procedure will remove the bump by shaving away bone that sticks out. It will not correct the underlying problem, which is the misalignment of the toe, but it may help —depending on the structure of your foot and the extent of the problem.

Don't expect your toes to be absolutely straight after bunion surgery. The achievable goal is restoring normal function, not appearance.

FUNGAL NAIL

When infected by fungus, toenails get thick, yellow and hard to cut. They may be raised from the toe and even fall off. The big toe is most commonly affected, but all are vulnerable. The infection is most common after the age of 50.

Fungi are everywhere and only need a breach in the body's defense to take hold. Even a minor injury can do it—such as you drop a can on your toe or someone steps on your foot. Ill-fitting shoes damage the nail and provide a damp, dark environment where fungi flourish.

If you think you have a fungal nail, see a doctor. *Medical attention is important for two reasons...*

• **Diagnosis.** Although fungus is the most common cause of thick, discolored nails, they can also result from psoriasis and other skin diseases or even illness elsewhere in the body, such as cancer or lung disease. To make the diagnosis, the doctor may need to back up his/her clinical judgment by culturing material from under the nail.

• **Treatment.** Because the fungus is entrenched deep within the root of the nail, it almost always needs more powerful treatment than is available over the counter.

Strong medicine: In recent years, anti-fungal medications of proven effectiveness have been developed.

Some, such as *ciclopirox* (Penlac), are applied directly to the nail—painted on like nail polish or massaged in as a cream. At prescription strength, they often are enough to do the job.

Important: To be effective, the medication must be applied religiously, every day for four months or more.

Oral medication with drugs such as *terbinafine* (Lamisil) and *itraconazole* (Sporanox) may be preferable or necessary, particularly when several nails are affected or the infection is severe and has been going on for years.

Advantages: Oral treatment is usually briefer. Also, it is preferable for people who have difficulty bending all the way over to apply the cream.

Drawbacks: These drugs may impair liver function. They require blood tests to ensure that the liver continues to function properly, and they cannot be used by those with existing liver problems. They can interact with other medications, particularly cholesterol-lowering drugs, antidepressants and blood thinners.

Whether you treat fungal nail with topical or oral medication, be patient. It may take months before the damaged nail grows out and is replaced by healthy tissue.

To prevent fungal nail...

•**Don't go barefoot,** especially outside and in athletic facilities, such as health clubs.

•**Avoid prolonged contact with sweat** by changing socks frequently.

•**If excessive perspiration is a problem,** seek medical help for it.

CHRONIC HEEL PAIN

Heel pain is often caused by plantar fasciitis, an inflammation of the fascia, a fibrous band of connective tissue that stretches across the bottom of the foot from heel to toes. Plantar fasciitis is typically a deep ache that feels like a bruise in your heel, most severe when you first get out of bed. The foot may feel better during the day, but become sore again after your foot has been resting—such as if you sit for a long period or when you first wake up.

People often attribute the pain to a heel spur—a spiky protuberance of the bone on the bottom of the heel. But plantar fasciitis is usually involved here as well—the heel spur causes pain by rubbing against and inflaming the fascia.

•**Self-care.** If heel pain is unusual for you and hasn't lasted long, you might try treating it yourself with rest, ice and elevation. To the extent you can, stay off your feet and keep your foot raised to the level of your heart. Apply ice with an ice pack or cold towel to the heel and arch region for 10- to 15-minute periods, three to four times a day. If the pain persists for 48 hours, seek medical care. If the problem began with an injury, don't wait more than a day.

•**Medical care.** If pain is truly due to plantar fasciitis (arthritis or Achilles tendinitis might actually be responsible instead), the treatment may be simply a program of stretching exercises to be done at home or with a physical therapist. If a muscle imbalance is involved, the doctor may prescribe an orthotic to change the mechanics of your foot.

Since plantar fasciitis is an inflammation, treatment often includes an anti-inflammatory drug like *fenoprofen* (Nalfon) or *ibuprofen* (Motrin). In severe cases, for those who don't get better with oral medication, a cortisone injection may be necessary.

WHAT KIND OF DOCTOR?

Most foot problems that a family doctor can't treat should be seen by a podiatrist or orthopedist. Skin conditions such as fungal nail may need to be treated by a dermatologist.

Speedier Healing

To prevent scarring after an injury, wash the affected area with soap and water, not peroxide—which slows healing by preventing new cells from forming. Put a protective film, such as Aquaphor or petroleum jelly, over the wound—keeping the area moist speeds healing. Instead of an adhesive bandage, use an Adaptic bandage—its plastic coating prevents gauze from sticking to the wound. Or try a liquid bandage, which seals the cut like a scab for faster healing.

Jeffrey Dover, MD, dermatologist, SkinCare Physicians of Chestnut Hill, Chestnut Hill, MA, www.skincarephysicians.net.

Natural Ways to Care for Your Gums

Jamison Starbuck, ND, a naturopathic physician in family practice and a lecturer at the University of Montana, both in Missoula. She is past president of the American Association of Naturopathic Physicians and a contributing editor to The Alternative Advisor: The Complete Guide to Natural Therapies and Alternative Treatments. Time Life.

For years, I've observed that far too many otherwise health-conscious people neglect their oral health. That's a mistake. Gum (periodontal) disease occurs in 50% of people over age 55. Even though we all know the importance of regular brushing and flossing, it often takes more than conventional tooth and gum care to keep our mouth tissues healthy. The mildest form of periodontal disease is gingivitis. This inflammatory condition, which is primarily caused by poor oral hygiene, typically leads to red, swollen gum tissue that often bleeds.

If you have these symptoms, see your dentist for a checkup. If you've got periodontal disease, and it is left untreated, surgery may be needed. The first step I recommend is to reduce your sugar intake. Sugar increases plaque formation and feeds the harmful bacteria that dwell in your gums.

Taking the right nutritional supplements also can help reverse gingivitis, often within three months. This could eliminate the need for costly periodontal surgery. *My favorite supplements for gum health...*

•**Vitamin C.** It strengthens gum tissue and enhances your white blood cells' ability to fight inflammation-promoting microorganisms in your mouth. To restore gum health, take 3,000 mg daily in divided doses for three months. If this amount of vitamin C causes diarrhea, cut back on the dose. If you have high iron levels, do not take a vitamin C supplement—it increases iron absorption. For healthy gum maintenance, take 1,500 mg of vitamin C daily.

•**Zinc.** Like vitamin C, zinc improves gum health by enhancing white blood cell activity. This mineral also inhibits plaque buildup (which increases inflammation) and speeds the healing of bleeding gums. To treat gingivitis, take 40 mg of zinc daily for three months. For healthy gum maintenance, take a daily dose of 20 mg of zinc.

•**Folate.** A deficiency of this B vitamin is common and increases risk for gingivitis. To treat gingivitis, add a daily dose of 1 mg of folic acid along with 500 micrograms (mcg) of vitamin B-12 to your supplement regimen for three months. Taking folic acid alone can mask a possible B-12 deficiency. Bleeding gums also improve with a 0.1% solution of liquid folic acid, which is available at health-food stores. Brush your teeth, then swish one-half ounce of the solution in your mouth twice daily for 60 seconds and then spit it out. For optimal gum absorption, do *not* eat or drink anything for at least 15 minutes after swishing. To maintain gum health, take 800 mcg of folic acid along with 400 mcg of vitamin B-12 daily.

•**Coenzyme Q10.** This powerful antioxidant helps our cells function efficiently. Studies show that CoQ10 not only protects the heart and brain, but also the gums. For periodontal disease, take 100 mg of CoQ10 daily for three months. Take 60 mg for gum maintenance. It is available wherever vitamins are sold.

Canker Sore Treatment

There is no way to prevent a canker sore, a small lesion in the mouth. The cause of canker sores is unknown, but stress or dental trauma may play a role. Canker sores begin innocently but ulcerate after a few days and can become painful.

Self-defense: If you get a canker sore, clean it frequently with hydrogen peroxide dabbed on a cotton swab. Use a prescription topical corticosteroid ointment such as *triamcinolone*, e.g. Kenalog in Orabase, which may help reduce healing time by one to two days. A canker sore typically heals on its own in seven to 10 days. Avoid spicy and acidic foods, such as vinaigrette, orange juice or tomato juice, which can worsen the pain.

Alan Winter, DDS, a periodontist in private practice in New York City.

Hate to Floss? What to Do Instead...

Matthew Messina, DDS, a practicing dentist in Fairview Park, OH. He is a consumer adviser for the American Dental Association.

D aily flossing removes plaque, bacteria and food particles from between teeth where toothbrushes can't reach. It's the best way to protect teeth and gums.

Flossing can even protect your overall health. Research has clearly shown links between periodontal (gum) disease and heart disease and diabetes and, very recently, possible links to Alzheimer's disease and pancreatic cancer. Yet about half of Americans don't floss each day.

Nonflossers often complain that flossing is painful, awkward or time-consuming. *If you can't bring yourself to floss, consider these alternatives...*

FLOSS ALTERNATIVES

•**Water picks.** Water picks use small, high-powered bursts of water to flush debris from between the teeth. This is not as effective as daily flossing, and the sensation takes some getting used to, but it's a lot better than nothing. Water picks are particularly useful for those who have braces or other dental work that makes flossing difficult.

Important: Set your water pick to its medium pressure setting, not the highest. Excessive water pressure can blast bacteria further under your gum line.

•**Mouthwash.** Antibacterial mouthwashes cannot remove plaque from between your teeth, but they can at least kill bacteria. Swish with mouthwash for at least 30 seconds—a full minute is even better. Select a mouthwash with the American Dental Association seal of approval to ensure that it is truly antimicrobial.

You also can fill a water pick with a diluted mouthwash solution (one or two parts water to one part mouthwash). The water pressure will dislodge much of the debris from between your teeth, and the mouthwash will kill most of the bacteria that remain.

•**Interdental cleaners.** These plastic tools are similar to toothpicks, only their blunted ends are less likely to damage the gums. Though not as effective as floss, they can remove much of the debris from between the teeth when used carefully. Ask your dentist to show you how to use one.

BETTER FLOSSING

These floss products can make flossing more pleasant...

•**Floss holders.** Arthritis sufferers and others with limited dexterity often find it difficult or painful to maneuver dental floss around the mouth. A floss holder, available at any drugstore, solves this problem by supplying an easy-to-grip handle.

•**High-quality flosses.** Premium flosses, such as Crest's Glide, are slicker and stronger than economy brands, making flossing easier, especially between tight teeth.

Temporary Fixes for Dental Problems

U ntil you can see your dentist, here are five ways to fix dental problems.

•**If a tooth is sensitive to cold or sweets,** rinse with warm water.

• **If you have swelling from an injury,** apply ice—a half-hour on, a half-hour off.

• **If swelling is from infection,** apply a heating pad or hot washcloth, or hold hot salty water in your mouth—the heat stimulates blood flow to the area, which helps remove toxins.

• **If you lose a filling,** rinse your mouth with warm water and place cotton dipped in oil of cloves in the cavity—the clove oil eases pain.

• **If a crown pops off,** use denture adhesive or tooth cement—available at most drugstores—to reattach it temporarily. See a dentist as soon as possible for any of these problems.

Irwin Smigel, DDS, president and founder, American Society for Dental Aesthetics, and a dentist in private practice, New York City, *www.smigel.com.*

Relief for Eczema— Steps to Prevent and Treat Dry Skin

Marianne N. O'Donoghue, MD, associate professor of dermatology at Rush University Medical Center, Chicago, and dermatologist in private practice for more than 30 years in Oak Brook, IL. She is past president of the Women's Dermatologic Society and a member of the American Academy of Dermatology.

Eczema, the chronic, dry skin condition that afflicts 15 million Americans, accounts for at least 20% of my practice, especially in winter, when the humidity is low. Men and women of all ethnic groups are equally vulnerable to the disease, but children under the age of six are slightly more likely to develop it.

The term *eczema* is broadly used to describe a variety of noncontagious conditions characterized by dry, red, scaly, itchy patches on the skin. It most often targets the arms and legs.

There are many different types of eczema, and the disorder can have many causes and occur in many forms. The most common kind of eczema—*atopic dermatitis*—is caused by an allergic reaction. It usually occurs in people who have a family history of hay fever, asthma or other allergies. I recently treated a little girl whose eczema was made worse because she was allergic to the nickel snaps on the front of her pants.

Eczema cannot be cured—but it can be controlled. *Here's how...*

PREVENTION

If you're prone to eczema, don't wait for a flare-up to take these steps, especially in the winter...

• **Use mild cleansers.** Use bar soaps that are meant for the face on your entire body. They are gentler on the skin. Good brands include Dove, Aveeno, Basis, Oil of Olay and Camay. Avoid antibacterial soaps and deodorant soaps, all of which aggravate eczema.

• **Lubricate skin twice a day.** Emollients are necessary to decrease the loss of water from the skin and prevent it from becoming too dry. Lotions won't do the trick. They are too watery and won't seal in moisture as ointments will. I recommend Vaseline Petroleum Jelly and Aquaphor to my patients.

• **Take no more than one shower a day.** People who shower at home, then go to the health club and take a second shower, particularly during the winter, are going to have more trouble with eczema than people who shower just once a day. It's even better not to shower daily—three or four times a week is optimal. And when you shower or bathe, make sure the water is lukewarm, not hot. Hot water dries out the skin more than cooler water.

If you swim in a pool for exercise, be sure not to shower before getting in the pool. After getting out, rinse only long enough to get the chlorine off—and don't use soap.

• **Avoid animals.** Many people are allergic to the shed skin—the dander—of animals, such as cats, dogs and rabbits. Animal dander floats in the air and gets on furniture and clothes. Without even touching an animal, you still can come in contact with its dander.

• **Watch what children eat.** Children under the age of six who have eczema should avoid orange juice, egg whites and peanuts—including peanut products, such as peanut butter and foods that contain even traces of peanuts. Children usually outgrow these allergies, and adults usually don't have to worry that something they eat will trigger their eczema.

TREATMENT

If you have a flare-up, patches of skin may become itchy. Avoid scratching. You will likely complicate the eczema by infecting it with bacteria and germs from your fingernails.

To relieve the itching, you may need medication. *The most effective medications include...*

• **Oral antihistamines.** I encourage my patients to use an oral antihistamine to help break the itch/scratch cycle. Topical antihistamines don't make the grade. They contain ingredients that may irritate your skin. Stick with oral antihistamines, and follow the directions on the label.

There are many over-the-counter oral antihistamines, including *chlorpheniramine maleate* (Chlor-Trimeton) and *diphenhydramine hydrochloride* (Benadryl), both of which can make you drowsy. Another oral antihistamine is *loratadine* (Claritin), which doesn't have this particular side effect. Or you can ask your doctor to prescribe an antihistamine for you.

Children who are prone to being itchy and have a habit of scratching should take an oral antihistamine when they take a nap or go to bed at night, so they don't scratch themselves while they sleep.

• **Cortisone ointment** has been used since the 1950s to help relieve symptoms of eczema. Over-the-counter steroids often are not strong enough, and you may need prescription strength.

Downside: Skin can get thin if cortisone is used too often.

• **Calcineurin inhibitors.** Patients who don't want to use topical steroids or who have used them without success can try effective, new prescription drugs called calcineurin inhibitors. These are applied topically and may sting slightly. They can be given to people over the age of two to control eczema. If you don't have insurance, be aware that calcineurin inhibitors are a lot more expensive than cortisone.

Don't Mix Sunscreen and DEET

In a new study, combining the insect repellent DEET with certain sunscreens causes skin to absorb DEET three times faster than it would otherwise. DEET is safe and has a low risk of side effects on its own.

Edward A. Ross, MD, associate professor of medicine, University of Florida, Gainesville, and leader of a study of DEET absorption, published in *Drug Metabolism and Disposition.*

Good Old Soap And Water

Ordinary soap and water get rid of germs better than alcohol rubs and antimicrobial wipes. Hand wipes and alcohol rubs provide some protection if you can't get to soap and water easily—but wash your hands as soon as possible after using wipes.

Emily E. Sickbert-Bennett, MS, public health epidemiologist, School of Public Health, University of North Carolina Health Care System, Chapel Hill, and leader of a study of hand-hygiene agents, published in *American Journal of Infection Control.*

How to Get Rid of Toenail Fungus

Jeffrey T.S. Hsu, MD, adjunct assistant professor in medicine (dermatology), Dartmouth Medical School, Hanover, NH.

Toenail fungus, also called onychomycosis, is a relatively common condition that disfigures the nail. About 2.5

million Americans see podiatrists annually for treatment of toenail fungus. People who wear tight-fitting shoes or tight hosiery are likely to develop toenail fungus, especially if they also have poor foot hygiene—not washing and thoroughly drying their feet every day...not changing socks daily...and/or not keeping their toenails trimmed. When a toenail is infected, it typically turns yellow or brown and becomes thickened, crumbles and separates from the nail bed. Toenail fungus rarely heals on its own.

What to do: Nail fungus can be difficult to treat, and recurrent infections are common. Over-the-counter antifungal nail creams are available, but they are rarely effective. If the infection is mild, your doctor may prescribe a medicated nail polish, which should be applied twice a week until the nail is cured. If the infection is more severe, your doctor will prescribe an oral antifungal medication, such as *itraconazole* (Sporanox) or *terbinafine* (Lamisil). These medications are typically taken for six to 12 weeks, but you won't see the end result of treatment until the nail grows back completely, usually in three to six months. In rare cases, both drugs may cause side effects, such as skin rashes or liver damage.

Germ-Fighting Secrets—from A Leading Microbiologist

Philip M. Tierno, Jr., PhD, director of clinical microbiology and immunology at New York University Medical Center, and associate professor, departments of microbiology and pathology at New York University School of Medicine, both in New York City. He is author of *The Secret Life of Germs*. Atria.

Everyone knows about the disease-causing potential of germs. Yet few people realize that microorganisms are essential for human health.

Of the 65,000 known species of germs, only about 1,400 cause disease. The rest are "good" germs, which establish our immune response, help us digest food and protect our bodies from potential pathogens. However, the germs that do promote disease can be deadly. Infectious diseases, such as pneumonia and septicemia (blood infection), are leading causes of death in the US.

Foodborne germs have made headlines due to the recent outbreaks of *Escherichia coli*-related illnesses. Even so, a surprising number of people are still not aware of the best ways to guard against infection through proper hygiene. Fortunately, most infections—everything from colds and the flu to life-threatening Legionnaires' disease—usually can be prevented. *My germ-fighting secrets...*

•**Wash properly.** The Centers for Disease Control and Prevention (CDC) estimates that proper hand-washing could prevent thousands of deaths annually, but studies show that less than 10% of people wash their hands as long or as thoroughly as they should.

To effectively remove germs: Wash with warm water and soap for about 20 to 30 seconds (roughly the time it takes to sing "Happy Birthday" twice) and rinse. Warm water dissolves soap more readily and makes it easier to remove germs. Rub the soapy water all over your hands—including the wrists, between the fingers and under the fingernails. (Use a fingernail brush, if possible.)

Best: Wash your hands several times a day—always before eating...after using the bathroom...after coughing or sneezing, especially when using your hands or a tissue... after shaking hands...and after handling anything touched by many people, such as door handles and automatic teller machines (ATMs). If soap and water aren't available, use an alcohol gel containing at least 62% alcohol.

•**Use antibacterial products when necessary.** Our hands pick up *millions* of potentially harmful organisms during daily activities—handling raw meats, poultry and/ or fish...changing diapers...picking up pet wastes in the yard, etc. Washing with soap and water removes (rather than kills) most germs, but some are left behind—potentially causing illness.

Interesting: Some experts worry that the regular use of antibacterial soaps will promote the emergence of antibiotic-resistant organisms, but there is no evidence that links these products to resistance. More study is needed to determine the long-term effects of antibacterial soaps.

Best: After washing your hands with soap, use an antibacterial cleaner if you've handled materials such as those described above. Some antibacterial products (such as Dial Complete hand wash) contain *triclosan*, a germicide that kills virtually all harmful bacteria.

Also important: Never allow a pet to lick your mouth, nose, eyes or an open wound. Many people believe that the mouths of dogs and cats are relatively germ-free—however, dogs and cats can carry *Pasteurella*, a bacterium that can cause skin infection in humans. And turtles, frogs and snakes can harbor *Salmonella*, a bacterium that causes gastroenteritis and other illnesses.

• **Limit kissing to close friends and family.** Mouth-to-mouth kissing clearly spreads germs, but even face kissing (kissing anywhere on the face, except the lips) can be dangerous if someone is ill. Flu viruses, for example, can be spread by an infected person during face kissing up to three days before full-blown symptoms develop and five days after they subside, depending on the germ.

Here's how: Before the kiss, the infected person may have touched his/her mouth or nose, then touched his face, contaminating it with infected saliva or mucus.

Best: Instead of kissing someone who may be sick, hug him. That way, you'll avoid face-to-face contact.

• **Air-dry toothbrushes and razors.** Bacteria thrive on toothbrushes and razors that stay damp. Bacteria on a razor could cause a staphylococcal infection of the skin, while a contaminated toothbrush can spread cold or flu viruses. Rinse and let them air-dry after every use—and store them upright so that they dry completely. To sanitize a toothbrush, put it in a cup of antiseptic mouthwash or 3% hydrogen peroxide (enough to cover the brush head), leave for one minute, then rinse and air-dry. Razors should be replaced after two or three uses...toothbrushes should be replaced when the bristles become worn.

• **Clean your showerhead.** The *Legionella* bacterium causes a potentially fatal, pneumonia-like condition called Legionnaires' disease, which is contracted by inhaling infected water droplets. The organism feeds on *cysteine*, a substance produced by a wide variety of waterborne organisms and bacteria found in potable water. Legionella can survive in tap water for many months, and showerheads provide a hospitable environment.

Best: Remove showerheads once a year. Disassemble and clean them thoroughly with a wire brush to remove any organisms that might be present. Use a solution of one ounce of bleach mixed with one quart of water.

Also important: Replace the standing water in humidifiers with fresh water at least once a week. Before adding fresh water, clean the filters/trays according to the manufacturer's directions.

• **Close the toilet lid.** Flushing an older toilet with the lid up can hurl droplets of water that contain fecal matter (and potentially other disease-causing organisms) up to 20 feet. The droplets can then contaminate toothbrushes, combs, faucets, etc. The risk for disease is even higher if the toilet bowl isn't cleaned regularly. Among the diseases that can be transmitted by fecal matter from an infected person are stomach flu and hepatitis A.

Best: In addition to closing the toilet lid, sanitize the bowl weekly with a commercial cleaner or a mixture of one ounce of bleach added to one quart of water.

• **Launder with hot water.** Bath towels can harbor fecal bacteria, including E. coli, along with hepatitis A and other harmful viruses—and these germs aren't necessarily killed by running them through a cold- or warm-water wash.

Warning: Because washing in cold or warm water doesn't kill germs, it's possible to get infected just by removing wet clothes from the washer if you then touch your nose, mouth or eyes.

Best: Use a "hot" washer setting (150° F or hotter) to kill most germs. Another option is to add bleach to the wash, which is effective even in cold or warm water. If you live in a sunny climate, consider line-drying clothes rather than using the dryer. Like the hottest cycle of a clothes dryer, the sun's ultraviolet rays will kill most germs.

Also important: Launder underwear separately in hot water to avoid contaminating other clothes. For added safety, use bleach to ensure that germs are killed when washing underwear.

More from Dr. Tierno, Jr. ...

The Best Way to Combat Germs in a Public Bathroom

Avoid germs in public bathrooms by using the first stall—it tends to be the least popular. Flush the toilet with your foot, then leave the stall quickly to avoid airborne bacteria. To be sure you are washing your hands long enough, sing the song "Happy Birthday to You" to yourself twice. Wash with comfortably lukewarm water—hotter water does not kill more germs. Use a paper towel to turn off the faucet and pull the door handle so that you don't pick up more germs after cleaning your hands.

A Sweet Solution

Honey acts as a natural antibiotic. *Here are instructions to help you make the most of the benefits of honey...*

How it works: Honey's natural acidity creates an inhospitable environment for germs ...and it contains a small amount of germ-killing hydrogen peroxide.

Important: Heat can destroy honey's beneficial properties, so buy the raw and unpasteurized kind. Honey can be used on most

wounds. If you have a puncture wound, consult your doctor.

What to do: Work one tablespoon of warmed honey into a four-inch by four-inch gauze pad, then place it on the wound. Change the dressing at least twice daily until the wound heals.

Caution: Infants younger than age one should not eat honey.

Peter Molan, PhD, professor of biological sciences, University of Waikato, Hamilton, New Zealand.

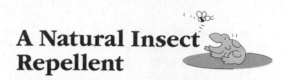

A Natural Insect Repellent

Oil of lemon eucalyptus is the only plant-based insect repellent on the Centers for Disease Control and Prevention's recommended list. But it must be reapplied more often than DEET or *picaridin* (frequency depends on the concentration).

Warning: Just one mosquito bite can transmit West Nile virus or other infections. Apply repellent to exposed skin whenever you are outdoors, especially between dusk and dawn.

Emily Zielinski-Gutierrez, DrPH, a behavioral scientist, Division of Vector-Borne Diseases, Centers for Disease Control and Prevention, Fort Collins, CO.

To Prevent Foot Odor

There are five ways to prevent foot odor, and we've outlined them below for you.

•**Apply a natural antiperspirant** that has buffered aluminum or aluminum chloride, such as Certain Dri Antiperspirant Roll-On, to the bottom of your feet.

•**Wear natural fibers**—socks made of cotton, which wicks away the moisture and allows greater circulation, and shoes made from cotton canvas or leather.

●**Don't wear the same pair of shoes two days in a row.**

●**Go barefoot** whenever possible.

●**Cut back on all caffeinated beverages**—sweating can sometimes be caused by consuming too much caffeine.

Natural Health, Box 37474, Boone, IA 50037.

What You May Not Know about Diarrhea

Douglas L. Seidner, MD, director of nutrition in the department of gastroenterology and hepatology at the Cleveland Clinic.

D iarrhea—bowel movements that are looser and more frequent than usual—is the second most common medical complaint (after respiratory infections) in the US.

Most people associate a bout of diarrhea with a viral infection or food poisoning.

Now: Researchers are identifying new—and sometimes surprising—triggers, including the use of some medications.

Latest development: The *Journal of the American Medical Association* published a study that links the use of acid-lowering heartburn drugs, such as *omeprazole* (Prilosec), *lansoprazole* (Prevacid) and *ranitidine* (Zantac), to increased infection with the bacterium *Clostridium difficile*—a cause of severe and persistent diarrhea.

In an unexpected finding, the same researchers identified an association between diarrhea and regular use of nonsteroidal anti-inflammatory drugs (NSAIDs). More study is needed to confirm this NSAID-diarrhea link.

HOW DIARRHEA DEVELOPS

What's left of food after most of it has been digested reaches the large intestine as a sort of slurry. There, the body absorbs water from this material, creating a solid mass to be excreted. Normal stool is 60% to 90%

water. Diarrhea occurs when stool is more than 90% water.

When stool does not remain in the large intestine long enough, it is excreted in a watery form. This "rapid transit" diarrhea can be caused by stress, overactive thyroid (hyperthyroidism) and certain drugs, such as antacids and laxatives that contain magnesium, and chemotherapy for cancer.

Other types of diarrhea...

●**Osmotic diarrhea** occurs when too much food remains undigested or unabsorbed. Water is drawn into the colon to dilute unabsorbed chemicals, which makes the stool looser.

Large amounts of certain fruits and beans as well as sugar substitutes (sorbitol and xylitol) that are used in some brands of fruit juice, chewing gum and candy are common causes of osmotic diarrhea. When the diarrhea sufferer stops eating the offending food, the condition stops.

Lactase deficiency—a lack of the enzyme needed to break down milk sugar (lactose)—is another cause of osmotic diarrhea. Most people know if they have this deficiency and avoid milk products.

Osmotic diarrhea also may develop in people taking antibiotics. That's because the drug eliminates beneficial bacteria that live in the intestinal tract, allowing harmful bacteria to proliferate. The beneficial microorganisms normally help the body process and absorb the small amount of food that hasn't been digested yet. Diarrhea usually develops within a few days of treatment. If it's bothersome enough, your doctor may prescribe a different antibiotic.

More rarely, diarrhea develops toward the end of antibiotic treatment—or even up to a month later. This may be caused by C. difficile or another bacterium that can flourish and cause inflammation of the large intestine when beneficial bacteria are eliminated.

Helpful: This infection is usually treated with the antibiotics *vancomycin* (Vancocin) or *metronidazole* (Flagyl).

●**Secretory diarrhea** occurs when an excessive amount of water, salt and digestive fluids are secreted into the stool. Viral infections,

261

bacterial toxins that cause some types of food poisoning and rare tumors of the small intestine and pancreas can trigger the secretions that lead to secretory diarrhea.

With food poisoning, excess secretions are stimulated by chemicals produced by bacteria that have contaminated something you ate. This diarrhea usually lasts for 12 to 24 hours and stops without treatment. If it persists, your doctor may order tests, such as stool cultures, to determine whether a virulent bacterium, such as *Salmonella, Shigella* or *Campylobacter*, is involved and will require medication.

Travelers' diarrhea has a similar cause. The culprit is generally a mild strain of a toxin-producing bacterium, such as *Escherichia coli*, that is present in food and/or water. Natives of the region you're visiting have been exposed to the microorganism for years and usually are immune to it. You're not. Travelers' diarrhea typically goes away within one to two days.

• **Exudative diarrhea** occurs when the large intestine's lining becomes inflamed. This triggers the release of blood, mucus, proteins and other fluids. Infection with the bacterium Shigella can cause this type of diarrhea. Crohn's disease (chronic inflammation of the small bowel or colon) and ulcerative colitis (chronic inflammation and ulceration of the colon) can also cause exudative diarrhea.

An antibiotic is sometimes used to treat a bacterial infection. Medication, such as the corticosteroid *prednisone* (Deltasone), and sometimes surgery are used to treat the inflammatory conditions.

BEST RELIEF STRATEGIES

In some cases, diarrhea can be a sign of a serious infection and should be treated by a doctor. *Even though most types of diarrhea run their course within a few days, the following steps can hasten the process and ease your discomfort...*

• **Eat right.** If food poisoning is the problem, you should abstain from all food until symptoms resolve, usually one to two days.

For other acute diarrhea, follow the "BRAT" diet: bananas, rice, applesauce and toast. Bananas and applesauce contain *pectin*, a water-soluble substance that helps firm up the stool...the carbohydrates in white rice and white toast are easy to digest. If you eat other foods, stick to small portions and avoid dairy products.

Yogurt is an exception. If it's made from live and active cultures, such as *Lactobacillus bulgaricus* and *Streptococcus thermophilus*, yogurt may replace beneficial bacteria in the colon, helping to relieve antibiotic-related diarrhea and stave off yeast infections.

When the diarrhea subsides, return to your normal diet cautiously. For the first few days, avoid fatty foods (they're harder to digest).

Important: Drink 64 ounces of fluids daily to replace what you're losing. Choose weak tea, water and/or small amounts of clear juice or soda, such as apple juice or ginger ale.

If diarrhea is severe: Drink "replacement fluids," such as CeraLyte, Pedialyte or Enfalyte. These contain salt and simple sugars that help the body retain water. Diarrhea-related dehydration isn't a danger for most adults, but it is a danger for children and many adults over age 65. Young children do not have as large of a reserve of water in the body as healthy adults. Older adults may have heart or kidney disease, which can be exacerbated by dehydration.

• **Medication.** Several over-the-counter preparations can help relieve diarrhea...

• *Loperamide* (Imodium) is a semi-synthetic narcotic that slows food as it passes through the bowel, allowing more time for water to be absorbed. Try loperamide if diarrhea is mild and hasn't been resolved in one to two days. It should not be taken if you have a fever or the stools are bloody.

• *Bismuth subsalicylate* (Pepto-Bismol, Kaopectate) absorbs toxins—it's quite effective for travelers' diarrhea. It should not be taken with aspirin. Do not take it if you have a fever or bloody stools. Children should not take this product.

CALL THE DOCTOR...

Seek medical attention if any of these danger signs appear...

•**The diarrhea is severe** (six or more stools a day), especially if there are signs of dehydration (parched lips, sunken eyes).

•**The diarrhea is bloody or includes mucus, rather than just water.**

•**It has lasted more than two days**—if mild, two weeks.

•**You have a fever over 101.5°F.**

•**Diarrhea is accompanied by severe abdominal pain** (anything more than moderate cramping).

Eliminating Body Odor Naturally

Jamison Starbuck, ND, a naturopathic physician in family practice and a lecturer at the University of Montana, both in Missoula. She is past president of the American Association of Naturopathic Physicians and a contributing editor to *The Alternative Advisor: The Complete Guide to Natural Therapies and Alternative Treatments.* Time Life.

As a physician, I pay attention to many details about my patients, including body odor. If I detect anything other than a mild, almost neutral scent, my medical curiosity is piqued. Body odor tells me about a patient's health status, dietary habits and hygiene. People with liver disease may have a musty odor…infections anywhere on the body usually emit a foul smell…uncontrolled diabetes often creates a smell best labeled as sweet fermentation. People who are on high-protein diets or who eat a lot of fatty and/or fried foods, onions, garlic or curry, or drink coffee or alcohol excessively, also have particular body odors. Poor hygiene leads to its own recognizable scent.

If you're worried about your body odor, ask a trusted friend or family member to do a sniff test.

What to do: Ask the person to stand within one inch of you and inhale. If the body odor is new, quite strong or confined to a specific part of your body—for example, your mouth, ears or genitals—see your doctor for an exam and evaluation. *If body odor is a familiar, long-standing problem that's not related to an illness, try the following suggestions for 10 days (if they help, continue as needed)…*

•**Eat right.** Fresh, whole foods give your body a fresh, wholesome scent. Eat a salad daily made with dark, leafy lettuce, sprouts, raw veggies and two tablespoons of olive oil. Avoid mayonnaise and cheese-based dressings, which contain odor-producing fat. Choose brown rice or a baked potato instead of fried potatoes. Reduce protein putrification in the digestive tract by eliminating meat—or consuming no more than three ounces of red meat or poultry per day. Drink one-half ounce of water for every pound of your body weight daily.

•**Take three saunas.** Saunas make you perspire, which has a detoxifying effect that reduces body odor.

What to do: Brush your dry skin with a loofah or other skin brush. Enter the sauna and stay there until you perspire all over your body, then leave the sauna and rinse with cold water for 30 seconds. Brush your skin again and return to the sauna. End with a brisk 30-second skin brush, then wrap up in soft, warm clothing. Repeat this process two more times over the next several days.

Caution: People with high blood pressure or heart disease should avoid saunas.

•**Use chlorophyll.** This chemical compound, which is responsible for the green pigment in plants, has astringent properties and can help control the type of body odor that comes from the fermentation of food in the digestive tract. Add one tablespoon of chlorophyll (available at health-food stores) to four ounces of water and drink it at the end of each meal. If you prefer, you can eat one-eighth cup of fresh parsley daily as a substitute for liquid chlorophyll.

•**Eliminate oral bacteria.** In addition to brushing your teeth at least twice daily and flossing at least once a day, gargle each morning with a cup of warm chamomile tea mixed with one teaspoon of hydrogen peroxide. This mixture will kill bacteria living in the throat and mouth, a common cause of bad breath. After the 10-day period, gargle with the chamomile/peroxide mixture as needed for sore throats.

Heartburn Relief

Ara DerMarderosian, PhD, professor of pharmacognosy (the study of natural products used in medicine) and Roth chair of natural products at the University of the Sciences in Philadelphia. He also is the scientific director of the university's Complementary and Alternative Medicines Institute.

Many people who suffer from heartburn take over-the-counter antacids or expensive prescription medication, such as *esomeprazole* (Nexium) and *lansoprazole* (Prevacid). These treatments can help but often cause side effects, such as diarrhea and dry mouth.

Heartburn, a sharp, burning pain under the rib cage, occurs when stomach contents "back up" (reflux) into the esophagus.

Chamomile, ginger and deglycyrrhizinated licorice have long been used (in tea, extract and tincture) to relieve heartburn as well as indigestion and intestinal irritation. Their effectiveness is supported by anecdotal evidence.

For relief proven in clinical studies, try pectin, a substance found in the outer skin and rind of fruits and vegetables. Apples and bananas are among the best sources of pectin. If you suffer from heartburn, try eating an apple (do not choose green or other tart varieties) or a banana to see if it relieves your symptoms.

Pectin supplements, which are available at most health-food stores, are another option. Take at the onset of heartburn until it subsides. For dosage, follow label instructions. Pectin supplements are generally safe but may interfere with the absorption of some medications, so check with your doctor before trying this supplement.

Caution: Chronic heartburn (more than twice a week) may indicate gastroesophageal reflux disease (GERD), a condition that should be treated by a gastroenterologist.

Herbal Remedies For Flatulence

Anil Minocha, MD, professor of medicine and director of the division of digestive diseases at the University of Mississippi Medical Center in Jackson. He is author of *Natural Stomach Care*. Penguin. For more information on gastrointestinal health, go to Dr. Minocha's Web site, *www.minochahealth.org*.

Eating certain foods, such as beans and some fruits and vegetables, can lead to flatulence (gas or air in the stomach or intestine that is expelled through the anus). Fortunately, dozens of carminative (gas-reducing) herbs can help relieve flatulence. Use them one at a time or in combination. *Best choices...*

• **Chamomile** relaxes the bowel, which reduces intestinal spasms. Steep a tea bag in hot water for about 10 minutes. Drink one cup before bedtime.

• **Ginger** is an antispasmodic that reduces the force and frequency of intestinal contractions. It's good for most digestive complaints, including gas. Peel and slice one inch of ginger root and boil in three cups of water for 20 minutes. Drink one to three cups daily. Or take 500 mg of ginger capsules or powder three times a day.

• **Fennel seeds** calm an upset stomach and reduce gas. Munch on a handful of seeds to ease or prevent gas. They're available at health-food stores. *For additional relief...*

• Massage your abdomen when you have painful gas. With moderate pressure, use your palms to massage your abdomen clockwise—the direction that food moves through the gastrointestinal tract—for five to 10 minutes. Massage pushes out gas and relieves discomfort.

• Try a simple yoga posture to help purge gas from your intestine.

What to do: Lie on your back, pull your knees to your chest and gently rock back and forth.

• Perform daily exercise to help move gas out of the intestine and reduce painful pressure.

Best: Walking, tai chi and bicycling.

Heartburn Help

Prone to heartburn? Stop drinking soda. Consumption of carbonated beverages is a risk factor for nighttime heartburn—which can cause more damage to the esophagus than daytime heartburn. Acid that comes up into the esophagus is not cleared as easily by the body during sleep. Even people who usually don't have heartburn should stop drinking soda at least three hours before bedtime to reduce the chance of nighttime acid reflux.

Stuart F. Quan, MD, professor of medicine, University of Arizona, Tucson, and coauthor of a recent study of 3,806 people with nighttime heartburn, published in Chest.

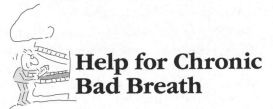

Help for Chronic Bad Breath

If you have bad breath, the first step is to identify the underlying cause. Bad breath can result from poor oral hygiene, infection, periodontal disease, poor-fitting dentures and crowns, or dentures that aren't cleaned regularly. Professional dental care is needed to treat periodontal disease and infection and to correct ill-fitting dentures and crowns. Proper tooth brushing, flossing and brushing or scraping of the tongue daily are important to remove food particles, which breed bacteria that can cause bad breath.

Medical conditions that can lead to bad breath include sinus or upper respiratory infections, uncontrolled diabetes, xerostomia (dry mouth) and gastroesophageal reflux disease (chronic backup of stomach acids into the esophagus).

Medications also can be to blame, especially drugs that dry out the mouth and prevent saliva from washing away bacteria and particles—such as antihistamines and some antidepressants, including *sertraline* (Zoloft) and *bupropion* (Wellbutrin).

If your bad breath persists despite good dental hygiene and professional dental care, see your internist to determine if a medical condition or medication is the cause.

Sheldon Nadler, DMD, dentist in private practice in New York City.

Natural Remedies For Constipation

Mark A. Stengler, ND, a naturopathic physician and leading authority on the practice of alternative and integrated medicine. He is director of the La Jolla Whole Health Clinic, La Jolla, CA, and adjunct associate clinical professor of the National College of Natural Medicine, Portland, OR. He is author of the newsletter *Bottom Line Natural Healing, www. DrStengler.com.*

Regular use of certain laxatives can make constipation worse by damaging the large intestine, making it "lazier" and even less efficient.

Most patients who experience constipation can prevent it permanently with dietary changes and other natural approaches. Even patients who have had constipation for years often can restore normal bowel function within two weeks.

WHAT'S NORMAL?

In a healthy body, waste travels through the digestive tract in a predictable, regular cycle, over a period of six to 24 hours. Most people have one to three bowel movements daily. Others have as few as three bowel movements a week. There's a lot of individual variability—what's normal for you might not be normal for someone else.

Red flag: Any change in your normal bowel habits. See a doctor if the frequency of bowel movements changes…you have blood in your stool…or you are experiencing intense abdominal pain. Constipation by itself is rarely dangerous, but it may be a sign of other problems, including colon cancer.

Stool in the intestine contains bacteria, fungi and metabolic by-products of digestion. If it remains in the colon for too long, these harmful substances cause a number of uncomfortable symptoms, such as bloating, painfully hard stools and a general sense of fatigue.

SUPPLEMENTS & FOODS

The right diet and supplements can relieve constipation. *Best choices...*

•**High-fiber foods,** including brown rice, whole-wheat bread, oatmeal, fruits, vegetables and legumes, such as beans and lentils. Fiber absorbs water in the intestine, which makes the stool bulkier. This triggers the intestinal contractions that cause bowel movements. Fiber also makes the stool softer, so it is easier to pass.

If you don't eat a lot of plant foods, you can supplement with an over-the-counter product containing *psyllium* (such as Metamucil), following the directions on the label. Or take one teaspoon of ground psyllium seed husks twice daily. Psyllium acts as a bulking agent and increases the frequency—and comfort—of bowel movements. Be sure to drink plenty of water or juice to avoid making constipation worse.

Ground flaxseed also works. It's a highly concentrated source of fiber, with the added benefit of supplying healthful omega-3 fatty acids. Have one to two tablespoons of ground flaxseed daily. You can sprinkle it on yogurt or cereal or just eat it plain. Be sure to drink at least 10 ounces of water with it. Don't eat whole flaxseed. It has a tough outer coating that is not broken down during digestion.

Some people take stool softeners. Common ones, such as *docusate* (Colace), are not laxatives and not habit forming, but you can get similar results with flaxseed oil. Take one to two tablespoons daily. The oil can go in a shake or on a salad.

•**Magnesium.** People with constipation often are deficient in this mineral. Magnesium helps in three ways—it increases the strength and regularity of the intestine's muscular contractions...it relaxes the nervous system...and at higher doses, it promotes the accumulation of water in the intestine, which boosts bowel function.

Foods high in magnesium: Green, leafy vegetables (such as spinach), brown rice, avocado, berries, cabbage, broccoli and bananas.

If you have acute constipation, take 250 mg of magnesium two to four times daily. Don't take supplemental magnesium for more than about a week. It can lead to dependence—reducing the colon's natural ability to contract—and can interfere with the normal absorption of nutrients. Don't take supplemental magnesium if you are pregnant unless authorized by your doctor.

•**Fermented foods.** People who eat sauerkraut, live-culture yogurt and/or kefir (a fermented milk) are less likely to experience constipation because fermented foods contain probiotics. These beneficial organisms crowd out harmful microbes that may impair digestion and elimination.

Eat fermented foods daily, or take a probiotic supplement. Look for a product that provides at least four billion active organisms, preferably a combination of *Lactobacillus acidophilus* and *bifidus bacteria*.

•**Milk thistle** (Silybum marianum). A traditional remedy for hepatitis, milk thistle improves the flow of bile, a digestive juice that breaks down fats in the intestinal tract. Bile improves the colon's motility (the ability of the colon to contract and eliminate wastes).

Dose: 200 mg to 250 mg of a product standardized to 80% *silymarin* (the active ingredient) with meals twice daily for six to eight weeks. Don't take it if you are pregnant or breastfeeding.

GIVE UP DAIRY

A *New England Journal of Medicine* study of 65 children with chronic constipation reported that cow's milk was the cause in two-thirds of cases. It contains the protein *casein*, which has been shown to cause constipation.

Also, reduce the amount of saturated fats in your diet. A diet high in saturated fat slows motility—and the longer the stool stays in the intestine, the more likely it is to harden and interfere with normal bowel movements.

DAILY EXERCISE

Mild-to-moderate aerobic exercise—a 30-minute brisk walk, for example—helps stimulate intestinal contractions. It also reduces stress and relaxes the nervous system, which improves muscle movements in the intestine and helps prevent or treat constipation.

STRESS CONTROL

Yoga, Pilates, meditation and other stress-reducing activities can reduce constipation. Studies show that people who experience high levels of stress often have reduced intestinal efficiency. In addition, people with high stress levels often have hectic lifestyles and don't take the time for regular bowel movements. Every day, set aside time for mental and physical relaxation.

Hidden Dangers Of Indoor Air Pollution

Richard J. Shaughnessy, PhD, program manager for the University of Tulsa's Indoor Air Program, a center dedicated to improving indoor air quality in homes, schools and workplaces. He served as the principal adviser to the Environmental Protection Agency on development of its Indoor Air Quality Diagnostics course. Dr. Shaughnessy has also conducted air quality research in China, South Africa and Australia.

When you hear the words "air pollution," you may think of a smog-filled metropolis.

What most of us do not realize: The concentration of air pollutants inside people's homes and other indoor spaces may be up to 100 times higher than outside pollutant levels—even in large cities.

WHAT'S IN YOUR AIR?

Many indoor pollutants cause a musty, noxious or otherwise unusual smell. But some offenders may cause no odor. The only sign of trouble may be the development of symptoms (such as those described on page 268). Older adults are at especially high risk since their bodies process and eliminate toxins less efficiently.

Among the most common indoor air pollutants are dust, pollen, animal dander, dust mite droppings, tobacco smoke, molds, and fumes from your stove, furnace or car. Pollutants that are less well-recognized include those from household products containing volatile organic compounds (VOCs)—for example, pressed-wood products, paints and paint strippers, varnishes, carpeting, degreasers, air fresheners and pesticides. Depending on the product and other factors, household products can emit VOCs for days, weeks or even years.

Frightening report: The EPA has found that concentrations of about a dozen VOCs —such as *terpenes* and *formaldehyde*—are typically two to five times higher inside people's homes than outdoors. Many of these chemicals are known to irritate the lungs, skin and eyes. Some, including formaldehyde, *benzene* and *perchloroethylene* (a chemical used in drycleaning and spot removers), are identified by the EPA as known or suspected carcinogens.

Radon, a radioactive gas that comes from the natural breakdown of uranium in soil, rock and water, is also a common indoor air pollutant and is believed to cause or contribute to approximately 20,000 lung cancer deaths annually in the US.

GOING TO THE SOURCES

Eliminating or reducing air pollutants at their sources is your first step. For example, to protect your family against carbon monoxide, having your flues, chimneys and furnace or boiler inspected and cleaned at the start of each winter is one of the best actions you can take.

Also recommended: Install a carbon monoxide detector in the hallway outside bedrooms. If your house has an attached garage, place a carbon monoxide detector nearby inside your home.

Other sources—and solutions…

For VOCs: Use latex instead of oil-based paints for interior walls…properly discard old paints and varnishes (which can release gaseous compounds even from closed containers)…avoid potentially harmful household cleaners, such as ammonia and chlorine bleach…and consider using all-natural cleaning products (such as those from Shaklee and Seventh Generation).

Caution: Pressed-wood products, including particleboard, hardwood plywood paneling and medium-density fiberboard, may emit formaldehyde.

For "greener" remodeling or construction materials, look for items approved by either the Greenguard Environmental Institute (*www.greenguard.org*) or Green Seal (*www. greenseal.org*). These two nonprofit organizations test and certify low-VOC-emitting furnishings, flooring, paints, lumber and other household products.

Helpful: If you want carpeting or rugs in your home, look for the Carpet and Rug Institute's Green Label or Green Label Plus certification. This ensures that the brand meets certain standards for VOC emissions (for more information, consult *www.carpet-rug.org*).

For pollens and pesticides: Keep windows closed during high-pollen season (roughly March through October) or when pesticides are being sprayed nearby…put doormats outside each entrance and leave your shoes at the door to avoid tracking in pollen and pesticide residues…and limit indoor pesticide use (instead, use baits and preventive steps, such as caulking cracks). According to the EPA, Americans get about 80% of their pesticide exposure inside their homes or other buildings.

For mold: Use a dehumidifier or air conditioner to keep indoor humidity levels below 50% (as measured by a hygrometer, a mechanical or electronic device available at hardware stores, starting at $15)…properly clean water catch trays in dehumidifiers every few days…promptly repair water-damaged walls, ceilings or floors…keep gutters clear and make sure they channel water away from your foundation…and take necessary steps (such as installing a sump pump) to ensure a dry basement.

For radon: Home owners should test their indoor air for radon. Do-it-yourself tests are available at most hardware stores for about $20. If you detect an unacceptable level of radon gas, contact a radon remediation specialist.

IMPROVING VENTILATION

When addressing indoor air pollutants, adequate ventilation is also important. Open your windows and doors (unless you have allergies and it's high-pollen season).

Other steps…

• **Install kitchen and bath exhaust fans that vent to the outside.**

• **To keep air circulating throughout your home,** use attic or whole-house fans, if possible.

USING AIR CLEANERS

If you follow the steps described earlier but continue to suffer symptoms, air cleaners may help. Air cleaners use either a mechanical filter that traps particulates as air passes through it…or an electronic setup that draws in air, gives particulates an electrical charge and then collects them on a plate or filter—or a combination of both methods.

Important: Air cleaners do not eliminate gases or particulates that have settled on surfaces.

Main choices…

• **Portable air cleaners** can be effective for individual rooms. Ensure that the cleaner is adequate for the room size and check the clean air delivery rate (CADR)—the volume of filtered air delivered by the unit. The CADR should be at least two-thirds of the room's area (for example, 80 for a 120-square-foot room).

• **In-duct filters** provide whole-house air cleaning. When selecting an in-duct filter, check the minimum efficiency reporting value (MERV) rating that tells you how efficiently a filter removes airborne particulates. If you have allergies, asthma or other respiratory problems, your best bet is a medium-efficiency pleated or extended surface filter with a MERV rating of 10 to 13.

More from Dr. Shaughnessy…

Signs of Trouble

If you regularly experience any of the following symptoms at home or in the workplace—but nowhere else—poor indoor air could be to blame…

- **Coughing or congestion** (not due to a cold).
- **Headaches, dizziness.**
- **Itchy, watery eyes.**
- **Itchy or sore throat.**
- **Unexplained fatigue.**
- **Difficulty concentrating.**

A Quick Flu Diagnosis

A new test diagnoses flu the same day. That is especially important for older people and those with compromised immune systems or chronic diseases, and it could help prevent complications.

Cost for the test: About $30. Antiviral medicines generally shorten the course of the flu by one day if taken within 48 hours of initial symptoms. The best defense against flu is vaccination.

Katherine A. Poehling, MD, assistant professor of pediatrics at Monroe Carell Jr. Children's Hospital, Vanderbilt University, Nashville, and leader of a study of influenza in more than 4,500 preschoolers, published in *The New England Journal of Medicine.*

Cough Relief

A llergy medications soothe coughs better than over-the-counter (OTC) cough remedies, such as *dextromethorphan* and *guaifenesin*. OTC allergy medications, such as those that contain *diphenhydramine*, *chlorpheniramine* and *brompheniramine*, help to quiet a cough due to the common cold by drying the secretions in the back of the throat.

Downside: These allergy medications may cause drowsiness as well.

Also helpful for a cough: Pain relievers, such as Advil (ibuprofen) and Aleve (naproxen)—they may lessen the severity and frequency of the cough by inhibiting chemicals that cause inflammation.

Richard Irwin, MD, professor of medicine, University of Massachusetts Medical School, Worcester, and editor-in-chief of the American College of Chest Physicians guidelines for treatment of cough.

Best Way to Blow Your Nose

U se paper facial tissues, not handkerchiefs, in which bacteria can grow. Also, use a tissue once, then throw it away. Blow gently—too much pressure can push infectious fluid into ears and sinuses. Press a finger outside one nostril, then blow through the open one. Repeat on the other side. Wash your hands after blowing. Wait 10 minutes after waking in the morning before blowing your nose—congestion decreases after you get up from a prone position.

Murray Grossan, MD, otolaryngologist, Towers Ear, Nose and Throat Clinic, Cedars-Sinai Medical Center, Los Angeles.

10
Natural Healers

Feed a Cold, Starve A Fever and Other Nutrition Myths

Many commonly held beliefs about the health impact of certain foods are based on hearsay, not on scientific research. *Here are the realities behind some often-cited nutrition myths...*

***Myth:* Feed a cold, starve a fever.**

Reality: Both a cold and a fever—and you can have both at once—are associated with inflammation, which increases metabolic rate, allowing you to burn calories at rest more quickly. However, eating more or less will have no real effect on how long you remain sick. There is no evidence that food shortens a cold's duration or reduces symptoms.

It's often believed that vitamin C can help a cold, but there's no firm evidence to back that claim. Last year, researchers reviewed 55 previous studies. Most showed that taking vitamin C did not prevent colds—a few showed that colds were slightly shorter with vitamin supplementation, but usually by only one day or so.

Zinc may reduce a cold's duration, but it must be taken early on—before full-blown symptoms strike. The benefit comes from zinc gluconate lozenges (see the label for the correct dosage). Zinc acetate lozenges or zinc-rich foods, such as oysters and beef, have no impact on a cold's severity or duration.

Bottom line: The real goal is to stay hydrated and loosen mucus by increasing your intake of liquids, such as water, clear soups and tea.

***Myth:* Fiber prevents colon cancer.**

Reality: A high-fiber diet keeps your bowel movements regular and can lower

Edward Saltzman, MD, chief of the division of clinical nutrition and medical director of the Obesity Consultation Center at Tufts–New England Medical Center, and a scientist at the Jean Mayer USDA Human Nutrition Research Center on Aging at Tufts University, both in Boston.

cholesterol and reduce risk of insulin resistance, a precursor to diabetes. But there is no consistent evidence that fiber protects against colon cancer.

A study in *The Journal of the American Medical Association* reviewed data on 726,000 people over 20 years and found that high-fiber diets did not reduce the risk of colon cancer. Another study determined that people eating 33 grams of fiber per day—roughly 6.5 servings of fruits and vegetables—had no fewer polyps (benign growths in the colon that may become cancerous) than those eating roughly half as much fiber. Even high-fiber cereals seem to strike out when it comes to protecting against colon cancer, although they may have benefits for cardiovascular health and prevent constipation.

Bottom line: Continue to eat fiber-rich foods, such as fruits, vegetables and whole grains, for their proven health benefits, including cardiovascular health and weight control. Also, while fiber-rich foods do not protect against colon cancer, they do protect against other types of cancer—including those of the breast, mouth, throat and esophagus—probably because of their phytochemicals, protective compounds found in some foods.

Myth: Soy relieves hot flashes.

Reality: Most scientific studies have not found that soy-rich foods or supplements offer relief from hot flashes. While soy is a good source of phytoestrogens (chemicals occurring naturally in plants that act like the hormone *estrogen*), it provides an extremely weak estrogenic effect. Some menopausal women may benefit from a soy-rich diet, but most do not—at least not on a consistent basis.

Bottom line: Soy-rich foods are nutritious, low in fat and may help lower cholesterol and improve prostate health (so far, studies have produced mixed results). And a recent analysis of 18 previous studies found that soy may slightly lower the risk of breast cancer. To control hot flashes, however, you're better off adjusting room temperature…wearing "breathable" fabrics, such as cotton…and drinking cool beverages when a flash starts. At this time, there are no dietary supplements known to be both safe and effective for hot flashes.

Myth: Eating after 8 pm causes weight gain.

Reality: It's not *when* you eat that causes weight gain—it's how much. There is no evidence that calorie "burn" is slower at night. Weight gain results from overeating and lack of activity, whether that occurs in the morning, afternoon or night.

This myth likely stems from the fact that many people eat little during the day but then overeat at night, when they're relaxing at home—but these people won't gain any more weight than those who overeat earlier in the day. Some research has suggested that people who eat breakfast are less likely to gain weight or become obese—though the reason for this is unclear.

Bottom line: Watch portion sizes more than the clock. Don't go for long periods without eating, because you are more likely to overeat when you are ravenously hungry.

Myth: Olive oil is the healthiest oil.

Reality: This foundation of the Mediterranean diet is among the healthiest cooking oils—and certainly gets the best publicity—but other oils may be just as good. For example, just a few months ago, the FDA decreed that canola oil, like olive oil, can carry a health claim for its ability to reduce the risk of coronary heart disease due to its unsaturated fat content. The important thing is to limit saturated fats, which are most often found in animal products, such as red meat, poultry, butter and whole milk.

Bottom line: Choose oils high in mono- or polyunsaturated fat, such as olive, canola, safflower, flaxseed and walnut oils. If you choose olive oil, select extra-virgin. Extra-virgin olive oil comes from the first pressing of olives, so it's less processed and contains higher levels of antioxidants, substances that slow down the natural process that leads to cell and tissue damage.

Myth: Honey is more healthful than sugar.

271

Reality: Honey contains more fructose than sugar—and fructose is becoming public enemy number one among some cardiologists.

Bottom line: Honey and sugar offer "empty calories"—a tablespoon of honey has 64 calories and a tablespoon of sugar has about 45 calories. Neither is a good source of any nutrient. You would need to overeat honey to an unhealthy level in order to benefit from its micronutrients or other purported health benefits.

Diet for a Pain-Free Life

Harris H. McIlwain, MD, a rheumatologist and pain specialist with Tampa Medical Group, and adjunct professor at University of South Florida College of Public Health, both in Tampa. He is also coauthor, with Debra Fulghum Bruce, PhD, of *Diet for a Pain-Free Life*. Da Capo.

As many as 150 million Americans suffer with ongoing pain. This usually is caused by such problems as arthritis or injuries to the neck or back.

Being overweight and having a poor diet are crucial factors, too. Fatty tissue is an endocrine (hormone-producing) organ, just like other organs in the body. Studies indicate that patients who are overweight produce high levels of *cytokines, C-reactive protein* and other proinflammatory chemicals (substances that promote joint and tissue damage and increase pain).

Good news: Losing as little as 10 pounds can significantly reduce inflammation, pain and stiffness—regardless of the underlying cause of the discomfort. A patient who combines weight loss with a diet that includes anti-inflammatory foods (and excludes pro-inflammatory foods) can reduce pain by up to 90%. The effect rivals that of *ibuprofen* and similar painkillers—without gastrointestinal upset or other side effects.

PAIN-FREE DIET

The saturated fat in beef, pork, lamb and other meats is among the main causes of painful inflammation. People who eat a lot of meats (including poultry) consume *arachidonic acid*, an essential fatty acid that is converted into inflammatory chemicals in the body.

Although a vegetarian diet is ideal for reducing inflammation and promoting loss of weight (no more than 6% of all vegetarians are obese), very few Americans are willing to give up meat altogether.

Recommended: A plant-based diet that includes little (or no) meat and poultry...at least two to four weekly servings of fish...and plenty of fiber and anti-inflammatory foods. Patients who follow this diet and limit daily calories to about 1,400 can lose 10 to 25 pounds of excess weight within three months.

Helpful: It takes at least two to three weeks to establish new dietary habits. People who give up meat entirely usually find that they don't miss it after a few weeks—while those who continue to eat some meat may find the cravings harder to resist.

My favorite cookbooks: *Vegan with a Vengeance* by Isa Chandra Moskowitz (Da Capo) and *Pike Place Public Market Seafood Cookbook* by Braiden Rex-Johnson (Ten Speed Press).

Here are the best painkilling foods and beverages. *Try to include most of them in your diet...*

RED WINE

Red wine contains *resveratrol*, the chemical compound that blocks off the activation of the COX-2 enzyme, one of the main substances responsible for pain and inflammation. Resveratrol may be more effective than aspirin at relieving pain from osteoarthritis and other inflammatory conditions.

Other beverages made from grapes, such as white wine and grape juice, have some resveratrol, but not as much as red wine.

Servings: No more than two glasses daily for men, and no more than one glass for women.

Alternative source of antioxidants for nondrinkers: Two or more cups of tea daily. Both green and black teas contain *epigallocatechin-3 gallate* (EGCG), a chemical that blocks the COX-2 enzyme.

BERRIES

Virtually all fruits contain significant amounts of antioxidants, which prevent free radical molecules from damaging the cell membranes and causing inflammation. Berries—particularly blueberries, cranberries, blackberries—are among the most powerful analgesic fruits because they are rich with *anthocyanins*, some of the most effective antioxidants. One-half cup of blueberries, for example, has more antioxidant power than five servings of green peas or broccoli.

Servings: One-half cup of berries daily, fresh or frozen.

Bonus: Berries are very high in the antioxidant vitamin C, a nutrient that builds and protects joint cartilage.

PINEAPPLE

Fresh pineapple contains the enzyme *bromelain*, which is in the stem and fruit of the pineapple and inhibits the release of inflammatory chemicals. It has been shown in some studies to decrease arthritic pain. I advise patients with sports injuries to eat pineapple because of its healing powers.

Servings: At least two half-cup servings weekly, more if you're suffering from injuries or an arthritis flare-up. Bromelain also can be taken in supplement form—200 milligrams (mg) to 300 mg, three times daily before meals.

GINGER

Ginger contains potent anti-inflammatory substances and was found in one study to reduce knee pain in 63% of patients.

Servings: One teaspoon of ginger each day. Fresh and powdered ginger are equally effective and can be added to food.

FISH

I advise patients to substitute oily fish (such as salmon, tuna and sardines) for meats. Fish has little saturated fat (the main pro-inflammatory nutrient in the American diet) and is high in omega-3 fatty acids. Omega-3s increase the body's production of *inhibitory prostaglandins*, substances that decrease levels of inflammatory chemicals found in the body. And this can help reduce arthritis pain.

Servings: Two to four three-ounce servings of fish weekly or 1,000 mg to 2,000 mg of fish oil (available in capsule form) daily. If you don't like fish, omega-3s also are found in flaxseed, walnuts and soy foods.

WHOLE GRAINS AND BEANS

These are among the best sources of B vitamins—especially important for people who eat a lot of processed foods, which are usually deficient in these nutrients. Studies suggest that vitamins B-1 (*thiamin*), B-6 (*pyridoxine*) and B-12 (*cyanocobalamin*) may reduce inflammation.

Other B vitamins, such as B-3 (*niacin*), also reduce inflammation and may increase natural steroid levels and reduce the risk of osteoarthritis.

Servings: Consume at least one-half cup of whole grains and/or beans daily.

Good choices: Brown rice, lentils, chickpeas, black beans and kidney beans.

Bonus: Grains and beans are high in fiber. High-fiber foods promote loss of weight by increasing a sense of fullness and maintaining optimal blood sugar levels.

Whole Grains Good For Your Gums

In a recent finding, people who ate an average of three servings a day of whole grains, such as whole-grain breads and cereals, had a 23% lower risk of developing gum disease than those who ate few or no whole grains. Whole grains help control blood sugar and reduce the risk of developing type 2 diabetes, both of which increase the severity of gum disease.

Anwar T. Merchant, DMD, ScD, assistant professor, clinical epidemiology and biostatistics, McMaster University, Hamilton, Canada.

Cranberry Antibiotic

A traditional remedy for urinary tract infections, cranberries are now being studied for their ability to fight other infectious diseases. New research shows that *proanthocyanidins*, compounds found in cranberries, may actually change the structure of some types of bacteria, making it harder for them to attach to human cells.

Worcester Polytechnic Institute.

The Healing Power of Spices

David Winston, a Washington, NJ, registered herbalist (RH) and a founding member of the American Herbalist Guild, the only peer-reviewed organization of herbalists in the US. He is a coauthor of *Herbal Therapy and Supplements.* Lippincott.

Traditional healers have recognized the medicinal properties of spices for thousands of years.

Now: A growing body of scientific evidence supports the use of spices to prevent —and even help treat—various diseases, such as arthritis, diabetes, cancer and Alzheimer's.*

New findings…

CAYENNE PEPPER

What it does: Lowers cholesterol…helps to prevent atherosclerosis…and decreases allergic responses. An extract from the pepper, called capsaicin, can be used in a topical cream to treat pain from arthritis, shingles, bursitis, low-back ache and neuropathy (or nerve pain). Cayenne's benefits can be attributed to all the antioxidants, flavonoids and carotenoids that it contains, all of which have anti-inflammatory effects and enhance circulation. Capsaicin depletes the nerve endings

*Check with your doctor before using spices for medicinal purposes, as they can interact with prescription medication.

of *substance P*, a neurotransmitter that facilitates nerve transmission of pain.

Scientific evidence: One four-week study published in the *Journal of Rheumatology* found that individuals with osteoarthritis of the hands who applied capsaicin cream four times a day experienced reduced pain and tenderness.

Typical dose: Cayenne can be bought as a supplement in capsules and tincture. Take one capsule of cayenne pepper up to three times a day…or place three to eight drops of cayenne tincture in four ounces of water and drink two to four times a day. Apply a topical cream containing capsaicin to painful areas, as directed on the label. You also can season your food with powdered cayenne pepper or hot sauce.

Possible side effects: Cayenne pepper can cause gastric upset. To avoid pain and burning, do not let topical capsaicin come in contact with your eyes or other mucous membranes. If you take *warfarin* (Coumadin), do not use cayenne pepper supplements.

CINNAMON

What it does: Helps prevent heart disease and type 2 diabetes.

Due to its antioxidant properties, cinnamon helps people with metabolic syndrome (a cluster of factors, including excessive abdominal fat, high blood sugar and elevated blood pressure, which increase the risk for cardiovascular disease and type 2 diabetes) use the hormone insulin in their bodies more efficiently.

Scientific evidence: A US Department of Agriculture clinical study found that consuming capsules containing 1 gram (g), 3g or 6g of cinnamon daily (about ¼ teaspoon, ¾ teaspoon or 1¼ teaspoons, respectively) for 40 days lowered blood levels of glucose and triglycerides (fats in the blood) by about 25% in adults with type 2 diabetes. It also reduced LDL "bad" cholesterol by up to 27%.

Typical dose: Use one-half to one teaspoon of powdered cinnamon daily on cereal or toast or mix into yogurt…take one capsule twice a day…or add 20 to 40 drops of tincture to one ounce of water and drink three times daily.

For tea, mix one-fourth to one-half tea-spoon of powdered cinnamon with eight ounces of boiling water. Steep for 10 to 15 minutes, covered. Drink a four-ounce cup up to three times a day.

Possible side effects: Because cinnamon can affect blood glucose amounts, people with diabetes should carefully monitor their blood sugar and ask their doctors if their medication needs to be adjusted.

GINGER

What it does: Reduces the pain and swelling caused by rheumatoid arthritis and osteoarthritis...helps to prevent the nausea and vomiting associated with motion sickness or pregnancy...enhances digestion and circulation...and eases intestinal gas.

Scientific evidence: In two clinical studies ginger relieved pain and/or swelling in 75% of arthritis patients.

Typical dose: Take one to two capsules with meals two to three times daily...or add 10 to 30 drops of the tincture to one ounce of water and drink three to four times daily.

For tea, mix one-fourth to one-half teaspoon of powdered ginger (or use a ginger tea bag) with eight ounces of boiling water. Steep for 10 to 15 minutes, covered. Drink four ounces up to three times daily.

Possible side effects: Ginger can cause a blood-thinning effect, so check with your doctor before using it if you take an anticoagulant, such as *warfarin* (Coumadin). Ginger may cause an upset stomach in people who take larger doses than those described above.

TURMERIC

What it does: Helps prevent atherosclerosis, some types of cancer and Alzheimer's disease...decreases the pain and stiffness of rheumatoid arthritis and osteoarthritis...can eliminate indigestion...and eases the symptoms of inflammatory bowel disease and of irritable bowel syndrome. The beneficial effects of turmeric (also present in curry) are due to its anti-inflammatory compounds known as *curcuminoids*, as well as the essential oils and carotenoids it contains.

Scientific evidence: In a double-blind, placebo-controlled study, 116 people with indigestion took either a 500-milligram (mg) capsule of curcumin (the substance that gives turmeric its yellow color) or a placebo four times a day. Nearly 90% of those taking curcumin experienced full or partial relief after seven days.

Typical dose: Take 250 mg to 500 mg of curcumin (standardized to 80% to 90% curcumin) three times daily...or add 40 to 60 drops of the tincture to one ounce of water and drink three to four times daily.

For tea, mix one-half teaspoon of powdered turmeric with eight ounces of boiling water and steep for 10 to 15 minutes, covered. Drink four ounces up to four times a day.

Possible side effects: Turmeric can stimulate liver function, so it should be avoided by anyone with gallstones or any other bile-duct obstruction. Preliminary studies show that curcumin may lessen the effectiveness of chemotherapy drugs, such as *doxorubicin* (Rubex) and *cyclophosphamide* (Cytoxan). If you are undergoing chemotherapy, talk to your doctor before taking curcumin.

Up to 70% of Cancers Can Be Avoided

Melanie Polk, MMSc, RD, director, nutrition education, American Institute for Cancer Research, 1759 R St. NW, Washington, DC 20009.

People often assume that cancer is out of their hands because it is "genetic." In fact, lifestyle decisions are much more important in determining who gets cancer—and who doesn't.

Even if your genes place you at risk for cancer, 60% to 70% of all malignancies can be avoided by paying attention to four lifestyle factors—diet, weight control, physical activity and not smoking.

IF YOU MAKE JUST ONE CHANGE...

Eating a plant-based diet is the single most important thing you can do to help lower your cancer risk.

275

Foods should be minimally processed and eaten as close to their natural state as possible. Processed foods may have lost some of their nutritional value.

Example: Eat a potato rather than potato chips or french fries.

Also limit intake of foods with added sugar, such as soft drinks and sweetened cereals.

If you eat red meat, have no more than three ounces per day.

Eating at least five servings—about one-half cup each—of fruits or vegetables every day can decrease your risk of cancer by 20%.

OTHER IMPORTANT STEPS

●**Maintain a healthful weight,** and be physically active. Try not to gain too much weight after reaching your full height (at about age 18 for women...24 for men).

Start by walking every day—working your way up to a brisk, one-hour walk daily. In addition, work up a sweat by engaging in some form of vigorous physical activity for at least one hour each week.

●**Drink alcohol in moderation**—if at all. There is no evidence that alcohol reduces cancer risk, though some evidence suggests that moderate alcohol consumption helps prevent coronary artery disease in men and possibly women. If you do drink, limit your consumption to one drink a day for women...two drinks a day for men.

Avoid alcohol entirely if you are a woman with an increased risk of breast cancer.

●**Select foods that are low in fat and salt.**

Limit your intake of fatty foods. Use a moderate amount of monounsaturated oils, such as olive and canola.

Avoid animal fat and hydrogenated fat, which is commonly found in shortening, margarine and bakery items.

Watch those snack foods, salty condiments and pickles.

●**Prepare and store foods safely.** Keep cold foods cold and hot foods hot.

If you eat meat, avoid charring it. Limit your intake of cured or smoked meat. Take precautions when grilling—trim fat from meat, marinate it, then microwave it for half the cooking time before grilling.

●**Avoid tobacco in any form.**

CANCER RISK FACTORS

Anticancer precautions are particularly important for individuals at increased risk for cancer. *These risk factors include**...

●**Family history of genetically linked types of cancer,** such as breast, ovarian and colon cancers.

●**Inflammatory bowel disease.**

●**Human papillomavirus (HPV) infection.**

●**Alcoholism.**

●**Hepatitis B or C virus (HBV/HCV).**

Additional risk factors for women...

●**First menstrual period before the age of 12.**

●**First child born after age 30.**

●**Childless and over age 50.**

●**Postmenopausal and on hormone-replacement therapy.**

*This information is based on a major study by the American Institute for Cancer Research that reviewed more than 4,500 studies to determine the relationships among diet, lifestyle and cancer risk.

Nuts and Seeds For Lower Cholesterol

Nuts and seeds contain cholesterol-lowering compounds.

New finding: In a study of 27 popular nuts and seeds, the levels of *phytosterols* (plant chemicals shown to lower cholesterol) were highest in wheat germ, sesame seeds, pistachios and sunflower seeds.

Helpful: Add wheat germ to cereal or yogurt...eat tahini (ground sesame seeds), an ingredient in hummus...or snack on a handful of unsalted sunflower seeds or pistachios.

Katherine M. Phillips, PhD, research scientist, department of biochemistry, Virginia Polytechnic Institute and State University, Blacksburg.

The Best Cancer-Fighting Foods

Karen Collins, MS, RD, a registered dietitian and nutrition adviser to the American Institute for Cancer Research (AICR) in Washington, DC. She is author of *Planning Meals That Lower Cancer Risk* (AICR), available at many college libraries, and "Nutrition Notes" and "Nutrition-Wise," weekly columns syndicated to more than 700 newspapers nationwide. She maintains a private practice in Jamestown, NY.

Only about 10% of all cancers are due to genetics. The remaining 90% of malignancies are related to diet, weight and exercise…smoking…and/or environmental factors.

Even though most people realize that diet can affect cancer risk, few regularly consume a variety of the foods that contain large amounts of *phytochemicals*, substances that actually can inhibit the cellular damage that leads to cancer.

Eating a combination of cancer-fighting foods is the best approach because no single food supplies all the available protective substances—vitamins, minerals, phytochemicals and fiber.

BLACK BEANS

Beans (legumes) have high levels of a cancer-fighting compound called *phytic acid.* They're also rich in fiber and *saponins*, chemical compounds that reduce the ability of cancer cells to proliferate.

The landmark Nurses' Health Study found that women who ate four or more servings of legumes weekly were 33% less likely to develop colon polyps than those who consumed one or fewer weekly servings. In people already diagnosed with colon polyps, those who ate more beans reduced their risk for a recurrence by 45%, compared with those who ate fewer beans.

Bonus: Beans are very high in protein. They're a good substitute for people who want to reduce their consumption of red meat—a major source of saturated fat, which can increase cancer risk.

Other cancer-fighting legumes: Small red beans, red kidney beans, pinto beans and garbanzo beans.

Helpful: If you don't want to spend time cooking dried beans, you can get many of the same benefits by eating canned. To reduce the sodium in canned beans, empty them into a colander and rinse thoroughly with cold water.

Recommended: Eat one-half cup of beans at least four times weekly.

BLUEBERRIES

Berries are rich sources of vitamin C and other antioxidants. People who regularly eat berries have a lower risk for malignancies of the colon, bladder, esophagus and prostate. Berries also may lower the risk for lymphoma and premenopausal breast cancer.

Blueberries are an excellent choice for cancer prevention because they are among the richest sources of *antioxidants*, chemical compounds that protect cells from free radicals that can damage cell DNA—the first step in cancer development.

Much of this nutritional power comes from their high levels of *anthocyanidins*, a type of antioxidant that reduces the ability of carcinogens to damage DNA.

Bonus: Because berries are both filling and low in calories, they can be substituted for other sweet snacks to promote weight loss—which further reduces the risk for many cancers.

Other cancer-fighting berries: Blackberries, strawberries, raspberries and cranberries.

Helpful: Keep frozen berries in the freezer. They can be kept almost indefinitely without spoiling and provide virtually the same nutritional benefits as fresh berries.

Recommended: Aim for at least one half-cup serving of berries per week.

BROCCOLI

Broccoli is a cruciferous vegetable that is rich in *isothiocyanates*, a family of phytochemicals linked to a reduced risk for colon, prostate, lung and premenopausal breast cancer. One of these phytochemicals, *sulforaphane*, reduces the ability of carcinogens to cause cell damage—and may increase the tendency of cancer cells to self-destruct, a process called *apoptosis*.

A study published in the *Journal of the National Cancer Institute* reports that men who consumed three or more weekly servings of broccoli (raw or cooked) were 41% less likely to get prostate cancer than those who consumed less than one weekly serving.

Other cancer-fighting cruciferous vegetables: Cauliflower, brussels sprouts, cabbage and kale.

Helpful: If you don't like the strong taste (and smell) of cooked broccoli and other cruciferous vegetables, eat them raw or lightly sauté them in olive oil or canola oil for three to four minutes.

You also can microwave or steam them. (Long cooking, such as boiling for 15 minutes or more, causes the release of strong-smelling/tasting sulfur compounds.)

Recommended: Aim for three to five half-cup servings per week of cruciferous vegetables.

GARLIC

Garlic is an allium, which is a family of plants that contain *allyl sulfides*, phytochemicals not found in any other foods.

The Iowa Women's Health Study found that people with the highest intake of garlic (at least one serving weekly) had a 32% lower risk of developing colon cancer than those who never ate garlic. Garlic has also been linked to a lower risk for prostate, lung, breast and skin cancers.

Bonus: Garlic can be used as a flavor enhancer to make healthful foods—vegetables, beans, whole grains, etc.—more enjoyable…and it reduces the need for unhealthful flavorings, such as salt and butter.

Other cancer-fighting alliums: Onions (all types), leeks and chives.

Helpful: To reduce the strong taste, use cooked garlic (by sautéing or roasting it, for example) rather than raw. The flavors mellow with long cooking. Wait 10 to 15 minutes after chopping garlic before cooking, to allow the active form of the protective phytochemicals to form. The cancer-fighting properties of jarred garlic are unknown.

Recommended: Aim to eat one to three cloves of garlic per week.

WALNUTS

Walnuts provide fiber and are rich in omega-3 fatty acids, the same healthful, anti-inflammatory fats that are found in fish. Reducing inflammation in the body helps prevent cell damage that can lead to cancer.

Other cancer-fighting nuts: Almonds and hazelnuts.

Helpful: Buy packaged or bulk shelled, unsalted nuts (raw or roasted). Substituting nuts for other snacks improves the body's ratio of omega-3 to omega-6 fatty acids—important for lowering inflammation and cancer risk.

Recommended: Eat three to five one-third-cup servings weekly.

WHOLE-GRAIN BREAD

Whole-grain bread is high in fiber. As fiber and certain starches resistant to digestion are fermented in the colon, substances are produced that block the cancer-promoting effects of the body's bile acids. In addition, whole grains are higher in antioxidant vitamins (including vitamin E) and phytochemicals called *phenols*, than are refined grains.

When scientists analyzed and combined the results from 40 different studies, they found that people who ate the most whole-grain bread and/or other whole grains had a 34% lower risk for cancer overall than those who consumed less.

Other cancer-fighting whole grains: Whole-wheat pasta, whole-grain breakfast cereal, brown rice, bulgur, kasha and quinoa.

Helpful: When shopping for whole-grain bread or cereal, don't be misled by terms like multigrain, which merely means that more than one type of grain is included… and don't judge by brown color, which can result from added caramel coloring. Check the ingredients list to make sure a whole grain is listed first, such as whole wheat or whole rye. "Flour" or "wheat flour" means that the product contains refined flour made from wheat—not whole-grain flour.

Recommended: Aim for three daily servings—one-half cup of whole grains or a slice of whole-grain bread counts as one serving.

Spice Cure for Cancer?

A powdered form of ginger kills ovarian cancer cells, according to a new laboratory study. Ginger may be unique because it causes cells to die in two distinctly different ways. This could aid in the development of therapies for treatment-resistant cancers.

University of Michigan Health System.

Cancer Cure?

Experimental vaccines made from patients' own tumors can stimulate the immune system to destroy deadly cancers.

Finding: In 18 of the 22 lung cancer patients who were studied, the vaccine stimulated immune response and caused fewer side effects than conventional cancer treatments.

Journal of Clinical Oncology, 330 John Carlyle St., Suite 300, Alexandria, VA 22314.

A Red-Hot Cancer Fighter

Red chili pepper contains *capsaicin*, an anti-inflammatory that is effective against cancer cells. In tests, capsaicin caused cancer cells to die without damaging normal ones. Though clinical trials are needed before a recommendation to eat chili pepper can be made, it can be enjoyed as part of your regular diet.

Sanjay K. Srivastaya, PhD, assistant professor of pharmacology, University of Pittsburgh School of Medicine, and leader of a study of capsaicin and pancreatic cancer cells.

The Healing Power of Mushrooms

Robert B. Beelman, PhD, professor of food science and chair of the Plant and Mushroom Products Impact Group at Pennsylvania State University in University Park. His current research focuses on the nutritional and medicinal values of mushrooms.

For centuries, Asian physicians have used mushrooms for medicinal purposes, but only recently have the fungi become a focus of research in the US.

Latest findings: In addition to being highly nutritious, mushrooms contain chemical compounds that appear to lower the risk for elevated cholesterol, cancer and other serious conditions.

Studies on the medicinal properties of mushrooms—in whole food as well as supplement and extract form—are under way at the National Cancer Institute and other medical organizations.

It's not yet known whether mushroom extracts and supplements are more beneficial than the whole food. Some medicinal mushrooms, such as reishi, have a tough, woody texture and can be taken only as an extract. But most—shiitake, maitake, etc.—are edible and available at supermarkets and specialty stores.

Caution: It's best to avoid wild mushrooms and to eat only those that have been proven safe—that is, store-bought mushrooms.

Aim to eat three to six ounces daily of a variety of mushrooms. Raw and cooked mushrooms contain equal levels of nutrients.

Important health benefits...

CHOLESTEROL CONTROL

High cholesterol is among the main risk factors for cardiovascular disease. Studies have shown conclusively that patients who lower LDL "bad" cholesterol with statin drugs can reduce their risk for heart attacks by 25% to 50%.

New finding: The oyster mushroom contains significant amounts of statin-like compounds, which suppress the activity of *HMG-CoA reductase*, an enzyme used to make cholesterol in the body.

Bonus: It's possible that oyster mushrooms can lower LDL without suppressing HDL "good" cholesterol.

All mushrooms contain *chitin*, a structural material that strengthens the cell walls in people who eat them. Chitin, which accounts for 25% to 30% of a mushroom's dry weight, binds to cholesterol molecules in the intestine and prevents them from passing through the intestinal wall into the bloodstream.

ANTIOXIDANT ACTIVITY

The white button mushrooms that dominate the produce bins at American supermarkets were once thought to be insignificant sources of disease-fighting antioxidants—but new research shows that they're high in *L-ergothioneine*, an antioxidant that's produced only by fungi.

Crimini and portobello mushrooms contain even more L-ergothioneine than white button mushrooms, and have the highest overall antioxidant content. What's more, all three of these mushrooms contain about 15% more L-ergothioneine than wheat germ or chicken liver, which previously were thought to be the richest sources.

The body has a chemical transport system dedicated solely to L-ergothioneine, which suggests that it's critical for normal metabolism.

In addition to L-ergothioneine, most mushrooms are also rich in selenium. Depending on the variety, one serving of mushrooms (about three ounces) provides about 10% to 20% of the recommended daily intake of this mineral—55 micrograms (mcg) for women and 70 mcg for men. Selenium is a very powerful antioxidant that inhibits blood-fat oxidation and the accumulation of arterial plaques.

Important: Most "specialty" mushrooms, such as oyster, shiitake and maitake, contain only trace amounts of selenium because they are grown on hardwood or sawdust, rather than selenium-rich soil. White button and crimini mushrooms are good sources of selenium.

ANTICANCER ACTIVITY

As far back as the 1950s, studies showed that laboratory animals with cancer that were given mushroom extracts had higher survival rates.

Increasing evidence now suggests that mushrooms contain chemical compounds and nutrients with anticancer properties.

Those anticancer chemicals…

• **Lentinan,** a substance in shiitake mushrooms, has been found in animal studies to increase levels of immune cells (such as T- and B-lymphocytes) that suppress tumor development.

• **Aromatase inhibitors** suppress the enzyme aromatase, which converts androgens (the so-called "male" hormones) into estrogens (the so-called "female" hormones). Lower estrogen levels may reduce the risk for prostate cancer and some kinds of breast cancer. White button, crimini and portobello mushrooms have the highest levels of aromatase inhibitors.

• **5-alpha-reductase,** an enzyme found in white button mushrooms, suppresses the conversion of testosterone to *dihydrotestosterone* (DHT), a hormone that promotes the development of prostate cancer.

WEIGHT CONTROL

An average serving of mushrooms has only about 28 calories and 0.4 g of fat—nearly ideal for a weight-loss diet. The high water (more than 90%) and fiber (up to 1.8 g in shiitake mushrooms) contents make mushrooms more filling than many other low-calorie foods. The chitin in mushrooms is also beneficial for weight loss because it reduces the absorption of fats.

Eat Your Veggies

Reducing risk of diabetes is the latest reason to eat vegetables.

New study: High blood levels of carotenoids—the powerful antioxidants found in yellow-orange vegetables, such as carrots, sweet potatoes and squash, as well as in dark green, leafy vegetables, such as spinach and kale—were associated with a 38% reduction in diabetes risk among nonsmokers.

David R. Jacobs, Jr., PhD, professor of epidemiology at University of Minnesota School of Public Health, Minneapolis, and coauthor of a study of the link between carotenoid levels and diabetes, published in *American Journal of Epidemiology*.

Surprise—Dark Chocolate Is Good for Your Skin

Cocoa, the main ingredient in dark chocolate, improves skin's texture, thickness, blood flow and hydration. It also contains antioxidants that help protect against sun damage—although you still need sunscreen. However, since chocolate is high in fat and calories, don't eat too much!

Ulrike Heinrich, PhD, professor, Institute for Experimental Dermatology, Universität Witten/Herdecke, Witten, Germany.

Cholesterol-Lowering Foods

In a new finding, 30% of 66 people who adhered to a diet rich in soy protein, oats, barley, margarine with plant sterols, and almonds for one year lowered their LDL "bad" cholesterol by more than 20%—the same drop seen in those who took a cholesterol-lowering statin for one month.

Reason: Soy protein reduces cholesterol production by the liver...fiber in oats and barley washes out metabolized cholesterol...plant sterols block its absorption...and almonds do all of the above. This food combination is especially well suited for people with slightly elevated cholesterol levels.

David Jenkins, MD, PhD, Canada Research Chair in nutrition and metabolism, University of Toronto.

Diet Is Linked to Lung Disease

In a study of more than 50,000 men and women, those who ate a diet high in sodium, saturated fats, meats and refined carbohydrates, such as noodles and white rice, were 43% more likely to develop bronchitis symptoms (cough with phlegm) than those who ate a more healthful diet. Chronic bronchitis often precedes or accompanies chronic obstructive pulmonary disease (COPD), persistent airway obstruction.

To improve lung health: Eat more foods with lung-protecting antioxidants, such as fruits, vegetables, soy foods and whole grains.

Stephanie London, MD, senior investigator, National Institute of Environmental Sciences, Durham, NC.

Cherries Fight Inflammation

In a recent study, 18 healthy men and women ate 280 g of bing sweet cherries (about 50 fresh cherries) daily for 28 days. Researchers measured levels of *C-reactive protein* (CRP), a marker of inflammation associated with diabetes and cardiovascular disease, in participants' blood during the study and for one month afterward.

Result: After one month, CRP levels dropped by 25% on average.

Theory: Cherries are rich in polyphenols that have strong antioxidant and anti-inflammatory properties.

Darshan S. Kelley, PhD, research chemist, Western Human Nutrition Research Center, US Department of Agriculture, Davis, CA.

10 Foods that Boost Sex Drive

Foods rich in vitamin E, magnesium, niacin, potassium, zinc and the amino acid L-arginine all increase libido, boost sexual stamina and improve performance.

Top 10 "sexiest" foods...

1. Celery.

2. Asparagus and artichokes.

3. Avocados.

4. Onions and tomatoes.

5. Almonds.

6. Pumpkin and sunflower seeds.

7. Romaine lettuce.

8. Whole-grain breads.

9. Fruits and nuts.

10. Chilies, herbs and spices, such as mustard, fennel, saffron and vanilla.

Barnet Meltzer, MD, founder of the Meltzer Wellness Institute and a physician in private practice in Del Mar, CA. He is author of *Food Swings*. Marlowe and Company.

Lower Blindness Risk

In a study of 4,170 people, those who ate the most foods rich in beta-carotene, vitamins C and E and zinc were 35% less likely to develop age-related macular degeneration (the leading cause of blindness in people over age 65) than those who ate less of these nutrients.

Theory: The antioxidants in these foods help protect against free radical damage to the retina.

Self-defense: Eat generous amounts of foods that contain the above nutrients, such as whole-grain cereal, eggs, poultry and olive oil.

Redmer van Leeuwen, MD, PhD, resident in ophthalmology, Erasmus Medical Centre, Rotterdam, the Netherlands.

Tomato Extract Lowers Blood Pressure

In a study of 54 adults with moderately high blood pressure (above 135 mmHg/80 mmHg), a dietary supplement derived from tomatoes reduced average systolic (top number) readings by 12 mmHg and diastolic (bottom number) readings by 6 mmHg after two to four weeks. The 250-mg capsule given daily was equivalent to eating four medium tomatoes.

Theory: High levels of lycopene and vitamins C and E improve function of the arterial wall, which can lower blood pressure.

Esther Paran, MD, head, hypertension unit, Soroka University Hospital, Ben-Gurion University of the Negev, Israel.

Herbal Tea Healers

Brigitte Mars, an adjunct professor of herbal medicine at Naropa University in Boulder, CO. She is author of 12 books, including *Healing Herbal Teas*, Basic Health, and a professional member of the American Herbalist Guild (AHG).

Herbal teas, which are generally rich in vitamins, minerals and other healthful compounds, have been used as healing agents for thousands of years.

However, because of the prevalence of over-the-counter and prescription medications, most Americans don't think of drinking tea to treat common ailments. That's a mistake.

Dozens of scientific studies have supported the use of herbals for a wide variety of health problems.* Herbal teas have the same active ingredients as herbs sold in capsules, powders and extracts. Herbal teas also have fewer side effects than medication and can be much less expensive.

Loose tea herbs, which are available at health-food stores, tend to be more potent than tea bags. To prepare tea with loose herbs,

*Check with your health-care practitioner before drinking herbal tea, especially if you are a pregnant woman.

use one heaping tablespoon of dried herb or three tablespoons of fresh herb in eight ounces of boiling water. Steep for 10 minutes.

For best results, drink four eight-ounce cups of herbal tea per day until the problem subsides. If you are age 65 or older, do not exceed three cups daily…or two cups daily if you are age 70 or older.

Best teas for treating common health conditions…

COLDS AND FLU

Echinacea, which has an aromatic, earthy flavor, promotes white blood cell production…acts as an anti-infection agent…and stimulates the immune system.

How to use: Echinacea should be used for no more than 10 consecutive days, because it loses its effectiveness when taken continually. Drink echinacea tea at the onset of cold or flu symptoms, such as sore throat, sneezing and/or nasal congestion.

Caution: Echinacea stimulates the immune system, so people with autoimmune diseases, such as lupus, should consult a doctor before using this herb. People who are allergic to plants in the daisy family, such as ragweed, are more likely to have an allergic reaction to echinacea.

Other teas that fight colds and flu: Elderflower and elderberry.

DIGESTIVE DISORDERS

Peppermint, which has a zesty, fresh taste, calms muscle spasms…eases intestinal cramping…contains antibacterial compounds …soothes ulcers…and freshens breath after a meal.

Caution: Do not drink peppermint tea if you are suffering from an acute episode of a digestive disorder, such as a gallstone attack. Seek immediate medical attention.

Other teas that fight digestive disorders: Cardamom, ginger and cinnamon.

HEADACHE

Lemon balm, which has a gentle lemon flavor and aroma, acts as an anti-inflammatory and antispasmodic…and contains magnesium, which acts as a muscle relaxant.

Caution: This herb may inhibit thyroid function. If you have low thyroid function (hypothyroidism), avoid lemon balm tea.

Other teas that fight headache: Feverfew and rosemary.

INSOMNIA

Linden flower, which has a sweet flavor and jasminelike aroma, is rich in vitamin C…calms nerves…and promotes rest. In Europe, linden flower tea often is given to patients before surgery to help them relax.

Other teas that fight insomnia: Chamomile and passionflower.

LOW LIBIDO

Oat seed, which has a slightly sweet, milky flavor, relaxes the nerves…and is often used as an aphrodisiac.

Caution: Oat seed contains gluten, so this herb should be avoided by people with gluten intolerance.

Other teas that fight low libido: Cinnamon and raspberry leaf.

Whole Grains To the Rescue

Joanne Slavin, RD, PhD, food science and nutrition professor at the University of Minnesota in St. Paul. She is the author of dozens of medical articles on dietary fiber.

Everyone knows that eating ample amounts of fruits and vegetables can lower cholesterol, promote weight control and help prevent heart attack, stroke, diabetes and some types of cancer. But few people realize that whole grains are just as good as fruits and vegetables—and sometimes even better—at fighting many of these serious illnesses.

Fiber gets most of the credit for the healthful properties of whole grains, but studies have found that the phytochemicals, antioxidants, vitamins and minerals found in whole grains, which contain all parts of the grain, are just as important. The whole grains described below can be found at most health-food stores and many grocery stores…*

*For recipes using whole grains, read *Whole Grains Every Day Every Way* (Clarkson Potter) by Lorna Sass or visit the Web site of the Whole Grains Council, *www.wholegrainscouncil.org.*

AMARANTH

What it's good for: This tiny grain with an earthy, faintly grassy taste may protect against heart disease and cancer. It is also an excellent source of complete protein—that is, one that contains all eight essential amino acids.

Major effective ingredients: Vitamins E and B. Amaranth is also rich in calcium, phosphorus and iron.

How to add it to your diet: As it cooks, amaranth releases a glutinous starch that adds body to soups and stews.

BROWN RICE

What it's good for: Helps fight eye disease (macular degeneration) and certain cancers, including lung cancer.

Major effective ingredients: Vitamin E and other antioxidants.

How to add it to your diet: Season brown rice as you would white rice, or it can be added to soups, casseroles, stir-fry dishes and salads.

CORN

What it's good for: Helps fight heart disease and cancer…and may guard against cataracts.

Major effective ingredients: Of all the grains, whole-grain corn is the richest source of antioxidants. It's also a good source of insoluble fiber, which cannot be digested but adds bulk to the stool.

How to add it to your diet: Choose whole-grain corn-based cereals, whole-grain cornmeal breads and cornmeal tortillas.

OATS AND BARLEY

What they are good for: Lowering cholesterol.

Major effective ingredient: Soluble fiber. When soluble fiber is digested, it changes to a gummy consistency that lowers blood cholesterol. The exact mechanism of this effect is not yet known.

How to add oats to your diet: Choose an oat cereal or oatmeal or make oatmeal cookies.

How to add barley to your diet: Use it to thicken soups and make creamy risottos, or cook it with carrots.

RYE

What it's good for: Protects against heart disease and hormone-dependent cancers, such as breast and prostate malignancies.

Major effective ingredient: Rye is a rich source of lignans, a class of phytoestrogens (plant compounds that help protect against the harmful effects of excess estrogen).

How to add it to your diet: Use whole-grain rye bread or whole-grain rye crackers.

WHEAT

What it's good for: It has a laxative effect that aids digestion and also is high in vitamins, minerals and antioxidants.

Major effective ingredient: Insoluble fiber.

How to add it to your diet: Replace white bread with whole-wheat bread…and highly processed cereals with whole-grain cereals.

Helpful: To ensure that a bread product contains whole grain, the label must include the word "whole."

Example: For whole wheat, look for whole-wheat flour or whole-wheat grain. Breads that contain seven, 12 or even 15 grains are not necessarily whole-grain breads.

Don't Fall for the Hype Of "Functional Foods"

Rebecca Shannonhouse, editor, *Bottom Line/ Health*, Boardroom Inc., 281 Tresser Blvd., Stamford, CT 06901.

Supermarket shelves are now filled with "functional foods"—products designed to provide health benefits beyond the food's basic nutritional value.

Examples: A new version of Tropicana orange juice contains 3 g of fiber per serving…a spread called Benecol contains cholesterol-lowering plant stanols…and a yogurt called Activia contains a strain of beneficial bacteria that helps promote regular bowel movements.

Some cereals, breads and other staples have been fortified with vitamins and minerals for decades. But the new functional foods have some nutrition experts worried.

"People who start adding foods to their diets because they're 'good for them' could end up consuming more calories if they do not eliminate other foods," says Alice H. Lichtenstein, DSc, professor of nutrition sciences at Tufts University in Boston. The health risks from obesity could far outweigh any of the likely benefits, she explains.

Other potential drawbacks…

• **Foods that are clearly bad for people,** such as soft drinks, could be marketed as "healthy," once they're spiked with vitamin C, calcium or other nutrients.

• **Foods can be less reliable and/or less convenient than supplements for getting some substances,** such as plant stanols.

Even though functional foods may be tempting to try, you're better off following the tried-and-true nutritional advice we all know—Eat a diet rich in vegetables, fruits and whole grains…include cold-water fish, such as salmon or mackerel, two times per week…and balance the calories you eat with those you burn.

Best and Worst Cooking Oils

Mark Hyman, MD, editor-in-chief of the medical journal *Alternative Therapies in Health and Medicine* and medical editor of *Alternative Medicine* magazine. He is author of *Ultrametabolism: The Simple Plan for Automatic Weight Loss* (Scribner) and coauthor of the best-seller *Ultraprevention: The Six-Week Plan That Will Make You Healthy for Life* (Atria). Formerly co–medical director of Canyon Ranch, a health spa resort in the Berkshires, in Massachusetts, he is in private practice in Lenox, MA.

For most health-conscious Americans, olive oil has become a dietary staple. It is a central feature of the Mediterranean diet (an eating plan that emphasizes fruits, vegetables, legumes, nuts, whole grains and fish) and has been shown in numerous studies to help guard against heart disease when used as a substitute for butter, margarine or oils that are higher in saturated fat.

The most healthful variety of olive oil is extra-virgin olive oil, which is extracted from olives without the use of chemicals. It is the least processed and contains the highest levels of disease-fighting antioxidants. But olive oil is not the only oil that is good for you.

ALTERNATIVES TO OLIVE OIL

Among the oils that provide health benefits similar to those of olive oil are almond, flaxseed, walnut and macadamia-nut oils. These oils are available at health-food stores (and even at many supermarkets) and can be used in cooking and/or baking as well as on salads.

Although these nut- and seed-derived oils usually are more expensive than vegetable oils—a 16-ounce bottle of flaxseed oil costs about $15 versus about $5 for the same size bottle of refined soy oil—a little goes a long way, and their distinctive flavors will add variety to your cooking.

SOURCES OF DIETARY FAT

To function properly, our bodies require dietary fat. It serves not only as an energy source, but also helps our bodies absorb fat-soluble vitamins, including vitamins A, D, E and K, from the food we eat. When used properly, cooking oils can be an excellent source of healthful dietary fat.

Most of the fats in your diet should be monounsaturated and omega-3 fats. For the greatest health benefit, a combination of the fats described below should be consumed, since each provides a different nutritional component.

Best sources of dietary fat…

• **Omega-3 fatty acids** are found in fatty, cold-water fish (salmon, herring, sardines and anchovies)…walnuts…some seeds (pumpkin seeds, hempseeds and flaxseeds)…and flaxseed oil.

According to some studies, as many as 70% of Americans are deficient in these essential fats. Omega-3s have been shown to reduce the risk for heart attack, depression and stroke, and perhaps help protect against prostate and breast malignancies as well as some types of dementia.

• **Monounsaturated fat** is found in avocados, some nut oils and olive oil. This fat boosts immunity and helps lower blood pressure, blood sugar and cholesterol levels. Monounsaturated fat, in the form of olive oil, is the primary source of fat in the Mediterranean diet.

• **Unrefined polyunsaturated fat** is found in walnut oil and natural vegetable oils that have not been chemically processed. This fat is a source of omega-6 fatty acids, which can be harmful when consumed in the high amounts that are typical in the American diet. However, small doses (no more than one tablespoon daily) of unrefined polyunsaturated fat are necessary to provide a healthful ratio of omega-6 to omega-3.

Important: When selecting an unrefined vegetable oil, be sure that it is "expeller-pressed" or "cold-pressed"—this means that the oil has been processed without chemicals, using pressure rather than heat.

Caution: Commercially available, refined "vegetable oils," including corn and soy oils, are commonly used in restaurant food and still can be found in the kitchen cabinets of many Americans. However, these oils are best avoided, due to the harmful compounds that are produced in the process of refining.

Food products that typically should be avoided include those that contain saturated fat, which is found in beef, pork, lamb, chicken and dairy products—as well as all foods with trans fat, partially hydrogenated oil that is widely found in cookies, crackers and other processed foods.

WHAT ABOUT CANOLA OIL?

Although many Americans use canola oil, I do not recommend it at this time. There have been no long-term medical studies of canola oil, a relatively new food made from a plant similar to the rapeseed plant, which is part of the mustard family. Moreover, animal studies have linked canola oil with reduced platelet count, shorter life span and

increased need for vitamin E. In contrast, olive and nut oils have been used for centuries…and have proven health benefits.

HOW MUCH IS ENOUGH?

Even though cooking oils can be a healthful addition to your diet, they are pure fat. All oils contain about 14 g of fat or 126 calories per tablespoon. This should be factored into your total daily intake of fat.

Helpful: Cooking oils have different smoke points—the temperature at which heated fat begins to break down, releasing smoke and giving a burned taste to food. Oils that have smoke points of about 350° F or higher and therefore are good for sautéing and stir-frying (cooking quickly over high heat while stirring continuously) include almond oil, macadamia-nut oil and sesame oil. Oils with low smoke points—about 225° F—include flaxseed oil and unrefined sunflower oil. They are best used raw and/or in baking.

Frozen OJ Is a Healthier Choice

Frozen orange juice has about 25% more vitamin C than ready-to-drink juice.

Reason: At refrigerator temperatures, oxygen slowly destroys vitamin C in ready-to-drink juice. This reaction is prevented by the colder temperatures needed to store frozen juice. Once a container of any type of citrus juice is opened and exposed to air, it may lose all of the vitamin C within a month.

Carol Johnston, PhD, RD, professor of nutrition, Arizona State University, Mesa.

Best Way to Clean Fruits and Vegetables

To remove pesticides and wax from fruits and vegetables: In a bowl or a basin, mix four tablespoons of table salt, four teaspoons of lemon juice and one quart of cool water. Soak fruits and vegetables for five to 10 minutes.

Exceptions: Soak leafy greens for two to three minutes...berries, one to two minutes. After soaking, rinse produce in plain cold water and dry.

Alternative: Veggie Wash. Made of 100% natural ingredients, it is available at supermarkets, health-food stores and on-line at *www.veggie-wash.com* (800-451-7096).

Joan Wilen and Lydia Wilen, authorities on folk remedies, New York City, and authors of *Bottom Line's Healing Remedies* and *Bottom Line's Household Magic. www.BottomLineSecrets.com.*

Pecans, Almonds And Walnuts Protect The Heart

Pecans and walnuts are high in a form of vitamin E called *gamma tocopherol*...almonds are high in *alpha tocopherol*. These powerful antioxidants help reduce risk of hardening of the arteries and heart disease. They also lower total and LDL (bad) cholesterol and raise HDL (good) cholesterol.

Best: Eat a moderate-sized handful of nuts every day.

Ella Haddad, DrPH, associate professor, department of nutrition, School of Public Health, Loma Linda University, Loma Linda, CA, and leader of a study published in *Nutrition Research.*

Grape Seed Extract Lowers Blood Pressure

In one recent study, 24 patients with metabolic syndrome (a cluster of heart disease risk factors, including high blood pressure, excess abdominal weight and elevated blood

sugar) took a 150-mg or 300-mg capsule of grape seed extract or a placebo daily for one month.

Result: Those who took either dose of the extract experienced an average drop in systolic pressure (top number) of 12 and 8 in diastolic pressure (bottom number).

Theory: Grape seed extract boosts the production of nitric oxide, a heart-protective enzyme.

If you have prehypertension (120 to 139 systolic and 80 to 89 diastolic), ask your doctor if you should try grape seed extract.

C. Tissa Kappagoda, MD, PhD, professor of cardiovascular medicine, University of California, Davis.

Fountain of Youth?

Two studies involving mice have shown that *resveratrol*, a component of red wine, can dramatically increase endurance when given in high doses...and can prolong life by offsetting the negative effects of a high-fat diet when given in moderate doses.

Caution: Resveratrol is available in health-food stores but has not yet been studied in humans—neither the optimal dosage nor side effects have been determined.

Johan Auwerx, MD, PhD, team leader, department of physiological genetics of nuclear signaling, Institute of Genetics and Molecular and Cellular Biology, Illkirch Cedex, France.

The Water You Drink

Steven Patch, PhD, authority on drinking water safety and director, Environmental Quality Institute, University of North Carolina, Asheville.

Here is important information about water, and how you can enjoy it more....

• **Don't try to drink an arbitrary daily amount of liquid,** such as eight glasses of water. Urine color is a good indicator of hydration—it should be light yellow. Other beverages, such as juice, milk and soda, are treated as water by the body—even if they contain caffeine.

• **It is fine to drink tap water**—the US has some of the safest tap water in the world, and many bottled waters are simply filtered tap water.

• **If your home was built before 1986,** have your water tested for lead contamination.

• **If your water comes from a well,** have it tested for arsenic.

• **Use a filter if you find that your water contains contaminants** or has a taste you dislike.

Bottled-water caution: Reusing plastic bottles that have not been sterilized can expose you to high bacteria levels. Wash bottles in hot, soapy water or run them through a dishwasher. Store unopened bottled water in a cool, dark place to prevent damage to the containers from heat and light.

Ginger Relieves Arthritis Pain

Ginger supplements soothe osteoarthritic joints by inhibiting production of pain-causing prostaglandins.

Best: Take a 100-mg supplement, such as GingerForce, one to three times a day.

Sung Woo Kim, PhD, associate professor of nutrition and digestive physiology, department of animal and food sciences, Texas Tech University, Lubbock, and leader of a study published in *Journal of Medicinal Food.*

Almonds May Improve Memory

In a recent study, mice with a disease similar to Alzheimer's that were fed an almond-rich diet fared better on memory tests than mice fed a diet without almonds. Almonds contain substances similar to those found in drugs used to treat Alzheimer's.

Neelima Chauhan, PhD, assistant professor of anatomy and cell biology, University of Illinois, Chicago, and leader of a study presented at the annual meeting of the Society for Neuroscience.

Aromatherapy Relieves Anxiety, Fights Headaches, Even Helps You Lose Weight

Alan Hirsch, MD, founder and neurological director of the Smell & Taste Treatment and Research Foundation in Chicago, *www.scienceofsmell.com.* He is a neurologist and psychiatrist, and is author of *Life's a Smelling Success* (Authors of Unity) and *What's Your Food Sign?: How to Use Food Cues to Find True Love* (Stewart, Tabori & Chang).

Aromatherapy can be a remarkable remedy. When a patient smells a particular odor, scent molecules bind to the surface of cell walls at the top of the nose. This triggers the release of neurotransmitters and other chemicals that stimulate different parts of the brain.

Scents that patients enjoy are more effective remedies than those that they find unpleasant.

Example: One study found that patients with claustrophobia who enjoyed the smell of green apple felt less anxious when they smelled it, but patients who didn't like the smell had no improvement.

Intermittent bursts of a particular scent are more effective than smelling it continuously. Patients who use aromatherapy are advised to limit their scent exposure to about three minutes or less at a time—by putting an essential oil on a handkerchief and smelling it briefly, for example, or by walking in and out of a room where an aromatherapy candle is burning. Essential oils and aromatherapy candles are available at most health-food stores and many grocery stores. Or you can sniff the actual food or flower, such as green apple or jasmine.

Many health conditions can be improved with aromatherapy. Whether or not these problems can be *prevented* with aromatherapy is still being researched.

ANXIETY

Some scents appear to calm the limbic system, the "emotional" part of the brain involved in anxiety. Also, patients who smell a pleasing odor feel happy—and this crowds out feelings of anxiety and stress.

Proven effective: Green apple and/or cucumber have been shown to reduce anxiety by about 18%. Also, patients who sniff lavender have an increase in alpha waves, a sign of heightened relaxation.

MIGRAINE HEADACHE

Most migraines are caused in part by inflammation and alternating cycles of dilation/constriction of blood vessels in the brain. Aromatherapy changes the electrical activity in the brain, which can help relieve migraines. Aromatherapy appears to be effective for other types of headaches as well, such as muscle contraction headaches. It also promotes feelings of relaxation, which can reduce both the frequency of headaches and a patient's sensitivity to pain.

Proven effective: Green apple. It has effects similar to that of *sumatriptan* (Imitrex), a leading migraine drug, and can reduce the severity and duration of migraines by about 16%.

Caution: About 15% of migraine sufferers have *osmophobia*, a hypersensitivity to odors that can make migraines worse. Also, about 18% of migraine patients have a reduced sense of smell and don't respond to aromatherapy.

CIGARETTE ADDICTION

A number of studies have shown that smokers given cigarettes infused with a pepperlike smell have reduced cravings. More recently, smokers who were exposed to both pleasant and unpleasant odors found it easier to quit smoking, but the pleasant odors were somewhat more effective.

Proven effective: Any odor that you find particularly pleasant—lavender, mint, etc. Smell the scent whenever you feel an urge to light up a cigarette.

Also helpful: People who were born prior to 1930 tend to respond better to natural smells—citrus, the odor of baking bread, etc. Younger patients often respond better to artificial smells that evoke strong positive memories, such as Play-Doh or Pez candy.

LOW ENERGY

Odors that stimulate the trigeminal nerve (which has receptors in the nose and eyes and is the same nerve that makes people cry when they cut an onion) cause increased activity in the part of the brain that is involved in wakefulness.

Proven effective: Peppermint. People who smell a peppermint scent or chew a piece of peppermint gum or candy experience a sudden burst of energy.

Also helpful: The smell of strawberries or buttered popcorn. Both cause an increase in energy as well as metabolism.

OBESITY

A number of studies have shown that particular odors can help people lose weight. Some scents stimulate the part of the hypothalamus that controls appetite. Odors also may act as a displacement mechanism—a reminder to eat less.

Proven effective: Peppermint and green apple. One large study found that people who sniffed either one of these scents when they felt hungry lost an average of 30 pounds over a six-month period.

Also helpful: Take frequent deep sniffs of food while eating. Odor molecules, regardless of the food they come from, can fool the brain into thinking that more has been consumed, which helps suppress the appetite.

REDUCED MEMORY/ CONCENTRATION

Many adults find that they don't remember new information—telephone numbers, plot twists in a novel, etc.—as well as they used to. Aromatherapy can be used to accelerate learning speed and promote better concentration and memory.

Proven effective: Floral scents. Sniffing a floral essential oil triggers the release of *norepinephrine* and *adrenocorticotropic hormone* (ACTH), hormones that increase attention. Floral scents have been shown to improve memory and learning speed by about 17%.

In one study, people were exposed to different scents prior to bowling. Those who smelled jasmine knocked down 28% more pins, probably because it improved their concentration and hand/eye coordination.

Strategy: Sniff a floral scent when the material to be learned is initially presented, and repeat exposure to the same odor when the material must be recalled.

CHEMOTHERAPY-INDUCED NAUSEA

It's common for cancer patients who are undergoing chemotherapy to develop an intense aversion to the foods they ate immediately prior to treatments. There's little evidence that aromatherapy has a direct effect on nausea, but it can help prevent patients from developing a lifelong aversion to specific foods, which they may need for good health.

Proven effective: Smelling artificial cherry flavoring prior to chemotherapy. The best way to do this is to suck on a cherry candy. (This has the added benefit of stimulating saliva and helping to reduce hunger pangs.) Some patients will later associate the smell (and taste) of cherry with the treatments, but they can avoid cherry flavoring and continue to eat healthful foods, important for maintaining good nutrition.

Natural Remedy For Bloating

Boil two tablespoons of fennel seeds in two cups of water for at least three minutes. Strain the seeds, add honey to taste and drink. Bloating should be relieved in one to two hours. Fennel promotes gastrointestinal motility and acts as an antispasmodic. Fennel seeds are available at health-food stores.

Birgit Rakel, MD, integrative physician, Jefferson-Myrna Brind Center for Integrative Medicine, Thomas Jefferson University Hospital, Philadelphia.

Diet and AMD

Diet can reduce the risk of age-related macular degeneration (AMD)—a leading cause of blindness among people over age 55. There's no cure for AMD, but the right foods may help prevent it. A new study of more than 5,000 people over age 55 found that those who had above-average intake of each of four nutrients—vitamin C, vitamin E, zinc and beta carotene—reduced their AMD risk by 35%.

Best sources: For vitamin C, oranges and fruit...for vitamin E, almonds and peanut butter...for zinc, turkey, chicken and fortified cereal...for beta carotene, sweet potatoes, apricots and peaches.

Jacqueline C. M. Witteman, PhD, Department of Epidemiology & Biostatistics, Erasmus Medical Center, Rotterdam, the Netherlands.

Improve Your Health with Honey

Jamison Starbuck, ND, a naturopathic physician in family practice and a lecturer at the University of Montana, both in Missoula. She is past president of the American Association of Naturopathic Physicians and a contributing editor to *The Alternative Advisor: The Complete Guide to Natural Therapies and Alternative Treatments.* Time Life.

As a physician, I've long known of the medicinal benefits of honey. Even though skeptics dismiss honey's beneficial effects as little more than a placebo, current research supports its medicinal properties. For example, studies conducted at the University of Illinois and the University of California confirm that honey is a potent source of antioxidants—those much-touted healthful substances found in some foods, such as fruits and vegetables, that defend against disease-causing free radicals. Typically, the darker the honey, the higher the antioxidant content, according to these scientists. Buckwheat honey is among the best. However, high levels of antioxidants are also present in light honey, depending on the crop. I recommend adding one to two tablespoons daily to tea or hot cereal—or eat it directly off a spoon.

Caution: If you are diabetic, eat no more than one teaspoon daily. Do not give honey to children under age one. Honey can contain trace amounts of deadly *botulinum toxin*, which cannot be eliminated by an infant's digestive system.

Honey also can be used as a topical antiseptic for cuts, scrapes, surgical incisions and fungal infections, such as athlete's foot or a red, flaky, fungal inflammation of the ears or eyelids. Honey is acidic and does not provide the nutrients that bacteria and fungi need for growth. Clinical studies focusing on honey derived from the flowers of the New Zealand/Australian manuka tea tree (*Leptospermum scoparium*) show that it is effective even against antibiotic-resistant *Staphylococcus aureus*. If you want to use honey as a topical antiseptic, apply it three times daily as you would an antibiotic or antifungal cream. Always monitor skin lesions for any sign of infection, such as swelling, redness, discharge, heat or pain. If any of these occur, see your doctor.

Because of its antiseptic properties, honey is an excellent remedy for upper respiratory ailments, such as sore throat or laryngitis. You may speed your healing from these conditions—even strep throat—by drinking tea liberally dosed with honey, which also has a soothing effect. Add two tablespoons of honey to a cup of tea and drink at least three cups daily throughout the course of a sore throat or upper respiratory ailment.

Eating local honey is an effective treatment for pollen allergies. Start by eating one tablespoon of honey daily in early March (or six weeks before pollen season in your area) and continue throughout the allergy season.

Honey also can be used to naturally preserve the nutritional value of food. For example, researchers have found that honey extends the storage time of meats and slows the browning of cut fruit. Substitute honey for sugar when you make a fruit salad, or add it to green salad or veggie dressings. Use honey glazes on roast meats.

And don't worry about gaining weight from honey use. Because it is rich in enzymes and nutrients, it is a very satisfying food. My patients find that when they regularly use honey instead of sugar, a little bit goes a long way.

Live Longer, Feel Great—Simple Strategy Of 100-Year-Olds

Bradley J. Willcox, MD, clinical assistant professor of geriatrics for the University of Hawaii as well as a physician-scientist for the Pacific Health Research Institute, which conducts research on aging and chronic disease, both in Honolulu. He is also co-author of *The Okinawa Diet Plan: Get Leaner, Live Longer, and Never Feel Hungry.* Clarkson Potter.

It *is* possible to eat more and live longer. Just ask the Okinawans. My brother and I (both of us researchers at Harvard Medical School at the time) pored over 50 years of research on the inhabitants of Okinawa, a chain of islands in Japan that touts the world's highest concentration of centenarians.

We discovered that their rates of killer diseases, such as cancer, heart disease and stroke, are among the lowest in the world, largely because of their diet, physical activity and close family relationships.

Now: New analysis of dietary data has uncovered additional details on the Okinawans' healthful eating habits.

CALORIC DENSITY

Foods differ in the ratio of calories to weight. The more calories per gram (g) or ounce a food contains, the more fattening it will be. This principle is known as caloric density (CD).

Here's the trick: If you consume two to three pounds of food a day, you'll probably feel satisfied. This is true whether the food contains 2,100 calories (as it will if you eat like most Americans) or 1,600 calories (as it will if you eat the low-CD Okinawan way).

That's because humans are programmed to eat a set amount of food—not just a quota of calories. Okinawans actually eat *more* than the Americans—an average of 2.5 pounds a day versus two pounds for Americans.

The traditional Okinawan diet includes some foods familiar in America (such as sweet potatoes and watermelon)…some that have made inroads into many American kitchens (such as tofu and shiitake mushrooms)…and others that might require a sense of adventure and a trip to a specialty-food store, including daikon (Japanese radish), adzuki beans and edible seaweed, such as wakame and hijiki.

GO THREE TO ONE

It isn't only what's in the Okinawan diet that counts—it's also the proportions.

Just follow this simple rule: Since animal products have higher CDs than vegetables, legumes, fruits and grains, consume at least three times more plant-based foods than meats and seafood or dairy products.

Another three-to-one rule applies to your plant-based foods: Eat about three times more "featherweight" plant-based foods than denser ones. A featherweight food contains fewer than 0.7 calories per gram (g).

Example: Eat plenty of fresh strawberries, grapefruit, broccoli, carrot sticks and cantaloupe…and as much tofu, salsa, vegetable soup, fat-free cottage cheese and low-fat plain yogurt as you want. But have smaller portions of high-CD foods, such as bread (even if it's whole-wheat) and nuts.

GET ENOUGH PROTEIN

Because protein is vital to maintaining all the cells, muscles and other tissues of the body, nature made this nutrient more satisfying than fats or sugars. Without sufficient protein—no matter how much fat and sugar you eat—you'll still be hungry. Adults should get 0.4 g of protein per pound of body weight daily.

Example: A 180-pound man needs 72 g of protein per day.

Once you adopt a low-CD diet and your calorie intake drops, you'll be eating a higher proportion of protein. Meat is a rich source, but it comes packaged with fat. Fish is less calorie-dense, and its fats are healthful omega-3s.

Helpful: Get most of your protein from plant sources, such as legumes and grains, and the rest from fish. Soy, a legume, is particularly valuable. It contains all the necessary amino acids.

KEEP FIBER IN MIND

Fiber, the nondigestible substance found in plants, adds bulk without calories to foods—so the more fiber, the lower the CD. High-fiber foods keep the edge off your appetite longer.

Bonus: Fiber aids digestion and reduces cholesterol. The phytonutrients (plant-based chemicals) found in fiber appear to lower the risks for cancer and diabetes.

The easiest way to increase your fiber intake is to start the day with a breakfast cereal that contains at least 5 g per serving.

Also: Substitute whole-wheat bread and pasta and brown rice for refined grain products. Add high-fiber beans and lentils to salads.

CHOOSE WATER-RICH FOODS

Like fiber, water adds volume without calories. Foods with high water content fill you up just as effectively as those that are loaded with fats and sugars.

To decrease the CD of your meals, water must be in the food.

To add more water to your daily diet…

•**Start your meals with soup whenever possible.**

• **Steam vegetables rather than baking or grilling them.** This will keep their water content high.

• **Eat water-rich stew as a main dish.**

EAT FREQUENT MEALS

Six small meals and snacks a day will keep your energy level up and your hunger down. You eat less, overall, when you graze rather than gorge.

Especially important: Never skip breakfast. A healthy, high-fiber morning meal that includes some protein, such as yogurt, makes it easier to resist fatty, sugary foods throughout the day.

DON'T DEPRIVE YOURSELF

Completely swearing off foods you really love won't work in the long run—sooner or later, cravings win out.

Instead: Meet yourself halfway. Eat just half a pastrami sandwich, and cut the meal's CD with vegetables. Finish with fresh fruit.

If you feel the urge for sweets, have a piece of hard candy. Drink hot cocoa to satisfy your chocolate craving—an eight-ounce serving has a low CD of about 120 calories, while a 1.5-ounce chocolate bar has about 220 calories.

11

Best Medicine

What You Say to Your Doctor Can Save Your Life

Not long ago, a colleague told me about a woman in her 50s named Ellen B. who went to her doctor because she often felt hot all over, experienced excessive sweating and suffered from terrible headaches.

"Menopause," the doctor concluded. So did four other doctors she had seen. After all, Ellen was the right age and appeared to be in otherwise good health. But she'd had hot flashes before, she said, and these were worse. *Much* worse.

It took a sixth doctor, who was determined to look further, to order a urine test. The test unexpectedly showed signs of a rare endocrine tumor that was confirmed with a computed tomography (CT) scan. The correct diagnosis led to surgery that relieved Ellen's symptoms. Had the condition not been properly diagnosed, Ellen could have suffered a stroke, heart attack or kidney failure.

Medical mistakes do happen—surveys say that about 15% of diagnoses are wrong. Most people assume that technical errors, such as mislabeling an X-ray or blood test, are to blame, but in up to 80% of cases, it's a flaw in the doctor's reasoning that leads to the wrong conclusion.

Here's how to protect yourself…

TELLING YOUR STORY

A doctor diagnoses an ailment by analyzing the history of your medical problem, the results of a physical examination and the findings of appropriate tests. With each step, the doctor looks for patterns that fit an illness.

The whole process begins with your account of the problem—the fatigue or

Jerome Groopman, MD, a professor of medicine at Harvard Medical School and chief of experimental medicine at Beth Israel Deaconess Medical Center, both in Boston. He is the author of four books, including the recently published *How Doctors Think*. Houghton Mifflin.

294

dizziness, the pain or the unexplained lump. *To help your doctor arrive at an accurate diagnosis, your account should include...*

- **How your symptoms began.**

- **The setting where they occurred—** were you at home or at work? Active? Hungry or tired?

- **What seemed to make the symptoms better or worse.**

- **The treatments,** including self-treatment, that already have been tried.

- **Your own thoughts about what might be causing the problem.**

DETOURS AND BLIND ALLEYS

In the diagnostic process, doctors match symptoms and their clinical impressions against a model that explains the symptoms. This is usually an efficient and accurate method—the facial flushing, sweating and severe headaches in a woman in her 50s are probably due to menopause, not a rare endocrine tumor.

A misdiagnosis can occur, however, if the cause of medical symptoms is immediately attributed to a stereotype—what doctors call an "attribution error." For example, stress or nerves are a convenient explanation for recurrent headaches, stomach upset and back pain. But the same symptoms may have a physical origin instead, such as a brain aneurysm, ulcer or kidney stones, respectively.

A related mistake can occur when a doctor pays close attention to facts that support his/her tentative diagnosis and ignores those that don't. Doctors are trained to look for a single cause that explains all or most symptoms. But stopping too soon in the diagnostic process—known as "premature closure"—may allow other problems to go undetected.

Example: Persistent abdominal pain can be caused by stress and diverticulitis (inflammation of a pouch—diverticulum—in the intestinal wall).

Self-defense: Preempt mistaken conclusions by admitting—humorously, if possible—what the doctor may be thinking. "I suppose I seem like the classic hypochondriac, and I am under a lot of stress, but is it possible that there's another reason for my headaches?"

START FROM THE BEGINNING

When symptoms persist despite treatment, it's typically wise to seek other medical opinions. When reviewing your case, each doctor starts with the previous one's tentative diagnosis.

In some cases, a wrong diagnosis can gain momentum as each doctor seeks evidence that confirms early suspicions. The previous doctor's credentials and hospital affiliations also may influence subsequent doctors' opinions.

Self-defense: If it appears that a doctor is simply rubber-stamping an earlier diagnosis, offer to retell your story from the beginning. After all, if the conclusions of earlier clinicians were entirely satisfactory, would you still be seeking help? Make sure the doctor is listening closely as you tell your story. You also might ask, "How did you arrive at your diagnosis?"

GETTING THE BEST CARE

Not all diagnostic errors can be avoided, and a complex, ambiguous illness may elude effective treatment for a long time.

To get the best care possible...

- **Find a doctor who knows how to listen.** Communication between you and the doctor is essential for an accurate diagnosis. Checking credentials and getting advice from other health professionals can tell you a lot about a doctor's clinical abilities, but you need to evaluate the human factor yourself.

In the course of an office visit, the average doctor interrupts his patient's recital of symptoms after just 18 seconds. Some doctors are better listeners than others. Look for someone with whom you feel encouraged to tell your story and who welcomes questions.

- **Be aware of "chemistry."** Professional as they try to be, doctors like some patients more than others. Most doctors are prone to take less time, listen less closely and dismiss more quickly the complaints of patients who rub them the wrong way. If you feel negative vibes, get another doctor.

Positive feelings can be even more insidious. We want our doctor to like us, but affection and empathy can discourage him from going all out and subjecting you to potentially unpleasant experiences, such as invasive tests. Since the doctor wants things to work out well for you, he may—without knowing it—shy away from investigating the more ominous possibilities. If you have an especially friendly relationship with your doctor—and even if you don't—tell him not to hold back on tests and/or physical exams.

•**If you think your doctor has overlooked something, tell him.** Initiating a dialogue reopens the doctor's thinking. Questions need not seem adversarial.

"What else could it be?" is always appropriate when the first diagnosis doesn't lead to effective treatment—or even before treatment begins. Knowing that standard medical reasoning looks for patterns, "Is there anything that doesn't fit?" can suggest a fresh approach.

Similarly, "Could it be that I have more than one problem?" raises the possibility that the single-cause explanation doctors usually opt for may need to be reexamined.

•**Offer your own suggestions.** As scientifically advanced as modern medical education may be, most doctors still have little interest or expertise in some crucial areas, such as nutrition. If your own reading and knowledge suggest this sort of explanation, don't hesitate to ask: "Could my problem be due to a nutritional deficiency? And if so, can you recommend an appropriate expert with whom I can consult?"

•**Think the unthinkable.** When people go to the doctor to have a symptom checked out, they're usually hoping for the best but may harbor the dread of something really dire. Don't keep such fears to yourself. Sharing your concerns may prompt more probing questions that highlight key details in your story and lead to an earlier, possibly lifesaving diagnosis—or a reassuring explanation.

Stay Safe in the Hospital—11 Ways to Prevent Medical Errors

David J. Sherer, MD, a board-certified anesthesiologist in clinical practice at Falls Church Ambulatory Surgery Center in Falls Church, VA, affiliated with Mid-Atlantic Permanente Medical Group. He is author of *Dr. David Sherer's Hospital Survival Guide: 100+ Ways to Make Your Hospital Stay Safe and Comfortable*. Claren.

As many as 195,000 patients die each year in US hospitals because of medical errors, according to a recent study by HealthGrades, a leading health-care rating company. Here's how to stay safe next time you're in the hospital. If you're too incapacitated by your illness or injury to do these things for yourself, a family member can do many of them for you.

1. Keep a list of prescribed medications with dosages. You can get this list from the attending physician (the doctor in charge of your case), an intern, resident or nurse. Receiving the wrong medication is one of the most common—and dangerous—hospital errors. When a hospital staff member hands you a pill or starts to hook an intravenous (IV) bag to your arm, ask what you're being given. *If the drug isn't on the list of medications you have been prescribed...*

•Ask "What does this treat?" If the answer isn't a condition that you think you have, double-check that the drug provider knows your name and birthday, to confirm you're the patient he/she thinks you are.

•Make sure it's not a drug with a similar name. If you've been prescribed Zantac and someone's trying to give you Xanax or you take Celebrex but the nurse shows up with Cerebyx, someone may have misheard the instructions and provided the wrong medication.

Also, if it is a drug you've been prescribed but you previously received a different dosage, make sure the change was intentional.

2. Label yourself. If you're in the hospital for an operation on a limb, a lung or anything else that you have more than one of on or in your body, use a marker or ballpoint pen to write "this arm," "this leg" or just "yes" on the side that should go under the knife, so there is no confusion in the operating room. (At some hospitals, your surgeon will sign his initials to the body part in advance of your operation.) Don't use an "X" to mark the spot, because an "X" is ambiguous—it could be misinterpreted as "not here."

•If you're allergic to any medications, make a sign to this effect and post it over your hospital bed.

Example: "Allergic to Penicillin."

3. Schedule your hospital stay wisely. New interns, residents and medical school students begin assignments at teaching hospitals in early July. If possible, postpone elective procedures until a different time, when young medical professionals have more experience.

If you can't avoid a July stay in a teaching hospital, be wary about what you let interns and medical students do. If one wants to draw blood, insert a catheter or perform another common hospital task, ask how many times he/she has done it before. If the answer doesn't fill you with confidence, insist that a nurse or resident take over.

Also, at any time of the year, try to schedule your surgery for early in the day. By the end of a long day, even the most skilled surgeons aren't at the top of their game. Also, because patients aren't allowed to eat or drink before surgery, a late operation means extra hours of hunger, thirst and worry.

4. Get to know the staff. A wide range of doctors, nurses, physician's assistants, interns, residents, orderlies and others might be involved in your care. Whenever a new face arrives, politely ask his name and what his role is, unless his name tag makes this obvious, then engage in some friendly conversation.

If you make a personal connection with everyone involved in your care, it reduces the odds that you'll be mistaken for a different patient with potentially dangerous results. It also increases the odds that you'll get prompt care. Because most hospital patients

are preoccupied with their health problems, the few who remain composed, personable and interested in the hospital staff often are treated more favorably.

5. Know who should do what. Find out when you can expect your attending physician to visit your bedside, and save any questions you have until then. Answers you receive from anyone else might not be definitive.

Don't let a UAP (also known as unlicensed assistive personnel or nurse assistant) insert an IV or catheter, change a sterile dressing, give you a shot or feed you through a tube. Such tasks should be handled by trained medical staff, such as a registered nurse. Check the person's name tag. If there's no designation, such as RN, ask what his training is.

6. Select the right surgeon. Unless it is an emergency, you shouldn't necessarily settle for the first surgeon you're sent to. *When you meet with a surgeon for a consultation, ask...*

•Are you board-certified in this specialty? Or check this on the Web site of the American Board of Medical Specialties (*www.abms.org*). You will have to register, but it is free.

•How many times have you performed this exact procedure? You want someone who has done it hundreds or even thousands of times. If the procedure is less common, you at least want a surgeon who performs it dozens of times per year.

7. Find the right hospital. If your surgeon has privileges at more than one hospital in your area, the annual "America's Best Hospital Guide" of *US News & World Report* (*www.usnews.com* and click on "Best Hospitals" at lower left) can help you decide which facility is best for a given procedure. Be aware that your health insurance might limit you to a particular hospital or restrict your choice of surgeons.

8. Plan for the unexpected *before* you wind up in a hospital. Ask your doctor now which emergency room in your region he considers the best, assuming that there's more than one. (Of course, in situations where every second counts, the closest ER is almost always the best choice.)

9. Speak up. Make no effort to conceal your pain in a crowded emergency room—the ER staff might equate a quiet patient with a low-priority medical problem and treat others ahead of you. If you must wait, let the staff know if the pain gets worse…you have trouble breathing…feel increasingly light-headed…or lose feeling in, or control over, part of your body.

10. Encourage bedside visitors. Visitors don't just keep you company in the hospital. They can keep an eye on the quality of your care when you're unable to do so yourself. And because hospital employees know that family members keep an eye on what's going on, more visitors tend to mean more attention from the staff.

11. Warn your anesthesiologist of any loose teeth. A loose tooth could be knocked out during intubation (when a breathing tube is placed in your windpipe), causing a potentially serious infection if the tooth reaches your lungs. Also, ask your doctor about removing any dentures or artificial teeth before you're taken to the operating room.

Best Time to Take Your Aspirin

Heart attack prevention may be enhanced by taking low-dose aspirin in the late evening. Heart attacks occur most often in the early morning, when platelet activity (tendency for clotting) increases because of the body's natural circadian (24-hour) rhythm. If your doctor has prescribed aspirin therapy, taking it around 10 pm provides peak anti-clotting action by early morning.

Jack M. Rosenberg, PharmD, PhD, professor of pharmacy and pharmacology and director of the International Drug Information Center, Long Island University, Brooklyn, NY.

How to Survive A Trip to the ER

Joel Cohen, MD, has practiced emergency care, urgent care and internal medicine for 15 years and is author of ER: Enter at Your Own Risk—How to Avoid Dangers Inside Emergency Rooms. *New Horizon.*

To experience true chaos, just visit an emergency room. Through those metal doors is a busy, often disorganized place that can be hazardous to your health.

ERs are overcrowded and understaffed. You may be treated by an overworked medical student, an exhausted intern or a doctor trained in a field unrelated to your problem.

Obtaining high-quality emergency care fast can be vital after an accident or when a chronic illness, such as heart disease or asthma, suddenly becomes life threatening. But in a surprising number of situations, you'll have enough leeway to *choose* your ER.

Key: Know how to go to the right place at the right time for the right reasons—and be treated by the right caregiver. *Here's how…*

PREPARATION IS IMPORTANT

Get ready for the ER visit that you hope you'll never need. *Do your homework…*

• **Visit all ERs within 30 minutes of your home.** If your condition demands exceptional treatment, arriving in a half hour may be better than being transferred from another hospital later.

Look around. Do you think you would feel well cared for?

Snowbird alert: If you have multiple homes or travel to the same places frequently, also do this exercise in these locations.

• **Identify facilities geared to your health problems.**

Example: If you have a heart condition, locate the ER with the best cardiac service. Your ultimate plan will be to ask an ambulance driver to take you there if your condition, such as symptoms of a mild heart attack, permits.

It surprises many people to learn that you often can get an ambulance crew to take you to the hospital of your choice. If the ambulance must go elsewhere or your condition demands faster treatment, the paramedic will say so.

Find the best ERs: Ask your primary care doctor, pulmonologist, cardiologist or other specialist where to find local high-level trauma or teaching hospitals. Ask the public relations departments at nearby hospitals for brochures promoting the hospitals' areas of expertise. Read hospital Web sites. Consult Castle Connolly Medical Ltd., a guide to top doctors and hospitals (212-367-8400, ext. 16, *www.castleconnolly.com*). *Cost:* $24.95 for a one-year membership.

• **Wear a tag, necklace or bracelet identifying your medical status.**

Examples: Diabetes, medication allergies, need for dialysis. Wearing this information on a medical alert tag will help ensure that you receive appropriate care. Also, medical personnel will be able to retrieve your health information by calling the tag sponsor.

Information: MedicAlert (888-633-4298, *www.medicalert.org*)...Bodyguard Medical I.D. Tags (800-383-7790, *www.medicalidtags. com*).

• **Research your health insurance plan's emergency coverage.** Must you report an ER visit within 24 hours? What if you're out of town or taken to an out-of-plan hospital? Having this information on hand will save precious time when admitted to an ER.

• **Maintain a relationship with a trusted physician.** In an emergency, your doctor may help you decide whether an ER visit is warranted...meet you there or consult by phone...recommend a specialist if you need one...find you a local doctor if you're out of town.

KNOW WHEN TO GO

For flu, a twisted ankle, longtime bad back or repeat kidney stone pain, call your doctor for an appointment. Consider going to a good walk-in urgent-care center (their quality varies tremendously) if your doctor isn't available and your insurance covers it. If you can, avoid ERs on Mondays and on Friday and Saturday nights, the busiest times.

Do head for the ER if you're experiencing unbearable or worst-ever pain...profuse bleeding...unfamiliar or severe chest pain, shortness of breath or abdominal pain... sudden arm or leg numbness or weakness ...any other signs of a stroke or heart attack (see below).

STEALTH SYMPTOMS

If you are having a stroke or heart attack, the sooner you reach an ER that has the appropriate technology and expertise, the better. When given within about three hours for stroke, six hours for a heart attack, clot-busting drugs may save your life or reduce disability. Optimal stroke treatment can make the difference between paralysis and a little weakness.

Little-known symptom: In older women, shortness of breath is a more common primary heart attack symptom than chest pain.

Other subtle heart symptoms: Weakness...fatigue...unfamiliar indigestion...jaw or upper back pain.

Information: American Heart Association (800-242-8721, *www.americanheart.org*)... National Heart, Lung, and Blood Institute (301-592-8573, *www.nhlbi.nih.gov*).

Subtle stroke symptoms: Severe headache...facial tingling...drooping mouth...unexplained dizziness.

Information: American Stroke Association (888-478-7653, *www.strokeassociation.org*).

THE BEST CARE ONCE THERE

At the ER, contribute to the quality of your care. *Be sure to...*

• **Enter riding.** Patients arriving by ambulance get much faster attention than walk-ins. Don't let a friend drive you unless waiting for an ambulance would take too long.

• **Focus on one or two chief complaints.** The more vague you are, the less seriously your problem will be taken.

Example: Mention the new sharp pain in your side, not your arthritic hip.

• **Help the staff to help you.** Don't accept every test or treatment suggested without a discussion. Ask the doctor treating you in the ER to help you decide whether the potential gains of any proposed intervention justify possible risks.

• **Identify yourself and your circumstances often.** Ask what you're being given and why. To a nurse adding medication to your IV line, say, "Do you know about my drug allergies?" Don't assume that everyone has read your chart.

• **Be wary.** Reject medications and prescriptions proposed without logical, compelling reasons. Refuse any risky or unnecessary test or treatment.

Reasons: Older people are especially vulnerable to complications from invasive procedures...standard adult drug dosages can be too strong for older people.

If you are sensitive to drugs or you have kidney or liver problems, tell every ER staff member who treats you.

• **Don't leave too soon.** An ER staff eager to "clear the board" may want to send you home although you feel the same as or worse than when you arrived. Explain that you still feel bad. Ask the person discharging you, "Are you an attending physician here? Will you discuss my case with my family doctor?" You can also ask to speak to the attending physician yourself, but he/she may not be available.

TAKE AN ADVOCATE

It's hard to advocate for yourself in the midst of a health emergency. A relative, friend or neighbor can make sure your needs are met...scrutinize your care...discuss options...make phone calls...take detailed notes. Staff are more vigilant when someone is watching.

Your advocate can request the business card of every doctor who sees you...the name of every nurse who treats you...the name of every test that you're given. You may need these details later in the day or for your records.

Self-defense: With an "ER buddy," visit ERs together and compare notes. Show each other where your relevant medical papers are kept, such as health-care proxies naming the person who can make health decisions for you. Agree to accompany each other to the ER if needed.

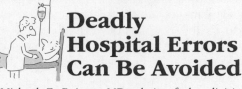

Deadly Hospital Errors Can Be Avoided

Michael F. Roizen, MD, chair of the division of anesthesiology, critical care management and comprehensive pain management at the Cleveland Clinic, OH. He is the author of *RealAge* (Collins) and coauthor, with Mehmet C. Oz, MD, of *You: The Smart Patient*. Free Press.

The hospital is one of the most dangerous places you'll ever go. Patients are exposed to bacteria and viruses...subjected to tests and procedures that have high risks...and given medications that need to be closely monitored—but sometimes aren't.

Between 44,000 and 98,000 Americans die annually from hospital errors. Although patients can't control everything that happens in the hospital, they can lower their risks more than they realize.

Example: Use only a hospital that's accredited by the Joint Commission on Accreditation of Healthcare Organizations. Accreditation means that a hospital is evaluated every three years to ensure that it meets the best standards in cleanliness, infection control, drug administration guidelines, etc. Nearly 15,000 health-care facilities are accredited—but many are not. To check, go to *www.qualitycheck.org*, or call 630-792-5800. *Other ways to stay safe...*

PICK THE BEST HOSPITAL

Teaching hospitals affiliated with major medical universities tend to have the latest technology and best-trained staff. If you require major surgery (such as a transplant operation) or have a life-threatening condition (such as an aortic aneurysm or pancreatic cancer), a teaching hospital is your best option. Smaller hospitals are fine for patients with "routine" health problems, such as pneumonia or a broken leg.

Warning: After July 1st, teaching hospitals are largely staffed with new residents and interns. Their dearth of experience can adversely affect care of patients. If you can, avoid teaching hospitals during the first two weeks of July, when the new school year begins. *Other points to consider...*

• **Is it a "magnet" hospital?** Medical centers with outstanding nursing programs receive this designation from the American Nurses Credentialing Center (800-284-2378, *www.nursecredentialing.org*). Patients in these hospitals benefit from improved care...less staff turnover...and high-quality physicians, who are more likely to work at a hospital with magnet status.

• **Are there full-time intensivists and hospitalists?** Intensivists are doctors who specialize in treating critically ill patients. Hospitalists are doctors who advise only hospital patients. Both types of specialists provide superior hospital care and don't maintain private practices "on the side."

• **How often does the hospital perform the procedure you're undergoing?** The best outcomes usually occur at the hospitals where a given procedure is performed most often, on average.

Examples: A top-flight hospital will perform at least 500 open-heart procedures annually ...100 carotid-artery grafts or surgeries...and 25 mastectomies.

CHOOSE THE BEST SURGEON

Only use a surgeon who is board certified in the specialty related to your operation—neurosurgery, cardiac surgery, etc. Look for the letters "FACS" (Fellow, American College of Surgeons) after his/her name. This means that the surgeon has been evaluated for competence and ethical standards.

Helpful: Call the hospital anesthesiology department, and ask one of the anesthesiologists which surgeon he would pick. (Anesthesiologists often are free between 3 pm and 5 pm.) They know all the surgeons and have no reason not to give a straight answer.

Once you compile some recommendations, choose a surgeon who does only a few types of procedures. Research has shown that surgeons who specialize—in nerve-sparing prostate surgery, for example—have better results and fewer complications than the national average.

Caution: Don't shave your surgical site before surgery. You'll wind up with thousands of invisible nicks that increase the risk for infection. Let the operating room staff do it. They use special creams that prevent nicks.

Important: Ask the anesthesiologist to provide a blanket (if it will not get in the way) to keep you warm during surgery. Patients who maintain *normothermia* (normal body temperature) have a lower risk for infection and other complications.

PREVENT HOSPITAL INFECTIONS

Each year, an estimated 2 million hospital patients develop an infection. With the emergence of antibiotic-resistant bacteria, even a minor initial infection can be fatal.

We all know the importance of hand washing, so insist that all visitors (including nurses and doctors) wash their hands before touching you. A quick rinse doesn't help. Studies show that you must wash vigorously with soap and warm water for at least 15 seconds to remove bacteria. As an alternative, hand-sanitizing gel, which is now provided outside many hospital rooms, may be used by visitors.

Other self-defense strategies...

• **Keep a bottle of hand-sanitizing gel at your bedside.** Use this hand cleanser yourself before eating.

• **Beware of the TV remote control.** One study found that remote controls in hospitals have three times more bacteria than doorknobs or nurse call buttons. To protect yourself, cover the TV remote with a new hospital glove. You'll still be able to change the channels.

• **Ask about the stethoscope.** Doctors and nurses are supposed to clean their stethoscopes with alcohol between patients, but some get too busy and simply forget. Uncleaned stethoscopes have been linked to hospital infections.

DRUG PROTECTION

Drug mistakes—giving the wrong drug, a dangerous drug combination or the wrong dose—often occur in hospitals. Ask your primary care doctor to supervise *all* of your

301

health care, including drug prescriptions. If that isn't possible, ask one of the hospitalists to do it. Patients with one supervising doctor face fewer risks.

Each time you're given medication: Show your ID bracelet. To ensure that you're getting the right drug (medical test or procedure), ask the nurse to check your ID wrist bracelet.

Also, ask the nurse to tell you what each drug is and why you're taking it. Don't take a drug unless you're sure it's the one that you're supposed to be taking. If you're receiving a medical test or procedure, confirm that it's the correct one.

Finally, ask a family member or friend to help monitor your daily care. This is especially important if the patient is not able to do so.

Help Your Doctor Avoid a Fatal Mistake

Mark Graber, MD, vice chair of the department of medicine at Stony Brook University, New York, and chief of medicine at Veteran's Administration Hospital in Northport, NY. Dr. Graber is widely recognized as a leading authority on diagnostic errors in medicine, and his scientific papers on the topic have appeared in *Archives of Internal Medicine, Academic Medicine* and other journals.

As many as 15% of medical diagnoses are wrong. You're told you're fine when you're really ill or that you have a disease you don't really have. Either result can be fatal.

In a study reported in *Annals of Internal Medicine*, doctors at Harvard School of Public Health analyzed more than 300 incorrect diagnoses. They found that 59% of these misdiagnoses seriously harmed the patient in some way, and of those, 30% were the cause of death.

In the study, the most commonly missed diagnoses were breast and colorectal cancers, fractures and infections. These probably were reported most often because they

are common problems that have significant negative consequences if missed.

Other health problems missed were those with vague symptoms—such as fatigue—that make it difficult for the doctor to quickly arrive at a precise diagnosis. Diseases in this category include multiple sclerosis, thyroid disease and certain cancers.

Here's how to help your physician make the correct diagnosis…

TELL YOUR STORY WELL

Doctors are medical detectives. They decipher clues from evidence, such as a physical exam or laboratory tests. Much of that evidence is rooted in your medical history—the story you tell your doctor about your health. Don't try to diagnose yourself. Simply tell your story clearly, completely and accurately. *Include the following…*

• **Timing.** When did the problem start? How long has it been going on?

• **Symptoms.** Describe your symptoms in detail. For example, is pain localized or general…mild or severe…intermittent or constant? What seems to make your symptoms better or worse—eating, activity, time of day?

• **Tests.** Explain the tests that have been done and the results.

• **Treatments.** Which treatments have you tried? Did they help?

Trap: A nurse or health technician may interview you before you see the doctor. Don't assume that he/she will relay your story to the doctor completely. Instead, let the doctor hear all of the information firsthand.

KEEP CAREFUL RECORDS

Maintain your own medical records by writing down relevant facts about your condition. Include test results, an accurate list of all current medications (prescription and over-the-counter) and supplements, reports from specialists and hospital admissions. Bring your records to every doctor's visit. Even if you're seeing the same physician, it's not unusual for your records to be unavailable for one reason or another.

If you're seeing a new doctor, even one within the same health-care system, don't assume that he/she will get your medical records. Confidentiality rules make it difficult to move records from one doctor to another.

GET TEST RESULTS

Ask for your test results. No news might *not* be good news. Perhaps the doctor is out of town or sick, and your results are sitting in the office—this can be dangerous if you have a life-threatening disease. Know when test results are due. If you don't receive them on time, call the doctor's office.

Even better: Ask your doctor if the lab can send the results to you as well as to the doctor.

KNOW WHAT'S NEXT

A doctor might say, "I'm pretty sure this is what you have." At that point, ask what is likely to happen to you next if his diagnosis is right. If what the doctor expects to happen does not happen, the diagnosis may be wrong.

Example: A longtime smoker catches a cold, and the cough persists for two weeks after the other symptoms have disappeared. The doctor might say, "I think you have bronchitis, which should resolve itself over the next two to three weeks. If not, get back to me." If the cough persists, the patient may have another more serious problem, such as heart failure or lung cancer.

ENCOURAGE YOUR DOCTOR TO THINK BROADLY

Experts who study misdiagnosis are fond of the following joke—What is the most commonly missed fracture?

Answer: The second fracture.

In other words, when a doctor finds a fracture or some other type of health problem, he may stop looking. This type of error has been dubbed *satisficing*—a doctor feels satisfied by finding one problem and stops looking for other problems. Satisficing is a common error. To help prevent it, ask your doctor, "What else do you think this could be?"

GET A SECOND OPINION

Give your primary care physician the first opportunity to diagnose and treat your problem, but if symptoms persist, you might want to get a second opinion. Ask your primary care physician for a recommendation.

Help everyone involved in your care to know what the other providers are thinking and planning. Don't assume that health professionals are coordinating your care behind the scenes—they probably aren't. You are the most reliable person for that job.

What Nurses Know—And Doctors Don't Tell You

Patricia Carroll, RN, quality-management coordinator, Franciscan Home Care and Hospice Care in Meriden, CT. She also is the author of *What Nurses Know and Doctors Don't Have Time to Tell You: Practical Wisdom for Everyday Home Health Care* (Perigee) and *The Surgical Nurse's Managed Care Manual* (Total Learning Concepts).

Medical doctors are trained to treat illness, injury and disease with medication, surgery and/or hospitalization—but they rarely have time to give detailed self-care advice.

Nurses are usually the best people to offer this type of advice and help patients avoid dangerous medical mistakes.

Common mistakes…

• **Relying exclusively on an ear thermometer.** Ear thermometers use an infrared beam to gauge the temperature of the eardrum. They are accurate when trained nurses use them on unconscious patients, who aren't moving. Getting an accurate reading on a conscious patient, who is almost certain to move slightly, is less likely. When a patient moves, the infrared beam may shift off the eardrum, making the reading unreliable.

Rectal thermometers are still the gold standard for getting an accurate temperature reading. Digital oral thermometers also are reliable. But, according to a new study conducted at the University of Virginia Health System, you should not eat or drink anything for 15 to 25 minutes before taking the reading.

Forehead thermometers gauge the temperature in the temporal artery, which supplies blood to the temple and scalp, and are considered less reliable because proper placement and use can be tricky. Follow label instructions carefully.

• **Using silverware to measure liquid medicines.** Daily doses of certain medications—for example, the heart drug *digoxin* (Lanoxin) and anticonvulsant drugs, such as *phenytoin* (Dilantin)—must be measured precisely because there is a narrow range between optimal and toxic doses. Liquid drug doses are prescribed in milliliters but often are translated into teaspoons and tablespoons for convenience. However, the size of silverware teaspoons and tablespoons varies widely.

Ask your health-care provider to skip this translation. Measure out your prescribed dose in milliliters in a needleless syringe or a dosing spoon (a plastic device with a spoon on one end and measurements along the handle).

Check with your health-care provider for a needleless syringe. Or buy a dosing spoon, available at a drugstore for about $2. If you're not sure how to use these devices, ask a pharmacist or nurse for a demonstration.

• **Storing medicine in the bathroom medicine cabinet.** The humidity that commonly develops in a bathroom with a shower or bathtub increases the chances that your prescription or over-the-counter (OTC) drugs will break down quickly, losing their efficacy and possibly causing unwanted side effects, such as stomach upset or skin rash.

A box, placed in a linen closet near the bathroom, is the best place for your drugs because it keeps the medication cool and dry. (If you have children in your home, place the box on the top shelf, where it is out of reach.)

• **Taking pain relievers that contain caffeine instead of getting it from coffee.** The OTC pain reliever Excedrin contains *acetaminophen*, aspirin and caffeine. Anacin, another OTC pain reliever, contains buffered aspirin and caffeine. These drugs cost up to three times more than plain aspirin or acetaminophen.

Caffeine is added because aspirin and acetaminophen are absorbed up to 40% faster when taken with caffeine. However, a cup of

caffeinated coffee contains about 135 mg of caffeine—compared with 64 mg to 130 mg per dose of pain reliever—and works just as well. Black tea, which contains 40 mg to 70 mg of caffeine per cup, also can be used.

If you use aspirin or acetaminophen, take it with a cup of coffee or tea in the morning to boost the drug's absorption. To avoid unwanted side effects, such as restlessness, do *not* drink coffee or tea at night.

Many people with arthritis suffer the most severe pain when they wake in the morning. Taking a pain reliever without caffeine allows you to take it at bedtime so it lasts until morning, without keeping you up at night.

Great Second Opinions— Without Leaving Home

Rebecca Shannonhouse, editor of *Bottom Line/ Health,* Boardroom Inc., 281 Tresser Blvd., Stamford, CT 06901.

What if you had a variety of cancer or another disease that local doctors had little experience treating? You would need a second opinion—but the quality of that opinion would vary widely in different communities. The Internet now makes it possible for patients to get second opinions from world-class specialists.

The specialists at the Cleveland Clinic and the Harvard-affiliated teaching facilities Brigham and Women's Hospital and Massachusetts General Hospital now offer second opinions on the Internet. Top-rated radiologists, pathologists, etc., review computed tomography (CT) scans, pathology slides and other laboratory and imaging tests. Then they share their findings with the patient's primary care physician.

"A doctor in a local hospital or even a regional medical center may see only a few cases of a particular disease in his/her entire career. With on-line programs, a primary care physician can tap the expertise of specialists who see several cases a *day*," explains Joseph C. Kvedar, MD, the founder and director of Harvard's on-line second-opinion program, Partners Telemedicine.

A first-year analysis of the Harvard program found that specialists arrived at different diagnoses in 5% of cases and recommended different treatments—such as newer drugs or more up-to-date approaches—90% of the time.

Typical cost: $350 to $750.* Insurance may cover some of this cost.

Visit eCleveland Clinic, *www.ecleveland clinic.org*, or the Center for Connected Health, *www.connected-health.org*, to learn more.

More from Rebecca Shannonhouse...

Premium Medical Care

If you are tired of crowded waiting rooms and rushed doctor appointments, you're definitely not alone.

Latest approach: Concierge medicine, in which physicians drastically reduce their patient loads in order to offer personalized attention, including longer office visits... same- or next-day appointments...and 24/7 availability by phone, e-mail or pager.

Doctors in concierge practices charge each patient a fixed annual fee, ranging from $1,500 to $20,000* per year. In addition, patients retain their usual insurance coverage and pay for services just as they would in a traditional doctor's practice.

Not long ago, Richard Goldman, MD, an internist and founder of a concierge medical practice in Wellesley, MA, handled 3,500 to 4,000 patients a year in an HMO. "Now I see 300 to 400 patients," he says. "This is the way medicine used to be practiced."

There are about 100 concierge medical practices in the US. This type of service isn't practical (or affordable) for everyone, but it can be a solution for people who...

•**Maintain hectic schedules** and cannot afford to spend time in a waiting room.

*Prices subject to change.

•**Feel rushed and depersonalized in an HMO.**

•**Suffer from chronic conditions** that require frequent care and/or want 24-hour access to their physicians.

To find a concierge medical practice in your area, consult the Society for Innovative Medical Practice Design's Web site, *simpd.org*.

How to Make Your Lab Tests More Accurate

Kandice Kottke-Marchant, MD, PHD, clinical pathologist, the Cleveland Clinic.

An employee who recently had her annual physical decided to have her cholesterol levels measured again at an employer-sponsored health fair. To her surprise—and dismay—the reading on the second cholesterol test was almost 20% higher than the first. Which results should she believe?

Many factors can influence test results. These include diet, medications, differences between laboratories, even season (cholesterol counts tend to increase in winter). Patients can't control all of these factors—but there are ways to increase lab test accuracy. *Steps to take in advance...*

•**Make sure the lab is accredited.** The physician and the insurance carrier dictate where a test is performed. Labs are typically accredited by reputable organizations, but it is a good idea to check that the lab has accreditation.

•**Use the same lab every time,** if possible, since there can be significant testing differences between laboratories. In my colleague's case, only the first test actually involved lab work. The health-fair test was the "instant" kind—so inaccurate results were more likely.

•**Follow all instructions**—for example, eating a meal exactly two hours before a two-hour postprandial blood sugar test or abstaining from sexual intercourse for two days prior to a prostate-specific antigen (PSA) test.

• **Review your medications, dietary supplements and herbal remedies** with your doctor. These can affect lab test results. For example, high levels of vitamin C interfere with certain tests...birth control pills can increase blood sugar...some antidepressants and blood pressure medications can decrease blood sugar. Generally, these factors can be taken into account when interpreting the test results, but your doctor may advise a change in your regimen prior to the test.

• **If you have experienced significant stress recently or exercised strenuously,** tell your doctor. Those factors can increase blood levels of *C-reactive protein* (CRP), an inflammation indicator associated with heart disease.

• **To avoid bacterial contamination,** clean yourself with soap and water before giving a urine sample, or particularly for women, use the special wipes available at testing facilities.

Dr. Kottke-Marchant warns that patients should keep a watchful eye during a test, too. *For example...*

• **If blood flows too slowly as it is drawn,** clots may form, invalidating the results for some tests, especially hematology and coagulation tests (drawn in tubes with purple or light blue tops). A simple tilt of the tube back and forth may detect a clotted sample.

• **Check that the sample is labeled accurately.** Confirm your name, type of test, date drawn and, if at a hospital, patient ID number.

Treatment decisions generally should not be made on the basis of a single out-of-range reading. A second test, drawn from a new sample, helps to confirm whether an out-of-range result is in line with prior results.

Sometimes trends can be more important than absolute numbers. A Johns Hopkins University study, for example, suggests that the annual rate of increase in PSA may be more significant than simply looking at

whether the numbers are within the normal range.

After the employee's elevated cholesterol readings, her physician decided to change her cholesterol-lowering medication. Her total cholesterol count is now lower, and she expects it to continue to drop.

What You Must Know Before Having Surgery

Charles B. Inlander, a consumer advocate and health-care consultant based in Fogelsville, PA. He was founding president of People's Medical Society, a consumer health advocacy group. He is the author of more than 20 books, including *Take This Book to the Hospital with You*. St. Martin's.

Each year, more than 80 million Americans undergo some type of surgery. Over the last 35 years, I have advised thousands of surgical patients on the information they should give their doctors and the questions that must be asked to ensure the best possible odds for a successful operation and recovery. *Here are the areas that are most often overlooked or cause confusion among patients...*

• **Medications and/or supplements before surgery.** If you take a blood thinner, such as *warfarin* (Coumadin), you will likely need to stop taking it three or more days before any major surgery, such as a coronary bypass or a hysterectomy, to prevent excessive bleeding. You will probably need to modify your medication schedule even for less invasive surgery, such as knee surgery or removal of a growth.

Caution: Do not assume that your surgeon knows the drugs and/or supplements you are taking. In fact, he/she probably doesn't. Give him a list of all your prescription and nonprescription drugs, such as aspirin or antacids, as well as all vitamins and other supplements that you take.

Self-defense: When your surgery is scheduled, ask your surgeon to write down the specific drugs and/or supplements you should stop taking before surgery and exactly how many days prior to the operation you should discontinue them. Also, be sure to mention any chronic conditions you have, such as diabetes, heart disease or allergies, which may affect the outcome of your surgery.

•**New drugs before surgery.** It's not uncommon that the surgeon will ask you to take an antibiotic (to prevent infection) or an anticoagulant drug (to prevent blood clots) several days before surgery.

Self-defense: Don't wait for the surgeon to tell you this. As soon as your operation is planned, ask about presurgery medications. Get this in writing as well.

•**Fasting.** Many types of surgeries require that you fast or go on a liquid-only diet the day prior to the procedure. Among other reasons, fasting is necessary to prevent the patient from vomiting and possibly choking. You also may need to take a laxative to empty your bowels before the operation.

Self-defense: When surgery is scheduled, ask your surgeon for a written schedule of when you should stop eating solid foods …when you should take a laxative (if necessary)…and when you must stop ingesting anything, including liquids.

•**Medical tests.** Presurgical tests may be required a few days before the operation to rule out any reasons to delay, alter or cancel the surgery. However, often, those same tests were performed only a week or two earlier to diagnose your condition.

Self-defense: Ask the surgeon or his staff to check whether you need to repeat a recently performed test. You have enough to do prior to surgery without going for unnecessary tests.

•**Conflicting instructions.** Your surgeon may tell you that it's okay to take a certain drug prior to surgery while one of your other doctors says to stop it.

Self-defense: When your surgeon gives you instructions that differ from what one of your other doctors has told you, ask that the doctors speak with each other and give you their joint recommendation.

More from Charles Inlander…

Avoid Unnecessary Surgery

Few things are worse than having an unnecessary surgical procedure. Yet every year, millions of Americans have operations they do not need. In fact, the Congressional Committee on Energy and Commerce reports that 20% of all surgeries performed in the US are unnecessary. *Surgeries you may not need…*

•**Removal of the prostate.** The most common treatment for prostate cancer is removal of the prostate gland, but clinical studies show that the operation is of little benefit to men who have a life expectancy of 10 years or less because the cancer grows very slowly. This means that most men over age 75 have nothing to gain and may suffer from side effects of the surgery, such as incontinence and infection. Regardless of a man's age, he should seek several medical opinions (including that of a urologist who does not perform surgery).

•**Cataract removal.** More than a decade ago, the Agency for Healthcare Policy and Research warned that many of the operations performed to remove a cataract were not necessary. The National Institutes for Health suggests that cataract removal is best performed if your vision has been reduced to at least 20/150—even with eyeglasses.

And yet each year, hundreds of thousands of Americans have the surgery even though their eyesight is far better than that. In many cases, surgery will not improve sight and can cause infection. For a more impartial view, get a second opinion from an optometrist (a health-care provider licensed to provide a broad range of eye-care services), rather than a surgical ophthalmologist (a medical doctor who specializes in eye disease).

•**Gallbladder removal.** Since the late 1980s, the number of gallbladder operations has increased by about 40%. The reason is the advent of minimally invasive laparoscopic surgery. This procedure can be done in an outpatient setting and is quicker (conventional surgery typically requires three days in the hospital), more convenient and more profitable for doctors. But it is often not necessary.

Before agreeing to gallbladder removal, consult an experienced internist about nonsurgical options, such as a special diet or the gallstone-dissolving medication *ursodiol* (Actigall).

•**Wisdom tooth extraction.** This procedure is the granddaddy of all unnecessary surgeries, as about half of all wisdom tooth extractions are unnecessary. For decades, major dental organizations and journals have criticized the removal of wisdom teeth that are symptom free. To protect yourself, any time a dentist recommends having your wisdom teeth removed, get a second opinion from another dentist. If wisdom teeth are impacted, infected or are causing other teeth to shift, surgery may be necessary. But many times they will not cause any problems, and you can save yourself a lot of time, money and pain.

Also from Charles Inlander...

Unexpected Sources of Lethal Infections

According to the Centers for Disease Control and Prevention (CDC), infections that are acquired in the hospital kill approximately 100,000 patients every year, seriously harm almost 2 million additional people and add more than $5 billion to annual health-care costs. The CDC also estimates that up to half of these infections are preventable, if only hospital personnel would take infection control more seriously—primarily by washing their hands.

However, hospitals aren't the only place that an unsuspecting medical consumer can acquire a deadly infection. You also can get an infection from outpatient surgical and emergency centers, nursing homes, assisted-living facilities—even your doctor's office.

Not one single state routinely inspects their nonhospital medical facilities for infection-control practices, nor do states require these facilities to report infections that might have been caused by treatments received there. That means it's up to you—the patient—to take steps that will lower your risk for infection. *Best strategies...*

•**Check for clean hands.** You may have heard it before, but you cannot afford to ignore this advice. In fact, the CDC reports that staff not washing their hands is the number-one reason that infections spread. Do not let anyone—not even a doctor or a nurse—touch you unless he/she has washed his hands in your presence. If a health-care worker comes into the examining room with gloves on, ask him to remove those gloves, wash his hands and put on new gloves. It has been found that, in rare cases, personnel wear the same gloves all day long!

•**Insist on clean equipment.** For example, make sure a doctor or nurse wipes the flat surface (diaphragm) of his stethoscope with alcohol before listening to your chest. Studies show that stethoscopes can be contaminated with *staphylococcus aureus* and other deadly bacteria if the equipment is not cleaned.

•**Beware of urinary catheters.** Infections triggered by urinary catheters are a problem, especially in nursing homes and assisted-living facilities. The longer the catheters stay in, the greater the risk for infection. Too often catheters are inserted in patients for the convenience of the staff, simply because they do not have the time (or desire) to bring a bedpan or change a diaper. Unless there is a medical reason for a urinary catheter, insist on a bedpan or diaper. It can save your life—or that of a loved one.

•**Ask about presurgical antibiotics.** When it comes to infection, outpatient surgery is just as risky as inpatient surgery. Research now shows that many patients should be given an antibiotic within one hour of surgery. Unfortunately, busy health-care workers often forget to administer it. So when your surgery is scheduled, talk to your doctor about receiving a presurgical antibiotic. If it is recommended, ask about the antibiotic as soon as you arrive at the facility.

Have Surgery in The Morning

Patients who have early surgery are less likely to develop complications of anesthesia than those who have surgery at 4 pm or later.

Possible reasons: Fatigue of doctors and other health-care workers by late afternoon…shift changes…higher case loads later in the day.

Good news: Even when postsurgical problems do develop, they are usually minor ones involving nausea or pain management.

Melanie C. Wright, PhD, assistant professor of anesthesiology, Duke University Medical Center, Durham, NC.

Keep Your Medical Records At an On-Line Site

The free iHealthRecord service lets you set up and modify your history of health conditions, allergies, medications, etc. Doctors anywhere in the world can access the information with your permission. Or you can print out data before going to a new doctor. You can update information and set up secure records for people you care for, such as children and aging parents. The system also can alert you to problems.

Example: An FDA warning about a previously unknown risk of a drug you use.

Details: *www.ihealthrecord.org.*

James Rohack, MD, past chair, American Medical Association (AMA), Chicago. The AMA and other medical societies formed Medem, which offers the iHealthRecord service.

Give Your Medical Bills a Checkup

Charles B. Inlander, a consumer advocate and health-care consultant based in Fogelsville, PA. He was founding president of People's Medical Society, a consumer health advocacy group. He is the author of more than 20 books, including *Take This Book to the Hospital with You.* St. Martin's.

My mother-in-law recently spent 20 days in the hospital with a near-fatal bout of pneumonia.

Her bill was more than $30,000. Although the hospital had billed her insurers directly, when she checked out, I insisted that we be given a fully itemized hospital bill—one that listed *every single charge.* After reviewing the bill, I discovered at least $3,000 worth of questionable charges. I called the hospital's billing office and challenged the bill. It was changed. I'm still waiting to see if Medicare and my mother-in-law's supplemental insurer got the correct bill.

Companies that review hospital bills report finding errors in at least 80% of them. Not surprisingly, most errors favor the hospital or doctor. Hospitals are not the only culprits. If you receive a medical bill for a visit to your doctor or an outpatient surgical procedure, chances are good it is incorrect. And don't assume that it's only your health insurer's problem. These errors contribute to skyrocketing health-care costs that are passed on to *you* in the form of higher insurance rates and out-of-pocket costs. *Most common errors to watch for…*

• **Double billing.** Getting charged twice for the same service, product or medication is by far the most common error in both doctor-office and hospital bills. This can happen because a nurse or doctor writes the same thing twice on a record or a clerk hits the wrong computer key.

• **Up-coding.** This frequently happens in hospitals when the charge for a lower-cost service is shifted to one that costs more. For example, you are charged for the brand-name medication when you were given a generic drug.

• **Unbundling.** This happens when a doctor performs just one procedure but charges for two separate ones. A dermatologist did this when my father had two small growths removed from his forehead. The doctor snipped both of them off in less than 30 seconds. When we got the Medicare benefit explanation, he had charged the government $400 for the two separate surgeries. What he did was illegal, and we reported him to the federal government. In such cases, doctors can be dropped by their insurance companies and Medicare—and lose their licenses.

• **Services never rendered.** Frequently, doctors and hospital personnel order a medical service and then decide against it—but they fail to correct the record. If you are hospitalized, you can guard against this by asking for a daily bill.

To protect yourself against these errors, question any billing that you think may be wrong. If the doctor or hospital ignores your inquiry, contact the fraud department of your insurance company to report the problem. If you are a Medicare beneficiary, call 800-633-4227 and say that you want to report a billing problem. Both the insurer and Medicare will look into it. If you suspect major fraud, contact your state's attorney general's office to report it.

Save Hundreds Of Dollars Buying Drugs On-Line

Rick Melcher, RPh, a registered pharmacist in Yakima, WA, and coauthor of *Smart Buys Drug-Wise.* Harbor.

Internet pharmacies can provide big savings for people who require prescription drugs. Prices average 18% less than even discount retail store prices. For some drugs, the savings are as high as 45%.

How it works: A patient orders a drug on-line. The patient or his/her doctor sends a written prescription to the Internet pharmacy. The pharmacist reviews and fills the prescription medication, which then is shipped through the mail.

Many over-the-counter products are available at Internet pharmacies, too. Most Internet pharmacies also accept phone orders if you do not have computer access…or you can go to your library and use the computer there.

Both the convenience and savings of Internet pharmacies have led many patients to abandon brick-and-mortar stores—but you have to make sure the pharmacy is reputable and shop wisely to get the best deals. *Here's how…*

• **Look for the VIPPS seal.** Internet pharmacies that advertise themselves as Verified Internet Pharmacy Practice Sites (VIPPS) have been inspected by the National Association of Boards of Pharmacy (NABP). NABP evaluates participating pharmacies on the quality and consistency of their procedures.

Caution: Some unscrupulous Internet companies display the VIPPS seal even though they haven't been inspected. Check out a company's status at *www.nabp.net.* Some reputable pharmacies are not VIPPS members—be sure you are familiar with the company's reputation.

• **Check insurance participation.** Most Internet pharmacies work with a limited number of insurance companies. Some bill the insurers directly…others do not. You can find this information on the pharmacy Web sites, or call your insurance company to find out which, if any, Internet pharmacies are part of its network.

• **Figure in extra costs.** Some Internet pharmacies offer free shipping for standard ground delivery. This usually takes two weeks, so order well in advance. Fees for overnight delivery can be high.

A few Internet pharmacies, such as AARP's, charge patients annual membership fees. If you need many prescriptions over a year, the savings can more than offset the extra fee.

• **Buy in bulk.** Some insurance companies allow people to get a three-month supply of medication for a single co-payment when they order from Internet pharmacies, cutting costs by 67%.

Patients also can save by buying up to a year's supply at a time.

Example: One woman ordered a year's supply of the thyroid hormone *levothyroxine.* She skipped her insurance company entirely—and still saved $80. In addition, some pharmacies offer free shipping on big orders.

• **Pick a company that has a "live" pharmacist.** Avoid any Web-based pharmacies that don't provide customer support. Look for one that has a pharmacist available to answer questions, either via e-mail or telephone.

•**Ask a pharmacist.** Some drugs, such as the anticoagulant *warfarin* and the heart drug *digoxin,* are sensitive to extremes in temperature and so can degrade while they're in the mail. Ask the Internet pharmacist whether your medications can withstand all the rigors of mail travel before ordering on the Internet.

Quality Medical Care For Thousands Less— A Guide to Safe Surgery Abroad

Rudy Rupak, cofounder of PlanetHospital, a foreign-medical-treatment company based in Calabasas, CA, that arranges affordable surgeries overseas and offers free evaluations to those seeking surgery abroad, *www.planethospital.com*, 800-243-0172.

More and more Americans are traveling to Europe, the Far East and Mexico for medical treatment.

Key reason: Low prices on top-quality care.

In the past, this kind of medical tourism has been associated with elective plastic surgery and experimental treatments not available in the US. But last year, more than 55,000 Americans went abroad for necessary but nonemergency operations, such as angioplasty, knee replacement and cataract surgery.* Less expensive labor and administrative costs make foreign treatment 50% to 75% cheaper. That can be a bargain even with the additional costs of airfare and accommodations. *Costs of medical procedures vary widely, within the US and internationally, but here are a few examples…*

•**Cataract surgery** in the US costs about $3,000 an eye…in Eastern Europe, it costs $1,200 an eye.

*US insurance companies currently do not pay for overseas surgery if it is not an emergency.

•**Repairing a herniated disk** in the US can range from $30,000 to $90,000…in Bangkok, Thailand, it starts at $3,500.

•**A total knee replacement** in the US is about $48,000…in India, $5,500.

•**Angioplasty** in the US, around $80,000 …in Singapore, $15,000.

•**Root canal** in the US can range from $500 to $900…in Mexico, less than $300.

FINDING THE BEST

Flying thousands of miles from home for an operation is not for everyone, but it's worth exploring if you don't have adequate health insurance. Of course, you would want to use only top-quality foreign hospitals and physicians. *Here's how to find them…*

•**Start by word of mouth.** Ask friends and associates who have had medical procedures overseas for recommendations. Also ask doctors who specialize in the type of surgery you need.

•**Check with Harvard Medical International** (HMI). This is a self-supporting, not-for-profit subsidiary of Harvard Medical School. Its role is to extend internationally the school's tradition of improving the quality of health care. HMI is affiliated with dozens of overseas medical institutions and hospitals. (617-535-6400, *www.hmi.hms.harvard.edu*)

•**Contact the Joint Commission International** (JCI), the global arm of the institution that accredits US hospitals. JCI hospitals have to meet rigorous standards of patient care, medication safety and infection control. (630-792-5000, *www.jointcommission international.org*)

•**Choose a hospital with an international patient coordinator on staff.** He/she will help you coordinate doctor's appointments, diagnostics and treatment at the hospital, as well as arrange postoperative recuperation. He also can help with practical matters, such as airport pickup, currency exchange, hospital meal choices and interpreters if necessary.

•**Ask the foreign doctor/hospital for references** from Americans who have had the same type of treatment.

311

TOP FOREIGN HOSPITALS

These are foreign hospitals I would trust for myself and my family...

- **India**
  - Apollo Hospitals has hospitals in Delhi, Chennai and Hyderabad that cater to foreigners and specialize in heart-related procedures. *www.apollohospitals.com.*
  - Wockhardt Hospitals Group has hospitals in Mumbai (formerly Bombay) and Bangalore that specialize in heart, eye, bone, brain and spinal surgery. Associated with HMI. *www.wockhardthospitals.net.*
  - The Max Hospital, New Delhi, offers state-of-the-art surgery for brain and pituitary tumors, aneurysms and vascular malformations. *www.maxhealthcare.in.*
- **Thailand**
  - Bumrungrad International Hospital is Bangkok's leading health-care institution. Specialties include endocrinology, nephrology and neurology. *www.bumrungrad.com.*
  - Samitivej Hospitals has branches in Bangkok and Chonburi. Specialties include cardiac and cancer surgery. *www.samitivej.co.th.*
- **Singapore**
  - Parkway Group Healthcare. Three hospitals specializing in cardiac surgery and neurosurgery—East Shore, Gleneagles and Mount Elizabeth. *www.parkwayhealth.com.*
- **Belgium**
  - AMC-Gent specializes in hip-related surgery. *www.hip-clinic.com.*
- **Mexico**
  - Hospitales Angeles has six hospitals in cities such as Tijuana and Juarez. Specializes in neurosurgery and dental surgery. *www.mediks.com* (site is in Spanish only).

GETTING QUALITY CARE

- **Ask for a full diagnosis from your own doctor first.** Develop a treatment plan you both feel comfortable with. Your doctor should be willing to forward all diagnostic information and communicate with the foreign surgeon to discuss your condition. Once you arrive, the foreign doctor also will evaluate you prior to surgery.
- **Bring a family member or friend.** You need someone for emotional support and to serve as your advocate. That person should bring with him/her your health-care power of attorney, which will be honored by international hospitals. This document allows him to make health decisions for you if you are unable to communicate your own wishes.

While a second person doubles the cost of the airfare, most foreign hospitals will allow a companion to stay as a guest in your room for no extra charge.

- **Know the costs.** Most international hospitals and/or health-care providers expect 50% of their fee to book the surgery and the rest of the cost of treatment at the time of admission. If complications prevent you from returning home immediately, hospitals will accommodate you longer, but ask for the rates so that you can plan accordingly. Also, you should be able to change any airfare you book multiple times with minimal penalty.

Important: Check with your insurance company to make sure it will pay for the treatment of any complications once you arrive home.

- **Confirm that the hospital gives you the same rights** that you have in the US. Reputable hospitals and surgeons will guarantee these rights in writing before you travel overseas. *You should have the right to...*
  - Receive complete and current information concerning your diagnosis, treatment and prognosis in terms that you can understand, including serious side effects or risks, problems related to recovery and the likelihood of success.
  - Have access to all information contained in your medical records.
  - Accept or refuse any treatment and be informed of the consequences of any such refusal.
  - Request consultation with the hospital ethics/oversight committee regarding complaints and ethical issues involved in your care.
  - Be transferred to another facility at your request or when it is medically appropriate.
  - Examine your bill and receive an explanation of the charges.

• **Understand that your legal rights are limited** if medical malpractice is committed overseas. You cannot sue in American courts, and most foreign countries strictly limit malpractice damage awards.

Helpful: If your overseas doctor has a medical board certification in the US, you can complain to the board and seek sanctions.

Relax Before Your Next Visit To the Dentist

Try relaxation techniques to calm yourself at the dentist...

• **Progressive muscle relaxation**—tense and relax each muscle one by one until every body part is relaxed.

• **Guided imagery**—imagine a happy scene.

• **Paced breathing**—breathe slowly and evenly.

• **Meditation**—focus on a soothing thought and repeat it to yourself.

Information: *www.dentalgentlecare.com*, *www.saveyoursmile.com* and *www.colgate.com*.

Robert F. Kroeger, DDS, dentist in private practice, Cincinnati, *cincinnatismiles.com*.

Boost Your Medication's Healing Powers

Leo Galland, MD, director, Foundation for Integrated Medicine, New York City. His latest book is *The Fat Resistance Diet*. Broadway. *www.fatresistancediet.com*. Dr. Galland is a recipient of the Linus Pauling award.

If you're among the millions of Americans taking medication for pain, asthma or allergies, hypertension, high cholesterol or depression, research shows that you may be able to maximize the benefits...curb the side effects...and maybe even lower the dosages of your drugs by combining them with the right supplements.

Important: Consult your doctor before adding a supplement to your drug regimen. Some supplements can interact adversely with medications—for example, some research shows that fish oil can reduce the time it takes for blood to clot and should be used with caution by people taking a blood thinner, such as warfarin (Coumadin).

Supplements (available at health-food stores) to consider using if you are taking any of the following...

ANTIDEPRESSANT

Supplement with: 1,000 mg to 2,000 mg daily of *eicosapentaenoic acid* (EPA), an omega-3 fatty acid found in fish oil. (Ask your doctor which dosage is right for you.)

What it does: Omega-3s are believed to enhance the ability of the brain chemical *serotonin* to act on the nervous system. In a recent British study, when depressed patients who were taking a prescription antidepressant, such as *fluoxetine* (Prozac) or *sertraline* (Zoloft), added 1,000 mg of EPA to their daily regimen for 12 weeks, they reported significantly less depression, anxiety and suicidal thoughts, as well as improved sleep, libido and energy.

Most standard fish oil supplements contain only 200 mg to 300 mg of EPA, so you'd need up to 10 capsules daily to get the recommended 1,000 mg to 2,000 mg of EPA. If you don't want to take that many capsules, take liquid fish oil—in an amount equal to 1,000 mg to 2,000 mg daily of EPA.

Helpful: To avoid "fishy-tasting" burping (the most frequent complaint), try taking the capsules on an empty stomach with a large glass of water. Some people also find that this unpleasant aftertaste is less likely to occur with liquid fish oil.

Also try: 500 micrograms (mcg) daily of folic acid, which promotes proper functioning of the nervous system. Low levels of folic acid have been linked to depression. Harvard Medical School researchers report that depressed patients who had achieved remission with fluoxetine were 13 times more likely to relapse during a six-month period if they had low blood levels of folic acid.

Caution: Supplemental folic acid may mask a vitamin B-12 deficiency, which can lead to nerve damage. Take a 500-mcg to 1,000-mcg B-12 supplement daily to prevent worsening of a B-12 deficiency.

NONSTEROIDAL ANTI-INFLAMMATORY DRUG

Supplement with: 350 mg of *deglycyr-rhizinated licorice* (DGL), three times daily.

What it does: Studies show that DGL may reduce or prevent the gastrointestinal (GI) inflammation, bleeding and ulcerations caused by aspirin and other nonsteroidal anti-inflammatory drugs (NSAIDs)—prescription and over-the-counter.

Caution: Whole licorice extract also protects the stomach, but it contains *glycyrrhetinic acid*, which even in small doses may raise blood pressure. Stick with DGL.

Also try: 1,000 mg to 2,000 mg daily of vitamin C (in two divided doses) and 7 g of powdered glutamine (one heaping teaspoon dissolved in water, three times daily). Studies suggest that taking 1,000 mg of vitamin C twice daily may help prevent aspirin-induced inflammation of the small intestine.

Meanwhile, the amino acid glutamine, long used to help heal ulcers, may decrease the intestinal toxicity of other NSAIDs.

ASTHMA OR ALLERGY DRUG

Supplement with: 1,000 mg daily of *gamma-linolenic acid* (GLA) and 500 mg daily of EPA.

What it does: GLA, an omega-6 fatty acid derived from evening primrose oil or borage oil, may inhibit production of *leukotrienes*, molecules that trigger inflammation and constriction of the bronchial airways. The asthma drug *montelukast* (Singulair) also works by inhibiting leukotrienes.

Important: Most omega-6 fatty acids (including those found in many processed foods) *increase* inflammation, unless they're balanced by sufficient amounts of anti-inflammatory omega-3s. GLA, however, is an anti-inflammatory, but at high doses—and in the absence of omega-3s—it can become inflammatory. The recommended 500 mg of EPA daily creates an optimal balance of omega-6s and omega-3s.

Also try: Quercetin, a bioflavonoid derived from red onions, apples and other foods. In laboratory studies, quercetin has demonstrated antihistamine and anti-allergenic properties. Clinical trials are needed, but given its safety, I often recommend quercetin to my asthma and allergy patients. Try using 500 mg to 600 mg, twice daily, of quercetin—taken on an empty stomach for maximum benefit—as an adjunct to your antihistamine and/or GLA.

BLOOD PRESSURE DRUG

Supplement with: 1,000 mg of arginine, twice daily.

What it does: Arginine (also called L-arginine) is an amino acid used by the body to produce nitric oxide (NO), a molecule that helps keep blood vessels flexible and able to dilate—both of which stabilize blood pressure. Legumes (such as lentils, black beans and kidney beans) and whole grains (such as brown rice) contain some arginine, but you'll need a supplement to get the 2,000 mg daily that is recommended for blood vessel health.

Caution: Because some research has shown that arginine can be dangerous for people who have suffered a heart attack, it should not be used by these individuals. If you have the herpes simplex virus and want to take arginine, you may need to add 1,500 mg daily of lysine, another amino acid. The virus grows in the presence of arginine but is inhibited by lysine.

Also try: 100 mg daily of *Pycnogenol*. This plant extract appears to enhance NO synthesis in blood vessels. In a recent placebo-controlled trial, Chinese researchers found that hypertensive patients who took 100 mg of Pycnogenol daily for 12 weeks were able to significantly lower their dose of a calcium channel blocker, a popular hypertension drug.

STATIN

Supplement with: 100 mg daily of co-enzyme Q10 (CoQ10).

What it does: Cholesterol-lowering statins deplete the naturally produced molecule coenzyme Q10—this depletion may lead to muscle damage.

Researchers at Stony Brook University in Stony Brook, NY, found that patients taking statins who added 100 mg of CoQ10 daily for one month reported a 40% reduction in severity of muscle pain, a common side effect of statins.

CoQ10 also may prevent oxidation of LDL "bad" cholesterol—an unfortunate side effect of statins that occurs to LDL cholesterol particles not eliminated by the drug.

Also try: Fish oil that contains 1,500 mg of EPA and 1,300 mg of *docosahexaenoic acid* (DHA) daily. Studies show that these essential fatty acids raise HDL "good" cholesterol and lower dangerous blood fats known as triglycerides—making EPA and DHA a valuable adjunct to statins, which mainly target elevated LDL cholesterol.

Examples: The cholesterol-lowering drug *atorvastatin* (Lipitor) and the anemia drug *epoetin* (Procrit). Even common antibiotics such as penicillin have been faked. *How to protect yourself…*

• **Sign up for free e-mail alerts on fake drugs** at *www.safemedicines.org*, the Web site of the nonprofit Partnership for Safe Medicines.

• **Become familiar with the shape, color and, if applicable, taste of the drugs that you take.** Some counterfeits appear and/or taste slightly different from the real medication.

• **Note if your medicine seems to stop working or causes new side effects.**

If you suspect that a drug is a counterfeit, tell your pharmacist and physician immediately—and report it on the FDA Web site (*www.fda.gov/medwatch*).

Counterfeit Drug Watch

Rebecca Shannonhouse, editor, *Bottom Line/ Health*, Boardroom Inc., 281 Tresser Blvd., Stamford, CT 06901.

M ost people know there's a risk of buying counterfeit drugs on the Internet.

Problem: Even drugs purchased from US pharmacies might be fake.

According to an FDA estimate, about 1% of the nation's drug supply—about 35 million prescriptions annually—is believed to be counterfeit.

What happens: Drugs are typically sold by manufacturers to wholesalers, who then sell them to pharmacies. However, some dishonest wholesalers tamper with drugs before selling them. Often, they buy cut-rate—sometimes phony—drugs from unlicensed or suspicious sources, explains Katherine Eban, an investigative journalist who has documented counterfeit drugs in her book *Dangerous Doses* (Harcourt).

The drugs most vulnerable to counterfeiting are commonly used and/or expensive.

Read This Before Taking a New Prescription

Rebecca Shannonhouse, editor, *Bottom Line/ Health*, Boardroom Inc., 281 Tresser Blvd., Stamford, CT 06901.

N early half of all Americans take one or more prescription drugs. You may assume that doctors would routinely explain the basics—what a drug does, how long to take it, etc. Don't count on it.

A new study based on audiotapes of 185 patient-doctor visits and published in *Archives of Internal Medicine* found that doctors do a poor job of explaining critical information related to medication.

Doctors discussed drug side effects in only 35% of cases…told patients how long to take a drug just 34% of the time…and were remiss in telling how many pills to take in 45% of the taped visits.

Prescription drug misuse accounts for thousands of deaths annually—and poor communication from doctors may be a contributing factor, says Derjung Mimi Tarn, MD, PhD, assistant professor of family medicine at the University of California, Los Angeles, and the lead author of the study.

Patients can get some information from pharmacists, medication labels, package inserts and/or the Internet.* But doctors are more likely to understand a patient's individual needs—and should know what other drugs a patient may be taking.

Before leaving your doctor's office, make sure that you understand…

- **Why the drug is being prescribed.**
- **The generic and brand names.**
- **How and when to take it.**
- **How long to take it.**
- **Whether it's likely to cause side effects or interact with other drugs.**

Don't settle for any less from your doctor!

*Consult the Physicians' Desk Reference Web site, *www.pdrhealth.com.*

The Worst Time to Fill Prescriptions

Don't fill prescriptions at the beginning of the month. Deaths due to mistakes—the wrong drug, the wrong dose—tend to rise by as much as 25% at the start of any month. This is probably due to a surge in orders received by pharmacies when government assistance payments are made to seniors and Medicaid patients.

Self-defense: Review your prescriptions with your doctor—know drug names, dosages and purposes. At your drugstore, double-check the information with the pharmacist, including your name and address.

David P. Phillips, PhD, professor of sociology, University of California, San Diego, LaJolla, and leader of a study of medication deaths, published in *Pharmacotherapy.*

Can I Crush My Pills To Make Them Easier to Swallow?

Crushing a pill makes it easier to swallow when mixed with food or liquid but may reduce its effectiveness. A crushed pill releases its active ingredients immediately, which may not be appropriate for some extended-release drugs. Also, some tablets contain a coating for easier swallowing and to help mask the taste. If the pill is crushed, it may be more difficult to swallow due to the bitter taste. If your pill has a small line called a score etched in it, this indicates that you can split the tablet, and it is probably safe to crush. Ask your pharmacist first to be sure.

Susan C. Winckler, RPh, vice president, policy and communications, staff counsel, American Pharmacists Association, Washington, DC.

Should I Get Rid of a Drug that Has Passed Its Expiration Date?

Jack M. Rosenberg, PharmD, PhD, professor of pharmacy and pharmacology and director of the International Drug Information Center, Long Island University, Brooklyn, NY.

Yes. Once you open an over-the-counter drug container or receive a medication dispensed by a pharmacist from a sealed bottle that had been opened in the pharmacy, the original manufacturer's expiration date cannot be relied upon. The US Pharmacopeia (USP) recommends that pharmacists add a one-year expiration date on the prescription label, called a "beyond-use date," on solid oral drugs (tablets and capsules)—provided the original container had an expiration date of at least one year from the date the medicine was dispensed. However, most solid medications that have passed their expiration date generally will cause no harm, though they may lose potency and may no longer dissolve readily. Liquid drugs, on the other hand, are not as stable as solid medications, and eyedrops and eardrops are more likely to become contaminated if used after the beyond-use date. To ensure maximum potency of any medication, abide by the expiration date and carefully follow the storage instructions on the container. Never place a drug in a cabinet above or near a sink, as humidity and high temperatures reduce the potency of medications and/or their ability to dissolve properly.

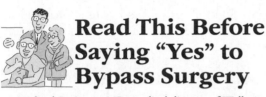

Read This Before Saying "Yes" to Bypass Surgery

Michael D. Ozner, MD, medical director of Wellness & Prevention at Baptist Health South Florida. He is author of *The Miami Mediterranean Diet: Lose Weight and Lower Your Risk of Heart Disease.* Cambridge House. Dr. Ozner's Web site is *www.cardiacoz.com.*

About 1.6 million Americans now undergo heart bypass surgery, angioplasty or stent procedures annually, even though there's no evidence that these procedures prolong life or prevent future heart attacks in the majority of patients.

The three-year survival rate for most patients who have had bypass surgery is almost exactly the same as it is for patients with heart disease who don't have surgery.

Good news: With medications and lifestyle changes, the vast majority of patients with heart disease can reduce the risk of a future heart attack by up to 80%—without undergoing expensive and risky procedures.

FLAWED APPROACH

More than half a million Americans die each year from heart disease. The majority suffer from coronary artery disease (CAD).

Many doctors view CAD primarily as a plumbing problem. When imaging tests reveal blockages in the arteries, their first instinct is to clear out the "gunk," whether or not a patient is experiencing troublesome symptoms.

This approach is often flawed. Most bypass and stent procedures are the equivalent of cosmetic cardiology. They make blood vessels appear healthy but do little to reduce heart attack risk. In fact, most heart attacks are caused by tiny blockages that can be hard to detect—and these blockages often are not in the blood vessels that triggered all the concern in the first place.

Surgical procedures are risky. The mortality rate from bypass surgery ranges from 3% to 5%. More than 50% of patients may experience cognitive difficulties after surgery, and patients who have bypass surgery are nearly four times more likely to suffer a subsequent stroke. Those are poor odds for procedures that don't necessarily prolong life or make patients healthier.

MEDICAL BYPASS

Some patients—those with unstable CAD—do require intervention, such as bypass surgery or a stent procedure.

Example: A person with critical blockages in multiple coronary arteries and a weak heart muscle.

Most patients with CAD, however, are stable and unlikely to benefit from a bypass or stent. They are the best candidates for what might be termed a *medical bypass.* With medications and lifestyle changes, most of these patients can eliminate symptoms (if any) and reduce heart attack risk. Only in rare cases, if symptoms get worse, would one of these heart patients need to consider medical intervention.

One key factor in cardiovascular health is to have an ongoing relationship with your doctor—he/she can advise you on the best steps to take to prevent and treat heart disease. *He may recommend that you...*

● **Follow the Mediterranean-style diet.** Eat lots of fruits, vegetables, whole grains and the legumes...olive oil instead of butter or margarine...several servings of fish weekly... and no more than a few weekly servings of lean meats. The landmark Lyon Diet Heart Study showed that people who ate a Mediterranean diet instead of a typical American diet had a 50% to 70% reduction in recurrent cardiovascular disease.

• **Relax with yoga, meditation, exercise, etc.** Doctors do not always ask patients about stress—which is why it is sometimes called the "forgotten" risk factor for heart disease. People who successfully manage stress can significantly lower blood pressure and the risk of heart disease. Stress management also lowers the risk for arrhythmias (heart rate irregularities).

• **Exercise daily for 30 to 45 minutes.** It is one of the best ways to maintain a healthy weight and prevent or control diabetes and high blood pressure. Regular exercise raises levels of HDL "good" cholesterol. It also can contribute to weight control—which can reduce inflammation in the blood vessels, a risk factor for CAD.

All forms of exercise are beneficial. Aerobic exercise, such as brisk walking, is the best choice for most people because it doesn't require a high level of fitness to do it.

• **Get your cholesterol checked annually**—and take cholesterol-lowering medication if necessary. Research indicates that an aggressive lowering of LDL cholesterol helps reduce risk of heart disease and death from CAD.

• **Take a baby aspirin daily.** It helps prevent platelets from clumping together and forming clots that can block blood flow to the heart. The anti-inflammatory effects of aspirin are also beneficial. Since aspirin may cause gastrointestinal upset, talk with your doctor before initiating aspirin therapy for CAD prevention.

• **See your dentist twice per year.** Studies have shown that patients with periodontal disease—gum inflammation that can result in tooth loss—have a higher risk of heart attack as well as stroke.

• **Get more omega-3s.** Most Americans are deficient in omega-3 fatty acids. Omega-3s lower inflammation and triglycerides, a fat that can put you at risk for heart disease. Omega-3s reduce the risk of arrhythmias and heart attack. Sources include cold-water fish, such as salmon, and walnuts and flaxseed. Or ask your doctor about taking a fish oil supplement.

Misconceptions That Increase Your Risk for Heart Disease

Barry L. Zaret, MD, Robert W. Berliner Professor of Medicine and professor of radiology at Yale University School of Medicine in New Haven, CT. He served as chief of the section of cardiology at Yale from 1978 to 2004. He is coauthor of *Heart Care for Life*. Yale University Press.

One out of every five Americans has some form of heart disease. Literally *millions* of cases could be prevented if people had better information about the best prevention and treatment strategies.

Despite the abundance of health information reported in the media, many people are endangering their health because they are still ill-informed about key aspects of heart disease. To learn about the most common misconceptions regarding heart disease, we spoke with Barry L. Zaret, MD, one of the country's leading specialists in cardiovascular health.

Misconception 1: **High cholesterol is the main risk factor for heart attack.**

Fact: While high cholesterol does increase risk, recent studies show that elevated levels (3 mg per liter or higher) of *C-reactive protein* (CRP), a protein that circulates in the bloodstream, may have an even stronger link than high cholesterol to heart attack and stroke.

Everyone has at least a small amount of CRP in the bloodstream. At higher levels, it indicates the presence of inflammation—possibly caused by an underlying bacterial or viral infection that may damage the linings of blood vessels and promote the development of atherosclerosis.

Every patient with a high risk for cardiovascular disease—smokers and/or those with a family history of heart disease, for example—should have a high-sensitivity CRP blood test. This test, unlike the standard CRP test, distinguishes between inflammation due to cardiovascular disease and other inflammatory conditions, such as arthritis. The high-sensitivity CRP test is particularly important for patients who have had a previous heart attack or who have unstable angina (chest pain caused by lack of blood to the heart). An elevated CRP level in these patients indicates a very high risk for heart attack—even if cholesterol levels are normal.

Misconception 2: All adults should take a daily aspirin.

Fact: Daily aspirin therapy is often recommended for patients who have an elevated heart disease risk due to family history, smoking, obesity, diabetes and atherosclerosis. Studies show that it can curb heart attack risk in *men* by more than 40%.

For women, the evidence is less clear. New research indicates that women who take aspirin are more likely to experience gastrointestinal upset or bleeding problems than men. Although research shows that in women age 46 or older aspirin protects against stroke, it does not reduce heart attack risk in all of these women. Aspirin has been shown to lower heart attack risk only in women age 65 or older, whether or not they have risk factors for the disease. Women of any age who smoke or have a family history of heart disease or other risk factors may benefit from aspirin therapy. The standard recommendation for women is 81 mg daily.

There's no evidence to suggest that aspirin helps prevent a heart attack in healthy women who are under age 65. For these women, not smoking, controlling body weight, getting regular exercise and maintaining a healthful diet are the best ways to guard against the development of heart disease.

This also is true for men age 64 and younger who are healthy and have no risk factors for heart disease. However, men age 65 or older, even if healthy, should take 81 mg of aspirin daily to protect against heart disease.

Misconception 3: The greatest danger of smoking is lung cancer.

Fact: Lung cancer is obviously a concern for smokers, but the risk for cardiovascular disease is actually higher. Of the approximately 440,000 premature deaths caused annually by smoking, the majority are due to cardiovascular disease, according to the Centers for Disease Control and Prevention.

Smoking increases levels of carbon monoxide in the blood, which damages artery linings and promotes atherosclerosis. It appears to lower HDL "good" cholesterol and increase blood levels of *fibrinogen*, a substance in the blood that promotes clotting.

Good news: One year after quitting, the risk for heart disease drops to one-half that of current smokers—and within 15 years becomes about the same as for someone who never smoked.

Misconception 4: Exercise is dangerous if you've already had a heart attack.

Fact: Heart attack patients *especially* benefit from regular exercise. An analysis of 22 different studies that followed more than 4,000 patients for three years found that the death rate among patients who participated in a cardiac rehabilitation program that included exercise was 20% to 25% lower than among those who didn't exercise.

Heart patients who exercise have increased endurance, fewer chest or leg pains and improved heart function. Regular exercise also lowers blood pressure, raises HDL cholesterol and lowers resting heart rate.

Patients who have heart disease or have had a heart attack, or those who have been sedentary, should get a thorough checkup before starting an exercise program. This should include a treadmill stress test, which evaluates blood flow to the heart. Once your doctor determines that it's safe to exercise, aim for 30 minutes at least three to five days a week. Aerobic exercise—fast walking, swimming, etc.—provides the most benefits for heart patients. If you've had a heart attack or other cardiac event, start your exercise routine at a rehabilitation center, if possible. Ask your cardiologist to recommend one near you.

Misconception 5: Reports saying that chocolate is good for the heart are mostly hype.

Fact: The cocoa beans used to make chocolate are extremely rich in *flavonoids*, plant compounds that appear to relax small blood vessels and lower blood pressure. Some of the flavonoids in cocoa also appear to inhibit the ability of platelets to form clots in the arteries.

Harvard researchers recently studied residents of Kuna (an island off Panama), who drink an average of three to four cups of cocoa a day. (They consume even more cocoa in other foods.) Hypertension among these people is almost nonexistent—until they leave the island and forgo their cocoa-rich diet. At that point, their rates of hypertension and heart disease rise.

Of course, there is a downside. The high levels of fat and sugar in chocolate can lead to obesity and elevated blood sugar. But one to two small squares daily of dark chocolate that's at least 70% cocoa and low in added sugar does appear to be good for the heart.

How to Use Statins Safely

Jay S. Cohen, MD, adjunct associate professor of family and preventive medicine and of psychiatry at the University of California, San Diego. He is the author of *What You Must Know About Statin Drugs & Their Natural Alternatives.* Square One. Dr. Cohen has published more than 15 journal articles on the safety of medication. His Web site is *www.medica tionsense.com.*

In the fight against heart disease, statin drugs are heavy artillery. Their cholesterol-lowering power has the potential to reduce heart disease, stroke and cardiac deaths by 25%.

Yet these medications aren't for everyone. In two surveys recently published in *The Journal of the American Medical Association,* 60% to 75% of 100,000 people who started taking statins said they stopped them within about eight months.

What goes wrong? When a patient has no insurance, cost is a factor—one month's supply of some statins exceeds $300. More often, people discontinue this medication because of side effects, which are largely avoidable—if the drugs are prescribed properly.

STATINS AND SIDE EFFECTS

To reduce cholesterol levels, statins alter liver metabolism. Cholesterol is manufactured in the liver, and statins inhibit an enzyme needed for cholesterol production. These drugs also prevent the inflammation that lodges cholesterol deposits inside arteries.

Although statins have fewer side effects than other cholesterol-lowering drugs, an estimated 15% to 30% of people taking them experience abdominal discomfort, muscle or joint pain, muscle weakness and/or memory problems.

More serious side effects occur in 1% to 2% of statin users, whose liver enzymes rise—a warning of possible liver damage when uncorrected. Rhabdomyolysis, a breakdown of muscle tissue, is an extremely rare side effect but can be fatal. Approximately one in 2,000 long-term (more than five years) statin users develops a painful nerve condition known as peripheral neuropathy.

These adverse effects—both uncomfortable and dangerous—are dosage-related. The more powerful the statin and the greater the dosage, the greater the risk.

The side effects can be minimized, if not avoided altogether, by following a simple principle: Take the lowest effective dosage.

MORE ISN'T BETTER

Many people are now getting excessive doses of statins because of the way the FDA assesses new drugs for approval. To gain FDA approval, a drug manufacturer must show that its medication works for the majority of people who take it—so manufacturers design clinical trials with doses high enough to meet that benchmark.

But people respond very differently to medication. Women may require less of a particular drug than men, and people who weigh less often don't need as much as those who weigh more. Older people often respond to lower dosages. And some people need less—or more—just because everyone's biochemistry is different.

Result: Many people could do well on far less than the "recommended" dosage that was proven to be most effective in clinical trials.

What's more, not everyone needs the same amount of cholesterol reduction.

PRECISION PRESCRIBING

The main question in prescribing a statin is, how much cholesterol reduction do you need? Depending on your risk for heart disease, aggressive treatment with statins may—or may not—be a good idea.

To determine your optimum cholesterol level, check with your doctor. National Institutes of Health guidelines advise LDL "bad" cholesterol levels of 100 to 160, depending on cardiovascular risk factors, such as family history of heart disease, age, HDL "good" cholesterol below 40 milligrams per deciliter (mg/dl), etc.

Regardless of your LDL level, it's prudent to make lifestyle changes. A diet that is low in saturated fats (10% or less of total calories) and high in fruits and vegetables (at least nine daily servings) and whole grains often can lower cholesterol as much as a moderate statin. Regular exercise also helps. Walking 45 minutes per day reduces cardiac mortality by 50%. And if you do go on medication, a healthy diet and regular exercise will enable you to use a lower dosage.

To be sure that you are being prescribed the appropriate amount of medication, ask your doctor what percentage of LDL cholesterol reduction you need.

Example: Your LDL cholesterol is 165, and your target is 130 (a 21% reduction). A daily 10-mg dose of *lovastatin* (Mevacor) or *pravastatin* (Pravachol) is a good place to start.

After one month, have your cholesterol tested again. If it hasn't dropped enough, you may need to increase the statin dosage. Or, if it has decreased to desired levels, particularly if you also have made dietary changes, you may be able to decrease your dosage.

This approach can identify your lowest effective dosage and minimize side effects.

WHICH STATIN?

All statins work the same way, so the key difference among them is potency. LDL reductions of 50% to 60% are possible if using *atorvastatin* (Lipitor) and *simvastatin* (Zocor), compared with an average of about 40% with older statins, such as lovastatin, pravastatin and *fluvastatin* (Lescol). The newest, strongest statin, *rosuvastatin* (Crestor), is also the riskiest. There have been reports of rhabdomyolysis, kidney damage and kidney failure in some patients. I recommend it only if no other drug lowers cholesterol adequately.

If you do need a significant reduction in cholesterol, particularly if you currently have heart disease or risk factors, one of the high-potency statins makes sense. Zocor is available in generic form and can be used as a less expensive alternative to Lipitor.

For a more modest reduction, you may well consider an older, less powerful drug. Lovastatin or pravastatin are particularly attractive choices if cost is a factor—since they are available in generic form and cost up to four times less than the other statins.

Statin Helper

Boost the effect of cholesterol-lowering statins by adding a B vitamin.

New finding: Taking 1 g of Niaspan ER, a prescription formulation of the B vitamin niacin, boosted HDL "good" cholesterol levels by 21% in patients taking a statin. This is the first study to show that the combination therapy can have benefits over taking a statin alone.

Self-defense: If your HDL level is lower than 40 mg/dl (for men) or 50 mg/dl (for women), ask your doctor about prescription niacin.

Allen J. Taylor, MD, director, cardiovascular research, Walter Reed Army Medical Center, Washington, DC.

Never Pay Full Price For Medicine Again

Marvin D. Shepherd, PhD, director of the Center for Pharmacoeconomic Studies and professor and chair of the Pharmacy Administration Division at the College of Pharmacy, University of Texas, Austin.

Although the increasing costs of drug development continue to drive drug costs up, most people can save *at least* 50%.

Secret: Smart shopping, plus inside information on how to get the most medication for your money.

Whether you pay for drugs out-of-pocket or have drug coverage, here's the top money-saving advice...

PRICE SHOP

Prescription drug prices can vary by 25% or more from one pharmacy to the next. Don't assume that big chains have the best prices. Some smaller pharmacies scout out the cheapest drug wholesalers and pass the savings to consumers.

Smart idea: Price shop via phone. Call in the evening or weekday afternoons when pharmacists are typically less busy.

BUY ON-LINE

You can save anywhere from 20% up to 50% buying drugs from on-line pharmacies, which have low overhead costs. It's a smart strategy for patients with chronic conditions, such as arthritis or high cholesterol, who use large quantities of the same drugs over time.

For computer users, the most reliable on-line pharmacies include Medco, *www. medco.com*, and Drugstore.com, *www.drug store.com*.

Important: Buy only from on-line pharmacies that display the Verified Internet Pharmacy Practice Site (VIPPS) seal. The seal means that the company has been inspected and accredited by the National Association of Boards of Pharmacy. Also, avoid on-line pharmacies that don't require a prescription. This is a sign that the company may be foreign or sells drugs illegally.

REQUEST OLDER DRUGS

Doctors don't admit it, but they're just as likely as patients to be influenced by slick drug marketing campaigns. Studies have shown that doctors are more likely to prescribe new drugs than older ones—even when there's clear evidence that the older drugs are just as effective and much less expensive.

Example: Millions of Americans with osteoarthritis switched to Cox-2 inhibitors, such as *celecoxib* (Celebrex), when these drugs were introduced. For most patients, Cox-2 inhibitors are no more effective than aspirin, acetaminophen or ibuprofen. Now studies show that these drugs may even increase risk for heart attack or sroke. What's more, a single dose of Cox-2 inhibitor might cost more than $2, compared with pennies for aspirin.

Smart idea: Ask your doctor to write prescriptions for older, less-expensive drugs unless there's a compelling medical reason to take a newer medication.

GENERIC DRUGS

The average price of a brand-name prescription for 2007 was $119.51, compared with $34.34 for a generic, according to the National Association of Chain Drug Stores.

If your doctor prescribes a specific brand-name drug, your pharmacist is permitted under state law to substitute a less-expensive generic.

To find out if a generic is available: Go to the FDA's Web site, *www.fda.gov/cder*, for a list of all FDA-approved drugs and generic equivalents. Or use a drug reference book, such as the *Physicians' Desk Reference* (Thomson) or *The Pill Book* (Bantam), available in bookstores and libraries.

MEDICARE DRUG COVERAGE

Everyone with Medicare coverage is now eligible to join a Medicare prescription drug plan and get insurance, which covers both brand-name and generic prescription drugs. For more information, visit the Medicare Web site at *www.medicare.gov* or call them at 800-MEDICARE.

BUY IN BULK

Check with your insurance plan to see if you can get a 90-day supply of your medications. You may be able to save the co-pay charges and dispensing fee charges.

Caution: Buy drugs in bulk only if you've already been taking them and know they work for you.

SPLIT PILLS

You can double the quantity of the doses in a single prescription by getting a higher-strength tablet and using a pill splitter to cut the pills into halves. A 100-milligram (mg) tablet often costs about the same as a 50-mg tablet of the same drug.

Important: Capsules cannot be split. Pills that have enteric coatings or other time-release mechanisms also should not be split. Ask your doctor or pharmacist if the pills that you take can be split.

Do *not* use a kitchen knife to split your pills. Use a pill splitter, sold in pharmacies for about $5.

Examples: EZY Dose Tablet Cutter and Deluxe Pill Splitter.

How to Get Drugs Not Yet FDA Approved

Medicines that have not yet been approved by the US Food and Drug Administration (FDA) may be available for patients who demonstrate real need. The patient's doctor has to recommend the patient, and the drug has to be in the human-testing stage or beyond.

Find out about compassionate use programs, for conditions ranging from lung cancer to obesity, at drug manufacturers' Web sites or search at *www.clinicaltrials.gov.*

Charles B. Inlander, a consumer advocate and health-care consultant based in Fogelsville, PA. He was founding president of People's Medical Society, a consumer health advocacy group. He is the author of more than 20 books, including *Take This Book to the Hospital with You.* St. Martin's.

Free Family Health History Tool

Your family's medical history may contain information that would be important to your doctor and to doctors who provide treatment to other family members.

New and useful: The US Surgeon General has devised a computer-based tool, *My Family Health Portrait,* which can be used to collect and organize a group health history focusing on illnesses that have a genetic tendency to run in families or that are of particular interest to the family.

The tool provides an organized printout that can be taken to a doctor. Until then, all information remains securely under the family's control on a home computer or saved to a disk if using an outside computer, such as at a library.

Visit *www.familyhistory.hhs.gov.*

How to Get the Same Quality Care As Your Doctor

Christine Dumas, DDS, and Kevin Soden, MD, medical correspondents for NBC's *Today* show. They are coauthors of *Special Treatment: How to Get the Same High-Quality Health Care Your Doctor Gets.* Berkley.

It's a fact—doctors do receive better medical treatment. Our experience with the health-care system gives us a big advantage when it comes to finding first-rate physicians, getting the most accurate diagnoses and avoiding unnecessary risks. *You, too, can get the same superior treatment...*

HOW TO FIND THE BEST PRIMARY CARE PHYSICIANS

To find a top physician, be sure to follow these four steps...

•**Get names from other doctors—** your ophthalmologist, dentist, etc. Also, ask friends, neighbors, colleagues and nurses at your local hospital.

• **Cross-reference your list with physicians in your health insurance plan.** Doctors join and leave insurance plans all the time, so save the recommendations that you don't use for future reference.

• **Be sure the doctor you select is board certified,** licensed in your state and has no disciplinary actions against him/her.

Resource: www.docboard.org provides free background and disciplinary information, including links to state medical boards.

• **Schedule an appointment with the doctor.** He/she should perform certain tasks, such as listening to your chest with a stethoscope. Physicians who leave these routine but important procedures to a nurse or physician's assistant may have trouble making an accurate diagnosis.

The doctor should explain what he is doing and learning about you during the examination. He also should listen respectfully to what you are saying. He should not interrupt you or make you feel rushed.

HOW TO GET THE BEST TREATMENT

To ensure an accurate diagnosis and effective treatment...

• **Document symptoms so you don't forget.** Note them as soon as they occur.

• **Organize your thoughts.** Rambling on with vague complaints makes it difficult for a doctor to help you in the standard 15-minute office visit. Make notes ahead of time about what concerns you.

• **Be honest about pain.** Men especially tend to downplay pain, causing the doctor to underestimate the problem.

• **Use the term** *we* **when talking about your health problems,** as in, *What do you think we should do?* The distinction is subtle, but there's a psychological impact on your doctor when you make it clear that you are a team working together.

• **Ask the golden question—***If you or someone in your family had a similar problem, which medical options/treatments/ other doctors would you choose?* This will most likely prompt your doctor's honest opinion.

• **Compare treatments.** Doctors will often use *www.guidelines.gov*, compiled by the US Department of Health and Human Services and the American Medical Association. It provides guidelines for treating hundreds of conditions.

HOW TO APPROACH SURGERY

• **Select an experienced surgeon.** Look for one who often performs the procedure that you need. He is likely to have much lower patient complication and death rates.

Resource doctors use: www.healthgrades. com, which provides report card ratings on hospitals and doctors specializing in such surgeries as coronary bypass, hip or knee replacement and cosmetic.

Helpful: Your health insurance plan may limit your choice of surgeons. If your research reveals that an out-of-network surgeon is far superior, ask your primary care physician to write a letter to your insurer making a case for that surgeon.

• **Have a postoperative plan.** Surgeons often define their success as repairing the problem, but your goal is to get back to your previous state of health. Rehabilitation is particularly important after cardiac surgery and joint/orthopedic operations, such as those involving rotator cuffs, knees and wrists. Find out from your surgeon where he has sent other patients for rehab, and ask those patients for their opinions.

HOW TO HANDLE MEDICATIONS

• **Ask the doctor three questions about medications...**

• Does my age, sex, weight or height affect the standard dosage of this medication?

• What are the serious side effects of this drug, and what would need to be done to counteract those side effects?

• Could this medication interact with any other medications I'm taking?

Resource: *www.healthsquare.com* provides detailed information on hundreds of prescription medicines.

• **Choose one pharmacy to fill all your prescriptions.** Learn the pharmacist's name and, whenever possible, try to deal with him—not assistants—when you order a new medication. Pharmacists often are more experienced than doctors at spotting potential drug interactions and staying abreast of the latest studies and government warnings.

• **Never cut pills in half without checking with your doctor or pharmacist.** You may save money by asking for larger-dose pills and splitting them, but the medicine may not be uniformly distributed. Also, cutting pills that are coated to prevent stomach irritation or extend the release of medication can trigger adverse reactions.

THREE MEDICAL TESTS TO INSIST ON

• **C-reactive protein (CRP) test.** This test measures inflammation in the body. Men with high CRP levels have twice the risk of heart attack…women, four times the risk.

Recommended for: Anyone over age 35.

Cost: $50,* covered by some insurance plans. Ask your physician how often the test should be done.

• **Apolipoprotein (apo) test.** The amount of apo—tiny fat particles floating in your blood—is an accurate predictor of clogged arteries and of heart attack risk.

Recommended for: Anyone over age 40.

Cost: $80, covered by some insurance plans. Ask your doctor how often you should have this test.

• **Colonoscopy.** Colorectal cancer kills more people than breast or prostate cancer. A colonoscopy—in which a fiberoptic scope is inserted in the intestine—detects most polyps.

Recommended for: People age 50 and over, every three to five years.

Cost: $1,200 to $1,500, covered by most insurance plans.

*Prices may vary by doctor and location.

How to Get Your Doctor to Return Your Phone Call

Marie Savard, MD, an internist in private practice in Philadelphia and author of *How to Save Your Own Life: The Eight Steps Only You Can Take to Manage and Control Your Health Care.* Grand Central.

Why is it so difficult for some doctors to return patients' phone calls? Although returning calls is part of the practice of medicine, calls are a nightmare for physicians. Errors are more likely by phone than in face-to-face consultation. Doctors are rushed. They may not have the information they need to give the best advice. And few physicians are reimbursed for the time spent talking on the phone.

Advice on getting your doctor to return your phone call…*

• **Communicate your symptoms and concerns.** State your worst fear in a serious way—for example, you are worried about your sore throat because you recently were exposed to someone with strep.

Helpful: Write down what you need to say beforehand. If you are concerned about being able to express yourself adequately, consider having someone else speak on your behalf.

The most dangerous thing patients do is trivialize their own complaints. For example, saying that abdominal or chest pain may be merely indigestion. If the problem is perceived as only minor, you are less likely to be called back in a timely fashion. And don't make a tentative diagnosis or propose treatment. The more you sound like you need help, the more likely you will be called back.

• **Make the "gatekeeper" feel important.** The more you tell the front desk about your concerns, the better you will be served. Often a nurse will return your call instead of the doctor. If you still are concerned,

*If you suspect a serious health emergency—such as heart attack or stroke—call an ambulance or go to the emergency room. Don't wait at home for a callback from your doctor.

explain that you have lingering questions and would like the doctor to call you back as soon as possible.

• **Be persistent—but respectful.** Ask when the physician will call you back. If the seriousness of your problem does not appear to be understood by the receptionist or nurse, repeat your concern.

Reminder: Keep the phone line open when waiting for the callback. Otherwise, it may be another hour—or even another day—before you make contact.

Patients need to talk with their doctors about phone calls before problems arise. When are calls returned? Who generally returns them? Under what circumstances would a phone consultation work as well as an appointment? Are there situations in which payment for the phone consultation would be appropriate? An agreement to pay may prompt a quicker response. And the charge may be covered by insurance (check with your provider).

Another vital topic to work out up front is how to deal with the on-call doctor when your own physician is not available.

Example: When suffering from an asthma attack on a weekend, you may be shocked to hear that the covering physician will not refill the medication that had worked for prior attacks—nor will he contact your primary physician for confirmation of the prescription.

Doctors who are not familiar with callers are less likely to prescribe over the phone. If you have a chronic condition subject to flare-ups, ask your doctor in advance what to do—including how to get the treatment you need—when he is not on call.

High-quality medical care demands an active partnership between doctor and patient—but it starts with you.

Read This Before Having Outpatient Surgery

Charles B. Inlander, a consumer advocate and health-care consultant based in Fogelsville, PA. He was founding president of People's Medical Society, a consumer health advocacy group. He is the author of more than 20 books, including *Take This Book to the Hospital with You.* St. Martin's.

Very few areas in medicine have changed more radically in the last 20 years than the location where people go for surgery. More than 1,500 different surgical procedures that previously were performed only on an in-patient basis, including the removal of cataracts and colon polyps, now can be performed on outpatients who enter a facility in the morning and leave later the same day. Although outpatient surgeries are cheaper and often safer (largely because of significantly lower infection rates), a successful outcome typically depends on the type of outpatient facility you choose for your procedure.

Key points to consider...

• **Doctors' offices.** You are not paying the high overhead associated with a hospital or freestanding surgical center, so procedures performed in a doctor's office can cost up to 50% less than those in the other settings—but they come with greater risk. That's because doctors' offices are not accredited by any private or government oversight agency. In fact, under current state laws, any licensed doctor (physicians must be licensed by the state in which they practice) can perform just about any surgical procedure in his/her own office without getting any special approval. Because of this, insurance companies and Medicare may not pay for a procedure performed in a physician's office. Check to see if your insurer will pay for the procedure you need with the doctor you are considering. If not, ask the company for a list of offices that are approved for payment.

• **Freestanding surgical centers.** Often called "surgi-centers," these usually are a better choice than a doctor's office. These facilities, often independently owned by physicians or by entrepreneurs, tend to be better regulated. Most states require them to be licensed, usually by the state health department. That means they are inspected and must meet certain standards for safety, infection control and other quality-related factors. These centers also can be accredited by the Accreditation Association for Ambulatory Healthcare or the Joint Commission on the Accreditation of Healthcare Organizations. Although accreditation is voluntary for surgi-centers, it's smart to choose a facility that is accredited by one of these organizations.

●**Hospital-owned outpatient facility.** This generally is the best place to have outpatient surgery. Since it is a part of a hospital, it must meet the same regulatory standards and accreditation requirements as the rest of the hospital (even if it is not located at the hospital site). These standards and requirements are much more strict and comprehensive than for other settings. Unlike a physician's office or a surgi-center, hospital-owned outpatient facilities will collect important data, such as infection rates. Many hospitals now are making that information publicly available. Ask for the annual surgical and outpatient report. If it's not available, consider another facility.

How to Get VIP Treatment In a Hospital

The first thing an admitting clerk does when you're brought into a hospital is slip a plastic tag with an identity number onto your wrist. From that point on, like it or not, you are a number to most of the hospital staff.

Being a number instead of a name can be an awful shock. It means that you may be treated as if you have no identity—except for your symptoms, vital signs and medical treatment.

Fortunately, there are steps you can take to improve that treatment. And those steps, if successful, not only will make you feel more comfortable and human during your hospital visit, they could dramatically affect your state of health by the time you're ready to be discharged. In fact, it may be the issue that determines whether you leave alive or dead.

WHAT YOU CAN DO

Think of a hospital as a sort of huge, complex hotel—however, one that dispenses more than food, entertainment and lodging.

As you obviously know, a hospital dispenses both life-saving and life-threatening services. A moment's inattention at a hospital can lead to tragedy.

So how do you get the hospital to treat you like a person instead of a number?

In general, you've got to use the same techniques you use in other aspects of your personal and business life. The key word is assertiveness. That's not to say you should complain and be demanding—although, as you'll see, that may be necessary under certain circumstances.

FINDING THE RIGHT DOCTOR

The first step in getting VIP treatment in a hospital should be taken long before you're admitted—and that's finding a doctor who can provide the leverage you'll need. You want someone with more than an MD after his name.

Every community has a clique of doctors who have "political" clout. Usually these are physicians who serve on the local hospital's board of directors. Be aware, however, that a doctor with clout doesn't necessarily have the skills or any other attributes that make a physician a superior healer. Do you want such a person as your personal physician? Generally speaking, the answer is no, but there are exceptions. If you're satisfied that such a doctor can serve double-duty, so to speak, then you need go no farther.

THE DRAWBACKS

Aside from the possibility that such a doctor may be more expert in a boardroom than an operating room, there are other potential problems.

The most serious: He may be more interested in keeping his professional calendar and the institution's beds filled than in your welfare. Of course, there are ways to get around that. If he wants to admit you to the hospital for treatment, and there is any doubt in your mind about this decision, ask for a second opinion.

Generally speaking, it's always wise to get a second opinion for any complex medical procedure—and the likelihood is that the procedure he's recommending is relatively complex if he wants to hospitalize you. So by asking for a second opinion, you're not showing lack of faith in your doctor.

Caveat: However, we've heard of many instances where doctors are annoyed when a patient announces that he would like a second opinion. If you ever face a less-than-cooperative response to such a request, it would be prudent to seek out another doctor immediately. It's well within your rights to consult with as many physicians as you wish.

THE PERSONAL TOUCH

To guarantee better attention once you know that you're going to spend time in the hospital, make a date with the hospital administrator. He may or may not be a doctor—but in any case, he is a businessman, so you can be sure he speaks the same language as you. Introduce yourself. Tell him that you're a little concerned about your hospital stay and that you'd appreciate it if he'd take a personal interest in your case.

He'll get the message, and in all likelihood, he'll take steps to be sure that you're well cared for. Now that you've made your presence known, he will probably, out of courtesy, call the head of nursing and the admitting office and tell them you are coming to the hospital and that they should be expecting you. It's just such words, without pressure, that may make all the difference in the way you're subsequently treated.

ONCE YOU'RE IN THE HOSPITAL

Even if you've failed or haven't had the time to take the above steps, there are still things you can do to ensure good treatment, if not VIP treatment.

If you're not physically up to it, your spouse or a friend or relative may have to help you, but if you're feeling well enough, you can take the following steps yourself.

• **During the admission procedure,** ask what rooms are available. You may prefer a private room, or for the sake of company, you may want to share a room with someone else. If you do want to share, ask about your potential partner's medical status to be sure that you can deal with his illness.

• **After settling into your room,** ask to see the dietitian. Explain that you understand that the hospital is not a hotel, but within reasonable bounds, and limited by doctor's orders, there are foods that you do and do not like. Itemize them. If you present your request with tact, the dietitian will probably try to meet your reasonable requests.

• **Go out of your way to be polite to the nursing staff.** They are your lifeline—literally. If the nurses take a dislike to you, the recuperation period will not be smooth.

• **It's not tacky to provide small favors,** such as a box of candy, and even flowers, on each of the three nursing shifts. The 8 am to 4 pm, the 4 pm to midnight, and midnight to 8 am. Don't offer a gratuity until you're ready to be discharged. Nurses are professionals, and most would resent the offer. But if you received extra-special care from a nurse during your stay, a tasteful gift isn't inappropriate.

• **Make it clear that you'd like to know what medication or treatment is being given to you** *beforehand*. That will require a discussion with your doctor. Some doctors work on the premise that patients don't want to know too much, and so only provide information as it's necessary or if the patient specifically requests it.

WHY YOU SHOULD
WANT THIS INFORMATION

Unfortunately, mistakes are made now and then, but if you ask the nurse, "What are these pills?" or, "What exactly will you be doing to me?", and he/she has orders from your doctor to provide that information on request, then it gives the staff the opportunity to double-check what they are doing, and it gives you a chance to say, "Wait a minute!" if an obvious error is being committed.

HOW TO COMPLAIN

If you're not happy with your care, explain your complaint firmly and politely to the nurse. If that gets you no place, ask to speak to the head nurse. And if that fails, you may have to speak to either your doctor or the hospital administrator. Usually, when you reach that level, and you're not being unreasonable, steps will be taken to satisfy your complaint and resolve your problem.

How to Get Faster Emergency Medical Care

Harry Alberts, MSW, a certified social worker, formerly with the New York State Department of Health.

These days, most emergency rooms (ERs) are characterized by confusion and chaos. But inside knowledge of how the system works can get you better treatment.

First step: A triage ("sorting") nurse will assess the priority of your medical need. This person will look you over and then ask several questions. Be prepared to give your medical history succinctly and descriptively.

Planning: Before a medical emergency strikes, prepare a card that lists your medical history, including allergies or other chronic conditions and previous operations or serious illnesses. Keep it handy and, in an emergency, take it to the hospital.

Organize your thoughts so that you're able to describe, clearly and accurately, symptoms, time of onset and medications taken. Don't draw conclusions or give opinions unless you're a physician. And don't selectively omit information. If you have

breathing or bleeding problems, indicate these first, firmly and clearly.

Reason: Life-threatening conditions are given priority.

After seeing the triage nurse—and sometimes even before—you must make arrangements for payment.

Helpful: On your medical history card, include information about your medical insurance coverage, date of birth, Social Security number and the name, address and phone number of your employer.

For complex conditions: Go to a large teaching hospital.

Advantage: University affiliation…best-trained staff…advanced technology that most other hospitals can't afford to provide.

Hospitals in general, including teaching hospitals, come in three varieties: Private for-profit, private not-for-profit and government-run public hospitals.

Myth: Public hospitals are the worst… some are, in fact, excellent.

Advantage of for-profit hospitals: They're usually less crowded since they generally turn away those who can't pay. Private not-for-profit hospitals, many of which receive funding that obligates them to serve the poor, and public hospitals tend to be crowded. If you're a high-priority case and your public hospital is a teaching hospital, you may get the best care there.

Important: Location of a hospital…and contracts that it may have to care for special groups. Hospitals that receive admissions from "combat zones" or are convenient to public transportation are likely to have a crowded emergency room. Hospitals that have a contract to treat emergency cases from a local mental hospital, center for the retarded, prison or shelter are also apt to be more crowded…often with high-priority cases. A low-priority case, such as a broken arm, might be treated faster at a walk-in emergency medical center—where it would be a high priority.

Hospitals that take Medicaid and Medicare (almost all) are always more crowded in areas where few doctors accept these types of insurance.

Reason: People simply go to the ER in lieu of a doctor's office.

Especially crowded time in all ERs: Saturday nights.

Inside information: If you arrive at a hospital by ambulance, you will usually receive a higher priority, even if you could have gotten to the hospital without the ambulance. If your condition is serious enough that taking an ambulance isn't frivolous, it's a good idea to call one.

Best: Arriving in the hospital's own ambulance, because you then automatically become one of the hospital's patients...and its patients receive priority.

Caution: If your insurance company determines that an ambulance was not medically necessary, you could be stuck with a huge bill.

For the same reason, the ambulance of a local volunteer unit or fire district is a good choice. These people know the local ER personnel, and they are your neighbors. Contribute to their fund drives and post contribution stickers.

If your condition is very serious: Call the police—always dial 911. Police response with an ambulance—or transport by the police, if no ambulance is available—will facilitate matters at the hospital.

Helpful: Call the ambulance a *bus*, an inside term used by police. They may assume that you or a close relative is a cop and render service accordingly.

The Alzheimer's/TV Association

Risk of Alzheimer's disease increases by 30% for each hour of daily TV viewing. Watching TV doesn't cause Alzheimer's, but it is a marker of an inactive lifestyle, which can contribute to the disease. Both mental and physical activities enhance brain health and help to prevent diseases associated with aging.

Robert Friedland, MD, professor and chief of neurogeriatrics at Case Western Reserve University in Cleveland, and leader of a study of activity level and Alzheimer's incidence in 551 people, presented at the International Conference on Alzheimer's Disease and Related Disorders.

New Hope for Alzheimer's Disease

Alzheimer's may be slowed with cholesterol-lowering drugs. In one three-year study of 300 Alzheimer's patients, the disease progressed more gradually (loss of 1.5 points in a 30-point mini mental status cxam, or MMSE) in people who took a cholesterol-lowering drug than it did in those not taking the medication (loss of 2.5 points in MMSE).

Theory: High cholesterol levels increase the deposition of proteins, which can impair brain function.

Florence Pasquier, MD, PhD, professor of neurology, University Hospital, Lille, France.

12

Household Help

Best Ways to Accident-Proof Your Home

f you need motivation for making your house a safer place to live, take just a moment now to read over the surprising facts that are outlined below...

• **Home accidents cause about seven million injuries a year.** According to recent statistics from the American College of Emergency Physicians, about 28,000 of those accidents result in death.

• **Falls are by far the most common of home accidents.** The cost of treating a hip fracture can exceed $30,000.

Additional incentive: Making your house safer can cut homeowner's insurance premiums and will almost certainly boost the value of the house if you decide to sell it. Safer homes also reduce the chance of guests having accidents (and subsequently suing).

Many home owners, however, are so accustomed to their houses that they overlook the areas where accidents are most likely to occur. Though eyesight deteriorates with age, for instance, we often don't fix safety problems at home because we get used to the layout and to obstacles being in familiar places.

To make your house safer, take a look at four key areas...

LIGHTING

The big problem with home lighting is that it's not always available when you need it.

Example: Entering the house at night.

Solution: A remote light switch that lets you turn on an inside light from your car or as you approach your house on foot. Or when you're in one room of the house, remote switches can turn on lights in another room.

Ella Chadwell, vice president of Life@Home, Inc., a home-safety consultancy based in Nashville, TN, that provides information on home accident prevention and also markets products for home safety, particularly for the senior market (800-653-1923, *www. lifehome.com*).

Remotes work at a maximum distance of approximately 50 feet and operate much like a TV channel changer.

Remote light switches are available at most large hardware and home-appliance stores.

Typical price: $30 to $50. They're not difficult to install, but if you need assistance, hire an electrician.

Other areas where lights are often not available when you need them...

•**Bedrooms.** There may be a strong overhead light and a table lamp with a bright bulb. But the lights are useless if one of them can't be turned on easily when you get up in the middle of the night.

Solution: Install a low-wattage night-light that will stay on throughout the night. These typically cost about $3 to $10 and plug directly into wall sockets.

Alternatives: Install a remote switch, and keep the transmitter within reach. Or install a touch sensor on the table lamp. Touch sensors are devices placed between the lightbulb and socket, making it possible to turn on the lamp by touching any part of it. They usually cost less than $25.

The advantage is that you can turn on the lamp without the risk of knocking it over by fumbling for the switch.

In case of power failures, also keep a flashlight within reach of the bed, and check the batteries at least once every six months.

•**Halls, stairs and large rooms.** Be sure to have light switches at both ends of stairs and hallways. In rooms with multiple entries, install switches close to each door.

Typical price: About $125 each, installed, depending on the type of light switch and the rate that electricians charge in the area where you live.

•**Porches.** Install motion-sensor lights that automatically go on when they detect motion within about 30 feet. They reduce the chance of tripping over porch steps and have the added advantage of deterring intruders.

Typical price: Approximately $50, plus cost of installation.

In addition to lights, make sure that handrails are in good repair on porches and stairs. (Strangers, such as the mailman or delivery people, who come to your door might sue if a faulty handrail causes an injury.)

BATHROOMS

You can cut the risk of accidents by spending thousands of dollars on a relatively new type of bathtub and shower designed so that you enter through a low door instead of climbing into it.

But unless you can't step over the side of the tub, there are simpler and much less expensive solutions...

•**Install one or two "grab bars" to hold on to when stepping into the tub.** Also install one near the toilet area, because it is easy to slip as you sit down. A stainless steel grab bar 1.25 inches in diameter typically costs $125 to $150 installed.

Today, grab bars are becoming popular in homes with children. That means if you sell your house, these devices may make it more attractive not just to seniors but to younger buyers as well.

•**Put a nonskid surface strip in the tub and/or shower area.** Nonskid strips usually cost less than $25 and last at least two years.

•**If you replace an old bathtub,** get a new one with a slip-resistant surface.

FLOOR COVERING

Loose rugs and carpets are especially dangerous because they're easy to grow accustomed to. If you've tripped harmlessly over a loose section of carpet, for instance, you are likely to be on guard against doing it again—until, perhaps, you're groggy from medication or distracted by a noise.

Myth: Carpeting is safer than wood flooring because, if you fall on a carpet, the injury won't be as severe.

Reality: Any fall from a standing position can be severe, particularly for older people.

As a general rule, natural wood creates the safest floor as long as it's not coated with a slippery finish. Low-pile carpeting is also generally safe except when there are bulges caused by improper installation. High-pile carpeting might look luxurious, but it often causes people to trip or lose their balance.

If you want an area rug instead of carpeting, put a slip-resistant mat under it. Secure both the rug and mat to the floor with carpet tacks. Slip-resistant mats usually cost about $3 to $4 a square yard.

Double-sided adhesive tape can also secure rugs to a floor, but frequent wear and temperature changes often cause it to come loose after a year or so.

WALKWAYS

When you clean house, get in the habit of moving electrical cords from lamps, computers, etc., far away from any area where people walk. If a cord is in an area with frequent traffic, tack it down out of the way.

Other items in pathways are often more difficult to spot because, as with poor lighting, home owners often get accustomed to them.

Examples: A pile of magazines on the floor in the den, an oversized coffee table in the living room, the dog's feeding bowl in the middle of the kitchen.

Smart move: Ask a friend or relative to walk through your house once or twice a year to spot obstacles that might be a hazard—especially at night or to guests who are unfamiliar with the house.

You might try teaming up with one or more neighbors so you can spot-check each other's houses, not just for cluttered walkways but for other hazards.

Home Maintenance— A Month-by-Month Guide

Danny Lipford, host of the nationally syndicated program *Today's Homeowner with Danny Lipford* and home-improvement expert for the Weather Channel and CBS's *The Early Show.* Based in Mobile, AL, he has worked as a remodeling contractor for nearly 30 years and has renovated more than 3,000 homes. His Web site is *www.dannylipford.com.*

Invest a few hours each month, and you can keep your house looking great and avoid expensive repairs down the road. *Here's my smart home owner's maintenance calendar...*

JANUARY

This is a good time to address some interior issues...

• **Start a to-do list.** Walk through your home, jotting down projects and maintenance problems you notice or that have been on your mind. Carry a screwdriver and a can of machine oil so you can immediately take care of minor issues, such as loose door handles and squeaky hinges.

• **Declutter your closets.** Throw away anything you don't need. Buy additional shelves, hooks and boxes to organize everything that remains. *Next:* Declutter the laundry room, another often disorganized, small space.

• **Consider your flooring.** January is a slow month for carpet sellers and floor refinishers, so it is a good time to get a deal on a replacement or spruce-up.

FEBRUARY

Tackle more indoor tasks before the warmer weather arrives...

• **Examine bathroom and kitchen caulking.** If you find gaps between the tub or shower and the floor and walls, or between the countertop and backsplash, recaulk.

• **Check under sinks and around toilets and showers for signs of leaks.** Also repair dripping faucets—if you don't know how, a local handyman may do the job at about half the price of a plumber. Save plumbers for bigger, complex jobs.

• **Call to have your central air-conditioning serviced.** Set up the appointment now for March or April to avoid the summer rush. The service will make sure that your compressor and air handler are working well and that the condensate drain is clear.

MARCH

Winter's ending. It's time to...

• **Search for peeling exterior paint.** Harsh winter weather can cause paint to chip, peel or flake, exposing wood to the elements. Touch up bare spots now to prevent moisture problems later. First, scrape and sand any loose paint, then prime and add at least one top coat.

•**Prep your lawn.** Apply a preemergent fertilizer to your grass in March (or as soon as the snow melts), and you'll have fewer weeds and healthier grass come April. A local nursery can recommend a fertilizer appropriate for your yard.

•**Examine the foundation.** Take a walk around the exterior and interior of your foundation (if accessible) in search of cracks. Small cracks should be filled with caulk and monitored to make sure they aren't widening. If you see large cracks, call a building contractor or structural engineer to inspect. Check cement walkways and driveways. If you find a crack, use a leaf blower to clear out debris, then seal with caulk made for your type of surface (asphalt, concrete, etc.). Use mortar only if the crack is more than a half-inch wide.

•**Replace the batteries in your smoke and carbon monoxide detectors** when you change the clocks for daylight saving time.

APRIL

Start your spring cleaning…

•**Wash your windows, both inside and out.** Also scrub the window frames and shutters. Replace storm windows and doors with screens.

•**Pressure-wash all outside surfaces.** Spray sidewalks, driveways, exterior siding, decks and fences. Pressure washers can be rented for $50 to $75 a day—split the rental cost with a neighbor.

Important: Sometimes high-powered pressure washers can damage siding and decks if used improperly. Read the unit's operating instructions carefully.

•**Test your underground lawn sprinkler system.** Monitor the system through a full cycle to make sure it survived the winter in good shape. Some sprinkler heads might need to be cleaned or adjusted.

•**Degrease your barbecue grill with a stiff brush and detergent.** Gas grills require disassembly to clean burners. Use a soap solution to check the regulator and hoses for leaks (see your owner's manual).

•**Clean and check gutters.** Remove leaves and other debris from gutters. If you find any cracks or leaky seals, clean the area and use a putty knife to apply a thick coat of butyl rubber caulk. When the caulk dries, flush out your downspouts with a garden hose. If the downspouts don't effectively divert the water away from your foundation, buy splash blocks and place one under each gutter downspout.

MAY

•**Make sure the dehumidifier is working properly** if you live where it's humid and your entire home isn't air-conditioned.

•**Vacuum window air conditioners,** then make sure there is no air leakage around them (use removable rope caulk if necessary) and they are operating properly.

•**Examine your deck for signs of deterioration.** Tighten screws and railing bolts, and hammer down any exposed nails. Clean and reseal wood surfaces. Also check patio furniture for rust. Scrub rusted areas with a wire brush, then prime and paint.

•**Check and repair weather stripping and caulking.** Gaps around your doors and windows inflate energy bills.

JUNE

Time to make some final preparations for the hot weather…

•**Change the filters at all air returns** of your air-conditioning system. While you're at it, vacuum out the cavity behind the filters.

•**If you have a fan in the gable end of your home to evacuate hot air from your attic,** make sure it is working. Confirm that the turbine vents spin freely. While you're in the attic, look for signs of moisture that might indicate the roof is leaking.

•**Hire a chimney sweep.** If you use your fireplace regularly, you should have the chimney cleaned at least every other year. The best time to schedule an appointment is early summer, when business is slow for chimney sweeps.

JULY

The month for outdoor projects…

•**Paint.** July is warm and relatively dry (in most regions), making it a good time for exterior painting projects.

•**Inspect your roof shingles.** If you don't want to risk climbing on your roof, use binoculars to carefully scan it for damaged and missing shingles.

•**Care for your garage door.** Tighten screws and bolts. Make sure the auto-reverse is working. Use a light grease recommended in the owner's manual to lube the rollers.

Important: Don't use a spray-on lube, which will sprinkle down on the car when you open the door.

AUGUST

August is the time to tackle those remaining outdoor projects or head inside if you've had enough sun...

•**Mend fences.** Replace broken or rotting boards. Repaint fences if necessary. Oil hinges on gates.

•**Trim bushes and shrubs around your house.** Your home has an increased risk of mold and mildew problems if you let plants grow within 12 inches of its exterior walls.

•**Clean your dryer vent system.** Disconnect the vent from the dryer and remove built-up lint. A leaf blower attached to the inside end of the vent can quickly clear it out.

•**Call to have your gas or oil furnace or boiler serviced.** It is best to set up the appointment before the cool weather comes. For forced-air furnaces, install a new filter every month during peak heating season.

SEPTEMBER

Summer's over. *Time to...*

•**Protect your firewood.** Cover your woodpile with a tarp, or move a winter's worth of wood into the garage or under an overhang, where it will stay dry.

•**Drain and refill your water heater.** Cleaning out sediment once a year will improve efficiency and extend the life of the unit. Check the manufacturer's instructions.

•**Clean bathroom exhaust fans and kitchen vent hoods.** Dust, dirt and mold can build up, reducing efficiency and air quality. Vacuum the fan assembly. Clean the grille and vent hoods with a mild detergent, and dry with a soft cloth. Never use abrasive cleansers.

•**Shut down dehumidifiers for the year.** Empty the reservoir completely, and wipe it down with a bleach solution to kill any mold growth.

OCTOBER

Cold weather's on the way...

•**Take in or cover outdoor equipment.** Clean and store the barbecue and patio furniture. Change the mower's oil, clean its blades and drain the gas. Call your town to find out about disposal points for the drained gas.

•**Test your snowblower.** Make sure that all winter equipment is working.

•**Drain your lawn sprinkler system.** Follow your system's winterization instructions. Also, store hoses and turn off the water to outside faucets, but leave them slightly open so that they drain.

•**Rake often.** Aim for every week or so when leaves are falling. If you wait until the end of the season, the job will be much harder, and your lawn will be starved for sun. Buy a leaf blower if raking is too hard on your back.

•**Service your generator if you have one.** Stock up on flashlights, candles, canned food and water in case of power outages.

NOVEMBER

Late-fall chores...

•**Tidy up your yard.** Trim plants, remulch gardens and rake up the last leaves to keep your yard looking nice through March.

•**Clean and stow lawn and garden tools.** Use a wire brush to remove any rust, and apply a thin film of oil to metal-on-metal surfaces.

•**Replace batteries in fire and carbon monoxide detectors.** Do this when you adjust clocks for the end of daylight saving time.

DECEMBER

Winter is here...

•**Make sure extension cords for holiday decorations that are used outside are rated for this use.** All outdoor lights should also be plugged into a ground-fault-interrupter (GFI) receptacle.

•**Add adhesive-backed nonskid strips to stairs and other dangerous areas,** because you will be indoors more. Keep walkways free of ice.

Secrets for a Perfect Lawn from the Boston Red Sox Groundskeeper

David R. Mellor, master groundskeeper at Fenway Park in Boston and author of *The Lawn Bible* (Hyperion) and *Picture Perfect: Mowing Techniques for Lawns, Landscapes, and Sports* (Wiley). He also has cared for grounds for the San Francisco Giants, the Los Angeles Angels at Anaheim, the Milwaukee Brewers and the Green Bay Packers.

If you think that you've lost the battle with your lawn, do not surrender! You can give your yard a first-class makeover without investing a lot of time or money. *Here are simple steps from David Mellor, master groundskeeper for the Boston Red Sox...*

•**Be wise when you fertilize.** Fertilizing your lawn is an important step, so do it at the right time—in the fall for cool-season grasses, such as Kentucky bluegrass and perennial rye...and twice (once in spring and once in early fall) for warm-season grasses, such as Bermuda grass. It's best to fertilize when the lawn is dry and water afterward. Use a rotary or broadcast spreader to apply the fertilizer. Ask your garden center to recommend a quality product for your area, and follow label directions carefully. Don't use a handheld crank spreader unless your lawn is small—it won't provide an even application.

Caution: Fertilizing too frequently can lead to explosive lawn growth, which may look great temporarily but will stunt growth over the long term. You'll end up with a shallow root system that won't be able to last through drought or other difficult weather.

•**Don't "scalp" your lawn.** Never cut more than one-third of the height of grass blades when mowing—if grass is three inches tall, cut no more than one inch.

Scalping harms the lawn's ability to support its own root growth. In general, you want grass to be at least three inches tall for the cool-season grasses or three quarters of an inch tall for Bermuda grass.

Tall grass retains moisture, so you will not need to water as often. Higher grass also shades the surface of the soil, minimizing the growth of weeds.

•**Water at dawn.** For the best results, water between 4 am and 7 am. If you water later, the water will evaporate quickly. There is no need to get up early—if you don't have in-ground irrigation, buy timers for your spigots.

•**Do not bag clippings.** I leave them on the field at Fenway Park and on my lawn at home. They release nitrogen into the newly cut grass, making your lawn healthier and more lush.

•**Check your lawn mower blade.** The Red Sox grounds crew checks the blade every week. For home owners, every month should suffice. The blade can become dull from use or be dented when the lawn mower rolls over branches and children's or pets' toys.

If your blade is dull, the tips of your grass blades will look gray and dried up. Disconnect your lawn mower's spark plugs, and remove the blade with a wrench. Place the blade in a vise, and sharpen with the beveled edge of a file, or get the blade sharpened at a hardware store or lawn center.

•**Test your soil.** A soil test will determine the levels of pH, phosphorus, potassium and organic matter in your soil, as well as the percentage of sand, silt and clay. The test will also tell you if your lawn's nutrients are unbalanced and explain what you need to add to your lawn.

Test soil every two or three years because its composition can change.

Best: Your local agricultural extension service, found in the blue pages of your phone book, can supply an inexpensive test kit with instructions on how to collect soil samples.

The Biggest Remodeling Mistakes Home Owners Make

Steve Gonzalez, a residential building contractor based in Fort Lauderdale, FL. Mr. Gonzalez is a frequent radio and TV guest and author of several books, including *Before You Hire a Contractor: A Construction Guidebook for Consumers*. Consumer Press.

Remodeling your house can make it more comfortable, more beautiful and more profitable when it comes time to sell. But modifying your house is tricky, and many well-intentioned projects turn into disasters. *Successful remodeling depends on avoiding the following pitfalls...*

***Pitfall:* Ignoring basic problems.** Time and time again I see home owners who want to spend money on remodeling when just repairs are actually needed. In a way, that's understandable. Guests aren't likely to look at your newly refurbished plumbing, and a beautifully remodeled kitchen is something to show off.

However, when you put the house up for sale, prospective buyers routinely hire an inspector who will look at the plumbing. If the inspector finds that the pipe fittings are too old and may soon need replacing, buyers may demand immediate repairs or a reduction in price.

Ignoring repairs can have more immediate consequences. A faulty roof, window or plumbing can lead to serious interior damage. Flooring and stairs that go without repairs can cause accidents.

Solution: Take care of any fundamental problems as you become aware of them. To find out about problems, hire an expert to look over the house.

Example: A building inspector from the local government authority that enforces housing codes. Inspectors often do this type of work on weekends or after regular office hours. When they work on their own, they don't report problems to the local government. The problems they find, however, may be ones that you want to tackle before considering remodeling—not just questions about windows, roofs and flooring, but also those dealing with the foundation, siding, woodwork and supporting beams.

To find an inspector, phone the city or county government and ask how to contact the appropriate department.

Cost: Less than $250, unless your house is unusually large or far out in the country.

Alternatively, consider using a retired contractor for an analysis (those still in business might have a self-interest in offering advice). You can often find one by phoning your county or state home builders association. Almost any contractor can tell you the name of the local association.

***Pitfall:* Making add-ons obvious.** Too often home owners add a room or raise a roof in a way that calls attention to itself—different materials or a different style from the rest of the house.

This becomes important when the house goes on the market—the remodeling job will detract from "curb appeal," either lowering the value of the house or keeping it on the market longer.

Solution: Tell the contractor that you want the new bedroom or sunroom, for example, to look as though it's part of the original house—in both style and materials. Consider hiring a designer or architect to draw up specifications for the contractor. This typically costs $2,000 to $10,000, but you're likely to recoup the expense when you sell the property.

Another safeguard: Ask prospective contractors if they've done similar types of projects in your area. Then check out the remodeling jobs to make sure they look like the quality you want.

There's no way, of course, to know exactly how a remodeling project will affect the resale value of your house. In fact, you rarely get back as much as you spend on remodeling. *But it helps to...*

• **Ask several real estate agents for their advice.** Agents know the local market and have an interest in providing accurate information in order to get your business later on.

•**Go to the Web site of *Realtor* magazine** (*www.realtor.org/rmomag.NSF*). The site lists typical remodeling costs and compares them with the value they will likely add to a house in their "Cost vs. value report."

Example: Replacing 1,250 square feet of old, low-grade siding with new, high-quality fiber-cement siding costs an average of $10,289 in the eastern part of the US, where the magazine says it typically increases the value of a house by $11,822. That's because fiber-cement siding resembles wood but is termite-resistant, durable and noncombustible.

In a more typical example, a home owner in the Midwest spends an average of $53,114 to remodel a basement with construction of a 20-by-30-foot entertainment area and a five-by-eight-foot bathroom. This major remodeling job usually adds only $38,767 to resale value.

***Pitfall:* Eliminating a bedroom. After the kids move out,** it's tempting to combine two bedrooms—or a bedroom and bathroom. That's a mistake because, as a general rule, the more bedrooms and bathrooms a house has, the easier it is to sell and the more it fetches.

If you're willing to accept that drawback, go ahead and combine bedrooms. But before you do, consider an alternative, such as adding on to an existing bedroom. The cost will probably be similar, and as long as the addition is in the same style as the rest of the house, the expanded bedroom will probably make the property more salable.

Two potential disadvantages: When you add on to an existing bedroom, you'll decrease the size of your yard. And, you may boost your property taxes because you've added square footage. Check with the local tax office that assesses property values.

***Pitfall:* Going with a fad.** Dark kitchens are the rage—dark flooring, dark stone countertops, dark wood cabinets and dark-colored appliances to match. In most parts of the country, all these can easily cost more than $80,000 for a 10-by-20-foot kitchen—much more, in fact, if remodeling includes top-grade granite countertops.

However, dark kitchens may be passé in a few years and depress the resale value of a house. A more immediate concern could be safety unless a home owner also installs additional lighting in a dark kitchen.

You don't have to avoid fads. Just be aware of the potential drawbacks before you start a remodeling project. If you have any doubts, wait awhile and see whether it's merely a fad or a long-term trend.

Example: Not long ago, fireplaces seemed to be a fad in South Florida, where they're rarely needed. But since then, fireplaces have become a common feature in Florida houses. They might not be necessary, but they add a coziness that home owners are likely to want for many years to come.

***Pitfall:* Overpersonalizing.** While fads are one trap, turning your house into a personal design statement can be another. We all like our homes to reflect our individual personalities, but it's easy to go too far.

Examples: Building a wine cellar or turning a bedroom into a library.

If you'll actually enjoy features like this—and as long as you understand that they limit the market for your house—go ahead and add them.

Better: Install personalized features in a way that lets future owners convert them back to a more traditional use. Instead of putting built-in shelving into a library, for instance, consider stand-alone cabinets that would be easy to remove if a buyer wanted to convert the room back to a bedroom.

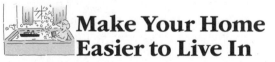# Make Your Home Easier to Live In

Laura N. Gitlin, PhD, director, Center for Applied Research on Aging and Health (CARAH), and professor, department of occupational therapy, Jefferson College of Health Professions, Thomas Jefferson University, both in Philadelphia.

More than one-third of adults age 65 and older struggle to perform one or more activities of daily living, such as bathing, climbing stairs, etc. Home designs and fixtures that work well for younger adults can cause problems for those with age-related health problems.

Possible result: An eventual loss of independence and, for many seniors, the need to move into a nursing home or assisted-living facility.

Good news: Most older adults can continue to live independently at home if they make simple changes that result in a safer, more comfortable place in which to live.

Example: Replacing round doorknobs with levers. They're much easier to manipulate for those with arthritic hands.

Extensive home renovations can easily cost tens of thousands of dollars—but in most cases, you can greatly increase home safety and convenience for less than $500, or for nothing at all.

Eliminating clutter is one of the best ways to prevent accidental falls in the home. If remodeling, consider installing additional closet and shelf space to hold knickknacks, extra clothes, etc. *Other important changes you might want to consider...*

BETTER LIGHTING

A senior needs about twice as much light to see clearly as someone in his/her 40s. Yet many homes are poorly lit, which makes it hard to perform daily tasks—and greatly increases the risk of accidents. *Important...*

• **Increase general, ambient light** by using ceiling fixtures with two to three bulbs of at least 60 to 75 watts.

• **Use plenty of task lighting**—under kitchen cabinets, on desks, next to reading areas, etc. Task lighting should shine directly on whatever you're working on. Use 100-watt bulbs for task lighting.

• **Arrange lamps to minimize glare** on tile floors and other hard surfaces. Glare can diminish depth perception, which increases the risk of falls and other accidents.

• **Use night-lights liberally** throughout your home so that you never have to move around in total darkness.

Important: Dust lamp shades and ceiling fixtures regularly. A thick layer of dust can significantly reduce lighting output.

SAFER BATHROOMS

Most home accidents occur in the bathroom—and a broken hip from falling is among the main precipitating factors that can result in a loss of independence and subsequent admission to a nursing home.

Bathing and using the toilet require substantial strength and balance. They're the two activities that often challenge seniors who have experienced functional changes, such as dizziness, or significant declines in muscle mass. *Helpful...*

• **Grab bars in the tub and/or shower.** They're among the best ways to prevent falls—and will give you something to hold on to should you start to fall. They add safety for everyone of any age or condition.

Important: There isn't a standard height for grab bars. Ask your doctor to recommend an occupational therapist. He will assess your strength, balance needs, etc., and determine the optimal bar placement based on your requirements.

• **Transfer bench/tub chair.** If you already are experiencing difficulty bathing or showering, the bench allows you to get into the tub by swinging your legs over the side, rather than attempting to stand and balance on one leg. The tub chair allows you to bathe while sitting, which also minimizes the risk of falls. A handheld shower device can be positioned on or near the tub chair.

• **Raised toilet seat.** If you have minimal leg strength or problems with balance, this type of toilet seat makes it easier to sit and stand. Raised seats typically add two to four inches of height. Some are placed over the existing toilet seat...others require removing the original seat first.

• **No-skid bath, floor and shower mats.** These are among the most important bathroom accessories—for all members of the family, not just seniors.

• **Reverse door "swing."** Have a carpenter change the bathroom door so that it swings out of rather than into the bathroom. That way, the door won't be blocked should you or a loved one slip and fall in the bathroom.

CONTRASTING COLORS

Seniors need more time for their eyes to adjust to changing light levels than when they were younger. Combined with other age-related eye changes, such as cataracts, this can make it difficult to distinguish shapes and objects with similar colors.

Example: White steps at the edge of a white tile floor can become almost invisible.

Solution: Use contrasting colors in high-risk areas. For example, don't put a white toilet against a white floor. The hardest floors to walk on safely are monochromatic ones, so go for patterns instead.

Examples: An alternating, checkerboard pattern...different-colored tiles or carpeting to signal transition areas, such as between a bathroom or hallway.

Important: Mark the edges of stair treads (the part that you walk on) so that they stand out. You can do this with a strip of aluminum/rubber, available at hardware stores. This can work even with carpeting. Another option is to have an electrician install lighting on stair risers.

Cost: About $26 to $130 per step, depending on type and style of lighting.

THE EASY KITCHEN

Bright light is a must in the kitchen.

Equally important: Cabinets and work areas should be set at comfortable heights. Older adults often suffer from osteoporosis, arthritis or other conditions that make it difficult to stand comfortably for long periods, or to reach cabinets and counters set at conventional heights. *What to do...*

• **Install upper cabinets a little lower than usual.** Instead of the usual 18 inches above the counter, have them placed at 14 inches or 16 inches. This makes it easier for people with shoulder pain and/or balance problems to reach what they need.

• **Make kitchen countertops a few inches lower** (most are 36 inches high). Or try removing a section of cabinet/countertop and replacing it with a 30-inch-high surface to allow you to work without raising your arms as high. The lower countertops will help when washing the dishes or cooking, if your stove is part of your counter.

Helpful: Place a stool in front of a lowered section of countertop and work while seated.

• **Set aside a section of countertop** for a microwave and other small appliances. They'll be easier to operate than if they're placed on an elevated shelf or suspended beneath cabinets.

• **Install a wall rack for pots, pans and utensils.** You can place it at a height that feels comfortable—as opposed to bending over to retrieve pans from lower cabinets.

Give Your Home The Look of Luxury Without Spending a Lot

Bill Keith, a remodeling contractor for 25 years in the St. John, IN, area and now host of the *Home Tips Show* on Chicago PBS-TV and radio stations. His Internet site, *www.billkeith.com,* offers free answers to remodeling questions.

You can make your home look more luxurious, even when you are on a budget. *Here are eight inexpensive items that can add elegance...*

INTERIOR

• **Ceramic tile flooring.** In entryways, hallways, kitchens and bathrooms, no flooring offers a more luxurious look per dollar spent than ceramic tile. Quality tiles typically cost $2 to $3* each, but home-improvement stores usually have discontinued or overstock tiles marked down to as little as 65 cents per tile. If you are handy, you can lay the tile yourself. If you aren't, installation typically is $2.50 to $3.50 per square foot.

Buy tiles that are at least 12" × 12" in size —big tiles make rooms appear larger. Neutral colors, such as beige, tan or taupe, never go out of style. Avoid white tile, which shows dirt and looks institutional.

*Prices subject to change.

• **New kitchen cabinet handles and knobs.** Give your kitchen a classy, fresh look. For timeless elegance, favor handles and knobs that have simple, clean lines and a brushed nickel finish. Prices start at $2 per piece at home centers.

• **Crown molding.** Adding molding where walls meet the ceiling brings an air of old-fashioned elegance. New polystyrene crown molding looks like wood, and do-it-yourself kits make it easy to install. Corners are premade, eliminating the need for a miter saw. Fill any gaps with painter's caulk before painting. A kit large enough for an average-sized room costs less than $200 at a home center.

• **Fresh coat of store-brand paint.** Despite what you may have heard, store-brand interior paint available at a reputable store is every bit as attractive and long lasting as a brand-name product. A five-gallon bucket starts at $30, about the cost of one gallon of designer paint.

Helpful: Home-improvement stores often offer free classes on techniques such as rag or sponge painting, which give walls a stylish, textured look. Or search the Web for "faux painting."

• **Off-brand overhead light fixtures.** For every designer lamp that costs $200 or more, there likely is an attractive imitation for much less. Because overhead lights are on the ceiling, no one is ever close enough to see that yours is made of plastic or plated metal. "Contractor packs" of four to six fixtures are available at big home-improvement stores for about $10 per fixture.

EXTERIOR

• **Entryway planter.** Put a large planter by your home's entryway. Use it to grow several plants, such as tall grass with ivy hanging over the side. Home stores sell large plastic planters that mimic limestone or terra-cotta for less than $50 each. Bigger is better here—it looks more luxurious. The planter should be at least 18 inches tall. Don't clutter your entryway with hanging plants or other small decorations.

• **Asphalt sealer.** Applying a coat of jet-black sealer to your asphalt driveway for about $100 to $200 (more for long driveways) makes your home look neater and more expensive.

If you have a concrete driveway, rent a pressure washer every year or two to remove grass stains and tire marks. A one-day rental costs $50 to $80. It shouldn't take more than a few hours to clean a driveway, so you may be able to split the cost with one or two neighbors.

• **Shutters.** Today's high-quality vinyl shutters look like wood and add a wonderful accent for about $35 a pair (installation averages an additional $50 per pair). They come prefinished in myriad colors. A good pair of wood shutters costs about $100 and needs to be painted or stained every six to eight years.

The color of your front door usually is the best color to select for shutters. If you would like to test a few colors, use a digital camera to take a picture of the front of your house, then print out a few copies. Using markers or colored pencils, draw in the colors you're considering. Post the pictures on the fridge, and see which you like at the end of a week. Don't waste money putting shutters on side or back windows—few people see them.

Restore Vinyl Siding

R estore vinyl siding's appearance with *Restora*. Vinyl is cleaned with a spray-on solution and scrub brush...then a revitalizer is applied, which goes on milky white and dries clear. Also works on vinyl shutters and doors.

Cost: About $270* for a 2,200-square-foot house if you do it yourself. You can restore about 16 shutters a day.

Information: Flood Company, 800-321-3444, *www.floodco.com*.

Home, 1633 Broadway, New York City 10019.

*Price subject to change.

Dangerous Toxins May Be Lurking in Your Home

Mitchell Gaynor, MD, clinical professor of medicine at Weill-Cornell Center for Integrative Medicine, and founder and president of Gaynor Integrative Oncology, both in New York City. He is the author of *Nurture Nature/Nurture Health: Your Health and the Environment*. Nurture Nature.

As long as you breathe, eat and drink, you cannot entirely escape environmental toxins. Research on the risks associated with these toxins is ongoing, but many scientists believe that existing evidence suggests that toxic buildup in our bodies contributes to the development of Parkinson's disease and may increase risk for some types of cancer and other serious conditions.

A Centers for Disease Control and Prevention study that tested 10,000 men and women for the presence of 116 chemicals, including *phthalates* and *dioxin*, concluded that most Americans carried some combination of these toxins in small amounts in their blood.

TOXICITY IN THE HOME

Household sources of toxins that are under investigation...

•**Home furnishings.** *Polybrominated diphenyl ethers* (PBDEs), the common ingredients in flame retardants that are used to treat upholstered chairs and sofas, foam mattresses and cushions, may be carcinogenic. PBDEs also may disrupt thyroid function and brain development.

What to do: When buying foam mattresses, upholstered furniture, etc., ask whether PBDEs were used during manufacturing.

•**Pressed wood and fiberboard,** which often are used in furniture and shelving, are common sources of *formaldehyde,* a gaseous compound that is used as a disinfectant. Formaldehyde has been found to be a probable carcinogen.

What to do: Look for solid-wood products or those carrying the seal of the American National Standards Institute (ANSI), which certifies that the item is low in formaldehyde emissions.

To find furniture and other products that are low in potentially dangerous chemical emissions, consult the Greenguard Environmental Institute, a nonprofit, independent organization that certifies low-emitting products, 800-427-9681, *www.greenguard.org.*

•**Cleaning products.** Most people utilize a wide variety of cleaning products and many of these do contain toxic chemicals. Chlorine bleach is potentially carcinogenic and can damage the respiratory system. Among its by-products are the *chlorinated hydrocarbons, chloroform* and *trihalomethanes,* all of which act like weak estrogens and can cause breast cells to divide more rapidly. These by-products have been shown to cause breast tumors in animals.

What to do: Use commercial cleansers that are free of chlorine and most chemicals. Seventh Generation and Sun & Earth are two brands that are widely available at health-food stores.

Or use natural cleaning alternatives—baking soda to scrub sinks, tubs and toilets... white distilled vinegar in a pump-spray bottle to clean mirrors and windows. If you really need to use chlorine-containing cleaners, make sure that the room is well-ventilated.

•**Pesticides.** Research has shown that pesticides increase risk for Parkinson's disease—and may be a cause of some cancers.

What to do: Use baits and traps instead of sprays. Try organic alternatives to toxic bug killers, including oil sprays, such as SharpShooter, an all-natural insect killer containing plant oils...Burnout II, a natural herbicide that contains vinegar, clove and lemon...and corn gluten meal, a natural weed killer. All of these products are available at most garden centers that carry organic products.

For more information on pesticides and other toxic household products, visit the Web site of Earth Share (a nationwide network of environmental organizations) at *www.earthshare.org.*

•**Cosmetics.** *Paraphenylenediamine,* which is found in some darker hair dyes, increases the risk for bladder cancer in humans, according to a finding in the journal *Carcinogenesis. Other toxic ingredients used in cosmetics…*

•*Phthalates,* typically used as a solvent and plastic softener, have been linked to cancer and to birth defects of the male reproductive system. They are found in many shampoos and other hair products, cosmetics, deodorants and nail polish.

•*Talc,* in talcum powder, has been linked to a 60% increase in the risk for ovarian cancer in women who use it in the genital area.

•*Propylene glycol,* an ingredient that's found in some moisturizing products and skin creams, is absorbed through the skin, and high levels may damage the kidneys and liver.

What to do: Read labels carefully. By law, cosmetic ingredients must be listed on the label, starting with those in largest amounts. Choose all-natural alternatives, such as products made with olive oil, safflower oil or oatmeal, whenever possible. Go to the Environmental Working Group's Skin Deep cosmetic safety database at *www. cosmeticsdatabase.com* to search more than 25,000 products for 50 definitive toxins.

SELF-DEFENSE

Antioxidants, such as vitamins C and E, are known to promote health by scavenging free radicals (harmful by-products of metabolism), which damage our cells and contribute to cancer and other diseases.

But antioxidants have another role that is possibly even more important in protecting against environmental toxins. The antioxidants stimulate an area of the DNA known as the *antioxidant responsive element* (ARE), which activates a gene that produces detoxifying enzymes. This is the body's way of breaking down carcinogens and other toxins.

In addition to commonly known antioxidant sources, such as brightly colored produce (carrots, beets, kale and tomatoes), make sure your diet contains…

•**Cruciferous vegetables,** such as cauliflower and brussels sprouts, which contain the potent enzyme inducer, *sulforaphane.*

•**Green tea,** an antioxidant source that is 20 times more potent than vitamin E, according to the American Chemical Society. Try to drink two to five cups daily.

•**Rosemary,** a source of *carnosol,* which has antioxidant and anticarcinogenic properties. Use rosemary in cooking, or drink one cup of rosemary tea daily.

•**Curry,** which contains curcumin and turmeric, two potent cancer-fighting herbs. Cook with curry three times a week.

Some Air Cleaners Can Be Unhealthy

In a recent study, some ionizing air filters expose users to high levels of ozone. Experts agree that exposure to ozone in excess of 80 parts per billion for eight hours or longer can cause coughing, wheezing and chest pain, and deaden the sense of smell. In a recent test, five ionizing room air cleaners performed poorly, and some emitted potentially harmful levels of ozone—Brookstone Pure-Ion V2, Sharper Image Professional Series Ionic Breeze Quadra S1737 SNX, Ionic Pro CL-369, Ioniz Air P4620 and Surround Air XJ-2000.

Best air cleaners: Friedrich C-90A and Whirlpool 45030—both effectively clean air and emit little ozone.

Mark Connelly, senior director of appliances and home-improvement department, *Consumer Reports,* 101 Truman Ave., Yonkers, NY, and leader of a test of five ionizing air cleaners, one electrostatic precipitator and one HEPA air cleaner.

No Room for the Car? Very Simple Ways to Organize Your Garage

Barry Izsak, president of the National Association of Professional Organizers, Austin, TX. He is author of *Organize Your Garage in No Time*. Que. His Web site is *www.arrangingitall.com*.

The garage is typically the most disorganized area in the home. A survey by Peachtree Consulting Group, a product development research company, found that 40% of people who have garages fill them so full of junk that they no longer have enough room for the car. *Here's how to organize even the messiest garage...*

BEGIN AT THE BEGINNING

The first step is to throw away, donate or sell anything that you don't need. Get rid of any broken items that you've been meaning to fix but haven't gotten around to for a year or more. *Also...*

• **Move from the garage to the attic or basement** the things that you can't bring yourself to dump but don't use more than once a year.

• **Group by category**—such as lawn and garden...sporting goods...tools...automotive supplies...barbecue accessories...children's toys...and bikes. Collect small items, such as nails and screws, in small bins and label the bins if they're not translucent.

• **Put items used most often near the garage door.** Anything used frequently— or used by young children—must be easily accessible, or it will never find its way back into its designated spot.

• **Recycle old dressers, kitchen cabinets, bookcases and filing cabinets.** They make great storage units in a garage. Or buy simple, inexpensive metal shelving units at home centers.

• **Hang pegboard from garage walls.** This time-honored solution is often overlooked by today's home owner. If your garage is unfinished, just nail the pegboard to the studs. If it is finished, first attach one-inch-thick strips of wood on top of the studs in the walls and attach the pegboard to them. The wood strips create enough space between the pegboard and the wallboards to insert hooks.

GREAT PRODUCTS

There are hundreds of products on the market to help you get organized. *My favorites...*

• **Bunjipegs** use straps of elastic cord and unique pegs to hold small items in place on a pegboard without hooks. A set of 40 pegs and 18 feet of elastic cord costs around $10 and can hold as many as 80 items in place. 800-871-8158, *www.leevalley.com*.

• **Sports Station** by Rubbermaid has a mesh basket for small sporting goods and racks for bats and other tall items. $19.99, *www.target.com*.

• **FastTrack,** an adjustable system of tracks and hooks, lets you hang garage clutter from the walls without pegboard. The FastTrack Supreme Garage Organization Kit lists for $129, or you can buy the components à la carte direct from Rubbermaid (866-271-9249, *www.rubbermaid.com*) or at the Home Depot.

• **Deluxe Tool Tower** storage unit holds long-handled items, such as shovels and rakes. $29.99, *www.target.com*.

• **The Grook Holder** is a simple yet effective device that hangs on the wall and uses nonslip rubber rings to grip rake and broom handles. It costs between $20 and $30, depending on the model selected. 800-841-4140, *www.casabella.com*.

• **Coleman's Tuff Duty** modular storage system looks great and has many of the features of high-priced systems, including quality cabinets and shelving. It is available at home products stores, such as Lowe's, for up to $198 per cabinet. *www.lowes.com*.

• **Whirlpool's Gladiator GarageWorks** has sleek, tough cabinets and other components. It comes with a 10-year-to-lifetime warranty, depending on the component. Prices range from $98 to $498 per cabinet. 866-342-4089, *www.gladiatorgw.com* (click on "Locate a Dealer").

• **GarageTek** is a top-of-the-line customized, adjustable garage organization system. It costs $5,000 to $10,000 for a typical garage, including installation by technicians. The system is made of a very durable thermoplastic. 866-664-2724, *www.garagetek.com*.

Relocating Know-How

Here are six ways to help you when you must relocate…

• **When relocating,** sell first, buy later. Rent a furnished apartment, and put your belongings in storage. This gives you time to hold out for a better price on the old house and shop for a new one.

• **Research the new area.** Talk to local residents, and check out neighborhoods.

• **Visit *www.schooltree.org*** for details about public schools nationwide.

• **Use a national bank,** so you don't have to close old accounts and open new ones.

• **Get change-of-address forms in on time** so you can stay up to date on bills.

• **Sign up for a cell-phone plan with unlimited in-network calling** so that family members who must stay behind to take care of unfinished business can be in contact without incurring high phone bills.

Money, Time-Life Bldg., Rockefeller Center, New York City 10020.

Looking for an Interior Designer?

To find an interior designer who best meets your needs, ask these questions during a phone interview before your first meeting: Do you have a signature style? Is my budget enough for what I want to do in my home? What should I bring when we meet? Are you willing to start with a smaller project…or do you always decorate the entire house? Are you willing to use my furnishings?

Home, 1633 Broadway, New York City 10019.

How an Air-Quality Expert Protects His Own Home…from Mold, Mites and More

Jeffrey C. May, principal scientist with May Indoor Air Investigations, LLC, an air-quality assessment company in Tyngsborough, MA, *www.mayindoor air.com*. He is author of three books on indoor environments, including *My Office Is Killing Me! The Sick Building Survival Guide* and *Jeff May's Healthy Home Tips: A Workbook for Detecting, Diagnosing and Eliminating Pesky Pests, Stinky Stenches, Musty Mold, and Other Aggravating Home Problems* (both from Johns Hopkins University).

Jeffrey May solves home air-quality and allergen problems for a living. He's also a lifelong allergy sufferer himself, as are his now-grown children. *Bottom Line/Personal asked May what he uses to improve the air quality in his own home…*

• **High-quality vacuum.** Most vacuums —even some expensive ones with high-efficiency particulate air (HEPA) filters—leak air while in use. Rather than collect dust and other allergens, these leaky vacuums actually churn up allergens and recirculate them throughout the home, reducing indoor air quality. Miele's HEPA Sealed System vacuums use high-quality filters and gaskets to dramatically reduce this problem.

Cost: $450* to $1,250, depending on the model. 800-843-7231, *www.miele.com*.

• **Dust mite covers.** Dust mites are microscopic organisms that thrive in warm, humid environments, such as bedding. A dust mite cover prevents mites from taking hold in your mattress—and kills dust mites that are already there by cutting off moisture. There are several varieties of covers on the market. The type I use—and the only

*Prices subject to change.

type that works reliably—is a plastic mattress cover. My choice is Allergy Control Products' Economy Mattress Encasing.

Cost: $39.95 to $61.95, depending on mattress size. A standard-size Economy pillow cover costs $12.95. 800-ALLERGY, *www.allergycontrol.com.*

If you don't like the feeling of sleeping on plastic, place a mattress pad over the dust mite cover. Wash and thoroughly dry this mattress pad every week or two to kill new dust mites. We also wash our blankets and quilts monthly and run them through the dryer on the regular setting every two weeks. Twenty minutes of drying should kill any dust mites living inside.

• **Leather couches and chairs.** Dust mites can infest fabric-covered couches and chairs, but they can't penetrate leather. All the chairs and couches in our home that we use regularly are leather. In less frequently used rooms, we have futon-style fabric couches, but we have encased the mattress portion of the futons in plastic dust mite covers, with the fabric futon covers over the plastic covers.

We also change our clothes immediately upon returning from places where we might have been exposed to pet dander, pollen or other allergens so that we don't contaminate our couches, chairs or beds.

• **Hot-water radiators rather than a forced-air duct system.** When you have a forced-air ventilation system, there's no way to know what's inside your ducts. Mold could be growing and spreading throughout the home whenever the system is used. Even professional duct cleaning is no guarantee that all allergens will be removed.

The only air-quality challenge presented by hot-water heat is dust building up on and behind radiators and/or baseboard units. We use a vacuum attachment called a flat crevice tool to remove dust from tight spots, such as behind radiators and refrigerators. Mid America Vacuum's 36-inch Exten-Vac Crevice Tool fits most vacuums.

Cost: $21, plus shipping. 800-649-7996, *www.vacuumstore.com.*

If you live in a home with a duct system, have the ducts cleaned at least once every five years. (Make sure the person you hire to do this cleans your coil and blower as well as the ducts.) In the summer, we use portable air conditioners, which we clean with a solution of one-third bleach and two-thirds water yearly. We also replace the filters every year. Use high-quality air-conditioner and furnace filters with a Minimum Efficiency Reporting Value (MERV) no lower than eight. If you have serious allergy issues, use filters rated at least 11.

• **Hardwood floors.** Carpets collect dust and other allergens, and not even the best vacuum can remove them all. For people like me who suffer from severe allergies, switching from carpets to wood or tile floors can be like flipping a switch from chronic bad health to good. That's particularly true in the winter, when we spend more time inside with the windows closed.

We do have a few small rugs in our home. They are synthetic, not wool or cotton, and I subjected each of them to a sniff test at the store before I brought them into my home. I put my face close to the carpet and inhaled deeply. If I didn't experience any allergic reaction, I purchased the rug.

• **Dehumidifier in the basement.** The relative humidity in our basement was above 50%, creating the risk of mold and mildew growth. I measured the humidity with a hygro-thermometer. Extech (781-890-7440, *www.extech.com*) makes good ones, ranging from $30 to $60. Don't buy a cheap one—it won't be reliable. I then purchased a Therma-Stor Santa Fe dehumidifier, and we keep it set to lower our basement's relative humidity level below 50%. Therma-Stor makes the most powerful and reliable dehumidifiers on the residential market.

Cost: $975 to $1,375, depending on the model. 800-533-7533, *www.thermastor.com.*

I attached the dehumidifier to a condensate pump, a device available in hardware and home-goods stores for around $50. The condensate pump automatically transfers water collected by my dehumidifier to a sink in the basement.

• **Face mask when I travel.** I carry a face mask with me so that when I start to feel allergy symptoms, I can put it on. I use an N95 mask made by 3M, available in hardware stores.

Cost: About $20 for a box of 20.

Cleaning Out Your Closet? Where to Donate Unwanted Items

Daniel Borochoff, president, CharityWatch.org, Chicago, a charity watchdog and service that helps donors make better giving decisions.

Most people know that they can give unwanted items to Goodwill and the Salvation Army, but there are other, smaller charities that make use of specific items, including...

• **Children's and teen's books.** *Reader to Reader* (413-256-8595, *www.readertoreader. org*) gives them to schools and libraries.

• **Prescription eyeglasses.** *Give the Gift of Sight* (513-765-6000, *www.givethegiftofsight. com*) sends used glasses to developing countries. Drop them at LensCrafters, Pearle Vision, Sears Optical, Target Optical, BJ's Optical or Lions Club.

• **Cell phones and rechargeable batteries.** *Call2Recycle* (877-273-2925, *www. rbrc.org/call2recycle*) refurbishes and resells them, and part of the proceeds goes to the Boys and Girls Clubs of America and the National Center for Missing and Exploited Children. *Drop-off sites include:* Stop & Shop, Radio Shack, Home Depot, Lowe's and Sears.

• **Coats.** *One Warm Coat* (877-663-9276, *www.onewarmcoat.org*) distributes outerwear to those in need.

• **Musical instruments.** *Hungry for Music* (202-674-3000, *www.hungryformusic.org*) distributes used musical instruments to underprivileged children.

• **Computers.** *National Cristina Foundation* (203-863-9100, *www.cristina.org*) gives laptops, desktops and printers to charities, schools and public agencies.

• **Business clothing.** *Career Gear* (212-577-6190, *www.careergear.org*) provides clothing for job interviews to low-income men. *Dress for Success* (212-532-1922, *www. dressforsuccess.org*) does the same for women.

• **Gowns and shoes.** *Fairy Godmothers Inc.* (215-675-9391, *www.fairygodmothersinc. com*) gives dresses and shoes to needy high school girls for their proms.

• **Luggage.** *Suitcases for Kids* (*www.suit casesforkids.org*) gathers luggage for foster children who move from home to home.

Electrical Outlet Warning

Outlets with ground fault circuit interrupters (GFCIs) may need to be replaced if they are 10 or more years old. GFCIs, the outlets with "test" and "reset" buttons, are designed to prevent electrocution. The circuitry in older GFCIs may no longer protect.

Solution: Most hardware stores carry GFCI testers, which will tell you if an outlet needs to be replaced.

Cost for a tester: About $10.

The Family Handyman, 2915 Commers Dr., Eagan, MN 55121.

When Looking for A Repair Person

Money, Time-Life Bldg., Rockefeller Center, New York City 10020.

You don't need to break the bank on home improvements. *To get a good price from a repair person, here are some helpful hints...*

•**Ask a friend for a referral**—a company is less likely to overcharge the friend of a good customer.

•**During your initial phone call, explain what's broken**—this helps to narrow the scope of the repair.

•**Tell the repair person** if there has been a history of problems with this appliance.

•**Ask if you can try to fix it yourself**—sometimes a repair person will tell you how to make the repair, particularly if he/she is busy.

•**Ask about the company's rates and if there is a minimum charge**—most companies have a base charge of $50 to $100, plus an hourly rate.

•**Offer to e-mail a photo of the problem**—this may save you the cost of a visit if the repairman is the wrong person for the job.

•**Offer to buy the supplies yourself**—you could save yourself the 20% markup and the hourly rate for shopping time.

Safeguard Your Home Against Hidden Health Hazards

Alfred Moffit, senior project manager, Environmental Waste Management Associates, LLC, a full-service environmental consulting company that tests soil, air and water quality, Parsippany, NJ.

Buy a home that has hidden health hazards, and you could lose your life savings to a massively expensive cleanup. Ignore the problem, and you might be the target of a lawsuit by a neighbor or the home's next owner. Also, as time passes and environmental regulations tighten, problems may become even more expensive to fix.

Here are five major environmental risks and what to do about them...

UNDERGROUND OIL TANKS

Buried fuel tanks often leak as they disintegrate. Tank removal can cost $1,200 to $2,000, depending on the size and where the tank is located. Fixing a significant leak that impacts soil and ground water can cost you $50,000 or more. If neighbors test their well water and discover that it is contaminated because of your leak or there are oil vapors in their home, you can be sued.

The only clue that a tank is leaking is a dramatic, unexplained increase in your heating bills or a heating failure due to water entering the system.

Helpful: Some homeowner's insurance policies cover cleanup costs. Some insurers and tank-installation companies sell tank insurance. Or check with your state's department of environmental protection—it might have programs that help pay for cleanups.

Example: New Jersey has a "Petroleum Underground Storage Tank (UST) Remediation, Upgrade and Closure Fund."

•**Home sellers.** To expedite a sale, present contractor certification from your town which proves your tank has passed a pressure test to detect leaks...or the permit documentation that a former owner removed or properly buried a tank and filled it with sand.

•**Home buyers.** The purchase should be contingent on removal of a buried oil tank or passing of a pressure test.

Cost of a pressure test: About $400 to $500.

ASBESTOS

Homes built before 1980 may have asbestos fibers in floor tiles, pipe insulation, roof material, sheetrock—even caulking. Asbestos can cause potentially lethal lung diseases, including asbestosis, mesothelioma and lung cancer. Professional removal costs up to several thousand dollars, depending on the amount of asbestos that's present.

You might not need to act. As long as the asbestos-containing tile or insulation is intact, there's no immediate health risk. If items containing asbestos begin to deteriorate and must be removed, hire a licensed asbestos abatement contractor.

• **Home sellers.** Disclose to potential buyers that you have removed asbestos and whether any asbestos remains.

• **Home buyers.** If the home was built before 1980, make the deal contingent on an asbestos test.

Cost: About $750.

LEAD PAINT

Homes built before 1978 usually have lead paint on walls, doors, trim and window frames. Lead in paint chips or dust can cause developmental problems in children. And, in adults, it can cause anemia, kidney damage, sterility and damage to the central nervous system.

If lead paint is in good condition, it usually is sufficient to paint over it.

Caution: Repainting is less effective on the edges of doors and windows. It might be necessary to remove lead paint from these high-wear areas. Sanding kicks up a huge amount of lead dust, so it's best to hire licensed lead abatement professionals if the paint is flaking throughout the home.

Cost: Up to several thousand dollars, depending on the extent of contamination.

• **Home sellers.** You must disclose the presence of lead-based paint in a home that was built before 1978.

• **Home buyers.** If a seller claims not to know about the existence of lead-based paint, be sure to make the deal contingent on a lead paint inspection.

Cost: About $400 to $700, depending on the home's size and age.

UNDRINKABLE WATER

Nonpotable well water can dramatically affect quality of life—not to mention a home's resale value. Many water-quality problems can be corrected with a contaminant filter, which costs from a few hundred to several thousand dollars, plus monthly maintenance fees. Culligan (800-285-5442 or *www.culligan.com*) is one popular filter company. If the problem cannot be corrected, it might be necessary to drink only bottled water.

• **Home sellers.** Few states require sellers to test well water, but if you know of a problem, you should inform buyers.

• **Home buyers.** Make the purchase contingent on a water-quality test by an environmental firm.

Cost: About $350 to $500.

RADON

This naturally occurring radioactive gas is linked to increased risk of lung cancer. Homes sometimes have dangerous levels of this colorless and odorless gas in the basement or on the first floor when there is no basement. The problem can be alleviated with a venting system, but retrofitting one into an existing home can cost up to $10,000, depending on the size of the house and the concentration of radon.

• **Home sellers.** You can present proof that your home has a safe level of radon. However, the buyer probably will perform his/her own inspection. Most mortgage lenders require that this test be done.

• **Home buyers.** A home inspector can test for radon for as little as $50. Do-it-yourself tests are available in home stores, but follow instructions to make sure that the house is "sealed" properly. A reading of more than 4 picocuries per liter of air means that action is required.

Cheap and Easy Ways to Cut Your Home Energy Bills

Harvey Sachs, PhD, director of buildings program, the American Council for an Energy-Efficient Economy, Washington, DC, a nonprofit organization that promotes energy efficiency, *www.aceee.org*.

You can easily shave hundreds of dollars off your energy bills next winter by taking a few no-cost and low-cost energy-saving steps.

SAVE ON HEATING BILLS

Furnace and fans...

•**Use ventilating fans in the kitchen,** bath and other areas prudently. In just one hour of use, they can pull out a houseful of warm air.

•**Check furnace filters monthly and clean or replace filters.** Dirty filters block airflow, increasing your energy bill and shortening the equipment's life.

•**Clean registers, baseboard heaters and radiators with a damp rag** or vacuum cleaner about once a month. Don't block them with furniture, carpeting or drapes—leave at least a few inches of space.

Thermostats...

•**Set your thermostats to the lowest comfortable level**—a good target is 65°F during the day and 60°F for sleeping.

•**Turn your thermostats down to 55°F in little-used rooms** if the system includes multiple zones.

•**Install a programmable thermostat** that you can set to lower the heat to 55°F when you are not at home.

Cost: About $35 to $100 for certified Energy Star (*www.energystar.gov*) models. (Energy Star is a government rating program—it shows which items are more efficient than typical models.)

Windows and doors...

•**If you have old single-pane windows, add storm windows.** They can decrease heat loss by 25% to 50%. For a quick, temporary fix, insulate your windows with plastic sheeting, sold for this purpose in home-supply or hardware stores, taped on the inside. Or replace single-pane windows with Energy Star–qualified windows. An Energy Star–qualified window has at least two panes and a low-emittance (Low-E) glass coating, and some have odorless, nontoxic gases, such as argon or krypton, between the panes to improve the insulating property of the window.

•**Seal up your windows and doors with weather stripping** if there are air leaks.

Ducts...

•**Use mastic (a gooey substance that will not degrade or shrink and is applied easily with a paintbrush) to seal seams and gaps** in all exposed ductwork in areas such as the attic, crawl space and basement. The mastic seals the joints and protects against warm air loss. If your pipes are not already insulated, add preformed pipe insulation that can be cut to fit your hot water and steam pipes.

•**After sealing, insulate ducts** that are in the attic and crawl spaces. Duct-wrap insulation is available at home-supply and hardware stores.

Other helpful things to do...

•**Keep draperies and shades on south-facing windows open** during the day, to admit solar heat, and closed at night to reduce heat loss and keep you from feeling chilly.

•**Keep the damper closed on your fireplace when not in use.** Use fireplaces sparingly—they suck heat from the house and send it up the chimney.

•**Consider buying a small electric space heater** that's approved by Underwriters Laboratories Inc. (*www.ul.com*)—with the UL symbol—to supplement inadequate heating in a room.

SAVE ON ELECTRIC BILLS

Appliances...

•**When using the washing machine and dishwasher, do only full loads.**

•**Clean out your dryer's lint filter after every load** to improve air circulation.

•**In the winter, circulate the warm air** that would otherwise stagnate at the ceiling, using a ceiling fan with the blades moving in reverse.

Lighting...

•**Energy for lighting accounts for about 10% of your electric bill.** Incandescent lightbulbs are out of date—95% of the power used to light them is wasted as heat (and they add unwanted heat to your home in the summer).

Substitute the five most used lightbulbs you have with Energy Star compact fluorescent bulbs. These are four times more efficient than incandescent bulbs and provide the same light levels. As other bulbs burn out, consider replacing them with compact fluorescents.

• **Use timers and motion detectors** on both indoor and outdoor lighting.

• **Maximize the power of daylight by keeping window shades and blinds open during the day,** and consider light wall colors to minimize the need for artificial lighting.

Water use…

• **Wash clothes in cold water.**

• **Take a quick shower instead of a bath.**

• **Install low-flow aerating showerheads,** which cut water use in half.

• **Check the temperature on your water heater**—it should be turned to "warm" —a thermometer held under running hot water should show a reading of no more than 120°F.

• **Hot-water tank insulation wrap costs about $20 and helps hold heat**— it will pay for itself in about one year. (This is not as important on very new, highly insulated models.)

• **Add preformed fiberglass pipe insulation to hot-water pipes** coming out of your water heater.

• **Turn off everything not being used** —lights, televisions, stereos, computers.

FREE COST-CUTTING GUIDE

The American Council for an Energy-Efficient Economy publishes the *Consumer Guide to Home Energy Savings* ($16.95), which includes tips, diagrams, charts and explanations on nearly every facet of home energy use—insulation, dish washing, laundry, cooking, heating and cooling, food storage, windows, lighting and more.

This guide also lists which investments in energy efficiency pay for themselves, which energy-saving products work and which are more hype than savings. Call 202-429-0063 to order or visit *www.aceee.org/consumer guide* for a free condensed on-line version.

Save Money on Next Winter's Fuel Prices

Emily Schiller, director of Public Interest Research Group Fuel Buyers, a nonprofit heating-fuel–buying cooperative in the greater Philadelphia region that is now a member of the Energy Cooperative, *www. theenergy.coop*. The Energy Cooperative has been in operation for more than 25 years and has more than 6,500 members.

Many heating-oil suppliers offer customers the option of locking in a price long before winter. Some allow lock-ins at any point during the year, though they might not aggressively advertise these programs until summer.

Deciding whether and when to try to lock in prices for home-heating oil, however, resembles betting on a roulette wheel. Predicting prices has been very difficult in recent years because political and economic forces have had as much effect as the weather. Hurricanes and a growing world economy helped drive up heating oil and natural gas prices to record levels in the winter of 2007–2008. Then, just when everyone was expecting the worst, prices pulled back, due in part to warmer-than-usual temperatures early in the season.

For consumers, the result is confusion. Where are heating-fuel prices headed? Is it wise to lock in a price for next year? Even professional oil analysts hesitate to make predictions this far in advance.

Co-op director Emily Schiller explains home-heating–fuel price options…

BEST TIME TO LOCK IN

As a rule, locking in a rate annually is most appropriate for those who don't sleep well when faced with financial uncertainty …and for those who are on fixed incomes and can't afford to risk ultrasteep heating bills. For the rest of us, the best policy is to play it by ear each spring or summer, locking in a rate when fuel prices are low relative to recent years…and not bothering when they're high.

If you wish to lock in a rate, April and early May, following a warmer-than-usual winter, often are good times to do it. Excess heating oil and natural gas from the previous winter most likely remain in storage tanks, pushing down prices. Heating-fuel prices could drop a bit further by summer, though there are no guarantees.

Important: A locked-in price is not ironclad. Fuel suppliers include clauses covering disasters and "acts of God" in their lock-in contracts. If a major hurricane or war in the Middle East were to cause massive disruptions to the fuel supply, suppliers might increase locked-in rates.

FINDING THE BEST DEAL

Since the deregulation of the natural gas industry in many states, even home owners who heat with gas can choose among several suppliers that charge different prices. In some states, such as Ohio (800-686-7826, *www. puco.ohio.gov*), the public utilities commission provides a list of certified gas suppliers that are actively enrolling customers and a price comparison. For heating-oil dealers, review price comparison sites and ask neighbors for recommendations. Don't jump at the first lock-in price you're offered. Rates can vary greatly among a region's fuel suppliers, so call as many as possible. Ask each company for its best lock-in price for the coming winter. Let each know that you're shopping around, because this encourages competitive bids.

Once you choose a supplier, read the lock-in contract before signing…

•**Is there a termination fee for canceling the agreement?** Are there any extra fees if you don't have automatic delivery and run out of oil? If you can avoid these fees, do so.

•**Does the contract include an "automatic renewal clause"?** You'll have to call next year to cancel if you don't want to be locked in again.

•**What's the length of the agreement?** If you sign your contract in April or May, get a 12-month agreement…but if you're locking in your price in September or later, an eight-month contract will allow you to refill your tank once next summer at the typically lower off-season heating-fuel rate.

Many heating-fuel suppliers also offer customers a "capped-rate" option, which is not the same as a lock-in rate. Here, the customer agrees to pay a premium over prevailing heating-fuel prices in exchange for a guarantee that the price will not exceed some predetermined maximum and will drop if market prices plunge. Unfortunately, the premiums tend to be very steep, and customers' capped rates may not drop much even if market prices do.

Example: Many capped-rate customers in the Philadelphia area paid $2.59 per gallon for heating oil this January, though it was available in the region for as little as $1.92. That's a difference of $469 for a typical home using 700 gallons over a winter.

The US Department of Energy tracks heating oil and natural gas prices nationwide at *www.eia.doe.gov* (click on "Petroleum," then go to "Reports" and click on "US Retail Gasoline Prices"). There are local sites, too. *Examples…*

•**For Maine home-heating oil users,** Energy Data Corporation has a Web site that compares prices within six regions in the state. *www.maineoil.com.*

CO-OPS OFFER ALTERNATIVES

In the Northeast, another way to trim heating-fuel costs is to join a heating-fuel–buying cooperative if one exists in your region (check heating-oil suppliers in the *Yellow Pages*). These co-ops negotiate fuel prices for their members, typically 10 to 30 cents per gallon below market rates for heating oil. There's usually an annual membership fee of $15 to $35, though this might be reduced for seniors and low-income individuals. Most co-ops offer a lock-in option. *Co-ops include…*

•**Mass Energy Consumers Alliance** in eastern and central Massachusetts. 800-287-3950, *www.massenergy.com.*

•**New Jersey Citizen Action Oil Group.** 800-464-8465, *www.njcaoilgroup.com.*

•**NYPIRG Fuel Buyers Group** in greater New York City, also serving portions of northern New Jersey, offers savings on either heating oil or natural gas. 800-695-4645, *www. nypirg.org/fbg*.

• **PIRG Fuel Buyers** in greater Philadelphia, including portions of Delaware and New Jersey has joined forces with the Energy Co-operative, 800-223-5783, *www.theenergy.coop*.

SERVICE CONTRACTS

If you sign up for automatically scheduled delivery, your oil supplier may offer a service contract to maintain your heating system. Prices and levels of service vary greatly, but if the base-level plan costs $200 or less, it can be a very good deal. Sometimes a dealer will even agree to forgo the service contract fee for one year to win your business.

This plan should include 24-hour emergency service and an annual cleaning. The cleaning alone can improve the efficiency of your heating system by 5% to 15% and may justify the entire cost of the service plan. (Similar "heater protection plans" are offered by many natural gas suppliers.)

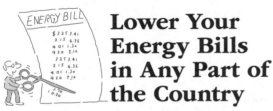

Lower Your Energy Bills in Any Part of the Country

Joe Schwartz, executive editor and CEO, *Home Power* magazine, which for 20 years has covered solar technology and other renewable energy sources for home owners, *www.homepower.com*. Mr. Schwartz lives in Phoenix.

No matter which area of the country you live in, now is a good time to look into solar energy for at least part of your home energy needs.

Situation now: Most experts say that natural gas, heating oil and electricity prices are likely to rise—however sporadically— over the next few years. Meanwhile, the cost of a home solar system has *fallen* and is likely to keep doing so.

Moreover, the federal government gives a lifetime income tax credit (in 2006 and 2007 only) of up to $2,000 for home owners who install most types of solar equipment, and many state and local governments have additional incentives.

For people at or near retirement age, these savings can be significant because they help stabilize expenses at a time when income may be holding steady, or even falling.

Still, it's often difficult to decide whether a solar system makes economic sense for your home. First of all, don't assume that the biggest factor is the amount of sunshine in your area. That's important, of course, but there are at least four other major variables—the cost of the system...the expected price of conventional electricity, gas or oil in your area...the financial incentives...and the expected increase in the value of a solar-equipped house.

Helpful: FindSolar.com, a Web site sponsored by the US Department of Energy, the American Solar Energy Society, the Solar Electric Power Association and Energy Matters, a group that promotes renewable energy in the US and Canada. By entering the location of your home and the name of the utility company into a form on the Web site, you can calculate the estimated savings of solar equipment, based on the major variables.

Example: If you live on Long Island in New York State, FindSolar.com estimates that installing a solar water heater for a household of three to four people will cost about $2,450 after federal tax credits. If water is currently heated with an electrical system, a solar system will cut utility bills by an estimated $36 to $55 a month over the expected 15-year life of the system with a payback of 4.5 years. The value of the property will rise by an estimated $4,815 to $7,223, but in most states, solar systems are exempt from property taxes.

The estimates, of course, are based on many figures that will almost certainly change, such as energy costs and government incentives. And while a solar system can increase the value of your house in the eyes of some buyers, it can deter others who are leery of new technology.

It all depends on how well solar is being accepted where you live. Right now, the odds seem to favor growing enthusiasm for solar, not just because energy prices are likely to rise, but also because governments are promoting solar and well-known companies like GE and British Petroleum have entered the field.

Also helpful: To find tax incentives in your area, ask contractors, contact your state energy department or access the Web site, Database of State Incentives for Renewables & Efficiency at *www.dsireusa.org.*

WATER HEATING

Solar water heaters are relatively simple devices—rooftop collectors that typically measure four feet by eight feet by six inches. The collector contains copper tubing, in which water or antifreeze is heated by the sun.

After this fluid is hot, it's pumped downstairs, where it heats the water in a secondary solar storage tank that's pumped in line with your conventional hot water tank. With this new source of heat, your conventional tank will sit idle much of the time, while 100%-solar-heated water will go directly to your appliances—reducing your gas, oil or electricity use by 50% to 100%, depending on the season.

Cost: $3,500 to $5,000, including installation, for a two- or three-bedroom house. The life expectancy of most systems is about 20 years. Within three to five years, the cost is usually exceeded by savings from lower utility bills. For an estimate of savings in your specific area, consult FindSolar.com.

Like any other mechanical device, home solar hot-water systems may require maintenance and repairs. These costs are usually similar to those for conventional systems and don't affect the payback estimate.

Major solar water heat manufacturers include SunEarth Inc. (909-434-3100, *www.sunearthinc.com*) and Heliodyne (510-237-9614, *www.heliodyne.com*).

Solar heating systems are also available for swimming pools, though they don't qualify for most tax credits. Using power from the filtration pump, these devices circulate pool water to and from the roof, where it's heated by the sun. The cost is about $1,500 to $2,500 if you install it yourself—or $3,000 to $5,000 if a professional does it.

Major manufacturers include Heliocol (800-797-6527, *www.heliocol.com*) and King Solar (800-589-5560, *http://kingsolar.com*).

SOLAR ELECTRIC

If you have a light-powered handheld calculator, you have seen a photovoltaic cell in action. That's the device that converts light into electricity. When thousands of more sophisticated photovoltaic cells are installed on a roof, they can generate enough electricity to run all or most appliances in your home.

Energy-efficient houses will typically require between 40 and 120 square feet of roof-mounted solar modules to supply the majority of the electricity needed on an annual basis. That might seem like a lot of space, but it actually measures just 10 feet by 12 feet.

Solar panels are usually installed on a south-facing side of the roof, but they can also hang on the house like an awning or even be mounted on the ground.

The panels save you money because they're connected to your conventional electricity lines. On a sunny day, you might get all of your electricity from the cells on the roof, but only a small percentage on cloudy days.

Cost: $10,000 to $20,000, including installation. In areas where sunshine is plentiful, such as the Southwest, the cost will be on the low end of the range because fewer modules are needed. The opposite is true in areas such as the Northwest, where there's less sunshine. Most panels are warrantied for 25 years.

Depending on how much sunshine your region gets and the level of incentives offered in your state, the payback is generally seven to 12 years.

Major manufacturers include GE Energy (*www.gepower.com*), BP Solar (301-698-4200, *www.bp.com*), Sharp Electronics (*http://solar.sharpusa.com*), Mitsubishi (*http://global.mitsubishielectric.com*) and Sanyo Electric (*www.sanyo.com/solar*).

FINDING THE PROS

To locate a contractor to install solar devices, ask friends or neighbors who have home solar systems, or look in the *Yellow Pages* under "solar."

FindSolar.com, the Web site mentioned earlier, has a very helpful directory of solar installers throughout the country and also lists customer complaints about those on the list.

HomePower.com has a "Business Directory" and "Installers Directory" that list installers, distributors and other types of solar businesses nationwide.

When you interview contractors, ask for at least two references. Don't work with a contractor who won't supply them or who isn't licensed by your local building codes division. Then contact the references and ask if they were satisfied with the work and whether the contractor's estimate differed significantly from the final bill.

If possible, deal with a solar contractor who is a member of the North American Board of Certified Energy Practitioners (800-654-0021, *www.nabcep.org*). To become members of the group, contractors must pass exams that require them to be knowledgeable about the latest solar technology and methods for installing it.

Important: For the lowest utility bills—and greatest savings from solar equipment—try to choose appliances that have been awarded an "Energy Star." This is the federal government's designation for products that are the most energy efficient. For a list of qualified products, visit *www.energystar.gov.*

Cool Your Home for Much, Much Less

Ray Kamada, PhD, energy conservation expert and contributor to Cyberhomes.com. Dr. Kamada, who holds a PhD in atmospheric science, currently remodels and retrofits homes in the Pacific Northwest for greater energy efficiency.

Home owners with central air-conditioning typically spend hundreds of dollars on electricity each summer to keep cool. (Those with window air conditioners typically spend half as much.) It's often possible to cut these cooling bills substantially without sacrificing comfort.

One way to save is to replace an old central air-conditioning unit with a new Energy Star model. A new unit could save you 30% to 50% in operating costs compared with one that is 10 years old or more. Modern Energy Star window units offer similar savings. Many local utility companies offer rebates or credits for installing high-efficiency equipment, but a new central-air unit still will cost at least $3,000 installed.

Fortunately, not all savings come at such a steep price. *Among the simple, inexpensive things you can do...*

SUN-PROOF YOUR HOME

Your air-conditioning won't have to work as hard if you keep the hot air outside...

●**Insulate your attic.** Install insulation with at least an R-30 value between the attic space and the living space.

Cost: As little as 35 cents per square foot. You even can do the job yourself.

Avoid attic fans—if a fan that is away from your living space burns out and shorts, there's a significant fire hazard.

●**Keep furniture and drapes clear of air-conditioner vents.** Your air conditioner must work harder if vents are blocked.

●**Limit use of major appliances on hot days.** Ovens, ranges, dryers, dishwashers and other appliances add significant heat to your home.

●**Let nature be your air-conditioning on cool nights.** Even when temperatures drop to comfortable levels, some people keep their homes sealed up so as not to "waste" cool air, but it's cheaper to turn off air-conditioning and open windows until morning.

●**Close the drapes on the sunny side of your home** before you leave for work.

COOL YOUR HOME'S SURROUNDINGS

The surrounding landscape can affect the energy efficiency of your air-conditioning. *Steps to take...*

•**Put mulch on the south side of your house**—a layer at least one inch thick. Mulch retains moisture. When this moisture evaporates in the sun, it lowers the temperature slightly in the surrounding area—including inside your home. (Mulching in the sunniest spot—the south side—produces the greatest benefit.) You can purchase mulch at any garden center.

•**Shade the south side of your home with deciduous trees.** They'll cool your house in summer but won't block the sun in winter, after they have shed their leaves.

MAINTAIN AIR-CONDITIONING UNITS

Well-maintained equipment will keep you cool for less, whether it's a central air conditioner or a window unit.

•**Clean the coils.** Dirty or dusty coils can reduce efficiency by as much as 20% for central and window air conditioners. Once a year, cut the power at the fuse box to the outdoor section of your central air-conditioning unit and hose off the coils. Then turn off the power to the indoor part of the system, remove the cover plate and wipe down the coils with a moist cloth. The coils on a window air conditioner should be easy to reach—they might not even be covered. Just unplug the unit, and wipe off the coils with a moist cloth.

•**Replace or clean the filter.** For central-air units, replacing the filter every month during cooling season can reduce operating costs by 5% to 15% and improve your home's air quality, according to the US Department of Energy. Replace or clean filters on window units as recommended in the owner's manual.

OTHER STRATEGIES FOR CENTRAL AIR-CONDITIONING

•**Get your ducts sealed.** As much as 30% of the cool air produced can escape through improperly sealed ducts. Duct tape isn't as effective at solving this problem as a quality sealant, such as mastic (a form of caulk), since duct tape can dry out and lose its grip when subjected to the changing temperatures of ventilation ducts. If you can feel cool air leaking out of the seams in your ducts, purchase mastic at a home center for a few dollars per tube and fill the gaps around your ducts.

If your ducts are difficult to reach, you may need to call in a professional, who might charge a few hundred dollars or more, depending on the accessibility of your duct system.

•**Insulate attic ductwork.** Temperatures in your attic might climb to well over 100 degrees in summer. Adding a layer of fiberglass insulation around ductwork should make a noticeable difference in your system's efficiency.

Cost: Less than $1 per square foot of ductwork if you do it yourself.

•**Shield your outdoor central air-conditioning unit** to keep it out of direct sunlight. A central air-conditioning unit that is left in the sun can use 10% more energy. If you can't easily move it to a shady spot, install an awning over it.

ENERGY-SMART RENOVATIONS

If you're planning some home improvements, keep these energy-saving strategies in mind...

•**When replacing windows,** choose ones with fiberglass or vinyl frames. Aluminum is an excellent conductor of heat, so aluminum window frames bring outside heat into the living space. Fiberglass or high-quality vinyl window frames can cut your cooling bills. (Avoid bargain-basement vinyl—it can become warped in higher temperatures. A quality vinyl window should be reinforced with fiberglass or metal inside the vinyl to help it keep its shape.)

•**For driveways on the sunny sides of homes in warm climates,** favor dark asphalt over light-colored cement. Lighter-colored driveways reflect more sun and heat onto your home. If a driveway doesn't reflect sun onto the home—perhaps because it's on the north side—lean toward a light-colored cement driveway.

•**When replacing your roof,** favor light-colored shingles. A dark roof absorbs tremendous heat on sunny summer days. Studies by the Florida Solar Energy Center and the Florida Power and Lighting Company found that switching from a black roof to a white one can reduce cooling bills by as much as 40%. (Your savings will be lower than 40% if your attic ductwork is well insulated, so it isn't worth replacing your roof until your old one is ready to go. Some towns have ordinances restricting roof-color options, so check the rules before making this change.)

It's true that your home will absorb less heat during cold months if it has a light-colored roof, but the amount of money added to heating costs is significantly less than the amount saved on cooling.

Helpful: Painting your home's exterior a light color also can reduce cooling bills.

Beware of These Contractor Tricks

Bill Keith, a home-remodeling contractor for 25 years in St. John, IN. He is now host of *The Home Tips Show* on Chicago-area PBS-TV and radio stations, *www.billkeith.com*. He is president of SunRise Solar, which designs and manufactures solar-powered attic fans.

Having a new home built or doing some renovation? Odds are, you're not getting everything you have paid for. On many home construction projects, a contractor or a subcontractor is cutting corners at your expense.

There are honest building professionals, but many will play every angle to increase their profits. They might use low-end building supplies instead of quality components…instruct workers to use one nail where two would be better…or inflate the charges on invoices.

Strategy: To get the home materials and workmanship you've paid for, include specific details in the contract. Spell out specific brands, model numbers and dimensions of each component. (Some large home-building companies include such details in their contracts as a matter of course, but most contractors don't.)

Examples: Instead of "kitchen faucet," write "Kohler Vinnata kitchen sink faucet in brushed nickel, model number K-690-BN." Instead of "14 double-hung windows," you might write "14 Andersen Windows 400-Series Woodwright Double-Hung Windows with oak finish, 3' 1⅝" x 4' 8⅞"."

Make sure the contractor agrees to these details *before* he quotes you a price. Otherwise, he might inflate his quote to account for your "upgrades."

Visit the building site (or nose around the project if you're still living in the home) at least every few days during construction to make sure the contract is being followed. If you spot a potential problem, mention it to the contractor as soon as possible. *Areas that deserve your attention…*

LAMINATE FLOORING

Low-quality woodlike flooring that sells for about 80 cents a square foot can look just like high-end, $4-a-square-foot laminate flooring when new—but it will wear out much sooner.

Strategy: To be sure that you get high-end, long-lasting laminate flooring, specify a particular product in your contract. Pergo (888-393-5667, *www.pergo.com*) and Mohawk (800-266-4295, *www.mohawk-flooring.com*) are among the most reliable brands today. Before the flooring is installed, check the packaging. If the label doesn't say Pergo, it isn't Pergo. (If you're not at the site when the flooring goes in, check the Dumpster for the packaging.)

CARPETING

Since the padding can't be seen once a carpet is installed, some contractors may use a subpar product.

Strategy: Specify in the contract a rebond carpet padding of six pounds or higher (or felt padding for Berber carpets). For information on padding, check the Carpet and Rug Institute's Web site (*www.carpet-rug.org*).

PAINT

Painting subcontractors frequently pour cheap paint into high-end paint buckets, reducing their materials costs by as much as $20 per gallon. This ruse is difficult to prevent.

Strategy: Specify an inexpensive paint in the contract, and adjust your price downward. There isn't much difference between high-end and low-end paint. Or simply buy the paint yourself.

TRIM

A subcontractor might substitute less expensive plastic or medium-density fiberboard trim for solid-wood trim. While this is fine in most spots, solid wood is better for exterior trim and high-moisture areas, and it is more attractive for staining. Once trim has been painted, it is hard to tell the difference between wood and medium-density fiberboard.

Strategy: Check the end of a cut piece of trim that has been discarded. The end of a piece of real wood is easy to tell from a man-made product.

SIDING

A high-end, brand-name vinyl siding might cost a contractor $100 for 100 square feet. He can get a low-end product for one-third the price. These thinner sidings are prone to buckling or flying off in high winds.

Strategy: Specify a brand and style of siding in your contract. Check the packaging label as the siding goes up to confirm what you're getting.

Helpful: If your contract calls for cement composite siding, specify that you want James Hardie (888-542-7343, *www.jameshardie.com*), the most reliable brand. This siding—a mix of portland cement and wood fibers—is a versatile and sturdy alternative to vinyl siding.

ROOF SHINGLES

A roofing contractor can save from $500 to $1,500 by substituting low-end shingles for higher-quality brands.

Strategy: Your contract should require a 25- or 30-year algae-resistant architectural shingle from a leading manufacturer, such as Owens Corning (800-438-7465, *www.owenscorning.com*), CertainTeed Corporation (800-782-8777, *www.certainteed.com*), GAF Materials Corporation (973-628-3000, *www.gaf.com*) or TAMKO Building Products (800-641-4691, *www.tamko.com*). Package labels will

tell you if the shingles are the ones requested. Spell out in the contract that four nails should be used per shingle (specify six or eight nails for an especially steep roof). Visit the site when the roofers are at work. Watch for a few minutes to see that they're using the specified number of nails.

Helpful: If you live in an area that gets lots of snow and ice in winter, make sure your contract calls for "ice and water shield." (It's required by building codes in some, but not all, cold-weather regions.) You should see the roofers apply a dark material, most likely pulled from a cellophane backing, over the plywood at the eaves and "valleys," where two rooflines meet, before they start nailing down shingles.

SUBCONTRACTORS

Independent subcontractors do most of the work on construction sites. Some contractors pick subcontractors who are willing to work for the lowest wage—even if they're not qualified.

Strategy: Before you sign a contract, ask your contractor for the names of subcontractors he will use for various tasks—electric… plumbing…roofing…framing…windows… masonry…siding, etc. Contact your town's building department to ask about these subcontractors' work. Building inspectors often are willing to issue off-the-record warnings when appropriate.

If your town's building inspector won't help, call the building inspectors in neighboring towns.

Helpful: If you're not satisfied with the subcontractors, find another contractor or insist that the contractor pick better subs. Have the names of the subcontractors you agree to written into your contract.

DUMPSTERS

Renting a standard 15- to 20-cubic-yard Dumpster should cost your contractor about $300 to $500. (You usually can keep Dumpsters until they are filled.) Yet contractors often charge their clients more than $500 for trash removal.

Strategy: If your invoice lists more than $500 for Dumpster rental and there's one Dumpster on the site, ask your contractor why you're being billed more than the Dumpster costs.

MUNICIPAL FEES

Your contractor might charge you more for permits and other municipal fees than he pays the town.

Best: Call the town offices, and ask the building permits department about building fees. If they're lower than the amounts you've been charged, ask your contractor to adjust your invoice.

When It Pays to Fix an Appliance

Dan O'Neill, founder of Appliance411.com, a home appliance information Web site. He has 15 years of experience in the appliance-service industry in Ontario, Canada, and has been assisting US and Canadian consumers through his Web site since 1997.

A basic appliance repair that might have cost $50 or $60 in the early 1990s now is likely to run $100 or more, including parts and labor. (Repairmen typically charge $50 or more just to diagnose a problem.) That's a lot of money considering that many new appliances cost only $300 to $400.

When does it pay to repair an appliance? In general, if a repair costs less than half as much as buying a new appliance of equal quality, it's worthwhile—but there are exceptions.

Here's a guide to deciding whether to fix household appliances, plus some repairs you can easily do yourself...

REFRIGERATORS

If your fridge is more than 10 years old, you're probably better off replacing it than repairing it. Refrigerators can be expensive to repair, since key components such as the compressor—the heart of the refrigeration system—are enclosed in sealed systems and require special tools to service. What's more, a new fridge with a favorable Energy Star rating will save at least $40 a year in electricity, compared with a refrigerator from the early 1990s—you will save more than $100 a year if your old fridge dates to the 1970s.

If a fridge is less than 10 years old, repairing it can make sense, especially if it is a high-end model. Compared with other appliances, fridge problems are tricky to diagnose. *Common problems...*

• **Leaking.** If the area under the fridge is wet, there might be a clog in the drain tube. If water is on the inside roof of the refrigerator portion of a freezer-on-top model, the leak might be from the freezer drain tube.

Repair cost: $80 to $100.*

• **Stops running or stops cooling.** Any number of components can cause these problems, including broken thermostats, defrost timers, compressors and condenser fan motors. Or it could be as simple as a faulty wire.

Repair cost: $100 and up, depending on the problem.

Do-it-yourself repair: If your refrigerator still cools but not very well, unplug it and thoroughly clean the dust and dirt from the condenser coils with a bottle brush. This should improve the appliance's heat-transfer ability and could solve the cooling problem. You might need to remove the grill or move the fridge to get at the coils from the back. Home owners also might be able to unclog drain tubes and solve some refrigerator leaks. It depends on how easy it is to reach the fridge's drain tube—at least some disassembly of the appliance will probably be required.

WASHING MACHINES

Any repair that can be done for $100 or less is worth doing unless the washer has had repeated problems or is showing signs of rust on its internal parts—rust suggests that water is getting into places it isn't meant to be, meaning that the washer might not have many years left. *Common problems...*

• **Fails to drain or drains slowly.** This might mean that the pump has failed or the drain line is clogged.

*Repair costs are estimates. Actual costs will vary based on skilled labor rates in your region and the cost of parts for your specific model.

Repair cost: $100 to have a new pump installed or $80 to unclog the drain line.

• **The motor is working, but the tub doesn't spin.** The problem might be a broken or worn belt. (If your washer uses multiple belts, the "drive" belt connecting the motor to the tub is the likely culprit.)

Repair cost: Less than $100. (All modern Whirlpool and most modern Kenmore washers use plastic motor couplings instead of belts, but they, too, should cost less than $100 to replace.)

• **The motor is broken.** The cost of the repair will vary. Ask for an estimate before you commit to the job.

• **The electronics system fails.** If the system fails on a computerized washer, it may be time for a new one. A repair could cost hundreds of dollars. If the washer is high-end and only a few years old, it might be worth the expense.

Do-it-yourself repair: If water is leaking, it could be a hose. Try tightening the connection or replacing broken pieces of hose. If the hose still leaks, a pro often can fix it for less than $100.

DRYERS

It's usually wise to repair broken dryers. Most fixes are inexpensive, and there's no reason that the repaired dryer can't keep running for many years. My dryer was made in 1969, and it's still going strong. Newer dryers don't do a much better job drying than older ones, and they're not much more energy efficient. In fact, many dryers made 20 years ago are more solidly built than today's models. *Common problems...*

• **The motor fails.**

Repair cost: $200. True, you can get a new low-end dryer for a little more than that, but it might be worth $200 to repair a higher-end unit—one that has more than two heat settings and the ability to sense electronically when clothes are dry.

• **The dryer is operating, but clothes remain cold and damp.** The heating element may need to be replaced.

Repair cost: $150—higher if it's difficult for the repairman to get to the part.

Do-it-yourself repair: If your dryer is drying very slowly, the problem might be a clogged dryer vent. If the vent hose isn't hidden in your wall, you should be able to clear it yourself by disconnecting the hose and removing anything that has built up inside. Whether you do this yourself or call a professional, don't put it off—a clogged dryer vent is a fire hazard.

DISHWASHERS

It's often worth repairing a broken dishwasher if it is a midrange to high-end model that is less than 10 years old. *Common problems...*

• **Drainage.** The cause could be simply a clogged internal or external hose, or it could be something major, such as a broken pump or motor.

Repair cost: $80 to clear a clog or replace a belt...$100 to $300 to correct a simple malfunction—prices vary by model. It's worth calling a serviceman for an estimate unless it's a low-end dishwasher.

• **Leaks.** These can be caused by failed seals or overfoaming due to excessive use of a rinse agent.

Do-it-yourself repair: Before you call a repairman, check the rubber seal around the interior perimeter of the door for signs of deterioration or displacement. If you find deterioration, you can replace the seal yourself. The new one should just slide or clip in. Also, try reducing your rinse agent use, particularly if your region has soft water. If leaks still occur, a broken pump might be the problem.

Repair cost: $15 to $100 for a new door seal. Add another $80 if you hire a pro to install it. The cost of replacing the pump varies with the cost of the part.

Caution: Fix any leak quickly to prevent damage to the motor. If the pump and the motor must be replaced, it may be time for a new dishwasher unless the current one is newish and high-end.

Other do-it-yourself repairs...

• **The dishwasher still runs through its cycle but no longer cleans well.** Detergent residue or hard-water deposits could be blocking water flow. Try a cleanser such as Dishwasher Magic, Glisten Dishwasher Cleaner or Glass Magic. The label will have directions, but it's usually as simple as adding a little to your usual dishwashing detergent for one or two cycles. If that doesn't work, there might be a clogged hose or broken water-inlet valve. Either problem can be repaired for $100.

•**Rusty dish rack.** Dishwasher makers charge $50 to $150 for replacement dish racks, so beware of signs of rust, such as blistering of the vinyl coating. Instead of replacing the rack, sand the rusted area and at least one inch on either side, then recoat the metal with a vinyl touch-up kit, available from manufacturers for $10 to $20.

OVENS/COOKTOP RANGES

It might pay to fix a high-end unit but not a low-end one unless the problem is minor. *Common problems...*

•**Electronic ignition systems** for gas ovens or cooktops. These often become slow to light or fail to light at all after five years of use.

Repair cost: $100.

•**Failure of the digital control system** for a gas or electric range. This is a costly problem. Repairs can run $100 to $250 for parts, plus $100 or more for labor.

•**No gas coming through.** The problem could be one of the gas valves in your range. If the main gas valve is turned on, the range may require service. A gas appliance technician may be needed rather than one from your local gas utility. Call the utility only if you suspect a problem with the home gas supply, which usually would affect all gas appliances.

Repair cost: $150 to $250 for a new gas valve or to have an oven igniter replaced. Considering that new gas ranges cost $500 to $2,000, they often are worth repairing.

Do-it-yourself repair: With an electric range, a reasonably handy home owner can replace the heating elements when they burn out—they're located right in the oven itself (typically at the top and bottom). Expect to spend $35 to $55 for each part. It will cost $80 to $100 more if you call a repairman.

Avoid Getting Ripped Off by Repair People

Tim Carter, a master licensed plumber and former contractor in Cincinnati, who writes "Ask the Builder," a nationally syndicated newspaper column on home-improvement projects. His Web site is *www.askthebuilder.com.*

Allan Gallant, a master electrician and owner of Gallant Electric in Bedford, MA. During the past eight years, he has appeared regularly as a guest expert on the PBS TV show *This Old House.* Mr. Gallant also appears regularly on *Ask This Old House.*

Leonard Geffner, founder and president of Abbey Locksmiths, a leading provider of locks and burglar-alarm systems to homes and office buildings in New York City for more than 50 years.

When you hire plumbers, electricians and locksmiths, always get a written estimate before any work begins and a final bill after completion. Also ask for a written warranty for any repairs. *Other ways to avoid costly rip-offs...*

PLUMBING
Tim Carter, "Ask the Builder"

Finding a reputable plumber...

•**Ask for a referral from neighbors or a real estate agent.** Realtors know plumbers—nothing derails a home sale faster than watermarks on the ceiling.

•**Ask to see the plumber's license from the state** and a certificate of workers' compensation insurance. Generally, a professional will offer you copies of these documents when the bid is presented. If he/she does not, find one who will.

Avoiding problems...

•**Find a plumber before an emergency.** You will pay top dollar for last-minute service from someone you find in the *Yellow Pages.* For example, some plumbers triple their prices on weekends.

Best: Find a plumber who charges flat rates for specified services. It's almost always cheaper than paying by the hour.

•**Don't buy parts yourself.** Your plumber knows which brands he prefers and can purchase them at a professional discount of up to 35%. Besides, if you buy the parts yourself, the plumber may not warranty his work.

To compare products: *Try these sites: www.keidel.com…www.ferguson.com…and www.faucet.com.*

• **Check the plumber's work before he leaves your home.** Look for leaks…turn new valves on and off to see if they work… check for adequate water flow volume and pressure. Also check for damage to household surfaces—countertops and floors. Hold him responsible if his tools scratched or tore the wallpaper.

ELECTRICITY
Allan Gallant, *This Old House*

Finding a reputable electrician…

• **Ask for a recommendation from a general contractor** who has done work around your house. He sees the electricians' work before it is hidden by walls.

Ask a candidate these questions…

Have you done a job that is somewhat similar to mine? If the answer is yes, call at least one reference. Ask if the job was completed on time, within budget and neatly, with minimal disruption in the home. If the answer is no, try to locate an electrician who has done similar work.

Will you be driving a truck stocked with tools and materials? Electricians who do save you time and money.

Also: Ask for the electrician's license number and how long he has been licensed— you want one who has been licensed for at least two years.

Avoiding problems…

• **Use an electrician only when it is absolutely necessary.** Learn how to reset a circuit breaker or change a blown fuse. Always check that a tripped circuit breaker or blown fuse is not the cause of your electricity loss, especially in summer, when air conditioners are running. It takes less than five minutes and can save you a $100 service call.

For instructions on simple electrical projects: *Wiring 1-2-3: Install, Upgrade, Repair, and Maintain Your Home's Electrical System* by the Home Depot (Meredith)…and *http://homerepair.about.com.*

• **Don't pay an inflated permit fee.** When your electrical work requires new circuitry, the electrician is required to obtain a permit from your municipality. The expense of the permit is based on the estimated cost of the job—generally about $25 per $1,000 of work. Some electricians might charge an hour or so of labor for the time it takes to get the permit. Anything more is unreasonable.

• **Make sure repairs are itemized in the estimate.**

Examples: The cost of cutting holes in walls or digging trenches for outdoor lighting. You might save money by having a handyman do such work. It's usually your responsibility to replace drywall, repaint or relandscape.

• **Make sure the electrician labels circuit breakers** or fuses and electrical panels before he leaves. It will save you time and money in the future.

Note: To report poor workmanship or fraud, call your local city hall and ask for the local and/or state wire inspector. Inspectors have the power to fine or withhold permits from electricians who rip off consumers.

LOCKS
Leonard Geffner, *Abbey Locksmiths*

Finding a reputable locksmith…

• **Ask your local police department to recommend a locksmith** and/or alarm specialist. Many locksmiths today also are in the alarm business.

• **If you find a locksmith in the *Yellow Pages,*** make sure that he has a physical location at the address listed.

• **Be sure the alarm system qualifies for discounts** on your homeowner's insurance. Installing a monitored system should reduce your annual premium by 15% to 20%. Adding dead-bolt locks should trim another 2%.

Avoiding problems with locks…

Common scam: You lock yourself out and call a locksmith, who quotes you $50 for a service call. He should be able to pick open the standard mortise lock without damaging it. Instead, he damages your lock on purpose and then charges $400 for a replacement.

To prevent a locksmith from ruining your lock, get an estimate before he starts his work. Ask him if he can avoid damaging your lock and exactly what it will cost if damage occurs.

Avoiding alarm-system problems...

•**Beware of offers of alarm systems installed for "free" or "$99."** These offers are not free or low cost because there are likely to be add-on charges and you're typically required to sign a five-year contract to use the company's central monitoring service.

Cost: About $1,500.

Better: Only hire a qualified locksmith, or shop among several alarm companies. Request that the professional use only Ademco and/or Napco products, the best in the industry. Also, insist on instruction in using the system, and keep your notes handy.

•**Contract with a central monitoring service on a flexible basis,** preferably month to month.

13

Leisure Time

How to Get Tickets to (Almost) Anything

**D**on't believe it when you see a "Sold Out" sign. In fact, there is hardly a game, concert, show or any other event to which tickets aren't available. *How to get them…*

●**Join a fan club.** Members often get first crack at tickets for a wide range of performances. Today, most fan clubs are Web-based.

Cost: $10 to $40 a year. Advance ticket offers generally become available as soon as you join.

Example: The Barry Manilow International Fan Club (*www.barrymanilow.com*) offers members tickets for tours several weeks before they're available to the public. *Membership fee:* $10.

Other performers, such as John Mellencamp (*www.clubcherrybomb.net*, $40 per year),

reserve a limited number of seats near the stage for fan club members. Some clubs also have phone numbers that members can call for last-minute tickets. To find a fan club, enter the performer's name and "fan club" into an Internet search engine.

●**Contact event sponsors.** Most sporting events, including playoff games, are sponsored by major corporations that make tickets available to customers and suppliers. Individual teams often have business partners that do the same.

Examples: Business partners of the Miami Dolphins football team include DHL, Publix, Verizon and Wachovia. Major theatrical productions, including many at New York's Radio City Music Hall, also have corporate sponsors.

If you're lucky enough to know an executive of a sponsoring company, ask him/her

Mark Andrew Zwartynski, former senior vice president of ticket sales and administration for the Dallas Mavericks and Indiana Pacers. He is coauthor of *Two on the Aisle: How to Get Tickets to Any Event, Anytime, Anywhere*. Masters.

to help you buy tickets. Or ask if your own employer does business with a sponsor that may be able to help you.

Don't hesitate to ask for assistance. Most sponsors and their trading partners enjoy helping out.

Helpful: Names of corporate sponsors of shows, events and teams are often included in print ads for the events or on the events' Web sites.

●**Search on-line brokers.** Not long ago, few companies competed with Ticketmaster (*www.ticketmaster.com*). Today, there are dozens of on-line ticket sellers, including *www.stubhub.com, www.tickets.com, www. ticketsnow.com* and *www.ticketsondemand. org*. Such brokers were formerly known as "scalpers," but local and state laws have allowed them to become legitimate businesses. On-line brokers often have tickets to top events, but brokers charge hefty fees, often 10% to 20%. (Many state governments are investigating this practice.)

Important: Do business only with members of the National Association of Ticket Brokers (630-510-4594, *www.natb.org*) or the firms listed above.

You also can buy tickets at auction at *www. ebay.com*.

●**Phone early, phone late.** When you see an announcement that tickets will go on sale at, say, 10 am, phone an hour early and you'll often reach someone to take your order.

Don't call only the 800 number listed in ads. Call the local number, too. Local agents often have tickets when national agents don't.

Also, call on the day of the event or, better yet, show up at the box office. A few tickets may have been returned.

●**Buy season tickets.** Most season ticket holders for sports events, theatrical productions, symphonies, etc., are offered the opportunity to buy additional tickets to postseason events and playoff games. If you don't want to buy a season ticket yourself, split the cost with friends and take turns attending.

She's Won Over 450 Contests— How She Does It

Carol Shaffer, author of *Contest Queen*. Truman. This book has helped many readers win prizes in local and national contests. She is based in Columbia, IL.

Carol Shaffer was over age 50 when she decided to get her degree in marketing. While at Southwestern Illinois College, she chose to do her thesis on contests and promotions, a subject that few people had studied. Ms. Shaffer's thesis led to more than a degree. She has won more than 450 contests in seven years and has written a book that shares her strategy with others. *Some of her best advice is outlined below...*

●**Think twice before you pass up an opportunity to enter a contest or sweepstake.** Your chances of winning are often far better than you imagine.

●**Apart from cash, you can win automobiles,** computers, dinner out with a celebrity, gift certificates, tickets to shows and games, toys, trips and chances to appear on television.

●**The myth is that so many people enter contests that the odds of winning are very long.** But in reality, organizations that hold sweepstakes often have trouble convincing people to enter.

Advantage: A large number of contests are free, while it costs money to enter the lotteries where you have only a remote chance to win.

Reminder: Taxes are due on the fair market value of your prizes.

GREAT OPPORTUNITIES

Here's where your odds of winning prizes are best...

●**Local contests and sweepstakes.** National events may have bigger prizes, but they usually attract many more entrants than local contests, some of which have surprisingly few entries.

Exception: National contests with a long list of prizes. The top prize might be a

365

vacation for two in Hawaii, for instance, but there could be dozens of lesser prizes.

Many would-be entrants stay away because they know chances of winning the top prize are slim. They forget that the overall odds are much better for winning one of the many smaller prizes. And as a general rule, the shorter the entry period is, the better your chances are because there's less time for competitors to get in the game.

• **Essay contests and competitions that require you to fill out a questionnaire.** Despite the allure of prizes, many people do not want to spend the few minutes that it takes to meet the requirements.

WINNING TACTICS

A couple of years ago, I entered a contest sponsored by CBS and Venture Stores, a regional discount chain. To win a top-of-the-line TV set, contestants had to answer questions about CBS television shows. The winner was then selected by a random drawing of correct entries.

Because there were nearly a dozen Venture stores in the area, I entered at each one. I won *three* TV sets.

This contest is a great example of two winning strategies…

• **Enter the contests that allow duplicate entries** or entries at more than one location. Sure, some other contestants may also submit more than one entry, but you'll have an edge over the vast majority who don't.

Advertisements for contests often ask you to fill out an entry form supplied with the product. The fine print, however, may explain that you don't actually have to buy the product to enter. That makes it easier to enter many times, which increases your odds of winning.

• **Read the rules very carefully,** and stick to them. Just by doing that, you can boost your chances enormously.

If the Venture contest was like most others, about 25% of entries were disqualified for not following the fine print.

Typically overlooked: Requirements to list your zip code, to use an envelope of a certain size or to print instead of writing in longhand.

BEATING THE ODDS

More winning strategies…

• **Choose contests that require long essays** over those that ask for short essays. Long-essay contests have better odds because there are generally fewer entrants. Also, in an essay of 100 to 200 words, judges are more likely to spot phrases they like than they are in an essay of, say, 25 words.

• **Go beyond the obvious.** One of my local TV stations, for example, held a contest for viewers to write about their favorite soap opera. I won with an essay on *The Young and the Restless*—because I was the only one who wrote about the female villain on the show, rather than the main characters as everyone else had done.

The prize? I got to tape an actual TV commercial for the local station—and they even used passages from my essay in the commercial!

And when National Foods held a recipe contest in the St. Louis area, I won $100 for using the company's ranch dressing—not in a salad, which would have been obvious, but in a hot side dish of potatoes, green beans, bacon and cheddar cheese.

• **Give your essay a title.** If a contest requires you to write an essay, put a short title on your entry that can catch the judges' attention. (Titles usually aren't included in the word count, but check the rules to make sure.)

If an airline, for instance, asks all contest entrants to write an essay on why they like to fly, you could write about flying to baseball games and then improve your chances with a title like "Take Me Out to the Ball Game."

The title is upbeat, mentions a national pastime and suggests a reason to fly that airlines may have overlooked. It could go a long way in making your entry stand out from the others.

Smart move: Pick up brochures of the sponsoring company, which are typically available where its product or service is sold. Or go to the company's Web site. Then try to make your entry a part of the marketing strategy that you read about. The baseball theme, for example, would be appropriate for an airline that's trying to attract families, especially during summer months. Football could work in the fall.

Be careful, however, not to mimic the exact words that a company uses in its ads—you will lose originality points.

• **Make your entries physically stand out.** Instead of mailing an entry in a standard white envelope, use a colored one of an odd size.

Caution: Make sure your entry conforms to the rules.

Or for a drawing, fold some of your entries like an accordion, or crumple them so they stand out to the touch when someone reaches into the container. Entries prepared in these ways are also less likely to settle unnoticed at the bottom.

I used the crumpled-entry strategy a few years ago in a big contest sponsored by the Sherwin-Williams Co. I won a Chrysler LHS sedan.

Similarly, don't submit all your entries on the same date in sweepstakes where the winner is drawn from a bowl or other container. By staggering entries, you cut the risk that all of yours will be in one section of the container.

And unless rules specify otherwise, consider writing your entry in colored ink or on colored paper. A small drawing at the top of the page can also make it stand out, and so can writing the entry in a unique style.

My grandson, for example, won a trip to the St. Louis Cardinals' spring training camp in Florida by writing an essay on why his mother was a good soccer mom. He wrote it as a poem!

To find out about contests, check local papers, ask store managers, tune in to the local radio and TV stations or go to their Web sites. A listing of nationwide contests is provided at *contests.about.com.*

Caution: The number of Web-based contests is soaring. Though most are legitimate, beware of scam contests with the purpose of collecting e-mail addresses and personal data.

Safeguard: Don't enter a contest unless it's sponsored by a company you've heard of and have no reason to distrust.

Better Ways to Win a Sweepstakes

Steve Ledoux has won hundreds of sweepstakes prizes. He is author of *How to Win Lotteries, Sweepstakes, and Contests in the 21st Century.* Santa Monica. He is a realtor living in California.

Boost your odds of winning a sweepstakes by following this very smart advice from a proven sweepstakes winner…

• **Enter local sweepstakes.** Local drawings are much easier to win than well-promoted national contests because they attract fewer entrants. Prizes include gift certificates, merchandise, dinners for two, etc. Look for entry boxes in area stores and ads in regional newspapers.

• **Opt for short-term sweeps.** The longer a sweepstakes runs, the more entries it will attract and the lower your chances become. Your odds are best in sweepstakes that last less than a month. These tend to be tied to promotional campaigns for new products, movie releases or special events.

Example: Albertson's supermarket chain held a sweepstakes that was open for just two weeks. The grand prize included two tickets to the Emmy Awards.

• **Stagger your entries.** All winners might be pulled out of the same mailbag. If your entries arrive all at the same time, they could wind up together in the wrong bag, leaving you with no shot at a prize.

If you can enter only once, do so toward the end of the entry period. This increases the chance that your entry will be near the top of the pile. You may be able to enter for friends and relatives, but make sure that you receive their permission first and an agreement to share the prize.

• **Make your entry stand out.** For in-store drawings, fold your slip of paper into an accordion or tent shape so that it will be easier for a judge to grab on to. For mail-in local sweeps, use brightly colored oversized envelopes.

• **Enter on-line sweeps.** It's easy, and you can save on postage. Read the rules carefully. You may find that you also can mail in entries, increasing your odds.

Favorite resources: Sweepstakes Advantage at *www.sweeps.ws* and Sweep the Net at *www.sweepthenet.com* list the current on-line sweepstakes.

Caution: Only enter sweepstakes that are sponsored by companies you know. Avoid the sweepstakes that require you to purchase anything, pay a fee or give personal information beyond your name, address, phone number and age.

Smart Lottery Playing

In lotteries that are fair, each number has the same chance of coming up—but some numbers are picked by lottery players much more often than other numbers.

Examples: "Lucky" numbers like seven numbers in a sequential pattern, and numbers corresponding to calendar dates (one to 31). If you wager on such popular numbers, you're more likely to share any prize you win with a number of other people.

Instead, choose unpopular numbers—your chances of having the winning numbers will be just the same, but since you'll be less likely to share a prize, if you do win, you will win much more.

Larry Lesser, PhD, associate professor of mathematics, University of Texas at El Paso.

See New Movies For Less

Ask your human resources director whether your employer has a corporate program with a movie theater company—you may be able to get discounted tickets. If you're self-employed, see whether your home business can get in on a corporate purchase plan by becoming a member of the National Association for the Self-Employed. You may have to buy tickets in bulk, but if you see movies frequently, you will save money.

Also: Go to the movies before 5 pm, when most theaters offer matinee tickets for up to half off the full ticket price.

ConsumerSavvyTips.org, on-line consumer advice and tips to help save money.

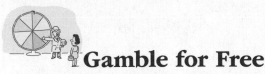

Gamble for Free

Max Rubin (*www.maxrubin.net*), professional gambler and a member of the Blackjack Hall of Fame. A former casino executive, Rubin is the expert analyst on CBS's *Ultimate Blackjack Tour.* He has been featured on the Travel Channel's *The Pro's Guide to Vegas,* and is author of *Comp City: A Guide to Free Casino Vacations.* Huntington.

Is it possible to win every time you gamble? Yes—if you play for comps, the more than $1 billion worth of favors that casinos give away every year. Even if you lose at a gaming table, you can get back more than you spend in the form of free drinks, meals, entertainment, etc.

Comps (short for complimentaries) occur on two levels. There are classic comps—cocktails, parking and other low-end giveaways—available to just about everyone who gambles.

Better: Premium comps—tickets to shows, limo rides and rooms and meals—are given only to qualified players. While comps are available no matter what kind of game you play, blackjack is the only game where you'll get back more than you're likely to lose. People who know how to take advantage of these rewards can get the equivalent of a free vacation with little or no risk.

You don't have to be a skilled gambler to come out ahead.

Why: In blackjack, the casino wins, on average, about 2% of every dollar that's bet. This means that an average player betting $5 a hand probably loses about $5 an hour over time. If you drink two complimentary cocktails (which would normally cost at least $5 each) during that time (and don't make boneheaded playing decisions), you earn twice as much as you spend.

GET RATED TO GET COMPS

Most comps are based on a player's *rating* —a formula that predicts the casino's potential to win that gambler's money. The way comp systems are set up, a casino typically plans to give back in comps about 30% of what it expects to win.

Most casinos use the same basic formula —the average bet multiplied by the hours played multiplied by the house advantage— to determine a player's rating.

Example: A player who makes an average bet of $100 in blackjack and plays for one hour (about 60 hands) will be expected to lose $120…and will be given a rating that provides the equivalent of about $36 in comps.

Important: Request your free card for the VIP club, something every casino has, though the name may differ. It's the first step to getting rated. Once you have the card, show it to the casino supervisor (floorman) when you sit down at a blackjack table. He/she will write down your name, how many chips you bought and how much you're betting per hand on a rating ticket. When you leave, the amount that you won or lost will also be recorded. This goes to the casino's marketing department, which decides what kinds of freebees you're entitled to.

TO GET MORE

Players can manipulate their ratings by making the casino think that they're spending more money than they really are. Suppose you're playing blackjack and the casino thinks you're betting $100 a hand 60 times an hour…when in fact you're only betting $40 a hand for about 45 hands. On average, you'll be losing about $36 an hour—but could be getting back $36 an hour in comps! *How to boost your rating…*

•**Get noticed.** The floormen are authorized to give small comps even to unrated players, and their supervisors (the pit bosses) can give comps for rooms and for more expensive restaurants. But first, you have to get their attention.

How: Buy in for a few hundred dollars when you sit down at the blackjack table. The dealer will notify the floorman, who has to OK all buy-ins over $100. When the pit boss looks your way, call him over and ask for a drink— even if you don't really want one. Ordering a drink really lets him know you're there.

Important: Make your largest bets when you see that the floorman is watching. When he's not, bet the table minimum (to keep your overall wagering down). After you've been playing for an hour, make another large bet or two—then ask the pit boss to buy you a meal. Just say, "May I have two tickets to the buffet or coffee shop, please?"

•**Play the busiest tables.** To maximize comps while minimizing losses, play slowly. The fewer hands you play, the less money you're likely to lose. A blackjack dealer can deal up to 250 hands per hour to a single player. At a busy table, he might deal as few as 50 hands per hour.

Best: Look for a table with six other players—preferably a friendly table where people (including the dealer) are telling jokes and laughing. Stall as often as possible—but don't be obvious. Show your hand to other players and ask how they'd play it…sit out a hand now and then…and take your time when it's your turn to cut the cards. All this lets you play fewer hands, but still log plenty of gambling time—an important key to comps.

•**Coast during boss breaks.** Pit bosses take two 20- to 30-minute breaks during an eight-hour shift, and a longer break for lunch or dinner. You can pad your rating (gambling less than the bosses think) by scaling back to the table minimum while the boss's relief is on the floor, then increasing your bets when the boss returns.

This way, you could have an actual gambling average of $25 an hour, but an "official" average of $150. If you do the above once during every shift you play, you'll increase your comp rating while reducing the risk of losses.

•**Look like a loser.** Casinos like losers —and give them better ratings/comps. Even if you're a winner, you want to look like you're losing. The only way to do this is to hide chips. Casinos frown on this (it raises suspicions of cheating), but the fewer chips you have on the table after you've been gambling awhile, the more generous the bosses are likely to be with perks.

Try this: Cup your hand over a stack of chips…squeeze one or two in your palm…and casually drop them into an inside jacket pocket while pulling out a mint. A woman can drop chips into an open purse in her lap.

• **Play with a partner.** Some casinos will combine two people on a single VIP card. This allows you to buy in with more front money—one of the keys to better comps. When you play together, the floorman will credit both bets on one rating slip, giving you a higher rating and more freebies.

• **Ask for what you want.** Many people are too embarrassed to ask for a free meal, a discount on a room, a suite upgrade or other comps. When playing any game in a casino, never hesitate to ask the boss for free drinks or other amenities. If he says no, ask how much more you need to be betting to qualify for additional comps. More often, you'll be given something, even if it's not exactly what you're asking for.

Example: You ask for an unlimited coffee shop comp—you get two buffet tickets.

Important: Always be friendly—and tip often. Even if you're only handing out the occasional dollar (or chip) to the dealer, you'll stand out for your attitude, which will translate into better comps.

Strategies: Tip when the boss is watching. People who seem to be big spenders get better ratings. Or, make a bet for the dealer on your first bet. He'll be more likely to say something positive when the boss later asks about your average bet.

Casino Savvy

To get freebies and discounts at casinos, don't hop from casino to casino. If you spend your gambling budget at one casino, you're more likely to get comps. Casinos give about 25% of their gross revenue back to gamblers this way.

Examples: Put $1,000 into play and you could earn a free lunch at the coffee shop…put $10,000 into play and you could get a free room. But don't ask the dealer for comps. Ask the floor manager who has been observing your play or a casino host.

Richard Armstrong, Washington, DC–based author of *Get Paid to Gamble: The Inside Story of Casino Complimentaries.* Slot Detector Co. For a free instant PDF download of his 55-page e-book, go to *www.goddoesntshootcraps.com.*

Insider's Guide To Playing Slot Machines

Frank Legato, a founding editor of *StrictlySlots* magazine and author of *How to Win Millions Playing Slot Machines!…Or Lose Trying.* Bonus Books. Legato is currently managing editor of *Casino Connection* magazine, 6625 S. Valley View, Las Vegas, NV 89118.

Josephine Crawford of Galloway Township, NJ, didn't believe the casino employee when he told her in 2006 that she had just won $10 million. But when bells kept ringing and people gathered around her, the 84-year-old former waitress soon realized that the employee at Harrah's Atlantic City was right. Her bet on the Megabucks nickel slot had paid off.

The odds are infinitesimal that you'll ever duplicate Crawford's success at the slots, but you can still have lots of fun. And who knows? You just might get as lucky as she was—especially if you know the ropes in playing slot machines.

Besides, playing slot machines requires little or no skill. You can play at your own pace and bet as little or as much as you want. *What you need to know…*

THE ODDS

Casinos try to take your mind off the odds. They introduce a constant stream of new slot games and offer eye-catching jackpots, such as new cars displayed on turntables in full view of the machines.

Regardless of the enticements, the majority of slot machines give an edge of 1% to 10% to the house, a term used for the owner of the machine, whether it's a casino or a convenience store in Nevada. This means that most slot players "win" back only 90 cents to 99 cents of every dollar they play.

These payback rates are calculated over the long run, which can be many thousands of games. So don't be misled when you see a player win several times during an hour's play at a particular machine. There eventually will be enough losses to bring the odds back in the house's favor. And you never know when those losses will occur.

The more it costs to play a slot, the higher the payback rate usually is. Games that cost $5 or $10, for example, might pay back 99%, while nickel games often return no more than 90% and penny games pay even less.

Caution: Slot games on the Internet are becoming popular.

My advice: Stay away from Internet slots. They're illegal to play in the US, and there's no way of knowing what the payback rate is.

Also, keep in mind that even the best odds at slots aren't as good as the odds with other games, such as blackjack, that require skill, concentration and a good memory.

IMPROVING YOUR CHANCES

The best slot machine odds are in Las Vegas—but not on the city's famous Strip. Casinos on the Strip—including Bally's, the Mirage, the Stardust and the Tropicana—don't need player-friendly slots because they enjoy a steady stream of tourists. The payback on 25-cent machines at Strip casinos is 93% or 94%, and on dollar games, it's 95% or 96%.

Casinos off the Strip rely more on local residents who demand the incentive of better odds to play the slots. That's particularly true in the suburbs of Henderson and North Las Vegas, where the payback at such casinos as Sunset Station, Fiesta Station and Green Valley Ranch is one or two percentage points higher than it is on the Strip.

In Atlantic City, nickel slots usually have a payback rate of only 90%, while 91% or 92% is typical for quarter games and 94% for dollar slots. Casinos elsewhere in the country have similar payback rates.

Slots at most casinos pay out bonuses to players who bet two or three coins at a time.

Example: If you put one quarter in a classic Double Diamond slot and three "wild" symbols come up, you'll win 1,000 quarters. But if you bet three quarters and the same symbols line up, you'll win 15,000 quarters—15 times the payback for three times the bet. Each slot machine has a written explanation of its winning combinations and prize amounts for various sizes of bets.

Today, video slots are popular, and they have the same payback rates as traditional mechanical machines, known as reel slots.

Some of the worst paybacks are at Nevada's airports and convenience stores, where the payback rate can be as low as 75%.

To find slots with the best payback rates, look at one of the gaming publications that regularly report on them. Two magazines with monthly payback reports are *Casino Player* (800-969-0711) and *StrictlySlots* (800-969-0711)—both at *www.casinoplayer.com.*

In any one casino, all slots that cost the same usually have the same payback rate, regardless of the particular game that's featured on the machine.

Example: If you put $1 in a Blazing 7s slot machine, you'll get the same payback rate as you would by putting $1 in a machine that features Tabasco, another popular game.

Nevertheless, many players believe that some games are luckier than others, and *StrictlySlots* regularly polls players to find out which games have that reputation. Be aware, however, that these polls are based on anecdotal evidence, and there are no statistical data to back them up.

Biggest game in town: Progressive slots, a game where machines are connected to one another and the jackpot rises as more people play. A huge overhead meter lets players keep track of the jackpot, which has reached more than $20 million in some cases. Two of the most popular wide-area progressive slots are Quartermania and Megabucks.

While prizes continue to rise, the odds of winning them remain long—very long. Ms. Crawford, for instance, was playing the nickel Megabucks slot, where the odds of winning the jackpot are about one in 40 million.

Important: To win the top prize, you must put the maximum number of coins in the slot, usually three. If Ms. Crawford had been playing with fewer coins, she would have won a few thousand dollars instead of $10 million.

MAKE THE SLOTS MORE FUN

Set a limit on how much to wager during any one session at the machines. Then stop playing when you've reached your limit or—if luck is with you—when you've won more than the amount you started with.

This exercise in self-discipline makes sense because no matter how long you play the slots, you're likely to lose many more games than you win. By quitting when you're ahead, you'll avoid the risk of a losing streak that takes away your winnings. Remember that the odds always favor the house. If you play long enough, you're certain to lose more money than you win.

Guidelines to establish a spending limit: At 10 spins a minute, it costs about $9 an hour to play a nickel machine with a three-coin maximum. A quarter machine would cost about $45 an hour and a dollar machine $180 an hour.

If setting a limit is difficult, remember Ms. Crawford. On the day she won, she had set a limit of $40 for the session and was down to her last $5. But if she had gone over her limit on the previous day, she might never have played on the day she struck it rich.

More from Frank Legato...

Most Winning Slots

When *StrictlySlots* asked readers to name the reel slot games where they experienced the most success, they listed...

- **Double Diamond**

- **Wheel of Fortune**
- **Blazing 7s**
- **Red White & Blue**
- **Triple Diamond**

Luckiest video slots...

- **Jackpot Party**
- **Wheel of Fortune**
- **Monopoly**

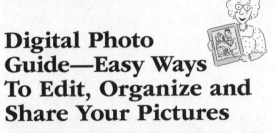

Digital Photo Guide—Easy Ways To Edit, Organize and Share Your Pictures

Barbara Brundage, a digital photography enthusiast, who is author of *Photoshop Elements 6: The Missing Manual* and coauthor of *Digital Photography: The Missing Manual* (both from O'Reilly Media, Inc.). She lives in Jensen Beach, FL.

Digital photography opens a range of new options for saving, organizing, editing, printing and sharing snapshots, but these new options can be confusing. *How to make the most of your digital photos...*

ORGANIZING

- **Use keywords to tag digital photos** as soon as you import them from your camera to your photo software.

Examples: Sante Fe Vacation, 70th Birthday, Wedding Flowers. Otherwise, pictures will be saved under the alphanumeric titles they are assigned by your camera, and you'll have to sort through hundreds of shots to locate the one you want. Once you tag photos, to see a picture or a group of pictures, all you have to do is use your software's search function to find the relevant keywords.

Helpful: When you import your pictures onto your computer, also burn them to a backup disk (you will need a CD or DVD burner). Disks can be stowed in a bank safe-deposit box or given to relatives. There they will be protected even if a fire or natural disaster destroys your home.

- **Use a photo-organizing computer program,** such as…

  - Adobe Photoshop Elements. This scaled-down version of the professional photography program *Photoshop* is the best of its type for PCs. Its list price is $99.99,* but it often can be found on sale for as little as $50. *www.adobe. com/products/photoshopelwin*

  - Picasa. Google's digital photo organization program for PCs might not be as versatile as *Photoshop*, but it's free. *picasa.google.com*

  - Apple iPhoto. A wonderful photo editing and organization program for the Macintosh. If you bought a Mac with the OS X operating system, your computer already has it installed. *www.apple.com/ilife/iphoto*

EDITING

Flawed digital photos often can be fixed—distracting elements can be erased, the red can be removed from eyes, and pictures can be trimmed and reshaped, etc. Digital editing software makes all of this quick and easy.

Top programs include *Adobe Photoshop Elements* and *Corel Paint Shop Pro Photo* for PCs (*www.corel.com/paintshop*, $79.99) and *iPhoto* for Macs.

PRINTING

Virtually any modern color computer printer can print digital pictures, but ink and high-quality photo paper are so expensive that printing pictures at home is just as pricey as leaving it to the pros. The best deals are on-line. Internet digital photo printing companies charge as little as 9 cents per 4-x-6 print. You upload photos using their software or directly from software programs, such as *Elements* or *iPhoto*.

Leading film processors include…

- **Snapfish.** Prices start at 9 cents for a 4-x-6 print. *www.snapfish.com.*

- **Kodak EasyShare.** Prices start at 15 cents for a 4-x-6 print. *www.kodakgallery. com.*

*All prices in this article are list prices, but discounts may be available.

DISPLAYING

You don't have to print your photos—you can view them as shows on a computer screen. There are programs that will help you create a digital slide show and even add music.

Or transfer pictures to a DVD and view them on your television (assuming that your computer is capable of recording to DVD). Macintosh users can do all of this with the *iPhoto, iMovie* and *iDVD* software that came with their OS X–equipped computers. A free program called *Jalbum*, available for PC and Mac, also offers digital picture display options (*http://jalbum.net*). Or PC users can create slide shows using Photodex's *ProShow* (*www. photodex.com/products/proshow*, $29.95).

FRAMING

There are high-tech picture frames designed to display digital photos. You don't print the images. You upload them into the frame, which is actually a display monitor, and change them whenever you like. Some frames also allow you to view pictures as a slide show, so you can see all the photos easily. If you have a relative who doesn't own a computer but would like to see your pictures, give him/her one of these frames as a gift, then send him camera memory cards containing your pictures. He can insert the memory card into the back of the frame and display the pictures he likes best. Type "digital picture frame" into Froogle.com or Amazon. com, or visit an electronics or photography store to find a selection of digital frames.

Cost: About $75 and up.

SHARING

Upload your digital photos onto a photo-sharing Web site, then e-mail the link to friends and family members. *Best sites that allow digital photo uploading and sharing include…*

- **dotphoto** (*www.dotphoto.com*)
- **Flickr** (*www.flickr.com*)
- **Kodak EasyShare** (*www.kodakgallery. com*)
- **Shutterfly** (*www.shutterfly.com*)
- **Snapfish** (*www.snapfish.com*)

How to Take Better Digital Photos

Scott Kelby, president of the National Association of Photoshop Professionals, training director of the Adobe Photoshop Seminar Tour and editor in chief of *Photoshop User* magazine, Tampa Bay, FL. He is author of *The Digital Photography Book,* Peachpit, Amazon.com's best-selling photography book of 2006. His Web site is *www.scott kelby.com.*

You don't need an expensive camera to take digital photos like a pro. You just need a few tricks…

BETTER BASICS

●**Avoid using your camera's LCD screen to take your shot.** You have to hold the camera away from your face to do this, and that often leads to shaky hands and blurry shots. If your digital camera has an optical viewfinder, use that instead, so you can brace the camera against your face. This helps keep the camera steady and makes your photos sharper. If you insist on using the LCD screen, at least buy a camera that has image stabilization (sometimes called "vibration reduction" or "antishake").

For even greater image sharpness, mount your camera on a tripod. You also can set the camera to shoot on a two-to-three-second delay, to eliminate any shake caused by pushing the shutter button.

●**Avoid shooting subjects in direct sunlight.** Direct sunlight washes out colors, creates unflattering shadows and makes subjects squint. Whenever possible, position your subjects in "open shade"—outdoors, but out of the direct sun. The best light of all is at the very edge of a shaded area—close to, but not in, the sun.

●**Evaluate shots on your LCD screen before subjects walk away.** Digital cameras let photographers instantly view their pictures. Ask everyone to stay put while you make sure they all look good.

●**Set the camera to "cloudy" for outdoor shots**—even on sunny days. The cloudy setting adds richness and warmth to outdoor photos.

ARTISTIC SHOTS

●**Think off-center.** Position your subject toward the left or right of the picture, not in the middle. The horizon line in a landscape should be either one-third or two-thirds of the way up, not across the dead center of the picture. The general rule is to choose one-third up if the sky or backdrop is beautiful, two-thirds up if the foreground is more appealing.

●**Try different angles.** Most amateurs take all of their pictures while standing. Instead, lie on the ground and take a picture of a flower from the flower's height. Get up close to a building and take a picture up its side, rather than straight on.

●**Position your subjects' eyes about one-third down from the top of the frame.** This is an old trick used by photographers and painters to create portraits with better balance. In a close-up, that might mean losing the top of the head or some hair—which is acceptable—but avoid cutting off the chin. If you crop midbody, do so between the joints, not close to the elbow or the knee.

●**Take landscape photos during the "magic hours."** The most beautiful light is usually during the 30 minutes before sunset until 30 minutes after sunset…and during the 15 minutes before sunrise until 30 minutes after sunrise.

It's Time to Make Music Again

Jerry Hendricks, president, New Horizons International Music Association, *www.newhorizonsmusic. org.* Mr. Hendricks lives in Lacey, WA.

For more than 40 years, Jerry Hendricks wanted to pick up the clarinet again. He had played in high school, but, since then, a demanding career in engineering hadn't left much time for music.

Several years ago, his wife pointed out a newspaper article about a band that was forming for people over 50 in their town of

Olympia, WA. Hendricks leaped at the opportunity and began playing with the band as often as possible. Today, several years later, Hendricks is retired, is a regular clarinetist with the Olympia New Horizons Band and is head of the international organization to which the band belongs.

Music has given Hendricks as much energy as he ever had in high school. *It can do the same for you...*

BENEFITS

Making music can have valuable benefits. Studies at George Washington University show that music and other community cultural activities promote physical and mental health. Research at the Albert Einstein College of Medicine and Syracuse University suggests that playing an instrument may lower dementia risk.

It's also fun—a chance to socialize, to experience the joy of performing and to challenge yourself in an activity that gives you pleasure.

GETTING STARTED

If you want to take up an instrument for the first time, rent one from a music store—or dig your old instrument out of the basement, if you used to play one years ago. Ask the store staff to recommend a teacher. Even if you're an accomplished player, a teacher can help get you back in form after a long absence from music.

Instrument rentals typically go for $30 to $50 a month, and part or all of the amount can often be applied to a subsequent purchase. Most commonly used band instruments sell for approximately $400, depending on condition. Pianos, bassoons, tubas and French horns, however, are likely to be more expensive. For example, a full electronic keyboard (88 keys, as on a standard piano) might cost about $1,000 new. For a small group, that would be adequate. However, for a larger ensemble, you will need to add a speaker system.

To find a teacher, it also pays to contact local schools that have music departments. Those teachers often give private lessons. In choosing a teacher, pick one who seems enthusiastic about giving lessons to a student over age 50.

Frequent question: If someone has never sung or played an instrument before, how much study does it take in order to perform with a local group?

Answer: Sometimes no more than a few months, but that depends on many variables, including your own talent and perseverance and the demands of the group.

In fact, the more you enjoy playing an instrument or singing a particular type of music, the easier it will be to learn. Once you start performing, making music usually becomes sheer pleasure.

Good news: There are increasing opportunities to perform with amateur and semiprofessional groups. Many community orchestras, bands and choirs depend chiefly on amateur musicians in their area. Religious, civic and alumni organizations often sponsor musical groups that may or may not be limited to their own members.

The most knowledgeable information sources on groups are local music teachers and stores. Many of them are likely to recommend a New Horizons band if there's one in the area.

New Horizons (360-754-9777, *www.new horizonsmusic.org*) is an international organization that helps communities establish musical groups—mostly bands but also orchestras and choirs—for people age 50 and over. There are now 130 New Horizons groups in the US, Canada and Ireland.

TAKING A BOW

New Horizons invites prospective members to sit in on a rehearsal and to talk with members of the band. If they like what they hear, they can join for about $20 a month.

Most New Horizons bands have about 30 to 50 members, and though the organization targets people age 50 and older, some local groups allow younger members to join. There is no upper age limit. Many musicians are in their 80s and some are in their 90s.

Rehearsals, under the direction of an experienced conductor, are typically held weekly and last two hours. No matter how little time a person has studied an instrument, a conductor will try to find music suitable to his/her competence level. For that reason, there are no auditions or minimum skill requirements. Virtually everyone who wants to play will have an opportunity.

The mainstay of most New Horizons organizations are concert bands that consist of wind instruments (flutes, clarinets, saxophones, French horns, trumpets, trombones, euphoniums and tubas) and percussion instruments (drums and cymbals). Many local bands include bassoons and oboes. There are also a few groups (swing, jazz, chamber music) that include keyboards.

In addition, local organizations often have side groups for members who sing or who play the violin and other stringed instruments, as well as for members who play instruments that are heard less often, such as the accordion, harp and bagpipe.

Most New Horizons groups are in big demand to perform. They play at many local events and regularly go on the road. One band recently toured Europe and another went to the Tournament of Roses in California.

Throughout the year, New Horizons sponsors camps where members can socialize and take group lessons from top professional musicians.

Example: At Chautauqua, NY, in October 2007, members and nonmembers can take tutorials in band performance as well as in string orchestras, percussion ensembles, the blues, jazz, fiddling, chamber music, Dixieland, choral singing and conducting.

Cost: $170 to $350, not including meals and lodging for the five-day camp.

Information: Call 360-754-9777, or click on the "Events" icon at the New Horizon Web site.

While learning and socializing are big advantages of being involved in music, the greatest thrill nearly always comes in performing. A few years ago, I was involved in a group that formed a Dixieland band that, today, often plays around town. When we played recently at a senior center, the music was so rousing that several people got out of their wheelchairs and danced.

It was great to see the joy in their faces—and an even greater joy to know that it was our band members who inspired them.

Dance Your Way to Fun and Health

Bonnie L. Vorenberg, a former professional dance instructor who is now president of ArtAge Publications, a Portland, OR–based supplier of resources for senior theater (800-858-4998, *www.seniortheatre.com*).

Using treadmills and stationary bicycles at home might be convenient, but they're not what most people would call fun.

Alternative: Dancing—a way to have fun with others and get great exercise, almost without realizing it.

Today, there are more opportunities to dance than ever before, thanks to public organizations and dance schools that are putting a new emphasis on senior participants. That includes opportunities to take up dancing for the first time or brush up on moves that you might have learned back when you "rocked around the clock."

MORE THAN JUST FUN

When you're dancing, you have so much fun that you forget about the physical effort you're putting into it. That effort, however, can have a big payoff. The American Heart Association recently reported a study that showed health benefits—including a stronger heart—from 21 minutes (alternating between slow for five minutes and fast for three) of waltzing three times a week.

The *Mayo Clinic Health Letter*, in fact, encourages people of all ages to try ballroom dancing as a way to burn calories and improve the cardiovascular system.

A study by California State University shows that ballroom dancers can easily burn 250 calories to 300 calories an hour. And another study at Albert Einstein College of Medicine in New York concluded that dementia is less likely when people over the age of 75 dance regularly. According to the study, the lower incidence of dementia is associated with executing complex dance steps and moving in rhythm to the music.

Though there may not be any formal studies on the subject, it's clear that dancing can also improve your balance, and that can be important in preventing falls. When people learn specific dance steps and rhythms, they become more aware of their physical movements and their range of motion as well. That, too, can help prevent accidents.

Most dancers also improve their posture, a move that gives them a younger, more vibrant appearance.

If all of these benefits aren't enough to convince you, consider that dancing…

• **Puts you in touch with music,** which has benefits of its own. When in a grouchy mood, for instance, if you hear an upbeat tune, your mood is likely to change.

• **Is a route to socializing.** As we grow older, there's a tendency to isolate ourselves. Dancing provides an enjoyable way to get together with others—often younger people with whom we might not otherwise socialize.

THE BEAT GOES ON

Most seniors grew up in an era when there was a new dance craze every few months—the Bristol stomp, fly, jerk, locomotion, loop de loop, Madison, mashed potato, pony, shake, stroll, twist and Watusi, just to name a few.

If you were a little old for those steps, you may have grown up in an earlier era of great dances—the fox-trot, Jersey bounce, jitterbug, Lindy and boogie-woogie. Or your parents may have taught you some of their own favorite moves, such as the Charleston or the shimmy.

If you like more traditional dances, there are dozens to choose from—the rumba, slow fox-trot, square dances, tango and waltz. Today, people of all ages are often interested in dances associated with particular cultures—Balinese, German, Irish, Israeli, Latin American, Polish and Russian, for instance.

And even ballet and tap dancing are becoming popular with seniors who are willing to put in the effort to learn.

Don't worry if you don't have a partner. Line dancing lets singles move to the music in an ever increasing number of ways. And for women, belly dancing, which is great exercise because it strengthens stomach muscles, is increasingly popular with a growing number of dancers throughout the US—yes, even among seniors.

TAKE THE LEAD

To find inexpensive dance classes, contact your local parks and recreation department, senior center or adult education program. Or consult the *Yellow Pages* for commercial dance studios, more of which now have classes specifically for people age 50 and older.

Helpful: Find dance studio directories on the Internet at *www.centralhome.com/dance-studios.htm*. And by using Google or another Web search engine, you can find instructors for specific types of dances.

Example: Belly dance classes are listed at *www.orientaldancer.net/belly-dance-instructors* and hula instructors at *www.mele.com/resources/hula.html*.

Smart move: Before you sign up for lessons, ask to observe a class and also talk with some of the students. Consider enrolling only if you like what you see and the students believe they're getting value for their money.

Courses taught at senior centers, local government facilities or religious organizations are usually inexpensive.

Examples: The Senior Center in West Covina, CA, charges $25 for six one-hour tap dance classes. A package of 10 ballet lessons at St. Mark's Episcopal Church in Washington, DC, costs $90.

Commercial dance studios charge more.

Typical: A Fred Astaire Dance Studio in Manhattan charges $75 for two half-hour introductory private lessons plus a practice session. A package of five private follow-up lessons costs $475 for an individual or a couple. Fees are similar at Arthur Murray studios, the other major chain of dance schools.

Though the best way to learn dancing is from an instructor, videos can also be useful, particularly those produced for seniors.

Examples: *Nick Felix's Swing Dancing for Seniors* and *Paul Merola's Most Popular Line Dances for Seniors.*

These and other dance-instruction videos and DVDs are usually available at Internet retailers such as *www.amazon.com, www.centralhome.com* and *www.activevideos.com/seniors.htm.* Videos and DVDs typically range in price from $14.95 to $25.95.

There's a thin line between actual dancing and exercising to music. Straddling this line are *Rise and Shine* and other videos by dancer Ann Smith. This kind of movement is a fine choice for people who, for whatever reason, don't actually want to dance. Smith's videos and DVDs are available from most Internet retailers and at *www.annsmithvideos.com.*

STEPPING OUT

Dance instructors and schools usually know about places where you can dance, and there are probably more of them than you realize—social organizations, nightclubs, cruise ships, religious groups, community events and senior centers. In addition, ballet and tap dancing schools often hold recitals where students perform.

There may be even more opportunities to dance onstage whenever a local theater group produces a musical with roles for older dancers. The best sources of information are the theater departments at local colleges and universities. My own organization, ArtAge Publications, also provides information about senior theaters throughout the country.

For specific types of dances, it's often helpful to contact the associations that promote them. The World Swing Dance Council, for instance, provides contact information for nearly two dozen organizations that hold regular swing dances throughout the country.

After a few turns on the dance floor, you'll get a good idea of whether you want to continue. If you decide that dancing isn't for you, at least you won't have spent hundreds of dollars on a treadmill that soon gets stored in a closet. But who knows? There's a time for every wallflower to bloom.

More from Bonnie Vorenberg...

Dances You'll Love

Organizations that can provide information on instruction, clubs and other opportunities to get out there and dance...

- **Ballroom.** USA Dance, 800-447-9047, *http://usabda.org.*
- **Belly dancing.** International Academy of Middle Eastern Dance, 818-343-4410, *www.bellydance.org.*
- **Bop, jitterbug and shag.** American Bop Association, *www.americanbopassociation.com.*
- **Country western, including line dancing.** United Country Western Dance Council, *www.ucwdc.com,* and Country Western Dance Information, 559-784-2341, *www.cwdi.org.*
- **Folk.** Folk Dance Association, *www.folkdancing.org.*
- **Hustle.** International Hustle Dance Association, *www.i-h-d-a.com.*
- **Square dancing.** United Square Dancers of America, *www.usda.org.*
- **Swing.** World Swing Dance Council, *www.swingdancecouncil.com.*
- **Tango, rumba, salsa, merengue, cha cha and other Latin dances.** LatinDance.com, *www.latin-dance.com.*

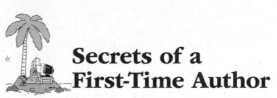

Secrets of a First-Time Author

Arthur Schechner, author of *The Second Son.* He is chairman of Schechner Lifson Corporation, an insurance and financial services company based in Summit, NJ, *www.slcinsure.com.*

Just after his 72nd birthday, Arthur Schechner thought his children and grandchildren should know about their family. The result is *The Second Son,* a memoir about births, deaths, World War II, high school adventures, business success, vacations in Italy and many other events that make families what they are. *For anyone who has considered writing a book, the experiences of Arthur Schechner are inspiring...*

● **I had never written a book before** and was faced with two immediate challenges. First of all, thoughts came in a disjointed pattern. Some memories would occur to me about events that took place when I was 20 years old, and then my memory would jump ahead to things that happened when I was in my 40s. That made it impossible to work from an outline, as I had originally planned.

I read about a system of putting thoughts on 3 x 5 cards that could later be organized into a logical order for the book, but this didn't work for me, either. I found myself writing so much on the cards that I might as well have been writing the book itself.

● **The second challenge** was how to deal with the two types of recollections I had. There were memories about the actual events in my life, and there were also thoughts about the events. For example, a significant part of my life was spent living in a three-generation household headed by my grandfather. But I also had many thoughts about how spending time with my grandfather was important in forming my own life.

There are probably many ways of reconciling these two types of recollections, but in my case, I did it by splitting the book into two parts. One part is a recollection of my life as I remember it, and the second is a series of essays and comments that I put at the end of each chapter.

This system also solved the challenge of organization, because it gave me a pattern to follow throughout the book.

WRITING IT ALL DOWN

I don't use a computer, so I wrote in longhand in a three-ring notebook. Then, my secretary transcribed what I wrote onto a computer disk. I have a bias against computers because they're converting the world into typists. But don't let my views discourage you from using a computer, an old-fashioned typewriter or any other means of getting your thoughts down on paper.

In writing the book, I discovered that one recollection would trigger the memory of other events, and those would lead to still more. So, whenever I had a chance, I would grab my notebook and write.

If you write a book about your life, don't make the mistake of hiring an editor who changes your style. In my own case, I first asked my wife—a college professor—to edit the book. She edited the first few pages and made dozens of changes in structure and grammar. When I protested, she pointed out that some of my thoughts weren't expressed in complete sentences. I said that was OK because that's how I wrote it.

I also decided not to ask friends and relatives to help me recall events because, if they did, the book would turn into a collaborative project. I wanted it to be strictly my own story.

So, I worked on my own, and my wife did nothing more than correct misspellings. As a result, some repetition occurs, and events aren't always in chronological sequence. But who cares if something happened in 1941 and I said it was in 1942? To me, that wasn't important.

Several people who have read the book tell me it's written the way I talk. And that's exactly how I wanted it to be.

THE STORY

Anyone who reads *The Second Son* will know that my family is the center of my life.

The story begins with my earliest memories as a child in Newark, NJ, and takes the reader through the events that shaped my life—attending Weequahic High School (where, for a reason I don't remember, I was known as the Sheik), seeing my grandfather for the last time as he lay dying in a hospital, my wonderful marriage, the evolution of my business, working with my father and other grandfather and the births of my two children and six grandchildren.

By the way, the Weequahic section of Newark was also home to some well-known people, including author Philip Roth and Marty Edelston, whose company produces the publication you're reading.

At the end of the book, I list some of the lessons and truths I've learned in the last 75 years. *Here are three of them…*

•**We all have a role in *tikkun olam*,** Hebrew for "repairing the world."

•**I learned that I am not the brightest,** nor the strongest, nor the fastest, nor the richest of my friends and brothers and, in fact, I never was.

•**I still like to win.**

GETTING IT IN PRINT

I first looked into some of the new self-publishing companies that print books as they're needed—on demand—instead of charging the author for a large initial press run. I did not feel that on-demand publishers were right for me, because most of them market to the general public. For now at least, I wanted to give my book only to people I knew would be truly interested in it.

I went to the printer that my company uses. The on-demand publishers might have charged $15 to $16 per book, and I paid about $28 a piece for 75 books.

The Second Son has 335 pages, including 31 pages of black-and-white photographs, a table of contents and a three-page prologue.

A lot of people tell me it's a fun read, so maybe someday I'll publish it for a wider audience.

ADVICE TO OTHERS

If you want to write a book about yourself and your family, the best advice I can give is this: Just sit down and start. Then, don't be discouraged if the first pages don't measure up to your expectations. Put the book aside for a while, and set a specific time for resuming work on it—in two months, for instance.

During that time, don't file the first pages away. Instead, keep them in sight. You might wake up in the middle of the night with something you want to add.

I believe that, like me, many others will find it easier to write in their own voice instead of trying to imitate the style of other writers.

As you continue to write, I predict that you'll face another problem—knowing when to end the book. There is no solution for that except to realize that most people don't want to read a personal history that's more than 300 pages or so.

It also helps to keep focusing on your objective. For me, I felt that if I could write about my life, then my children, grandchildren and maybe my great-grandchildren yet to be born will have a document—written as I spoke—that will answer the question, "Who is that guy?"

More from Arthur Schechner…

Self-Publishing Is Easier Today

Arthur Schechner opted to print his own book, but other writers may want to take advantage of the dozens of companies that use digital technology to print books inexpensively.

Fees vary widely but generally range from about $1,000 to $4,000, depending on the extent of editing, the length and design of the book and the number of marketing services included in the publishing agreement. In addition, printing costs are typically $5 to $15 per book (softcover, up to 250 pages).

Major on-demand publishers include Author House (888-519-5121, *www.authorhouse. com*), BookSurge (866-308-6235, *www.book surge.com*), iUniverse (800-288-4677, *www. iuniverse.com*) and Xlibris (888-795-4274, *www.xlibris.com*).

Keep Family in Contact Via the Internet

A "family blog" is a private Web site that any family member can update with written messages, pictures, video and sounds at any time for all others to enjoy. It is password protected to bar unauthorized visitors.

Simplest: Use the free Blogger utility provided by Google at *www.blogger.com*— there's no charge for the Web site.

Other ways: E-mail can be used to send pictures, video and sounds as well as text messages. Instant messaging can let family members "chat" in real time.

All of these can keep family members in close contact even when they are located on different continents.

Patricia Robison, president, Computing Independence, Box 2031, New York City 10011.

How to Find Anything On the Web

Guy Hart-Davis, author of more than 30 computer books, including *Windows XP Professional: The Complete Reference…PC QuickSteps…*and *Mac OS X Panther QuickStep*s (all from McGraw-Hill).

Finding quality content on the Web can be frustrating and tedious. If you can't find what you are looking for by using your favorite search engine, it may be time to try searching on another site. *Among the best ones today…*

•**Ask.com** began as a question-answer Web site, but now it also offers conventional keyword searches. At *www.ask.com/webadvanced*, searches can be restricted to a Web site, geographical area or time period when a page was last modified.

•**Google** (*www.google.com*), the current search engine king, covers more than 8 billion Web pages. Special features include local business lookups…"SafeSearch," which blocks sexual content (click "Preferences," then check "Use Strict Filtering")…and many other advanced tools for narrowing your search.

•**MSN** (*www.msn.com*), the Microsoft Network, has both a search engine and an Internet portal—a site that organizes information so that you can click on a category (such as movies or sports) to browse rather than search the entire Internet.

•**Yahoo!** (*www.yahoo.com…search.yahoo.com*) is a veteran search engine combined with an Internet portal.

Also: Click on "Advanced Search" to search by domain (.org, .gov, etc.), for pages updated within a certain time frame and more advanced features.

Beware: Many Web services, including Google, insert cookies, or tracking files, into users' computers. People with privacy concerns can use Scroogle (*www.scroogle.org*) or another Web-based "Google scraper," which lets you search with Google but blocks its cookies.

•**Specialized search engines** can speed searches in subject areas or for specific content. *Examples…*

•Singingfish (*www.singingfish.com*) offers free audio and video content—songs, music videos, radio shows and more.

•BookFinder.com (*www.bookfinder.com*) searches more than 100,000 sellers for new and used books.

•Technorati (*www.technorati.com*) specializes in finding information posted on Web logs ("blogs") about everything from news stories to recipes.

Alternative: Use a metasearch engine, which delivers results from several search engines, to get an overview of the range of information available on a subject.

Among the best: Ixquick (*www.ixquick.com*) and SurfWax (*www.surfwax.com*).

Amazing Cell Phone Tricks

Dylan Tweney, a technology journalist located in San Mateo, CA. He has contributed to many publications, including *PC World* and *Business 2.0.*

Modern cell phones can do much more than simply make calls, thanks to text-messaging technology. (Instructions are on your phone provider's Web site or in your owner's manual.) *Here is how to use your cell phone to…*

•**Communicate even if the cellular network is overwhelmed.** Most cell phones sold since 2002 let users send and receive short text messages. In an emergency, these messages may be your best way to communicate.

Example: London's cellular phone system was so overwhelmed following terrorist bombings in July of 2005 that many voice callers got only busy signals—yet text messages still made it through.

You might have to pay a few cents per message if text messaging isn't included in your cellular calling plan. Typing on a cell phone takes time, so practice using text messaging periodically. In an emergency, try calling out before resorting to text messaging.

•**Get helpful information.** Google's Short Message Service (*www.google.com/sms*) will send you driving directions…local business listings…stock quotes…weather forecasts…and even word definitions to any cell phone equipped with text-messaging capability. To get any of the following, type the information listed and send it as a text message to the number 466453.

•Store or restaurant. Want to find a nearby Thai restaurant or hardware store? Just type the word "Thai" or "hardware" and the local zip code into your phone as a text message and send it. (If you don't know the local zip code, Google will accept the town/city and state instead.)

•Weather report. Type and send "weather" and zip code for a forecast.

•Directions. Type and send "from" and an address and "to" and an address for driving directions (include city and state in each address).

•Movie times and theaters. Send the film's name and your zip code.

•Stock price. Send a ticker symbol to get a stock quote.

•Word definition. Just send "define" and any English word.

A text message that contains the information will be sent to your cell phone within a minute. A printable, wallet-sized "tips sheet" with details is available on the Google SMS Web site. The service is free, but your service provider might charge a few cents per message.

•**Take a memo.** Most cell phones do contain some variety of voice recorder or a text memo function. Your phone's manual should have details on locating and using these tools, or just scroll through the phone's menu. If your phone doesn't include a memo tool, you can use its address book or calendar to save notes to yourself as text messages.

•**Identify a song.** Want to know the name of the song you're enjoying on the radio or in a store or restaurant? Dial 866-411-SONG on your cell, and hold the phone up to the music for 15 seconds—the call will disconnect on its own. You'll get a text message back from 411-Song (*www.411song. com*) identifying the artist and title. The first ID is free—subsequent song IDs cost 99 cents each. There's no charge if a song is too obscure or its sound quality is too poor for an ID.

Holiday Tricks from a Party Planner

Denise Vivaldo, a party planner and consultant in Los Angeles for 20 years and author of *Do It for Less! Parties*. Terrace. Her company, Food Fanatics, provides food-styling services for Hollywood television shows and movies. Go to *www.diflparties.com* or *www.foodfanatics.net* for more information.

A holiday open house is a great way to entertain friends and family without spending a lot of time and money. *Here, a longtime professional party planner reveals her secrets…*

SMART SCHEDULING

•**Opt for the third weekend of December.** This tends to be best for holiday parties—the first two weekends are usually overbooked with competing parties, and the fourth weekend falls too close to Christmas. Your holiday decorations should be up by the third weekend of the month, which means less time decorating for the party.

A late Sunday afternoon open house, say from 2 pm to 5 pm, will cause fewer conflicts than one on Friday or Saturday evening. Sunday night is not a wise choice, because guests will fret about getting up for work on Monday.

Schedule three to four hours for the open house—anything longer and you'll be exhausted by the end.

•**Send out invitations three weeks in advance.** Provide details about your open house on the invitation. Is dress casual or fancy? What food will be served? (You could say, "Hors d'oeuvres and drinks" on the invitation.) Are kids welcome? Should guests skip a gift? Where should they park? If there's an important game the day of your party, your invitation should reassure sports fans that the game will be shown, perhaps in a side room. Also, ask guests to let you know in advance if they have special dietary needs so that you can adjust your menu accordingly.

Helpful: If your friends are Internet savvy, you can e-mail invitations and track responses for free at Evite.com.

FOOD

In addition to cheese and fruit plates or crudités with dip, provide at least one hearty hors d'oeuvre. Beef or chicken satay is usually a big hit at parties. Or you can opt for the traditional sliced, roasted turkey breast or ham, with rolls, mayo, Dijon mustard and other fixings for do-it-yourself sandwiches.

Hot foods are a challenge at open houses because they won't stay hot for long, but meatballs and cheese fondue (served with cubes of French bread) are two hot dishes that typically hold up well in chafing dishes. Think twice about serving other hot foods that force you to run back and forth to the oven every few minutes.

DRINK

You don't need to provide a full bar at an open house, but do have a number of drink options—not everyone likes eggnog. Offer beer, wine, sparkling water, soda and perhaps a pitcher of a popular mixed drink, such as cosmopolitans or mojitos. Cold beverages should be set out in ice-filled tubs or coolers so your guests don't have to open your refrigerator every time they're thirsty.

If some of your guests are big drinkers, ask a friend to serve as the designated driver to get inebriated guests home safely…keep the phone number of a cab company handy…or hire a pair of responsible teenagers from your neighborhood to be on call as drivers—one to drive the guest's car home, the other to follow in his/her own car for the trip back. You

could be liable if a guest has an accident after drinking alcohol at your home.

TROUBLESHOOTING

•**Make sure you have enough plates and glasses.** Open houses often run short of glasses and hors d'oeuvre plates—one guest can go through four or five of each. Rent extra plates and glasses, or buy quality plastic ones.

•**Prevent used plates and glasses from piling up all over** by putting a large tray near the kitchen. Place one or two dirty dishes on it before guests arrive so they can tell that it's the busing station. You might have to clear the tray several times.

•**Don't overdo the cleaning.** Turn down the lights, and bring out the candles. (Use hurricane candle shades to reduce risk of fire.) No one will notice the floors weren't scrubbed.

•**Spread thick, clear rug-runner plastic by the door** for guests to leave wet boots and umbrellas. You might even buy a few dozen pairs of thick socks and ask your guests to leave their shoes by the door and help themselves to your holiday gift of a pair of socks.

Gift-Giving Dos and Don'ts

Peggy Post, great-granddaughter-in-law of etiquette pioneer Emily Post. She is a director and spokesperson for the Emily Post Institute in Burlington, VT, and author of *Emily Post's Etiquette, 17th Edition.* HarperCollins. The institute's Web site is *www.emilypost.com.*

Every holiday season, we receive hundreds of letters at the Emily Post Institute asking about the etiquette of gift-giving. *Here are the questions we get most often…*

•**Is it OK to "regift"?** *Sometimes—but proceed cautiously and follow these guidelines…*

•The item must be brand new and in its original package.

•The gift should be something the recipient would love.

•It should not be something the original giver took great care to select or make for you.

•Regifting a nice bottle of wine to a wine lover is fine. Regifting the crystal vase that your mother gave you is not. If in doubt, don't do it.

•**Someone with whom I wasn't planning to exchange gifts gave me one. Do I have to reciprocate?** No. Just thank the gift giver sincerely and leave it at that. Otherwise, you may start a new gift-giving tradition that can be very difficult to break. Of course, if that's what you would like to do, reciprocate!

•**My parents gave me a very expensive television—but it is not the one I wanted. Can I ask them if I can exchange it for a different one?** Just be honest, especially since the gift was extravagant and your parents will expect to see you use it.

First, thank them enthusiastically for the very generous gift. Try to point out something specific that requires you to return it. For example, if it's missing a feature that you were hoping for, gently suggest an exchange. Say something like, "Mom, Dad, this is an amazing gift—but this model doesn't include the surround-sound feature that I think we would especially enjoy. Would you mind terribly if I exchanged it?"

•**I've been invited to a holiday party. Should I bring a gift for the host?** Yes, but don't bring anything that distracts the host—food or flowers that need to be taken care of immediately are not the best choices.

Keep the gift simple and under $20—a bottle of wine…a small potted plant…an arrangement of flowers already in a vase…a box of holiday cookies or chocolates.

There is one exception. An open house is an informal way to celebrate and doesn't require a gift for the host, though you can certainly bring one if you choose.

•**I mail my grandchildren their holiday presents, but they never send me thank-you notes. This really bothers me. Should I talk to my son?** Start by calling and asking your son or daughter-in-law—or even better, ask your grandchildren directly—whether all their gifts arrived safely. If the answer is yes, drop a hint with, "Well, I'm glad to hear that. Since I didn't hear from you, I was starting to wonder if the packages made it there. Did you like the gifts?"

If you don't think that you got your message across, you will have to be more direct. Talk frankly to your son—or if the grandkids are age eight or older, speak to them. Tell them politely that it's important to you that they express appreciation when you give them a gift.

If this doesn't work, you may choose to stop sending gifts. That should get their attention—and teach your grandchildren that thank-you notes mean a lot.

•**Should I give my boss a holiday gift? What about the people who report to me and other coworkers?** Generally, you should not give a gift to the boss. It could be seen as an attempt to win favor. However, an inexpensive gift that isn't too personal from you and other employees is fine. If you and your boss have worked closely together for years, it's OK to give a small gift.

When you're the boss, it's up to you whether or not to give gifts to your staff. It's certainly a nice gesture and a great way to acknowledge those who work for you.

If you do decide to give gifts, give across the board—don't give to only one department head but not to the other two.

Good gift ideas include a nice bottle of wine, gift certificates, CDs and food items.

As for coworkers, a Secret Santa (in which each employee draws a name and gives a gift to that person) or a holiday grab bag are two of the easier ways to handle gift giving.

Food gifts also are a good idea—bring in a batch of homemade cookies or a box of chocolates to share with colleagues.

More from Peggy Post…

When Guests Stay Too Long

Even the best parties have to end sometime—but some guests just don't take the hint when it is time to leave. If starting to clean up and other tricks don't work, it is OK to let guests know that the party is winding down.

Tell them that you have had a nice time but that you have to get up early the next day. Or say, "I have to 'close down' in 15 minutes," which allows them to depart in a relaxed fashion.

For house guests who stay too long: Define the length of their stay from the beginning. If you haven't done that and you are ready for guests to leave, tell them, "I have enjoyed your visit, but I must return to my regular schedule." Offer a farewell breakfast as a send-off.

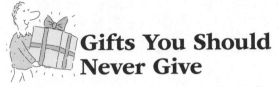

Gifts You Should Never Give

Sherri Athay, coauthor of *Present Perfect: Unforgettable Gifts for Every Occasion.* Mobius. She and her husband, Larry, founded Present Perfect Gift Consultants, gift selection advisers, Essex, CT, *www.giftelan.com.*

The best gifts can nurture the relationship between the giver and recipient. The worst gifts "say" inappropriate things. *Don't give gifts that are...*

• **Inducements to improve.** Although you might think such gifts are exactly what the recipient needs, he/she may resent their implications—and you.

Examples: A treadmill given to a couch potato...time-management classes to someone who is disorganized.

• **Beneath the recipient's standards.** If your sister wears only solid gold jewelry, don't present her with costume jewelry. Just because you can't tell the difference doesn't mean she will appreciate an impostor.

• **Assembly required**—unless you're certain the recipient is willing or able to do the job (or you'll do it for him). You wouldn't give a child an unassembled bicycle, and you shouldn't leave Uncle Ned's bookshelf in pieces in the box.

• **Living creatures.** Giving any pet to a child without consulting his parents or to an adult without being certain the animal is wanted can backfire. The recipient might resent having to take care of the pet and may give it away.

• **Intended for family use,** or your own use, but disguised as a gift to an individual. The recipient will be on to you as soon as the wrapping is off.

Example: A high-definition TV to your wife when you're the one who loves to watch TV.

A Guide to Fine Scotch

Kevin Erskine, creator of The Scotch Blog (*www.thescotchblog.com*), which offers Scotch whisky industry news, Richmond, VA. He is author of *The Instant Expert's Guide to Single Malt Scotch.* Doceon.

Scotch is growing in popularity in America, but many people still find selecting a Scotch intimidating. *Here's help...*

SINGLE MALT VS. BLENDED

To be legally called Scotch, a whisky must be distilled and aged in Scotland. Scotch is made from barley, water and yeast and is aged for at least three years. In the malting process, barley is soaked in water and allowed to germinate—germination allows enzymes in the barley to turn starch into sugar, which converts to alcohol.

Single-malt Scotch is made from malted barley at one distillery. Blended Scotch is a combination of malted barleys (often from different distilleries) and other nonmalted grain whiskies (usually from two to 50 varieties). In general, single-malt Scotch has stronger flavors than blends, which are smoother and lighter. Blends are best for mixed drinks, such as a whiskey sour or Rob Roy, or if you're adding soda water, cola, fruit juice or ice.

TASTE TEST

To determine what you like in a Scotch, taste a variety of brands. A good way to sample different Scotches is to buy miniature bottles or try a glass at a bar or restaurant.

- **Smell the Scotch** to detect its signature scents. For example, you may notice vanilla and caramel, a peaty (earthy) aroma or floral, spicy or fruity scents. If possible, sample the Scotch in a tulip-shaped glass or a brandy snifter, which allows the aroma, or "nose," to gather in the bell of the glass.

- **Notice the color.** Scotch ranges from very pale gold or yellow to bronze or amber. When first distilled, Scotch is clear in color. It is then placed into oak casks previously used to age bourbon or sherry. Scotch gets all of its color during the aging process. Lighter colors generally denote bourbon casks, while darker colors indicate sherry casks.

- **Cup the glass in your hand** to warm the whisky before drinking it. Many connoisseurs also add a bit of bottled water to their Scotch. Adding water "opens up" the whisky, releasing new scents and flavors. Start with a few drops—let your taste dictate how much. In general, older or lighter-flavored Scotch requires less water than younger (eight-to-12-year-old), very peaty Scotch.

- **Take a large sip,** and let the whisky roll over your tongue. Observe the feel of the Scotch—is it smooth, light, oily, thick, astringent, dry? Identify the primary tastes—sweet, salty, sour or bitter. Most whiskies have a mixture of tastes. Next, try to detect the flavors—you may recognize citrus, apple, vanilla, honey, wood and grass or any of a dozen other flavors. Swallow and notice whether the flavor disappears immediately or lingers, changes or is replaced by a new flavor (this is called "the finish").

- **Recap the bottle tightly,** and store it in its carton in a cool, dark place. Exposure to light could adversely affect the flavor. As a rule of thumb, an open bottle of whisky that is more than half empty should be finished within 18 months because air in the bottle can affect the flavor as well.

BRANDS TO ENJOY

Scotch can cost hundreds of dollars. *Here are quality affordable choices...*

Single malts...

- **The Balvenie Double Wood** (pronounced bal-VEH-nee). A sweet, bourbonish taste. $40.*
- **Bruichladdich 15** (brewch-LADDIE). A balanced sweet barley malt with a touch of peat. $65.
- **Glenfiddich 12** (glen-FID-ick). Light-bodied, sweet taste. $32.
- **Glenmorangie 10** (glen-MOR-angee). Fruity, spicy notes. $50.
- **Laphroaig 10** (la-FROYg). Full-bodied, dry, pungent. $49.
- **The Macallan 12** (ma-CAL-en). Full-bodied, rich and creamy. $45.

Blends...

- **The Famous Grouse.** Peppery with light honey undertones. $40.
- **Johnnie Walker Gold.** This mix of rare single malts has a creamy taste. $70.

*Prices subject to change.

Greetings from The White House

Christie Parell, White House spokesperson, Washington, DC.

The White House will send greetings signed by the president to US citizens who are celebrating their 50th wedding anniversary and beyond...80th birthday and beyond...weddings...and other special occasions. Requests should include the name, title (Ms., Dr., etc.) and address of the honoree(s)...name and daytime phone number of the person making the request...month, day and year of the special occasion...age of the recipient (for birthdays)...how long the couple has been married (for anniversaries). Mail requests for anniversaries and birthdays at least six weeks before the event. Mail to The White House, Attn.: Greetings Office, Washington, DC 20502-0039...fax them to the White House Greetings Office at 202-395-1232...or send them on-line through the Web site *www.white house.gov/greeting* (click the second "Guidelines" under "Invitations and Greetings").

Real-Time Answers From Librarians

Available 24/7 at *www.massanswers.org*, librarians from participating institutions nationwide offer free question-and-answer sessions on any topic. This will save a trip to your local library and is helpful if your Internet searches aren't finding the answers.

Real Simple, 1271 Avenue of the Americas, New York City 10020.

The Secret to Improving Your Golf Swing—Don't Believe the Pros

Michael Yessis, PhD, professor emeritus of kinesiology at California State University, Fullerton, and president of Sports Training, Inc., a sports fitness and consulting company in Escondido, CA. He is author of several books on sports training, including *Sports: Is It All B.S.? Dr. Yessis Blows the Whistle on Player Development* (Equilibrium) and *Explosive Golf: Using the Science of Kinesiology to Improve Your Swing* (McGraw-Hill), *www.dryessis.com.*

Golf pros and golf magazines are full of suggestions for improving one's swing, but sports fitness consultant Michael Yessis, PhD, believes some of the most common advice is wrong. He has studied the golf swing, using high-speed photography, to determine what works and what doesn't.

Here are six common myths...

Myth 1: **The backswing is the key to your swing.**

Reality: The backswing means less than most people believe. Golf instructors harp on the backswing simply because it's the only part of the swing that is slow enough for them to follow, but as long as your backswing is consistent, comfortable and gets you to a starting point that lets you generate power, its fine details are not a problem. Instead, focus on your down swing—that's where you get both your power and accuracy.

Myth 2: **Hands and arms should start your downswing.**

Reality: If your hands and arms are leading your downswing, you're sacrificing a tremendous amount of power. Your downswing should begin with a forward weight shift of the hips, followed by hip rotation. Only when hip rotation is nearly concluded should shoulder rotation even begin, starting the hands in motion. By rotating the hips before the shoulders (and arms and hands) start to move, you stretch the abdominal oblique muscles so that they can contract with greater force when your upper body does come through.

Even during your shoulder rotation, your hands should be following the shoulders, not driving the action. Only when shoulder rotation is virtually complete should your hands and arms be powering the swing.

Bottom line: Think of your swing as a step-by-step process of transferring force from your midbody to your shoulders and only then to your arms and hands and then onto your club.

Myth 3: **You'll get more power if you drive your knee forward during your swing.**

Reality: You'll get more power if you drive your hips forward and let your knee and leg simply follow them forward as a result. The heavier the body part, the greater the power it can convey to your club head. Shifting your hips will transfer a lot more weight and power than shifting your knee.

Myth 4: **Wrist break happens naturally during a good swing.**

Reality: Golf instructors say it's natural because it feels natural to them. For many amateur golfers, wrist break doesn't automatically happen at the proper moment. The wrists should break as the club head nears the ball.

Myth 5: **A slice is the result of an outside-inside swing.**

Reality: Outside-inside swings—which loop out and then back in again—are very uncommon. If you really did swing this way, you would be off-balance and falling backward. It's far more likely that your slice is the result of striking the ball with an open clubface—when the club head strikes the ball at an oblique angle rather than a square angle—probably because of weak wrist break or arm action.

Exercise: You can improve your wrist and arm action by improving your wrist and arm strength. Attach a 2.5- to five-pound weight to one end of a short bar, such as a dumbbell bar. Stand normally with your arms at your sides and your palms facing your legs, holding the bar in one hand with the weighted end extending behind you. Without moving your arm, turn your wrist to lift the weight (and your little finger) up toward the side of your forearm, then ease it back down and repeat. Perform this exercise with each wrist for a few weeks, and you might cure your slice.

Myth 6: **The longest hitters in driving competitions stand up very straight,** so you should stand up straighter, too.

Reality: Stand up straight, and you will have trouble keeping your eye on the ball, causing frequent mis-hits. The competitors in driving competitions are willing to sacrifice accuracy and consistency for distance. In all other circumstances, it's smarter to lean over the ball.

Helpful: Lean from the hips, not from the waist. Your drives will be longer and your back healthier if your spine is straight, in its normal, slightly arched lumbar curvature, during your swing. This might feel uncomfortable at first, but stay with it and you'll get used to it.

Batter Up—Vacations With Baseball Heroes

Marjory Abrams, publisher, *Bottom Line* newsletters, Boardroom Inc., 281 Tresser Blvd., Stamford, CT 06901.

When Patrick Netter, our longtime fitness expert, heard that a friend had signed up for a Yankees' baseball camp, it didn't take him long to do so, too. Ever since he was young, Patrick has loved baseball—especially Yankees baseball. He used to hide a radio under his blanket so he could listen to games long after his bedtime.

The opportunity to meet some of his heroes—and maybe feel like a boy again—was just too good to pass up. Heroes In Pinstripes Yankees Baseball Camp* (*www.heroesinpinstripes.com*), started more than two decades ago by Mickey Mantle and Whitey Ford, more than met his expectations...

• **There was plenty of time to schmooze** about baseball and life with such old-timers as Bucky Dent, Ron Guidry, Tony Kubek and Don Larsen, who graciously signed autographs.

• **There was lots of baseball**—two nine-inning games every day and a two-inning game with the old-timers on the last day. What could compare with being coached by Mickey Rivers? Patrick even had the chance to be the commentator during the old-timers-versus-campers game at Fort Lauderdale Stadium.

• **He batted over .400.** Though he gives himself some of the credit, Patrick explained that the pitchers—the real Yankee training pitchers—were not trying to strike you out. Also helpful were pregame stretches and the Yankee trainer who soothed any overused muscles.

Patrick's professional life revolves around fitness. He reviews and introduces sports, health and fitness gear on TV and his Web site, *www.gearguru.com*. But fantasy campers don't have to be fitness buffs or, for that matter, young—except young at heart. The minimum age to participate is 30. Some campers are well into their 60s (Patrick is in his 50s). Wives, children and girlfriends may attend games and some events, but the camp is for men only.

This particular Yankee fantasy camp, now run by Moose Skowron and Hank Bauer, is scheduled for November 9 to November 16, 2008, in Fort Lauderdale, FL. If pinstripes don't suit you, check out the camps offered by other Major League teams, including the Boston Red Sox (Florida in February), the

*There also is another Yankees fantasy baseball camp called Pride, Power, Pinstripes. *newyork.yankees.mlb.com.*

Detroit Tigers (Florida, January and February) and the San Francisco Giants (Arizona, January). For more details, look for the team's Web site via the Major League Baseball Web site, *www.mlb.com* (search for "camp").

Baseball camp isn't cheap—but it can make a great gift for a special occasion. The five-day Heroes In Pinstripes experience costs about $5,000 and includes first-class accommodations, ground transportation and most meals—plus an authentic team uniform (with bench jacket, socks and belt), an autographed ball and other souvenirs. One of the best "perks," included in the price, is the camp reunion that takes place at Yankee Stadium the following summer...the continuation of a dream come true.

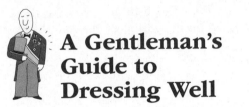

A Gentleman's Guide to Dressing Well

Bob Mitchell, copresident of high-end clothiers Mitchells of Westport, CT, and Richards of Greenwich, CT. Mitchells was started by his parents in 1958. *www.mitchellsonline.com*.

Many men say they don't care about fashion, but dressing well isn't just vanity—how we look affects how we're perceived and how we feel about ourselves. *To make a great impression...*

●**Opt for a trim look.** The fit of a garment can be even more important than its quality. Suits and shirts feel most comfortable when they're cut a bit loose, but the extra fabric can make you look overweight or rumpled. You'll look best if your suits and shirts are cut trim (but not tight), even if you're carrying extra pounds. *Also...*

●Narrow-bodied men should ask their tailors to take in the sides of their shirts.

Cost: About $20* per shirt.

●Short-armed men should have a tailor shorten the shirt's arms—the cuff bottom should come to the end of the wrist.

*Prices subject to change.

Cost: About $20 per shirt.

Helpful: You also can order custom-made shirts starting at about $50.

●**Match your shirt collar to your neck.** Men with long necks look best in dress shirts with high collars...men with wide necks look best in wide collars...and men with short necks look best with short, narrow collars.

●**Favor long sleeves over short.** Short-sleeved shirts are fine for lounging by the pool or playing golf on warm days, but choose long sleeves for most other occasions. If it gets really hot, a long-sleeved shirt with rolled-up sleeves still looks sharper than short sleeves.

●**When selecting a tie, stick with solids and simple stripes.** Ties may be bright but never busy. If you would like to make a bold fashion statement, go ahead and choose a boldly colored tie, perhaps in yellow, pink or teal, but don't select a busy tie with a complicated pattern—these are distracting and appear undignified.

●**Buy timeless, not trendy.** If you purchase classic-style suits and sports jackets, you don't have to worry about looking dated or keeping up with the latest styles.

●Navy and gray...solids and very subtle stripes...in medium-weight wool are always in style.

●Two- or three-button jackets are preferable to four or five buttons.

●Medium-width lapels are better than noticeably thin or wide ones.

●**Choose white or light blue solid dress shirts** unless you're confident of your fashion sense.

●**Skip pleated pants.** Flat-front pants are flattering and stylish for men of all body types.

●**Match your belt and your shoes.** Black belts go with black shoes, brown with brown. Ideally, your shoes and belt would match your briefcase as well.

●**Pick socks that bridge the gap.** Your socks should split the color difference between your shoes and your pants.

Example: If you're wearing dark brown shoes and tan pants, select medium-brown socks that fall roughly midway between those shades. Socks should either be solid in color or have only a subtle pattern.

•**Dress with class even when you don't need to dress up.** Many men are at a loss for how to look good when they're not in a suit. *If you want to look sharp even when casual...*

•Wear wool pants instead of cotton. Cotton pants wrinkle easily. They're fine for the golf course but not for most outings. Mid-weight wool pants with a pressed crease are always appropriate and can be worn most of the year...lightweight wool pants can be worn in summer. Choose conservative colors—black, gray, navy or olive.

•Favor a classic loafer over boat shoes or sneakers.

•Bold-colored shirts are acceptable when you're not wearing a tie, but avoid busy, distracting patterns. Solids and subtle stripes or checks are best.

•**Skip the ski jacket unless you're skiing.** Ski jackets are particularly inappropriate when you're wearing a suit or sport jacket. Wear a three-quarter- or full-length coat instead.

Poker Whiz Andy Bellin's Rules for Winning

Andy Bellin, who left graduate school—where he was an astronomy and physics student—10 years ago to become a semiprofessional poker player. A former contributing editor at *The Paris Review*, he is also author of *Poker Nation*. HarperCollins.

Most people are terrible poker players because they are really not at the table to win, but to socialize. To become a better player, you've got to follow a few rules, which you can do without spoiling your fun or alienating your friends. *Here's how...*

•**Stay focused.** Be as sociable as you want at the table—but only *between* hands. As soon as the cards are dealt and until you fold, avoid conversation.

Keep your eyes on the action around you. What cards do you have in your hand? What are the odds of turning it into a winning hand? What clues can you pick up from other players' body language?

Don't drink too much alcohol, either. The more attention you pay to the game, the more often you'll win.

•**Play fewer hands.** The easiest way to make money in poker is to avoid losing money on bad hands. To achieve that, you must be willing to fold your hands early and often.

Most players think it's rude to fold early in a hand, so they will bet at least once no matter what cards they're holding. I've seen poor players raise four times on nothing hands just because they didn't want to appear timid or tight with money.

My advice: Don't bet at all unless you think you have a potentially winning hand. Instead, fold and let others make the bad bets. If other players tease you and say, "Hey, it's only a dollar," ignore them.

Don't bet wildly even if you think you do have a winning hand. The worst hand in poker is the second-best hand in the game. You'll keep feeding money into the pot, which eventually will go to the player whose hand trumps yours.

Strategy: Analyze the betting. If someone who is normally cautious keeps raising, he/she may have a better hand than you. If visible cards in your hand show strength and another player isn't frightened, fold. Save your money for the next hand.

•**Expect to lose some hands.** Bad poker players obsess over every hand. They know, to the penny, how much they're up or down for the night. They'll say, "I'm down 20 bucks and I have to get even."

If you put yourself under that kind of pressure, you will push too hard and make dumb bets. You'll finish the evening down a lot more than $20.

Right mind-set: Expect to lose some hands. Sometimes you will lose even great hands—

because someone else had even better cards. Do not beat yourself up if you fold and find out later that you would have won the pot. It's OK to get bluffed. Dropping out when it looks like you won't win means that you are a discerning player—you're taking all of the factors of the game into account, not just calling every bet. That's a good thing. If you win every hand you have the cards to win, you're probably losing even more on games where you should have folded but didn't.

View poker with a long-term perspective. Accept your losses for the night, without punishing yourself. You'll be the winner another night.

● **Don't overestimate your skills.** You may not want to admit that you are a poor poker player, but the surest way to lose money is by thinking that you are better than you really are.

Example: Poor players think the way to win at poker is by bluffing. In fact, few hands in a low-stakes game are won by bluffing out another player.

Just play your hand, and don't try anything fancy. If you have a great hand, bet it hard. If you don't, fold quickly.

● **Play games where you have an edge.** When you're the dealer and can choose the game, pick one in which your position has an advantage.

Example: In games where cards are visible, such as "seven-card stud," the betting usually begins with the high card. As dealer, you could be the first to bet, the last or somewhere in between. In "draw or hold 'em," however, where all cards are face down, betting starts to the left of the dealer and then goes around the table. That offers you, as dealer, a tremendous advantage because you will get to see everyone else bet before you do.

If you have a strong hand and there have been few, if any, raises, you can think about calling and playing a little longer. The more that other players have raised, the more you should fold with anything but a very strong hand.

● **Know the odds of drawing to a hand.** Billions of poker games have been played over hundreds of years. Over that time, it has been established to a mathematical certainty the odds of drawing to a given hand. *Here are the odds...*

YOUR HAND	ODDS AGAINST DRAWING
No pair	1 to 1
One pair	1.25 to 1
Two pair	20 to 1
Three of a kind	46 to 1
Straight	254 to 1
Flush	508 to 1
Full house	693 to 1
Four of a kind	4,164 to 1
Straight flush	64,973 to 1
Royal straight flush	649,739 to 1

Knowing the odds of drawing to a given hand is an essential part of becoming a winning poker player. Say there's $10 in the pot and you must bet $1 to stay in the game. Based on your study of other players, you believe you need three jacks to win. But the odds against finishing with three jacks are 46 to 1, while the most you can win if you take the pot is $10. Common sense tells you to fold the hand.

Important: Just knowing the odds is not enough. You must use the knowledge to keep from making bad bets. If you're the kind of player who says, "I know I'm going to lose this hand but I'm going to take a chance anyway," knowing the odds won't do you a bit of good.

● **Beware of games with wild cards.** Home poker games are filled with gimmicks, such as wild cards. Avoid them, unless you are a truly sophisticated player.

Reason: All those odds of drawing to a given hand are based on basic, straight poker. Whenever you add wild cards into the mix, the math changes. Unless you're confident you can recalculate the odds when there are four or eight wild cards in the game, stick to meat-and-potatoes poker. Let other players throw their money away on gimmicks.

14

Car Smarts

Is Your Auto Mechanic Ripping You Off?

Although most auto mechanics are honest, some are scam artists who will try to trick car owners into paying for unnecessary repairs. Such disreputable behavior is particularly common at service stations near highway exits, since most customers are only passing through. But even a local mechanic may "manufacture" a problem when you bring your car in for an inspection or some other reason.

MOST COMMON CONS

• **Loosening spark plug cables.** A garage mechanic loosens your spark plug cables, then tells you that your engine is running sluggishly and recommends a tune-up or some other pricey fix.

Solution: Before you let a mechanic service a suddenly rough-running engine, make sure your spark plug cables are all tightly connected.

• **Faking a failing alternator.** A mechanic surreptitiously splashes antifreeze on your alternator, causing it to give off smoke when the engine is hot. He warns you that when an alternator smokes, it needs to be replaced.

Solution: If there wasn't smoke before you pulled into the gas station, the problem might have been caused by the attendant. Try wiping down the smoking part with a moist rag to see if the smoke is eliminated.

• **Cleaning up an old part** and telling you it's new. A mechanic tells you that your car needs a new part, such as a starter or air filter. After you agree to let him do the work, he pulls out the old part, cleans it up or repaints it, then puts it back into your car and tells you it's new.

Solution: When you are handed a repair bill that includes replacement parts, insist on seeing the garage's purchase receipt from

---

Sid Kirchheimer, an investigative reporter and author of the "Scam Alert" column in *AARP Bulletin*. He is author of *Scam-Proof Your Life: 377 Smart Ways to Protect You & Your Family from Ripoffs, Bogus Deals & Other Consumer Headaches.* Sterling.

the auto-parts store. (If the work was done at a dealership where the part was in stock, there won't be a purchase receipt.)

Keep a bottle of correction fluid, such as Wite-Out, in your glove compartment. When a mechanic tells you that a part must be replaced and the part is easily accessible, put a dot of Wite-Out on it when he isn't watching, preferably on the side or bottom so it isn't obvious. Once the repair has been done, ask for your old part back. If the part you're handed lacks your Wite-Out mark, the original part might have been used.

Also put a dot of Wite-Out on the sidewall of one tire when you bring the vehicle in for a tire rotation. If the dotted tire is still in the same position when you return, the work wasn't done.

• **"Short-sticking" the oil.** A service station attendant doesn't push the dipstick all the way in, creating the impression that your oil is low. He sells you a few quarts of oil—but the oil bottles he appears to pour into your engine actually are empty.

Solution: Check the oil yourself unless you trust the garage.

• **Poking holes in radiators or tires.** A sneaky mechanic might jab radiators or tires with a screwdriver to cause leaks, then charge you to fix them.

Solution: Radiators don't often suffer small puncture holes—cracks and corrosion are more common problems. Be suspicious when a mechanic "discovers" a hole if your vehicle showed no previous signs of radiator problems.

When tires are punctured, the nail or other debris that caused the hole usually remains embedded in the rubber. If there's no nail and the tire seemed fine before you pulled into the station, you might be the victim of a scam.

Of course, the problem must be repaired. If the car is still drivable, head to another repair shop or, if you are a member of an auto club, have your car towed.

• **Spraying oil on the shock absorbers.** With a few squirts of oil on your car's shock absorbers, a mechanic can make it appear as if your shocks are leaking and need to be replaced.

Solution: Examine this "leaking" oil closely—if it is really from your shocks, it should look grimy and old, not clean and fresh. If you have any suspicions, don't be pressured into replacing your shocks immediately. Even if they are failing, this doesn't pose a danger—you will just have a bumpier ride. (Driving with worn shocks does somewhat increase tire wear and braking distances, however.) Wipe the suspect oil off the shocks, and check them over the coming days. If the oil returns, you probably do need new shocks.

FINDING A MECHANIC YOU CAN TRUST

To find a trustworthy mechanic, ask friends for recommendations. Also, check the garage recommendations in your area on the Car Talk Web site (*www.cartalk.com/content/mechx*).

Avoid shops that…

• **Have lots of municipal vehicles parked out front.** Governments often take the lowest bids, which usually don't equate to top-quality work.

• **Have had the same cars sitting in front for months.** This might mean ongoing lawsuits about repair bills.

• **Have only cars of different eras or makes than yours out front.** For example, a garage that mainly works on domestic cars might not have the expertise to deal with an import.

Those Knocks, Clicks And Strange Smells Could Mean Danger

Eric Peters, Washington, DC–based automotive columnist and author of *Automotive Atrocities! The Cars We Love to Hate.* MBI.

Cars often give their owners plenty of warning—in the form of new noises, odors and other signs—before a mechanical failure occurs. *Here are some danger signs and what they may mean…*

NOISES

•Metallic tapping/clicking from the engine. If you hear a new sound such as this, it probably means you're low on engine oil—a condition that could burn out the engine. Check your oil, and fill it up if necessary. If the metallic tapping/clicking persists, you might have a failing oil pump or a problem related to the valve train, such as a collapsed hydraulic lifter. (Lifters actuate the valves, which let fuel into and exhaust out of your engine.) Take your car to a shop as soon as possible to avoid potentially serious damage.

Comfort: If the sound has been there a long time, it just might be an indication of a heavily worn, high-mileage engine.

•Underhood screeches. If you hear screeching when accelerating or turning the steering wheel, you might have a loose or worn-out drive belt...low power-steering fluid ...or a failing water pump, a device that circulates coolant through the engine to keep it from overheating. Major damage can occur quickly from overheating, so stop driving the car if a problem of this sort crops up.

If you are a bit handy, you can top off your power-steering fluid by following the instructions in your owner's manual. Otherwise, take the car to a repair shop.

If the power-steering fluid is too low, the power-steering system will eventually fail, the car will be much more difficult to steer and you might not be able to maintain safe control.

Drive belt and water pump problems need a mechanic's attention. Don't wait long. If the water pump fails (or the "serpentine" belt that drives it and other accessories fails), the engine will quickly overheat—and you will lose the use of all power-assisted devices, so pull over as fast as you safely can.

•Clunking or "ka-thumping." If, when you put your car into drive (or put a manual transmission car into a gear), you hear a fairly loud clunking or ka-thumping sound, you may have a worn-out universal joint—the flexible joint that connects the transmission to the driveshaft and the driveshaft to the axle. This is not necessarily an emergency, but if you let it go on too long, the joint could fail. Then your driveshaft could come loose, possibly striking the ground and even pole-vaulting the vehicle into the air.

•Knocking. Many late-model cars with modern engines keep running smoothly regardless of whether you put in regular (low-octane) or premium (high-octane) fuel, so you won't hear the knocking or pinging that is a classic sign of too-low-octane fuel. (You will, however, suffer decreased fuel economy and less horsepower if you use the wrong gasoline.)

With cars built before electronic controls became commonplace in the late 1980s, gas with an octane rating below the recommended minimum may cause premature combustion, and you'll hear the knocking or pinging. That is a sign of great stress on internal engine components. In these cars, extended use of low-octane gas can cause severe engine damage.

Another kind of knocking: If you ever hear very loud knocking coming from the engine compartment—so loud that it's impossible to drown it out with, say, the radio—it could signal a major problem, such as a "spun" (loose) crankshaft bearing or connecting rod failure, either of which can cause major—perhaps irreparable—damage. A sudden loss of oil pressure (caused by, say, the oil drain plug falling out) could also cause a racket.

When your car makes any very loud noise, immediately pull over and turn off the engine—that may limit the damage. Then arrange for a tow.

•Undercar sputtering. This usually means a leaky exhaust system. Typically, the sound gets more obnoxious the harder you push on the gas pedal—and in particular, when you suddenly lift off the gas. Get this checked out quickly because a leaking exhaust system can allow dangerous fumes into the car's interior.

•Whining or screeching that's not from the engine. This could indicate a problem with the automatic transmission's internal pump, which circulates hydraulic fluid that lubricates and powers the transmission. The noise might be accompanied by late or erratic shifting from gear to gear or "slipping" (you press on the gas and the engine revs, but the car doesn't move forward right away).

On manual-transmission cars, a worn or out-of-adjustment clutch may "chatter," sending vibrations through the clutch pedal. When it is very worn, it will cause the same kind of gear slippage that you might experience with a worn automatic.

SMELLS

•**Oily-sweet.** This is the smell of engine coolant—and if you smell it inside your car, you could have the beginnings of a real mess. It could be a leaking heater core—a small, radiator-like part buried deep inside your car, often in between the engine and the passenger compartment. When it fails, it can allow hot, smelly (and oily) engine coolant to seep into the car's interior and soak the carpet.

Another clue: An oily/foggy film on the inside surface of the windshield and the front passenger window, near those windows' defroster ducts. In a pinch, a mechanic might be able to stop the leak by redirecting coolant away from your heater core—leaving you without a working heater. Ultimately, your heater core will have to be replaced.

•**Rotten eggs.** An occasional rotten egg smell may not be a problem. However, if this smell persists, it typically is a sign of an emissions-control problem, usually having to do with the car's catalytic converter. As this is expensive, you want to have the source of the trouble located and dealt with as soon as possible, before you face a bill for a ruined converter.

DRIPS

Fluid slowly leaking from your car—other than water that has condensed when you run your air conditioner—is often a sign of a serious issue. See a mechanic right away.

•**Reddish brown drip.** You may have a leaking transmission—maybe just the pan gasket (from overtightening) or maybe because of something more serious, such as a leaking front seal.

•**Green or orange-red drip.** This suggests cooling system trouble—generally a leaking radiator or hose.

•**Molasses-to-blackish–colored, thick drip.** This is probably engine oil. If your car is more than two or three years old and/or has more than 20,000 miles or so on it, and you're seeing just a few drops per day, it's probably nothing to worry about. All engines eventually drip a little oil. But when you see more than that—especially anything that could be described as a "puddle"—it could be a sign of a serious problem. Also, if your car does drip oil, be sure to check the oil level frequently and top it off when necessary. And when you drive, keep a close eye on your oil-pressure gauge (or dashboard oil warning light). If the pressure drops unusually low or the light comes on, turn off the car immediately (in a safe spot), and check and add oil. Never run an engine with low oil pressure or an oil warning light on—unless you don't mind paying for a new engine.

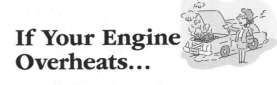

If Your Engine Overheats...

To cool an overheating engine, shut off the air conditioner, and avoid riding the brake in traffic. Race the engine to increase coolant circulation and dissipate heat. Turn on the heater to draw heat away from the engine. If overheating continues, shut off the engine and open the hood. If necessary, bring the car to a service station.

Car & Travel, 1415 Kellum Place, Garden City, NY 11530.

Buying a Car? Avoid the Latest Dealer Rip-Offs

Remar Sutton, president and cofounder of the nonprofit Consumer Task Force for Automotive Issues, Atlanta, *www.autoissues.org.* He is author of *Don't Get Taken Every Time.* Penguin.

Some auto dealerships sell cars at fair prices and provide good service, but some others are always thinking up ways to take advantage of car buyers. *Among the latest rip-offs...*

MANDATOR ARBITRATION AGREEMENTS

After you have agreed to terms, the salesman insists that you sign a "Dispute Resolution" or "Conflict Resolution" agreement. This says that if a problem develops, you will settle through arbitration, not take the dealership to court. Sounds reasonable—unless you bother to read the fine print. The agreement may stipulate that the dealer chooses the arbiter...you pay the fee...you can't appeal the decision, but the dealership can...and you can't participate in class-action lawsuits against the dealer.

Strategy: Before you begin to negotiate, ask a salesman if the dealership requires an arbitration agreement. If so, shop elsewhere. Many dealerships that require these agreements are disreputable ones that would face frequent lawsuits without them.

SPOT DELIVERY

You have decided on a vehicle and filled out an application with the dealer's finance department. Though your loan hasn't been officially approved, you are told you can drive the car home. A few days later, the dealership calls and says that you were not approved for a loan at the interest rate discussed. Instead, you were approved for a loan at a higher rate. This means that your new car might cost you thousands more than you expected over the life of the loan. If you try to call off the deal, the dealership says it has already sold your trade-in model, so there is no going back. If you didn't have a trade-in to begin with, the dealership might threaten to sue you if you don't agree to the new terms. *You have no recourse*—buried in the fine print of the loan agreement is something called a "writ of rescission." You unknowingly agreed to pay a higher interest rate if you failed to qualify for the loan at the agreed-upon rate.

Strategy: Don't sign any application containing a writ of rescission, and don't agree to take delivery of your new vehicle until the dealership approves your loan. Better

yet, get a loan from a credit union or bank. You'll probably get a better rate, and you'll certainly have fewer worries about unethical practices.

"ENVIRONMENTAL" FEES

After you have settled on a price, the salesman or finance manager hands you a contract containing additional fees that had not been previously mentioned. Among them is an "environmental fee." When questioned, the salesman might imply that it is a government charge that cannot be avoided. In truth, it is just the latest made-up fee that dealerships invented to coax a few extra dollars out of car buyers. Other common rip-offs include "protection packages," with unneeded rust-proofing...fabric treatment... and overpriced extended warranties. Advertising fees may even be added—though the cost of advertising beyond the amount included in the invoice price is the dealership's problem, not yours.

Strategy: Refuse to sign. If the salesman doesn't back down, walk out.

"ZERO, ZERO, ZERO" DEALS

A dealership advertises what sounds like a great offer—nothing down, no interest, no payment for the first year. What the "zero, zero, zero" ads don't say is that very few buyers ever qualify for these offers. The rest must pay some interest, and once interest is added to the mix, the deals suddenly become unattractive. You pay nothing for a full year, but interest still compounds on the full purchase price. You could wind up owing more than your vehicle is worth.

Strategy: If the "zero, zero, zero" deal is what you want, get preapproved for a loan at your credit union or bank. That way a car salesman will be hard-pressed to show your credit isn't strong enough to qualify for the offer.

Get a Great Deal On a New Car

Ken and Daria Dolan, authors of five books on personal finance, including *Don't Mess with My Money.* Currency Doubleday. They are frequent guests on national television news programs, including NBC's *Today* show. They were money editors on *CBS This Morning* and *CBS News Saturday Morning* for several years and also hosted their own show on CNBC. Their Web site is *www.dolans.com.*

Toward the end of the year is the perfect time to give yourself a gift—a new car at a great price. Reason? This is crunch time for dealers who want to make their sales quotas for the whole year. And, this puts them in the mood to move cars off the lots—even if it means selling them cheaper than they would like.

Here are the steps to gaining control of the entire car-buying process so that you can get a better deal…

• **Decide between a 2008 and 2009 model.** Dealers want to clear old models off their lots to make way for new ones, so automakers will offer plenty of rebates and low-interest financing on 2008 models.

Many people may hesitate to buy a 2008 model late in the year because of concerns about resale value. They think buyers will see the car as a year older than it actually is. But savings on 2008 models versus comparable 2009 models can range from a few hundred to a few thousand dollars or more.

If you plan to keep the car longer than five years, the difference in resale value between a 2008 and a 2009 of similar condition will be minimal. If you plan to keep your new car for fewer than five years, buy a 2009 model.

• **Check financing options before you go car shopping.** If you think that you will need financing, compare rates on car loans at *www.bankrate.com* or get quotes from local lending institutions. Their rates generally are one to two percentage points below those offered by car dealers. If your credit score is 650 or higher (out of 850), you should ask for the lowest available interest rate, whether you decide to finance with the dealer or a local lender. If your score is below 650, be prepared to pay at least one or two percentage points more.

Request a free copy of your credit report from *www.annualcreditreport.com,* or phone 877-322-8228. You can also purchase a copy of your credit score here or through one of the three credit reporting agencies.

• **When considering a specific car, check the white label on the driver's-side door or doorjamb**—it shows the month and year in which the car was manufactured. In most cases, the older the car is, the more anxious the dealer will be to sell it. In fact, you can save money by looking for "slow sellers"—models whose national "days' supply" (a projection of how long the current on-hand inventory will last) exceeds 60 days. You can locate this figure in *Automotive News,* a trade publication available at major newsstands and in large public libraries. Or you can subscribe for $155* per year (52 issues). 888-446-1422, *www.autonews.com.*

• **Drive a hard bargain.** Salespeople know that most new-car buyers walk into dealerships unprepared to negotiate one of their largest purchases ever.

Smart strategy: Instead of negotiating *down* from the sticker price, negotiate *up* from the car dealer's invoice (what the car costs the dealer).

Some dealers might sell you a car *below* invoice price. How is this possible? Some invoice prices quoted in car-pricing guides are above the actual cost to the dealer because they include holdbacks (a portion of the manufacturer's suggested retail price or invoice price repaid to the dealer after the sale) and dealer rebates from the manufacturer. However, if the invoice price includes regional marketing fees—which increase the dealer's cost—you may have less negotiating room. For pricing information, go to *www.edmunds. com* or check the *New Car Buying Guide 2008–2009* (Consumer Reports), available at *www.consumerreports.org.*

Other sources: www.carsdirect.com, www. autousa.com and *www.invoicedealers.com.*

*Prices subject to change.

• **Don't be a "turnover"**—a customer who is passed along to another salesperson because the first one couldn't get you to sign a contract. A more aggressive salesperson will then try to close out the sale. To better control this process, keep negotiating with the salesperson you started with—or go to another dealership.

• **Don't trust a dealership to give you a fair trade-in price for your old car.** To get the best price, do your best to sell your car to a private party. Check out prices that thousands of other sellers are asking for different cars at *www.kbb.com* and *www.auto trader.com*.

• **Don't give your Social Security number to a salesperson.** He/she often will use that information to check a shopper's credit history. Unnecessary credit checks can hurt your score.

• **Hand over your driver's license only when you go for a test drive,** and then only for it to be photocopied. Write on the copy, in bold letters, *Credit Checks Not Authorized!* The Federal Trade Commission forbids unauthorized credit checks. By doing this, you have made it clear that you won't allow one. Your credit rating is none of the dealer's business unless you decide to discuss financing.

Important: Don't let anyone from the dealership hold on to the original license. You can't make a quick exit without your license in hand.

• **Explore dealer financing only after you have settled on a price.** Don't be suckered by the question, "How much of a monthly payment can you afford?" Many times, the salesperson is trying to divert your attention from the actual price of the car. By manipulating the loan terms, he can get you the monthly payment you ask for and still get the highest overall price for himself.

Nor should you fall prey to "If you spread out the payments over 72 months (or more), you'll be able to afford this beauty." If you can't afford to pay off the car in 36 or 48 months, it's probably beyond your budget. Find a less expensive car.

Important: If you don't need financing, don't sit down with the "F&I" (finance and insurance) person. One of his/her jobs is to sell you expensive—and often unnecessary—add-ons, such as undercoating, an overpriced extended warranty, a security system or paint sealant.

• **Put your deposit on a credit card.** Don't use cash or a check. If something goes wrong between contract and delivery, it might be hard to get back your cash or check. With a credit card deposit, you can get the card issuer in your corner in the event of a dispute.

• **Never forget the ultimate weapon**—every salesperson's greatest fear—your ability to walk out of the showroom.

LEASE OR BUY?

Consider leasing if…

• **You are willing to pay extra,** in the long run, for a new car every three or four years.

• **You have a legitimate business use for the car**—some auto-related costs may be tax deductible.

• **Your priority is to keep up-front costs down**—they may be lower for a lease than for a purchase.

More information at *www.leaseguide.com*.

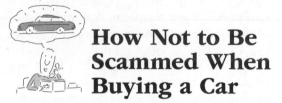

How Not to Be Scammed When Buying a Car

Bernard Brown, a Kansas City, MO, attorney as well as cofounder of the National Association of Consumer Advocates, 1730 Rhode Island Ave. NW, Washington, DC 20036.

Car scams are increasing, not just with sales of used vehicles but also new vehicles. While it may be possible to sue if you're the victim of a scam, lawsuits are expensive and lengthy. *It's much wiser to avoid scams at the outset…*

THE YO-YO SCAM

Typical scenario: The dealer asks the buyer of a new or used car for, say, a $1,500 or $2,000 down payment and mentions that interest will be 5%.

The salesperson spreads a handful of documents on a desk and asks the buyer to sign in several places. Among these papers is a document that says the buyer's purchase isn't final until all financing is confirmed by the lending company with which the dealer does business.

Often, the buyer is so eager to close the deal that he/she doesn't read each form carefully. Moreover, unscrupulous dealers try to rush customers and handle documents with what they call a "five-finger fold" to cover up the contents.

The buyer drives off the car lot with his purchase, but then a week or two later, the dealer telephones to say that the financing didn't go through. The car dealer asks for an additional $2,000 on the down payment and says the interest rate will now be 9%.

If the buyer objects, the dealer points out that he signed an agreement saying that the purchase wasn't final until financing was confirmed. Car dealers may also apply pressure by saying the buyer's trade-in has already been sold (which is usually untrue). The buyer sees little choice and then reluctantly agrees to the new terms.

Protection: After you tell a salesperson that you will purchase a car at the offered price, refuse to sign an agreement that makes the sale contingent on financing, and insist that the car dealer arrange for the financing while you wait. Never sign over your title until the financing is confirmed.

Most dealers will agree to these terms. Stay away from any that won't. But even if a dealer agrees, study everything you sign to make sure that there is no language that makes the sale contingent on financing.

Yo-yo scams exist because auto dealers make a large part of their profit by selling loan agreements to large, nationwide finance companies.

Example: An auto dealer may get a 5% loan approved by a finance company but then charge the customer 9%. The dealer pockets the difference.

Such transactions themselves *may* be legal, but few customers are aware of this practice. Yo-yo scams, however, are illegal because they involve deceiving customers.

DISGUISED PROBLEMS

Many unscrupulous car dealers are experts at covering up evidence that a car has been in a wreck. A vehicle that was structurally damaged can be unsafe, and cars involved in collisions may not last as long as others.

Similarly, unethical dealers often try to hide high mileage by rolling back the odometer. Or they conceal flood damage or a vehicle's use as a delivery vehicle by sprucing up the car.

Protection: Ask the dealer to let you take a used car to a body shop, which can spot signs of a wreck, and to a mechanic who can check out the vehicle for other problems.

Many body shops and mechanics will not charge for inspecting the car because they hope to get your business later. Even if they do charge, the fee is usually less than $50.

Don't conduct business with any automobile dealer that won't let you have a used car inspected. Insist on inspection even at large national chains or if the vehicle is still under the manufacturer's warranty.

It's been my experience that most auto information services, such as on-line search services, are often not reliable for checking on whether a car has been wrecked, which is why it's especially important to have a car checked by a body shop and a mechanic before you buy it.

Reasons: You may be dealing with an honest salesperson at an unethical dealership, and evidence of a wreck can invalidate a manufacturer's warranty.

If you discover evidence that the car has suffered minor damage, negotiate the price down if the repair shop believes it's safe to drive. Otherwise, take your business to another dealer.

When shopping for a late-model used car, it's nearly always best to buy a vehicle with only one previous owner whom you can

399

ask about any wrecks or problems that may have occurred. However, less-than-straightforward dealers often conceal a car's ownership history.

Protection: Refuse to buy a car unless the dealer lets you speak with the previous owner. That might seem like an excessive precaution, but it really isn't. If the dealer refuses to let you contact the previous owner, there is a good chance he's trying to cover up a problem.

Some dealers claim that privacy laws prevent them from disclosing owners' names, but this is untrue. In fact, after you buy a car, you'll see the previous owner's name on the title.

OVERPRICED FINANCING

While not engaging in anything illegal, many dealers charge high interest rates, often taking advantage of a buyer's eagerness to drive off the lot with a newly acquired vehicle.

To find cheaper financing: Check with your bank or credit union for the going rate on automobile loans. If the auto dealer charges more, tell him that you'll buy the car but only at whatever you discover to be the going rate. Most dealers will quickly agree for fear of losing the sale. Alternatively, tell the dealer that you'll handle the financing through your bank or other lending institution.

Smart negotiation tactics: When you first speak with a salesperson, never say that you intend to pay cash or finance the vehicle yourself. If you do, the dealership may quote a high sticker price to make up for its lost profit on financing.

It's also wise to stay away from any service contract that a dealer might offer. Evidence shows that the cost of these contracts is usually greater than the amount that will likely be paid out to the owners.

If you're concerned about future repair bills, shop for a car that's still under the manufacturer's warranty.

PHONY ADS

Today, a growing number of unethical dealers disguise their identities by placing classified ads in newspapers and local magazines.

This practice, known as "curbstoning," is often used to sell cars that have been in accidents or that have other problems. Curbstoners rely on unwary buyers who are more trusting of individuals than of dealerships.

Protection: Insist on seeing the title, which will tell you whether an individual or dealership owns the car. Don't do business with a dealership that disguises itself as an individual. The car may well have problems.

Automaker Secret

From the editors of *Bottom Line/Personal*, 281 Tresser Blvd., Stamford, CT 06901.

One of the best-kept secrets of the automobile industry is the existence of *informal warranties.*

How they work: When a significant number of new-model cars are reported to have the same mechanical problem, the manufacturer may inform regional sales offices and car dealers that it will cover the cost of repair—beyond the standard warranty.

Problem: Manufacturers and dealers won't publicize these warranties.

Solution: If your car has a malfunction that may be covered under one of these warranties, write to the Center for Auto Safety,* an auto-complaint clearinghouse that tracks corporate memoranda, bulletins to regional offices and dealers, and car-owner complaints to deduce which components are likely to fall under informal warranties. Tell the Center the automobile's year, model, and problem, and they will send you pertinent information.

If the malfunctioning component appears to be covered, speak with the dealer's service manager for repairs…and if he or she won't fix the problem, contact the factory's

*Send a self-addressed stamped envelope together with descriptive information to The Center for Auto Safety, 1825 Connecticut Ave. NW, Suite 330, Washington, DC 20009, or go to *www.autosafety.org* and click on "file/view complaints."

regional office and ask the factory representative to mediate.

Last resort: Take the dealer to small-claims court or seek arbitration through the Better Business Bureau. You'll have a good chance of winning if you're armed with documentation.

You Can Save Thousands of Dollars On a Used Car

Eric Peters, Washington, DC–based automotive columnist and author of *Automotive Atrocities! The Cars We Love to Hate*. MBI.

I f you're in the market for a used car or truck, vehicle auctions may be your best low-cost alternative to dealerships, used-car lots and classified ads. The auctions used to be "insider-only" events—restricted to buyers representing dealerships and other professionals. Cars would be bought wholesale, then resold to consumers with a dealer's markup. Now, with a glut of used vehicles for sale as they come off leases, many vehicle auctions are open to the public. *The main types…*

• **Government auctions.** Federal, state and even some local governments hold auctions to dispose of cars that they no longer need or vehicles that have been seized. Auctions are advertised on local radio and TV stations, or you can contact town officials for information. For information on federal auctions, access the US General Services Administration's auction Web site, *www.autoauctions. gsa.gov,* or write to GSA Fleet Vehicle Sales, 2200 Crystal Dr., Arlington, VA 22202.

• **Charities** such as Goodwill Industries (800-741-0186, *www.goodwill.org*) and The Salvation Army (800-725-2769, *www.salvation armyusa.org*) auction cars they have received as donations.

• **Car wholesalers** auction dealer trade-ins as well as excess inventory.

Attending most auctions is free, although you may have to register in advance. If you do buy a car, you typically take it home the same day.

ADVANTAGES

Why buy at an auction? In most cases, you'll pay less for a given make and model than you would elsewhere. The bidding generally starts at or below the average wholesale value of the car or truck in question. At a lot or dealership, your starting point for negotiation is the full retail price. The savings at auction can be as much as 40% off the dealer price, depending on the car and the number of bids.

DRAWBACKS

• **Potentially shabby appearance.** An auction company's costs are lower than a dealership's, in part because it doesn't service, clean up or otherwise "detail" the vehicle to make it presentable.

• **Hurried pace.** You have to make a quick decision when the moment arrives.

• **Mechanical problems.** You will have a few hours at most to check out a vehicle. You can start the engine and hear it run, but test drives are seldom granted, so it is difficult to gauge a vehicle's mechanical condition. There are legal protections and, depending on the auction, there even may be a guarantee of some kind—but if you are not satisfied with the car, it's harder to seek redress against an auction firm, which is likely to be based out of state, than a local dealership or private seller in your community.

AUCTION STRATEGIES

To boost your chances of getting a fair deal at an auction…

• **Arrive early.** This will give you time for a thorough "walk-around" inspection of any car you're interested in. (You can open up the hood, crawl underneath the auto, etc.) Jot down the car's make, model, vehicle identification number, year of model, mileage, features and other information that might affect its price. If you are not familiar with cars and where to look for signs of trouble, bring a car-savvy friend or ask a mechanic to accompany you for a fee—say, $100 for two hours.

- **Bring a laptop computer or a personal digital assistant,** if possible, so that you can research cars on the Internet.

Alternative: Arrange for a friend to look up helpful information when you call from your cell phone. Never bid on a car until you have checked its value with such sources as the National Automobile Dealers Association's used-car pricing guides (800-252-6232, *www.nada.com*).

- **Run a check with Carfax.com** to instantly find evidence of odometer fraud, flood damage, accidents, etc.

Cost: $24.99.*

- **Check out the car's title** before any money changes hands. Don't buy a car that lacks a clean, lien-free, transferable title.

- **Keep a clear head**—don't overbid.

ON-LINE AUCTIONS

On-line auctions, such as those on eBay Motors, have increased in popularity. They run for several days—giving you ample time to check a car's vehicle identification number. You can make arrangements with a buyer to see a car before purchase, but that might involve traveling. You can use the site's escrow service to hold your down payment, which will vary by lender, and pay the balance when the car and paperwork are transferred.

*Prices subject to change.

Test Drive Without The Salesperson

Do you want to test-drive a new car without the salesperson in the car? Convince him/her that you are a serious buyer. Explain why you like that specific car and what competing models you're considering. Be prepared to show your driver's license, explain where you work and give your phone number. If the dealership limits test-drives to a specific route with a salesperson in the car, take that drive—then, after returning, explain that you like the car and would like to drive it again alone. If considering an expensive or exotic car, visit the dealership first and expect to return another day for a test-drive.

Consensus of car salespeople and dealership managers, reported in Car and Driver.

Cars that Prevent Collisions

Toyota and General Motors are working on a new technology that can anticipate a collision. Toyota's radar-based system detects if the car is going to be rear-ended. It flashes warning lights to signal the oncoming vehicle, and if that car does not stop, it adjusts the driver's headrest to prevent whiplash. General Motors' system works through radio transmissions and global positioning technology. It also can detect an imminent crash and blinks the lights as a warning, but this system can apply the brakes if your car is coming up too fast on another car.

Automotive News, 1400 Woodbridge Ave., Detroit.

Get a Vehicle History Report

Vehicle history reports for used cars are more important than ever. These reports, which document accident and repair records of used cars, are becoming increasingly popular among used-car buyers. They are even more important now after the widespread flooding caused by Katrina and other Gulf Coast storms damaged huge numbers of cars that could be in the used-car market today. About 30% of manufacturer franchise dealers now provide history reports at no charge to potential buyers of used cars.

Jane Crane, director of automotive retail research, J.D. Power and Associates, 2625 Townsgate Rd., Westlake Village, CA 91361, www.jdpower.com.

Consider Buying a Diesel Car for Better Gas Mileage

Diesel cars typically get up to 30% better fuel mileage than cars with gasoline engines of equivalent size.

Snag: Antipollution regulations have limited their availability until now. But today new "clean" diesel fuel—for example, with 97% reduced sulfur content—is becoming available across the US. As a result, more diesel-powered car models are being introduced. Mercedes and Volkswagen already offer diesel car models...Jeep now offers a diesel model...Mercedes has a diesel SUV and Land Rover will offer one soon...Volkswagen offers several models.

Eric Peters, Washington, DC–based automotive columnist and author of *Automotive Atrocities! The Cars We Love to Hate.* MBI.

Eleven Ways to Save at the Pump

Nancy Dunnan, editor and publisher of *TravelSmart* at *www.travelsmartnewsletter.com.* She also is a financial adviser and the author of numerous books, including *How to Invest $50–$5,000.* HarperCollins.

High gasoline prices make it more important than ever to save on fuel. Most people do know to avoid higher octane fuel than their cars require and to keep their cars tuned up and tires inflated. *Other money-saving ideas that you might not have thought of...*

- **Check the gauge.** Be aware of the amount of gas in your tank. When the tank is half full, start looking for a gas station. This gives you time to comparison shop. Avoid interstate and highway gas stations—gas on a busy highway costs 10 to 15 cents more per gallon than the same brand and grade in less-trafficked areas. Buying self-service gas saves 10 cents or more per gallon. Compare prices on-line at *www.gaspricewatch.com* and *www.gasbuddy.com.*
- **Buy big-box gas.** Some wholesale clubs sell discounted gas at member-only pumps. Their gas averages about 12 cents a gallon less than gas at regular stations. Try BJ's (*www.bjs.com*).
- **Get a gas card.** Major gas companies offer a 1%* to 6% discount if you use their MasterCard or Visa when buying their brand of gas. Sunoco and ExxonMobil both have cards and rebate programs. The BP Visa Card, for example, has no annual fee and gives an introductory 10% rebate on gasoline for the first two months, 5% thereafter (*www.bp.com*, 800-278-4721).

The Visa card cosponsored by AAA gives one point for every dollar spent on retail purchases, plus double points for every dollar spent on gas for the first 12 months, regardless of brand. Points can be redeemed for merchandise, gift cards, cash and more (no annual fee, 800-551-0839, *www.aaa.com*). Pay your bill in full each month so interest costs don't wipe out the savings.

- **Don't let your car idle.** If you're going to be at a standstill for more than a minute, turn off the engine. Idling consumes up to one gallon of gas per hour. It also wastes more gas than restarting the engine.
- **Map unfamiliar routes in advance,** so you won't get lost and waste gas.
- **Drive strategically.** Combine errands to avoid shorter trips. Use cruise control—it cuts down on gas as well as speeding tickets. Avoid roads that have a long string of traffic lights. Don't slam on the brakes or accelerate rapidly—this lowers gas mileage by 33% at highway speeds and by 5% around town.
- **Buy gas early in the morning or late in the evening** when it is cool outside to reduce the amount of evaporation.
- **Take alternative forms of transportation.** Use public transportation, or even walk or bike. Get a scooter—Vespas and other scooters get 40 miles per gallon (mpg) to 60 mpg. Consider a diesel-powered car—they have 20% to 40% better fuel economy than gas cars. Look into a gas-electric hybrid.

*Percentages are subject to change.

•**Park in a shady spot in hot weather** so you don't need to blast the air-conditioning as soon as you get back in your car. Air-conditioning reduces fuel economy dramatically.

•**Keep the windows closed.** When traveling on highways on long trips, open windows can create air drag and reduce your mileage by as much as 10%.

•**When renting a car, choose the model that gets the best gas mileage.** Most Hondas, Toyotas and Hyundais as well as the Pontiac Vibe and Dodge Neon get 29 mpg or more in highway traffic.

To compare fuel economy among cars: *www.fueleconomy.gov.*

More from Nancy Dunnan...

Which Cars Have the Best Fuel Economy?

The Department of Energy (DOE) has a special section addressing your concerns at its Web site, *www.fueleconomy.gov.* Two DOE tools posted there will help you make an informed decision: "Find and Compare Cars" and "Our MPG." You'll learn, for example, that among the 2008 models, the Toyota Prius is overall the most efficient, getting an estimated 48 miles per gallon (mpg) in the city and 45 mpg on the highway.

You'll also see a list of the least-efficient cars—Aston Martin, Mercedes-Benz and Bentley—also among the most expensive cars.

Save Money at Gas Stations

Here are three ways to save money when filling up the gasoline tank...

•**Don't use your debit card.** Some gas stations require banks to automatically set aside $50 or $100 for each purchase to make sure that the customer has the funds to cover them—you may not have access to that money for up to three days.

•**Don't use gasoline credit cards.** Their annual percentage rates often are high, and many don't offer rebates on gas purchases. Check GasPriceWatch.com and GasBuddy.com regularly to find the best gas prices in your area.

•**Don't shop at gas station convenience stores**—most inventory is vastly overpriced, although some high-volume goods, such as cigarettes, beer and coffee, may be competitively priced.

SmartMoney, 250 W. 55 St., New York City 10019.

To Improve Fuel Economy...

Replacing a car's dirty air filter can improve fuel economy by up to 10%.

Carmakers' recommendation: Change the filter annually or every 12,000 miles if you tend to drive over dusty roads...every two years or 24,000 miles for normal conditions.

Car & Travel, 1415 Kellum Place, Garden City, NY 11530.

Fuel Efficiency— The Basics

Autobytel, *www.autobytel.com.*

Here are seven easy adjustments that will help to make your fuel last longer...

•**Use fuel with the octane rating recommended by the manufacturer**—buying higher-octane gas does nothing for performance and just wastes money.

•**Keep tires inflated to recommended levels.**

- **Change the oil regularly,** and have all scheduled maintenance done on time.

- **Avoid high speeds on the highway.** Driving 62 miles per hour instead of 75 can lower fuel use by 15%.

- **Use air-conditioning only when needed,** and then keep it set at around 75 degrees.

- **Keep windows closed**—open windows cause extra drag, reducing fuel economy by up to 10%.

- **Shut off the engine if you will be idling for more than one minute.** Restarting uses less fuel than idling.

Don't "Top Off" Your Car's Gas Tank

Today's cars have an antipollution evaporative emission (EVAP) system that includes a charcoal-containing canister that absorbs gasoline fumes from a full tank. When gas runs low, the system sucks the fumes out of the canister and injects them into the fuel mix. But if the gas tank is overfilled, liquid gasoline may pour into the canister. This can destroy the charcoal, trigger a warning light on your dashboard and lead to a costly repair of your car's EVAP system.

MotorWatch, Box 123, Butler, MD 21023.

Find Lowest Gasoline Prices on the Internet

It now pays more than ever to go on-line and check gasoline price-monitoring Web sites before filling up. Use them to locate the lowest prices at gas stations in your area.

Examples: *www.gaspricewatch.com* and *www.gasbuddy.com*.

Jean Chatzky, financial editor for *Today* on NBC. She is author of *Pay It Down*. Portfolio.

How to Make Your Car Sparkle

Eric Peters, Washington, DC–based automotive columnist and author of *Automotive Atrocities! The Cars We Love to Hate*. MBI.

Professional automotive detailers who work at higher-end car washes and car dealerships use more than just elbow grease to make cars sparkle—and they charge as much as $150 for "the works."

Many of the products that the professionals use are readily available at automotive-supply and hardware stores. *Here's how to spiff up your car like a professional—for a lot less money...*

- **Spray cleaner/bug remover.** These products safely spot-clean most painted surfaces—often without water. Plexus Plastic Cleaner, Protectant & Polish is available at motorcycle dealerships, and it works on cars, too.

Cost: About $13 for a 13-ounce can.

Alternative: Griot's Speed Shine (available for $9.99 at 800-345-5789, *www.griotsgarage.com*), which comes in dispenser form, with individual 5-x-8¾-inch cleaning/polishing pads. Both products can be tucked in your glove compartment or trunk.

- **Adhesive remover.** Goof Off spray gets rid of the sticky residue left on your bumper or windshield after removing a sticker, as well as tar and other difficult-to-remove stains—without harming the surface.

Cost: About $6 for a 12-ounce can.

- **Tire cleaner.** Westley's Bleche-White restores the like-new look to white letters on tires. *Cost:* About $4 for a 22-ounce spray bottle (800-416-1600, *www.westleys.com*). It quickly dissolves the grime that builds up on tire sidewalls. Just spray it on, wait a minute, then wash it off. Follow up with a light wipe of Armor All or a similar rubber treatment/protectant.

Cost: About $3 for a four-ounce bottle.

- **In-line water softener.** If your tap water has a high mineral content, after-wash "spotting" of the finish can be a problem. Prevent it by installing an in-line water softener that plugs into your garden hose (available from Griot's for $129, including all necessary fittings). The internal—and easily replaceable—filter element demineralizes water before it hits your car and puts an end to spots and streaks.

●**Proper sponges/washcloths.** Using an ordinary rag to wash your car can result in surface scratches either because the rag is slightly abrasive or because the washing didn't lift away grime. Use Zymöl's nonabrasive sponge ($5, 800-999-5563, *www.zymol. com/carwash.htm*). Soft-bristle toothbrushes are excellent for detail work and hard-to-reach spots. To prevent streaking, dry the car with a chamois or a clean high-quality cotton towel made for cars.

●**Wheel and interior surface cleaners.** Cleaners for aluminum-alloy wheels safely remove brake dust and other grime without harming the wheel's delicate coated surface. There also are cleaners and conditioners for leather surfaces and carpets. Choose products from Griot's, Zymöl, Westley's and Armor All (about $5 for a 22-ounce bottle).

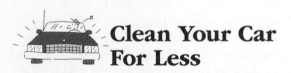

Clean Your Car For Less

Joan Wilen and Lydia Wilen, home-remedy experts in New York City. The sisters are coauthors of many books, including *Bottom Line's Household Magic: 2,022 Money-Saving, Time-Saving, Make-It-Last Solutions and Surprising New Uses for Everyday Products!*, from which this article was adapted. Bottom Line Books. *www.BottomLineSecrets.com/ store.*

Y ou don't need to spend a lot of money or time dealing with car-cleaning problems. *Cheap and easy tricks that really work...*

Caution: Always test any cleaning remedy on an inconspicuous area of your car to be sure that it won't harm the car's finish.

Never use scouring pads, steel wool or abrasive household cleaners on your car's finish.

●**Foggy windshield.** A thin coat of gel shaving cream applied to the interior of your windshield and other car windows can keep them from fogging up in the winter.

To apply: Spread the gel on the window, let dry, then use a clean cloth to rub it off. The glass should remain fog-free for days, if not longer. (This also works on bathroom mirrors.) Keep a blackboard eraser in your glove compartment to quickly wipe the glass clear without leaving streaks when it does fog up again.

If your windshield seems hazy even when it's not fogged up, pour white vinegar on a clean cloth and wipe down the glass inside and out. Then wash the windshield with water, and wipe it dry.

●**Grime-covered headlights.** Combine one cup of white vinegar, one quart of water and one tablespoon of cornstarch. Use a sponge to apply the mixture to your headlights, or you can use an old pair of panty hose. Let the cleaning solution sit for about 10 minutes, then rub off with a soft cloth.

●**Dirty windshield wipers.** Wipe the blades with a cloth soaked in rubbing alcohol. Besides cleaning the blades, the alcohol also will reduce the amount of ice that builds up on them during storms.

Also: Lightly run a folded piece of extra-fine sandpaper along the wiper-blade edges to remove stubborn gunk. This light sanding can help older wiper blades remain effective longer.

●**Bumper stickers.** Soak a cloth in white vinegar, then position the cloth so that it completely covers the sticker for 30 to 60 minutes. If the sticker is on a vertical metal surface, use refrigerator magnets to hold the cloth in place. The vinegar should dissolve much of the sticker's glue, allowing you to peel it off or very carefully scrape it off using an old credit card. (Favor peeling over scraping if the sticker is on paint.) If some of the sticker's adhesive remains after the sticker has been removed, pour some vegetable oil on it and the adhesive should become much easier to rub away.

If this doesn't do the trick, use a hair dryer to loosen the adhesive. Set the dryer on high, and check every few minutes to see if the sticker will peel free.

• **Nicks and scratches.** If your car dealer doesn't have touch-up paint for your car, crayons are the cheapest way to hide ugly nicks and scratches. Find the crayon color that most closely matches that of your car, and carefully work it into the nick or scratch. Use a clean, soft cloth to wipe away any excess. This won't be a perfect fix, but it should make the flaw much less obvious. If you can't find an appropriate-colored crayon, at least apply clear nail polish to the damaged area to prevent it from rusting.

• **Dead bugs.** Bugs and bird droppings (see below) contain acids that can damage a car's painted or chromed surface if they're not cleaned away quickly. To make bug removal easy, spray a light coat of vegetable cooking oil on your car's bumper, grille and hood before long drives. The slick oil should make it much easier to wipe away the bugs after the trip.

When dead bugs do get stuck firmly to your car, dip a scrunched-up mesh onion bag, nylon net shower sponge or old pair of panty hose in warm soapy water and gently scrub off the bugs.

• **Bird droppings.** Pour seltzer on the droppings as soon as possible. Once the seltzer stops bubbling, wipe the area with a microfiber or cotton cloth.

Helpful: Griot's Garage's Speed Wipes Travel Pack is a car-care product worth having. Keep these wipes in your glove compartment so you can clean off bird droppings when you don't have seltzer handy.

Cost: $9.99 for a pack of 20 wipes (800-345-5789, *www.griotsgarage.com*).

• **Tree sap.** The easiest way to remove sap is to wipe it off before it has a chance to dry. If the sap already has dried, coat it with mayonnaise, wait a few minutes for the mayo to reduce the sap's stickiness, then gently rub with a cloth. If this fails, pour rubbing alcohol on a soft cloth, hold it against the sap for a minute, then use the cloth to gently rub away the sap. If the sap still won't budge, spray WD-40 on it. Wait a few minutes, then rub it off with a cloth. Wash the affected area after the sap has been removed. To make sure these remedies won't harm your car's finish, test an inconspicuous area.

• **Road tar.** Put mayonnaise on the tar, wait two minutes, then wipe the area clean with a soft cloth. (Test on an inconspicuous area first.)

• **Grease.** Grease is not as sticky as sap and tar, but it can be difficult to wash away. A simple solution is to use baby wipes. Baby wipes also can be used to clean grime off a car's vinyl or cloth upholstery. Cloth upholstery should be allowed to air-dry after a baby wipe is used, but vinyl can be wiped dry with a paper towel. Baby wipes should not be used to clean leather car interiors—use saddle soap instead.

• **Bad smells.** A pet has an accident in the car...a child gets sick. You clean up the mess, but the smell's still there. Put shallow bowls of white vinegar on the car's floor, in front and back. Then close the windows and leave the car overnight. In the morning, remove the bowls of vinegar and open the doors and windows for a few minutes so that any lingering vinegar smell disappears.

More from Joan Wilen and Lydia Wilen...

Get More Gas for Your Buck!

There are many ways to make your gas last longer...we have listed two of them...

• **Fill up your tank in the early morning or late at night.** Gasoline expands with heat, so if the outside air temperature and the car's gas tank are cooler, you end up getting more for the same price.

• **Visit the Web site** *www.gasbuddy.com* and enter your zip code or the zip code of the area to which you're traveling. You'll be given a list of local gas stations, along with their current gas prices.

When Backing Up...

Don't depend on your mirrors when backing up your car—turn your head and shoulders in the direction you want to go. Don't stick your head out the window (you have more control of the vehicle when your head is inside), and never open your door while the vehicle is in motion.

To safely back up your car: Check for children and objects nearby and behind you. Lift yourself out of the seat a bit—the higher you sit, the better you will see out the back window. Move the car slowly—don't touch the gas pedal unless absolutely necessary. Otherwise, keep your foot on the brake pedal.

William E. Van Tassel, PhD, manager, AAA, Heathrow, FL.

Rx for Cold-Weather Car Problems

David Solomon, a certified master auto technician and chairman of MotorWatch, a consumer automotive membership organization, Box 123, Butler, MD 21023, *www.motorwatch.com.*

Here are four ways to get your car going on those frosty winter mornings...

•**Door frozen shut.** Spray silicone lubricant on the outer edge of the door. Wait one or two minutes until the silicone sinks in. Open the door gently. Don't yank on it— you could damage the weather stripping.

•**Emergency brake won't release.** Rock the car back and forth gently by putting it in forward and then reverse while trying to release the emergency brake. If this doesn't work, have the car towed somewhere warm so the cables underneath can thaw.

•**Ice buildup where the windshield meets the hood.** Clear this area before using the windshield wipers. Otherwise, the wiper motor will continue trying to put the windshield wipers back in their home position. This can burn out the wiper motor.

Also: Don't use wipers to clear snow or ice from the windshield—this also can burn out the wiper motor.

•**Frozen cooling fan.** Even in winter, you need this fan to keep the engine from overheating. Watch your temperature gauge. If it starts to climb into the red, stop...turn off the car...wait a few minutes...then try starting the car again.

Check Tire Alignment In Addition to Tire Pressure

Irregular tire wear can mean poor alignment—the tires are not facing exactly the right way. This leads to faster tire wear and extra fuel consumption. Have a mechanic check alignment if you are not sure how tires should look.

Also: Avoid wide tires if you want to keep fuel use as low as possible. Wider tires literally have more rubber on the road—which gives them better traction but more friction and higher fuel use.

David Solomon, a certified master auto technician and chairman of MotorWatch, a consumer automotive membership organization, Box 123, Butler, MD 21023, *www.motorwatch.com.*

Don't Get Overcharged When Your Lease Is Up

Eric Peters, Washington, DC–based automotive columnist and author of *Automotive Atrocities! The Cars We Love to Hate.* MBI.

Most car leases stipulate that the customer is responsible for any damage to the vehicle beyond "normal wear and tear."

When it's time for you to turn in a vehicle at the end of the lease, the lessor/dealer may charge you the full "retail" price of any repairs, even if he/she pays less than that to have them done.

It may be cheaper for you to have any minor damage repaired yourself before you turn in the vehicle.

• **Get estimates from two or three body shops and/or detailing centers.** Get at least one estimate from a new-car dealer that sells your type of car. This will give you an idea of what the lease issuer would charge you. It's best not to check with your own dealership —that will only alert the lessor that your car has damage.

If an independent shop offers to fix the damage for significantly less than a dealer's price, it may be smart to go ahead and have the work done.

Caution: Use a competent repair shop. Turning in a leased car with a shoddy repair (such as a repainted fender that doesn't match the rest of the car) is usually worse than just giving the car back without repairing it. You will have paid the repair shop and are likely to be charged by the dealer to have the car fixed properly. Check any shop you're considering with the Better Business Bureau (703-276-0100, *www.bbb.org*) and the Department of Consumer/Regulatory Affairs in your city/county (look this up in your phone book's business pages). Also, ask acquaintances for referrals.

• **Don't file a claim** with your auto insurer for lease-end cosmetic work. You may be tagged as a higher insurance risk and be subject to higher premiums.

More from Eric Peters...

Simple Rules for Winter Driving

Modern features, such as electronic stability control and air bags, have made cars safer than ever, but that doesn't mean drivers can afford to be complacent.

Here are basic driving rules that are commonly ignored. *Practice these, especially on icy roads in winter, and you will do more to avoid an accident than any of the new features can...*

THE RULES

• **Slow down.** When winter weather hits, the single most important thing you can do is slow down to give your car the additional time it needs to stop safely. Snow, ice and slush on the road can increase stopping distances by 50% or more.

Caution: Having four-wheel drive or all-wheel drive doesn't mean that your vehicle will be able to stop any better than a standard front-wheel-drive or rear-wheel-drive car.

• **Use your brakes properly.** If you need to stop quickly and your car has an antilock braking system (ABS), apply the brakes with force and don't let up. ABS will prevent the wheels from locking and help keep the car from skidding.

If your car doesn't have ABS, pumping the brake pedal will give maximum stopping power and prevent your wheels from locking up.

Caution: Electronic stability control— which automatically corrects overly aggressive braking and steering—doesn't always prevent skids. In fact, the risk can be higher because the system gives drivers a false sense of security. Instead of beginning to skid at 30 miles per hour (mph), a late-model car may not begin to lose traction until it reaches 50 or 60 mph. By that time, the skid will be more extreme, making it harder to recover.

Thus, if you have electronic stability control, it is just as important to drive slowly and carefully in bad weather.

• **Go with the flow of traffic.** In good weather, driving too slowly can be more dangerous than driving a little faster than the speed limit. In dense traffic, a dawdler creates what amounts to a rolling roadblock. If the driver of the car behind you clearly wishes to go faster than you and conditions permit, let him/her get by.

• **Obey the three-second rule.** Crowding the car ahead of you makes it more likely that you'll smash into it if the driver should suddenly brake, especially on slick roads. To avoid tailgating, heed the three-second rule—when the vehicle ahead of you passes a fixed object (such as a tree or a telephone pole), slowly count "one one-thousand, two one-thousand, three one-thousand." If you reach the object before completing the count, you're following too closely. Double your following distance in inclement weather, such as snow and rain.

DRIVING SCHOOLS

If you want to become a better driver —and really learn to handle emergency situations—you may want to attend a driving school with a closed-course track. These schools are not cheap, but they pay off in heightened ability and safety.

• **Bob Bondurant School of High Performance Driving,** Phoenix. Highway Survival Training (one day, $1,225), High Performance Driving (two days, $2,325 or three days, $3,275). 800-842-7223, *www. bondurant.com.*

• **Skip Barber Racing School,** nationwide one- and two-day programs for basic and advanced techniques range from $999 to $2,999. 800-221-1131, *www.skipbarber.com.*

• **Master Drive Driver Training School,** Denver area and Irvine, CA. Senior citizen, teen and high-performance courses (call for prices and dates). 719-260-0999, *www.master drive.com.*

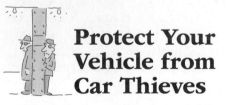

Protect Your Vehicle from Car Thieves

Michael Cherbonneau, co-principal investigator (with Richard T. Wright, PhD) of a research grant entitled "Auto Thieves on Auto Theft," funded by the University of Missouri Research Board. He previously took part in a study of incarcerated auto thieves while completing a master's degree from the University of Alabama–Birmingham.

More than 1.2 million vehicles will be stolen in the US this year alone. Most victims never come face-to-face with the criminals who drive off with their cars, but Michael Cherbonneau meets car thieves regularly. He is conducting a field-based study on how auto thieves carry out their crimes. So far, he has completed 30 face-to-face interviews with auto thieves recruited on the streets of St. Louis, MO. He previously assisted with a University of Alabama–Birmingham study that interviewed 54 incarcerated auto thieves.

We asked Cherbonneau to tell us what he has learned about how car thieves operate …which cars are at the greatest risk…and which theft-deterrent systems really work…

• **Who is the typical car thief?** The guys I have interviewed are hard-core street offenders. They live for the here and now, spend money as soon as they make it and consider life a perpetual party. Your car is probably safe in the daylight morning hours, say, between 8:00 am and noon, because most car thieves are still in bed asleep.

Most of these guys are not car-theft specialists—they're hustlers and opportunists. Today they might steal cars…tomorrow sell drugs or commit robberies. But when they're in need of quick money, they consider auto theft a reliable way to get it. Compared with their other endeavors, auto theft is safe and dependable. If they mug someone or break into a home, they don't know how much they'll get or how the victim will react. When they steal a car, they can pick exactly the vehicle they want and not have to deal with the victim.

Some thieves steal cars to sell to chop shops. A chop shop strips a stolen car and sells the parts or changes the vehicle identification number and sells the entire car. But not every thief has access to chop shops—in some areas, only a few are in operation or they don't exist at all.

• **How much are stolen cars worth?** Thieves can get anywhere from $50 for a part to $3,500 for a stolen car. That might not seem like much, but thieves want to make money fast while avoiding detection, so they are willing to let cars go for "street prices." Newer cars generally fetch more than older ones. Thieves also get more for cars with high-end audio systems and flashy aftermarket wheels that can be easily removed and sold. In major port cities, cars usually are stolen for export, and that can increase the thief's profits.

● **Which cars are most likely to be stolen?** Generally, the more popular a car is with buyers, the more popular it will be with thieves. Chop shops pay more for popular vehicles because parts removed from common cars are sure to be in demand. Stealing common cars also makes it less likely that the thief will be caught. If a gray Honda Accord or white Dodge Ram is stolen, the thief is relatively safe, because the police can't pull over every one that drives by. Also, some cars are easier to steal than others because of their ignition design. Favorites among thieves include many older General Motors vehicles and most of the new low-to-mid-range Dodge, Chrysler and Pontiac models.

● **How effective are engine-immobilization security devices?** These computerized security systems block the ignition or fuel flow if someone lacking the proper key tries to hot-wire the car. This "smart key" technology is a very effective theft deterrent, but many American cars—especially low-end and mid-range models—don't come with factory-installed immobilizers. If I drove a car without engine-immobilization technology, I would consider having an aftermarket system installed. Your auto insurance provider might even offer a discount if you do.

Be aware that thieves who can't beat an engine-immobilization system may try to steal your key. Some female thieves steal car keys from men in bars. Other thieves loiter around gas stations waiting for customers to leave their keys with their cars when they head inside to pay.

● **What other automotive security devices deter thieves?** No security product will make your car 100% theft-proof, but anything that makes it more difficult for the thief is worthwhile. *Car thieves are not known for working any harder than necessary...*

● Alarms. Most thieves claim to be able to disable auto alarms. Even when they can't,

it isn't clear that alarms are effective deterrents for vehicles parked on crowded streets—the sound of a car alarm is so common that people tend to ignore it. Still, if your car is parked in a driveway or in front of a home in a quiet neighborhood, the sound of the alarm might send some would-be thieves running.

● The Club. The Club locks onto your steering wheel, making the vehicle impossible to operate. It can be defeated by sawing through the rim of the steering wheel with a hacksaw, but that can be time-consuming, increasing the risk of being caught.

More information: 800-527-3345, *www.theclub.com*.

● LoJack. LoJack is a small radio transponder hidden in your vehicle to track it when it's stolen. Many of the thieves I spoke with had never heard of LoJack, which is more likely to be on higher-end vehicles not targeted by these thieves. LoJack is of concern to thieves who target luxury cars, but these thieves know that LoJack is effective only when the victim reports the theft quickly. Many thieves simply time their crimes so the loss won't be noticed until after the car has been torn apart and the transponder smashed at the chop shop. For example, thieves target business park parking lots in the afternoon. Car owners are back from lunch and won't notice that their cars are missing until after 5 pm.

More information: 800-4LOJACK, *www.lojack.com*.

● **Of the three deterrents you listed, which is most effective?** Based on my conversations with car thieves, I would say The Club is probably the most cost-effective deterrent, aside from engine-immobilization devices.

● **What about carjackings? Are they common?**

Victimization surveys and auto insurance data indicate that carjacking is a rare event, accounting for roughly 3% of vehicles stolen each year. Carjackings are more likely to occur in urban areas and are carried out in a spontaneous and very opportunistic manner. From the offender's perspective, if he does not act when the opportunity is presented, that opportunity may be lost forever.

Lock Out Car Thieves

Stop car thieves with the AutoLock. The steel pedal-clamping system (which is impervious to drilling and sawing) fits around your brake or clutch pedal so that it can't be depressed. The lock has an encrypted, four-sided key that can't be duplicated.

Cost: $49.95* at auto-parts and hardware stores.

*Price subject to change.

AAA Isn't the Only Auto Club

Shop around. Some insurers will let you join their motor clubs even if you are insured by another carrier. *Better World Club* (866-238-1137, *www.betterworldclub. com*) matches AAA's rates, and owners of hybrids and diesels get 15% discounts. *GE Motor Club* (800-616-9286, *www.gemotor club.com*) offers group discounts for its services, including roadside assistance, legal defense reimbursement, hotel and rental-car discounts, etc. The standard annual fee for most auto clubs is $38 to $80.

SmartMoney, 1755 Broadway, New York City 10019.

Fight Parking Tickets On-Line

The parkingticket.com Web site employs former judges and police officers to assist its clients in getting tickets dismissed.

How: Ticket data is entered on the Web site and users then receive a customized dismissal request letter to file, citing the exact reason(s) why the ticket should be dismissed.

Guarantee: If the fine is not dismissed or reduced, you pay nothing. If it is, the fee is half the amount saved.

Service currently is available in New York City, Washington, DC, San Francisco, Boston and Philadelphia, and is expanding.

Shop Around

Shop for the best car insurance rates and benefits every year. The car insurance market is extremely competitive now, with the various insurers adopting differing price and benefit strategies (such as actual cash value vs. replacement value and first accident forgiveness). This means premiums and coverages will vary greatly from company to company.

J. D. Howard, executive director, Insurance Consumer Advocate Network, Branson West, MO. *www. ican2000.com*.

Insist that Your Car Insurer Pay Actual Repair Costs

The insurer may offer a cash settlement for what appears to be a minor repair.

Problem: After the car owner accepts the money, he/she may find that the cost to repair the damage is more than the settlement.

Self-defense: Get an estimate from an independent repair shop before accepting any offer.

David Solomon, a certified master auto technician and chairman of MotorWatch, a consumer automotive membership organization, Box 123, Butler, MD 21023, *www.motorwatch.com*.

My Fender Bender Blunder

Marjory Abrams, publisher, *Bottom Line* newsletters, Boardroom Inc., 281 Tresser Blvd., Stamford, CT 06901.

Several months ago, a man backed his truck into my car. No one was hurt, but my car's hood was damaged. The other driver, Scott, admitted he was at fault. Fearful of going through his insurer, he offered to pay for my repairs. The estimate from the repair shop was about $500. Scott said that he would put down a deposit with the shop the next day. He didn't, and despite several phone conversations during which he promised that he would make good, he never did, and he stopped returning my calls. I'm angry at Scott—and angrier at myself for trusting him.

San Francisco attorney Joseph Matthews told me that despite my experience, people often do take care of this sort of thing by themselves—but that I should have done more to protect myself. (I had done some things right but neglected other important steps.) Matthews is the author of consumer law books, including *How to Win Your Personal Injury Claim* and *The Lawsuit Survival Guide. His self-defense strategies if you're in a car accident…*

• **Always report to the police and your insurer accidents that involve personal injuries** or vehicular damage that amounts to more than your state's required reporting limit—check with your insurer for the limit.

• **Obtain information about the other party or parties:**

 • Names, addresses and phone numbers of the driver, passengers and vehicle owner if different from the driver (ask to see the insurance card and registration).

 • Insurer and policy number.

 • Year, make, model and license plate of the other vehicle.

 • Witnesses' names and their phone numbers.

• **Document the damage** to all vehicles and their contents. Keep a disposable camera in your car for this purpose…use your cell phone to take pictures…or write detailed notes.

If the other driver prefers to bypass insurance companies, wait several days before giving an answer.

Reason: Injuries and vehicle damage may not be immediately apparent. "Rear-enders" may cause back and neck problems days later.

• **Take your vehicle to a repair shop that you trust,** not one selected by the other driver or one you aren't familiar with. Once you have an estimate and you decide to settle without the insurance company, give the other party a deadline to pay you—in cash. If he/she doesn't meet the agreed-upon deadline, report the accident to your insurer. The company will then notify the Department of Motor Vehicles and settle the claim. Be sure to check with your insurance carrier on how long you have to report the accident.

Would it have been better—or, in the end, simpler—to report the accident to my own insurer? Matthews says that everyone has to make decisions like this on a case-by-case basis. My deductible is high enough that I would receive no reimbursement. Most likely, my monthly premiums would not have gone up (as long as I could show that the accident was clearly not my fault), but the incident would go on my record—which could cause problems if I try to switch insurers in the future. So I'll take the loss. However, next time around, I will certainly get all of the information to ensure it is adequately resolved.

Auto Insurance Trap

A big mistake when changing auto insurers is not filing a proper cancellation form.

Trap: If you just don't pay the old policy and let it lapse, the old insurer will cancel it for nonpayment of premiums. This will go in your credit record and may cause the new insurer to raise your premium—so you wind up moving to a new insurer with a higher premium.

J. D. Howard, executive director, Insurance Consumer Advocate Network, Branson West, MO, www.ican2000.com.

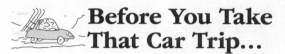

Before You Take That Car Trip...

Eric Peters, Washington, DC–based automotive columnist and author of *Automotive Atrocities! The Cars We Love to Hate.* MBI.

A pilot never takes off without running through a checklist. A road trip should be approached the same way. Even if your car is relatively new, it always is a good idea to make a quick check of vital systems before you leave for an extended trip.

●**Check that all four tires are properly inflated and in good shape.** The recommended tire pressure can be located in the owner's manual or on a sticker on the vehicle. Replace any tire that has bulges (which indicate a weakness in the tire wall that could lead to a blowout), visible cracks in the tread or sidewall, or a tread depth that is close to the wear indicators—the small bands that appear across the tread when the tire becomes worn.

●**Make sure you have all the equipment to change a tire.** This includes a properly inflated spare and all the parts of the jack. Toss an old blanket (at least 6' x 8') into the trunk along with a pair of heavy-duty gloves and an old shirt. Make sure you include a strong flashlight with fresh batteries and at least four flares so you can illuminate the vehicle if it becomes disabled.

●**Create an emergency kit.** You never know when you will have to patch a leaking hose or tie down a trunk that is too full. Round up a few basic hand tools—flat- and Phillips-head screwdrivers and an adjustable wrench—as well as duct tape and a few feet of rope. These things can get you out of a jam—or at least, to the next gas station.

●**Check that all routine maintenance has been performed.** That includes changing the oil and filter and checking the air filter, battery, brakes and cooling system. Check the belts that drive vital engine accessories for wear or cracks. Also check the condition of rubber radiator and heater hoses. These should be replaced every four years even if there are no obvious signs of wear. Install fresh wiper blades if yours are more than six months old. Top off the windshield washer fluid. Make sure headlights, turn signals and brake lights are working.

●**If you plan to pull a trailer or boat and the car has an automatic transmission,** consider having the transmission fluid and filter changed and an accessory transmission oil cooler installed if the vehicle does not already have one. The added heat created by pulling a trailer can dramatically reduce the service life of an automatic transmission and even lead to a failure on the road. The cost—about $150 to $200 installed—is far less than the $2,000 for a new transmission.

Smart Ways to Improve Your Safety on the Road

John H. Kennedy, executive director of defensive driving courses, National Safety Council, 1121 Spring Lake Dr., Itasca, IL 60143, *www.nsc.org.*

More than 2.5 million people are killed or seriously injured in road accidents each year in the US. But there's good news—with only a little bit of effort, you can improve your driving skills enough to lower your chances of being among the victims. In the process, you may also lower your insurance premiums.

Learning to drive defensively is particularly important if you're over 50 because—like it or not—vision, motor skills and other abilities diminish with age.

EARLY WARNINGS

Unfortunately, problems with one's driving are often hard to spot because abilities diminish gradually. *Be especially concerned if…*

• **Cars often honk at you.** Other drivers may be trying to get your attention because you may be driving erratically. You might not be as alert as you once were. Medication can be one of the reasons, and not everyone realizes that it's against the law to drive when ability is impaired by medication.

Apart from making you vulnerable to accidents, violations can result in hefty fines, possible loss of your license and higher insurance premiums.

Essential: Whenever a physician prescribes medication, be sure to ask if it will impair your driving ability.

• **You squint to read road signs, or oncoming headlights look blurry.** Either of these can be symptoms of eye problems, many of which can be corrected.

Essential: Have an ophthalmologist examine your eyes yearly.

• **You are often startled by a car behind you, especially when you change lanes.**

It usually happens because you are distracted or have not adequately scanned your driving environment. It's recommended that you check your mirrors every three to five seconds.

People over age 50 often become less agile, which makes it harder to turn to check the blind spots. Also avoid driving in another person's blind spot. If you cannot see the other driver's rearview mirror through his/her back window, you are probably in his blind spot. Adjust your speed to move out of this position.

Solutions: Limit lane changes, slow down—and consider a physical exercise program to improve flexibility (check with your doctor).

Also: Park your car, and ask a friend to walk around behind it. Then look in your mirrors, and, when you can no longer see the other person in each mirror, turn in your seat and note where the blind spots are. Adjust the mirrors to the best position.

DEFENSIVE DRIVING

Defensive driving courses are available in every state. Most courses include four to eight hours of classroom instruction and cost less than $65.

Statistics show that drivers who have taken courses have fewer serious accidents, and in most states, they're eligible for a reduction in insurance premiums, usually about 10%. Completing some courses may also let you remove points from your driving record.

Even in states where a premium reduction is not automatic, individual insurance companies will often cut their rates if customers offer proof that they've taken a defensive driving course.

To find a course, ask your state motor vehicle bureau. *Some of the most popular courses…*

• **The National Safety Council's "Defensive Driving Courses" and "Defensive Driving for the Mature Driver."** The National Safety Council also provides an on-line driving course (630-285-1121, *www. nsc.org*).

• **AARP's "Driver Safety Program"** (888-227-7669, *www.aarp.org/driver_safety*).

• **AAA's Driver Improvement Program course, "Safe Driving for Mature Operators."** Information on courses is available from local AAA branches, which are listed in your phone book.

EXPERT SAFETY TACTICS

To reduce the chance of being involved in a serious accident…

• **Beware of intersections,** where a high percentage of accidents occur. Defensive drivers not only slow down but also scan ahead to anticipate problems as they approach an intersection. They also keep their left foot over the brake so they can stop quickly if necessary.

Another strategy is to avoid a busy intersection altogether by taking another route.

• **Keep to a three-second following distance.** Determine that distance by counting the time it takes your car to reach a light pole or other stationary object after the car ahead has reached it.

Add a second to the distance if it's dark, and another second if it's raining. Add yet another second if the road is icy.

• **When you are caught in the glare of oncoming headlights, do not turn your head.** Instead, avoid the glare by focusing on the road itself.

• **If another driver shows any signs of anger, get out of his way.** Trying to win an argument is often a route to a serious accident. Similarly, good defensive drivers slow down to let tailgaters pass.

• **Keep your hands on the wheel at the 9 o'clock and 3 o'clock positions, to have maximum control over the car.**

• **Fasten your safety belt.** If you need an incentive for using your seat belt, imagine your body crumpled against the dashboard after a crash. It's also illegal to drive without a safety belt fastened, and convictions could increase your insurance premiums.

• **Know your braking system.** Today's antilock brakes operate very differently from older systems. If you're unsure about how to use antilock brakes, review your owner's manual. Or you can experiment using them in an empty parking lot.

Most important: In an emergency, do not "pump" antilock brakes. Instead, apply steady pressure to the pedal until you stop. For more information, visit *www.nsc.org*.

• **Familiarize yourself with the dashboard controls.** Ironically, many otherwise excellent drivers do not know what each control does. That knowledge is important because it lets you manage lights, door locks and systems that can be vital in emergencies.

• **Don't use distracting devices while driving.** Using a cell phone, even a hands-free model, is dangerous because taking your mind off the road can result in an accident. Other distractions include eating, drinking, putting tapes or CDs into a player, even adjusting the heat. If you need to make a call or do anything else that might be a distraction, pull over to the side of the road and stop.

Smart move: With so many safety steps to remember, it's wise to ask for help from anyone who frequently rides with you. Tell these friends how you're trying to drive more safely, and ask them to remind you whenever you forget.

You can increase safety even more by driving shorter distances, avoiding trips at night and taking less congested routes, particularly at rush hours.

When these steps just aren't possible, ask a friend to drive or take a taxi. With today's high cost of operating a car, taxis make more and more sense, especially when two or more people can share the fare.

15

Travel Update

Ten Secrets that Hotels Don't Want You to Know

You want a hotel to be your home away from home, but many aspects of hotel pricing and policy are really anything but homey. *Here's what you need to know...*

GETTING A ROOM

• **You can get the best rate by calling the hotel's local number,** not the 800 number, which usually links callers to an off-site centralized call center. Instead of asking for the reservations desk, ask to speak with the manager on duty, the general manager or the director of sales. These people have the authority to negotiate room rates.

It's often possible to beat a hotel's best advertised price by 20%, particularly if you call just a few days before your visit. First, shop around for the best deal on a third-party Internet travel site, such as Expedia.com or Hotels.com. Don't take the deal—just jot it down for reference.

Then call the hotel and explain to a manager or director that you know these Web sites mark up room prices by 20% to 40%. Tell the manager you would like to split the difference—say you'll pay 20% below the price you found on-line. Unless the hotel is filled to capacity, the manager is likely to take you up on your offer.

• **Everything is negotiable.** Think parking is overpriced? If the lot looks half empty, offer less than the daily rate. Planning to make a lot of phone calls? Some hotels offer a per-day flat fee for long-distance in the US and local calling—usually about $9.95—but you must ask for it.

• **Rooms are available even when a hotel has no vacancies.** In any large hotel,

Peter Greenberg, travel editor of NBC's *Today* show and host of the nationally syndicated *Peter Greenberg Worldwide* radio show (*www.petergreenberg.com*). He is author of *The Traveler's Diet: Eating Right and Staying Fit on the Road*. Random House.

a few rooms usually are listed as "out of order" at any given time. The problem might be something as simple as a stain on the carpet or a chair that has been sent out for repairs. If you're desperate for a last-minute room in a hotel that claims to have none available, tell the manager you are willing to take an out-of-order room that has only a minor problem. You might even be able to negotiate a better rate, since the room would otherwise sit empty.

• **"Guaranteed" rooms really aren't guaranteed.** When you make a hotel reservation, you often are asked to "guarantee" your room with a credit card—but there's still a chance that the hotel will give away your room if you arrive late. Providing a credit card number improves the odds that your room will be held—but it still pays to call to confirm that you're coming if you won't arrive until after 9 pm.

SAFEGUARDING VALUABLES

• **A thief takes one credit card, not your entire wallet.** It's no secret that crime is common in hotels. The new twist is that some hotel thieves now take just one credit card when they find an unguarded wallet in a room—and leave everything else untouched. Frequently, a victim doesn't notice the card is missing until the credit line is maxed out.

Travel only with the credit cards that you really need, and check your wallet carefully if you accidentally leave it unattended.

• **Your bags aren't safe with the bellhop.** Even in elite hotels, luggage can be stolen right off the luggage carts in the lobby. Though these bags theoretically are in the possession of the bellhop, the hotel assumes no legal responsibility for the loss.

If your bag is going to sit for more than a few minutes, ask that it be placed in a secure room. Keep valuable items in the hotel safe.

Helpful: High-end luggage might impress fellow travelers, but it also impresses thieves. The cheaper or uglier your luggage looks, the greater the odds that a thief will target someone else.

• **It pays to tip the housekeeper every day.** Exchange a few pleasant words with the housekeeper if you see him/her—and leave a $2 or $3 tip each day. You'll receive better service—housekeepers are the most overworked, underpaid and underappreciated people in the hotel, so any gesture will be appreciated.

Knowing the housekeeper also reduces the chances that your room will be burglarized. Dishonest housekeepers are less likely to target guests they have met. If a burglar enters your room while it is being cleaned and pretends to be you—a common ruse—the housekeeper should be able to spot the impostor.

MORE INSIDER SECRETS

• **Hotel rooms are infested with germs.** Certain items in hotel rooms never get cleaned. The biggest trouble spots include the TV remote control, telephone and clock/radio. Travel with a package of antibacterial wipes, and be sure to clean these items when you arrive.

Also, while reputable hotels provide fresh linens, bedspreads might be cleaned only once every few months. Remove them from the beds as soon as you check in. Ask for clean blankets as soon as you arrive.

• **Lost-and-found is a great resource for cell-phone users.** If you have a cell phone, odds are that someday you'll forget to bring your recharging cord or lose it in transit. If you're staying at a hotel, there's no need to buy a replacement. Recharging cords are the number-one item left behind in hotel rooms. Most hotels are willing to lend cords from their lost-and-found—but guests rarely ask.

• **Not all concierges are really concierges.** A true concierge is the most connected person around town. He can obtain tickets to sold-out events…reservations to popular restaurants…prescriptions filled in the middle of the night…even a new heel on a shoe by 8 am. (A tip of $10 to $20 usually is appropriate—more if the concierge really worked miracles.) But not all hotels that advertise "concierge service" truly provide it.

Many simply assign a regular hotel employee the role each shift.

An elite concierge wears a gold key on his lapel. It's the symbol of Les Clefs d'Or—French for "Keys of Gold"—a prestigious international concierge organization.

More from Peter Greenberg...

Best Time to Call for Lower Hotel Rates

For the best hotel rates, phone the hotel after 4 pm on Sundays.

Reason: The yield/revenue managers—the people who dictate the sliding rates for hotel rooms—are off on Sundays, so you have a better chance of getting someone at the front desk who is anxious to fill unsold rooms.

Also from Peter Greenberg...

Travel Detective's Money-Saving Tricks

Airline passengers used to complain about the quality of onboard meals. Now they're lucky if they are fed at all. Here's how you can still find good deals on hotels, airlines, rental cars and more...

HOTELS

• **Call hotels at 4 pm on Sunday** to reserve a room for anytime within the next two to three weeks. You'll have a better chance of getting a low rate from a front-desk clerk who understands that an unsold room is revenue the hotel will never recoup. Don't call the hotel's 800 number—you are likely to be put through to a national reservation line. Look up the hotel's number in the city you plan to visit.

• **Request weekend rates.** At some hotels, weekend rates are one-third of regular rates. If you're staying through the week, ask that the cheaper weekend rate be extended. Make sure the room price reflects hidden charges, such as resort fees, as well as taxes.

• **Consider alternative lodging.** Many hostels have gone upscale and offer private rooms for $25 to $160 a night. For information,

contact Hostelling International USA (301-495-1240, *www.hiusa.org*).

Also: More than 70% of colleges rent dorm rooms at reasonable prices during vacation periods.

RENTAL CARS

• **Call the local rental location.** If you use a toll-free number to make a reservation, you may not get the lowest rate or the best car. Local operators can price cars to reduce a temporary surplus.

Avoid renting at airport lots, which can be more expensive than in-city ones. Compare local and national rates at RentalCars.com.

Helpful: Rent on Saturday. There is a good chance cars will be available because customers requested them for the weekend but never claimed them.

CRUISES

• **Book a cruise at the last minute.** Many routes have more berths than passengers. Some travel agents and consolidators offer great last-minute packages.

Warning: Cruise lines now charge for extras that used to be included, such as onboard recreational activities. Expect to pay about two-and-a-half times the basic cruise price, so a $600 cruise actually could cost $1,500.

AIRFARES

• **Be flexible.** When calling airlines, don't provide travel dates to reservation agents up-front. Instead, ask the agent to punch into the computer every fare for the itinerary you desire within a range of dates. Ask for the cheapest fares first. If you're flexible, you may be able to cut ticket costs.

• **Buy tickets after midnight on Tuesday** in the time zone where the airline is based. Typically, airlines start fare sales late Friday, and competing airlines match the lower fares. All the matching usually stops by Monday. Airlines usually give customers who book low fares 24 hours in which to buy them. All the low fares that were booked on Monday but not purchased by midnight Tuesday come back into the airline's computers at that moment.

Scoring a Reservation

Get a dinner reservation at a popular restaurant by phoning around lunchtime the day before. This is when many people call to cancel their reservations for the next evening.

New York, 444 Madison Ave., New York City 10022.

Much Safer Travel

Peter V. Savage, vice president and cofounder, Passport Health, a leading provider of low-cost immunizations and travel-related services to businesses and tourists, Baltimore, *www.passporthealthusa.com.* He is author of *The Safe Travel Book.* Lexington.

When you're on vacation, the last thing you want to worry about is your safety, but it's wise to be prepared. We asked travel author Peter V. Savage, a clandestine officer in the CIA for two decades, what to watch out for. *His travel advice...*

• **Contact the embassy.** Before you book a trip, call the American embassy in the country you will be visiting and ask for the Regional Security Officer (RSO). You can get the number by contacting the State Department at 202-647-4000 or *travel.state.gov.*

The RSO should be able to answer questions about disease outbreaks, high-crime areas, weather issues, where to get the best exchange rates and problems American travelers have had recently.

Example: A few years ago, I called the RSO in Ottawa, Canada, and asked about Montreal. The RSO told me that if I rented a sport utility vehicle (SUV) during my stay, I should keep it parked in a garage. Criminals were stealing SUVs off the streets, quickly stripping them and shipping the parts to China.

• **Don't dress like an American.** I shake my head when I see Americans in foreign countries wearing clothing that announces where they're from or where they went to college. I even saw an American oilman in Venezuela wearing cowboy boots and a cowboy hat with a turkey feather. Letting others know that you're an American may prompt crooks to assume that you are a wealthy tourist worth robbing or, even worse, worth kidnapping for a ransom.

Keep watches and jewelry—even costume jewelry that looks real—at home. If you must bring jewelry or other valuables, make sure they are insured. Also, avoid using expensive luggage. Keep cameras hidden when not in use.

• **Outsmart pickpockets.** I keep money, my passport and credit cards in a wallet that attaches to my belt and is concealed under my clothes. You can buy these at *www.austinhouse.com.*

If you use a fanny pack, keep the pouch in front. (A common trick of pickpockets is to bump into you front and back—pickpockets usually work in teams—and quickly slice the bottom of the fanny pack and catch the valuables as they drop.) Women should carry purses football fashion. Don't bother getting traveler's checks—these days, credit cards have wider acceptance. In your purse or pocket, carry enough cash to satisfy a mugger.

• **Prepare for medical emergencies.** Be sure you have the proper immunizations before heading out of the country. You can find a local travel medicine clinic at *www.istm.org* or at my Web site, *www.passporthealthusa.com.* Plan several months in advance—some vaccinations require multiple doses with weeklong intervals in between. If you take medication, bring extra in case you have to stay longer than planned. Before you leave, buy an emergency assistance medical and evacuation insurance policy. Providers have established medical contacts worldwide, can pay in cash on the spot and can bring you home if necessary.

Good source: www.travelguard.com.

• **Keep important information with your passport.** Write down the phone numbers of the American embassies in the countries that you intend to visit. Also, include your blood type and whether your blood's Rh factor is positive or negative.

Make copies of your passport and keep them with you in case you lose your original. Leave copies with friends or relatives at home as well.

Buckle Up

Vehicle-related accidents are a major cause of accidental deaths of US citizens abroad. Especially in developing countries, taxi and bus drivers may take far more risks than in the US—overloading vehicles, ignoring stoplights, driving recklessly on mountain roads and failing to use headlights.

Self-defense: Avoid traveling at night, especially in rural areas. Sit in the backseat, and buckle up. Don't ride in taxis that don't have seat belts in the backseat.

Road safety information: Road reports for individual countries are available from Association for Safe International Road Travel (*asirt.org*).

Stuart R. Rose, MD, president, Travel Medicine, Inc., Northampton, MA, and author of *International Travel Health Guide*. Elsevier. *www.travmed.com*.

How to Travel for Next To Nothing—or Free

Sue Goldstein, creator of The Underground Shopper, a multimedia outlet that includes a Dallas-area call-in radio show on shopping and an Internet shopping site, *www.undergroundshopper.com*.

Two of the best ways to travel all over the world on an exceptionally tight budget…

COURIER FLIGHTS

When a company needs to have an important document or package hand delivered, it might hire a courier to handle it. As a courier, you give up a portion of your check-on luggage allowance, which the company uses for its cargo. When you arrive, you deliver the package to the shipping agent's representative and your job is done.

Courier arrangements are most worthwhile for international flights. With nearly 40,000 courier flights every year, the destination choices are extensive. Flying from New York to Bangkok, for example, might cost you only $300 round-trip. A standard commercial flight to Bangkok typically costs more than $1,000. It's best to reserve at the last minute. The closer your desired departure date, the bigger your discount. There are times when a courier will be able to fly for free with just a few hours' notice.

Most courier companies expect you to stay for a specified period of time, usually anywhere from seven to 30 days. You are limited to one check-in piece of luggage and sometimes only one carry-on.

Tickets typically are nonrefundable and must be paid for in cash and picked up in person, often on the day of the flight. Most tickets are round-trip, and the return flights typically are open-ended. You can return anytime after your stint as a courier ends.

Courier flights depart from major cities, such as New York, Los Angeles, Chicago and Miami. Some courier flights charge a registration fee—$35 to $50—which gives you access to a wider range of ticket options and prices.

Where to book courier flights…

• **Air Courier Association/Cheap Trips.** $39 for annual membership (some memberships require a monthly maintenance fee). 800-383-6814, *www.aircourier.org*.

• **International Association of Air Travel Couriers.** $45 for annual domestic membership ($50 for international). 402-218-1982, *www.courier.org*.

FREE OR LOW-COST CRUISES

If you are a gentleman between the ages of 45 and 75 and are well-groomed and well-spoken, cruise ships want you.

Your mission: To dance with and otherwise accompany the many unescorted women passengers. You might also help with dance classes and act as an escort on shore excursions as well as to dinner.

Gentlemen hosts need to be able to fox-trot, rumba, cha-cha and waltz. Cruise lines might ask you to audition at a dance studio in a nearby major city—they have relationships with studios around the country. In return, you get to see the world, meet people and enjoy gourmet feasts around the clock.

Most important rule: You must act professionally at all times. If you're caught sneaking extra dances or otherwise romancing particular passengers, you'll be asked to leave the ship at the next port and will have to get home on your own.

A gentleman host is unpaid but receives a free cabin, discounts on drinks, laundry service and often free airfare. Booking agencies might charge a small fee—less than $30 per day. If you go directly to the cruise line, there's usually no fee.

To become a gentleman host…

•**Crystal Cruises.** 800-804-1500, *www.crystalcruises.com* (click on "Media Center," then "Fact Sheets," then "Ambassador Host Program for Singles").

•**Sixth Star Entertainment & Marketing.** 954-462-6760, *www.sixthstar.com.*

•**Compass Speakers.** 954-568-3801, *www.compassspeakers.com.*

Airline Pilot's Insider Information

Meryl Getline, a pilot in Elizabeth, CO, with 32 years of flying experience, including 15 years as a captain with a major airline. She now maintains the aviation Web sites FromtheCockpit.com and Flying Fearless.com. She is author of *The World at My Feet: The True (and Sometimes Hilarious) Adventures of a Lady Airline Captain* and the e-book *Ground School for Passengers* (both available at FromtheCockpit.com and FlyingFearless.com).

We trust our lives to airplanes and the pilots who fly them, but there is a lot that the average passenger does not realize about modern aircraft. *Here,*

a veteran airline captain answers some of the most common passenger questions…

•**Where is the best place to sit on an airplane if you are prone to airsickness?** The best spot is over the wing or a few rows in front of the wing. When a plane climbs or descends, it pivots on its center of gravity, which tends to be just in front of the wings. The closer you are to this point, the less you'll feel the movement, just as sitting in the middle of a seesaw subjects you to less movement than sitting at the end.

•**How do you prevent jet lag?** I really don't suffer much from jet lag. I always observe local time, though many pilots keep their watches set to their hometown time and try to sleep accordingly. If you're traveling on business, this may be impractical.

The best advice is to stay well-hydrated and rest on the plane if you are traveling overnight and arriving in the morning. If you are traveling during the day, plan to read or watch a movie en route so that you're ready to sleep that night after you arrive.

•**Could the "autopilot" fly or land a plane without the pilots?** Not really. Autopilot can't do much more than fly a programmed route or maintain the last heading or altitude entered by the pilots. Pilots are needed to manage the autopilot during the flight.

The autopilot sometimes plays a role in landings—it can keep the plane lined up with the centerline of the runway and it can even land the plane under certain conditions—but the pilot must control the air speed (even if autothrottles are utilized, they must be programmed and the speed monitored), flaps and landing gear. The autopilot plays no role at all during takeoffs, although some airplanes may employ autothrottles during takeoff.

•**How do I know that I can trust my pilot?** Airline pilots are among the most thoroughly trained and tested professionals in the US. They also must go through a rigorous retraining each year to remain certified. Any pilot at any airline in this country can be trusted to be a proficient flier.

The pilot certification process may not be as rigorous in some less developed countries, however. Before you board a flight on a small airline in another country, consider checking the airline's safety record on the Web site *www.airsafe.com.* You can view accident reports and other statistics and reach your own conclusions.

• **Are air pockets dangerous?** Not only are they not dangerous, they don't exist. The term "air pocket" was coined by a journalist during World War I, but he really just was referring to turbulence—irregular air currents that can shake aircraft around a bit.

When a plane "hits an air pocket" and seems to drop 1,000 feet, it really has just run into a little turbulence and probably dropped or climbed no more than 10 to 20 feet. Light turbulence is so common and inconsequential that experienced pilots scarcely notice it.

There is such a thing as "severe turbulence," which can be strong enough to injure passengers who aren't wearing their seat belts, but this is so rare that I have never encountered it in my 32 years of flying. Modern radar is advanced enough that pilots usually can steer clear of areas that have a high probability of moderate or severe turbulence.

Even when a plane does experience severe turbulence, it won't crash because of it. When was the last time you read or heard of an airplane accident blamed on turbulence? If you're worried that a little turbulence will bring down your flight, watch one of those Discovery channel documentaries on "hurricane hunter" planes that fly right into the middle of huge storms and come out unscathed on the other side. A modern passenger jet is just as sturdy.

• **In the movies, whenever a plane hits severe turbulence, the baggage compartments open up and luggage tumbles out. Would that happen in a real plane?** On occasion, if it gets really rough, an overhead compartment could open, especially if it isn't securely latched. I have never witnessed more than one compartment at a time come open due to turbulence, and I have only seen this once or twice.

• **How dangerous is it when a plane gets struck by lightning?** My plane has been struck at least three times in my career. There's sometimes a bang, like a cannon going off, but it's not all that dangerous. The lightning charge simply travels around the plane's metal exterior, then off the "static wicks" (pencil-like protrusions) on the trailing edges and tips of the wings and tail.

It is true that lightning can cause problems for a plane's electrical systems. Once, on a flight from Los Angeles to Denver, a lightning strike knocked out my plane's power, but only for a few seconds. Even if the plane's main electrical system had been permanently disabled, we still had standby power. Some modern planes are now outfitted with Ram Air Turbines (RATs), which use the airstream to power onboard electrical backup generators and hydraulic systems.

Between the emergency power systems and the extensive training that pilots receive, there's no reason to think that a plane would crash just because its main electrical system went out.

• **What advice do you have for people who are afraid to fly?** I suggest that you consider the statistics regarding flying. It really is true that the drive to the airport is many, many times more dangerous than the flight. Personally, I feel far safer in a plane than I do in a car.

• **Are some airports safer than others?** All US airports are safe, but some are more modern than others and thus probably a little safer.

Modern airports often have longer runways, easier-to-navigate approaches and more sophisticated electronics that allow pilots to land even with limited or no visibility. The ultramodern airports include Denver International Airport and Los Angeles International Airport.

Older airports, such as Chicago's Midway International Airport, Jackson Hole Airport, San Diego International Airport, New York City's LaGuardia Airport and Ronald Reagan Washington National Airport, are not this advanced, but I certainly wouldn't call them unsafe.

•**Has air travel security improved since 9/11?** Yes, mostly because the passengers themselves now are part of the security force. In the past, if a passenger started acting oddly, those seated near him/her would just mind their own business. These days, if a passenger starts doing anything halfway suspicious, other passengers quickly alert a flight attendant.

The Seven Best Tours in America

Mike Putman, founder of Travel Team Consulting, Inc., which advises airlines, hotel chains and others in the travel business, *www.travelteamconsulting.com*. He is president of Putman Travel, Inc., a Greenville, SC, travel agency that has been in business for 20 years.

O ne way to cut down on travel hassles is to sign up for a tour and leave all the driving, decision making and problem solving in the capable hands of the tour operator.

Tours can also be moneysavers. Tour companies negotiate group rates on hotels, meals, admission prices and transportation. In general, you can expect to spend approximately 30% less with a package tour than you would following the very same itinerary on your own in a rental car.

Tours are best for those who like to keep busy on vacation and enjoy meeting new people, not for those who prefer to relax on the beach or travel with only a few companions. Most people who sign up for tours are in their 50s or older, so younger vacationers might feel out of place (except on tours specifically designed for families or young people).

To make sure you are dealing with a quality travel organization, confirm that it is a member of the American Society of Travel Agents at 703-739-2782 or at *www.astanet.com*…it has been in business for at least five years…and there aren't numerous complaints about it lodged on travel Web sites, such as TripAdvisor.com, or with the Better Business Bureau.

Here, seven domestic tours that deliver a lot for the money…*

•**Yellowstone & Grand Teton National Parks.** See the wonders of the West, including the magnificent glaciers, forests and stone pinnacles of Grand Teton National Park …the dramatic canyons and geysers of Yellowstone National Park…and the grandeur of Mount Rushmore on this 10-day journey. You'll also explore some of the historic towns of the West and take a raft trip on the Snake River. Tauck World Discovery (800-788-7885, *www. tauck.com*). Trips are priced from $2,690.

•**Southern Charms and the Great Smokies.** This wide-ranging nine-day tour starts in Tennessee with stops in Memphis and Nashville, ventures north into Kentucky bluegrass country, then south through the Great Smoky Mountain National Park and finally east into Atlanta. Globus (866-755-8581, *www.globusjourneys.com*). From $1,869.

•**Rockies Rail Adventure.** Take a scenic nine-day rail tour through the Rocky Mountains, staying in quality hotels along the way. Rail lines go places that cars cannot, hugging the sides of mountains and tracing the course of rugged rivers. You'll tour spectacular Mesa Verde National Park and also explore New Mexico's enchanting Taos and Sante Fe. Maupintour (800-255-4266, *www. maupintour.com*). From $2,949.

•**California Coast Vacation.** The Pacific Coast Highway, also known as Route 1, is often called the most scenic driving road in America. This nine-day tour lets you sit back and enjoy the views. You'll visit some of America's greatest cities, including San Francisco, Los Angeles and San Diego, and explore picturesque towns such as Carmel, Monterey and San Juan Capistrano. The package includes a short cruise to Catalina Island and a dinner cruise in San Diego Bay. Globus, from $2,249.

*Prices are subject to change. Prices are also per person double occupancy and do not include travel expenses to and from the tour's departure point. Packages typically include some but not all meals. Contact the tour operator for details.

•**Alaska: A Family Adventure.** This nine-day family-oriented tour isn't cheap, but considering what you get, it's a good value. You take a private guided tour of Denali National Park…meet an Iditarod champion and his dog team…fly on float planes and bush planes…visit remote locations that are inaccessible by road…cruise the Kenai Fjords… and enjoy the whale watching, panning for gold and campfires. Abercrombie & Kent, Inc. (800-554-7016, *www.abercrombiekent. com*). $7,930 per adult/$4,530 per child under age 12, sharing with two adults.

•**The Best of Hawaii.** It isn't easy to see all of Hawaii in one visit—you have to arrange flights from island to island and secure a rental vehicle and hotel room on each island. This 12-day package offers an easy way to visit the four most popular islands—Kauai, Maui, Oahu and the Big Island. You will explore volcanoes, tour harbors and villages and visit coffee farms and historic sites, such as Pearl Harbor. Plus there's plenty of time for snorkeling, golfing and all the other things people associate with Hawaiian vacations. Tauck World Discovery, from $4,399 (with an additional charge for flights between islands).

Six Amazing American Gardens

Joan Rattner Heilman, an award-winning travel writer based in New York. She is author of *Unbelievably Good Deals and Great Adventures That You Absolutely Can't Get Unless You're Over 50.* McGraw-Hill.

Visiting beautiful gardens is a favorite American pastime. Below are some of the most memorable gardens in the US. All are open for visits year-round and offer guided tours.

OREGON: JAPANESE GARDEN, PORTLAND

Located on 5.5 acres of forested land in Portland's Washington Park, this is a "specialty" garden where plants, stones and water have been combined and arranged to represent five formal Japanese garden styles.

Designed by a Japanese landscape architect to be "a haven of tranquil beauty," with a variety of views and soothing scenes, it was opened to the public in 1967 and has become one of the Northwest's favorite destinations. Sinuous gravel paths meander over hills and hollows that include koi ponds, bridges, a teahouse, raked white-sand landscapes, waterfalls and sculptured stone lanterns.

Details: Washington Park, 611 SW Kingston Ave., Portland, OR 97205, 503-223-1321, *www.japanesegarden.com*. Open seven days a week except Thanksgiving, Christmas and New Year's Day.

Admission: Adults, $8…seniors age 62 and over, $6.25…students ages six to 17, $5.25…college students, $6.25…children age five and under, free.*

PENNSYLVANIA: LONGWOOD GARDENS, KENNETT SQUARE

This is a horticultural display garden showcasing not only rare and exotic plants but also common varieties displayed in extraordinary ways. Longwood was created on farmland just south of Philadelphia by industrialist Pierre S. du Pont in 1906. Today, it has 1,050 acres of plantings, woodlands and meadows, and four acres of indoor gardens. Its specialty gardens include a 600-foot Flower Walk and the fantastic Topiary Garden.

Longwood has more fountains than any other garden in the country and is noted for its illuminated fountain displays synchronized with music.

Details: Longwood Gardens, Route 1, Kennett Square, PA 19348, 610-388-1000, *www.longwoodgardens.org*. Open every day, 9 am to 5 pm or later.

Admission: Adults, $16…seniors age 62 and over, $14…students ages five to 22, $6 …under age four, free.*

THE NEW YORK BOTANICAL GARDEN, BRONX

This national historic landmark, one of the oldest and largest botanical gardens in the world, and probably the most popular, is

*Prices subject to change.

visited by hundreds of thousands of people a year. Its rolling terrain contains 50 gardens and plant collections, and a 50-acre tract of original forest. It also offers the Enid A. Haupt Conservatory, the nation's largest Victorian-style greenhouse, which holds a permanent exhibition of tropical plants and changing seasonal flower shows.

Created in 1891 on land owned by the Lorillards, a family of tobacco merchants, it was financed by such tycoons as Andrew Carnegie, Cornelius Vanderbilt and J. P. Morgan. Among its most outstanding displays are the Rose Garden and the Perennial Garden.

Details: The New York Botanical Garden, 200th St. and Kazimiroff Blvd., Bronx, NY 10458, 718-817-8700, *www.nybg.org.* Open Tuesday to Sunday (and on Monday if a federal holiday). Closed Thanksgiving and Christmas Day.

Admission: Adults, $6…seniors age 62 and older and students, $3…children ages two to 12, $1…under age two, free.*

FLORIDA: FAIRCHILD TROPICAL BOTANIC GARDEN, CORAL GABLES

With extensive collections of rare tropical plants, including palms, cycads, fruit trees, flowering trees and vines, this 83-acre garden was founded in 1938 by David Fairchild, a noted plant explorer, and designed by William Lyman Phillips, a landscape architect from the firm of Frederick Law Olmsted, the famed designer of New York's Central Park.

Among the most popular features are the Richard H. Simons Rainforest, an outdoor exhibit of tropical rainforest plants from around the world…the McLamore Arboretum that displays hundreds of tropical flowering trees and vines…and the Keys Coastal Habitat, which includes marshes and mangroves and species native to southern Florida. The conservatory's Windows to the Tropics is a two-level display of tropical trees and plants that can survive outdoors only in the deep tropics.

Details: Fairchild Tropical Botanic Garden, 10901 Old Cutler Rd., Coral Gables, FL 33156, 305-667-1651, *www.ftbg.org.* Open daily except Christmas.

*Prices subject to change.

Admission: Adults, $20…seniors age 65 and older, $15…children ages six to 17, $10 …under age six, free.*

ARIZONA: DESERT BOTANICAL GARDEN, PHOENIX

A 145-acre oasis set among the red buttes of Papago Park in Phoenix, this is the only botanical garden in the world whose mission is to focus solely on desert plants. Its collection of more than 50,000 plants emphasizes cactus, agaves, aloes and the flora of Arizona's Sonoran Desert, but it also includes many other rare, threatened or endangered plant species, a seed bank of desert species and an herbarium containing preserved plant specimens.

The garden is divided into five thematic trails—Desert Discovery displays desert plants from around the world…Plants & People of the Sonoran Desert explores how native plants were used for nourishment and tools… Sonoran Desert Nature shows the relationship between plants and animals…Center for Desert Living covers water and energy conservation…and Harriet K. Maxwell Desert Wildflower trail showcases colorful desert flowers.

Details: Desert Botanical Garden, 1201 N. Galvin Pkwy., Phoenix, AZ 85008, 480-941-1225, *www.dbg.org.* Open daily except July 4, Thanksgiving and Christmas.

Admission: Adults, $10…seniors age 60 and older, $9…students ages 13 to 18 and college students, $5…children ages three to 12, $4…under age three, free.*

NORTH CAROLINA: BILTMORE GARDENS, ASHEVILLE

Surrounding Biltmore House, a 250-room French Renaissance–style chateau and the largest privately owned home in America, these gardens were created by Frederick Law Olmsted for the grandson of industrialist Cornelius Vanderbilt. On what is now an 8,000-acre parcel of land, he created a large farm, planned woodlands, fields and gardens, both formal and informal. The formal gardens include a walled garden…a 16th-century Italian garden with three reflecting pools, classical statuary and walls enclosed by a hemlock hedge…a shrub garden…a rose garden…and

*Prices subject to change.

the Spring Garden, filled with forsythia, spirea, rhododendron and holly. The rest of the grounds were landscaped as well, making them a wooded park. The gardens and Biltmore House are open to the public.

Details: Biltmore Estate, 1 Approach Rd., Asheville, NC 28803, 800-543-2961, *www. biltmore.com*. Open daily.

Admission: Adults, $47 Sunday through Friday and $51 on Saturday…children ages 10 to 16, $23.50 to $25.50, depending on day…under age 10, free.*

*Prices subject to change.

Vacation at a Lighthouse

Many lighthouses are converting into hotels and bed-and-breakfast resorts as ship navigation becomes electronic. Located on coastlines—frequently rugged ones—they often offer beautiful views and access to nature. Some lighthouses continue to operate while hosting guests, and a few even have guests help tend their beacons.

Helpful: For an on-line directory of all New England lighthouses offering lodging, and a "lighthouse bookstore" providing information about such lighthouses nationwide, visit the New England Lighthouses Web site, *www.lighthouse.cc*.

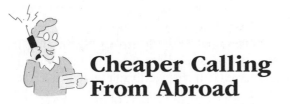

Cheaper Calling From Abroad

When traveling in Europe and Asia, consider using prepaid phone cards, such as Absolute Global (877-532-2737, *www. zaptel.com*) or MCI World Traveler (800-483-3805, *www.speedypin.com*). You call a toll-free number, then punch in a personal identification number (PIN) and the phone number of the person you are calling. Prices range from 10 cents to $2.50 per minute.

Alternative: A callback service, made through the American telephone network, such as United World Telecom (561-276-7156, ext. 301, *www.uwt4me.com*). You call a toll-free US number and let the phone ring once, then hang up. A computer "calls" you back, you enter the number you wish to call and you benefit from US phone rates anywhere in the world.

Example: A call from the UK can cost just four cents per minute.

The Wall Street Journal.

Passport Savvy

Kelly Shannon, press officer, Bureau of Consular Affairs, US Department of State, Washington, DC.

It's best to keep your passport up-to-date—even though the US government doesn't require its citizens to maintain valid passports. Some countries require a passport to have been valid for at least six months before your travel date. Others require that it be valid for at least six months after the date of your arrival. This is especially important if there is any chance that you may have to travel abroad with little notice.

Example: If you have ill or elderly relatives abroad and may have to get to them quickly. Countries' passport regulations change, so check with the embassy or consulate of each country you may visit.

Helpful: Register with the US Department of State prior to traveling so the government can more easily help you in—or notify you of—an emergency. Registration is free and secure at *https://travelregistration.state.gov*, and lasts for six months.

Note: Since January 23, 2007, Americans traveling to Canada, Mexico, Bermuda, the Caribbean and Central and South America are required to have a valid passport or other security document.

Information: *www.travel.state.gov*.

Beach-Sand Danger

Beach sand has five to 10 times more bacteria than adjacent water. Bacteria from bird droppings and human waste, such as *E. coli*, may survive longer in sand than in water because bacteria adhere to particles.

Self-defense: Wash hands after leaving the beach. Warn children not to put their hands in their mouths when digging in sand.

Walter McLeod, president, Clean Beaches Council, Washington, DC.

Water Dangers— How to Stay Safe When You Travel

Connie Lohsl, RN, BSN, nurse manager and travel-health specialist with Passport Health, a nationwide chain of travel-health franchises that provide low-cost immunizations and other travel-related services, based in Baltimore, *www.pass porthealthusa.com.*

Unprepared travelers who hope to enjoy exotic locales often spend their days in a hotel bathroom instead. About 40% of all travelers experience some form of stomach upset from mild to debilitating diarrhea. For those with underlying kidney or heart problems, the dehydration from diarrhea can be life-threatening.

Check the Worldwide Rating of Drinking Water Safety (*www.safewateronline.com*) to find out which countries have safe drinking water. *They're divided into five classes of risk...*

High risk: Parts of Africa, Mexico and Central America, South America, Asia and the Middle East, especially the rural areas. Hepatitis A has been a concern in Russia.

Intermediate risk: Portions of Eastern Europe.

Low risk: US, Canada, Japan, Western Europe and Australia.

To stay safe...

• **Drink bottled water, but inspect it first.** In some countries, a container of bottled water costs $4 or more. Unscrupulous vendors may refill empties with tap water. Always check that the factory seal is intact. Buy carbonated water, if available—it's harder to fake.

• **Wipe bottles and cans dry before drinking.** Bottled and canned beverages may be kept cold in tubs filled with ice water. Moisture on the outside may contain organisms that can get into your mouth when you drink. Of course, don't add ice cubes to beverages unless you are sure they are made from uncontaminated water.

• **Use bottled water for brushing teeth.** Stand your toothbrush upright between uses so it isn't contaminated with water from the sink.

• **Drink bottled water on cruise ships and airplanes.** Nonbottled water could be contaminated. Coffee and tea made with boiling water should be safe.

• **Sterilize your water.** *Two ways...*

• Boiling. Put the water in a clean pot, bring it to a rolling boil, then remove it from the heat and let it cool. Transfer to a sterilized container. Boiling is the most reliable way to kill most disease-causing organisms.

• Use a water-filtration bottle. This can protect against bacteria, protozoa and lead. Some also filter viruses, including hepatitis A. Check the product label. Available at my Web site, *www.passporthealthusa.com,* or at any local passport office or camping-supply store.

Cost: $40 to $100 or more.

• **Beware of swimming.** Swimming in the ocean is usually safe—few bacteria and parasites can survive in salt water. But lakes and other bodies of freshwater can have high levels of contamination—and some organisms pass directly through the skin.

Showering and toweling off soon after swimming will assist in removing parasites before they have a chance to burrow through the skin. Wearing swimming shoes can protect you from parasites and puncture wounds.

Well-maintained, chemically treated swimming pools generally are safe.

Beware of On-Line Travel Bargains

On-line travel deals may be too good to be true. Many hide handling fees, blackout dates and penalties for changes to your itinerary in the fine print.

Self-defense: Always read the fine print carefully before purchasing any on-line travel deal. It may be cheaper to book directly with the tour operator or the airline.

The New York Times.

Best Cruise Fares

Cruise ships are sailing full these days, so last-minute bargains are becoming rare. The best savings now come from booking early—and can be as much as 40% off.

Other opportunities: Travel during "shoulder season." This is at the edge of the busy season when demand for rooms falls off but weather is still good at your destination.

Or take a "repositioning cruise" on a ship as it moves between seasons from one cruise route to another.

Example: You could cruise from the Caribbean through the Panama Canal and up the Pacific Coast to Alaska.

Sherri Eisenberg, freelance travel writer, *Travel + Leisure*, 1120 Avenue of the Americas, New York City 10036.

International Rentals— Experience the World For Much Less

Lief Simon, real estate editor of *International Living*, a magazine and on-line information service that helps clients buy and rent property in more than a dozen countries in Europe, Latin America and Asia. *www.internationalliving.com.*

Would you like to live for all or part of the year on a tropical island, in a secluded countryside retreat or in a fashionable district of a world capital? Today's international rental market makes that possible and more affordable than you may have imagined.

Examples: A furnished condo on Mexico's Caribbean coast recently rented for $800 a month. For around $1,100 a month, you can rent an apartment in a charming Belgian village close to Brussels. In Paris, luxury apartments often rent for about $2,000 a month, but more modest ones are usually less than half that amount. And these prices are all for short-term rentals—usually less than six months.

The growing short-term rental market for apartments and houses is largely the result of demand from today's more sophisticated travelers who want to enjoy the area in much the way that local residents do. That means going to local shops, street fairs, community events and inexpensive, out-of-the-way restaurants and cafés to experience the real flavor of the locale. These rentals can also provide the opportunity to meet area residents.

Savings can be huge. For a month's stay, a rented apartment is likely to cost about half as much as a moderately priced hotel. In a rented apartment, you also save money by cooking for yourself.

HOW TO DO IT

In response to the demand, hundreds of companies have been started—many Internet-based—that specialize in overseas apartments and houses that you can rent for a few days to several months. Over the Internet, you can see pictures of apartments for rent.

Example: In New Zealand, a cottage-style apartment on a working cattle farm recently rented for $1,200 a month, including breakfast daily.

To find companies that deal in furnished short-term rentals, go to Google or another Internet search engine and enter the name of the city or country you're interested in, plus "short-term apartment rental."

Two major companies are Sublet.com (201-845-7300, *www.sublet.com*) and Vacation Rentals By Owner (*www.vrbo.com*), which list short-term furnished apartment rentals in nearly 100 countries. Craig's List, the Internet classified advertising company, also has extensive lists of rentals, but its Web site, *www.craigslist.org*, can sometimes be confusing because of the huge number of ads.

These three companies try to bar ads from unreliable property owners, but it's ultimately up to renters to check out landlords and their property. That can be difficult when they are located overseas. *The best strategy...*

• **Ask the landlord detailed questions about the property,** and don't deal with a landlord or real estate agent who hesitates to give you answers.

• **Ask for and contact US-based references** to see whether they were satisfied with the landlord. Many foreign landlords, however, won't have US-based references, and there's little point in contacting foreign references, because they may not be representative and can be expensive to contact.

• **Initially, rent the apartment for only a short period of time**—a week or two, for instance. That way, you'll be able to check it out for a subsequent longer rental period.

• **If you have lingering doubts about a rental, it might pay to retain an attorney in the country to check it out.**

Typical cost: $100 to about $500. (Attorneys can usually be located through the US embassy.)

Another way to find short-term rentals is through traditional real estate agencies in countries you're considering. To find them, ask for recommendations from a US real estate company that you know to be reliable. Most American real estate agencies know of reliable counterparts overseas.

My company, International Living, lists real estate agencies we know to be reliable in many countries.

Example: Tierra Yucatán Real Estate (*www.tierrayucatan.com*) recently listed a furnished house in Mérida, one of the safest and most picturesque cities in Mexico, for $550 a month.

At our Web site, *www.internationalliving.com*, you can also find information about such essentials as a country's cost of living,

climate, transportation, health care, culture, entertainment and sports.

Still another way to find a rental apartment or house overseas is to take a regular vacation in a place you like and stay at a hotel. While there, look for a residence that you can rent later for an extended stay. That strategy can also give you a chance to speak personally with the landlord and actually see the residence.

Helpful: American expatriates in areas you're interested in. They can often recommend real estate agents who deal in short-term rentals, and some expats themselves rent or sublet their apartments. To find expat organizations, contact American consulates in cities you're considering. Consulates can be located through the State Department at 202-647-4000 and on the Web at *http://usembassy.state.gov*.

RENTING THE BEST

There's no standard contract for short-term rentals overseas, but agreements usually are similar to what you would expect in the US, including a refundable advance (typically less than $200) to reserve the apartment.

Before signing a contract, ask the following questions...

• **What floor is the apartment on?** "First floor" overseas usually means what Americans call the second floor. Ask whether the building has an elevator (in many countries, older buildings often don't).

• **Will the phone be connected when you move in?**

• **Is there a TV with a hookup to English-language channels?**

• **Is the apartment air-conditioned?**

• **Will the electricity and water be turned on?** If you rent for three or more months, you may have to make arrangements with the landlord to deal with utility companies.

• **How close are grocery stores, pharmacies, transportation and other services you might need?**

• **Which furnishings are included?**

Examples: Linens, towels, cooking utensils, etc.

Safeguard: Ask the landlord to write or e-mail you with answers to the questions. The reason isn't to pin him/her down legally, because lawsuits usually aren't worthwhile if something goes wrong with an overseas rental. Nevertheless, landlords are much less likely to fudge answers that are in writing. In fact, landlords who regularly rent their apartments often provide instruction booklets that describe features of the residence as well as the neighborhood.

Negotiating tactic: When you look for rentals overseas, you may find quotes only for daily or weekly rates. But if you're interested in the residence for a longer stay, make an offer to rent it by the month for two-and-a-half times the weekly rate.

You might have to negotiate upward a bit, but many landlords will take your offer, especially in the off-season.

More from Lief Simon...

Where to Find Top-Value Rentals

Here are some fascinating places to consider for your upcoming overseas stay.

- **Argentina.** In Buenos Aires, one of the world's most sophisticated cities, prices start at about $750 a month for a one-bedroom apartment in Recoleta, an area known for cultural activities, nightlife, cafés and shopping.

- **Ecuador.** In this safe and charming country, a couple can typically live comfortably on less than $2,000 a month. The capital, Quito, has a springlike climate year-round, and furnished one-bedroom apartments are often as low as $500 a month.

- **Europe.** London, Dublin, Paris, Rome and major Scandinavian cities are expensive (typically more than $2,000 a month for a one-bedroom apartment), but even these cities have less expensive neighborhoods that are safe and colorful. You can generally find apartments for less than $1,000 a month in lesser-known cities within the expensive countries and throughout Spain, Portugal, Belgium and the former Eastern Bloc nations.

- **Mexico.** The country offers white-sand beaches, ancient colonial towns, a rich culture, affordable living and a variety of climates to suit nearly anyone. Houses in Guadalajara typically rent for as little as $600 a month.

- **Panama.** No matter where you rent, you'll have easy access to beaches and mountains. The coast offers fishing, scuba diving and boating while the mountains and forests are great for hiking and bird-watching. Ocean-view apartments are often less than $1,000 a month, and those in the mountains can be half that amount.

- **Thailand.** Thailand remains safe, inexpensive and beautiful. It's usually not hard to find a furnished apartment in Bangkok for about $500 a month.

Quick Ways to Learn a New Language

Trying to learn a foreign language before you visit a new country?

- **Find a language study partner** by visiting an exchange site, such as *www.my languageexchange.com*. Users can ask members from more than 130 countries to help them practice writing and speaking on-line in voice chat rooms.

- **Download language audiobooks** onto an MP3 player to listen to while traveling.

Example: Through iTunes (*www. itunes.com*), you can download "In Flight Spanish" for $8.95.

- **Listen to foreign-language news broadcasts** and other radio programs.

Example: Hear world news in French on the Internet at *www.rfi.fr.*

Newsweek, 444 Madison Ave., New York City 10022.

Defeat Pickpockets

Tourists are prime targets for pickpockets. *Here's how to protect yourself...*

Risk: When you receive change from a purchase and put it in one of your pockets, a pickpocket who is watching you can see where you keep all your money, strike to empty that pocket and quickly move on.

Self-defense: Divide your money among different pockets, wallet/purse, briefcase, carrying bag, etc. When on the street and in public places, don't use any money from your wallet/purse that holds most of your money—take it from one of your other pockets holding a lesser amount instead.

TravelSmart, www.travelsmartnewsletter.com.

Important Travel Vaccines

Carol DeRosa, RN, executive director of Passport Health, Inc., provider of immunizations and travel consultations, Baltimore. *www.passporthealthusa.com.*

Every traveler, regardless of destination, should get vaccinated against tetanus and hepatitis A. Hepatitis A virus is found in food and water, even in the US. Get revaccinated for tetanus every five years.

Also: *Typhoid* vaccination if going to Central or South America, Africa, India, Malaysia, Indonesia, Vietnam or the Mideast. *Yellow-fever immunization* if visiting tropical South America or subequatorial Africa. Polio booster if you haven't been vaccinated since childhood and are going to Africa, India, Pakistan, Malaysia, Indonesia or some parts of southern China. Influenza shot if visiting tropical areas in the southern hemisphere, where flu occurs year-round. *Tuberculosis testing* (PPD) should be done three to six months after travel to Central or South America, Africa, the Mideast, Eastern Europe and Russia.

Airplane Anxiety

If you get nervous on airplanes, try the homeopathic product Rescue Remedy ($10.50 for 10 milliliters), available at health-food stores. This combination of flower extracts reduces anxiety without causing drowsiness and has no side effects. Put 15 drops in an eight-ounce bottle of water, and sip it before and during the flight.

Mark A. Stengler, ND, a naturopathic physician and leading authority on the practice of alternative and integrated medicine. He is director of the La Jolla Whole Health Clinic, La Jolla, CA, and associate clinical professor of the National College of Naturopathic Medicine, Portland, OR. He is author of the newsletter *Bottom Line Natural Healing, www.DrStengler.com.*

Find Out About Your Flight

Find out if your flight is likely to be delayed or canceled at *www.flightstats.com,* a database from Conducive Technology Corp. that lists how often a flight is canceled, diverted or tardy and the maximum and average delays. The most troubled flights are those that are lightly booked and that travel into or out of big hubs. When faced with weather, crew or mechanical issues, airlines most often opt to cancel flights with the fewest passengers.

Travel Smart

Carry a local newspaper when on city streets abroad—especially when you go to use an ATM. The newspaper will make you look less like a vulnerable tourist. And, when using the foreign ATM, you can position the newspaper to shield your PIN from prying eyes as you type it into the keypad.

TravelSmart, www.travelsmartnewsletter.com.

Travel Insurance

Travel insurance may not cover airline bankruptcies. This insurance has been popular since the September 11 terrorist attacks, but many insurers modified coverage to avoid payouts to travelers if an airline files for bankruptcy.

Self-defense: Ask when buying insurance—you may have to buy from a different company or fly on a different airline to get full coverage. Airlines and other travel suppliers that are on the bankruptcy watch list may be found at *www.totaltravelinsurance. com/bankruptcy-insurance.asp* or by calling 866-226-7500.

Alex Velinov, president, Total Travel Insurance, New York City.

Keep Your Luggage Safe

Andrea McCauley, public affairs specialist, Transportation Security Administration, Washington, DC.

When preparing for a flight, take these precautions to make sure your belongings arrive at your destination intact...

•**Double-check pockets and bags,** particularly in carry-on luggage, to ensure no prohibited items were packed. For a list of prohibited items, check the Transportation Security Administration's Web site, *www.tsa.gov.*

•**Don't pack fragile or expensive items** or electronic devices, such as PDAs or iPods, in checked bags.

•**Don't overpack bags.** If screeners have to open bags, they may have difficulty closing them and your bags may be delayed until a later flight.

•**Get a TSA-accepted lock.** There are products on the market that have uniform locking systems that allow screeners to open and relock a bag. Available at Target or on-line at *www.safeskieslocks.com* and *www.*

nextag.com. If you don't have the right lock, consider leaving your bags unlocked.

•**Put undeveloped film in carry-on baggage.** Equipment used to screen checked baggage will damage film. If you use high-speed or specialty film, ask screeners to inspect it by hand.

Don't Be an Ugly American

Don't be viewed as an arrogant American when traveling abroad.

•**Speak lower and slower**—match your voice level and tonality to the environment and other people nearby.

•**Don't use slang**—most foreigners will not understand the meaning.

•**Listen as much as you talk,** and show an interest in the lives and culture of the people you meet.

•**Dress nicely**—in some countries, casual clothing, including jeans, T-shirts and sneakers, is a sign of disrespect.

USA Today.

Best Way to Get Foreign Currency

American Express charges a flat fee (usually $3*) for currency purchases at its branches or $15 for on-line orders. It has a wide currency selection and offers favorable exchange rates.

Alternative: Travelex, the biggest currency-exchange company, lets travelers pay $5 to guarantee the same exchange rate if they return the currency within 31 days after buying it. Travelex fees are higher—$5.50 or 1% of the total, whichever is higher—and exchange rates are not as favorable. AAA members receive a 25% discount.

More information: www.travelex.com.

*Prices subject to change.

How to Tip

Hotels in most countries typically charge a service fee—10% to 15% of the cost of your stay—that is distributed among the housekeepers, concierge and laundry and kitchen staff. However, most hotel service-staff members still expect individual tips. The amount varies, so ask the front desk about what is customary.

Exceptions: In Australia and New Zealand, tips are not expected at hotels and service fees are rare.

Most restaurants around the world add a service fee of 10% to 15%. If there is no service fee added to your bill, a 10% to 15% tip is acceptable—up to 20% in the US and Canada.

Exceptions: In Australia and New Zealand, it is customary to tip only 5% to 10%.

Travel & Leisure, 1120 Avenue of the Americas, New York City 10036.

Travel in Style

On your next European vacation, consider renting an apartment or a house rather than staying in a hotel. The Web site *Rentvillas.com* lists properties available for as little as three days or for months at a time. Prices are comparable—and sometimes cheaper—than hotel prices. Rentals are available from *Rentvillas.com* in France, Greece, Great Britain, Italy, Portugal, Spain and Turkey.

Cheaper than a Hotel

Renting a time-share often is cheaper than staying in a conventional hotel.

Best: Rent from individual time-share owners—they usually charge less than resorts.

Information: *www.redweek.com* offers extensive time-share rental listings, but you must be a member to contact owners.

Membership fee: $9.99 for a six-month subscription or $14.99 for 12 months.

Timeshare User's Group (904-298-3185, *www.tug2.net*) offers in-depth reviews of resorts, as well as rental listings and contact information.

Membership fee: $15 for a 12-month subscription.

Kiplinger's Personal Finance, 1729 H St. NW, Washington, DC 20006.

Rail Passes No Longer A Bargain

For decades, Eurail and other European train passes have been used for travel at bargain rates. But today's deregulated European discount airlines can take travelers between cities often at a fraction of the price of the railroads—and save travelers hours in doing so, allowing that much more time to spend at the destination. If you happen to enjoy traveling by rail, then a railway trip may be an attraction in its own right. But when low cost and more time at your destination are priorities, look at European discount airlines first.

Steve Venables, CTC, travel expert and columnist, *International Travel News*, 2628 El Camino Ave., Sacramento, CA 95821.

Don't Believe Quoted Car-Rental Prices

The rates do not always include airport fees or state and local taxes—which can almost double a low daily rate. And rental clerks are trained to push hard for extra-cost options, such as insurance, prefilled tanks of gas and larger or more fully equipped cars for "only" a few dollars more. These extras add up fast and are usually unnecessary.

Self-defense: Make your reservation, find out the required taxes and fees in advance, and refuse to pay more when you show up at the rental counter.

Mary Hunt, editor, *Debt-Proof Living*, Box 2135, Paramount, CA 90723. *www.debtproofliving.com.*

Save on Group Vacations

Groople.com caters to groups that need at least five hotel rooms. It offers discounted rates for hotels, flights, trains, cruises and rental cars. General discounts range from 10% to 20% but often can be higher based on availability, seasonality and event schedules. Caters to all sizes and kinds of groups—from family and military reunions to destination weddings. Groups design their own itineraries.

Slash Rental Car Costs in Half

Reduce rental car costs by as much as 50% by booking on-line. *Bnm.com* can help you track down and reserve the cheapest rental available whether you are traveling in the US or abroad. If driving a specific model is not important, you can check prices at *Bnm.com* or *Hotwire.com* and then go to *Priceline.com*'s car-rental page to bid for even steeper discounts.

Time, 1271 Avenue of the Americas, New York City 10020.

Best Ways to Get a Free Upgrade

To get a car-rental upgrade, book the cheapest car available. These small, inexpensive rentals are usually the first to go, so you have the best chance of getting a free upgrade to a larger car. If you are not offered an upgrade

for free, you often can get one by paying a small extra charge at the rental counter.

Nancy Dunnan, editor and publisher, *TravelSmart*, Dobbs Ferry, NY, *www.travelsmartnewsletter.com.*

Use Frequent-Flier Miles Quickly

Some airlines are cutting back the time before they expire. Delta miles will expire in two years in inactive accounts, and US Airways miles will expire in just 18 months. The industry custom had long been three years. To keep your account active even if you are not flying much, make transactions with airline partners, such as credit cards, banks and on-line merchants. For Continental, Delta, Frontier, Northwest and US Airways, you can earn miles by viewing and responding to Internet ads at *www.e-miles.com.*

Tim Winship, publisher, *The FrequentFlier Crier*, 2021 Hillhurst, Los Angeles, CA 90027, *www.frequent flier.com.*

Mile Maven

Get the inside scoop on airline promotions at *MileMaven.com*. The site provides information about frequent-flier promotions and special deals. You can search offers by city or by airline. Good deals also may be found on the site's "Countdown"—a list of promotions set to expire within 14 days at *www.milemaven.com/countdown.*

Nancy Dunnan, editor and publisher, *TravelSmart*, Dobbs Ferry, NY, *www.travelsmartnewsletter.com.*

Airfare Comparison

Compare airfare prices at ITA Software (*matrix.itasoftware.com*). The free site displays fares for specific days, weekends or even every day in an entire month. The color-coded

435

bar graph identifies particular airlines for an easy-to-read schedule of prices and times.

Fast Company, 375 Lexington Ave., New York City 10017.

Keep Luggage From Getting Lost

An estimated 30 million bags failed to arrive at their destinations on time last year.

What to do: Remove old baggage claim tags. Attach a sturdy ID tag to your bag with your phone number, your travel agent's business address, a post office box or your business address. Do not use your home address—it may alert thieves to your absence. Include your cell-phone number so that the airline can contact you if your luggage is misrouted. Put contact information on the inside of your bag in case the ID tag gets lost. Decorate your luggage with stickers or ribbons to make it easy to identify. Check bags at least 90 minutes before departure to ensure that they get through security in time.

Susan Foster, packing expert, Portland, OR, and author of *Smart Packing for Today's Traveler.* KSB Promotions.

Passenger Rights

The rules about overbooking, "bumping," lost luggage, canceled flights and other problems confronted by air travelers are explained in a new 58-page government publication, *Fly Rights: A Consumer Guide to Air Travel.* Read it or download it for free online at *http://airconsumer.ost.dot.gov,* or order a printed version by sending a check for $4 to the Citizen Information Center, Pueblo, CO 81009.

Valet Parking at Airports

Valet parking at airports can be a help to travelers arriving late for flights—or those who find standard airport lots full. Among the airports with valet parking are Cincinnati…Dallas–Ft.Worth…Denver…Detroit…Las Vegas…Los Angeles…Miami…Minneapolis–St. Paul…Newark…Pittsburgh …and Washington, DC—both Reagan and Dulles.

Cost: Starting at about $20 per day. Some airports also offer expedited car return and even such add-ons as car washes.

USA Today.

Buy Extra Leg Room When You Fly

Some airlines sell seat upgrades for people seeking additional leg room. United charges $349 for a one-year membership in its Economy Plus program, which gives you the chance to upgrade to seats with five inches of extra space. Northwest's Coach Choice program charges an additional $5–$35 for coach seats with extra space, such as bulkheads and exit rows. US Airways GoUpgrades program offers first-class upgrades for as little as $50. AirTran sells upgrades to business class for as little as $40.

Nancy Dunnan, editor and publisher, *TravelSmart*, Dobbs Ferry, NY, *www.travelsmartnewsletter.com.*

Special Tours For Age 50+ Travelers

Joan Rattner Heilman, an award-winning travel writer based in New York. She is author of *Unbelievably Good Deals and Great Adventures That You Absolutely Can't Get Unless You're Over 50.* McGraw-Hill.

Enterprising travel companies have discovered that there are plenty of people who would rather go places with their contemporaries than with a mixed bag of ages. The hundreds of trips available only to super-grown-ups are usually marketed to those "over 50," but if you go, you'll find the average age to be higher, perhaps 65 or so. No children, no college students, not even 30- or 40-somethings are invited.

SPECIAL ITINERARIES

The itineraries are planned to move along at an unhurried pace that allows ample time for relaxation and independent activities. On the typical group tour, everything's easy. Someone else makes the major decisions, solves the large and small problems, sees to it that your luggage miraculously arrives in your room before you do and transports you from hither to yon. On the other hand, some of the tours emphasize "soft adventure" in exotic and sometimes primitive places, and physical activity such as hiking, climbing or biking. So, if you prefer a more active trip, you can choose what suits you best.

Most senior trips give you at least two or three nights per stop so you're not always packing your bags and rushing off, and some even let you stay in one place for a week or more. Transportation and accommodations are chosen for comfort and convenience, even in the wilderness, and almost always include your own private bathroom.

Most of the participants in over-50 excursions will tell you that they prefer going with contemporaries because there's more to talk about, more experiences in common, more camaraderie. They like the leisurely itineraries and they don't have to worry about keeping up with the young folks.

Here are some of the companies that plan trips exclusively for the older crowd, and some of their best trips. All prices are from New York, unless otherwise specified.

• **Grand Circle Travel.** The first US company to offer international vacations to older travelers, Grand Circle markets a dizzying array of tours, all with unhurried schedules, in groups of up to 40 people with an average age of 73. Choices include classic escorted tours, extended vacations in one location, river cruises and ocean cruises with land-based stays in ports of call.

A really great one that runs year-round except in the winter is the 17-day "Best of Eastern Europe."

Cost: $1,795 to $2,745,* including airfare.

Information: Grand Circle Travel, 800-959-0405, *www.gct.com.*

• **Horizon & Co.** offers "luxury adventures" to unusual destinations from the Canadian wilderness to the Mekong delta. To appeal to two distinct segments of mature travelers, it has its "Classic Series" for older participants who are happier with all-inclusive, meticulously organized, worry-free, small-group tours that move at a relaxed pace. Its "Exploratory Series," escorted or independent, targets more energetic 50-plus travelers who look for unusual experiences, sophisticated cuisine and upscale accommodations.

Example: One of Horizon's high-end adventures expressly tailored for seniors is an escorted 16-day tour of South Africa and Botswana taking you to cities, scenic mountains and on safari for big-game viewing in Chobe National Park.

Cost: $12,902* (including domestic flights and gratuities), plus airfare.

Information: Horizon & Co., 800-387-2977, *www.horizon-co.com.*

• **Overseas Adventure Travel (OAT).** The sister company of Grand Circle, OAT takes groups of no more than 10 to 16 people with an average age of 58 on soft adventures all over the world. Its trips are more rugged than most and require that you be in reasonably good physical condition to participate. Destinations include such places as South America, China, Borneo and Tanzania.

Example: The 11-day "Amazon River Cruise and Rain Forest" trip spends a couple of days in Lima, Peru, then six nights aboard a riverboat that stops every day for shore adventures in the jungle.

Cost: $2,295 to $2,695, depending on the season, including domestic flights and airfare from New York City. From Miami, $1,995 to $2,395.*

*Prices quoted are per person, double occupancy, and subject to change.

Information: Overseas Adventure Travel, 800-493-6824, *www.oattravel.com.*

• **Globus and Cosmos Tours.** These affiliated companies specialize in over-50 travel. Globus, the upscale partner, has several varieties of escorted tours. "Cruise Vacations" combine land tours and cruises…"Platinum Collection Vacations" give you stays of two or three nights per city and include activities such as cooking classes and golf outings… "Independent Vacations" in the US and abroad allow you to explore whatever cities you wish to visit for as many days as you like with on-site hosts to offer advice and assistance.

Example: On a leisurely nine-day escorted getaway, you explore Paris for a few days, then travel to Normandy and the famous Mont St. Michel. Continue to Blois for two nights before returning to Paris.

Cost: Starting at $1,529, land only.

Cosmos specializes in traditional, moderately priced escorted bus tours all over the world.

Example: A favorite is the 14-day Blue Ridge Mountains trip that starts in Washington, DC, and travels to many destinations including Williamsburg and Lexington, VA; Gatlinburg, TN; Shenandoah National Park and back to Washington. Scheduled fall and spring.

Cost: $1,679–$1,689.

Information: Globus and Cosmos Tours, 866-313-2855, *www.globusfamily.com.*

• **Trafalgar Tours.** This company has been in the business of taking mature travelers on trips for almost 60 years. Its hundreds of itineraries are designed to be hassle-free, leisurely and comfortable and its fully escorted tours include comfortable buses and first-class or deluxe hotels. Everything is tailored to the needs and desires of an older group of participants. They go just about anywhere in the world, with a special emphasis on riverboat cruising and regional tours in the US and Canada.

Example: A perennial offering is the "Best of the Canyonlands," a seven-day trip that starts in Denver, travels to Arches National Park, Mesa Verde, Monument Valley and the Grand Canyon and ends with a couple of days in Las Vegas.

Cost: $1,050, plus airfare.

Information: Trafalgar Tours, 866-544-4434, *www.trafalgar.com.*

• **Grand European Tours.** On its leisure tours to Italy and other European countries, Australia, New Zealand, Mexico, South Africa, Asia and Russia, you stay a minimum of two or three nights in every location you visit. On its SuperLeisure vacations, the stays are four nights or more in each place, so you can see the world at a relaxing pace. This is the kind of relaxed itinerary that suits most seniors just fine. You travel by bus and stay in first-class hotels.

Cost: Starting at $2,500, including airfare.

Information: Grand European Tours, 800-552-5545, *www.getours.com.*

Travel with Fido

Information about pet-friendly accommodations…how to handle on-the-road emergencies…airline regulations…rules for national and state parks…and more is available at *www.petsonthego.com.*

Safer Hotel Stays for Women

Pick a hotel with fewer than 100 rooms, on a busy street and with active neighborhood businesses, such as restaurants and all-night food stores.

Important: A well-lit and secure parking lot. Ask for a room near the elevators, on an upper floor, away from catwalks and terraces. Use all available locks on doors. Put expensive clothing on hangers under other clothing. Lock up valuables in the room safe or hotel safe—and lock larger valuables in your suitcase.

Women's Travel Club recommendations, *www. womenstravelclub.com.*

Budget Hotels Are More Attractive Now

You can find the same amenities—or better—at economy motel chains as you can at more expensive chains. They can be a good choice for business travelers, as well as for travelers on a budget. Chains such as Days Inn, Econo Lodge, Motel 6, Red Roof Inns, Rodeway Inns, Super 8 and Travelodge are upgrading mattresses and towels. Some are offering loyalty points—redeemable at restaurants such as Denny's and Olive Garden and merchants such as Blockbuster and Home Depot. The chains usually offer breakfast but no other meals—however, low-cost restaurants are typically nearby. And budget chains often include amenities that more expensive chains charge for, such as high-speed Internet access.

Maria Chevalier, vice president, global business intelligence, Advito, the consulting division of BCD Travel, Atlanta.

Monty Python Star Shares His Travel Secrets

Michael Palin, London-based member of the Monty Python comedy troupe. His book, Himalaya, *Phoenix, was the subject of a TV series on the Travel Channel. His Web site,* www.palinstravels.co.uk, *offers travel information and free access to his books.*

Actor and comedian Michael Palin is an avid traveler whose journeys have been chronicled in books and on television. Since being bitten by the travel bug in 1988, he has visited more than 80 countries, logging enough miles to fill a half-dozen passports.

His latest journey was to the Himalayas— from the Pakistani-Afghan frontier through India, Nepal, Tibet, Assam, Bhutan and Bangladesh.*

While between trips, Mr. Palin shares some of his travel secrets…

• **Few people have the time or money to visit Tibet, Nepal or the headwaters of the Amazon, as you have done. Can you recommend some equally thrilling—but more accessible—locations?** Almost everyone lives within a short journey of out-of-the-way places that are fascinating because of their history, culture and natural beauty. To find these places, get a guide on local history or on a particular subject you are very interested in, such as folk art. Then plan a short trip.

Not too long ago, for instance, I discovered Glencoe in Scotland. Glencoe is one of the most pristine places in the British Isles—mountainous and beautiful. Whenever I hike around the area, I get the feeling that no one else has ever been there, much as I have felt in the middle of the Sahara. In fact, Glencoe is only a half-day trip from London and several other big cities.

• **Many travelers never see much more than their hotels and a few well-trodden tourist sites. How can they get a real understanding of a place?** Ask people you meet—local residents as well as other tourists—to suggest interesting side trips. Sometimes you'll be disappointed, but you'll often have the satisfaction of seeing people and places that others miss.

In Tibet, for example, a local resident recommended that we meet a yak herder who could show us more about their ancient way of life than any guidebook could. The yak herder even prodded me into milking one of the animals.

Of course, what anyone derives from a travel experience is up to the individual. In this case, I derived just enough yak milk for a cappuccino.

• **You have retraced the steps of Ernest Hemingway's journeys. Did you enjoy that? Is there another famous**

*US government travel advisories are available from the Department of State, 888-407-4747 or *www. travel.state.gov*, click on "Travel Warnings."

writer you would recommend following? Following in the footsteps of a famous person can be a great way to get insight into both the individual and the places he/she visited. I might never have thought to visit some interesting parts of Havana if I had not read Hemingway's accounts of them. After seeing the running of the bulls in (Pamplona) Spain, I gained a much better understanding of his novel *The Sun Also Rises.*

Robert Louis Stevenson is another writer who can point the way. In *Travels with a Donkey in the Cévennes,* he wrote wonderfully about journeying through the central southeast region of France. It remains a beautiful and fairly remote part of the country. I would strongly recommend his book as well as a visit to the Cévennes.

• **Which places are your favorite alternatives to the familiar tourist spots? What makes them special?** For some of the best music in the world, go to Dakar in Senegal, located on the west coast of Africa. For exotic scenery, you can't beat the interior of Colombia. Both countries don't attract many tourists, but it's not difficult to find comfortable accommodations.

Tricks for Turning Frequent-Flier Miles Into Tickets

Randy Petersen, editor and publisher of *Inside-Flyer,* Colorado Springs. He has earned more than 10 million frequent-flier miles and points. *www.inside flyer.com.*

Frequent-flier miles are supposed to earn free tickets for air travelers—but more often, the miles earn them hours on hold waiting for customer service representatives to tell them that no award seats remain on the flights they want. Various obstacles, many of which are set up purposely by the airlines, make converting hard-earned miles into tickets an increasingly frustrating chore.

The airlines finally have begun to respond to the mounting frustration with flashy new on-line tools and updated policies that make miles a little easier to redeem—but only for travelers who are savvy enough to understand their options. *The best strategies to help you turn award miles into flights…*

CHECK WEB SITES

All of the major airlines now offer Web sites that let frequent fliers secure award tickets without waiting on hold for a phone rep. If the date you initially select is sold out, color-coded calendars make it easy to identify alternative dates when tickets are available.

Unfortunately, these Web sites have some limitations…

• **They are not very good at finding alternate itineraries.** If no ticket is available for, say, Los Angeles to Denver on the day you want to fly, the site may not automatically check flights out of other LA area airports, such as Burbank or Ontario (California) International, or flights into Colorado Springs. You would have to run through all of the possible combinations yourself.

• **They don't always check for indirect flights,** which would require stops and possibly transfers to different planes along the way, particularly for shorter trips that normally would be direct flights.

• **They will not find available award tickets on all partner airlines.** All of the major airlines have partners, including many foreign partners, but the Web sites won't show you all their flights even if your frequent-flier miles make you eligible for them.

Solution: A good airline phone rep knows how to handle all of these problems, so it is worth calling if you can't find the flight you want on-line.

IMPROVING YOUR ODDS

• **Reserve six months in advance.** The best time to try to reserve a frequent-flier ticket is about six months before your travel date, not 331 days (about 11 months) before, as is widely believed. Though you're allowed to book up to 331 days in advance, airlines generally don't load all of the frequent-flier seats into the system that soon. If the award tickets you want are not available when you first call or check on-line, try again every week or two. Approximately one in five frequent fliers alters travel plans after making the initial reservations, putting the seats that were initially reserved back on the market.

•**Call after midnight.** Consider checking availability when it's shortly after midnight in the time zone from which the flight would be departing. Midnight local time is when tickets that were put on "hold" tend to return to circulation if the transactions are not finalized.

•**Travel on a Tuesday, Wednesday or Thursday.** That's when your odds of finding a seat improve by 20% to 30%. When your travel schedule is flexible, consider finding frequent-flier award seats before you pick a vacation week.

•**Consider connecting through an alternative airport.** If your travel dates are inflexible and the award tickets you need are not available for departure from a nearby airport, consider expanding your ticket search to include departure from an airport you could fly to for a small amount of cash before you start the award portion of your trip.

Example: You can't find a frequent-flier ticket from San Francisco to Burlington, Vermont, but one is available from Los Angeles to Burlington. Round-trip flights from San Francisco to Los Angeles are often available for nearly $100—$400 less than you would have to pay for the San Francisco to Burlington flight.

•**Don't bother with a waiting list.** They often don't exist. They're just something customer service reps offer to get unhappy customers off the phone. And while you're waiting for the airline to contact you, you could be missing out on newly available seats.

•**Check out first class.** When tickets are not available for the standard number of frequent-flier miles, do not automatically resort to paying double the number of miles, which airlines often suggest you do because more seats are available at that award level. First check whether a first-class award ticket is available. First-class round-trip award tickets for domestic flights typically cost 40,000 miles—10,000 less than double-miles coach tickets.

•**Split the difference.** "Split-award" redemption is an option on US Airways, Delta and Alaska Airlines. If you can find the frequent-flier seat you need for the standard number of award miles in one direction of your round-trip but not the other, you can opt to spend double miles for half the trip. For a domestic trip, that would mean 12,500 miles one way and 25,000 the other.

MAJOR AIRLINE PROGRAMS

The pluses and minuses of your airline's frequent-flier program and how to get the most out of it…

•**American Airlines AAdvantage.** It's the largest frequent-flier program, and it is among the best at getting members the award tickets they want. The Web site lets users view availability for months at a glance. On the downside, American's only domestic partners are Alaska Airlines and Hawaiian Airlines, and one of its major international partners, British Airways, does not let travelers earn or redeem American miles on flights across the Atlantic. Frequent-flier tickets typically can be placed on hold for 15 days. 800-882-8880, *www.aa.com.*

•**Continental Airlines OnePass.** Continental is mediocre at best when it comes to award-ticket availability, particularly on international flights. The airline's on-line ticket-finding tools are a bit clunky to use, and the airline requires a Saturday night stay with 25,000-mile award tickets. However, Continental does have an excellent partnership with Northwest, Delta and Alaska Airlines. (The Saturday stay rule also applies if you redeem your Continental miles on its partner airlines.) Award tickets usually can be kept on hold for five days. 713-952-1630, *www.continental.com.*

•**Delta SkyMiles.** Delta is toward the back of the pack in terms of ease of miles redemption but should improve now that the airline has emerged from bankruptcy proceedings. Delta offers many trans-Atlantic flights and has Northwest, Continental and

Alaska Airlines as partners. Its on-line award-ticket booking system is very good. It allows split bookings if you can find a seat for the standard number of miles in only one direction and for double miles in the other. Delta's on-line awards calendar covers an entire month at a time, in contrast to some that span only two weeks. Award tickets cannot be put on hold. 800-323-2323, *www.delta.com.*

• **Northwest Airlines WorldPerks.** Northwest does a reasonably good job of making award seats available, but its search technology is weak. Award-ticket seekers are better off calling a rep to access partner flights on Delta, Alaska Airlines or Continental. Northwest requires either a three-night minimum or a Friday or Saturday night stay on 25,000-mile tickets. Award tickets cannot be placed on hold. 800-447-3757, *www.nwa. com/worldperks.*

• **United Airlines Mileage Plus.** United has a good frequent-flier program overall. Its only domestic partner is US Airways (including the merged America West), but United is a member of the Star Alliance network, which includes AirCanada, Lufthansa and many others as partners. United's on-line frequent-flier reservations system is not as easy to use as Delta's or American's, because it does not have a rolling calendar to check on earlier and later dates. Award tickets can be held until midnight the next day. 800-421-4655, *www.united.com.*

• **US Airways Dividend Miles.** US Airways is the worst of the major domestic airlines in terms of frequent-flier seat availability. Its on-line award-ticket reservations system is not yet completely coordinated with that of America West, now part of US Airways Group. On the bright side, US Airways is partnered with the United Airlines frequent-flier program—and they both allow split bookings. Award travel reservations can be held for up to 72 hours. 800-428-4322, *www.usairways.com.*

SMALLER AIRLINES

These three airlines make lots of seats available to frequent fliers…

• **Alaska Airlines.** 800-654-5669, *www. alaskaair.com/mileageplan.*

• **Frontier Airlines.** 866-263-2759, *www. frontierairlines.com.*

• **Southwest Airlines.** 800-445-5764, *www.southwest.com/rapid_rewards.*

A different type of program…

• **JetBlue TrueBlue.** Instead of award miles, you earn points—ranging from two points for short flights to six for cross-country flights. For every 100 points, you get a free round-trip domestic flight. 800-JET-BLUE, *www.jetblue.com/trueblue.*

Offbeat Vacations For Adventurous Travelers

Joan Rattner Heilman, an award-winning travel writer based in New York. She is author of *Unbelievably Good Deals and Great Adventures That You Absolutely Can't Get Unless You're Over 50.* McGraw-Hill.

Paris, London and Venice are so old hat. And the Grand Canyon, Charleston, Russia and the Fiji Islands are so yesterday. Even Mongolia and Bhutan will soon be teeming with tourists. So where do you go these days if you're looking for a place that's relatively undiscovered and different, a place that will give you some great stories to tell that your friends haven't heard before? *Here are four offbeat destinations for seasoned travelers looking for something a little different…*

CROATIAN SUN

Croatia's Dalmatian Coast on the Adriatic Sea has been dubbed the new St. Tropez because it's now where chic Europeans go to relax on the white pebbled beaches, sit in charming seaside cafés and explore ancient ruins. Croatia lies alongside Serbia and Bosnia-Herzegovina.

Start with a couple of days in Split, a bustling city of old squares, outdoor cafés, shops and stalls set atop the remains of the summer palace built in 275 AD by the Roman Emperor Diocletian. Be sure to take a palace tour.

Ferry over to Hvar, the largest of the 1,000 or so islands off the coast, to sun and swim at its white-stone beaches, explore the fields of lavender and spend time exploring one of the best-preserved medieval towns in the region. End in the ancient walled city of Dubrovnik, which dates from the seventh century, with its stunning Old Town of white limestone buildings, terra-cotta roofs, ancient city walls, historic churches, monasteries, cobbled streets and marble squares.

A good way to visit Split, Hvar and Dubrovnik is on a 12-day "independent tour," where you're free to roam on your own, offered by Travel Time.

Included: Airfare from New York City or Boston, hotel accommodations, ferry tickets, airport transfers and two meals a day.

Information: Travel Time, 800-354-8728, *www.traveltimeny.com*. Costs vary according to the season—approximately $2,590* in April and October...$2,890 to $3,100 in June through September, per person, double occupancy.

CORSICA WALKING TOUR

This spectacular French island situated in the Mediterranean off the coasts of mainland France and Italy is made for walking. In just one day, you can cross from a pebble beach on the sea to lush green valleys and then rocky peaks. The landscape is dominated by coast-hugging mountains rising high above deep bays, tiny fishing villages, 17th-century watchtowers, Romanesque chapels and churches and Genoese towers. The interior is rustic, sparsely populated and unspoiled.

On a 10-day all-inclusive trip by Walking the World, a tour operator that caters exclusively to travelers age 50-plus, you start in Bastia, walk along the coastal road through ancient villages to the famous cliffs of Piana, take a boat to Scandola Natural Reserve—designated a World Heritage Site (worthy of preservation) by UNESCO because of its geographic significance—then head to the center of the island through conifer forests, ancient mountain villages and gorges and around lakes.

*Prices subject to change.

Walking at a leisurely pace for six to nine miles a day, you spend your nights in small hotels, drink wine and eat in the best restaurants on the island. Your group, led by two local guides, is limited to 14 participants and is accompanied by a van that carries the luggage and transports you to new locations.

Information: Walking the World, 970-498-0500, *www.walkingtheworld.com*.

Cost: Approximately, $3,595 per person, double occupancy, land only. Costs vary per annual package.

ANCIENT PUEBLOS IN ARIZONA

Canyon de Chelly National Monument is located inside the Navajo Reservation in northeastern Arizona. This unique desert park—entirely on tribal land—is jointly owned by the Navajo Nation and the National Park Service, and most of it is off-limits to visitors unless they are accompanied by a Native American guide. The guide, driving a heavy-duty six-wheel-drive vehicle, takes you off-road on a 60-mile round-trip through sandy red-walled canyons to see the ancient ruins of multistory, multifamily dwellings built into steep white limestone cliffs centuries ago by the ancient Pueblo people. On the way, he describes the geology, wildlife and current use of the land where the Navajos live, farm and graze livestock.

Cost: $70.30 per person, including lunch.

You can visit Canyon de Chelly for the day but, better yet, go for the two-night package offered by the rustic Thunderbird Lodge, the only overnight accommodations in the park. Available March through October, the package includes accommodations for two, breakfast, a 10% discount in the gift shop, the full-day canyon tour with box lunches and a DVD to take home with you.

Information: Thunderbird Lodge, 800-679-2473, *www.tbirdlodge.com*.

Cost: $395 for two people for the two-night package.

TREKKING IN BORNEO

For a really far-out adventure, take a trip to Borneo, located in Southeast Asia, to see the oldest jungle on earth, orangutans, sea turtles that come ashore nightly year-round to lay eggs, herds of elephants and proboscis monkeys. This 18-day journey, for travelers age 50 and older, takes you by longboat up the Lemanak River from the old colonial city of Kuching into the interior to pay a visit to former head hunters, the Iban tribe, who have lived in their communal longhouses in the jungle for thousands of years.

Flying aboard small jet planes, you go first to Mulu National Park to explore rainforests and the world's largest cave "tunnel," then to Sabah, the smaller Malaysian state on Borneo, in the far north to hike at the base of Mt. Kinabalu, Malaysia's tallest mountain. You'll also visit the small tropical islands of Gaya and Manukan with mangrove forests and jungle trails. Last is a river safari by longboat through lush jungles in search of the rare proboscis monkeys, hornbills and wild elephants.

Information: Eldertreks, 800-741-7956, *www.eldertreks.com.*

Cost: $3,495 per person, double occupancy, land only.

Less Waiting At Disney Attractions

RideMax (*www.ridemax.com*) PC software helps users plan trips to Disneyland in California and Walt Disney World in Florida. Users can select the attractions they wish to visit, and the program will create a personalized schedule that minimizes the amount of time spent waiting in line.

Recent example: A visitor rode six of Disneyland's most popular rides in just over two hours, with an average waiting time of only 13 minutes per ride.

Cost for Disneyland: $14.95 for a 90-day subscription or $24.95 for a one-year subscription to the program.*

Cost for Disney World: $16.95 for a 90-day subscription or $26.95 for a one-year subscription.*

*Prices subject to change.

Frequent-Flier Miles Can Be Used for Space Travel

Expected to begin in 2009, the flight costs two million Virgin Atlantic frequent-flier miles. This will land you a seat on the Virgin Galactic space flight which would cost approximately $200,000 without frequent-flier miles.

Information: *www.virginatlantic.com.* On the home page, enter "galactic" in the search box and then click on "Virgin Group Index."

Group Travel Trap

When you travel with others—even good friends—you may find yourself having "too much" of them as the trip goes on.

Remedy: Prearrange a few activities just for yourself.

Examples: Meeting other personal friends along the way…activities that appeal to you but not others (such as going to a special kind of museum or performance).

When traveling with friends, note your differences as well as common interests and plan to accommodate them.

Example: When a couple who are early risers travel with another who are night owls, they can agree to spend their days together from lunch through dinner and their early mornings and late nights apart. They'll all be happier.

Stacy Small, luxury travel consultant, Elite Travel International, West Palm Beach, FL, *www.elitetravel international.com.*

Make Overseas Dinner Reservations

You can make dinner reservations at popular restaurants in Europe and Asia on the

Internet at *www.eat2eat.com* for Asia…*http://cuisinenet.co.uk* and *www.toptable.co.uk* for the United Kingdom, Paris, Dublin, Barcelona and New York…and *www.restaurantrow.com* worldwide (which charges $4.95* for each reservation).

*Price subject to change.

Arrive on Time

To arrive on time, fly on a Saturday. That's the day on which flights are least likely to be late. Fridays are the worst days for late arrivals. Thursdays are second-worst.

Also helpful: Travel in September, the month with the best on-time record…always fly nonstop…consider nearby alternative airports instead of larger, busier ones.

Condé Nast Traveler, 4 Times Square, New York City 10036.

How Good a Deal Are Duty-Free Items at Airport Shops?

Duty free indicates that an item is being sold without the customs tax normally imposed by the country in which the shop is located.

Duty free applies to the merchant who sells the item to travelers—but only to take out of the country. This enables the merchant to charge you less for the item because his/her costs are lower. But there's no guarantee that a merchant will do so. Generally, items that would otherwise be subject to high duties are the best buys, such as perfume, liquor, tobacco products and luxury items.

Best: Determine what you would like to buy ahead of time, check the price at home

and then compare it with the price at the airport, port or cruise ship.

Nancy Dunnan, editor and publisher, *TravelSmart*, Dobbs Ferry, NY, *www.travelsmartnewsletter.com*.

Smart Airline Seating

Before booking an airline flight, compare seats on-line to find the one you want at SeatGuru.com. This Web site provides detailed seating information for 29 airlines, identifies "good" and "poor" seats and tells their location relative to exits, lavatories, galleys, etc. Request the seats you want when making your reservation—but realize that seating generally isn't final and may be changed until you obtain your boarding pass. So check in early to get it. Most airlines now provide on-line check-in through their Web sites up to 24 hours before flight departure.

Kiplinger's Personal Finance, 1729 H St. NW, Washington, DC 20006.

Does Travel Insurance Cover Bad-Weather Problems?

Nancy Dunnan, editor and publisher, *TravelSmart*, Dobbs Ferry, NY, *www.travelsmartnewsletter.com*.

Most people buy travel insurance so that they will be reimbursed for plane fare or cruise costs if they have to cancel their trip—say, because of a medical emergency. To cover a snow emergency situation, you would need a policy that covers problems *during* your trip.

Airlines aren't financially responsible for weather-related delays. If you fly in regions (or during seasons) when bad weather is a high probability, consider buying a policy that will cover your hotel room and meals should your flight be delayed or canceled.

Ask your insurance agent if he/she handles travel insurance. If not, compare quotes for more than 100 policies from *www.insure mytrip.com* (800-487-4722), a consumer-oriented site with information on plans from 19 different companies.

Fun and Easy Travel with Your Grandchildren

Joan Rattner Heilman, an award-winning travel writer based in New York. She is author of *Unbelievably Good Deals and Great Adventures That You Absolutely Can't Get Unless You're Over 50.* McGraw-Hill.

Traveling with your grandchildren—without their parents—is a wonderful way to grow closer to them, especially if you live far away and seldom have a chance to get together. It's a rare opportunity to get better acquainted, strengthen your relationships and have a very good time. You may even find that your grandchildren are the best travel companions you've ever had.

Whether it's a one-day tour of a nearby city, an overnight camping trip, a weekend at a farm, a week at the beach or a dude ranch, or a 10-day tour of the national parks or Europe, this is the kind of togetherness that really counts.

It needn't cost a lot of money, either, especially if you go somewhere near home and do your own driving.

Super money saver: Choose hotels that offer a good senior discount *and* a children-stay-free policy—or maybe an inexpensive "suite" hotel with a kitchenette, so that you can prepare some of your own meals. Cooking together can be part of the fun.

Even easier: If you don't want the responsibilities of traveling on your own with children, you can go with a tour company that specializes in intergenerational vacations. Everything is planned for you from morning until night, with most activities for the

two generations together but some just for the adults alone, so you'll get an occasional breather.

Some tours are designed for children in a certain age range, while others accept all youngsters ages seven or older, up to 17 or 18. Available in all price ranges, these tours are almost always scheduled in the summer, or sometimes during winter breaks, when the kids are out of school.

Some of the tour companies that will take you and your grandchildren on a fun, well-planned vacation...

• **Elderhostel.** For an educational, low-cost vacation, sign up for one of Elderhostel's intergenerational programs in the US or Canada. For example, next summer, you and your grandchildren ages eight to 12 could enjoy a six-night stay in Minnesota's north woods, hiking to spectacular overlooks, paddling a canoe under tall cliffs, looking for native animals or learning to climb rocks. Or choose a city, perhaps spending five nights in a hotel in San Francisco, riding cable cars, visiting all of its neighborhoods from Chinatown to Fisherman's Wharf, seeing a fortune-cookie factory, and visiting the Gold Rush Museum and the Exploratorium.

Cost: For Minnesota, $499 per adult, $454 per child ages eight to 12. For San Francisco, $798 per adult, $748 per child ages seven and older.*

Information: Elderhostel, 877-426-8056, *www.elderhostel.org.*

• **Sierra Club.** The largest environmental group in the country, the Sierra Club plans many affordable "outings." Among them is an annual six-day stay at the club's Clair Tappaan Lodge at Donner Pass in Tahoe National Forest, California, for grandparents and kids at least six years old. The activities include short hikes, fishing, swimming, picnics and a tram ride at Squaw Valley.

Cost: $525 per adult, $425 per child ages six and older.

Information: Sierra Club Outing Dept., 415-977-5522, *www.sierraclub.org/outings.*

• **Grandtravel.** The first company to send grandparents and grandchildren (ages seven

*Prices subject to change.

to 17) off on vacation together, Grandtravel offers intriguing five- to 15-day deluxe tours. These trips are educational (led by teacher-escorts), limited to 20 participants and expensive, with destinations ranging from New York City to Alaska, Kenya, Italy and Australia. Coming up next summer is a 12-day tour of Italy that starts in Venice, complete with a palazzo hotel, gondola ride, boat trip to the Lagoon Islands and a tour of the city. Then on to Florence by train to see the Duomo and its famous bronze doors, the statue of David, the Uffizi Gallery's art treasures, ending in the Tuscan countryside and an excursion to Siena. Last stop is Rome to explore the city, including the Forum, Colosseum, the Villa d'Este in Tivoli and Vatican City.

Cost: $6,995 per person.

Information: Grandtravel, 800-247-7651, *http://grandtravel.com*.

• **Generations Touring Company.** Another deluxe tour operator, this one offers tours in the US and other parts of the world from Costa Rica to England and Scotland, and the Galapagos Islands in Ecuador. Some of its trips are classified as "journeys" and aren't too physically demanding. Others are "adventures," for grandparents and children who especially enjoy physical activities.

An example of an adventure: A week in Ecuador, which takes you to Quito, the capital of the country, then to Guayaquil to travel by ship for a few days in the Galapagos Islands. Using small pangas (boats), you climb ashore on many islands for close encounters with giant tortoises, iguanas, blue-footed boobies, albatross and sea lions, among other creatures.

One of the company's more relaxing journeys: Eight nights in Costa Rica takes you to San Jose, the capital, and then to Tortuguero by bus and covered boat to view birds and sea turtles in this wildlife preserve. Fly to Arenal Volcano National Park and walk across the forest canopy on a suspended bridge. Visit the Cloud Forest Reserve in Monteverde, where you can see a butterfly farm and a local school to learn about Costa Rica's way of life.

Cost: For Ecuador, $3,199 per adult, $2,099 per child ages 11 and under. For Costa Rica, $2,599 per adult, $2,099 per child ages 11 and under.

Information: Generations Touring Company, 888-415-9100, *www.generationstouringcompany.com*.

X-Ray at the Airport

Full-body scans at airports expose travelers to only one-tenth the radiation of a chest X-ray. Current plans are to use airport X-ray machines on travelers who are selected for extra screening—beyond a standard metal detector. These travelers will be given the option of the full-body X-ray or being patted down by a screener.

If you travel frequently: Opt for the pat-down—effects of even low levels of radiation build up over a lifetime.

Everett M. Lautin, MD, FACR, radiologist in private practice and former professor of radiology, Albert Einstein Medical College, New York City.

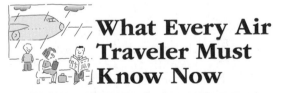 **What Every Air Traveler Must Know Now**

Terry Trippler, a leading expert on airline rules of operation who is based in Minneapolis, *www.cheapseats.com*.

With airlines trying to conserve every dime, the "friendly skies" aren't as friendly anymore. But if you know your rights, you can save money, avoid headaches and get more out of traveling. *Here is what you need to know...*

• **When you are involuntarily bumped from a flight,** federal law requires the airline to compensate you if your new flight is delayed an hour or more.

If it is scheduled to arrive one to two hours past your original arrival time (or between one and four hours for an international flight), you are entitled to receive a refund on your ticket price and a maximum cash payment of $400, as determined by new US Department of Transportation guidelines.

If you are scheduled to arrive more than two hours late (or more than four hours late for an international flight) or if the airline is unable to find you another flight, you are entitled to a refund plus up to an additional $800 in cash.

Helpful: The airline might encourage you to accept a voucher toward a future flight instead of cash. Voucher values must equal the amounts listed above, but they typically exceed them.

If you're interested in a voucher, negotiate for a better deal with the agent at the gate. If you're entitled to $400, try to get $1,000. Whether or not you get a greater amount generally will depend on the mood of the gate agent.

•**When you volunteer to be bumped from a flight,** the airline is free to offer any deal it wants. Once again, you have lots of leverage—airline personnel don't want to kick passengers off flights.

Example: My friends had tickets for an overbooked flight from Minneapolis to Anchorage. Since it was the last flight of the day, Northwest offered each of my friends $500 in cash, a $500 airline voucher, accommodations, ground transportation and seats on the first flight out the next day.

Helpful: Before you accept a voucher, scrutinize all the terms—expiration date, blackout dates and whether it can be transferred. The fewer restrictions, the better, but these generally can't be negotiated.

•**If your flight is delayed until the next day,** your rights depend on the cause...

•If the airline was at fault—in the case of mechanical problems or late connecting flights—you have a good chance of getting the airline to pay for a hotel room nearby. The airline is under no obligation to do so, but it's good for public relations. The airline will provide a voucher to pay for the room and generally a meal.

•If the delay was caused by weather, terrorism, a fuel shortage or a labor dispute, you are not entitled to compensation.

•**If the flight is canceled,** the airline will find another flight for you. If the flight is the next day, the airline may pay for your accommodations for the night, but it is under no obligation to do so.

•**If an airline loses your luggage,** the maximum reimbursement is $3,000 per passenger. The airlines will rarely pay the highest amount unless you can present receipts totaling that amount. You probably will have to file a claim under your homeowner's or renter's insurance to recoup the balance of the loss if it exceeds your deductible.

Self-defense: If you need to transport something valuable or very important, ship it.

Most missing bags are recovered within 48 hours. While you're waiting for your luggage, ask the airline for cash to buy necessities. If you're lucky, you might get $150, but $50 to $100 is more common. What you receive typically depends on the mood of the airline employee. You aren't entitled to anything if you have flown into your hometown.

Insider Tricks For Hassle-Free Air Travel

Marjory Abrams, publisher, *Bottom Line* newsletters, Boardroom Inc., 281 Tresser Blvd., Stamford, CT 06901.

Air travelers have not had it easy. Long security lines, extensive weather delays, lost baggage, canceled flights and other woes have turned dream trips into nightmares.

Rudy Maxa, known as public radio's *Savvy Traveler* (*www.rudymaxa.com*), is the ultimate frequent flier. I caught him en route from Los Angeles to the Caribbean—just a small fraction of the 100,000 miles or so that he flies every year. Rudy is not shy about getting his needs met when he encounters problems at the airport or in the air. *His secret strategies...*

•**If the security line is so long that you might miss your flight,** go to the front of the line, politely explain your situation to a security agent and ask him/her to move you right through the line.

•**If you need to get to a gate fast,** flag down a motorized cart—airport personnel use them to quickly navigate the facility—and hitch a free ride.

•**If you don't like your seat once you are on the plane,** look for a better seat. Move only after the doors are closed. You don't have to ask permission to change seats—but you must stay within the same class of service.

Rudy has great hassle-prevention strategies, too—beyond choosing nonstop flights...

•**Skip the check-in lines by getting your boarding pass at home.** Most airlines allow you to print them from their Web sites within 24 hours of your flight.

•**If it is clear that you will be stranded overnight,** book a hotel room right away. Airport hotels fill up fast during bad weather.

I also checked with Randy Petersen, publisher of *InsideFlyer* at *www.insideflyer.com.* "Despite all the publicity about enhanced security, people still don't get it," he says. "Passengers still are trying to go through security with knives, firecrackers, baseball bats and other prohibited objects. They hold up the line for everyone."

Randy advises travelers to check out the latest regulations of the Transportation Security Administration, on the Web at *www.tsa.gov* or call 866-289-9673.

New no-no: You are not allowed to carry a cigarette lighter or matches onto a plane.

Randy has his own trick for resolving flight-related problems quickly. On the way to the gate area, pay attention to the location of the customer service desk. If your flight is cancelled—or has a lengthy delay—go there to figure out alternatives. Don't wait at the departure gate with everyone else.

Finally, attitude matters. Yes, delays can be annoying...but they are better than flying in unsafe conditions.

What Never to Drink on a Plane

The tap water on more than 17% of planes recently tested contained disease-causing bacteria, including *E. coli.* At least 12 airlines in the US have agreed to new voluntary testing standards—they will test the water systems on each of their planes annually, give the results to the Environmental Protection Agency, flush onboard water systems four times a year and post signs to stop use of aircraft tap water if high levels of bacteria are found.

Best: Buy bottled water after you have cleared security.

Details: *www.epa.gov/airlinewater.*

United States Environmental Protection Agency, Washington, DC.

16

Safety Alert

Innocent Mistakes... That Can Get You in Trouble with the Law

**E**ven honest, well-intentioned people occasionally run afoul of the law through bad luck or bad judgment. *These five situations are among the most likely to cause problems...*

ENTERING INTO A "HANDSHAKE AGREEMENT"

An oral contract is as legitimate as a written one—it's just harder to prove, which can create legal hassles.

Example: Dan entered into an oral agreement to provide home-maintenance services to his neighbor in exchange for the neighbor's camping trailer. When a dispute arose regarding the maintenance chores, the neighbor called the police and reported the trailer stolen. The matter was eventually settled, but only after the police showed up on Dan's doorstep with a warrant for his arrest.

Self-defense: Even if you would rather not pay a lawyer to draw up a contract, write out and sign a statement summarizing your agreement and have it signed and dated by the other party and, preferably, witnessed.

FAILING TO REPORT A CRIME

There are many reasons people don't report crimes. The crime might seem too minor to bother the police...reporting it might expose illegal or embarrassing activities on the part of the victim...or the criminal might be a friend or relative of the victim.

Example: Susan had her wallet stolen, but she didn't bother to report the theft. There were only a few dollars in the wallet at the time, and she thought she knew who had taken it. She didn't want to get the police involved in what she considered a personal matter.

Joseph S. Lyles, an attorney in Greenville, SC, with more than 20 years of experience in the personal injury field, *www.joelyles.com.* He is author of *How You Can Avoid Legal Land Mines: A Layman's Guide to the Law.* R.J. Communications.

450

It turns out that Susan was wrong about who had stolen her wallet. Two years later, the police knocked on her door with a warrant for her arrest for writing bad checks. The thief had used her ID to open a checking account in a different county. Since the wallet had never been reported stolen, it was difficult for Susan to establish her innocence.

Self-defense: Always report a crime, no matter how minor it seems.

Even failing to report a minor car accident can lead to problems. Sometimes the two parties agree not to call the police to avoid damaging their driving records and raising their insurance rates. But if one of these drivers changes his/her mind, he could call the police and claim that the other party fled the scene of the accident, a serious offense.

Self-defense: At a minimum, exchange all information. Carry a disposable camera to photograph the cars, driver and the surroundings. Get names and numbers of any witnesses.

IGNORING A TRAFFIC TICKET

Even honest people sometimes forget to pay traffic tickets...or incorrectly assume that they won't be held responsible for a ticket from another state.

Example: A ticket for running a red light in another state arrives in your mail. The attached letter says that a computerized camera captured the violation. You don't remember committing this violation, so you stash the ticket in your glove compartment and hope no one follows up.

Self-defense: Never ignore a ticket, even one from out of state. These days, states share ticket information.

The fine print on a traffic ticket says that the recipient must either pay a fine or appear in court for a trial. Those who fail to do so by the designated date risk a misdemeanor charge of failing to appear for trial.

In the worst-case scenario, the court could issue a warrant for your arrest and your state's department of motor vehicles could suspend your license.

ALTERING A CHILD-CUSTODY AGREEMENT

When a court has made a ruling on a child-custody case, the parents do not have the right to alter the arrangement without the court's consent—even if both parents are in favor of the change.

Example: A father agreed to take charge of his children when their mother's job became too demanding. Both parents agreed to the new arrangement, but they didn't bother to inform the court, which had awarded the mother custody.

Later, the woman changed her mind about giving up the children and pressed charges against their father for violating the terms of the child-custody agreement—even though the new arrangement had been her idea. She also charged him with failing to pay court-ordered child support—though he was supporting the children.

It took a considerable amount of time and money for the father to sort out the situation.

Self-defense: Apply to family court before making changes to any custody agreement.

ENTERING INTO A BUSINESS PARTNERSHIP

You can be found financially responsible for the misdeeds of a business partner.

If your partner runs up a big debt, you might have to pay it. If the partner engages in illegal business activities, you might share responsibility for paying fines or making restitution.

You generally can't face criminal prosecution unless you were aware of your partner's illegal actions, but it can be difficult to prove a lack of knowledge. In certain situations, you could be prosecuted even if you were completely in the dark about your partner's wrongdoing.

Example: A federal statute makes it illegal to own the equipment necessary to pirate satellite broadcasts. The way the statute is written, it could be interpreted to mean that knowledge of ownership of the equipment is not necessary to establish guilt. So if your partner buys such equipment in the business's name, you could be guilty of a crime that you didn't know about.

Self-defense: Don't enter into a business partnership unless you're certain that your potential partner is a stickler for following rules. Keep a close eye on all aspects of your partnership, even those that fall under your partner's purview. Should you later decide to leave the business, legally disband the partnership through a written agreement—don't just walk away. If you signed forms personally guaranteeing lines of credit with suppliers or lenders, cancel them by following the forms' instructions.

To avoid legal problems, set up a small business as a limited liability company.

Don't Make These Mistakes With Your Will

Alexander A. Bove, Jr., Esq., partner, Bove & Langa PC, a law firm that specializes in trust and estate matters, 10 Tremont St., Suite 600, Boston 02108. He is author of *The Complete Book of Wills, Estates & Trusts: Third Edition*. Henry Holt.

The number of Americans who die without wills is estimated to be as high as 70%. And many people who do have wills have set them up improperly...allowed them to become outdated...have even forgotten exactly what they say. A poorly written will can bring turmoil and heartache to your loved ones—and cost your heirs lots of money.

Don't make the following common mistakes...

• **Not having a will.** If you die without a will, you die "intestate" and your assets will be distributed under state law. Generally, your state's intestacy law will not produce the results you would like.

Example: Some states require that 50% of a decedent's assets go to a surviving spouse and the other 50% to the children. Even if there are no children, 50% might go to next of kin such as parents or siblings.

This may deprive your surviving spouse of needed wealth.

Caution: You might think that your assets will bypass probate (the legal process in which a court oversees the distribution of a decedent's property) if you die without a will, but that's not true. There are many ways to avoid probate, but failing to execute a will is not among them.

• **Thinking your will alone is enough.** Assets that pass to heirs through your will must go through probate of your estate. Probate can be costly because of legal fees, adversarial because a will can be contested and time consuming because a court must oversee the process.

In addition, using a will as your entire estate plan may not provide adequate estate tax–planning opportunities.

Strategy: A will should be only one component of a comprehensive estate plan. Other components might include various trusts. Assets placed in trust during your lifetime can pass to others under the terms of the trust without going through probate.

Many types of trusts can offer estate tax reduction. A "bypass" trust, for example, may allow you to provide for a surviving spouse yet avoid estate tax on trust assets at the death of both spouses. Current federal estate tax law provides for a $2 million exemption, so anyone with $2 million–plus of assets should consider this strategy.

Also needed: Besides a will and trusts, other elements of an estate plan might include powers of attorney (to handle assets without going through probate), life insurance trusts (to make their proceeds estate tax free), health-care proxies and end-of-life directives.

A health-care proxy allows you to name someone who'll make decisions about your medical treatment if you become unable to make those decisions...end-of-life directives indicate whether you want to be kept alive by medical life-support systems in case of a terminal illness.

• **Creating your own will.** You can find "do-it-yourself" kits for writing your own will on-line and in bookstores. Executing your own will is promoted as a cost-saver because you'll avoid legal fees.

Reality: Your will is one of the most important documents you'll ever sign. Such a crucial document should be drafted by an experienced attorney so your heirs will avoid problems after your death. Legal fees need not be excessive—you might pay up to $3,500 for an entire estate plan, including a will.

• **Believing your will covers all of your assets.** Suppose you have a $1 million IRA, which you would like your two children to inherit. This desire may be expressed in your will, but such a bequest will be irrelevant.

An IRA will pass to a designated beneficiary, the person you name in IRA documents, no matter what it says in your will. The same is true for other retirement accounts, annuities, life insurance policies, transfer-on-death or payable-on-death accounts, and assets transferred into a trust.

In addition, property that is held jointly with right of survivorship will pass to the surviving co-owner or owners. Again, mention of such property in your will has no impact other than to incite a contest.

Bright side: The assets described above (items going to beneficiaries, jointly held property) will not be subject to the effort and expense of probate.

Important: Be sure to review all of your beneficiary designations periodically to confirm the choices you've made.

Trap: With IRAs and other retirement accounts, don't name your estate as beneficiary. This can result in the loss of valuable tax deferral and may even push your heirs into higher income tax brackets.

• **Not notifying your executor.** In your will you'll name your executor ("personal representative" in some states), the person who'll be responsible for handling the transfer of the assets that pass under your will.

This is a vital task, so it's important to get that person's consent to serve before naming him/her. You also should name at least one backup executor in case your first choice becomes unable or unwilling to serve.

Parents of minors: It's vital to name guardians for young children in case the remaining parent is unable to fill that role. Again, get the guardians' consent beforehand and name backups.

• **Leaving an outdated will in place.** Once you draft a will, you can't just forget about it. Your personal situation may change—births, deaths, marriages, divorces, changes in financial status, etc., all can have an impact on your plans.

Taxes, too: Changes in federal and/or state tax law also may suggest new strategies compared with the one outlined in your current will.

Thus, revisit your will and the other elements of your estate plan after each major change in your personal circumstances and after each change in estate tax law. Even without such events, take a look at your will every few years to make sure that it still reflects your current wishes.

• **Hiding your will.** Some people hide their wills because they don't want people to find them and know what they will (or won't) inherit. Unfortunately, a hidden will might very well *stay* hidden. Your will should be kept in a place that's both safe and accessible.

The best way to make your will both private and accessible is to leave it with the friend or relative you trust the most. If there's no one you trust, name an institutional executor such as a trust company and let this firm hold your will.

Even if you store your will elsewhere, your executor and other loved ones should know where you put it. The attorney who drafted your will should have a copy, as well as a note stating the location of the original.

• **Putting funeral and burial instructions in your will.** Most wills aren't read until days or weeks after death. Meanwhile, your survivors must make immediate decisions about a funeral or a memorial service.

Best: Use a separate document to spell out your final wishes and tell your executor where this letter may be found.

Why You Need a Power of Attorney

Martin S. Finn, Esq., CPA, managing partner in the law firm Lavelle & Finn, LLP, 29 British American Blvd., Latham, NY 12110-1405. Mr. Finn is co-author of *The Complete Trust Guide* (Professional Education Systems, Inc.) and *Cents & Sensibility: The Practical Guide to Money & Aging* (iUniverse).

Talk to any financial adviser about securing your future, and you're likely to hear the term "power of attorney" before very long. If you're like most people, your first reaction might be, "Wait a minute—isn't it risky to give someone power over my affairs? I would much rather keep control myself."

The concept of a power of attorney is often misunderstood. It is not a risky document when written properly—in fact, it can be critical to ensuring your financial safety and that of your family. *Here's what you need to know about the various kinds of powers of attorney, and some situations in which a power of attorney can help and/or protect you...*

Situation: You've retired and moved to a faraway state. Some of your financial affairs—a home that you have been trying to sell and an interest in a local business—remain in your former locale. You would rather not travel back and forth to deal with these affairs.

Solution: Rather than cede decisions to, say, an adult child of yours who still lives near your old home but who may be relatively uninformed (or who may not agree with your financial goals), you appoint a trusted adviser, such as your accountant or lawyer, to be your "agent" under a power of attorney. That person can then represent you and make and/or execute decisions on your behalf. *Two kinds of powers of attorney...*

• **A "general" power of attorney** gives a trusted person the right to act on your behalf in any financial matter if you're traveling or are otherwise unable to make a personal appearance.

• **A "special" power of attorney** limits the person's authority to a specific onetime transaction (say, a real estate closing) or for a limited period (for instance, while you're working or traveling overseas).

Situation: You become incapacitated, either temporarily or permanently, and are unable to make some or all of the decisions affecting your finances.

Many people are caught flat-footed—they haven't made any arrangements for someone to step in and handle their affairs.

Trap: You did set up a power of attorney, thinking it would help in case you became incapacitated. But sometimes general or special powers of attorney can have a flaw—they become invalid if you become legally "incompetent" (unable to handle your affairs). Therefore, a typical general or special power of attorney won't be effective when you most need help managing your finances.

Self-defense: For protection in case of incapacity, use a "durable" power of attorney. A durable power will remain in effect if you become incompetent. Therefore, if you reach the point where you can't handle money matters, your agent will be able to pay bills, sell securities, put your home up for sale, etc., if and when these actions are in your best interest.

Situation: You worry that by setting up a general and/or durable power of attorney, you would be giving up too much power. You don't want anyone else to have ongoing legal access to your assets.

Solution: In most cases, advisers, relatives and friends do end up doing the right thing when called upon as agents. But if you nonetheless are reluctant to have a power of attorney in force when it's not needed, you have another tool at your disposal—a "springing" power of attorney.

Such a power does not take effect when it's executed, so your agent will have no power to touch your finances. Instead, the power will "spring" into effect when certain events transpire, as described in the document.

Example: A qualified doctor attests to your incompetence. At that point, the document will become an effective durable power of attorney and your agent can manage your affairs.

Advantages: Until a springing power becomes effective, you will not have to worry that someone will use a power of attorney to take advantage of you. If you never lose your mental capacity, this springing power will never go into effect.

Disadvantages: If you become incompetent, the process of having a doctor examine you and attest to your incompetency might be time-consuming. In the meantime, you may mismanage your own affairs—and no one around you will have the legal right to stop you.

Bottom line: Springing powers of attorney are less useful, in my experience, than many people believe. If you are going to trust someone to manage your assets when you are incapacitated, why not trust him while you are capable of keeping an eye on your affairs—and on him?

Situation: **You and your spouse have divided the ownership of your assets** for estate planning or asset protection purposes.

This is commonly done to reduce estate taxes and to protect certain assets, such as a home, from creditors and/or lawsuits. In such cases, it probably makes sense for both spouses to grant powers of attorney.

Reason: If one spouse has not done so, his/her incapacity may leave some assets unprotected until a court can appoint a guardian. Usually each spouse names the other as agent. Be sure to also name successor agents in case a primary agent is unable to act.

NUTS AND BOLTS

A power of attorney is generally a very simple document—you can even buy a basic version in a stationery or office-supply store and fill it out yourself. But a do-it-yourself form may not cover all possible uses of a power of attorney and may leave the power open for abuse. Or it may be too narrow—failing to give an agent a specific power that you do want him to have, such as the right to make gifts on your behalf, to create trusts or to distribute funds from a 529 college savings plan for your grandchildren.

Best: Use an attorney to create your power. The fee generally will be modest, usually under $500, especially if you work with the lawyer who draws up your will and other estate planning documents.

After a power of attorney has been executed, you may want to send copies to your bank, your brokerage and certain other financial firms with which you do business so that your agent will be able to work with them. Some financial firms have their own power of attorney forms for clients to use and are reluctant to accept others. So when you send yours in, ask for a letter in response acknowledging receipt of the document and acceptance of its terms. This will reveal any problems right away, when they can be dealt with.

Any power of attorney document should be reviewed every few years with an eye toward any law changes or changes in the named agents.

Also, financial firms may be reluctant to accept the exercise of a power that was executed, say, 10 or 20 years earlier. Even though they may be legally required to honor the document no matter how old it is, if they stall while checking that it's still valid, it costs you time. Meanwhile, your financial affairs are not being administered.

How to Know If Long-Term-Care Insurance Is for You

Joseph Matthews, San Francisco–based attorney. He is author of *Beat the Nursing Home Trap: A Consumer's Guide to Assisted Living & Long-Term Care.* Nolo Press.

Many insurance companies will now pay nursing home reimbursements for geriatric conditions. And home health care coverage is typically part of all good long-term-care policies.

But does it pay to buy a policy?

WHEN COVERAGE IS A WASTE

A good policy's premiums may run as high as $750 a year for people in good health who are 50 years old—and $2,000 a year for people age 70. Such a policy will pay a $100 maximum daily benefit for three years—with a 100-day deductible. If you can afford to pay 20 to 30 years of annual premiums, you probably don't need long-term-care insurance.

Reason: You can afford nursing home or home health care if it becomes necessary.

A person's odds of spending a long period in a nursing home are relatively low. So—most people who purchase this insurance collect few, if any, benefits because they simply don't need a long stay at a nursing facility.

Better: Consider investing the money you would spend each year on premiums in a separate investment account. This way, if you don't need long-term care, you will have the assets for other things or for inclusion in your estate.

THE IDEAL CANDIDATE

Even though the likelihood that you'll need a lot of long-term care is low, insurance coverage may make more sense for some people than for others.

Examples: People in their 60s and 70s who can't afford care…or have a small family that wouldn't be able to care for them…or have family members who live far away.

When considering coverage, remember that national health care costs rise faster than inflation, and your policy may not keep up with the cost.

Helpful: Be sure your policy includes inflation protection, although rapidly rising health costs may require you to pay more out of pocket when you need care.

How to Prevent Crime… Against Yourself, Your Home and Your Car

Captain Robert L. Snow, retired commander of the homicide branch of the Indianapolis Police Department. He is also the author of *The Complete Guide to Personal and Home Safety: What You Need to Know.* Da Capo.

According to the FBI, one property crime occurs in the US every three seconds…and one robbery every 1.2 minutes.

However, you don't have to spend lots of money on security products to decrease the chance of being a crime victim. There's no need to turn your home into a fortress or to turn your automobile into a tank.

AT HOME

Make your house less of a target in the eyes of burglars…

• **Doors.** If given a choice, most criminals avoid a house with heavy doors and conspicuous dead-bolt locks. The back door is especially important because it's the preferred entry point for many burglars.

Often overlooked: An open garage door gives crooks an opportunity to steal its contents and also, if there's no car, it signals that the house may be unoccupied. The heavier the garage door, the more effective it is as a crime deterrent.

Important: Never open a door unless you recognize the person on the other side. Make sure all doors have peepholes. Don't rely on an inside chain lock. They can easily be broken.

• **Lights.** When you go out at night, leave lights switched on in a way that makes burglars believe that someone is home. It's not enough, for instance, to just turn on the back porch light every time you leave the house. If you do, burglars can easily spot the pattern and realize that you're not at home.

Instead, vary the pattern, leaving the lights on in different rooms on different occasions —or consider using a timer.

Even better, leave the television on and put a bowl of snacks on the coffee table. If the TV isn't visible from a window, place a radio near the front door instead and turn it up just loud enough to lead someone outside the door to believe there are people in the house. Tune the radio to a talk station.

Leaving home before sunset and forgetting to turn on lights or the television can be an invitation to burglars, who often drive through neighborhoods to spot easy targets. When they see a dark house at 2 am, crooks have no idea if the occupants are inside because few people are awake at that hour. But when a residence is unlit at 7 pm, they see it as a possible target.

• **Mail.** If you receive mail that contains your Social Security number, install a mailbox with a lock or rent a post office box.

Reason: Social Security numbers are gold to identity thieves.

If you regularly receive checks by mail, ask the sender to deposit these electronically in your bank account instead. Many organizations, including the Social Security Administration, offer this service.

• **Neighborhood watch.** Join or organize a neighborhood watch program in which volunteer residents are trained to patrol their areas. Almost every police department believes that neighborhood watch programs are the single most effective deterrents to crime.

Most local police and sheriffs' departments and some state attorneys general offices can help set up watch programs.

Helpful: The Neighborhood Watch Program of the National Sheriffs' Association (703-836-7827, *www.usaonwatch.org*).

• **Item ID.** Engrave your initials on valuable items in your home, such as TVs and cameras, to help with recovery if they are stolen. Many police departments and neighborhood watch organizations will assist with engraving.

Bottom line: If your house is burglarized…

• **Don't go inside.** If you already are inside, leave immediately.

• **Call 911.**

• **Resist the temptation to straighten up the house before police arrive.** You don't want to destroy evidence.

ON FOOT

The most effective way to prevent getting robbed or mugged is also the most overlooked—being observant. In today's fast-paced world, many people are too preoccupied to even notice their surroundings.

Examples: Two men are just sitting in an idling car near an ATM, or a person you don't know is walking unusually close behind you. In both cases, the people may have innocent and legitimate reasons for their actions. On the other hand, they could be looking for a victim to rob. By noticing suspicious actions, you can reduce the chance that you'll be that victim.

Increase your awareness by thinking like a policeman. Just as a cop might do, take a close look at passersby as you walk along. Try to spot people whose actions seem unusual, like the person who walks close behind you.

When you spot a suspicious person or situation, move away.

For more protection…

• **Appear to be alert by looking oncoming pedestrians in the eye.** (Do not stare, however.) This simple measure will often work because purse snatchers and muggers look for unobservant victims. Looking people briefly in the eye gives you the appearance of awareness.

• **Carry your wallet in an inside pocket.** If you have a purse, keep it close to your body. Most people know this, but will let their guard down if they are in a "safe" area, such as an upscale shopping mall. But that is the type of area where crooks are likely to prey.

• **Consider carrying a whistle or other noisemaker.** It can be useful if you're physically unable to move very fast or if you walk in areas where a shout or scream is unlikely to be heard.

If you are a victim…

• **Shout as loudly as you can.** Screaming or using a noisemaker is frequently effective because most crooks fear drawing attention to themselves.

• **Fight back.** Resist physically only if you are in imminent danger of serious injury. It's better to make lots of noise before things even progress to that point. Criminals know that they haven't done anything really criminal yet and will usually just flee before the noise you make brings a passerby or the police.

Myth: A course in self-defense will help you fight off an attacker.

Reality: Judo, karate and other techniques can bolster self-confidence, and that's important in helping you not look like a victim. But training in self-defense will rarely help an individual who is in a confrontation with a toughened streetwise attacker. Moreover, against an assailant with a weapon, it's often best not to offer any resistance.

BEHIND THE WHEEL

Just because your car hasn't been looted or stolen in, say, 30 years, don't assume it's safe. Criminals are more sophisticated and constantly searching for unsuspecting drivers and fresh areas in which to operate.

To protect yourself and your vehicle...

• **Stay in your car if you're rear-ended on the road.** Bumping the car ahead of him/her is often a crook's ploy to rob the driver of his money and car.

Instead of getting out, drive to the nearest gas station and signal to the other driver to follow you. Crooks will nearly always head in the other direction.

• **Don't rely solely on club-type devices to lock the steering wheel.** Clubs are effective against most small-time crooks, but sophisticated auto thieves can easily thwart them. For additional protection, install a reinforced steering collar.

Typical cost: Less than $25, available at specialty auto stores.

• **Use parking garages as a last resort.** Most of these are not nearly as safe as generally believed. Instead, park only in open lots or park on the street in well-lit and well-traveled areas. Those are the places criminals are less likely to be lurking.

Very Clever Ways to Hide Your Valuables

Detective Sergeant Kevin Coffey, who has 23 years of experience at a major US police department. He is founder of Corporate Travel Safety, LLC, which offers security products and seminars, Calabasas, CA, *www.corporatetravelsafety.com* or *www. kevincoffey.com.*

Most burglars like to get in and out of homes quickly. They will focus on closets and drawers and under mattresses. Their favorite targets include cash, jewelry, checkbooks, credit cards, handguns, cameras and laptop computers.

The safest place to keep valuables is in a safe-deposit box or a safe built into the wall or the floor of your home. If you decide to use another location, let a trusted relative know about your hiding spot or put a note in your safe-deposit box describing the location. Otherwise, your valuables could be lost if you pass away or forget where they're hidden.

If there are young children in your house, make sure your hiding place isn't somewhere that they're likely to discover.

SIMPLE HIDING PLACES

Here are simple hiding spots for small items, such as cash, jewelry and rare coins...

• **Dry goods jar.** Seal your valuables in small plastic bags, then bury them in a large jar of rice or flour. Store near the back of a kitchen cupboard.

• **Frozen with vegetables.** Defrost a package of frozen vegetables, put your valuables in a small plastic bag and put the bag in the package. Glue the package shut and refreeze. Even if a thief did look in your freezer, he wouldn't take the time to defrost your peas. This is appropriate only for items that won't be damaged by being in the freezer and that are used infrequently, because it will take some time for the valuables to thaw out.

• **Tennis ball.** Cut a small slit in a tennis ball, squeeze the ball to open the slit and insert your valuables. Put the ball back in its canister with two normal tennis balls. Make sure the canister doesn't rattle when moved, or you might tip off an alert thief.

• **Foam couch cushion.** Unzip a foam couch cushion, cut a slit into the foam, insert your valuables and rezip. This is appropriate only for durable and flexible valuables, such as cash.

• **Diversion safe.** This is a small container that looks exactly like an ordinary household item, such as a can of brand-name soda or shaving cream. My favorite diversion safe is a book, which can be kept with other books on a shelf. Type "diversion safe" into a search engine to find products, or check "Travel Safes" in the travel products section of my Web site, *www.corporatetravelsafety. com/catalog.*

458

DO-IT-YOURSELF "SAFES"

These hiding spots will take a bit more time and effort to construct. They might be worth the trouble if you have basic carpentry skills and you keep a significant amount of valuables in your home. Some are best for small items, such as jewelry. Others can hide larger items, such as a laptop computer.

•**Posts of a poster bed.** The tops of the bedposts usually unscrew. Take the tops off, then drill down into the wood posts to create hiding spaces for valuables (be careful not to drill into the grooves where the top screws in).

•**Fake pipe, vent or electrical outlet.** Add an unnecessary pipe or duct among the real pipes and ducts in your attic, basement, laundry room or kitchen, and store valuables inside. This pipe or duct should look as if it is part of the home's plumbing or heating, ventilation and air-conditioning (HVAC) system.

Or use a phony electrical outlet or vent to provide access to valuables hidden in the wall. The fake outlet or vent should match the color and style of the real outlets or vents in your home.

Caution: Remove valuables before having your plumbing, HVAC or electrical system serviced.

•**Below a bookcase.** The lowest shelf of a wooden bookcase often is a few inches above the floor. Turn the space below into a hiding area large enough for even a laptop computer by cutting a secret door into the wood facing.

HOTEL ROOMS

Your best security options are the front-desk safe and the safe in your room. If these are not available, there's often room to hide things beneath the lowest dresser drawer. Pull the bottom drawer out completely and stash your valuables below, or put them behind the television in the armoire.

Another possibility is to bring along a diversion safe that looks like a personal-care item, such as shaving cream or hair spray.

Or lock valuables inside luggage. Locks can be pried open with screwdrivers, but few hotel thieves carry screwdrivers. There also are portable safes and steel briefcases on the market.

CARS

Valuables left in parked cars are at risk no matter how well they are hidden. When this must be done, the safest spot is in the trunk, under or behind the spare tire.

Stow valuables in your trunk before you arrive at your destination. Otherwise a criminal could see you put something in the trunk, then break in when you walk away.

Don't Fall for E-Mail Scams

Bob Hopper, manager, computer crimes section, National White Collar Crime Center, *www.nw3c.org*. The center is a congressionally funded nonprofit corporation that helps law-enforcement agencies combat crimes, especially those in high-tech areas.

Think you'll never fall for an e-mail scam? You're just the kind of person the scammers are looking for. E-mail scammers aren't necessarily very clever. But they have learned to send out millions of bogus messages and hope that just a few recipients fall for their traps.

They're never disappointed. And the victims are usually people who let down their guard because they think they could never be caught in a scam.

At best, you might suffer the temporary inconvenience of having your e-mail account hijacked. At worst, your identity could be stolen, leading to a financial loss and a lot of inconvenience.

Good news: You don't have to go to extraordinary lengths to avoid scams. But you do need to be vigilant and take some relatively simple steps to cut the chances of being scammed to nearly zero. *What you should know...*

THE BAIT

How do scammers mislead even the wary?

One particularly successful scam starts with an e-mail that purports to be from a bank, credit card company or PayPal, the payment system used by many Internet marketers, or even from your own Internet service provider (ISP). The e-mail looks authentic and even displays a credible replica of the company's logo.

The message might say, for instance, that your credit card was inadvertently charged $127.83, but it assures you that the error can be corrected. All you have to do is send certain information to a certain e-mail address. This information includes confirmation of your credit card number, your Social Security number, street address and telephone number.

In reality, the e-mail is from a scam artist who uses your information to buy products with your credit card or to apply for credit in your name—in other words, to steal your identity. In a short time, you can wind up with thousands of dollars of debt and a severely damaged credit record.

MORE E-MAIL SCAMS

•**Premium rate phone calls.** You receive an e-mail that gives you a seemingly plausible reason to make a phone call—to collect a prize that you've won or to help a relative who's trying to get in touch with you.

But the number you're asked to phone is one that bills the caller several dollars a minute, as numbers for horoscope readings or gambling tips legitimately do. In this case, the person you phone runs up the bill by getting you to stay on the line for as long as possible.

In the US, these "premium rate" numbers are easy to identify because they usually have a 900 or 976 prefix.

Trap: A call may be surreptitiously forwarded to such a number, and you'll never know until you get the bill. Or you may be asked to phone overseas, where premium rate numbers can have many other prefixes.

•**Cheap prescription drugs can seem irresistible.** Scammers know this when they send e-mail that purports to be from a pharmacy that sells at a deep discount. To take advantage of the prices, you're asked to supply your address and credit card information. You never see the drugs—just huge charges to your credit card.

•**Work-at-home scams.** Want to make easy money by working at home? In one popular scam, you get an e-mail that promises quick profits if you agree to receive retail goods at your home, repackage them and send them on to other addresses.

Scammers say they need this service to make sure the products aren't damaged. In fact, the goods have usually been bought with fraudulent credit cards. The scam artist avoids detection by having them sent to your address, but needs your help in sending them on to him/her.

EFFECTIVE PROTECTION

•**Never open e-mail from an unknown source.** Even though the sender might not be trying to scam you, the e-mail could contain computer codes that can mean big trouble for your machine.

In reality, however, most people occasionally open unsolicited e-mail, especially if it appears to come from a legitimate source, such as a well-known company.

•**Always independently check with a company before responding to its e-mail.** Use Google or another search engine—not a phone number or Web address in the e-mail—to find the company's contact information. If it's a nationally known firm, phone and find out if it was actually the source of the e-mail. Or if you've previously received statements from the company, use contact information contained in that correspondence.

If it's a company that you don't know, contact the Better Business Bureau in the company's purported hometown to make sure that it has a clean record before dealing with it.

Similarly, check out any company that says it provides a way to earn money at home.

•**Don't give out your personal information**—phone number, address, etc.—to a company or person whom you don't know.

Also: When an e-mail asks for your password, assume it's a scam and delete the mail. The only parties who should know the password are you—and perhaps family members—and your Internet service provider. ISPs never ask because they already know.

•**Install security software** that protects your computer from e-mails that might contain viruses, spyware or other harmful programs sometimes referred to as "malware."

Most ISPs provide some degree of protection, which you can reinforce by installing your own security products from companies that include McAfee (866-622-3911, *www. mcafee.com*) and Symantec (408-517-8000, *www.symantec.com*).

Don't, however, be lulled into a false sense of security by thinking that even the best products will protect you from all harmful programs or from e-mail sent by scammers. Stay alert, and take the protective steps just mentioned.

•**Cut down on spam.** Sooner or later, nearly all e-mail addresses fall into the hands of spammers. To cut down on the amount of spam you receive, change your e-mail address once or twice a year. That might seem inconvenient, but you can make the procedure less troublesome by e-mailing friends and frequent correspondents whenever you change addresses.

Alternative: For family members and close friends, use an e-mail address that you rarely change. For others, use one that you change periodically.

•**Change passwords twice a year.** This will reduce the chance that your passwords will fall into the wrong hands.

If, despite these steps, you fall victim to an e-mail scam, contact the Internet Crime Complaint Center at *www.ic3.gov.* The organization, a partnership between the FBI, the National White Collar Crime Center and the Bureau of Justice Assistance, channels complaints to the appropriate law-enforcement agencies. Also contact your ISP, which can take legal action against scammers.

Sadly, however, it's highly unlikely that you'll ever recover any money you lose.

Reason: E-mail scams are usually short-lived, and the perpetrators quickly move on. Nevertheless, reporting the crime is important because it helps reduce the number of fraudulent e-mails that you and others receive.

Safest Banking

Many people are reluctant to use on-line banking because they think it is more risky than traditional banking, but just the reverse is true.

Why: Eliminating paper statements prevents identity thieves from stealing or intercepting them. Paying bills on-line eliminates credit card charges and paper bills that identity thieves may steal to get confidential information. Electronic statements that are always up-to-date inform about questionable transactions more quickly than do paper monthly statements. So if you are concerned about security, on-line banking should be attractive to you.

Chris Musto, general manager, WebExcellence division, Keynote Systems, a leader in Internet and mobile test and measurement services, San Mateo, CA, *www.keynote.com.*

Beware of On-Line Romance Scams

On-line romance scams have become so common that an entire Yahoo users group is devoted to them (*http://groups.yahoo. com/groups/romancescams*). The scams use phony postings at dating sites to ask for money. The postings usually involve claims of being stranded in a foreign country, such as Nigeria, and having trouble cashing paychecks. Scammers have a few chats with targets, claim to be falling in love, then ask for favors that always involve money.

Self-defense: Beware of anyone who seems too good to be true…claims to be in trouble overseas…starts saying "I love you" after a brief on-line acquaintance.

Social Security Scam E-mails

One e-mail with the subject line "Cost-of-Living for 2008 update" gives information about the 3.3% inflation adjustment to benefits in 2008, then directs the recipient to a counterfeit SSA Web page to enter information to "update" his/her account. Any information entered is used by the scammer to commit identity theft. The SSA urges recipients to report such scam e-mails by calling 800-269-0271, or on-line at *www.social security.gov/oig.*

Alert: The IRS says that many such fake e-mails have been sent in its name as well—so expect more invoking the SSA and other government agencies. Be wary of all such unsolicited e-mails.

Don't Apply for Store Credit Cards In the Store

An application for credit includes your name, address, Social Security number and other information that makes you vulnerable to identity theft. You do not know the person in the store who takes the application, and you do not know who else will have access to it.

Self-defense: If you want a store credit card, apply for it on-line or mail an application to the credit department.

Curtis Arnold, president and founder, CardRat ings.com, North Little Rock, AR.

Protect Your Identity

Nancy Dunnan, a New York City–based financial and travel adviser and the author or coauthor of 25 books including the best seller, How to Invest $50–$5,000. HarperCollins.

A security freeze stops thieves from getting credit in your name by blocking access to your credit report and your credit score. Without this data, no business, including banks, will issue new credit. Then, when the time comes that you need

new credit—say, for a car loan—you follow your state's instructions. In most cases, that means using a personal identification number (which will be sent to you) to unlock access to your credit file.

For more information on instituting a security freeze, go to the Consumers Union Web site, *www.consumersunion.org.*

Additional steps to protect yourself from ID theft…

•**Monitor your financial accounts for any signs of fraud or identity theft.** That means looking over your monthly statements very carefully. If you spot suspicious activity, contact one of the credit bureaus (by law, each must report information received to the other two)—Equifax (800-525-6285, *www.equifax.com*), Experian (888-397-3742, *www.experian.com*) or TransUnion (800-680-7289, *www.transunion.com*) to place a fraud alert on your credit report. A fraud alert puts a 90-day "watch" on your credit file. Creditors must contact you before they open a new account or make any changes to your existing accounts.

Note: Another advantage of requesting a fraud alert is that it entitles you to a free copy of your credit report—in addition to the annual free report to which everyone is now entitled. You may need more than one report every 12 months.

•**Close any account that's been tampered with** (ask for a new account with a new account number) and file a police report.

•**Contact the Federal Trade Commission,** which is tracking any fraud, by calling its identity theft hotline at 877-438-4338 or going to *www.consumer.gov/idtheft.* The VA will update information as it becomes available at *www.firstgov.gov* and at 800-333-4636.

Identity Theft Insurance

Identity theft insurance is now being offered by many employers to lower the cost of lost productivity when a worker is victimized. The average identity theft victim spends hundreds of hours restoring his/her credit, which requires time off from work. Insurance, which reimburses victims for the cost of restoring their identities and repairing their credit reports, can cost a few dollars per year per employee, depending on company size and level of coverage.

Nancy Callahan, vice president, AIG Identity Theft and Fraud Division, New York City, www. aigidtheft.com.

"Freeze" Your Credit— New Tool Against Identity Theft

Credit reporting agencies Equifax (888-766-0008, *www.equifax.com*), Experian (888-397-3742, *www.experian.com*) and TransUnion (800-916-8800, *www.trans union.com*) now allow consumers in every state to "freeze" their credit files.

Freezes prevent identity thieves from obtaining credit cards in your name. Fees for freezes vary by state, generally $10 per agency each time you initiate or lift a freeze.

Linda Foley, director of Identity Theft Resource Center, San Diego. www.idtheftcenter.org.

How to Remove Personal Info From the Web

Marjory Abrams, publisher, Bottom Line newsletters, Boardroom Inc., 281 Tresser Blvd., Stamford, CT 06901.

According to Philadelphia-based privacy expert John Featherman, the risks of Internet privacy are getting worse. More local governments are making their records available on the Internet—so it is even easier to steal people's identities—and data-harvesting companies are increasingly defending their rights.

John recommends finding out what information there is about you (and your loved ones) on the Internet. Each month, check in search engines such as Google.com, Whitepages.com, A9.com, Live.com, Yahoo.com, PrivateEye.com and Zabasearch.com. Search for variations of each person's name, and put the name in quotation marks ("Marjory Abrams," "Margie Abrams," etc.).

Even better: Set up a Google Alert (at *www.google.com/alerts*), which will inform you whenever the "crawler" finds old or new pages with your name. You can choose to be updated weekly, daily or as soon as a page is found. (John prefers to get the information when it is found.)

To remove your personal information from the Web…

• **If you have your own Web site**—for friends or business clients—you can create a block against most search engines. John suggests blocking Google and other popular search sites. For example, type "Removing information from Google" into Google Search, and click on "Web Search Help Center" for directions.

• **If your information appears on a public site**—say, in a phone directory—see whether the site has a mechanism for opting out. If not, contact the site and request that your information be removed.

Some local governments are reviewing their on-line documents so that Social Security numbers and other sensitive information can be edited out, but John says that it is up to individuals to make sure this is done. If you find information that you want removed, ask the agency in writing to do so.

If any kind of fraud or illegal business practice is involved, the fastest way to get action is to contact the National Association of Attorneys General (202-326-6000, *www. naag.org/ag/ful_ag_table.php*)…the Federal Trade Commission (877-FTC-HELP, *www. ftc.gov*)…the Federal Communications Commission (*www.fcc.gov*)…and/or your state's consumer protection office (*consumeraction. gov/state.shtml*).

Most job-search and dating services allow users to remove résumés and personal "portraits," but this doesn't mean that they will disappear from the Internet—other Web sites may have made the information accessible. Similarly, you can delete all or part of your own blog, but material from it still may be floating around, and you can't remove postings you have put on others' sites. People have been fired from jobs due to personal postings, particularly on social networking sites.

Of course, says John, the safest thing is to not post personal information in the first place—but if you are going to do so, check privacy policies carefully…and post cautiously.

To Prevent Credit Card Fraud…

Audri Lanford, PhD, cofounder and coeditor, ScamBusters.org, Boone, NC.

Lower your chances of becoming a victim. Here are eight easy ways to prevent credit card fraud.

•**Do not give out your account number on the phone** unless you originate the call to a known vendor.

•**Never provide your card number to a Web site that is not secure**—look for "https" in the site address and a padlock icon on the page.

•**Sign new credit cards as soon as you get them.**

•**Shred unwanted card applications.**

•**When using your card in public,** shield it with your hand so that people nearby cannot copy the number or use a cell phone or camera to capture it.

•**Carry only cards you really need.** Keep less-used ones securely at home.

•**Open bills promptly, and check each one for any charges you do not**

recognize. Report any unrecognized charges promptly.

•**Never respond to spam solicitations (unsolicited or junk e-mail) for credit cards,** and never send your credit card number via e-mail.

Check Fraud Protection

Protect yourself against a common check fraud scam.

How it works: A thief steals from your mailbox a check you've written, washes off your writing with a common household cleaner, then fills in the now blank check.

Protection: Use a Uni-Ball 207 to write checks (less than $2). It uses a pigment that bleeds into the paper so it can't be washed out by chemicals.

Frank Abagnale, secure-technology consultant and lecturer, Washington, DC, *www.abagnale.com*.

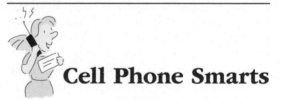

Cell Phone Smarts

If your cell phone is stolen, you pay for all calls that are made until you report the theft.

Example: One woman was stuck with a $26,000 bill when her phone was stolen while she was on vacation—the thief made a week's worth of international calls.

To reduce risk: Program a password into your phone so that only you can use it (check your owner's manual for instructions or call your phone service provider). Put a hold on your account when you notice the phone is missing, even if you think it's simply misplaced.

David Wood, formerly of DialingforDeals.com.

How to Keep an Eye On Elderly Family Members from Afar

Jim Miller, an advocate for senior citizens, writes "Savvy Senior," a weekly question-and-answer information column syndicated in more than 400 newspapers nationwide, *www.savvysenior.org*. Based in Norman, OK, he is a regular guest on the NBC *Today* show.

Many new technologies have been developed to help adults ensure that their older loved ones are safe...

HOME MONITORING

A basic form of this system—the personal emergency response system (PERS)—has been around for years. With a PERS, a person wears a device (panic button) that sends out a call for help if needed. The problem is that many who have such a device don't wear it or aren't alert enough to hit the button if they fall or become ill.

High-tech home-monitoring systems (which still offer the panic-button feature) require no input from the person being cared for. They work through wireless motion sensors placed throughout the senior's home and collect information on activities of daily living, such as getting out of bed, using the bathroom, eating and taking medicine. The system establishes the person's routines so it can detect when there are changes to those patterns, such as a person failing to leave the bedroom in the morning. Alerts are sent to the caregiver via phone or e-mail. Family members also can check on their loved one's patterns via the system's secure Web site. *Companies that offer this product...*

• **QuietCare.** A leader in the industry and the first to offer this service.

Cost: Less than $300*, plus about $90 a month for monitoring (varies by area). 877-822-2468, *www.quietcare.com*.

• **Healthsense.** Offers a more comprehensive monitoring system that allows you to keep an eye on just about everything.

*Prices subject to change.

With a variety of sensors, you can monitor such things as sleep patterns, shower and toilet use, whether the stove has been left on, when your loved one has left the house, etc.

Cost: $1,300, plus $60 for monthly monitoring, though prices vary depending on tier of service and size of the home. 800-576-1779, *www.healthsense.com*.

• **GrandCare.** In addition to monitoring, this system has a small computer that connects to the Internet and plugs into the TV, allowing family members to share pictures, e-mails, appointment reminders and more on a dedicated TV channel.

Cost: $2,000 to $2,500, plus a $30 to $50/ month monitoring fee, depending on the service. 262-384-4903, *www.grandcare.com*.

MEDICATION MANAGEMENT

Remembering to take medications is a challenge for many seniors. The MD.2 system can help organize medications and dispense them on schedule. It also provides multiple reminders to take the medication. Caregivers are alerted if necessary. The system can be monitored via the Internet.

Cost: $750, plus a $30 monthly monitoring fee, or it can be rented for less than $100 per month, but cost will vary by distributor. 877-563-2632, *www.imd2.com*.

Helpful: *www.epill.com* offers a full line of medication-reminder products and services. 800-549-0095.

VIDEO CHAT SERVICE

An on-line video chat service allows you to speak to and see each other. It is easy to set up, though both parties need a computer, webcam and high-speed or broadband Internet connection. Two services are Windows Live Messenger (*get.live.com*) and SightSpeed (*www.sightspeed.com*).

All-in-one videophones (from such companies as *www.packet8.net...www.viseon. com...*and *www.ojoservices.com*) also can provide this service.

Cost: About $400 per phone, plus $15 to $20 per month.

How to Disaster-Proof Your Belongings

Martin Kuritz, San Diego–based author of *The Beneficiary Book: A Family Information Organizer* and coauthor, with Alvin H. Danenberg, DDS, CFP, of *My Business Book,* a binder that has fill-in forms for business owners. Both are available from Mr. Kuritz's company, Active Insights, 800-222-9125, *www.active-insights.com.*

Several years ago, a wildfire threatened my family's home in California. We were caught unprepared, so we had to evacuate quickly without taking our photographs and important papers. Fortunately, we escaped safely and our home was spared, but I agonized about what could have been lost, including my father's letters home from World War II and my grandson's first work of art.

Last season's hurricanes served as reminders that the danger my family faced is hardly unique. Each year, many families confront earthquakes, floods and tornadoes.

To help protect important items, I developed a strategy that anyone can implement…

SECURING DOCUMENTS

Purchase a notebook, several portable plastic file boxes (available in legal and letter size) and a fireproof (and preferably waterproof) home safe. In addition, arrange for a safe-deposit box at a bank.

Make copies of all important items, including deeds, credit cards, insurance policies and health directives (living will, health-care proxy, etc.). Do not forget to copy keepsakes, including photos, diplomas, letters and children's report cards. Put these along with spare keys, valuable jewelry and irreplaceable objects, such as coin collections, in your home safe. (Don't keep loose photo negatives or stamp collections in the safe—conditions may be too moist. Consult an expert on collectibles for the proper storage.)

Keep the originals of documents in your safe-deposit box.

Off-site, perhaps at a friend's house, keep a current list of passwords and personal identification numbers, the combination of your home safe and a spare key to your safe-deposit box.

PORTABLE STORAGE

You can store digital or scanned photos on a CD. Copy this information from your computer frequently onto CDs, and store the CDs in your office or safe-deposit box.

Items that can't be copied and must be stored at home, such as family heirlooms, should be kept in portable file boxes. Mark the tops and sides of the boxes "Take." Store them where they can be reached if you must evacuate.

Keep an empty file box near the home safe in case you need to pack up the valuables quickly—or if there is room, keep them in a file box in the safe.

KEEPING TRACK

To prepare for any insurance claims, keep a room-by-room inventory or a video record of possessions. Don't forget items stored in garages, attics and basements. For major items, such as appliances and electronic gadgets, include the serial numbers, dates of purchase and prices. Store the inventory list or video record in your safe-deposit box.

In a notebook, keep instructions on where to find your documents and keepsakes, as well as names and phone numbers of emergency contacts, such as close family members, physicians, lawyers, insurance agents, etc. List all important family medical information and health insurance ID numbers. Make sure the notebook is accessible—say, on a shelf near the front door—so that you can grab it if you must evacuate.

Emergency Life for Your Cell Phone

Charge 2 Go is a reusable emergency cell-phone charger powered by one AA battery. Add a battery and plug the adaptor into your phone. Adaptors are available for most phone models. A two-hour charge provides up to three hours of talk time and 90 hours of standby time. Plastic or aluminum casing in black, blue, red or silver.

Cost: $19.50.

Information: Charge 2 Go, 800-248-4694, *www.charge2go.com.*

Your Home Emergency Kit

John H. Fenimore V, retired US Air Force Major General. He previously served as Adjutant General of New York State, and as chairman of the New York State Disaster Preparedness Commission and the National Guard Bureau's Weapons of Mass Destruction Advisory Board.

H ere's a listing of what you really should have at your home to be prepared for an emergency...

• **A survival kit.** Water is most important—one gallon per person per day for at least three days—but you also should have canned food (including food for pets), maps, water-purification tablets, medications, flashlights and batteries. Complete survival-kit instructions are now available from the US Department of Homeland Security (800-237-3239, *www.ready.gov*) or on the Internet sites of the Federal Emergency Management Agency (*www.fema.gov*) and the Red Cross (*www.redcross.org*).

• **Hand-cranked radio** that includes shortwave or TV audio band in addition to AM and FM. Shortwave transmissions carry such long distances that you may be able to get your information from overseas if necessary. Hand-cranked AM/FM radios, such as the Grundig FR200 with shortwave capability and Eton FR300, offer both light and unlimited reception time.

Cost: About $40 to $60.*

• **Cash.** In a box that's fireproof, put enough money for food, lodging and gas for a few days at inflated prices. Also keep a list of your bank and investment account numbers handy.

Helpful: Select a friend or relative who lives in a different part of the country to act as your emergency coordinator. Calling out

*Prices subject to change.

of a disaster area can be easier than making a local call. You might be able to exchange information through this person. All members of the family should have this information.

How I Reclaimed My Stolen Identity— A Lawyer's Story

Mari J. Frank, Esq., a lawyer and privacy and identity-theft expert in Laguna Niguel, CA, *www.identitytheft.org.* She is author of *Safeguard Your Identity.* Porpoise.

A s many as 10 million Americans become victims of identity theft each year. It is awful—and I know because I was one of the earliest victims.

Back in 1996, I was 48 years old and living in Southern California with my husband and two children. I was a successful attorney. I had no debt, kept excellent financial records and thought I knew how to protect my personal information. When my identity was stolen, I had no idea at first how to get it back and reclaim my credit standing. *I hope my experience can help others avoid the emotional and financial pain...*

MY STORY

One afternoon, a bank called me, wanting to know why I had missed the payments on my $11,000 Visa bill. I thought it was a prank call.

In fact, someone had opened new credit card accounts in my name and charged more than $50,000 over 10 months before anyone notified me. I found out that a Ford Mustang convertible had been purchased by using credit in my name, and a rental-car company was suing me for damages to a vehicle that my impostor had rented. Though I was not held responsible for the charges, my credit was ruined.

Worst of all, this wasn't just a financial crime—the thief was stealing my professional identity as well. She was handing out business cards with my name on them to people who were looking for an attorney.

Because of my legal expertise, I figured that stemming and repairing this damage would take several weeks. Instead, it wound up taking almost a year. I met resistance at every turn. The credit card issuer told me that the bills for the fraudulent charges had been going to an address in Ventura County, four hours north of my home, and that it would investigate. Instead, the card issuer turned over my account to a collection agency, which inundated me with threatening calls.

UPHILL BATTLE

Local police refused to take the case because I wasn't responsible for the charges. The FBI informed me that it does not get involved with financial crimes against consumers (a federal law that I lobbied for has since changed that). The US Postal Service was so slow to grant my request to cease delivery to the thief of preapproved credit card offers in my name that I approached the local mailman in the thief's neighborhood. I pleaded with him to stop delivering such mail. He said that he would try to help but couldn't guarantee what would happen on his days off.

In desperation, I called up the Ventura County Police Department again and got lucky. One of the officers I spoke with had been a victim of identity theft himself. He investigated and then arrested the thief—a paralegal who had stolen my credit report from a law office where she worked as a temporary secretary. The law firm had a subscription to an information service, enabling my impostor to download my credit reports. Eventually, the woman pleaded guilty to six counts of felony fraud. Because she had not committed a violent crime, she was sentenced to probation and community service.

Meanwhile, it took me $1,500 and 500 hours of work to clean up the problem. (The national average for identity theft victims is $1,400 and about 600 hours.) During that time, I was barraged with calls from creditors and was not able to get new loans or credit. *Here's what I learned from the experience...*

IF SOMEONE STEALS YOUR IDENTITY

• **Contact the three main credit-reporting agencies.** Ask that a notation called a "fraud alert" be attached to your accounts. It is free, good for 90 days and hopefully (if the creditor is diligent) means that you will be telephoned for verification whenever credit is applied for in your name. If you want to maintain the alert for up to seven years, you need to mail proof of identify theft, including a police report (see below) and affidavit, to each agency.

If you reside in a state that allows a security freeze, you can lock your report so that no one can get it without your permission secured by a password. To find out which states now have security freeze laws, visit *www.pirg.org/consumer/credit/statelaws.htm.*

While the reporting agencies, major banks and credit cards now offer credit-monitoring services that provide early notice of fraud, these services are quite expensive—as much as $200 a year. It's more cost effective to take advantage of a new federal law that requires each of the big reporting agencies to issue you one free credit report a year. That way, you can get a report every four months and monitor your credit record yourself. Visit *www.annualcreditreport.com* or call 877-322-8228 for more information.

• **Get an identity theft report** from the local police in your area documenting the fraudulent accounts and other illegal actions the thief has taken. It also should include the thief's address (if you know it). The police will take a full set of your fingerprints and your photo if someone committed a crime in your name.

Important: Few police departments have the resources to investigate identity theft, but every state gives you the right to get a victim's report "for informational purposes only." A report establishes the date that you became aware of the crime and makes it easier to get information and clear your name with financial institutions and government agencies. For example, federal law requires that once any creditor receives your identity theft report, it's illegal for it to sell, transfer or turn the debt over to a collection agency.

Caution: Do *not* contact the impostor yourself. He/she may be violent or may retaliate by threatening or harassing you. In addition, contacting him also could compromise any criminal case against him.

●**Contact the security/fraud departments at your bank** and all institutions from which you had credit—not just Visa and MasterCard issuers, but also stores, gas stations, brokerages, mortgage companies, etc. You also will need to contact any institutions that granted credit to the thief. All fraudulent accounts need to be closed and noted on your record as "Account Closed at Consumer's Request," not as "Lost or Stolen Card," which could lower your future credit score. Ask that new accounts opened by the perpetrator be "permanently removed" from your record, not simply closed—often, accounts are given a "soft" close, which means that they can be reopened with a request by phone.

Helpful: Identity theft victims tend to cancel all of their accounts to protect themselves, but you should keep open those that were not affected by the identity theft. Your credit record may be damaged due to the fraud, which will make getting new loans or credit almost impossible.

●**Reassert control of your bank accounts.** In addition to reporting stolen checks or account numbers to your bank, also report the theft to the major check guarantee/verification companies.

Reason: Merchants use these databases to learn whether you have a history of writing bad checks. Your bank may not update this information right away.

●**Conduct civil and criminal court checks** to make sure that the thief hasn't incurred any lawsuits, civil judgments or criminal charges in your name. For example, say that an impostor fails to pay his landlord, who sues and wins a case against "you" for past-due rent, or a large check bounces and a warrant is issued for your arrest. These problems are very serious because, for obvious reasons, they can escalate as time goes on.

To look up civil judgments, see *www.knowx.com* (free to search, reports cost $7.95*). If you discover a lawsuit against you, contact the court where the suit was filed to request a copy of the court records. Also contact the office of the attorneys involved in the case for instructions on resolving the matter.

For criminal cases, have your local police run a criminal background check on you. If your name surfaces, you'll need to hire an attorney to contact the police and/or district attorney's office where the crime was committed to get help. Also contact the US Department of Justice (202-514-2000, *www.usdoj.gov*) to check if your name is in the National Criminal Database. If it is, officials will tell you how to get it removed.

●**Do not pay fraudulent bills.** After months or years of fighting collection agencies and watching the interest and late fees on unpaid bills soar, many victims figure that it's easier to pay off false credit card charges or even declare bankruptcy. But doing so can damage your credit and hurt your case as a crime victim should other fraudulent charges surface. You must send harassing bill collectors the identity theft report issued by the police. Inform them that continuing to call you violates federal law and you will take legal action if they persist.

●**Log the time and expenses involved in clearing your name.** Any fraud losses, out-of-pocket costs and work time lost may be tax deductible under IRS Tax Code Section 165(c). You also could have a case against your credit grantors or the credit-reporting agencies if they violated the *Fair Credit Reporting Act* by committing willful or negligent acts in violation of the law, such as failure to investigate the fraud that resulted in the identity theft. Your action must be filed within two years of the date of discovery but no later than five years from the date of violation.

Finally, you can help prosecute the impostor and ask for restitution for out-of-pocket costs. In my case, the judge ordered restitution of several thousand dollars, but all I received was $60—my impersonator was subsequently incarcerated for committing identity theft again.

*Prices subject to change.

More from Mari Frank, Esq....

Resources for Identity Theft Victims

The following resources provide invaluable help to identity theft victims…

CREDIT-REPORTING AGENCIES

• **Equifax,** 888-766-0008, *www.equifax. com.*

• **Experian,** 888-397-3742, *www.experian. com.*

• **TransUnion,** 800-680-7289, *www.trans union.com.*

CHECK-GUARANTEE COMPANIES

• **Certegy,** 800-770-3792.

• **ChexSystems,** 800-428-9623.

• **CrossCheck,** 800-843-0760.

• **Global Payments,** 800-560-2960.

• **SCAN,** 800-262-7771.

• **TeleCheck,** 800-710-9898.

HELPFUL ORGANIZATIONS

• **Federal Trade Commission,** 877-438-4338, *www.consumer.gov/idtheft.*

• **Identity Theft Prevention and Survival,** 800-725-0807, *www.identitytheft.org.*

• **Identity Theft Resource Center,** 858-693-7935, *www.idtheftcenter.org.*

• **Privacy Rights Clearinghouse,** 619-298-3396, *www.privacyrights.org.*

Warnings from a Top Securities Cop— The Latest Financial Rip-Offs

Michael J. Byrne, chief counsel of the Pennsylvania Securities Commission in Harrisburg, PA, and head of the Enforcement Trends Project at the North American Securities Administrators Association (NASAA), *www.nasaa.org.*

The multiyear boom in energy prices is reviving the popularity of many shoddy investments. *Here, ones to be wary of now…*

SELF-DIRECTED IRAS

How they work: People who leave jobs and convert large employer-sponsored retirement accounts into IRAs are urged to set up "self-directed IRAs."

Self-directed IRAs are legal, but in the hands of scammers, they are used to divert funds from sound investments, such as mutual funds and bank CDs, into risky investments that might ultimately become worthless—such as fraudulent business ventures and some of the investments listed below.

Self-defense: If you want to establish a self-directed IRA, work with an adviser who is familiar with the tax complexities. Make sure both the investment and the person selling it are registered with the SEC.

OIL AND GAS LIMITED PARTNERSHIPS

How they work: Deals are promoted over the Internet or by phone.

Common ploys: A new drilling technology has been invented that can recover millions of gallons of oil left in old lines…the company pitching the partnership is operating on leased property next to a large reputable oil firm.

You buy $2,000 to $50,000 worth of shares of a limited partnership that promises attractive tax advantages. Once you invest, poor returns are blamed on equipment malfunctions and inclement weather. In some cases, the investment is a total sham—there is no well.

Self-defense: While some partnerships are reputable and offer big tax breaks, shady ones pop up when energy prices soar. Oil and gas exploration is so expensive that it's unlikely a little-known enterprise will strike it rich.

Check the company with your state's securities regulator. For links to state regulators, contact the North American Securities Administrators Association (202-737-0900, *www.na saa.org,* click on "Contact Your Regulator").

Ask to see the company's track record on past deals, and review offering documents with a financial adviser.

Be especially wary of offshore or foreign oil and gas ventures in which most wells are beyond the reach of state regulators.

EQUITY-INDEXED CDS

How they work: These CDs are sold by banks. Returns are tied to the average performance of a market index, such as the S&P 500, over a period of time, typically five years. The principal is FDIC-insured up to $100,000.

However, the CDs don't pay interest until maturity and carry penalties for early withdrawal. In rising stock markets, you don't get 100% of the gain of the index. In falling markets, you won't lose money, but you won't earn a return. One-year traditional CDs yield 4.5% risk-free, so it doesn't pay to tie up money for a long time based on the promise of only slightly higher returns.

Self-defense: Don't invest in an equity-indexed CD unless you are willing to tie up your money for several years. You can compare equity-indexed CDs at *www.personalyze.org*, a Web site by Premium Producers Group, a creator of software for financial professionals.

TIME-SHARE–TYPE AGREEMENTS

How they work: Investors are offered an opportunity to buy resort time-share units from a hotel company in Mexico or elsewhere in Central America. Investments generally start at $5,000. At the time you invest, you sign a contract leasing the time-share back to the company, which will act as the management and servicing agent. You're promised an annual return of 9% or more on your investment, plus a guarantee that the company will buy back the unit at your original purchase price after five years.

Often, the promised returns don't materialize. Then, when you want to get out of the deal, you learn that the time-share never existed or that the seller lacks the financial capacity to keep its repurchase promise.

Other variations on these agreements have involved investments in pay telephones, Web "booths" (in which users pay for Internet access) and mobile billboard advertising (for instance, on trucks and buses).

Self-defense: Make sure that any time-share is purchased from a licensed real estate agent. Review the terms with a real estate lawyer.

RECOVERY ROOM SCAMS

How they work: "Recovery" or "reload" telemarketers contact people who have already lost money on an investment and offer help—for a price. They frequently claim to be affiliated with the fraud division of an agency such as the FBI, IRS, the state district attorney's office or a public-advocacy group. They may offer to file the necessary complaint paperwork on your behalf and see to it that you are placed at the top of a list for victim reimbursement.

You are required to send a retainer—several thousand dollars. The firm promises a refund of the fee if it is unable to recover the lost funds.

The caller might appear legitimate because he knows a lot about your case, but he/she probably is working with the person who originally defrauded you on the investment.

Self-defense: To recover losses due to a fraudulent investment, contact an attorney or your state's securities regulator. Links can be found at *www.nasaa.org* (click on "Contact Your Regulator") or call 202-737-0900.

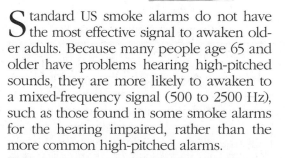

Fire Danger

Standard US smoke alarms do not have the most effective signal to awaken older adults. Because many people age 65 and older have problems hearing high-pitched sounds, they are more likely to awaken to a mixed-frequency signal (500 to 2500 Hz), such as those found in some smoke alarms for the hearing impaired, rather than the more common high-pitched alarms.

Smart: Use an interconnected system that includes an alarm in each bedroom to increase the chance of being awakened in case of fire.

Dorothy Bruck, PhD, associate professor, Victoria University, Melbourne, Australia.

Hotel Identity Theft Scam

Don't give credit card information over the phone to the front desk when staying at a hotel.

Scam: An identity thief calls a hotel, asking for a guest with a common name. He/she is then connected to the guest's room and pretends to be calling from the front desk. He says there's a problem with the credit card and asks the guest to verify the account number, expiration date and security code. The scammer then sells the information or uses it to run up charges.

Kevin Coffey, founder, Corporate Travel Safety, LLC, Calabasas, CA, which specializes in travel-safety seminars, *www.corporatetravelsafety.com* and *www. kevincoffey.com*.

Not All 800 Numbers Are Legitimate

Chuck Whitlock, a journalist whose work exposing scams has been featured on many television programs, including *Inside Edition* and *Extra*. He is author of several books about scams including *Mediscams: Dangerous Medical Practices and Health Care Frauds*. St. Martin's Griffin. *www.chuckwhitlock.com*.

Scammers frequently use call forwarding to send a phone call made to an 800 line to a 900 line at a different telephone company. The instant your phone call is connected, you start being charged as much as $25 per minute. Because this forwarding is done electronically and automatically, the phone companies don't know what is happening until the victims call to complain about the excessive charges on their phone bills. The criminals using this scam generally keep the forwarding in place for only a month or two, then move on to different phone numbers—but in just that short time, they can take in many thousands of dollars.

Self-defense: Call your phone company if you think that you have been scammed. Phone companies are not required to credit customers for these illicit charges, but they often will to avoid any bad publicity.

How to Win in Small-Claims Court— Mistakes Most People Make

Emily Doskow, an attorney in Alameda County, CA, who has served as a judge in small-claims court. She is legal editor at Nolo Press, publisher of do-it-yourself legal guides, and editor of *Everybody's Guide to Small-Claims Court*. Nolo.

In small-claims court, you can sue an individual or a company for money owed you without having the expense of hiring a lawyer. That's the good news. The bad news is that most people have little experience with small-claims courts and tend to make mistakes that can be damaging to their cases.

Here are six common mistakes and what to do instead...

PREPARATION

Mistake 1: Confusing "unfair" with "illegal." Just because someone makes you angry doesn't mean that you have a legal case against him/her. *You must be able to show that...*

• **You have suffered a loss.** You can't sue your neighbor just because she leaves garbage cans out every week for days after the trash has been collected. You've suffered no financial loss.

• **The defendant is legally responsible for your loss.** If your car is robbed while parked in a building's garage, your suit against the building owner won't succeed unless you can show that he promised that the garage would be secure.

Mistake 2: Being unable to explain how you calculated damages. If you're suing for the exact amount of an unpaid debt, this is clear-cut. If your damages are more complex, you should have detailed written calculations ready for the judge. Bring receipts and appraisal estimates to establish that your dollar figures are proper.

Example: You paid a garage to repair your car, but the problem soon recurred. Your calculations might indicate that you're suing for the amount it cost to have another garage redo the repair...plus the amount you paid for a tow...plus the amount you paid for a rental car while the work was being redone.

If you win your case, ask the judge to include the costs of court filing fees in the judgment as well.

Your state's maximum dollar limit for small-claims court suits could be as low as $1,500 or as high as $15,000. Ask the court clerk for details. Or use an on-line search engine, such as Google, to locate your state's small-claims court Web site—plug in your state name and "small-claims court" in the search window ("Connecticut small-claims court," for example).

If your damages are slightly above your state's limit, you can choose to waive the excess amount and sue for your state's small-claims limit to avoid the lawyer's bills, higher fees and more complex procedures of superior court. You may end up netting more in the end with less hassle.

Mistake 3: **Failing to properly serve the defendant.** The plaintiff must have a copy of the claim delivered to all named defendants after filing with the court clerk. Usually, for a small fee, the court clerk can do this for the plaintiff by mailing a certified letter with a return receipt requested. Some states, including Georgia, Mississippi and Montana, do not allow service through the mail...and most states do not consider a defendant served if he refuses to sign for the letter.

A plaintiff often shows up on the trial date ready to argue his case only to learn that the defendant wasn't properly served and the suit cannot proceed. It's usually possible to re-serve papers and reschedule the court date, but that means starting the process all

over again. It can take at least four weeks to set a court date after filing.

To avoid delays, call the court clerk a few weeks after the claim was mailed to make sure the defendant was served. If he/she wasn't, you might have to pay a sheriff or a private process server (typically $20 to $75) to hand the papers to the defendant. In some states, any adult other than the plaintiff can serve the papers. Ask the court clerk for details.

Important: Each defendant you name must receive his/her own copy of the claim, even if the defendants are family members or business partners.

DURING THE PROCEEDINGS

Mistake 4: **Rambling.** Launching into an extended speech detailing your troubled relationship with the other party—or making an emotional plea to the court to correct an injustice—will only muddle your legal argument and exasperate the judge. Stick to the facts. To the best of your abilities, calmly state what happened. If you're nervous about the presentation, you can read a prepared statement. If the judge wants more information, he'll ask for it.

Helpful: Try to determine which way the judge is leaning. If he seems to be on your side, shut your mouth and let him do the talking for you.

Mistake 5: **Being impolite to the other party.** If you let your anger at your courtroom opponent show, it could make you seem irrational. Don't interrupt this person to call him a liar, even if he is lying. Wait your turn...calmly state that much of what was just said is untrue...then do your best to prove it.

Mistake 6: **Trouble with witnesses.** If you have friends or family members appearing as witnesses, insist that they try to give an impression of impartiality—and make sure they are there on time. Don't make the judge wait while you dash out to the car or the diner next door to get your witness. It's best to have a witness appear in person, but if that's not possible, you can bring in a sworn statement or affidavit.

473

Wise Ways to Protect Yourself from Muggers, Carjackers, Pickpockets And More

Roger Shenkle, president of Survival Solutions, a security consulting firm, Box 476, Gambill, MD 21054. He is a former US Army counterintelligence agent.

There are more than a half million robberies in the US each year—and that figure doesn't include the 150,000 stolen purses and wallets…30,000 carjackings…and nearly 250,000 rapes, attempted rapes and sexual assaults. The numbers add up to almost one million victims.

How to protect yourself…

MUGGERS AND RAPISTS

Maintaining "situational awareness"—that is military-speak for paying careful attention to what's going on around you—is the best way to avoid street crime. People get so caught up in their own lives that they don't spot danger until it is too late.

Situational awareness is especially important in places *between* the places where you spend time—the deserted parking lot you traverse to get from the mall to your car…or the empty stairwell you descend to get from your office to the street.

When you leave a building and enter a parking lot or garage, look for lingerers. If you see anyone suspicious, go back and ask someone to walk you to your car. If no one is available, call the police and ask them to send a cruiser. It's usually a mistake to try to rush to your car because there often is not time to unlock the door, start the engine and drive away.

When you're in a potentially dangerous area, walk with a quick, confident gait. This makes you less appealing to criminals.

Caution: If the choice is between, say, walking confidently through a dangerous-looking group of teens or reversing course—it's best to reverse course.

Other high-risk situations…

●**Jogging.** Don't wear headphones unless you're certain your jogging route is safe. Headphones will reduce your ability to hear danger. When jogging on a sidewalk, go against the flow of traffic so a vehicle can't follow behind you. On city sidewalks, stay close to the road, not near buildings, to make it harder for a predator to jump you from a doorway. Always avoid secluded areas.

●**ATMs.** After dark or in crime-prone areas, go to an ATM that is located inside a store—not one that is visible from the street. Don't assume that an ATM is safe just because it is in a locked bank vestibule accessible only with an ATM card. Muggers carry stolen cards so that they can buzz themselves in and corner victims.

●**Unfamiliar locations.** If you don't know whether a certain part of town is safe, call the local police department's non-emergency number. They will tell you what neighborhoods you should avoid.

Important: If you're mugged, hand over your money immediately. Try to escape only if your instincts inform you that you might be attacked even if you do turn over your cash. If you do decide to flee, try a diversionary tactic. Throw some cash so that the mugger has to choose between pursuing you or retrieving the money. If your assailant tries to force you into a car in a public place, you're usually better off resisting right there rather than being driven to a more deserted site.

CARJACKERS

Most carjackings happen when vehicles are stopped at red lights or stop signs. If you're driving in a neighborhood that makes you uncomfortable, lock all your doors and roll up your windows. Also, turn off the radio to cut down on any distractions. When you come to a stop, leave enough room between your car and the one ahead so that you can maneuver quickly. Choose the lane farthest from the curb—you'll have more warning if someone on the sidewalk heads toward your car.

If you think you're about to be carjacked and no other cars are around, run the red light, blast your horn and flash your lights.

If a carjacker is beside your vehicle with a gun drawn, let him/ her have the car—aside from the engine block, no part of a car is likely to stop a bullet.

If confronted when you're unlocking your car, throw your keys to the side and run so that the pursuer must choose between following you and taking your car.

Carjacking gangs sometimes use a "bump-and-rob" technique—they cause a minor car accident, then steal the victim's car when he gets out to exchange insurance information.

Self-defense: If you're involved in a minor accident in a solitary area, stay in your car, keep the engine running and yell through the closed window for the other driver to follow you. Drive to the nearest police station or a well-lit, crowded area—an open gas station is a good option.

If possible, write down the other vehicle's license plate number and call the police on your cell phone to report the accident and where you're heading.

PICKPOCKETS AND PURSE SNATCHERS

A wallet is best kept in a front pants pocket. If you wrap a thick rubber band around it, you're more likely to feel friction if someone tries to slide it out. A purse should be held firmly against the body, not allowed to dangle freely. A fanny pack should be worn in front, with the zipper closed and secured with a safety pin.

Backpacks are the least secure and should be held against the chest when in high-crime areas.

The most secure spot to keep credit cards, passports or other light valuables is in a flat pouch worn under your shirt and attached to a chain or string around your neck.

The most common place to get pickpocketed is on a train or subway car while it is stopped at a station. The thief takes the wallet and makes a quick escape before the train departs. The victim usually is miles away before he notices his wallet missing.

From the time that you board a train or subway until the doors close, keep a hand in the pocket that contains your wallet.

Diversions are another common pickpocket technique.

Example: Someone bumps into you—or stops short in front of you so that you bump into him—while a partner picks your pocket.

Whenever you're jostled, always check for your wallet.

Be Financially Prepared for Any Disaster

Nigel B. Taylor, a CFP in Santa Monica, CA. His wealth-management firm, Taylor & Associates, serves individuals, families and businesses. He is former president of the Los Angeles Society of the Institute of Certified Financial Planners. His Web site is *www.protectassets.com.*

If you had just 10 minutes to evacuate your home during a natural disaster, what would you take with you? Where would you get cash if ATM and credit card networks were down? Would your insurance be adequate to rebuild your home?

Obviously, the safety of you and your family is your first concern—but ensuring your financial security is second. *As a certified financial planner based in disaster-prone Southern California, here's what I tell my clients...*

●**Keep enough cash in the house for a weekend away.** It can take that long after a disaster for merchants to be able to accept credit or bank cards.

Also keep $300 in one-dollar bills on hand.

Reason: Stores may not be able to make change. After the last earthquake in this area, some people had to hand over $20 bills to pay for a carton of milk or a bottle of water.

●**Keep important items in a secure,** fire-safe box near the front door—perhaps in a coat closet. (Keep all original documents in a safe-deposit box or a fireproof safe.) The box should be lightweight so that you can easily carry it to your vehicle in an emergency. *The box should contain...*

• Legal papers. Copies of titles to your home and vehicles, marriage and birth certificates, passports, insurance policies, military and medical records, Social Security cards, driver's license numbers, wills and powers of attorney.

• Extra supplies of medications if your doctor will prescribe them. Rotate them monthly so that the newest medication always is available. Also keep lists of medications, doctors' phone numbers, etc. People who have extreme allergies should include Epi-Pen injectors.

• Financial records. Copies of credit card and employee benefit statements, household budget, tax returns for the last three years, contact and account numbers for financial accounts.

• Key to your safe-deposit box, if you have a box.

• Extra checks.

• Inventory of your household possessions, including professional appraisals for valuables, such as jewelry and antiques, and receipts for the cost of major home improvements, like kitchen remodeling or a new deck.

Helpful: Use a digital camera or camcorder to record your home's contents for insurance purposes. Go room by room, giving an audio or written description of the approximate cost, condition and age of each piece of furniture, appliance and decorative element—even towels and clothing. Send a copy on DVD or CD to your insurance agent, as well as copies of receipts for big-ticket items, to expedite future insurance claims.

While many documents may also be stored in a bank safe-deposit box, keep in mind that your local bank could be closed for several days or weeks after a disaster.

Backup plan: Scan documents into a single electronic file, and save it on your computer hard drive. Also, regularly back up the file to a removable flash storage device that you can take with you in the event of a disaster. These portable storage devices are the size of a cigarette lighter and plug into your computer's USB port. They are available

for about $6 to $75, depending on its capacity, in electronics or office-supply stores. You can buy a scanner for under $50, or have your documents scanned at the office-supply store.

• **Maintain an emergency fund.** Keep three months' to a year's worth of basic living expenses—rent/mortgage, food, insurance, etc.—in safe, liquid investments, such as short-term CDs and short-term municipal bonds. This will protect you from a disaster as well as a loss of income—if your place of work is damaged, you may be without a paycheck for some time.

Also: Recent laws have forced all of the financial institutions to implement disaster-continuity plans. Obtain copies of these plans to learn how to access your money after a disaster.

• **Make sure your homeowner's insurance includes appropriate coverage for disaster.** Depending on where you live, you might need flood insurance through the US government's National Flood Insurance Program (annual premiums of $300* and up) and riders for hurricanes and/or earthquakes if you can purchase them ($2,500 per year and up for a $200,000 home with a $10,000 deductible). Such riders are expensive, but losing everything because you're not covered is more expensive.

Smart: Increase your deductible to $3,500. Premiums drop at that level, making riders more affordable. For more information, contact FEMA at *www.fema.gov.*

Make sure that you have "replacement value" coverage that pays you the amount necessary to replace articles with ones of similar quality at current prices. Also, check that you will be reimbursed for living expenses if your home is damaged and uninhabitable.

Cost: Less than $100 in annual premiums for $10,000 of coverage.

If you have a home office, you will need a commercial policy to cover damage to business-related equipment. (Homeowners' policies do not cover home-based businesses.) Many homeowners' policies limit replacement

*All rates subject to change.

of computer equipment to $2,500. You can double this coverage for $20 to $30 per year.

Helpful resources: *Disaster Recovery: A Guide to Financial Issues,* free from the Red Cross, *www.redcross.org/services/disaster/be prepared/finrecovery.* FEMA also provides a free guide *Are You Ready?,* which has helpful information on disaster preparation.

Be Your Own Private Eye

Steven K. Brown, a former FBI agent and current owner of Millennial Investigative Agency, a private investigation company in Ponte Vedra Beach, FL, *www.stevenkbrown.com.* He is author of *The Complete Idiot's Guide to Private Investigating.* Alpha.

Looking for an old love or maybe a long-lost friend? Suspicious about a potential employee? Want to check up on your doctor or lawyer?

I have been tracking down people for 31 years—first as an FBI agent and then as a private investigator. *Here are the most effective ways to find people, largely using the Internet...*

CHASE DOWN CLASSMATES

• **Classmates.com** compiles contact information on graduates. Its database currently contains information on about 60 million people from more than 200,000 elementary schools, high schools and colleges. Their database goes back more than 50 years.

Cost: Free to browse names...$39* annually if you want to contact classmates directly.

Alternative: Locate your school's Web site to get the alumni relations officer's e-mail address or phone number. He/she usually will forward messages to former classmates at your request. Or you can use the site's link to your school's alumni magazine, which lists contact information for your class's secretary, who can often help.

*Prices subject to change.

FIND A LOST FRIEND

• **Internet search engines offer tremendous power to locate people.** Conduct an advanced search on several search engines using the person's full name and any unique details. For example, try including a middle initial...city of residence...or occupation. The engines will search through millions of sites for any references to that person.

Important: For best results, use more than one search engine. *Below I've listed some of my favorites...*

- *www.google.com*
- *www.looksmart.com*
- *www.lycos.com*
- *www.webcrawler.com*

• **National white-page phone directories help you locate a person's name, address and phone number.** *My favorite free sites...*

- *http://directory.superpages.com/people.jsp*
- *www.whitepages.com*
- *www.canada411.com* (for Canadian directories only)
- *www.freeality.com/findet.htm*

Information on free sites tends to be a year old. If you think the person has moved, try a paid site—they are updated more frequently.

My favorite: *http://555-1212.com.*

Cost: $11.95* for 100 searches.

Unpublished versus unlisted numbers: An unpublished number is not printed in phone directories, but it is available from an operator if you request it. If a number is unlisted, operators don't have access to it. However, most operators will verify the address of a person who has an unlisted telephone number, so that you can write to him.

• **Dig up someone's e-mail address.** *My favorite free sites...*

- *www.theultimates.com/email*
- *www.iaf.net*

• **Search publications.** *www.findarticles. com,* owned by the search engine Look Smart, allows you to search 3.5 million

*Prices subject to change.

articles in 700 newspapers and magazines. Type the person's name into the search box, and click "Look."

• **Verify a death.** The Social Security Administration's Master Death Index contains more than 80 million names and records on the deceased. *http://ssdi.genealogy.roots web.com.*

CHECK UP ON YOUR DOCTOR

Disciplinary records often are available by calling your state's department of health and asking for the division that deals with medical disciplinary proceedings. Generally, you will be given a list of the actions and malpractice claims against the doctor. If you want more details, you have to request them in writing.

All the state licensing boards usually can be located through the American Medical Association (AMA) at *www.ama-assn.org/ ama/pub/category/2645.html.* However, the AMA's main Web site, *www.ama-assn.org,* also provides a wealth of information about individual doctors, including their training and specialties.

• **Federation of State Medical Boards** is a convenient nonprofit clearinghouse that allows you to find out about disciplinary actions taken against a doctor by medical boards. *www.docinfo.org.* Just go to "Order Options," and click on "Get Immediate Results" or "Mail in Request."

Cost: $9.95* per report.

EXAMINE YOUR LAWYER

Backgrounds of as well as disciplinary actions against lawyers are available from...

• **American Bar Association (ABA),** which publishes a Web link to the disciplinary agency in each state. Here you also can verify that your attorney has been appropriately licensed. Some state ABA Web sites will list disciplinary actions taken against lawyers. Others do not list these actions on their Web sites, but they will make the information available when you request it

Prices subject to change.

in writing. *www.abanet.org/cpr/regulation/ scpd/disciplinary.html.* Free.

• **Martindale-Hubbell,** a service providing biographies of practicing lawyers. They include explanations of their experience, specialties, education and major clients. Each attorney is rated by his peers for legal ability and ethics. *www.martindale.com.* Click on "Lawyer Locator." Free.

RUN A CRIMINAL-RECORDS CHECK

There is no single comprehensive government database of criminals that is accessible to the public. *However, you still can investigate prospective employees, business partners and household help...*

• **The Federal Bureau of Prisons** provides information on all current and former federal prisoners since 1982. *www.bop.gov.* Click on "Inmate Locator" to search. Free.

• **The Federal Bureau of Investigation** provides links to databases with the names and addresses of convicted sex offenders in each state. *www.fbi.gov/hq/cid/cac/registry. htm.* Free.

• **Criminal information.** Most states will provide you with some criminal records, but you must request them in writing. They usually cost less than $20. The amount and detail of information vary by state. For example, Florida offers a database of any current and past criminal on-line. And, Utah discloses only information about sex offenders. Even when a state does not make information available on-line, you often can get Web access to county courthouse records to learn about convictions. Do a search for the county government.

• **Background Check Gateway.** This company provides telephone numbers and Web sites, where you can learn each state's policy for making information available. *www.backgroundcheckgateway.com.* Click on "Step 3: Start Your Investigation," then "Criminal History: Does He Have a Criminal Record?" Free.

CATCH UP WITH VETERANS

• **The US Department of Veterans Affairs** will forward a letter to any veteran registered with them. Contact your local office. Free.

● **The US Department of Defense** will supply the mailing addresses for servicemen and women on active duty in the US Armed Forces. Free to immediate family members and government officials. For all others, $3.50* per inquiry. *www.usa.gov/topics/loca tors.shtml.*

● **VetFriends.com**—a national military membership organization—helps both past and present servicemen and -women find one another. Enroll on its Web site, and receive e-mail when someone from your unit becomes a member. Click on "Start Here." Free. For an annual fee of $39*, you can search the organization's registry and contact others.

● **The National Archives and Records Administration** provides much information, like dates of service...decorations... date and location of death...place of burial, on deceased servicemen and -women. This information generally is free but may incur a charge depending on the search. *www.ar chives.gov/veterans.*

LEARN ABOUT
YOUR NEIGHBORS

Public records kept by your town and county can tell you how much your neighbor paid for his home. And, thanks to the Internet, you can search those records confidentially.

Available: Date and amount of the last sale...who sold it...address where the property tax bill is sent. In some states, you also can get tax and property assessment information.

● **Links to county tax assessors records** from around the country are available at *www.netronline.com/public_records.htm.* Just click on your state, then your county. They also are available at *http://searchenginez. com/real_estate_usa.html* (scroll down to "Property Ownership—State & County")... and *www.blackbookonline.info* (click on "State Records," then your state, then "Real Estate Ownership"). Costs vary.

*Prices subject to change.

The Big Money Rip-Offs Facing Seniors Today

Sheryl Garrett, CFP, who was recognized by *Investment Advisor* as one of the 25 most influential people in financial planning for four straight years (*www. garrettplanningnetwork.com*). Based in Shawnee Mission, KS, she is author of several books, including *Personal Finance Workbook for Dummies.* Wiley.

Seniors are prime targets for scammers. Many have amassed impressive financial resources, while many others are struggling with the challenges of living on a fixed income. Scammers often jump in to exploit this situation. *Biggest rip-offs targeting seniors...*

MEDICARE POLICIES

Rip-off: **Unscrupulous insurance agents misrepresent Medicare policies.**

Medicare beneficiaries have a bewildering array of health insurance options now. They can choose from dozens of "Part D" prescription drug plans to supplement Medicare, and they can opt out of traditional Medicare and enroll in private Medicare Advantage Plans for their medical and drug coverage. *This is fertile territory for scam artists...*

● **Medicare Advantage.** To reap hefty commissions, some insurance agents push seniors into buying a type of private policy called a Medicare Advantage Plan without explaining the limitations of the plans.

Examples: You may use only doctors and hospitals in the plan's network...you may lose supplemental coverage from a former employer's plan. They've even been known to sign up people without their knowledge.

How: The agent says that he/she needs the senior's Social Security number, and the senior gives it to him. The agent then uses the number to enroll the senior.

● **Part D.** Posing as "Medicare representatives," unscrupulous insurance agents call and ask you about the Part D plan that you have already signed up for. Since you know that you do have Part D, you can be tricked into thinking that it's safe to give personal information to the caller, such as your Social Security number, which the scammer then uses for identity theft.

• **Drug discount cards.** An individual may be offered a plan from a licensed insurance agent that costs less than Medicare Part D, but the agent does not disclose that the plan provides much less coverage than Medicare.

Self-defense: Before buying any Medicare-related plan, card or policy, contact your state insurance department. Ask if the agent is licensed, if the product is legitimate and whether there have been any complaints against the agent or the company. If you have been fraudulently enrolled in a Medicare Advantage Plan, contact the State Health Insurance Assistance Programs (SHIP) at *www.shiptalk.org.* (Click on "Find a Counselor.") Also contact your state insurance department and attorney general's office, which can take action against agents for sales abuses.

TODAY'S PONZI SCHEMES

Rip-off: **Investment deals that are really Ponzi schemes.**

In a Ponzi scheme (named for a 1920s con artist), you are offered the opportunity to put money into a sophisticated investment—such as real estate, oil and gas leases, promissory notes for a start-up company or housing for the homeless—that will pay very high returns. You invest, and soon you're getting statements and the promised returns. But after a while, the statements and the payments stop coming. You can't get your money out because the scammer has disappeared.

There never really was an investment. You were paid with money that later participants "invested" in the scheme.

Beware: There are a variety of Ponzi schemes being used right now. *Examples...*

• **In New Jersey,** hundreds of investors so far have been defrauded of a total of $90 million because they invested in a real estate scheme to supposedly renovate and maintain certain rental properties. Investors are promised annual returns of 15% to 20%.

But: The properties don't exist.

• **In Washington State,** two oil firms falsely advertised themselves as being actively involved in the energy sector in Southeast Asia. To date, 200 people have invested a total of $54 million.

Self-defense: Be especially suspicious of an investment company that claims to be registered in one state, physically exists in a second state and sells to investors in a third state. It's likely the company does not exist.

Always check with your state securities regulator to verify an investment company's registration. You can find your state's regulator through the North American Securities Administration Association (202-737-0900, *www.nasaa.org/home/index.cfm*). At its Web site, click on the "Contact Your Regulator" link and the state where the business is supposed to be registered. Or go to the Financial Industry Regulatory Authority site (*www.finra.org*) to look up a securities firm or broker.

If you think you may be a victim of a Ponzi scheme, contact your state attorney general's office.

HIGH-YIELD INVESTMENTS

Rip-off: **International investment schemes that "offer" extremely high yields in a relatively short period of time.**

The con artist purports to have access to "bank guarantees" that he can buy at a discount and sell at a premium, producing exceptional returns. To make the schemes more enticing, con artists often refer to the "guarantees" as being issued by the world's "prime banks."

Legal documents associated with such schemes often require victims to enter into nondisclosure agreements, offer returns on investments in "a year and a day" and claim to use forms required by the International Chamber of Commerce (ICC). In fact, the ICC has issued a warning to all potential investors that no such investments exist.

Self-defense: Reject any investment that offers unusually high yields by buying and selling anything issued by "prime banks."

FORECLOSURE RESCUES

Rip-off: **Claiming to be able to prevent foreclosures.**

The scammer makes misleading promises that a victim's home will be permanently saved from foreclosure by signing the title over to the scammer. The victim ultimately loses his home, along with the money he paid to the scammer, who walks away with the title and equity in the home.

Because foreclosure filings are public information, scammers target already troubled home owners, repeatedly contacting them by phone or mail. *Self-defense…*

• **Check the credentials,** background and references of anyone offering to buy your home to save it from foreclosure.

• **Take your time.** Don't sign anything without checking with your lender. Never sign away ownership of your property to settle a default.

• **Have an attorney or a financial professional,** such as an accountant, review the paperwork before you sign anything.

• **Don't let anyone persuade you to cut off communication with your lender.** The lender should be your first contact if you're struggling to make your mortgage payments.

Beware of Scam Contacts "From the Government"

Increasingly brazen scam artists pose as being from the government (IRS, Social Security Administration, local police or courthouse) to cheat victims out of money and confidential information.

How: They offer to help with a problem (such as with one's taxes, or an "outstanding violation") or to provide something (a refund, extra benefit payment) if the victim pays a fee and/or provides confidential information (perhaps to "confirm identity").

Self-defense: Unsolicited contacts from government agencies are almost always scams. To find out for sure, call the agency at its publicly published phone number and ask.

Mark Huffman, contributing editor, *Consumer Affairs.com,* a free consumer news publication, Washington, DC.

To Ward Off A Dog Attack

If you encounter an unleashed dog that shows signs of aggression, stand still, be quiet and avoid eye contact. Running away may encourage its instinct to chase and attack. When the dog calms down, wait for it to walk away, then back away slowly. If the dog continues to approach, assert verbal dominance by giving commands such as "no," "sit" and "go home." If the dog still advances, try "feeding" him a jacket or other garment. If the dog bites, resist the instinct to pull back—it will cause the dog to bite harder to hold on and worsen any injury. If a bite breaks the skin, cleanse the wound with soap and water and get medical advice —especially if the dog is a stray.

UC Berkeley Wellness Letter, 6 Trowbridge Dr., Bethel, CT 06801.

To Avoid ID Theft Don't Make These Mistakes On the Internet

James Christiansen, former senior vice president of information security at Visa International and former chief information security officer at General Motors. He is author of several books on Internet security, including *Internet Survival Guide: Protecting Your Financial Information.* Sheltonix.

High-tech thieves can use the Internet to gather the account numbers and other personal data they need to steal your identity. You could be at risk if you shop, pay bills or access your bank accounts on-line—or even if you store personal data, such as your Social Security number or credit card numbers, on your own computer.

Here's how to steer clear of the Internet missteps that can lead to identity theft. *These include...*

Mistake: Sending e-mails that contain confidential information.

Even if the recipient of your e-mail is reliable enough to be trusted with your sensitive information (Social Security number, driver's license number, credit card number, date of birth, mother's maiden name), others could gain access to your message as well. E-mails do not transfer instantly from our computer to our recipient's computer. They make stops at several points along the way, where they could be read.

Alternately, if a criminal gained access to your computer or the message recipient's computer, he/she could find your e-mail stored in memory.

Self-defense: Convey sensitive information over the phone, not the Internet. If you *must* e-mail sensitive information, use the encryption program WinZip E-Mail Companion ($19.95, *www.winzip.com*).

Mistake: Providing personal details on social networking Web sites or chat groups.

The Internet is a great place to converse with people who share your interests, but sharing too much information could put you in danger. A criminal might decide that you make a good target for identity theft—or worse.

Self-defense: Keep personal details to a minimum when on-line. Never mention your address, phone number or financial institutions with which you have accounts. Use a nickname. Withhold personal information even in private e-mail exchanges with people you meet through the Internet. These people might not be what they seem.

Mistake: Downloading free programs from the Internet or clicking on pop-ups.

When you download a program from the Internet, you could unknowingly load spyware onto your computer in the process. This spyware could give a scammer access to any information you type into or save on your computer. Clicking on a pop-up could create similar problems. (There often is no way to tell the safe pop-ups from the unsafe ones, so the best policy is to skip them all.)

Self-defense: Download software from the Internet only if you're confident in the integrity of the site providing the program.

Internet security programs can help prevent spyware from reaching your computer and remove it if it does. ZoneAlarm Internet Security Suite is the most reliable and comprehensive ($49.95, 877-966-5221, *www.zone alarm.com*). However, ZoneAlarm has been experiencing problems with Microsoft's latest operating system, Windows Vista. Another good choice is Microsoft Windows Live OneCare that includes virus control, firewall and automatic backup software ($49.95 per year, *www.onecare.live.com*). Free spyware protection programs are available as well, and can do a reasonable job. The best of these include Ad-Aware Free (*www.lavasoftusa.com*) and Spybot Search & Destroy (*www.safer-networking.org*).

Best: Ask your Internet service provider if access to an Internet security program is included in your monthly fee.

If you have only one spyware program, download another one and run it every few weeks as a backup—no single security program catches every problem.

Mistake: Assuming e-mail messages are from who they seem to be from.

Scammers can make e-mail messages appear to have been sent by anyone, including people and businesses you know.

Examples: You receive an e-mail that appears to be from your bank. It asks whether you made a particular transaction and warns that you must respond immediately if you did not. Or, you receive an e-mail that appears to come from the IRS. It says you will be audited if you do not reply to the message quickly, then asks for your Social Security number or other personal information.

Self-defense: Be very suspicious of e-mails claiming to be from financial institutions or the IRS, particularly if these messages ask you to enter passwords, account numbers or Social Security numbers (or steer you to Web sites that ask for any of these things). These messages are likely to be from scammers. Instead, look up the phone number of the company or agency that the e-mail claims to be from (do not trust the phone number that might be included in the e-mail) and call to confirm the validity of the message.

If you receive an e-mail message that seems to be from a friend featuring an Internet link or picture and a simple message such as "you have to see this," it might have been sent by a scammer. If you click the link, it could load spyware onto your computer, opening the door to identity theft. Do not click the link or open the picture until you have contacted your friend and confirmed that he sent the note.

Mistake: **Entering important data or passwords into a public computer.**

The public computers in libraries and coffeehouses are often contaminated with spyware.

Self-defense: Assume that everything you type on these computers is being recorded. Never use public computers to make on-line purchases or to do on-line banking. Do not even check your e-mail—a scammer could learn your user name and password and gain access to personal information stored in your e-mail files.

Mistake: **Trusting Web sites that have weak security.**

Most Internet companies that accept credit card numbers or other sensitive data work very hard to keep this information secure. Unfortunately, some sites' security measures fall short, increasing the odds that a criminal could be monitoring your transaction and stealing your information.

Self-defense: Do not enter your credit card number or any other important data into a Web site unless its Web address begins "https," not just "http." The "s" indicates an added level of security. A small picture of a closed lock should appear on the Web address line as well.

Note: Never enter confidential information onto a site if you clicked on it from an e-mail, even if it has "https." Always type in a URL.

Mistake: **Picking obvious passwords.**

Scammers have software that can help them guess common passwords. If your password is a date, a name, a word or a repeating or progressive series of letters or numbers, such as "zzzz" or "2468," it could be cracked if a high-tech criminal targets you. If you use the same password for many accounts, this could give the criminal wide access to your personal and financial information.

Self-defense: The most secure passwords are multiple-word phrases. If the site permits, these should include numbers or symbols, such as "my2dogsareyellow" or "Ilikeham$alad."

Select phrases that are memorable to you. Use different ones for each account, and don't write them down near your computer. A program called RoboForm (*www.roboform.com*) provides an encrypted computer "password safe" that can remember up to 10 passwords for you for free. RoboForm Pro, which costs $29.95, can remember more than 10 passwords.

Walk Along Roads Safely

Walking is a superior exercise and the best for many seniors. But more than 170,000 pedestrians are injured walking along roads each year, and more than 4,700 died in 2006 (the last year for which information is available).

Safety: Walk on the sidewalk. If there is none, walk facing oncoming traffic.

To be more visible to drivers: Wear light-colored clothing and reflective accessories at night, and stay clear of obstacles such as parked cars and hedges. Cross streets only where drivers expect you to, at corners and crosswalks.

John Pucher, PhD, professor of urban planning, Rutgers University, New Brunswick, NJ.

How Safe Are Plastics? What to Do about Dangerous Water Bottles, Food Containers, More

Patricia Hunt, PhD, reproductive biologist and geneticist and Meyer Distinguished Professor in the School of Molecular BioSciences at Washington State University in Pullman. She is a recipient of the 2007 SciAm 50 Award (*Scientific American's* list of top 50 researchers).

The National Toxicology Program, a federal health agency, acknowledged for the first time in April that a chemical found in thousands of plastic products, including water bottles, is of "some concern."

The chemical, *bisphenol A* (BPA), is known to be an "endocrine disruptor." It has hormonelike effects that could potentially increase the risk for breast and prostate cancers. Studies indicate that it also might be linked to miscarriages, early puberty in girls and birth defects.

To learn more about the effects of plastics on foods and beverages, *Bottom Line/Personal* spoke with Patricia Hunt, PhD, a noted reproductive biologist and geneticist at Washington State University...

• What types of products contain BPA?

BPA, or chemicals that might have similar effects (such as *phthalates*), are found in some sports bottles, as well as some baby bottles, food wraps and storage containers. BPA also is used in the resins that coat the insides of many food and beverage cans. In addition, it is in a variety of plastic products, such as compact discs and eyeglass lenses.

• How dangerous is it?

Traditionally, the potential danger of a chemical has been assessed in dose response studies—this assumes that the higher the dose, the greater the risk. Thus small amounts usually are not cause for alarm.

BPA is different because it has powerful, hormonelike effects. Like the body's natural hormones, even trace amounts can produce profound changes in the body.

We entered into this area of research purely by accident. We were studying eggs from normal female mice when we suddenly noticed a huge increase in abnormalities. It turned out that our laboratory mice were being exposed to BPA—because their plastic cages and water bottles had been inadvertently damaged when they were washed with the wrong detergent.

About 10% of their eggs were chromosomally abnormal. (In mice not exposed to BPA, only 1% of eggs were abnormal.)

It's not yet known if humans exposed to BPA face similar threats. We suspect that they do. We do know that phthalates, chemicals that make plastics soft and pliable, have been linked to genital defects in newborn boys.

Exposure to chemicals such as BPA and phthalates that have hormonelike effects hasn't been conclusively shown to cause cancer. But the evidence is getting stronger that they might cause a variety of cancers or reproductive system abnormalities, including polycystic ovary disease.

Infants (and fetuses) face the highest risks from these chemicals because their brains and reproductive tracts are still developing. A bill was introduced in the Senate to ban BPA from all products intended for babies, including baby bottles.

• How much BPA is safe?

No one knows. The Environmental Protection Agency has estimated that an exposure of up to 50 micrograms (mcg) of BPA per kilogram of body weight per day is safe. But that calculation is based on older animal studies, and more recent studies suggest that much lower levels of BPA—as little as 0.025 mcg per kilogram of weight—induce a variety of adverse effects in rats and mice.

Researchers from the Centers for Disease Control and Prevention analyzed urine samples from 2,517 Americans six years of age and older. They found traces of BPA in nearly 93% of the population.

•Which products contain BPA?

It's hard to know. Some plastic containers are stamped with recycling codes that indicate the type of plastic used, but recycling codes are only a partial guide. For example, polycarbonate plastic—which contains BPA—doesn't have a specific recycling code. If it is coded, it will be stamped with the number "7." But this is the code for "mixed plastics," so seeing a "7" doesn't tell you for certain that the product contains BPA.

Some plastics are considered safer than others because they don't react as readily to heat or harsh cleaners. These include *high-density polyethylene* (used in milk and water jugs and marked "2")...*low-density polyethylene* (used in produce bags and some food storage containers and marked "4")...and *polypropylene* (used in yogurt containers and some food storage containers and marked "5").

I'm not sure what to say about *polyethylene terephthalate* (commonly abbreviated PET and marked with the number "1"). It is better than polycarbonate, but there is some concern that it may leach *antimony trioxide* (a heavy metal used in the production of plastic).

•Should we stop using disposable water bottles?

Many people already have. I have switched to Klean Kanteen stainless steel containers when I want to take water with me (530-345-3275, *www.kleankanteen.com*). Nalgene, an outdoor-products company that makes refillable bottles, already has phased out polycarbonates—the company now produces sports bottles from polymers that don't contain BPA (800-625-4327, *www.nalgene-outdoor.com*). Other companies also will be introducing BPA-free plastics in the months or years to come.

If you like to take water with you and prefer lightweight plastics, look for those made with polyethylene or polypropylene—or that say "BPA-free" on the label.

•Is it safe to microwave food in plastic containers or plastic wraps?

I'm not certain that anyone can tell you whether or not it is "safe." I can tell you that I don't do it. Heat is an invitation for chemicals to migrate out of plastic. We've all noticed the "plastic-y" taste that is sometimes present when we microwave foods in take-out containers or some storage containers. What we're tasting is chemicals. My rule at home is that plastics never go in the microwave. I also throw out any plastic items that are showing signs of wear.

•What about the washing of plastic containers?

Wash them by hand, and use only a mild dishwashing solution. The heat in many dishwashers is too hot for plastics—it accelerates the rate at which they break down and release chemicals. Strong detergents also can cause plastics to release more chemicals.

•Should we avoid canned foods?

Unfortunately, consumers can't know which products contain BPA, and for most people, it's unrealistic to give up all canned foods.

Be aware that once foods are canned, they're often subjected to high-heat sterilization. If a can is lined with a BPA-containing resin, the heat will cause more BPA to leach into the food. This means that canned foods might contain more BPA than, say, canned sodas. But this is just speculative at this point. In my opinion, consumers should demand that information about the lining be disclosed on the can label.

•What about baby bottles?

Formula-fed babies are potentially exposed to a lot of BPA. It's present in some baby bottles and in the linings of liquid and powdered formula containers. Federal officials have started asking manufacturers if they test routinely for BPA, but this is all very recent.

Right now, the best choices are baby bottles made from glass or BPA-free plastic, such as BornFree bottles.

•Are other plastics a risk?

We don't know. BPA is present in all sorts of plastics, including swing seats and PVC plumbing. The assumption has been that our main exposure to BPA is from foods and beverages. However, a new study suggests that foods alone can't account for the BPA levels in the US population.

It's possible—but not certain—that we absorb BPA through the skin from environmental exposure, such as dust or via bathwater that has traveled through PVC pipes.

Relief from Jellyfish Stings

Jellyfish Squish is a topical antidote that relieves the pain of a jellyfish sting within minutes of application. The product was invented by a Savannah, Georgia, entrepreneur in consultation with marine biologists and has proven in field testing to be more effective than home remedies, such as meat tenderizer or baking soda. More than 85% of sting victims tested reported relief within five minutes of applying the product.

Cost: $9.99 for a four-ounce spray bottle. Coastal Solutions, 912-353-3368, *www.jelly fishsquish.com.*

BJ Fisher, director of health and safety, American Lifeguard Association, Vienna, VA. *www.american lifeguard.com.*

Medical ID Theft Is on the Rise... Very Dangerous to Your Health and to Your Wallet

Joy Pritts, JD, founding director of the Center on Medical Record Rights and Privacy at Georgetown University's Health Policy Institute, Washington, DC. She has testified before Congress on privacy and the use of medical information, and is the prime author of *Your Medical Record Rights*, a series of publications available free on-line that explain patients' rights to their medical records in each of the 50 states and DC. *http://ihcrp.georgetown.edu/privacy/records.html.*

A growing form of identity theft known as medical ID theft can devastate victims' finances. It also can compromise

their medical records—and even put their health at risk.

With medical ID theft, criminals access victims' medical records rather than their bank or credit records. Medical records contain victims' Social Security numbers and credit card numbers (assuming that the victims have used credit cards to pay medical charges), so the criminal can make fraudulent charges and open accounts in victims' names, just as with standard ID theft.

The difference is that medical identity thieves also gain access to victims' health insurance policy information and medical histories. They can use this information to forge insurance ID cards that can be sold to uninsured people in need of expensive medical treatments.

The ID thief's "customers" receive medical treatment under the victim's name, Social Security number and health insurance policy, then disappear. Bills for co-payments or uncovered procedures are sent to the victim, who must sort out the mess.

GROWING PROBLEM

Medical identity theft currently is less common than standard financial identity theft—but it is becoming more common, in part because many health-care facilities do a poor job of protecting patient records. At least 13% of health-care providers have experienced a data breach, according to a 2008 survey. The ongoing digitalization of medical records will only make it easier for tech-savvy thieves to steal medical identities.

For victims, dealing with medical identity theft can be even more daunting than dealing with conventional identity theft. Victims not only must convince service providers and collection agencies that bills are fraudulent and repair their damaged credit histories, they also must correct the inaccurate medical information that is now part of their health records.

If someone else's medical problems are mixed in with your records, you could have difficulty obtaining life insurance or individual health insurance. The inaccurate medical history could cause a health-care provider to supply treatments or medications that are inappropriate for you, potentially endangering your health, even your life.

Medical ID theft even could lead to blackmail if medical records contain details about sensitive health conditions that patients don't want others to know about.

PREVENTING MEDICAL ID THEFT

It's important to guard your health insurance identification number just as closely as you do your Social Security and credit card numbers. Never leave your insurance card where it can be seen or lend it out, even to a seemingly helpful neighbor who offers to pick up your prescription.

Also, do not post your insurance identification number next to your phone or read the number out loud to a pharmacist if other customers are within earshot. Shred insurance documents before throwing them away.

Unfortunately, there is nothing you can do to prevent your medical records from being stolen from a hospital or doctor's office. *However, you can limit the potential damage if a theft does occur by taking these six steps...*

1. Open and read all medical bills and "Explanation of Benefits" (EOB) statements from your health insurer as soon as they reach you. If these describe treatments that you did not receive or name doctors or medical facilities that you don't remember visiting, immediately contact your insurance company or the health-care facility and request additional details.

2. If you're convinced that a bill or insurance statement refers to treatment you did not receive, ask to speak to the employee in charge of investigating fraud or medical ID theft at your insurance company and at the medical facility involved. Inform these individuals that there is a treatment in your records that was not provided to you and that you are the victim of either medical identity theft or a billing error.

Follow up your phone calls with letters sent directly to these employees via registered mail with return receipts requested. In your letters, describe the situation once again, then ask for any bills to be voided and your medical records to be amended to

state that you did not have this health problem and did not receive this treatment.

Important: Americans have the right under federal Health Insurance Portability and Accountability Act (HIPAA) rules to have any inaccuracies in their health records amended, but not to have inaccurate information completely removed, even in cases of medical identity theft. Medical service providers argue that if inaccurate information were completely removed from patients' files, health-care providers could be sued for improper treatments that they had prescribed in good faith based on the now-deleted information.

3. Report the ID theft to the police in the town in which the medical services were rendered and to that state's attorney general's office. Most police departments do not pursue identity thieves with much vigor, but reporting the crime could at least provide you with a copy of a police report, which you can send to bill collectors who contact you.

4. Contact every health-care provider you use, explain what has occurred and ask if the erroneous information has found its way into that provider's records. If it has, request that the records be corrected. If possible, provide some evidence of the crime, such as a copy of the police report or a letter from your health-care provider or insurance company. There is no centralized medical record bureau to correct errors.

5. Call the major credit bureaus to report the fraud and set up fraud alerts, just as you would with any case of identity theft. The three credit bureaus are Equifax (888-766-0008, *www.equifax.com*)...Experian (888-397-3742, *www.experian.com*)...and TransUnion (800-680-7289, *www.transunion.com*).

Request free copies of your credit reports, and make sure no fraudulent new accounts have been opened in your name.

If you have ever used a credit or debit card to pay a medical bill, the thief could have your account information. Contact your card issuers, ask to review recent activity for suspicious charges, then cancel the cards and request replacements.

6. Scan your medical records for errors every few years, assuming that it is not too expensive to do so. Inaccuracies are distressingly common, even without identity theft.

Patients have a legal right to receive a copy of their medical records from any doctor's office or hospital where they received treatment, but first ask how much this will cost. Some states allow medical facilities to charge fees, which could be $1 per page or more for potentially hundreds of pages of records.

Sneaky Supermarket Come-Ons... How to Avoid Spending More at the Store

Phil Lempert, food editor for NBC's *Today* show. Based in Santa Monica, CA, he is author of many books, including *Being the Shopper: Understanding the Buyer's Choice.* Wiley. *www.supermarketguru. com.*

Food prices are soaring, and stores are pulling out all the stops to create the illusion of savings, value and good deals. *Here's how grocery stores get shoppers to overspend—and how to defend yourself...*

•**Buy one, get one free.** These offers make you feel that you are getting two items for "half price." But it isn't really half price if the cost is more than that of a similar item— and you're getting no bargain at all if you don't want or can't use more than one of a product.

Self-defense: Ask the manager whether you can buy one item for half the price of two. Stores don't advertise this alternative, but it often is allowed.

•**Limit four per person.** Scarcity exerts a powerful effect on shoppers. Any time you're restricted from buying, a hoarding mentality kicks in and you are likely to buy more than you need.

Problem: Excess items can spoil, sit in your cupboard for years or simply get thrown out.

Self-defense: Purchase only the amount that you reasonably need and can use, no matter how good the price.

•**Double discounts.** *Quick:* If you were given a choice of buying a $100 item at 50% off or buying the same item at 25% off with an additional 30% discount given at the register, which would you choose? Most consumers add the 25% and 30% and think that they are getting 55% off the product. In reality, they are paying $2.50 more.

Self-defense: Look at the fine print on the shelves to see if the store does "unit pricing" breakdowns for you (showing the final cost per ounce, pound, piece or whatever the unit is). Or better yet, bring a calculator to cut through the number games.

•**Country-of-origin labeling.** With the recent scare over tainted products from China, stores know that consumers will pay more for food they trust. I've seen supermarket signs promoting "Live Maine Lobsters" or "Washington State Apples" with fine print that reads, respectively, "Imported from Chile" and "Product of Mexico."

Self-defense: Don't trust store signs for foods' countries of origin. Check origin labels on the products.

For organic foods, which often are priced higher, look for proof of authenticity. To be 100% sure that the product is organic, the packaging should carry a stamp that reads, "OTCO" (which means it is certified by Oregon Tilth, a national nonprofit organic certification organization) or "USDA Organic."

•**Alluring end caps.** These are stand-alone display cases at the ends of aisles. On average, shoppers are 30% more likely to buy end-cap goods than those in the middle of an aisle. End caps seem to have good deals—some say, "Stock up now!" or "Great price!"—but half the time, they're not. In fact, these prime spots often are reserved for high-profit, so-called gourmet foods.

Self-defense: Buy from an end cap only if it is truly a good deal. Be wary of freestanding (island) displays as well. They offer a different kind of impulse buy—expensive, "integrated" merchandise.

Index